Make the Grade.
Your Atomic Dog Online Edition.

The Atomic Dog Online Edition includes proven study tools that expand and enhance key concepts in your text. Reinforce and review the information you absolutely 'need to know' with features like:

- **Review Quizzes**
- Key term Assessments
- Interactive Animations and Simulations
- Notes and Information from Your Instructor
- Pop-up Glossary Terms
- A Full Text Search Engine

W9-CGK-959

Ensure that you 'make the grade'. Follow your lectures, complete assignments, and take advantage of all your available study resources like the Atomic Dog Online Edition.

How to Access Your Online Edition

If you purchased this text directly from Atomic Dog ….
Visit atomicdog.com and enter your email address and password in the login box at the top-right corner of the page.

If you purchased this text NEW from another source….
Visit our Students' Page on atomicdog.com and enter the **activation key located below** to register and access your Online Edition.

If you purchased this text USED from another source….
Using the Book Activation key below you can access the Online Edition at a discounted rate. Visit our Students' Page on atomicdog.com and enter the **Book Activation Key in** the field provided to register and gain access to the Online Edition.

Be sure to download our *How to Use Your Online Edition* guide located on atomicdog.com to learn about additional features!

This key activates your online edition. Visit atomicdog.com to enter your Book Activation Key and start accessing your online resources. For more information, give us a call at (800) 310-5661 or send us an email at support@atomicdog.com

194SGOK9F

PKG

*Some online Editions do not contain all features.

Midterm
1-4
6
7
14

International Logistics

The Management of International Trade Operations

Second Edition

International Logistics

The Management of International Trade Operations

Pierre A. David, Ph.D.
Baldwin-Wallace College

Richard D. Stewart, Ph.D.
University of Wisconsin-Superior

THOMSON

Australia · Canada · Mexico · Singapore · Spain · United Kingdom · United States

International Logistics
Pierre David ~ Richard Stewart

Executive Editors:
Michele Baird, Maureen Staudt, and Michael Stranz

Marketing Manager:
Mikka Baker

Managing Editor:
Kendra Leonard

Associate Developmental Editor:
Sarah Blasco

Marketing Coordinators:
Lindsay Annett and Sara Mercurio

Production/Manufacturing Manager:
Donna M. Brown

Production Editorial Manager:
Dan Plofchan

Custom Production Editor:
Jennifer Flinchpaugh

Rights and Permissions Specialists:
Kalina Hintz and Bahman Naraghi

Cover Image:
© Getty

International Logistics / Pierre David and Richard Stewart / Second Edition

BOOK ISBN 0-7593-9143-2
BOOK ISBN 978-0-7593-9143-7
PACKAGE ISBN 0-7593-9573-X
PACKAGE ISBN 978-0-7593-9573-2
LCCN 2006909685

International Divisions List

Asia (Including India):
Thomson Learning
(a division of Thomson Asia Pte Ltd)
5 Shenton Way #01-01
UIC Building
Singapore 068808
Tel: (65) 6410-1200
Fax: (65) 6410-1208

Australia/New Zealand:
Thomson Learning Australia
102 Dodds Street
Southbank, Victoria 3006
Australia

Latin America:
Thomson Learning
Seneca 53
Colonia Polano
11560 Mexico, D.F., Mexico
Tel (525) 281-2906
Fax (525) 281-2656

Canada:
Thomson Nelson
1120 Birchmount Road
Toronto, Ontario
Canada M1K 5G4
Tel (416) 752-9100
Fax (416) 752-8102

UK/Europe/Middle East/Africa:
Thomson Learning
High Holborn House
50-51 Bedford Row
London, WC1R 4L$
United Kingdom
Tel 44 (020) 7067-2500
Fax 44 (020) 7067-2600

Spain (Includes Portugal):
Thomson Paraninfo
Calle Magallanes 25
28015 Madrid
España
Tel 34 (0)91 446-3350
Fax 34 (0)91 445-6218

to Beth

to Kathleen

Brief Contents

Contents

Preface

A User's Perspective

We wrote this book with the idea that its content should be directed at the users of international logistics services. It covers all of the concepts that are important to managers who are actively exporting or importing goods or are otherwise involved in international trade operations. All of the relevant issues are thoroughly explained, including documentation, terms of payment, terms of trade (Incoterms), exchange rate exposure, international insurance, Customs clearance, agency and distributorship sales contracts, packaging, and transportation.

We strived to make this book accessible to the reader: We took great care to make certain that all of the concepts are clearly and accurately portrayed, and we spent a considerable amount of time ensuring that the vocabulary is precise and accurate, a perspective that we gained from years of experience teaching hundreds of students, including a fair proportion of non-native English speakers.

We have paid attention to the order in which the material is introduced, so that the approach is logical and that the reader can understand a concept without the need to refer to material presented later in the book. Given the interdependence of international logistics topics, this was a challenging undertaking, but we think we managed to achieve that goal. Nevertheless, we would strongly advise the interested reader to read the book once "quickly," before delving into some of its finer details.

Since the book introduces a number of topics that tend to be technical or unfamiliar to many readers, we included more than seventy illustrations, tables, and figures in the text to support the core content. All were chosen carefully to accurately depict the concepts presented in the text: We used our own photographs, but we also have to thank more than thirty professional and amateur photographers who let us borrow their work.

Feedback

It became quickly apparent that the first edition of this book clearly met a need. It received strong academic support and was adopted by most of the logistics programs in the United States and many abroad. It also became the official reference textbook for the international portion of the Certification in Transportation and Logistics offered by the American Society of Transportation and Logistics.

We are very thankful that our textbook, which presents the information from the perspective of the users of international logistics services, is a beneficial tool for courses taught in so many programs. Many faculty members and readers found that perspective useful and refreshing and told us so. Several recommended changes and improvements, and the material in the second edition has benefited from the feedback of many colleagues, who took a substantial amount of time to let us know how to improve it, and from hundreds of our students, most of whom are professionals engaged in international business, who helped us determine which aspects of the book needed to be revised.

What's New in this Edition

The second edition of this textbook includes many changes, all of which improve the text substantially. With the addition of a co-author and the incorporation of suggestions made by reviewers and adopters, the text has been entirely updated to reflect the changes in the practice of international logistics that have happened in the last few years, especially in terms of cargo security and Customs' rules. All examples, statistics, and illustrations have also been updated.

The first visible change in the second edition is the addition of the knowledge and talent of co-author Richard Stewart, a former sea captain (Master Unlimited) who currently teaches at the University of Wisconsin–Superior. We are very grateful for Richard's expertise in international ocean transportation and international insurance, and his contributions greatly strengthen those two chapters. He also adds an important practitioner's perspective throughout. Altogether, this book is much stronger because of his valuable expertise.

Another substantial change to this text is the expansion of this text to include two new chapters and the complete revision of another. Chapter 1 was added in response to those adopters of the first edition who wanted to see more of a review of international trade and international trade theory. It is written for those students who need a review of the historical development of international trade and of the creation of the institutions that facilitate international trade, as well as an overview of the drivers of international commerce and of the principal economic theories of international trade.

The greatest change in this text, which culminates in the new Chapter 16, is the inclusion in almost every chapter of a prescriptive section, which elaborates on the best practices of international logistics managers worldwide. In addition, Chapter 16 adds recommendations that are not specifically linked to international logistics but are fundamental to good international trade practices and good marketing.

Finally, Chapter 2 is fully revised and now includes a better theoretical background to frame the professional discipline of international logistics, and we think that this chapter summarizes accurately the evolution of the field, including the shift toward "Supply Chain Management" that permeates the industry. We hope we have correctly captured the current state of the discipline in this chapter, and we propose a framework within which we think that the discipline of international logistics can be studied.

Online and in Print

International Logistics: The Management of International Trade Operations, Second Edition, is available online as well as in print. The online version adds interactive media components that supplement the text and enhance presentation and understanding. For example,

- Chapter quizzes test students' knowledge of various topics and provide immediate feedback.
- Clickable glossary terms provide immediate definitions of key concepts.
- References and footnotes "pop up" with a click.
- Highlighting capabilities allow students to emphasize main ideas. They can also add personal notes in the margin.
- The search function allows students to quickly locate discussions of specific topics throughout the text.
- An interactive study guide at the end of each chapter provides tools for learning, such as interactive

key-term matching and the ability to review customized content in one place.

Students may choose to use just the online version of the text or both the online and print versions together. This gives them the flexibility to choose which combination or resources works best for them. To assist those who use the online and print version together, the primary heads and subheads in each chapter are numbered identically. For example, the first primary head in Chapter 1 is labeled 1-1, the second primary head is labeled 1-2, and so on. The subheads build from the designation of their corresponding primary head: 1-1a, 1-1b, etc. This numbering system is identical in the online version, to make moving between the online and print versions as seamless as possible.

Supplements

Atomic Dog is pleased to offer a competitive suite of supplemental materials for instructors using its textbooks. These ancillaries include a set of PowerPoint slides and an Instructor's Manual.

The PowerPoint slides available for this text are designed to provide instructors with comprehensive visual aids for each chapter in the book. These slides include outlines of each chapter and highlight important terms, concepts, and discussion points.

The Instructor's Manual offers lecture outlines and notes; in-class and take-home assignments; multiple-choice questions for each chapter; recommendations for multimedia resources such as films and websites; and long and short essay questions and their answers, appropriate for use on tests.

Also available are two compact discs of photographs that duplicate and supplement the photographs in this book. These photo CDs are available to faculty members upon request, by contacting Pierre David at pdavid@bw.edu.

About Atomic Dog

Atomic Dog is faithfully dedicated to meeting the needs of today's faculty and students by offering a unique and clear alternative to the traditional textbook. Breaking down textbooks and study tools into their basic "atomic parts," we were able to recombine them and utilize rich digital media to create a "new breed" of textbook.

This blend of online content, interactive multimedia, and print creates unprecedented adaptability to meet different educational settings and individual learning styles. As part of Thomson Custom Solutions, we offer even greater flexibility and resources in creating a learning solution tailor-fit to your course.

Atomic Dog is loyally dedicated to our customers and our environment, adhering to three key tenets:

Focus on Essential and Quality Content: We are proud to work with our authors to deliver you a high-quality textbook at a lower cost. We focus on the essential information and resources students need and present them in an efficient but student-friendly format.

Value and Choice for Students—Our products are a great value and provide students more choices in "what and how" they buy—often at a savings of 30 to 40% compared to traditional textbooks. Students who chose the online edition may see even greater savings compared to a print textbook. Faculty play an important and willing roll—working with us to keep costs low for their students by evaluating texts online and supplementary material.

Reducing Our Environmental "Paw-Print": Atomic Dog is working to reduce its impact on the environment in several ways. Our textbooks and marketing materials are printed on recycled paper, and we will continue to explore environmentally friendly methods. We encourage faculty to review text materials online instead of requesting a print review copy. Students who buy the online version do their part by going "paperless" and eliminating the need for additional packaging or shipping. Atomic Dog will continue to explore new ways that we can reduce our "paw print" in the environment and hope you will join us in these efforts.

Atomic Dog is dedicated to faithfully serving the needs of faculty and students—providing a learning tool that helps make the connection. We know that after you try our texts that Atomic Dog—like a great dog—becomes your faithful companion.

Acknowledgements

We are thankful for all of the help that we obtained in writing this second edition. First are the suggestions made by our colleagues: Yavuz Agan (Western Illinois University), Bud Cohan (Columbus State Community College), Angelica Cortes (University of Texas–Pan American), Frank Davis (University of Tennessee), Stanley Flax (St. Thomas University), Mary Jo Geyer (Robert Morris University), Tom Grooms (Northwood University), Jon Helmick (United States Merchant Marine Academy), Bill Jackson (Green River Community College), Michael Landry (Northeastern State University), Michael Munro (Florida International University), Steve Swartz (University of North Texas), and Peter Weaver (Ferris State University). Second are the suggestions made by the reviewers of the first edition: Syed Tariq Anwar (West Texas A&M University), Thuong T. Le (University of Toledo), Larry LeBlanc (Vanderbilt University), and Evelyn Thomchick (Pennsylvania State University). We could not have done it without your help.

We are also indebted to Steve Scoble, Kendra Leonard, Matt Walker, and Sarah Blasco at Atomic Dog–Thomson Publishing for their enthusiasm and support for this second edition. They encouraged us along, and this book would not have been possible without their considerable help.

Finally, Pierre would like to thank his wife Beth, and children, Natalie, Caroline, and Timothy, for their patience and encouragement during the long summer of 2006. Richard would like to thank his wife Kathleen Collins for her continuous strong support in this project.

Berea, August 16, 2006

About the Authors

Pierre A. David, Ph.D., Baldwin-Wallace College

Pierre David is a Professor of Business Administration at Baldwin-Wallace College, a liberal arts university located in Berea, Ohio. His teaching interests include marketing and operations management, particularly as these disciplines are applied to an international environment: His primary teaching focus are the courses in international logistics and international market research offered as part of the Baldwin-Wallace College International MBA program. His regular teaching schedule also includes courses in international marketing, marketing management, market research, and operations management at the graduate and undergraduate levels. In 1998, based upon student recommendations, he received the Bechberger Award for Excellence in Teaching.

Dr. David has also had the opportunity to conduct international logistics training sessions in the United States, France, Turkey, China, and Brazil. His research interests are in international logistics and international market research but also include statistics: He and other faculty members at Kent State University are doing very-large-scale computer simulations to determine sampling distributions of specific statistics.

He earned a Ph.D. from Kent State University, an MBA from the University of Pittsburgh, and an MBA from l'École de Hautes Études Commerciales du Nord in Lille, France, all of which were in marketing and operations management. He has lived in four different countries (Tunisia, Switzerland, France, and the United States) and visited a dozen more.

Dr. David is active in the Native Sons and Daughters' programs, the United Way, and his church. He is married to Beth, and they have three children.

Richard D. Stewart, Ph.D., University of Wisconsin-Superior

Richard Stewart is a Professor at the University of Wisconsin–Superior, the Director of the Transportation and Logistics Research Center, and the Co-Director of the Great Lakes Maritime Research Institute.

He earned his Ph.D. at Rensselaer Polytechnic Institute's Lalley School of Management, his Master's degree at the University of Wisconsin–Green Bay, and his Bachelor's degree at the U.S. Merchant Marine Academy. Dr. Stewart has commanded ocean going ships and was manager of a $300 million fleet of tankers and bulk vessels trading worldwide. He was a Captain in the U.S. Naval Reserve and holds a current Unlimited Ocean Master's License and STCW-95 certification.

Dr. Stewart has extensive teaching experience in undergraduate and graduate courses in the United States and overseas. He is an examiner for the American Society of Transportation and Logistics and is certified in Transportation and Logistics. His publications include research reports as well as books and articles on transportation management, port operations, transportation education, and marine environmental management. He is a consultant for law firms and transportation companies.

Dr. Stewart is active in Boy and Girl Scouts, several professional societies, and serves on public advisory committees and nonprofit boards. He is married to Kathleen Collins, and they have four children.

Introduction

Chapter One

Source: © 2007 JupiterImages Corporation.

The years since World War II have seen an unprecedented increase in international trade and a parallel improvement in the economic development of most nations. Countries that were barely able to feed their population sixty years ago are now economic powerhouses where inhabitants enjoy a modern standard of living and where companies trade internationally. In many developing countries, political concerns have shifted from famine and abject poverty to pollution and urban gridlock, once the concerns of developed countries only.

This increase in international trade was triggered by the realization that countries' economies benefit by trading with each other and that trade increases the overall well-being of the world's population. Figure 1-1[1] illustrates how much international trade has grown, and the respective shares of the twenty-five European countries, the United States, Japan, China, and of the remainder of the world in international trade.

Professionals in international logistics have been the main facilitators of that trade growth. They have been the managers responsible for the safe and timely deliveries of these millions of dollars worth of goods. They are responsible for:

- arranging transportation of these goods over thousands of miles
- understanding the trade-offs between the different modes of transportation available and making the correct decision
- making sure that the goods are packaged properly for their journey
- insuring the goods appropriately while in transit, and understanding the risks they face
- minimizing the risks associated with international payments by selecting the right payment currency or the right hedging strategy
- making sure that the goods are accompanied by the proper documents so that they can clear Customs in the country of destination
- defining properly who, between them and their foreign counterparts, is responsible for which aspects of the voyage and the documents
- determining which method is most suitable for payment between the exporter and the importer.

While all of these responsibilities of an international logistics manager will be covered in the remainder of this textbook, this chapter gives an overview of the extent of international trade, of the economic theories of international trade, and of

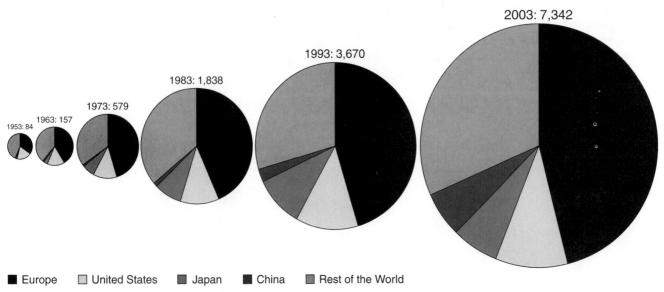

■ Europe   ☐ United States   ◧ Japan   ■ China   ◩ Rest of the World

Figure 1-1
Growth in World Trade, in Current U.S. $ Billions (1953–2003)

some of the difficulties associated with conducting business in an international environment.

1-1 International Trade Growth

In constant U.S. dollars, international trade has grown 2,400 percent between 1950 and 2005[2] (see Tables 1-1[3], 1-2[4], and 1-3[5]), and by more than 225 percent since 1980 an annual growth rate of 5 percent (the differences between exports and imports reflect the different ways in which the values of exports and imports are calculated).

This increase in international trade was triggered by a massive liberalization of international commerce following World War II and the creation of a number of international organizations designed to facilitate international commerce, as well as a

▶ **TABLE 1-1**	World's Total International Trade in Merchandise	
International Merchandise Trade Volume in US $ billions		
Year	**Exports**	**Imports**
1980	2028.53	2067.43
1985	1937.08	1995.84
1990	3388.15	3488.46
1995	4967.42	5078.02
2000	6245.47	6517.99
2004	6642.00	6985.00

▶ **TABLE 1-2**	World's Total International Trade in Services	
International Service Trade Volume in US $ billions		
Year	**Exports**	**Imports**
1980	364.30	400.40
1985	381.80	399.30
1990	783.20	817.90
1995	1190.80	1200.10
2000	1457.30	1453.10
2004	2125.00	2095.00

▶ **TABLE 1-3**	World's Total International Trade in Merchandise and Services	
Total International Trade Volume in US $ billions		
Year	**Exports**	**Imports**
1980	2392.83	2467.83
1985	2318.88	2395.74
1990	4171.35	4306.36
1995	6158.22	6378.12
2000	7702.77	7971.09
2004	8767.00	9080.00

significant decrease in transportation costs and transit times. During that period, a much greater consumer acceptance of things "foreign," from food to automobiles, allowed an increasing number of companies to expand their sales beyond their domestic borders.

1-2 International Trade Milestones

The development of international trade has been fostered over the years by several critical milestones, the ratification of several key international treaties, and the establishment of international organizations designed to facilitate and support international trade activities.

1-2a The Bretton-Woods Conference

In the last year of World War II, world leaders of the Allied nations met in July 1944 in the resort town of Bretton-Woods, a conference that led to the creation of several international institutions, two of which were specifically designed to facilitate world trade:

- The International Monetary Fund (IMF) on December 27, 1945,[6] which established an international system of payment and introduced stable currency exchange rates.
- The General Agreement on Tariffs and Trade (GATT), which through multiple negotiation periods (in Geneva [1948], Annecy [1949], Torquay [1951], Geneva [1956], the Dillon Round [1960–61], the Kennedy Round [1964–67], the Tokyo Round [1973–79], and the Uruguay Round [1986–94]), led to a decrease of duty rate from an average of over 40 percent in 1947 to an average slightly above 4 percent in 2006.

1-2b The World Trade Organization

The World Trade Organization (WTO) was officially created on January 1, 1995.[7] It "replaced" the GATT and is the organization that is essentially in charge of "enforcing" free trade. Since 2001, the WTO has been working on the Doha Round of multilateral negotiations, whose goal is to improve trade in agricultural commodities, which is impeded by a large number of nontariff barriers, and replete with agricultural subsidies in developed countries.

1-2c The Treaty of Rome

The Treaty of Rome in 1957 among Belgium, France, Germany, Italy, Luxembourg, and the Netherlands led to the eventual creation of the European Union and was emulated by countless other groups of countries that were more or less successful in designing their own common markets. The European Union expanded in 1973 (Denmark, Ireland, and the United Kingdom), in 1981 (Greece), in 1986 (Spain and Portugal), in 1995 (Austria, Finland, and Sweden) and in 2004 (Cyprus, Czech Republic, Estonia, Hungary, Latvia, Lithuania, Malta, Poland, Slovakia, and Slovenia). It totals twenty-five countries as of August 2006.

The creation of the European Union triggered many other regional economic groups and other bilateral or multilateral agreements: most notable are the Association of South East Asian Nations (ASEAN), Mercosur, the Andean Community, and the North American Free Trade Agreement (NAFTA). A number of examples are given in Table 1-4.

1-2d The Creation of the Euro

euro The common currency of twelve of the twenty-five countries of the European Union.

The **euro** is the European currency introduced in 1999 and put in circulation on January 1, 2002 in twelve of the twenty-five countries of the European Union (Austria, Belgium, Finland, France, Germany, Greece, Italy, Ireland, Luxembourg, the Netherlands, Portugal, and Spain). It has also become the currency of a number of smaller

TABLE 1-4	Economic Trade Blocs

Economic Group	Date of Creation	Current Membership (2006)
European Union	1958	Austria, Belgium, Cyprus, Czech Republic, Denmark, Estonia, Finland, France, Germany, Greece, Hungary, Ireland, Italy, Latvia, Lithuania, Luxembourg, Malta, Netherlands, Poland, Portugal, Slovakia, Slovenia, Spain, Sweden, United Kingdom
Central American Common Market	1960	Costa Rica, El Salvador, Guatemala, Honduras, Nicaragua
ASEAN (Association of South East Asian Nations)	1967	Brunei, Cambodia, Indonesia, Laos, Malaysia, Myanmar, Philippines, Singapore, Thailand, Vietnam
Andean Community	1969	Bolivia, Colombia, Ecuador, Peru
Caricom (Caribbean Community)	1973	Antigua and Barbuda, Bahamas, Barbados, Belize, Dominica, Grenada, Guyana, Haiti, Jamaica, Saint Kitts and Nevis, Saint Lucia, Saint Vincent and the Grenadines, Suriname, Trinidad and Tobago
ECOWAS (Economic Community of Western African States)	1975	Benin, Burkina Faso, Côte d'Ivoire, Gambia, Ghana, Guinea, Guinea-Bissau, Liberia, Mali, Niger, Nigeria, Senegal, Sierra Leone, Togo, Cape Verde
Gulf Cooperation Council	1981	Bahrain, Kuwait, Oman, Qatar, Saudi Arabia, United Arab Emirates
NAFTA (North American Free Trade Area)	1994	Canada, Mexico, United States
Economic and Monetary Community of Central Africa	1994	Cameroon, Central African Republic, Chad, Republic of the Congo, Equatorial Guinea, Gabon
East African Community	2001	Kenya, Tanzania, Uganda

countries not part of the European Union, and the currency on which a number of developing countries have pegged their currencies. It was the first multinational effort to replace twelve strong legacy currencies, and it has become one of the strongest currencies of the world.

1-3 Largest Exporting and Importing Countries

Figures 1-2[8] and 1-3[9] show the largest exporting and importing countries for 2004, most of which have liberal trading policies or free-trade agreements with many of their partners.

1-4 International Trade Drivers

There are many explanations for the enormous surge in international trade in the second half of the twentieth century. Companies found reasons to expand their sales in foreign countries, and others found reasons to purchase some of their raw materials and supplies from abroad. These international trade drivers can generally be divided into four main categories: cost, competitive, market, and technology.

1-4a Cost Drivers

For companies that require large capital investments in plants and machinery, there is a strong incentive to spread the costs of these fixed costs over a large number of units. For that reason, companies in the automobile industry have been among the first to seek customers outside of their domestic markets, and the companies that dominate that industry are present in just about every country: Ford Motor

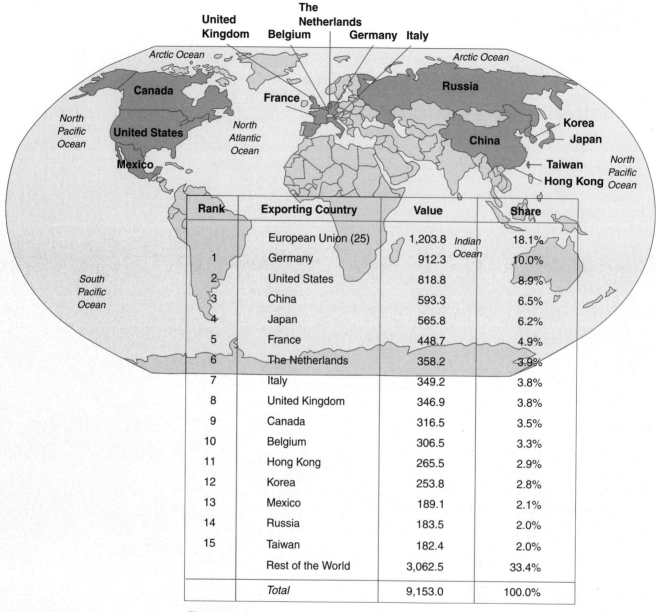

Figure 1-2
World's Largest Exporters of Merchandise in 2004 in US $ billions (includes re-exports)

Rank	Exporting Country	Value	Share
	European Union (25)	1,203.8	18.1%
1	Germany	912.3	10.0%
2	United States	818.8	8.9%
3	China	593.3	6.5%
4	Japan	565.8	6.2%
5	France	448.7	4.9%
6	The Netherlands	358.2	3.9%
7	Italy	349.2	3.8%
8	United Kingdom	346.9	3.8%
9	Canada	316.5	3.5%
10	Belgium	306.5	3.3%
11	Hong Kong	265.5	2.9%
12	Korea	253.8	2.8%
13	Mexico	189.1	2.1%
14	Russia	183.5	2.0%
15	Taiwan	182.4	2.0%
	Rest of the World	3,062.5	33.4%
	Total	9,153.0	100.0%

Company, Toyota Motors, and Volkswagen produce and sell automobiles in the most remote corners of the world. Those that do not have as strong of an international presence tend to be purchased by their competitors: Chrysler was purchased by Daimler-Benz in 1998 and Nissan was purchased by Renault in 1999. In late spring 2006, General Motors and Renault-Nissan were considering a similar arrangement.

Such cost drivers are not limited to plants and machinery. In industries where the developmental costs are very large and the costs of manufacturing are low, such as in the software industry, companies are keen to develop their international sales to dilute their developmental costs; such is the case for Microsoft, for example.

The other cost incentives to trade are found on the sourcing side; companies that assemble products from parts and subassemblies (called Original Equipment Manufacturers) seek suppliers that have the lowest possible prices. They will purchase their parts from companies located in countries that enjoy low labor costs or low energy

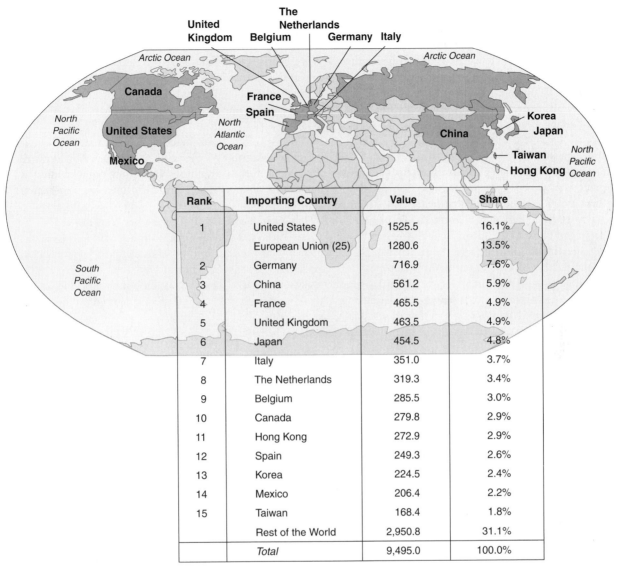

Rank	Importing Country	Value	Share
1	United States	1525.5	16.1%
	European Union (25)	1280.6	13.5%
2	Germany	716.9	7.6%
3	China	561.2	5.9%
4	France	465.5	4.9%
5	United Kingdom	463.5	4.9%
6	Japan	454.5	4.8%
7	Italy	351.0	3.7%
8	The Netherlands	319.3	3.4%
9	Belgium	285.5	3.0%
10	Canada	279.8	2.9%
11	Hong Kong	272.9	2.9%
12	Spain	249.3	2.6%
13	Korea	224.5	2.4%
14	Mexico	206.4	2.2%
15	Taiwan	168.4	1.8%
	Rest of the World	2,950.8	31.1%
	Total	9,495.0	100.0%

Figure 1-3
World's Largest Importers of Merchandise in 2004, in US $ billions (includes re-exports)

costs. Such a purchasing pattern is called **outsourcing**. For example, Royal Appliance Manufacturing, a producer of vacuum cleaners under the brand "Dirt Devil," used to manufacture all of its products in the United States. As of 2006, it produces none in the United States, having outsourced all of its production.

This outsourcing phenomenon is also called the "Wal-Mart effect" in the United States. Manufacturers are asked to provide products at certain prices, called "price points," and there is an unrelenting pressure to make these price points lower every year, in response to consumer preferences. Companies then seek the lowest-cost suppliers, invariably abroad.

The pursuit of lowest manufacturing costs has also caused a substantial shift in other industries as well, notably those that manufacture products that are sold to consumers at retail: textiles, toys, housewares, and so on.

1-4b Competitive Drivers

In some cases, it is a competitive incentive that drives companies to expand overseas. For example, if one of their domestic competitors ventures into a particular country,

outsourcing A practice that consists of a business contracting with other businesses to have them perform some of the operations that it used to handle in-house.

Global Business

The globalization of markets has become so ubiquitous that it is taken for granted. For example, it would not surprise anyone to observe a Canadian businessman, Tony, meet with his Indonesian counterpart, Juria, in a French restaurant located in London. Further scrutiny would reveal that one is dressed in an Italian suit and wears Brazilian shoes, while the other sports a Hong Kong suit and Thai shoes, although both of their shirts are made of Egyptian cotton. Tony is staying in an Indian-run hotel; Juria in one owned by a Palestinian businessman. The encounter could very well take place over a cup of coffee from the Ivory Coast accompanied by Syrian pastries and end with a Cuban cigar.

Tony might have flown to London on a European airplane owned by an American airline, while Juria arrived on an American plane owned by a Singaporean company, both using fuel derived from oil extracted in Saudi Arabia

and Nigeria. One would have traveled to the restaurant in a taxicab made by a Swedish firm, the other in a Spanish-made rental car. They would both have been there on time, one relying on a Swiss watch, the other on a Japanese one.

Their meeting, necessitated by the eventual purchase of a German machine tool for a plant in South Africa owned by Tony's Korean employer, resulted in a quickly drafted agreement on a computer made in Korea of components of myriad origins. After their meeting, they both agree to watch a game of football [soccer] between Brazil and Costa Rica on a Chinese-made large-screen television, on a channel owned by an Australian firm in a bar owned by an Irishman.

These examples of globalization not absurd; they are merely a stretch, although mostly made up of unfortunate stereotypes.

they may feel compelled to follow suit, so as to not lose overall market share. Examples of such competitive behavior are more common in industrial goods than they are in consumer goods; however, this is the drive for the intense competition between the two largest retailers in the world. Carrefour of France and Wal-Mart of the United States compete in many different countries; as soon as one enters a foreign market, the other feels compelled to follow suit.

In other cases, companies expand their sales abroad in response to moves made by their competitors. When a new overseas competitor enters their home market, they "retaliate" by going overseas themselves and competing in that newcomer's home market. An example of such behavior would be The Gap entering the Italian market after Benetton started competing in the United States.

Competitive drivers also exist on the sourcing side. If a competitor starts offering an entry-level product targeted at a segment of price-conscious consumers, a company may retaliate by offering a similar product in order to maintain its market share. Because the competitor's entry-level product tends to be manufactured in low-cost producing countries, the company has little choice but to source overseas as well.

1-4c Market Drivers

As international tourism has exploded, consumers have become increasingly global in their interests, and their tastes and preferences have become almost uniform worldwide. This phenomenon was originally observed for products that reflected this consumer mobility, such as camera film and hotel rooms. Should a consumer want film in any country, there are essentially only three choices everywhere (Kodak, Agfa, and Fuji), but they are easy to purchase with identical sizes, sensitivities, and processing technologies. For hotel rooms, the number of alternative brands is much greater, but the uniformity of choices is similar.

Firms faced with consumers who wanted to find their products everywhere had to expand overseas. In the 1970s, McDonald's restaurants in Germany, Great Britain, and France were mostly patronized by foreigners looking for an experience with which they were familiar. Although foreigners still represent a good portion of their sales today, McDonald's restaurants cater mostly to domestic consumers who have come to appreciate the convenience of fast food. This phenomenon of standardization of tastes is everywhere: television shows, clothing, books, music, food, sports, and so on.

Finally, as consumers become increasingly knowledgeable about the products they consume, they are more likely to purchase products with which they are unfamiliar. The wine industry is very typical in that aspect. French and Italian wines at one time dominated the higher segments of the market, but the way they were marketed demanded that the consumer learn a complex system of classification. When United States vintners "simplified" the industry by labeling the bottles with the name of the grape variety they used, it expanded the market by making it less intimidating to buy wine. Consumers were less likely to make mistakes and more likely to enjoy their wines. An unintended consequence of this simplification was a substantial increase in the sales of wines from countries that traditionally had sold exclusively domestically (Chile, South Africa, and New Zealand, for example).

1-4d Technology Drivers

Another reason people are more familiar with products is that the diffusion of information has become universal. Anyone with an Internet connection can quickly access *Wikipedia* or any other website that provides information. Consumers can conveniently purchase products everywhere, and it is just as convenient to purchase from overseas as it is to purchase next door. Companies that have a presence on the Internet are enticing consumers everywhere to purchase their products. Expanding on this concept of worldwide competition between companies, Thomas Friedman writes about how the world has become flat, and that individuals are now competing with each other on a worldwide scale for jobs: Easy communications and transfer of information have made one's location irrelevant.[10]

An easy example of the worldwide availability and sharing of information is the textbook that you are reading; in order to find good illustrations of certain concepts, the authors looked for photographs on the Internet. There are a total of forty-one different photographers, from nineteen different countries, who provided the illustrations for this book. In a similar fashion, companies can easily find suppliers for just about any product on the Internet as well.

1-5 International Trade Theories

On a formal level, economists have developed several theories to explain why countries trade, and all have empirical support. The following four theories are the ones most commonly used to explain bilateral trade between two countries.

1-5a Smith's Theory of Absolute Advantage

Adam Smith's Theory of Absolute Advantage was first defined in *The Wealth of Nations* in 1776: "If a foreign country can supply us with a commodity cheaper than we ourselves can make it, better buy it of them with some part of the produce of our own industry, employed in a way in which we have some advantage."[11]

The principle of **absolute advantage** is very easy to understand. Suppose companies, located in France, can produce 20,000 liters of wine for each year of labor they employ, and, using the same labor, can produce two units of machinery. Suppose companies in Germany produce, with the same amount of labor, 15,000 liters of wine and three units of machinery. It is obvious that the French enjoy an absolute advantage in making wine and that the Germans have an absolute advantage in making machinery, and therefore it is in the best interest of both parties to have the French companies produce wine and the German companies make machinery. The theory does not concentrate on labor alone, but on the sum of all of the resources that are needed to make the product. A company (country) has an absolute advantage if it produces more goods than another, using the same amount of input; in other words, a company enjoys an absolute advantage if it is more efficient.

absolute advantage An economic theory that holds that when a nation can produce a certain type of good more efficiently than other countries, it will trade with countries that produce other goods more efficiently.

There are many examples of absolute advantage in international trade; countries "specialize" in specific crops or manufactures because they enjoy a worldwide absolute advantage over all other countries. For example, Kuwait produces crude oil more cheaply than any other country and imports most everything else its economy needs. Taiwan produces most of the world's supply of Random Access Memory (RAM) chips, and uses these proceeds to import other products and goods it cannot produce as efficiently, such as soybeans from Brazil.

1-5b Ricardo's Theory of Comparative Advantage

Although most frequently attributed to David Ricardo, the Theory of Comparative Advantage was first outlined by Robert Torrens in his *Essay on the External Corn Trade* in 1815.[12] It was Ricardo, though, who illustrated it with a numerical example in *On the Principles of Political Economy and Taxation* in 1817[13] and who is responsible for its great acceptance.

comparative advantage An economic theory that holds that nations will trade with one another as long as they can produce certain goods relatively more efficiently than one another.

The principle of **comparative advantage** is not as simple as the Theory of Absolute Advantage. In this case, suppose that companies in Great Britain can manufacture, using one year of labor, five units of machinery and twenty-five tons of wheat. Companies in Brazil can manufacture, using the same input of labor, three units of machinery and twenty-one tons of wheat. In this case, Britain enjoys an absolute advantage in both machinery and wheat, and therefore the two countries would not trade, according to the Theory of Absolute Advantage.

However, Britain enjoys a comparative advantage in the production of machinery and Brazil enjoys a comparative advantage in the production of wheat. For Britain to manufacture twenty-five tons of wheat, it has to "give up" five units of machinery; in other words, the cost of a piece of machinery is five tons of wheat. For Brazil, in order to produce twenty-one tons of wheat, it has to give up three units of machinery. The cost to Brazil of producing one unit of machinery is therefore seven tons of wheat. Therefore, it makes sense for both countries to trade with one another; Britain can sell units of machinery in exchange for wheat from Brazil. Should the agreed-upon price be six tons of wheat for each piece of machinery, Britain is better off making machinery rather than growing wheat, and Brazil is better off growing wheat than making pieces of machinery.

The Theory of Comparative Advantage is present in most of the exchanges that companies make internationally. Most firms specialize in making certain products efficiently and these specializations give them a comparative advantage. At one point in its history, the Ford Motor Company built the River Rouge plant where, at one end, iron ore and coal were delivered, and at the other, finished automobiles rolled off the assembly line. Today, Ford has gained a comparative advantage in designing and assembling automobiles, and countless suppliers have made a business out of their own comparative advantage: Mittal Steel (India) in sheet metal, Alcan in aluminum products, TRW in airbags, and so on. Even though the Ford Motor Company is capable of producing these products, it chooses not to, and rather buys them from companies that can produce them relatively more efficiently than it can.

1-5c Heckscher-Ohlin Factor Endowment Theory

The Factor Endowment Theory was developed by Eli Heckscher and Bertil Ohlin in 1933[14] and builds on Ricardo's comparative advantage concept. Ricardo's explanation of **factor endowment** was based on comparing the effectiveness of a country at using its labor to produce goods, and it assumed different levels of technology to account for the differences in the countries' ability to manufacture goods.

factor endowment An economic theory that holds that a country will enjoy a comparative advantage over other countries if it is naturally endowed with a greater abundance of one of the factors of economic production.

The Factor Endowment Theory extends that idea by assuming that, even when technology is identical, some countries enjoy a comparative advantage over others because they are endowed with a greater abundance of a particular factor of production. Economists consider that there are four factors of production—land, labor, capital, and entrepreneurship—and therefore countries with a greater abundance of one of these factors enjoy an advantage over others.

This Factor Endowment Theory explains why certain countries specialize in the production of certain products. Argentina has abundant grazing land, and therefore enjoys a comparative advantage over other countries in beef production. India has abundant educated labor and therefore enjoys a comparative advantage in the staffing of call centers. The United States has an economic system in which entrepreneurship is handsomely rewarded, and it enjoys a comparative advantage in innovation and the development of intellectual property.

1-5d International Product Life Cycle

The **International Product Life Cycle** Theory was developed by Raymond Vernon in 1966.[15] This theory explains the development of international trade in three stages.

In the first stage, a company creates a new product to satisfy a market need. This generally takes place in a developed country, as the critical number of customers necessary for a new product launch is often only found in those countries. The product may also use proprietary technology that is only available in that country as well. The firm manufactures the product in the country of innovation because it needs to be able to monitor the manufacturing process carefully, because there are always unexpected problems in manufacturing a new product. As the product gains acceptance, the firm starts to export the product to other developed countries, where similar markets start to emerge.

In the second stage, sales in other developed countries start to grow, and local competitors see that there are enough customers to justify production of products that imitate the original product. Alternative processes or patents are developed. Sales grow further, and the product manufacturing process becomes much better controlled and somewhat standardized, and many companies master the intricacies of making that product. At the same time, the higher-income segments of developing countries' markets import the product from developed countries, and a market in those countries start to emerge.

In the third stage, the manufacturing process has become much better known and almost routine. There are pressures to lower production costs. At the same time, the markets in developing countries start to reach such sizes that entrepreneurs in developing countries start to produce the products, frequently under contract from firms in the developed countries. Because the manufacturing costs of a mature product tend to be mostly labor-related, these firms start to export massively toward developed countries, slowly replacing all of the manufacturing capacity in those markets.

There is much empirical evidence that supports the International Product Life Cycle Theory. The first televisions were first manufactured and sold in Great Britain. They eventually were manufactured in other developed countries in Europe, North America, Japan, and Australia-New Zealand. As their popularity increased, all of the manufacturing facilities in those developed countries were eventually replaced by manufacturing facilities in developing countries in Southeast Asia. As of 2006, there are no manufacturing facilities in the United States for televisions at all.

1-5e Porter's Cluster Theory

Michael Porter's Cluster Theory, developed in 1990,[16] is not a theory of international trade, but an explanation of the success of certain regions at developing a worldwide absolute (or comparative) advantage in a particular technology or product, despite having no particular advantage in any specific factor of production.

The **cluster** theory argues that it is critical to have a cluster of companies in the same industry, as well as their suppliers, concentrated in one geographic area. The companies feed on each other's know-how, and their competitiveness pushes them to innovate faster. In addition, when such a cluster exists, the best and brightest employees are eager to move to that location, as they know that they will easily find employment. As these employees move from firm to firm, they also take with them

International Product Life Cycle An economic theory that holds that, over its life cycle, a product will be manufactured in different countries.

the know-how they acquired with their previous employers and therefore innovation "travels" from firm to firm. In some cases, these employees develop technologies and ideas that their employers may not want to pursue further and they themselves then start a company to exploit these ideas. Innovation flourishes within the area.

There are several areas of the world where such clusters can be found. The most commonly mentioned location is "Silicon Valley" in California, where most of the innovation in computer technology took place in the latter part of the twentieth century. Porter studied the cluster of Sassuolo in Italy, which specializes in ceramic tiles and produces more than 30 percent of the world's ceramic tiles, and where more than 70 percent of the production is exported.[17]

1-6 The International Business Environment

On a more practical level, the international logistics professional should have some understanding of the particularities of the international business environment. While it is impossible to replace experience in dealing with people from different countries, it is often useful to know the relevant issues. These few paragraphs are no substitute for classes in international marketing, intercultural communication, international finance, and international economics, but neither are these classes substitutes for experience in world travel and frequent contact with people from different countries and the extensive study of a foreign language.

The international environment is often first described by differences in culture, which is a term that encompasses the entire heritage of the people living in a particular country or geographical area: their language, their customs, their traditions, their morals, their beliefs, and their relationships with one another. If there is one aspect of international business about which it is difficult to generalize, it is culture. Not only are there differences between countries, but there are often differences between regions of a country (in the United States, consider New York and Hawaii), between industries within a country (the bio-tech industry and the auto industry), and often between companies within an industry (IBM and Apple Computers). Therefore, stating that the normal business attire in the United States is a pin-striped suit, a white shirt, and a conservative tie is correct, but only in a certain industry, in a certain geographic location, and in a particular company. Making similar generalizations about certain countries is just as incorrect.

The best strategy for a person interested in a career in international business would be to become familiar with the different techniques for intercultural communications. A number of excellent textbooks have been written in this field.[18] For a person interested in conducting business with a firm in the United States, there are books dealing with the American business culture.[19] For managers interested in a specific country, Brigham Young University publishes the "Culturegrams," which are an excellent synopsis (a few pages) of a given country's culture.[20] Despite all of these tools, culture and cultural misunderstandings are probably the greatest sources of frustration for managers involved in international business. Several tools are presented in Chapter 16 to prevent some of these problems, but the best strategy is to be flexible and sensitive to other people's reactions.

The remainder of the international environment is simpler to understand; countries have different approaches to their legal system, to the way they run their governments, and to the way their economies function. Most information about a country can easily be found in the *World FactBook* published by the Central Intelligence Agency,[21] in the *Country Commercial Guides* published by the United States Department of Commerce,[22] and in the *Country Profiles* and *Country Reports* published by *The Economist*'s Intelligence Unit.[23]

Key Terms

absolute advantage (p. 9)

cluster (p. 11)

comparative advantage (p. 10)

euro (p. 4)

factor endowment (p. 10)

International Product Life Cycle (p. 11)

outsourcing (p. 7)

Review and Discussion Questions

1. Given the total volume and importance of international trade and international exchanges, describe the implications to someone's career in business, and to your education in particular.

2. Consider two countries' situations: Country A can produce either six automobiles or twelve movies with the same amount of resources. Country B, using the same resources, can produce either five automobiles or eight movies. Using Ricardo's Theory of Comparative Advantage, determine which country would produce automobiles, which would produce movies, and the range of relative prices within which these products would trade.

3. Wal-Mart is famous for requesting ever lower "price points" from its suppliers: If a supplier offers a product for $45.00, Wal-Mart will ask the supplier to consider introducing a similar product for $39.00. According to the Heckscher-Ohlin Factor Theory, what consequences do such requests have?

4. In addition to the clusters of Silicon Valley and Sassuolo, Michael Porter identified a cluster for printing presses in Heidelberg, Germany, and others have written about clusters in Limoges, France, for porcelain and in Valenza Po, Italy, for gold jewelry. What characteristics do industrial clusters have that other cities do not have? Can you think of another industrial cluster in the United States or abroad?

Endnotes

1. *World Trade in 2004—Overview*, World Trade Organization, 154 rued de Lausanne, CH-1211 Genève, Switzerland, http://www.wto.org/english/res_e/statis_e/its2005_e/its05_overview_e.pdf, August 5, 2006.

2. "The WTO in Brief: Part1: The Multilateral Trading System—Past, Present and Future," http://www.wto.org/english/thewto_e/whatis_e/inbrief_e/inbr01_e.htm.

3. *World Trade in 2004—Overview*, WTO Publications, World Trade Organization, 154, rue de Lausanne, CH-1211 Genève, Switzerland.

4. *Ibid*

5. *Ibid*

6. "The IMF at a Glance; A Factsheet," http://www.imf.org/external/np/exr/facts/glance.htm, October 27, 2002.

7. "The WTO in Brief: History," http://www.wto.org/english/thewto_e/whatis_e/inbrief_e/inbr00_e.htm, October 27, 2002.

8. *World Trade in 2004—Overview*, World Trade Organization, 154 rued de Lausanne, CH-1211 Genève, Switzerland, http://www.wto.org/english/res_e/statis_e/its2005_e/its05_overview_e.pdf, August 5, 2006.

9. *Ibid*

10. Friedman, Thomas, *The World is flat: a brief history of the twenty-first century*, Farrar, Strauss and Giroux, New York, New York, 2005.

11. Smith, Adam, *An inquiry into the nature and causes of the wealth of nations*, Bantam Classics, 2003.

12. Torrens, Robert, *The budget: On commercial and colonial policy*, London, Smith, Elder, 1840.

13. Ricardo, David, *On the principles of political economy and taxation*, Dover Publications, 2004.

14. Ohlin, Bertil, *Interregional and international trade*, 1933, reproduced in Samuelson, Paul A., *Heckscher-Ohlin international trade theory*, MIT Press, 1991.

15. Vernon, Raymond, "International Investment and International Trade in the Product Life Cycle," *Quarterly Journal of Economics*, May 1966, 80 (2), pp. 190–207.

16. Porter, Michael E., *The competitive advantage of nations*, The Free Press, New York, New York, 1990.

17. "Sassuolo cluster profile," United Nations Industrial Development Organization, http://www.unido.org/doc/4309, August 10, 2006.

18. Lustig, Myron W., and Jolene Koester, *Intercultural competence: Interpersonal communication across cultures*, Allyn and Bacon, Pearson Education, Boston, 2006. Beamer, Linda, and Iris Varner, *Intercultural communication in the global workplace*, McGraw-Hill-Irwin, Boston, 2001. Klopf, Donald W., *International encounters: the fundamentals of intercultural communication*, Morton Publishing Company, 2006.

19. Robinson, David, *Business protocol*, Atomic Dog Publishing, Cincinnati, 2006.

20. *Culturegrams*, http://culturegram.stores.yahoo.net/incul.html.

21. *The World Factbook*, Central Intelligence Agency, http://www.cia.gov/cia/publications/factbook/index.html.

22. *Country commercial guides*, United States Department of Commerce, http://www.export.gov/marketresearch.html.

23. *The Economist's* Intelligence Unit, http://www.eiu.com.

International Supply Chain Management

Chapter Two

Source: © 2007 JupiterImages Corporation.

Before presenting the different aspects of international logistics, it is useful to understand how this function is currently included in the management of a firm engaged in international business. It is essential for the international logistician to understand the responsibilities of that profession and the interactions that this function has with the other operational functions of a firm, such as marketing, finance, and production.

Over the years, the responsibilities of an international logistics manager have evolved substantially. This chapter introduces a brief history of the development of the profession of international logistician, the evolution of the activities that have become his or her responsibility, and the current status of this managerial position. It should be made clear that the responsibilities of an international logistician are still changing; it is not known whether the profession will eventually include a greater number of activities or whether its responsibilities will be curtailed, especially in the light of the creation of Supply Chain Management.

2-1 Historical Development of International Logistics

2-1a The Early, "Slow" Days

The globalization of markets is generally understood to be a recent phenomenon, triggered by the economic development explosion after World War II; however, while international trade has certainly increased dramatically in the second half of the last century, nations have engaged in international trade for eons. However, before the twentieth century and the advent of modern transportation, trade between nations had always relied on courageous traders who ventured in faraway places in the hope of earning a living. They were responsible for determining what goods they should take along as payment for the goods they hoped to bring back, negotiating with foreigners with whom they did not share a language, and arranging for the transportation and safekeeping of the goods while in transit. They were exposed to the risks of international travel, of market preferences, and of political instability. They were mostly adventurers and pioneers.

Can these early traders be considered to have been the first involved in international logistics? Undoubtedly. The word "logistics" comes from the Greek *logistike*, which translates as "the art of calculating"[1] using concrete items, in contrast with *arithmetike*, which was the art of calculating using abstract concepts. The latter eventually evolved into the modern concepts of arithmetic and algebra. The first gave birth to the modern term of "logistics," which has evolved into the art and science of determining eminently concrete aspects of business management, from transportation and packaging to warehousing and inventory management.

The first international traders were involved in logistics; they calculated how much their ships—or beasts—could carry, how much food to bring along, and how best to package the goods while in transit, decisions that parallel exactly what a modern logistics manager does. They had to decide which payment method was most appropriate, just as a modern exporter must determine what is the best way of ensuring it will get paid. While many aspects of international logistics have changed, the main concerns of people involved in this field remain similar; they have to ensure that goods manufactured in one part of the world arrive safely to their destination.

However, the modern interpretation of the term "logistics" has its origins in the military, where it was used to describe the activities related to the procurement of ammunitions and essential supplies to troops located at the front. It gave birth to the title of *Maréchal des Logis* in the French military, which is given to a sergeant in charge of a unit's supplies and housing. Interestingly enough, when the term applies to the branch of the military in charge of logistics on a large scale, the French use a different word altogether, "*le train*."

Initially, therefore what was understood as "business logistics" was based on the military concept and encompassed mostly the physical movement of goods (1970s). The term is now much broader and includes not only all the activities related to the physical movement of goods, both upstream (procurement activities) and downstream (sales) activities, but also the management of some of the relationships with suppliers and customers.

Over the last thirty years, the focus of logistics has evolved substantially: Early on, and probably until the mid-1980s, the main concern of logistics managers and specifically of international logistics managers, was to make sure that the goods arrived at their destination in good condition and at the lowest possible cost. Shorter transit times were considered, but generally only when the goods were perishable or because the goods were so urgently needed that the additional costs were justified; for most goods, however, long transit times were essentially considered normal. As time moved on, a transition was made to shorter transit times.

2-1b The Move Toward Speed

Containers—"boxes" in the logisticians' vernacular—changed the focus of international logistics. Even though they were introduced in 1956, containers had a limited impact on international trade until the early 1970s.

Before containers, the process of shipping internationally by ocean was cumbersome and very time consuming. The traditional method was to first pack the goods into a truck or a railroad car for their inland trip to the port. The goods were then unloaded in the port and loaded onto a ship using cranes and slings, as well as a large number of longshoremen who stowed them appropriately for their ocean voyage. The goods were then unloaded again in the port of arrival, loaded again in a truck or railroad car for their inland trip, and finally unloaded at their destination. Packages had to be small to accommodate being handled by humans in the ship's holds, and very sturdy to withstand their being handled numerous times. A transatlantic shipment took in excess of one month, the majority of that time spent in the ports.

With the advent of containers, shipments began to speed up. Instead of loading and unloading the goods several times, containers were loaded once in the shipper's plant and unloaded once at the customer's facilities. Packaging did not have to be as sturdy. Ship loading and unloading operations were much faster. Ships no longer had to be completely empty to load new cargo; as soon as a stack was empty, the crane could unload containers from the ship, place them on a waiting truck, and, instead of returning to the ship "empty," could immediately pick up another container to be loaded onto the vessel. The costs of ocean shipping came down: Port labor costs were lower, ships were more productive because they spent less time idling in ports, and some significant investments were made in new container ships that were ever more efficient.

Only a few years later, in the late 1970s and early 1980s, international logistics saw an explosion in the number of air shipments. Even though DHL had been founded in 1969 and Federal Express in 1973, neither of these services provided much coverage: DHL was strictly a San Francisco–Honolulu service until 1974, and Federal Express had only twenty-five domestic destinations until 1979. However, Federal Express sales rose quickly and by 1983, it had become a billion-dollar corporation strictly based on domestic shipments. It started international operations in 1984, and, by 2005, it had changed its name to FedEx, and became a $30 billion corporation. In the United States, the term "fedex" has become a verb.

Ocean Shipping before Containers

Before the advent of containers, stevedoring was backbreaking work. The goods to be shipped abroad would arrive to port in trucks or railroad cars in small packages or in pallets. They would then be unloaded in a warehouse located alongside the pier and counted. When the ship arrived, it would first have to be completely emptied of its current goods and that merchandise had to be removed from the pier before any loading could start. The merchandise to be loaded was then moved from the warehouse to the quay and counted once more. A loading plan was devised to determine what should be loaded first (the heavier, tougher items), and what should be loaded last.

Longshoremen would then assemble the goods into "drafts," which were larger parcels that could be loaded onto the ship by cranes. They did this by hand, carrying, dragging, and rolling the merchandise to a point where the crane could pick them up; they eventually placed slings under each draft before they were loaded. The merchandise was then lifted onto the ship where another gang of longshoremen would unpack the drafts, count the goods once again, and position them into the holds of the ship (still using muscle power), making sure that every piece of cargo was tightly braced against the others and would not shift during the voyage.

Many of these goods were not packaged to be handled easily; some were 100kg (220 lbs.) bags of grain or 60kg (132 lbs.) bags of sugar. A single longshoreman generally carried the bags of sugar, but two shared the work of moving a bag of grain. Bananas were regularly unloaded by walking down a gangplank on the side of the ship rather than by crane. Each weighed about 80kg (176 lbs.). Longshoremen accidents were common; every year, one in six was injured. Between 1947 and 1957, forty-seven longshoremen were killed in the port of Marseille.[2]

Unloading was not much different. The results of such labor-intensive work was that there were millions of longshoremen employed worldwide, as many as 50,000 in each of the ports of New York, London, and Marseille. Most of these men were employed only part-time, working whenever there was a ship, idle when they were none, competing for work when one was scheduled to arrive in port. They toiled in all sorts of weather, and had to learn to move anything; one day they would load and unload delicate goods, and the next, heavy, dirty, smelly bags.[3]

All this changed with the advent of containers, which allowed the mechanization of loading and unloading ships. The work of a stevedore has become much less physical; although some dockworkers still have to be aboard the ship to position the twist locks that tie the containers to one another and lash down the two lower containers in a stack, many of them drive trucks to position containers alongside the ship or pick them up, or operate a gantry crane.

In 2006, three books were published to celebrate the fiftieth anniversary of the creation of the container.[4] Their titles emphasized that containers have revolutionized international trade.

The costs of air shipments also dropped considerably during this period. In the beginning, Federal Express operated with Dassault's Falcon jets, which had limited cargo capacity. By the end of the 1970s, after a partial deregulation of the industry, it had acquired Boeing 727s and McDonnell-Douglas DC10s, which had much greater capacity. Further deregulation in the 1980s and open-sky agreements in the 1990s increased the number of aircrafts dedicated to freight, and air shipments became increasingly cost competitive with surface alternatives.

2-1c The Emphasis on Customer Satisfaction

By the early 1990s, the increased speed of ocean shipments and the availability of affordable airfreight services had effectively changed the focus of logistics managers: They began to consider the shortest reasonable transit time in response to customers' request for speedy deliveries. Although it was still very important to make sure that the goods arrived in good condition and at the lowest possible cost, the managers' focus had shifted from these process-oriented concerns to the satisfaction of customers' requirements.

The major reason behind this change of objectives in the management of logistics was the increased focus by large manufacturers on the reduction of inventories during the 1980s. Starting in the mid-1970s, but culminating in the early 1980s, interest rates climbed to unprecedented heights, triggering a concern about all the money immobilized in inventories. In the 1980s, companies emphasized reductions in their "static" inventories, or the goods they kept in their warehouses or plants. By the early 1990s, they had shifted their attentions to their "mobile" inventories, or the goods that were in transit between two of their plants or between their suppliers and their plants. The tools they used were **Materials Requirement Planning (MRP)** and **Manufacturing Resources Planning (MRP II)**, which allowed them to create **Just-In-Time** manufacturing processes. In turn, these processes triggered a need for "time-defined" deliveries of assembly parts; plants demanded to have parts delivered just before they were used on the assembly line, and not later. The number of goods that were "in transit" had to be curtailed as well.

By the mid-1990s, all manufacturers had adopted such techniques and were requiring their suppliers to ship just-in-time. At the same time, large retailers and other distributors jumped on the same idea. They started to use techniques derived from MRP and MRP II, which they called **Distribution Resources Planning (DRP)** techniques, which used final consumer sales data to "pull" products through the distribution channel. Consumer sales data were collected through the point-of-sale (POS) scanners. If the products were selling briskly, then the DRP program reordered the goods from the manufacturer and had them delivered just-in-time to the appropriate warehouse or retail store. If a product did not sell well, none were ordered again. This strategy forced logistics managers to shift their attention to transit times and to become adaptable to frequent changes in their work. This came to be known as "agile logistics."

Today, the requirements of most manufacturers and large retail chains are such that they penalize financially the suppliers that do not deliver on time (too early or too late) by withholding a portion of the invoice at the time of payment.

It is fair to say that customer satisfaction is now the primary concern of logisticians: Not only does the shipment have to be accurate (the right parts, in the right quantity), complete (no back-ordered parts), and the packaging appropriate so that the goods arrive undamaged and ready to be sold, but it must also be delivered within a very specific time frame.

While international logisticians must make sure that the shipment is accurate, complete, and arrives on time, they also have many additional responsibilities. They must make certain that their shipment's paperwork is in perfect order so that it can clear Customs without delay. They must make sure that the packaging is sufficient to protect the goods during their long (and often eventful) international voyage. They must ensure that they meet a myriad of security requirements and must manage the intricacies of a transaction involving different currencies and different laws. They must choose the right mode of transportation and must make sure that the goods are properly insured. In short, they have many challenges with which to contend for each shipment.

Materials Requirement Planning (MRP) A computer-based management tool that allows a manufacturing firm to determine what to produce, and in which quantity, in function of what it sells to its customers.

Manufacturing Resources Planning (MRP II) A computer-based management tool that uses MRP at its core, but also includes other functions in the firm, such as finance, procurement, and purchasing.

Just-In-Time A management philosophy that consists of planning the manufacturing of goods in such a way that they are produced just before they are

Distribution Resources Planning (DRP) A computer-based management tool that allows a retail firm to determine what to order from its suppliers in function of what it sells to retail customers.

2-2 Definitions of Logistics and Supply Chain Management

As the fields of logistics and international logistics evolved, the managers working in those fields changed the definitions that they used to describe their profession. Whereas "logistics" was the most commonly accepted term for all of the activities in which they engaged, the term was broadened, starting in the mid-1980s, to include additional activities; eventually, the profession was renamed "supply chain management" in the 1990s. Today, the term "logistics" is understood to encompass a number of activities that are a subset of the activities that constitute Supply Chain Management.

Materials Requirement Planning

In the late 1970s and early 1980s, Japanese manufacturers adopted a new manufacturing management philosophy that was based on reducing work-in-process inventory and delivering the goods to the assembly line just before they were needed. Such philosophy was called "Just-In-Time." Toyota's system for just-in-time (JIT) management was a technique using cards that it still uses today, called *kanban*. Other manufacturers adopted the JIT philosophy, starting in the early 1980s, but implemented it using a technique called Materials Requirements Planning (MRP), especially in the United States.

MRP is a computer-based system that determines what needs to be manufactured on a given day, in which quantity, and whether that order should be expedited. It creates a Master Production Schedule based upon what is currently in inventory (on-hand), what is required to be produced (orders and forecasts of sales for the final product), and bill-of-materials files that spell out precisely what each product's components are. It is a "pull" system: Nothing is manufactured unless there is an order for the final product (or a forecast of an order), and all parts and sub-assemblies are only manufactured to fulfill a particular order.

Although it was originally strictly a manufacturing program, MRP eventually expanded to include other functions related to production: purchasing, finance, and so on, and programs that included those functions came to be known as Manufacturing Resources Planning software, or MRP II. As of 2006, MRP II programs are present in almost all North American plants.

Another derivative of the MRP programs was the development of Distribution Requirements Planning (DRP) software. The idea behind a DRP is similar: Whenever a consumer purchases a product in a retail store, that purchase is captured by point-of-sale scanners, and the DRP program orders another one to be shipped from the distribution center, and one to be manufactured by the supplier. This also operates as a "pull" system: No product is manufactured or shipped by the supplier unless that product was sold by the retailer, and it minimizes the probability of unsold inventory in the supply chain.

Both MRP and DRP have strongly influenced the management of logistics; the traditional warehouse, which was once used to keep products in inventory until they were needed, has become a distribution center (DC), whose function is to take large shipments from manufacturers and separate them into smaller parcels to be delivered to retail stores. Such "cross-docking" operations, where trucks are being unloaded on one side and loaded on the other, are illustrative of the increased emphasis on just-in-time deliveries.

2-2a Logistics

As it stands today, the term "logistics" is defined by the professionals in the field as:

> Logistics is that part of the supply chain process that plans, implements, and controls the efficient, effective forward and reverse flow and storage of goods, services, and related information between the point of origin and the point of consumption in order to meet customers' requirements.[5]

From this definition, it is clear that logistics managers see that the focus of their profession lies in those activities that are related to the *physical aspects* of the movement of goods from supplier to customer. Logisticians are mostly concerned about the transportation, packaging, warehousing, security, and handling of goods that their firm purchases or sells, and they interact daily with managers who hold other responsibilities closely related to the movement of these goods; manufacturing and production, purchasing and procurement, marketing, inventory management, finance, customer service, and so on.

Figure 2-1 summarizes a slightly different opinion of the evolution of logistics, as seen by Alfred Battaglia.[6] In his view, the logistical function of a company came to include the management of materials and manufacturing somewhat earlier than the 1990s. What is clear is that most logistics professionals referred to their profession as "Supply Chain Management" by the early 2000s.

2-2b Supply Chain Management

In an international survey of logistics educators that was conducted in 2001, Larson and Halldorsson[7] found that there were four different viewpoints regarding the

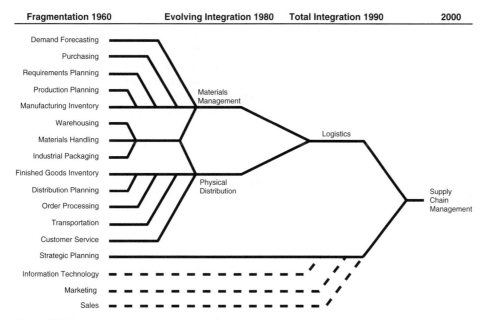

Figure 2-1

The Evolution of Logistics

Source: Diagram © Alfred J. Battaglia. Used with permission. Reproduced by Natalie David.

relationship between logistics and supply chain management, three of which are shown in Figure 2-2.

Nevertheless, it seemed that by 2004, the "inclusionist" viewpoint had prevailed, as the Council of Logistics Management changed its name to the Council of Supply Chain Management Professionals (CSCMP) to reflect what was perceived as the broader nature of the field, and produced a definition of the term "supply chain:"

> Supply Chain Management encompasses the planning and management of all activities involved in sourcing and procurement, conversion, and all Logistics Management activities. Importantly, it also includes coordination and collaboration with channel partners, which can be suppliers, intermediaries, third-party service providers, and customers. In essence, Supply Chain Management integrates supply and demand management within and across companies.

The most significant characteristic of this definition is that it reflects an extension of the concept of logistics to that of supply chain management. In the view of the CSCMP, the shift from logistics to supply chain management was a shift from an internal focus on the company's own processes to an external focus that includes all the firm's partners. The scope of Supply Chain Management is therefore much

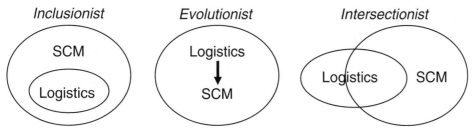

Figure 2-2

Three Different Perspectives on the Relationship between Logistics and SCM

Source: Adapted from Larson and Halldorsson. Reproduced by Natalie David.

broader than the scope of logistics; not only does it include all of the tactical and managerial decisions on which logistics and operations managers tend to focus, but it also includes strategic issues that are more traditionally the domain of the managers in those top management positions that are now colloquially referred to as "C-level" positions (CEO, Chief Executive Officer, CFO, Chief Financial Officer, COO, Chief Operations Officer, and so on). Several companies have created positions of Chief Supply Chain Officers, and the magazine *Chief Supply Chain Officer* was launched in February 2005.

2-3 Definition of International Logistics

The role of international logistics in the global supply chain mirrors that of logistics in the domestic environment: International logistics professionals focus on the tactical aspects of the global supply chain, those activities that are inherent to the movement of goods and paperwork from one country to another, those activities that constitute the basis for export and import activities and operations.

The definition of logistics provided by the Council of Supply Chain Management Professionals can therefore be logically modified to define international logistics by including the elements of the international environment:

International logistics is the process of planning, implementing, and controlling the flow and storage of goods, services, and related information from a point of origin to a point of consumption located in a different country.

The emphasis of international logistics is therefore on the creation of internal processes and strategies. These processes and activities are the focus of this textbook.

2-4 Definition of International Supply Chain Management

A characteristic of supply chain management is that it is inherently global in nature; just about every company outsources some percentage of its production abroad or sells to customers who are located abroad. If it does not, its suppliers or customers do. In 2006, *Forbes* Magazine reported that the percentage of the content of the quintessential American car (the Ford Mustang) that was made outside of the United States stood at 35 percent. In contrast, the Toyota Sienna, a Japanese minivan sold in the United States, was made of 90 percent American parts.[8]

It is not clear why the Council of Supply Chain Management Professionals did not include this global aspect of supply chain management in its definition. The Council's definition should more accurately read:

Supply Chain Management encompasses the planning and management of all activities involved in sourcing and procurement, conversion, and all Logistics Management activities. Importantly, it also includes coordination and collaboration with channel partners, which can be suppliers, intermediaries, third-party service providers, and customers, whether they are located in the United States or abroad. In essence, Supply Chain Management integrates supply and demand management within and across companies.

Figure 2-3 outlines the current state of the relationships among logistics, international logistics, and supply chain management as of 2006. The activities included in the logistical function are those that include physical transportation of the goods

Figure 2-3
Logistics, International Logistics, and Supply Chain Management
Source: Diagram by Natalie David. Used with permission.

from the supplier(s) to the company and from the company to its customer(s). Logistics also includes the warehousing and other inventory functions within the company that involve the products it purchases, manufactures, and sells.

International logistics works in a parallel form for foreign suppliers and customers. It includes additional activities, such as Customs clearance, documents handling, and international packaging, but the main function of international logistics is concentrated on the physical movement of goods from suppliers to the company and from the company to its customers. The fact that they are in an international arena makes fulfilling these activities much more complex.

Supply chain management is a much broader term; it includes both the domestic logistics and the international logistics functions, but it is also the management of the relationships with suppliers and customers (domestic or foreign) and, to some degree, of their relationships with their suppliers and customers. It deals with the entire supply chain, attempting to manage a smooth flow of goods from the first supplier to the ultimate customer. A possible example of a supply chain management activity is the management of quality by the large U.S. Original Equipment Manufacturers (General Motors, Ford Motor Company, Daimler-Chrysler, and General Electric), that implemented QS-9000, which includes a process by which they certify the quality function of their direct suppliers (called tier-one supplier), of these suppliers' suppliers (called tier-two), and of these firms' suppliers (called tier-three).

2-5 Elements of International Logistics

There are only a few activities that are exclusively specific to international logistics; however, the traditional logistical activities are managed differently in an international environment than they are in a domestic environment.

- The environment involved in international logistics is quite important. While there is obviously the issue of language and culture—neither of which should be underestimated, but which are more appropriately covered in an intercultural management textbook—the physical environment of international logistics is quite distinct. The differences in the infrastructure of international logistics and the challenges they represent are covered in Chapter 3.

- The decisions regarding international transportation are eminently more complicated. Because of the distances involved, there are different modes of transportation, different carriers, different transportation documents, and much greater transit times. Chapters 11, 12, and 13 cover these transportation alternatives.

- The number of intermediaries involved is greater. Banks, insurance companies, freight forwarders, not to mention the governments of the exporting country and of the importing country, all have different paperwork requirements. Chapter 9 covers the multitude of documents that are utilized in international trade.

- The inherent risks and hazards of international transportation are much more significant. In order to protect the goods while they are in transit, the logistics manager must have a good understanding of the packaging options that are available. Chapter 14 covers the choices and decisions surrounding packing for international transport.

- International insurance is much more complex. The contracts sometimes are written using archaic language and terminology that varies in meaning depending on the country in which the insurance company is located. Chapter 10 presents the different types of insurance coverage available in an international environment.

- International means of payment are more involved. The risks of nonpayment and currency fluctuations call for specific strategies that are never used in domestic transactions. Chapter 7 explains the different alternative means of payment and Chapter 8 presents the methods used by international traders to protect themselves against the risks presented by currency fluctuations.

- Terms of trade are much more complicated, as the greater number of nodes and links increases the number of possible alternatives for transfer of responsibility and ownership. The terms of trade used in international sales—the Incoterms of the International Chamber of Commerce—are presented thoroughly in Chapter 6.

- The crossing of borders represents specific challenges. Products sold abroad or purchased from abroad have to go through Customs, a complicated and paper-intensive process in most countries. The procedures involved in such a process are described in Chapter 15. In addition, when conducting business with foreign firms, issues arise in the contracts of sale, distribution agreements, and other legal documents. Chapters 4 and 5 present the options available to a firm engaged in international trade.

- Inventory is managed differently, as the risks of delays and variations in shipping times are increasing the challenges of Just-in-Time production. Safety stocks should therefore be created using slightly more complicated algorithms; a good primer on such methods can be found at http://www.international-logistics.info or in a good inventory management textbook.[9]

2-6 The Economic Importance of Logistics

In a yearly study of domestic logistics, Rosalyn Wilson calculates the percentage of the United States' Gross Domestic Product (GDP) that is spent on logistical activities (transportation, inventory, and other administrative costs linked to logistical activities). That percentage stood at 8.5 percent in 2004, but increased to 9.5 percent in 2005 due to increased interest rates and rising fuel costs.[10] Collectively, American businesses spend close to U.S. $1.2 trillion on domestic logistical activities.

Until 2005, though, logistical costs had been steadily decreasing as a percentage of GDP: While their share of the GDP was traditionally in the mid-teens in the 1960s

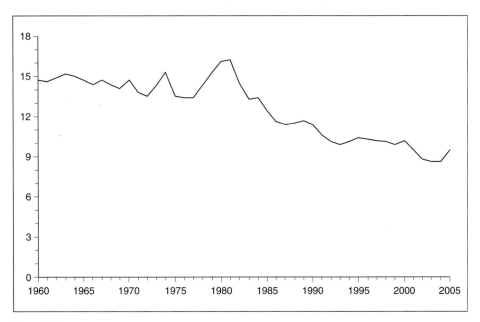

Figure 2-4
Logistics as a Percentage of U.S. Gross Domestic Product

and 1970s—with a high of 16.2 percent in 1982—they have steadily declined since the 1990s, as shown in Figure 2-4.[11] This decrease is mostly due to corporations becoming more efficient in their use of inventory; the advent of Just-in-Time, Manufacturing Resources Planning, and their subsequent derivatives have decreased inventory levels from 24 percent of the United States' GDP in 1981 to 14 percent in 2004[12] and 14.1 percent in 2005.

Some of this decrease can also be attributed to more efficient means of transportation—for example, the increased use of containers—and to the deregulation of the U.S. transportation industry, especially during the 1980s and early 1990s.

However, since the late 1990s, the costs of transportation have been slowly rising; increased fuel costs, a shortage of truck drivers, additional security costs, and a transportation infrastructure stretched to its limits have considerably increased what businesses spend collectively on transportation. Transportation costs rose 15.2 percent from 2004 to 2005, and represent 6 percent of the GDP of the United States.

2-7 The Economic Importance of International Logistics

While there are no comprehensive data illustrating the total value of international logistics activities, it can be conservatively estimated that the percentage spent on international logistics activities would be around 15 percent of the total volume of international trade. Because the total value of the world's merchandise trade is U.S. $9.5 trillion, the total expenditures on international logistics is approximately U.S. $1.4 trillion. This estimate takes into account the fact that the logistical infrastructure of the North American continent is particularly efficient and that international logistics activities are typically more cumbersome and costly due to less efficient infrastructures and procedures, as well as longer distances.

There is one aspect of international logistics, though, that distinguishes it from domestic logistics regarding its impact on the world's economy; not only are the profits of corporations involved in logistics taxed by their respective governments, but international trade also generates a considerable amount of additional government revenues, as most imports are subject to tariffs. A very conservative estimate of the "value" of duty collection and other taxes directly linked to international trade would be about 5 percent of the world's merchandise trade. International logistic activities therefore generate approximately U.S. $500 billion in additional government revenues.

Key Terms

Distribution Resources Planning (DRP) (p. 19)

Just-In-Time (p. 19)

Manufacturing Resources Planning (MRP II) (p. 19)

Materials Requirement Planning (MRP) (p. 19)

Review and Discussion Questions

1. What are the elements that differentiate international logistics from domestic logistics?

2. What are the principal distinct components of international logistics?

3. What are the major costs of international logistics? Given what you read in Chapter 1 about the World Trade Organization, what trend do you expect these costs to follow?

4. MRP and DRP have allowed manufacturers and retailers to carry less and less inventory. What consequences would a major snowstorm or disruption of transportation have on such Just-In-Time management systems?

5. Describe the impact of international trade on your own life, using the products that you own or have purchased in the recent past.

Endnotes

1. Klein, Jacob, *Greek Mathematical Thought and the Origin of Algebra*, translated by Eva Brann, Dover Publications, Mineola, New York, USA, reprinted October 1992. Original publication by MIT Press, Cambridge, Massachusetts, USA, 1968.

2. Pacini, Alfred, and Dominique Pons, *Docker à Marseille*, Récits de vie Payot, T.S. Simey, Paris, 1996.

3. Levinson, Marc, *The box; how the shipping container made the world smaller and the world economy bigger*, Princeton University Press, Princeton, New Jersey, 2006.

4. Levinson, Marc, *The box; how the shipping container made the world smaller and the world economy bigger*, Princeton University Press, Princeton, New Jersey, 2006. Cudahy, Brian J., *Box boats: how containerships changed the world*, Fordham University Press, New York, New York, 2006. Donovan, Arthur, and Joseph Bonney, "The box that changed the world," *The Journal of Commerce*, Commonwealth Business Media, New York, New York, 2006.

5. Council of Supply Chain Management Professionals, "Supply Chain Management/Logistics Management Definitions," http://www.cscmp.org/Website/About CSCMP/Definitions/Definitions.asp, March 8, 2006.

6. Delaney, Robert V., and Rosalyn Wilson, *13th Annual State of Logistics Report: Understanding Inventory—Stay Curious*, ProLogis and Cass Information Systems, Inc., June 10, 2002, http://www.cassinfo.com/2002 Press Conference Full.PDF, October 15, 2002.

7. Larson, Paul D., and Arni Halldorsson, 'Logistics vs. supply chain management: An international survey,' *Journal of Supply Chain Management*, March 2004, pp. 17–31.

8. Fahey, Jonathan, "The parts paradox," *Forbes*, May 8, 2006.

9. Silver, Edward A., and Rein Peterson, *Decision Systems for Inventory Management and Production Planning*, Second Edition, John Wiley and Sons, New York, New York, 1985.

10. Wilson, Rosalyn, *17th Annual State of Logistics Report: Embracing security as a core business function*, Council of Logistics Management, June 19, 2006, https://cscmp.org/Downloads/Memberonly/17State LogisticsReport.pdf.

11. *Ibid*

12. Wilson, Rosalyn, *16th Annual State of Logistics Report: securityreport card—not making the grade*, Council of Logistics Management, June 27, 2005, https://cscmp.org/Downloads/Memberonly/16State LogisticsReport.pdf.

International Logistics Infrastructure

Chapter Three

Source: © 2007 JupiterImages Corporation.

For the manager of international logistics, it is important to have a good understanding of the challenges presented by the different levels of infrastructure found abroad. It is always one of the first problems encountered by an international manager; things don't work abroad like they do at "home." There are different standards, there are different expectations of performance, there are things that work much better, and there are things that do not work as well—in some cases, not at all. Adapting to those differences, and anticipating problems before they arise, are part of the assets of an experienced international logistics manager.

The issue with learning how to manage these differences in infrastructure is that they are difficult to generalize in one particular comment or statement. Most challenges tend to be concentrated in some small geographic areas, and in most cases are limited to a single location: A specific port is not equipped with sufficient cold-storage warehousing space, does not have an appropriately sized crane, or is experiencing delays in getting the goods from the port to the remainder of the country; a road is particularly congested, a specific tunnel has recently been closed, or a railroad is experiencing shortages of appropriate cars. These challenges force the manager involved in international logistics to recognize the possibility of serious problems. The purpose of this chapter is to present enough information and examples to encourage him or her to ask questions at the onset of a transaction, so that there are no discrepancies between the expectations of the company and what can be achieved.

3-1 Definitions

Before going much further, it would be useful to determine what is meant by "infrastructure" in the context of international logistics. A few dictionary definitions would be a good start:

> The basic facilities, services, and installations needed for the functioning of a community or society, such as transportation and communication.[1]

> A collective term for the subordinate parts of an undertaking; substructure, foundation. The permanent installations forming a basis for military operations, as airfields, naval bases, training establishments, ... etc.[2]

In the field of logistics, the definition can be very broad: Infrastructure is a collective term that refers to all of the elements in place (publicly or privately owned goods) to facilitate transportation, communication, and business exchanges. It would therefore include not only transportation and communication elements, but also the existence and quality of public utilities, banking services, and retail distribution channels. To this list, it makes sense to add the existence and quality of the Court system, the defense of intellectual property rights, and the existence of standards. As these concepts are introduced in this chapter, their inclusion into the concept of infrastructure will become more acceptable.

The study of infrastructure is important because the movement of goods and of documents, as well as the movement of money and information, is dependent on these infrastructure components.

3-2 Transportation Infrastructure

The infrastructure that most obviously affects the movement of goods internationally is the transport infrastructure. Without a good understanding of the transportation infrastructure that a shipment will face, a manager may package a product inappropriately, may face delays, or may even be faced with unexpectedly damaged merchandise.

3-2a Port Infrastructure

Port infrastructure is made up of several items, most of which are interconnected, and obviously affect the type of ships that can call on a given port, as well as the type of merchandise that can transit through it.

With the advent of the much larger post-Panamax* containerships, ports have been faced with many challenges. Specifically, the size of those ships is stretching the capabilities of the ports: They are wider, longer, higher above the water, and have a much deeper draft. Between 2005 and 2007, it is expected that 150 vessels with a capacity in excess of 8,000 TEUs—twenty-foot equivalent units, or twenty-foot containers—will come into service, most of them on the transpacific routes between the United States, Japan, China, Singapore, and Hong Kong. Such large ships mean that as many as 4,000 forty-foot containers need to be loaded or unloaded in a single port.[3]

Depth of Water

The first issue is undoubtedly the depth of the water of a port, also called the **draft** of a port. In many ports, the depth of the channels and of the berths, which had been sufficient to accommodate Panamax ships, is not sufficient to accommodate the newer larger ships. Therefore, in a great number of ports, the port authorities have had to engage in dredging activities in order to allow ships with drafts exceeding forty feet (13.5 meters) to access the port.[4] Only a few ports with naturally deep channels have been exempt from this activity.

This dredging of channels and ports can be exceedingly expensive, but ports have little alternative but to undertake this improvement of their capabilities. Competition is such that ships would call on a different port if one were not expanding.[5]

In a parallel fashion, longer ships require longer turning circles, and therefore a redesign—and dredging—of different access channels. As ships become yet longer, wider, and heavier, the challenge for the ports will be to keep up with these ships' requirements and adapt.[6]

draft The minimum depth of water that a ship needs in order to float.

Bridge Clearance

Another factor of great importance in ports is the clearance under its bridges. In many older ports, such as New York-New Jersey, the bridges are too close to the water, leaving very little clearance for tall ships or ships carrying outsized cargo. In some cases, the cargo has to be partially dismantled or repositioned, or the ship lowered with ballast water and the delivery made at low tide so that it clears the bridge span.[7]

All of these factors (depth of channels and berths, as well as bridge clearance) are likely to affect how ports are used in the future. There is a strong likelihood that some ports will not be able to make the necessary infrastructure adjustments to accommodate the largest ships and that there will be a need to create large port hubs, to and from which mega-containerships will travel. Smaller ports would then be served by smaller "feeder" ships that would not tax the ports' infrastructure beyond their capacity.[8] Such ports were created in the 1990s in the Mediterranean Sea: Marsaxlokk in Malta and Cagliari in Sardinia (Italy) serve as trans-shipment ports, loading and unloading large containerships in a deep-water port and using feeder services to serve the local markets and shallower ports of France, Italy, and Spain.[9] In 2005, the Chinese government inaugurated the first phase of the deep-water Port of Yangshan, near Shanghai, to accommodate larger ships.[10] There have been discussions of a large port fulfilling the same function on the Atlantic Coast of

---

* A Panamax ship is a vessel whose dimensions allow it to cross the Panama Canal. A post-Panamax ship is a vessel too large to fit through the Panama Canal locks. For more information on the size of ships, please see Section 11-2.

the United States, to alleviate the constraints presented by the current older ports of New York and Philadelphia.

Cranes

Port terminals have found out that the width of those post-Panamax ships can also be a challenge for their cranes. Traditional Panamax ships can be loaded with up to thirteen containers in the width of a ship (see Figure 3-1). Some of the post-Panamax ships can be loaded with as many as eighteen containers side-by-side. This presents a problem for ports in which the cranes cannot reach the far side of the ship. Early on, ports managed their lack of crane capacity by loading ships from one side, turning the ships around, and then loading the remainder of the containers. The problem was one of balance, as the ships seriously list if they are heavier on one side. Today's ports have made considerable investments in new large-capacity cranes that can load these large ships.

Another obvious alternative is for ports to increase the reach of the cranes. This modification is also accompanied by a need to increase the height of the cranes, as the vessels are higher. These modifications can be quite costly for a port and new cranes capable of serving these ships can cost $50 million.[11]

Another alternative, chosen by the stevedoring company Ceres at the Port of Amsterdam's Paragon Terminal, is to create an indented **berth** to allow the ship to be loaded from both sides (see Figure 3-2). An advantage of this configuration is that it allows the ship to be loaded with up to twelve cranes rather than the maximum of six in a traditional port. This alternative speeds up the loading of the ship considerably, from a maximum of 160 containers per hour (the world record held by the Port of Singapore for a traditional berth) to up to 300 containers per hour, decreasing the time that a ship spends in port and therefore increasing its profitability.[12]

For shippers handling non-containerized cargo, the cranes' capacity is a major factor in deciding through which port to send a specific cargo. Cigna Insurance publishes a directory called *Ports of the World* that lists the equipment of any port in

berth The location, in a port, where a ship is loaded and unloaded.

Figure 3-1
A Traditional Container Berth and Gantry Cranes
Source: Photo © National Oceanic and Atmospheric Administration. Used with permission.

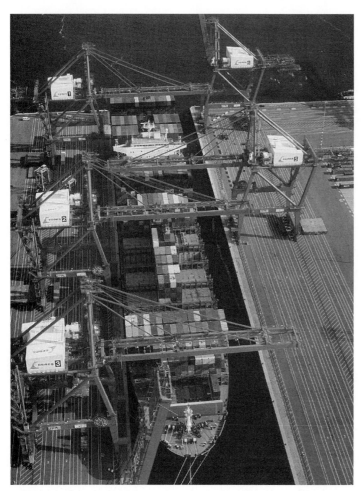

Figure 3-2
The Indented Container Berth of the Paragon Terminal in Amsterdam
Source: Photo © Ceres Paragon Terminals. Used with permission.

the world, specifically the capacity of its cranes (see Table 3-1).[13] It should be obvious that the crane at the port of destination should have at least the same capacity as the one that was used to load the cargo. Failure to pay attention to that fact is likely to lead to a dismantling of the cargo or to the use of an oversized crane, both of which could place the cargo in jeopardy.

Port Operations

Another issue in ports is the way the port is managed, particularly its work rules, which are often dictated by strong unions. Some ports, such as the Port of Long Beach on the Pacific Coast of the United States, only operate eight hours a day[14] instead of the much more efficient twenty-four hours a day, seven days a week of most Asian Pacific Rim ports. Work rules can also be mind-bogglingly complex and hamper the efficiency of ports to the point where they are less and less competitive:[15] In the 1950s, unions dominating the ports of South America were refusing to unload containers,[16] for example. When there are attempts at modifying these rules, strikes are common: Some Japanese and European ports are plagued with recurring work stoppages.

Warehousing Space

Finally, it is critical to understand the amount of warehouse storage space that exists in the port. In most instances, it is necessary for merchandise to be placed in some storage areas that are protected from the elements (specifically rain and sun). If these

TABLE 3-1	Typical Entries in *Ports of the World Booklet*

Piraeus, Greece

Facilities

Transportation Services	Truck, Rail, and Barge
Cargo Storage	Covered: 245,000 m^2
	Open: 1.6 million m^2
	Refrigerated: adequate
Special Cranes	Heavy lift: 130 tons
	Container: 2 with 40-ton capacity
Air Cargo	Hellinikon Airport: 14 kilometers

Cargo Handling

Containerized, bulk, and general cargo can be handled by existing port equipment. 2 RO/RO and 7 tanker terminal berths are available. Specialized handling is also provided for ore and bulk commodities.

General

Winters are mild (3°C to 4°C average) with summers hot (42°C) and relatively dry (40 cm annual rainfall). Container facilities are being expanded. Plans include the development of an open area of 320,000 m^2 for the Ikonion Container facility.

Takoradi, Ghana

Facilities

Transportation Services	Truck and Rail
Cargo Storage	Covered: storage adequate; transit shed accommodate 12,500 tons of general cargo.
	Open: 5,000 tons capacity
Special Cranes	Heavy lift capacity is 17.5 tons
Air Cargo	Accra Airport: 260 kilometers

Cargo Handling

Normal cargo can be handled through Takoradi. This port also has bulk, tanker, and RO/RO berths for specialized cargo handling.

General

Average rainfall is approximately 70 cm, with heaviest accumulations from April through August. Temperatures range from 16°C to 30°C. Fixed shore facilities are to be upgraded and new equipment provided.

storage areas are not available or are overcrowded, then it's likely that cargo will be left exposed, leading to possible damages. Cigna's *Ports of the World* lists the amount of covered storage space available in every port (see Table 3-1).

Even if the cargo can tolerate being left exposed to the elements, another concern is the possibility of flooding in the container—or cargo—staging area. It is not unusual, when bad weather strikes, to see a port's container yard flooded, and the containers at the bottom of a stack partially immersed, even in a modern port. During the Katrina hurricane of September 2005, hundreds of containers were submerged by the water surge in the port of New Orleans (see Figure 3-3). For shippers involved with refrigerated cargo, those issues are compounded with the need for reliable power supply, as well as proper reefer storage areas, equipped with power outlets and personnel competent enough to monitor the temperature charts of the refrigerated containers.

Connections with Land-Based Transportation Services

Yet another issue in ports are their connections to the remainder of the country's transport infrastructure, such as rail and road access. In some cases, there is so much congestion in the access roads to port terminals that cargo can be delayed substantially. This is a major issue in just about every port in the world, but particularly in North and South America and in China. Most ports are obviously located near the ocean, and the cities that developed around these ports are located between the port and the hinterlands, where the cargo eventually has to go. Therefore, every piece of

Figure 3-3
Containers Damaged by Hurricane Katrina in the Port of New Orleans (2005)
Source: Photo © Illinois.com. Used with permission.

cargo that is shipped through the port has to travel through the city, which creates a serious strain on road and railroad infrastructures to the port and engenders serious traffic jams and the resentment of the local population. Ports are actively looking at overcoming these bottlenecks.[17]

The Ports of Los Angeles and Long Beach inaugurated in 2002 the Alameda Corridor, a north-south, twenty-mile rail link between the ports and the transcontinental rail yards on the eastern edge of the city of Los Angeles (see Figure 3-4). The Corridor is a thirty-three-feet deep trench that cuts through the city's neighborhoods and is uninterrupted by road traffic.[18]

Port Capacity

Yet another issue in ocean transportation is the strained capacity of ports, as many ports are operating at capacity or very near their capacity. Because ports tend to be physically located between an ocean and a city, there are limits in the ways that they can expand as their traffic increases. Many ports add capacity by gaining on the sea with landfills or by purchasing real estate that is then transformed into port terminals, both of which tend to be quite costly. For example, the port of Santos in Brazil is located on a "river" that stretches between an island and the main land. The older port is located on the island, and it cannot expand because it is constrained by the city of Santos on one side and the river on the other side, on which it cannot gain because the river cannot be made narrower. All of the port expansion has been on the other side of the river, but, there again, it is limited by the river and suburbs that are growing along with the city.

In the United States, there is, for example, an increasing need for additional capacity in container terminals on the Pacific Coast, but it is highly unlikely that much capacity can be added economically. However, the greatest need is probably in Liquefied Natural Gas (LNG) terminals; in 2004, the United States imported only 2 percent of its needs in natural gas using a total of five terminals.[19] Several could be built in the northeast of the country or in California, but the coastal areas are heavily urbanized and popular opposition is substantial. Although they are much more

Figure 3-4
The Alameda Corridor between the Port of Long Beach and East Los Angeles

expensive, off-shore terminals may be the only alternatives to increase the United States' capacity to import LNG.[20]

3-2b Canals and Waterways Infrastructure

Maritime transportation is also quite dependent on the existence and proper maintenance of canals and other maritime channels. Their size, as well as the size of their locks, has a great influence on international trade. For example, ships sized to get through the Suez Canal are called Suez-Max ships, and those sized to get through the Panama Canal are called Panamax ships. The current trend in shipbuilding is to create ships that are much too large to fit through the Panama Canal: These vessels are called post-Panamax ships.

From an international logistics standpoint, several waterways are fundamentally and strategically important. However, these waterways have lost their monopoly, as alternatives were developed to circumvent their shortcomings.

- **The Bosporus Strait in Turkey:** Joining the Black Sea to the Mediterranean Sea, it is the only water link between the Black Sea and the oceans. A large percentage of the merchandise trade between Russia and the rest of the world transits through it, creating severe congestion and raising safety concerns for the city of Istanbul, which is built on both sides of the Strait. Several efforts have been made to convert some of that traffic to a network of pipelines.[21]

- **The Suez Canal:** It allows ships to avoid traveling around the entire continent of Africa when they are going from the Persian Gulf to Europe. When it was closed after the Six-Day War in 1967, oil companies started to build much larger oil tankers, to make the voyage around the Cape (South Africa) more cost-effective. Since its reopening in 1975, the Canal has recaptured some of the traffic it had lost, through a widening and deepening effort. However, the Canal is still too

The Panama Canal

The Panama Canal was started in 1882 under the leadership of Ferdinand de Lesseps, the Frenchman who built the Suez Canal. After many setbacks, the French abandoned the project and the Canal was finally dug by the United States under the leadership of President Teddy Roosevelt: It opened in 1914. On December 31, 1999, after almost a century of United States' management, the Canal's ownership was turned over to the Panamanian government.

The Canal was a massive undertaking, necessitating construction of a dam, which created the largest artificial lake in the world at the time (Gatun Lake) and provided water to six enormous locks (see Figure 3-5) that raise or lower ships eighty-five feet (26 m). The Canal is at least 300 feet wide (91 m), and allows ships with forty feet (12 m) of draft.

Transit times are approximately one day, as ships move slowly from one ocean to the other. The ships never negotiate the locks under their own power; they are handled by electric locomotives, called "mules."

In the years before the handover to Panama, the Canal started a massive plan of renovation and expansion. It scrapped most of the mechanical devices that opened and closed the locks and replaced them with hydraulic systems and adapted a computerized traffic management system. It expanded its watershed to increase its capacity. As ships move through the Canal, the locks that they traverse use an inordinate amount of fresh water. The Canal is currently using its reserve of fresh water to its maximum capacity. A widening and deepening project is expected to be undertaken, in order to increase the Canal's throughput. This expansion, including a new retaining lake and wider, longer locks, are in the works, and they are expected to boost the Canal's capacity by 40 percent by allowing ships as large as 10,500 TEUs—twenty-foot equivalent units.[22]

In 2005, the Canal handled upwards of 12,500 transits a year, representing almost 200 million tons of cargo, and the Panama Canal Authority collected U.S. $846 million in tolls.[23]

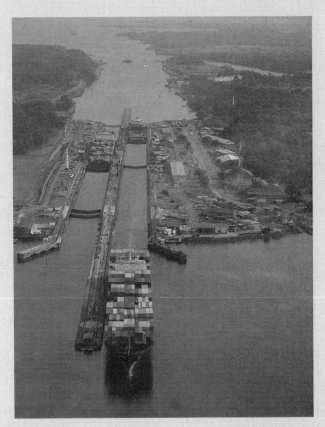

Figure 3-5
The Panama Canal: the Gatun Locks on the Atlantic Side
Source: Photo © Thorwald Westmaas, www.ilisa.com. Used with permission.

shallow for many ships, and its tolls are prohibitive. The cost of a round trip through the Canal can reach U.S. $500,000.[24]

- **The Panama Canal:** It allows ships to avoid traveling around South America. However, the Canal is remarkably "slow," because ships can only travel in one direction at a time, and it is essentially running at its maximum capacity. Wait times to enter the Canal average twenty-two hours.[25] However, despite the emergence of land bridges (see Section 3-2d) in the United States, and the emergence of post-Panamax ships, the Canal still retains its commercial importance and its tolls are competitive, averaging U.S. $67,000.

- **The Saint Lawrence Seaway:** It links the Great Lakes to the St. Lawrence River and the Atlantic Ocean. Unfortunately, the Seaway is narrow and few ships can pass through its locks. It is also plagued by ice, and the Welland Canal—which links Lake Erie to Lake Ontario and bypasses the Niagara Falls—closes from January to March. This has forced companies to find alternative means of transportation, and the traffic through the Seaway is down 45 percent from what it was twenty years ago.[26]

The absence of certain waterways is also detrimental to international trade and the efficient movement of goods. For example, there had been considerable talk about a canal through Nicaragua that would be "parallel" to the Panama Canal and be free of locks, an advantage that would speed up the transit time considerably.[27] A railroad "land bridge" was also once proposed for the same region. However, both of these projects have been abandoned, and the Panama Canal is, for the foreseeable future, the only water connection between the Atlantic and the Pacific. A canal through the Isthmus of Kra in Thailand—the Malay Peninsula—which would bypass the Strait of Malacca and the Port of Singapore would speed up the transit time between Europe and the Far East as well. This project has been in the planning stages on and off in the past decade within the Thai government and there is increased interest on the part of Malaysia, Indonesia, and China.[28] No decision had been made by summer 2006.

The same lack of infrastructure is found in freshwater passages. After the War in the Balkans, there was a period during which there was no freshwater communication between the Black Sea and Northern Europe, as many bridges were demolished on the Danube River[29] and barges could not pass. There is still no freshwater communication between the Mediterranean Sea and Northern Europe, as the construction of a canal between the Rhône River and the Rhine River is still being debated;[30] however, the Europakanal, a canal between the Rhine and the Danube, was completed in 1992, and is heavily traveled.

3-2c Airport Infrastructure

Airports are also a fundamental part of the transportation infrastructure. There are fewer critical issues in the management of an international airport than there are in a port, but they can be just as constraining.

Runways

The runways of an airport determine the type of aircraft that they can serve. The lengths of the runways are particularly relevant, as they generally determine whether the airport can support direct flights to faraway places. Many airports in the world cannot accommodate the large jumbo jets that serve international destinations because the runways were designed mostly for smaller aircraft. As the cities around the airports grew, they became landlocked, unable to extend their runways. Several cities have had to build airports far from their city centers, in order to build facilities that can accommodate international flights. Whereas Charles de Gaulle Airport in Paris, France, and Heathrow Airport in London, UK, (both built in the 1970s) are about fifteen miles (twenty-five kilometers) from the cities they serve, the airports built in the 1990s are much further away: Denver International is twenty-three miles (thirty-seven kilometers) from the city and Malpensa in Milan, Italy, is thirty miles (forty-eight kilometers) away.[31]

A second concern is the number of runways, which determines the capacity of the airport. Most airports have more than one runway, but the busiest airport—in number of passengers—in the world has four runways (Hatfield Airport in Atlanta, Georgia, USA), and both Chicago O'Hare and Dallas-Fort Worth International have seven. An airport can be quite constrained by its lack of runways; for years, Narita Airport in Tokyo had only one runway to accommodate its traffic. It was stretched to capacity, and there was no way to build a second runway as a number of small farmers refused to sell their land to the airport.[32] Because, by law, the Japanese government cannot expropriate them, the airport cannot build the runway on their land, and travelers and cargo shippers are inconvenienced as the number of flights in and out of Narita is limited, increasing the landing fees. Narita has finished a second runway that avoids the reluctant farmers' land, but it is too short to accommodate

The Legendary Kai Tak

Kai Tak Airport in Hong Kong was one of the most unusual airports in the world. As the airplanes landed, they flew a few hundred feet away from the high rises and the hills that surrounded the airport (see Figure 3-6). It was an uncomfortable experience for many passengers.

In 1998, its replacement, Chek Lap Kok Airport, opened. Dubbed the most expensive construction project in the world at U.S. $20 billion—the Chunnel under the English Channel cost "only" $15 billion—it is an artificial island on the outskirts of the city, with its own dedicated tunnel, its own suspension bridge, its own commuter railroad,[33] and the largest cargo facility in the world.[34] It operates twenty-four hours a day, a boon for cargo shippers involved in the South-East Asian market, because Kai Tak closed at night.

In addition to the challenges of building such a large infrastructure, the "transfer" from one airport to the other was attempted in one night. As Kai Tak closed at midnight on July 5, 1998, all of its equipment was moved to Chek Lap Kok with 10,000 vehicle trips, seventy barge voyages, and thirty flights, and the new airport opened on July 6, at 6:30 A.M.[35] Unfortunately, it did not happen as smoothly as expected, and the first couple of weeks were hectic, especially for cargo.[36]

Nevertheless, the new airport has become the busiest international cargo airport in the world, handling 3.4 million tons in 2004, an increase of almost 10 percent per year since its first full year of operation in 1999.[37]

Figure 3-6
The Approach at Kai Tak Airport in Hong Kong
Source: Photo: © Daryl Chapman. Courtesy of www.airliners.net. Used with permission.

jumbo jets, which constitute 90 percent of the Narita traffic, so it is only used for local traffic.

A single runway also increases the probability of delays as the slightest accident or malfunction will immobilize the entire airport.

Hours of Operation

Another concern of importance is the time frame during which airports are operating. Because most airports are geographically close to large cities, their hours of operations are generally limited by noise constraints and they operate only during "day hours." Because cargo tends to fly at night, specialized cargo airports that are located outside of large cities and can operate twenty-four hours a day, seven days a week, have started to emerge such as Prestwick in Scotland, Hahn in Germany, and Chateauroux in France.[38] To some extent, this development mirrors that of the Memphis airport, which has become the largest cargo airport in the world, with 3.6 million tons of freight in [39] even though it is not located near a large metropolitan center.

Warehousing Space

Another concern of importance for cargo shippers is the existence of appropriate warehouse space at an airport; cargo should be protected while it is in transit, and not left to the elements. This is particularly important as air cargo tends to be—erroneously—not as well packaged as cargo destined for ocean shipping.

The problem is even more acute for refrigerated warehouse space, which can be in very short supply.

3-2d Rail Infrastructure

Another element of the transportation infrastructure of a country is its railroad network. In the eighteenth and early nineteenth centuries, railroads became the most important means of long-distance land transportation. In Europe, the United States, India, Africa, and Asia, a dense network of railroads was built, sometimes under the impetus of colonizing forces who wanted to be able to move troops quickly. This historical development led to some decisions that, a century and a half later, are causing significant problems. To prevent possible invaders from using their railroad infrastructures, Spain, Brazil, and Russia developed railroad gauges (the width between the rails) that were incompatible with the rest of Europe. While it did prevent military troops from using the network, this decision is still causing trouble for any type of rail transportation between these countries and their neighbors. For example, most trains stop at the French-Spanish border so that cargo can be shifted to railcars that are appropriate for the gauge used in the other country; others—including passenger trains—slow down to a crawl while specially designed axles expand or contract.[40] For Brazil, the cost of the rolling stock is substantially higher as every car and locomotive must be adapted to its unusual gauge size, whether they are purchased new or used, and trains have to travel slower because the cars are much wider than what the rail was designed to handle and therefore are less stable.

Most countries have updated their railroad infrastructure as their economies grew. However, in a few countries, the economy has grown much faster and the infrastructure has not been able to keep pace. Such is the case in China, where demand far outstrips supply in terms of rail transportation. China's network satisfies only 60 percent of current demand.[41] The Chinese government has pledged to develop further links that will be vital to connect the port cities of the southeast to inland cities.[42] Such rail links are critical when the road infrastructure is not yet fully developed.

Over the years, though, as roads and trucks improved, many countries' railroads gradually lost their focus on shipping merchandise and shifted their efforts to high-speed passenger transportation; such is the case of Europe, where most merchandise is shipped by means other than railroad, but where intercity rail passenger transportation is commonplace, convenient, fast, and competes with airlines over small distances. The best examples are the French (now European) *Trains à Grande Vitesse* (TGV), which connect Paris to London in three hours

Figure 3-7
The Only "Merchandise" High-Speed Train, Used by the French Postal Service
Source: Photo © Peter Schokkenbroek. Used with permission.

(dubbed the Eurostar) and Paris to Brussels in an hour and a half (the Thalys). There is only one TGV dedicated to merchandise transport, and it is used by the French Postal Service ("La Poste") exclusively for mail transportation (see Figure 3-7). A similar switch from merchandise to high-speed passenger transport occurred in Japan; the Shinkansen train covers the 192 kilometers (120 miles) between Hiroshima and Kokura in less than forty-five minutes, for example. These high-speed trains run on dedicated tracks that are separate from the remainder of the slower rail infrastructure.

Multi-Modal Emphasis

In the last two decades, three factors have contributed to the renewal of merchandise traffic on railroads: The congestion of roads has worsened, concerns about pollution and noise have increased, and the creation of the multi-modal container has eliminated the need to load and unload merchandise from the traditional boxcars.

In the United States, railroads have invested heavily in the modernization of their rolling stocks; they have shifted from boxcars to piggy-back cars—allowing them to carry truck trailers—and to container cars. At the same time, they have improved their infrastructure by increasing the height clearances in tunnels and other areas, allowing trains to transport containers "double-stacked" (i.e., twice as many containers as a single-stack train would). Figures 13-8 and 13-9 illustrate these concepts. American trains tend to be exceedingly long, with at least 100 cars, allowing a crew of a few individuals to move in excess of 200 containers or truck trailers, making them particularly cost-effective. In addition, because passenger rail transport is almost nonexistent in the United States—with the minor exception of the northeastern part of the country—cargo trains have priority on the network and tend to be relatively fast.

Unfortunately, such improvements have not yet been made to the European infrastructure, which still consists mostly of aging boxcars.[43] Moreover, the emphasis on passenger transportation gives priority to passenger trains, and relegates cargo trains to second-class status, making them slow and inefficient cargo movers. Attempts to create high-speed cargo railroad links from ports in Northern Europe to ports in the Mediterranean have been made,[44] but politics and administrative delays are unlikely to make this corridor a reality for some years.[45]

In the same fashion, the success of North American railroads has enticed several developments in Asia. There are plans to significantly modernize the trans-Siberian railroad, which would allow cargo to be shipped from Asia (Vladivostok) to Europe by rail.[46] There are also plans to create a Trans-Asian railroad, which would connect Singapore and Seoul to Europe via Turkey.[47] However, the obstacles that remain to such a venture are substantial, and its completion is far from certain.

Land Bridges

A consequence of the increased efficiency of the railroads in the United States has been the creation of **land bridges**. The concept of a land bridge is based on the idea that containerized ocean cargo needs to "cross" some landmass; for example, cargo from South-East Asia needs to cross North America on its way to Europe. One alternative is to take the Panama Canal; however, it is a fairly long voyage south in the Pacific to reach Balboa, and a fairly long voyage north in the Atlantic onto Europe. Another alternative is to take the cargo around India and through the Suez Canal, which is inconvenient and expensive.

The best alternative is to cross North America on a land bridge; the cargo is unloaded from a large containership somewhere on the West Coast of the United States or Canada, and shipped by double-stack train to the East Coast. The journey is faster and cheaper than by ocean. In addition, it allows shipping lines to use post-Panamax ships on their trans-Pacific and trans-Atlantic routes, which is also more efficient. A consequence of this trend is that cargo going from Taipei to Barcelona is going to transit through Chicago. Such variations from the traditional itinerary of Taipei-Panama-Barcelona are said to be "transparent" to the shipper, which means that it is unaware of them. However, such a transparent voyage may expose the shipment to lower temperatures than those the shipper expected and a shipment may not be protected adequately enough for the extremes in temperature.

land bridge A term coined to describe the practice of shipping goods from Asia to Europe through the United States by using railroads.

3-2e Road Infrastructure

In addition to the infrastructure of ports, airports, and railroads, a great amount of shipping moves by road, especially on the last "leg" of the journey, from the port, airport, or rail terminal to its final destination.

The road infrastructure of a country is evaluated somewhat differently than the rest of its transportation infrastructure. In no country is there a shortage of roads, for example; however, there certainly are issues regarding the quality and maintenance of the network, its congestion, as well as the existence of high-speed links between major metropolitan areas. The concern therefore is not one of density, but one of usability.

Quality

The road infrastructure of a country is generally described in documents such as the U.S. Department of Commerce's *Country Commercial Guides*[48] or the CIA's *World Factbook*[49] in terms of total miles of road, and of the percentage of these roads that are paved. For example, the country of Argentina is listed as having 215,000 kilometers (134,000 miles) of roads, of which 63,500 kilometers (39,500 miles)—29.5 percent—are paved. Even in the United States, paved roads only represent 90 percent of the road infrastructure.[50]

However, this is somewhat misleading, as most of the traffic obviously utilizes paved roads, and the unpaved roads serve remote rural areas. In addition, the condition of a paved road makes a substantial difference in its usefulness; an over-crowded, two-lane highway riddled with potholes is not very conducive to the safe transportation of cargo. Such is the case with the roads in the countries of Belarus, Albania, Romania, Lithuania, and Latvia. The government of Poland estimates that 80 percent of its roads are in unsatisfactory or bad conditions;[51] cargo shipped under such conditions has to be particularly well packaged. Unfortunately, there is no statistical source that indicates the condition of the roads in a country, and because

Figure 3-8
Traffic Congestion in Lagos, Nigeria
Source: Photo © Onyisi Agalim, www.Galbe.com. Used with permission.

there are substantial variations from one region of a country to another, it is even more difficult to evaluate. China has a very good road infrastructure between Guangzhou and Shanghai, for example, but the interior of the country is plagued with deficient and outdated roads.[52]

Congestion of the road infrastructure is also endemic to certain cities: There are too many cars, trucks, and other vehicles on the road, and deliveries are difficult to make (see Figure 3-8). In Calcutta, India, the traffic is so congested that the average speed in the city is five mph (eight km/h); most people travel by rickshaw or by public transportation rather than by car.[53] In Delhi, the government has created a category of vehicles, called VVIP—Very Very Important Persons—that are allowed to zip through traffic with blaring sirens and flashing lights.[54] In many developed countries' cities, a system of alternating days for traffic has been instituted; vehicles with odd-numbered license plates are only allowed to travel on odd-numbered days, and vehicles with even-numbered license plates can only travel on even-numbered days. Such is the case in Lagos, Nigeria, for example. The problem is compounded by the fact that resourceful Nigerians obtain two license plates for every vehicle from corrupt civil authorities, and change the plates every morning.

Although congestion is a problem that is extreme in developing countries, it is certainly also present in large metropolitan areas in Europe, Japan, and the United States. As the number of automobiles increases, the situation will worsen further and make deliveries to customers more problematic and inefficient. Many delivery firms are now using motorcycles and mopeds, which are more maneuverable in large cities. London enacted a very effective tax system to prevent vehicles from entering the heart of the city; vehicles' license plates are monitored and recorded through a closed-circuit television system and commuters are charged £8.00 for each day they travel into the city. Residents receive a 90 percent discount of this daily rate. Traffic in the city has decreased approximately 15 percent since this measure was enacted, and congestion is said to have decreased 30 percent, although it is not known how the city of London measures congestion.[55]

Yet another issue in cities is the confusion that can be generated by the lack of signage and a different addressing system. While most Northern American cities have a "grid" of east-west and north-south streets, with a fairly logical numbering sequence of streets and buildings, European cities are plagued with a maze of different streets that change names at each—or so it seems—intersection. Mexico City has an extraordinarily confusing system of streets; there are nearly 800 streets named after Benito Juárez, 760 named for Miguel Hidalgo, and 300 streets renamed every year. To make things more interesting, 80,000 city blocks have no signage at all.[56] Japan has the tradition of numbering buildings on a street in the order in which they were built, and not in a sequential order based on location. Most of Bombay's addresses are not based on street names, but defined by a succession of smaller and smaller areas: A person's address will include the name of the house, the name of the street, the name of the block, the name of the city, and the city code. In addition, there will be an east or a west, depending of which side of the railroad track the block is, with parallel structures on either side. Such systems make it challenging to deliver goods to a new customer. The worst situation from this perspective is on the island of Saipan in the Northern Mariana Islands, with a population of 70,000, which still has no address system at all.[57]

To decrease the congestion in cities, countries have built a network of high-speed links that avoid smaller cities while connecting the larger ones. These limited access highways speed up considerably the transportation of goods between cities. Nevertheless, these highways are subject to a number of rules and regulations, some of which limit the size of the trucks that can travel on them and the speed at which they can travel. Because these rules vary from country to country, it can be a challenge to arrange international truck transportation of merchandise. In addition, in many countries, access to high-speed highways is limited to vehicles that pay a toll, making such roads an expensive alternative. In France, for example, the private company running the high-speed highway system charges approximately €0.20 per kilometer (€0.32 per mile) for semi-trucks.

Civil Engineering Structures (*Ouvrages d'Art*)

If the country is mountainous, these high-speed thoroughfares are built with numerous bridges and tunnels designed to "eliminate" the constraints of the landscape. A perfect example of such a highway is the Italian Autostrade, which runs along the Appennine Chain and is seemingly an unending succession of tunnels and bridges. Such engineering structures are called collectively (in French) *ouvrages d'art*—art structures—and it is an apt moniker; unfortunately, there is no equivalent in English, so the French term will be used.

The dependence of international trade on such *ouvrages d'art* cannot be underestimated: Most natural borders are either water (oceans or lakes) or mountains at the watershed separation. To cross these natural borders, bridges or tunnels have to be built. The Chunnel—the tunnel built under the English Channel, between France and Great Britain—is a case in point. Until its opening in 1994, shipping goods from one country to the other was delayed by a fairly lengthy ferry voyage, which sometimes could be delayed or cancelled due to bad weather. The Chunnel has substantially shortened shipping times between the two countries, although it is quite expensive.

Another international route that has been radically changed by *ouvrages d'art* is the trade between Western Europe and the Middle East, with the opening of the two suspension bridges in Istanbul, one in 1973 (Boğaziçi Bridge), the other in 1988 (Fatih Sultan Mehmet Bridge). These are the only two bridges that allow road transportation between Europe and Asia, save for an itinerary north of the Black Sea, through Bulgaria, Romania, the Ukraine and Russia. To date, there is no rail link from Southern Europe to Asia, as the Orient Express ends on the European side of Istanbul, and the Baghdad Railway starts on the Asian side. No rail link is available between the two stations, and passengers and cargo cross the Bosporus on the bridges or by using ferries.

The so-called Øresund Fixed Link between Copenhagen, Denmark, and Malmö, Sweden, is another example of an *ouvrage d'art* that has significantly altered the transportation landscape of an international border: It actually is a succession of three

Figure 3-9
The Millau Bridge

bridges and a tunnel, with a switchover on an artificial island in the middle of Flinte Channel It is the first terrestrial communication between the two countries, and it replaces a forty-five minute ferry ride with an eight-minute drive. More importantly, it is the first land link between Western Europe and the Scandinavian countries.[58]

The Millau Bridge in southern France opened in 2004 and is another highway bridge that significantly reduces transportation times (see Figure 3-9). It links two high plateaus that are bisected by a deep river gorge, for which the only crossing was in the middle of the small town of Millau. Before the construction of the bridge, vehicles had to travel down approximately 300 meters (1,000 feet) through a series of hairpin turns to the city, across the river, and then climb up the same distance on the other plateau. The town was infamous for its traffic jam, and it was not unusual to spend two hours to go from one plateau to the other. With the bridge, it takes less than one minute. The bridge is 345 meters above the river (1,150 feet), about twenty meters higher than the Eiffel Tower, and was built in a little over three years.[59]

Some bridges are much less architecturally noticeable but no less important to the economies of the countries they link. For example, the United States and Canada, for a significant portion of their common border, are only "connected" by a bridge and a tunnel in Detroit, Michigan (to Windsor, Ontario), and a few bridges near Buffalo, New York. At least one of those bridges, the Peace Bridge between Buffalo and Fort Erie, Ontario, is used at its maximum capacity and has not been expanded since 1927.[60]

Another example of the critical nature of bridges and other structures can be seen in the tiny island nation of Palau, where a bridge collapse between the capital city of Koror and the main island of Babelthuap created an economic nightmare. People on the main island used to commute to the capital via the bridge, which has been inadequately replaced with ferry services.[61] Only its reconstruction will allow the country's economy to recover. The building of a bridge can also alter the character of a region; for example, Prince Edward Island is now connected to the rest of Canada by a newly built bridge, and its residents are divided on its impact on their life and economy.[62]

Moreover, it is not just in developing countries that the failure of such infrastructures can be catastrophic: All *ouvrages d'art* are vulnerable. In March 1999, a deadly fire occurred in the Mont-Blanc tunnel between France and Italy, under the Alps; the tunnel was closed until April 2002. This forced trucks to use the Fréjus tunnel, the only other tunnel under the Alps between France and Italy, or to make a substantial detour along the Mediterranean coast, neither option being a good alternative. A fire in the Saint Gothard tunnel—the second longest road tunnel in the world, between Switzerland and Italy—forced its closure in October 2001; while the tunnel was reopened in December 2001, it was limited to half of its traffic capacity until April 2002, as traffic was only allowed in one direction at a time.

3-2f Warehousing Infrastructure

It is evident that transportation is dependent on an infrastructure that allows the movement of goods. However, it is equally important to realize that cargo is often stationary when it "waits" for the next transportation alternative to be available. Therefore, it is important for a shipper to obtain information about the warehousing infrastructure of the locations where a shipment will be in layover.

The issues revolving around the warehousing infrastructure concern the protection of the goods when they are waiting while in transit. Will they be protected from the rain? From the sun? From possible floods? From (unusual) cold? A savvy international logistics manager will attempt to determine the conditions under which the goods will be kept, and will then determine whether they are correctly packaged, or whether they need to be shipped through a different itinerary. The Cigna Insurance Company's *Ports of the World* booklet[63] (see Table 3-1) lists the warehouse space available in each port.

In many cases as well, shippers will use public warehouses for storage purposes, in order to deliver goods to their customers without having to resort to an international shipment. This enables the company to provide much better customer service by delivering goods with a much shorter lead time.

Unfortunately, the warehousing infrastructure of a country is difficult to evaluate, as there are no general sources of information on the availability and quality of public warehouses. Therefore, in those cases where a company is considering using a public warehouse to serve its customers, it would be best to plan an actual visit to the location considered, as the standards used in public warehousing management may be quite different than the ones expected.

3-3 Communication Infrastructure

In addition to the transportation infrastructure, the communication infrastructure is also of substantial importance to international logistics. The ability to communicate with customers and suppliers, either by mail, by phone, or through other electronic media, is very important to the smooth operation of an international transaction. Unfortunately, there are different expectations of service and performance in communication means from country to country.

3-3a Mail Services

The ability of the postal services to deliver mail on time and reliably should be a given in most developed countries. However, there is ample anecdotal evidence that it is not the case in all places. On many occasions, there are unacceptable delays and errors: While the European Union countries strive to deliver letters sent to a national address on the day after it is mailed—a so-called *D+1* policy—and on the second day if it is international mail within the European community, this is a difficult standard to achieve. Italy, especially before its national postal service was privatized, was notoriously unreliable. France has periodic strikes of its mail service and of its national railway service, both of which can substantially delay the delivery of mail. In South Africa, the mail service has become so unreliable that businesses and individuals no longer trust it enough to send payments, forcing them to make payments in person or through banks.[64]

Another issue is the safety of the mail: Will a letter or package make it to its destination, or will it be lost, damaged, or stolen in transit? Because postal services tend to be very large employers, it is difficult to screen all employees effectively. There have been countless documented instances of postal employees stealing the contents of parcels, removing the contents of letters—especially cash, checks, and credit cards—before they reach their destination. Developing countries have an even greater problem, as public employee wages tend to be modest, and the temptations are many.

Many firms intent on ensuring that their postal communications are safely delivered have switched, especially for international documents' exchanges, to private services such as DHL or FedEx. While the costs of private services tend to be much higher than the costs of the traditional postal services, these companies have gained much market share, thanks to their reputation for greater reliability. In particular, the customers' ability to track packages and documents online has increased this perception.

Another phenomenon is the exploitation (arbitrage) of the differences in prices and mail categories for international mail from one country to another. A direct marketer sending a substantial number of identical mail pieces internationally will determine in which country that particular mailing is going to cost the least amount; it will then ship the mailing materials in bulk to a company operating a remailing service in that country. The remailer will then place the individual items in the mail and so the overall mailing costs to the marketer will be lower. Commercial materials emanating from France have come to the author from Denmark, Great Britain, and the Netherlands; the lowest cost provider was probably determined by the fact that the weight of the materials being sent placed them in different price categories in different countries.

3-3b Telecommunications Services

Slightly different issues are facing telecommunication services; not only has the demand for voice telecommunication increased about 10 percent a year, but the demand for data telecommunication has essentially doubled every year for the past ten years, and shown no sign of slowing down. Some countries have been able to build a sufficiently large domestic infrastructure to carry this increased load, often by using their already existing infrastructure. Many gas and oil pipelines have been given the added responsibility of transmitting data through a fiber-optic line laid in their midst.[65] Many countries, though, have not been able to keep up with such growth, and telecommunications in those countries are slow and not very reliable: In 2001, Ghana, for example, had only 249,000 phone lines for 20,000,000 inhabitants, or one line for every eighty persons.[66]

This reliability is the primary concern in several countries where the economy has grown quickly; the domestic communication infrastructure did not follow. Phone service is notoriously unreliable, with phone conversations disconnected, phone calls regularly connected to wrong numbers, and dial tones all but absent.[67] Fortunately, in some of those countries, a phenomenon known as **leap frogging** has taken place. Because the "old" land-based telephone infrastructure is not working properly, people have switched to cellular phones very quickly and bypassed the land-based system. This switch is facilitated by the fact that many countries quickly adopted a single operating standard, which makes for easy portability and for increased convenience. Such is the case in places like the Czech Republic, where cellular phones now have a greater penetration rate than land-based telephones. In China, there are almost half as many cellular phones as there are land-based phones, and the rate of growth in cellular phones far surpasses that

leap frogging The idea that some countries will "skip" a particular technology to adopt the most recent one available.

Iridium

The Iridium project was the first attempt by a single company to put together a worldwide communication infrastructure. The idea was to make mobile telephone service available everywhere, even in areas where it is not cost-effective to build a cellular network, by using a total of sixty-six satellites through which all calls would be transmitted. The target market was composed of persons whose jobs took them to remote areas of the world, but who needed to be in touch with the rest of the world at any time.[72]

While Iridium's technical problems were extremely difficult to overcome, including an inability to use the service while in a building or an automobile, what ultimately prompted the demise of the entire project was its inability to secure enough customers in its first stages. To be profitable, the service needed 500,000 to 600,000 customers,[73] but despite over a million inquiries, very few of these turned into actual sales, as Iridium's sales partners were ill-equipped to follow up on those requests.[74] In addition, the cost of the service was very steep, around U.S. $3,000 for the phone and U.S. $7.00 per minute, which also discouraged some potential users. At its peak, Iridium had only 55,000 customers.[75] These were not sufficient to bear the cost of the entire infrastructure, and the firm declared bankruptcy in 2000. Its last act was to send all of its satellites tumbling toward the earth, where they burned up upon re-entry in the atmosphere.

of the traditional technology. Countries such as the United States, which have a strong land-based infrastructure, have been slower at switching to cellular phone usage. As of 2005, the United States was forty-first in the world when ranked by the percentage of its population that owned a cellular telephone. Although this ranking was due to the fact that the land-based infrastructure is very good (and people have less of an incentive to switch), it was also due to the fact that there are four different operating technologies competing for cellular phone customers, and therefore that there are four times as many towers to be built (and paid), making cellular phone service particularly expensive.

On the international side, telecommunications are heavily dependent on a network of underwater cables that run across the Atlantic, the Pacific, the Mediterranean Sea, or other large bodies of water. As telecommunication traffic has increased, the capacity of these cables has also increased dramatically. Altogether, though, there are still very few cables (only seven cross the Northern Atlantic), and their vulnerability is extraordinary. Although they are buried on the portion of their route that is located in shallow water, they are for the most part simply laid on the floor of the oceans, at the risk of being snagged by fishermen's nets and boat anchors.[68] When these cables cross land, they are just as vulnerable and at the mercy of a careless backhoe operator or other accident.[69] Whenever they are snagged or damaged, traffic on that cable seizes until it is repaired. In an outstanding article in *Wired* Magazine, Neal Stephenson followed the construction of the FLAG—Fiber-optic Link Around the Globe—and reported on the vulnerability of this network: For example, five of the major worldwide cables are routed through a single building in Alexandria, Egypt.[70]

Satellite telecommunications are no less dependent on a limited number of alternatives and therefore just as vulnerable; because satellites are increasingly heavily used for communications such as television programs, their capacity is entirely used, and the failure of a single satellite can wreak havoc on telecommunications. Such was the case when PanAmSat's Galaxy V failed in May 1998.[71]

Other telecommunication infrastructures are vulnerable; the Internet, although touted as "robust," is still very dependent on so-called "root-servers" that keep the list of addresses on the Internet. In the summer of 1997, Root Server A, located in Hernston, Virginia, the mother of all root-servers, "lost" its master list. Internet traffic was disrupted worldwide for several hours.

3-4 Utilities Infrastructure

Another area of concern for the manager involved in international logistics is the utilities infrastructure. While it is generally taken for granted that all utilities—electricity, water, sewage, gas—are available in most countries, experience shows that there is often a shortage of one or more of these commodities in many countries, including developed countries. And while utilities are not directly an issue in transportation, they can become critically important when a company is considering operating a warehouse or establishing a corporate office.

3-4a Electricity

The most common problem with utilities is the availability and reliability of electrical power. It is common in countries where the rate of economic growth outpaces the rate of growth in electricity production to have blackouts for part of the day. Actually, the situation is endemic in sub-Sahara Africa, where there are scheduled blackouts because the production of electricity is much lower than the demand for it; households and businesses therefore plan their days around the availability of electricity.[76] India and China are also affected by recurring blackouts,[77] and so is Saudi Arabia.[78] However, this is not a phenomenon that is limited to developing countries; the availability of electricity is sometimes also disrupted in developed countries. Such was the case in California in the summer of 2001, during which there were substantial supply and demand imbalances and numerous shortages. However, recent evidence has shown that, even though there were infrastructural shortages at the root of the problem, the speculative behavior of the Enron Corporation was mostly responsible for the wild price fluctuations that Californians experienced.

On the other hand, some countries have abundant electrical resources: Brazil and Paraguay share the Itaipu Dam (see Figure 3-10), which provides 82 percent of Paraguay's electrical needs and 26 percent of Brazil's. Nevertheless, for those areas of Brazil that are geographically far from Itaipu, there are still shortages and temporary blackouts.

In addition to problems of production, the utilities are sometimes the victims of theft; households and businesses bypass their meters or tap directly in the grid without the "inconvenience" of a meter, preventing utilities from collecting enough income to be able to invest in additional capacity. A World Bank loan to India to

Figure 3-10
The Itaipu Dam

build additional power plants was actually made conditional on the utility getting paid for a greater percentage of its production.[79] In Russia, an endemic problem is the theft of the electrical wires for scrap, a "business" that killed 500 thieves in 1999 and forced the Russian government to replace 15,000 miles of high-tension wires,[80] without mention of the disruptions to businesses and individuals

3-4b Water and Sewer

Water supply is also a concern in many countries in the world, leading to interruptions, rationing, and recurring water shortages.[81] It is not uncommon for cities to ration water in the middle of a drought period, on some occasions reducing the availability of water to a few hours a day or a few days a week.[82] As populations in cities increase, the infrastructure delivering water to the cities is often overtaxed, which can lead to potentially catastrophic problems, especially in cities with aging infrastructures. For example, New York City gets most of its water from reservoirs 125 miles away, and it is delivered by two tunnels that were built in 1917 and 1937. Neither of these tunnels has ever been shut down for repairs, as the city would not be able to function without the water they deliver.[83] A new water tunnel is currently under construction and is scheduled to start operating in 2020. Many cities have leaky pipes and lose a portion of their supply to those leaks; the city of Manila, in the Philippines, estimates it loses *half* of its water production through leaks and illegal siphoning of the water.[84]

The quality of the water is also a concern: In many cities, the water delivery infrastructure is not well protected, leaving a strong possibility of bacterial contamination, and forcing users to boil the water before they use it. This procedure is a common recommendation given by international travelers. The World Bank estimates that no more than 80 percent of the world population has "reasonable access" to clean water, defined as access to within one kilometer (0.62 miles) of the house.[85]

On the other end, the infrastructure designed to remove used water is also critical. Many countries have inadequate or overburdened sewer treatment facilities, resulting in the pollution of water tables and adjacent bodies of water, or problems with sewer backups at times of heavy rains, for example. While less critical than water availability to the proper operation of a warehouse or distribution center, sewer service is still important as it can be a nuisance to have employees deal with stench or frequent cleanups. The World Bank estimates that less than 60 percent of the world population has access to adequate sanitation.[86]

Similar observations can be made about refuse removal, a service generally provided by the municipalities, but which can be unreliable; strikes of municipal workers can take several days, during which no pickup is conducted, resulting in a problem in the operation of any type of business.

3-4c Energy Pipelines

The infrastructure of access to energy is also of importance. As most of the easily accessible oil and gas fields are near the end of their life expectancies, energy resources now come from remote areas that are difficult to operate and from where it is difficult to ship. Building energy pipelines from those areas is a challenge, and the obstacles include the weather—the Alaskan pipeline—natural barriers, political issues,[87] environmental challenges,[88] and bickering between the oil companies and the governments of the countries in which they were building.[89]

Nevertheless, the infrastructure of pipelines is growing and allows an ever-greater percentage of the energy needs of the world to no longer be transported by ships, trucks, and railroads.

Key Terms

berth (p. 32)

draft (p. 31)

land bridges (p. 42)

leap frogging (p. 47)

Review and Discussion Questions

1. What are the main elements of the maritime transportation infrastructure? How would the quality and dependability of the maritime transportation infrastructure affect an international shipment?

2. What are the main elements of the air transportation infrastructure? How would the quality and dependability of the air transportation infrastructure affect an international shipment?

3. What are the main elements of the land transportation and warehousing infrastructure? How would the quality and dependability of these infrastructures affect an international shipment?

4. What are the main elements of the communication and utilities infrastructure? How would the quality and dependability of these infrastructures affect an international shipment?

Endnotes

1. *American Heritage Dictionary*, Third Edition, 2000, Houghton-Mifflin Company, Boston, Massachusetts.

2. *Oxford English Dictionary*, Second Edition, online, http://www.oed.com.

3. Mongellluzzo, Bill, "Too Much, Too Soon," *The Journal of Commerce*, December 6, 2004, p. 12.

4. Lipton, Eric, "Beneath the Harbor, it's Dig or Else" *The New York Times*, November 23, 2004.

5. Verhovek, Sam Howe, "In the Northwest, a Fight to Deepen a Ship Channel," *The New York Times*, April 1, 2002.

6. Damas, Philip, "Big Ships. Big Problems," *American Shipper*, August 2001, pp. 12–22.

7. Journal of Commerce Staff, "Supercranes Arrive at Global Terminal," *The Journal of Commerce*, November 15, 1999, p. 15.

8. Machalaba, Daniel, "Maersk is Ready to Start on Giant Port," *The Wall Street Journal*, June 5, 2000, p. A4.

9. Porter, Janet, "Cagliari to Woo Med Box Trades," *The Journal of Commerce*, March 17, 1997, p. C1.

10. Tirschwell, Peter M., "Staying Ahead," *The Journal of Commerce*, November 21, 2005, pp. 32–33.

11. Mongelluzzo, Bill, "With Cranes, Size is Everything," *The Journal of Commerce*, December 31, 1996, p. 1B.

12. Bonney, Joseph, "Cranes to Work from Both Sides," *The Journal of Commerce*, August 25, 1999, p. 1.

13. *Ports of the World*, Fifteenth Edition, Cigna Insurance Corporation, available from Publisher, *Ports of the World*, Cigna Insurance Companies, P.O. Box 7716, Philadelphia, Pennsylvania 19192, USA.

14. Mongelluzzo, Bill, "Extending Terminal Hours," *The Journal of Commerce*, March 5, 1997, p. 1B.

15. Machalaba, Daniel, "Treading Water: U.S. Ports Are Losing the Battle to Keep Up with Overseas Trade," *The Wall Street Journal*, July 9, 2001, p. A1.

16. Davies, John, "Slow Passage to Progress," *International Business*, December 1996–January 1997, pp.14–17.

17. Smith, Jeremy N., "Breaking Through Bottlenecks at the Port," *World Trade*, June 2004, pp. 16–20.

18. Mottley, Robert, "Corridor Kicks Off," *American Shipper*, June 2002, pp. 50–54.

19. Romero, Simon, "Fears Drain Support for Natural Gas Terminals," *The New York Times*, May 14, 2004.

20. Fialka, John J., and Russell Gold, "Fears of Terrorism Crush Plans for Liquefied Gas Terminals," *The New York Times*, May 14, 2004.

21. Moore, Molly, "Is the Bosporus Taking On More Than It Can Handle?" *The International Herald Tribune*, November 17, 2000, p. 2.

22. Lyons, John, "Panama Takes Steps Toward Expanding the Canal," *The Wall Street Journal*, April 24, 2006, p. A8.

23. "Panama Canal Traffic—Fiscal Years 2003 Through 2005," Panama Canal Authority, http://www.pancanal.com/eng/maritime/reports/table01.pdf, May 25, 2006.

24. Jehl, Douglas, "Journal: Trying to Revive a Canal that Is Out of the Loop," *The New York Times*, April 30, 1997.

25. Carl, Traci, "Panama Wants a Bigger Canal for Bigger Ships," *The Cleveland Plain Dealer*, March 31, 2002, p. G5.

26. Urquhart, John, "U.S., Canada Try to Revive Once-Grand Waterway," *The Wall Street Journal*, March 12, 1998, p. A14.

27. *The Nicaraguan Canal Proposal*, Case No. 405, The American University, Washington, D.C., USA. http://www.american.edu/ted/NICCANAL.HTM, May 1997.

28. Corben, Ron, "Canal plan to Bypass Singapore is Revived," *The Journal of Commerce*, August 27, 1999, p. 13. Levett, Connie, "Thai Canal Plan to Save Millions," *The Age*, March 29, 2005, http://www.theage.com.au/news/World/Thai-canal-plan-to-save-millions/2005/03/28/1111862317996.html.

29. Kim, Lucian, "Danube Trade Blocked by Bridges," *Christian Science Monitor*, October 6, 1999, p. 6.

30. Trueheart, Charles, "Canal Plan in France Stranded," *The Washington Post*, July 30, 1997, p. A18.

31. *Airwise: The Airport and Air Travel Guide*, www.airwise.com/airports/index.html.

32. Kristof, Nicholas D., "Thanks to Farmers, Airport Grows like Bonsai," *The New York Times*, June 10, 1999.

33. Platt, Kevin, "Hong Kong's End to Close-Call Landings," *The Christian Science Monitor*, March 5, 1997, pp. 10–11.

34. Rapoport, Carla, "Seamless Airport Transfer Sought," *The Journal of Commerce*, May 7, 1998, p. 1A.

35. *Ibid*

36. Zhan, Sherrie E., "No Kudos for Chek Lap Kok," *World Trade*, October 1998, p. 32.

37. Putzer, Ian, "Balancing Out," *Air Cargo World*, June 2006, pp. 10–11.

38. Conway, Peter, "Taking the High Road," *Air Cargo World*, January 2000, pp. 62–67.

39. "The World's Top 50 Cargo Airports," *Air Cargo World*, June 2006, p. 7.

40. "Three Routes Lead to Iberia," *SBB Cargo*, http://www.sbbcargo..ch/en/index/sbbcargo_magazine/00_03/03_00_1.html, March 15, 2001.

41. Ting, C. L., "Intermodal Continues to Develop in China," *Inbound Logistics*, September 1996, p. 14.

42. Ting, C. L. "Strained Infrastructure Continues to Hamper Trade with China," *Inbound Logistics*, October 1996, p. 14.

43. Watson, Rip, "Europe Fails to Establish Intermodal Ties, Creating Barriers to Logistics Providers," *The Journal of Commerce*, April 22, 1999, p. 1A.

44. Carding, Tony, "Trans-European Transport Network to Link Ports in Marseille and Antwerp with Hinterlands," *Traffic World*, April 17, 1998, p. 32.

45. Barnard, Bruce, "France Vetoes Plan for Rail Freeways Outlined by the E.U.," *The Journal of Commerce*, June 4, 1997, p. 3B.

46. Helmer, John, "Russia to Overhaul Trans-Siberian Rail," *The Journal of Commerce*, April 21, 1998, p. A1.

47. Associated Press, "Asian Railway Chugging to Reality," *The New York Times*, October 20, 1997.

48. *U.S. and Foreign Commercial Service: Country Commercial Guides*, http://www.stat-usa.gov/mrd.nsf/vwCCG_Country, April 5, 2002.

49. *World Factbook*, Central Intelligence Agency, http://www.cia.gov/cia/publications/factbook/index.html, April 5, 2002.

50. *Ibid*

51. Feller, Gordon, "For Truckers, Polish Roads are a Deep, Dark Pothole on Route Linking EU and Russia," *Traffic World*, September 8, 1998, p. 18.

52. Conley, John, "Chinese Puzzle," *International Business*, July/August 1996, pp. 16–20.

53. Zubrzycki, John, "In City of Joy, Foot-Power Loses Pull with Rickshaw Ban," *The Christian Science Monitor*, December 11, 1996, p. 1.

54. Marquand, Robert, "Driving in Delhi: Chaos of Cars, Carts and Cows," *The Journal of Commerce*, August 18, 1999, p. 1.

55. Transport for London Fact Sheet, http://www.tfl.gov.uk/tfl/, May 25, 2006.

56. Dillon, Sam, "Can't Find Juárez Street? There are Hundreds!" *The New York Times*, January 12, 2000.

57. Faison, Seth, "Palm Trees and Sun (and Who Needs an Address)," *The New York Times*, February 23, 1999.

58. Aalund, Dagmar, "Bridge Soon Will Link Futures of Danes, Swedes," *The Wall Street Journal*, May 25, 2000, p. A20.

59. http://www.viaducdemillaueiffage.com, May 25, 2006.

60. Tower, Courtney, "The Peace Bridge? Hardly," *JoC Week*, August 28–September 3, 2000, p. 17.

61. Osmond, Warren, "Bridge Collapse Rips a Tiny, New Pacific Nation," *The Christian Science Monitor*, January 13, 1997, p. 6.

62. De Santis, Solange, "A Long Ferry Tale Ends, to the Dismay of Some Canadians," *The Wall Street Journal*, February 14, 1997, p. A1.

63. *Ports of the World, op. cit.*

64. Dellios, Hugh, "A First-Class Headache," *The Chicago Tribune*, July 10, 1997.

65. Ewing, Terzah, "Williams Cos. Seeks to Extend Its Information Pipeline," *The Wall Street Journal*, November 21, 1997, p. B4. Ransdell, Eric, "Rolling Out the Future," *U.S. News and World Report*, August 12, 1996, pp. 47–48.

66. Phillips, Michael M., "On Ghana's Tech Frontier," *The Wall Street Journal*, May , 2002, p. B1.

67. Goering, Laurie, "A City Hung Up by Too Many Hang-Ups," *The Chicago Tribune*, March 4, 1998.

68. Naik, Gautam, "Braving Sharks, Waves, to Lay Phonelines," *The Wall Street Journal*, September 12, 1997, p. B1.

69. Robinson, Sara, "Cut in Fiber Cable Disrupts Internet Traffic Nationwide," *The New York Times*, September 29, 1999.

70. Stephenson, Neal, "Mother Earth, Mother Board," *Wired*, December 1996, pp. 97–160.

71. Biddle, Frederic M., John Lippman and Stephanie N. Mehta, "One Satellite Fails and the World Goes Awry," *The Wall Street Journal*, May 21, 1998, p. B1.

72. Hardy, Quentin, "How a Wife's Question Led Motorola to Chase Global Cell-Phone Plan," *The Wall Street Journal*, December 16, 1996, p. A1.

73. Hardy, Quentin, "Global-Minded Iridium Has Down-to-Earth Need: Profit," *The Wall Street Journal*, January 26, 1999, p. B4.

74. Cauley, Leslie, "Losses in Space. Iridium's Downfall: The Marketing Took a Back Seat to Science," *The Wall Street Journal*, August 18, 1999, p. A1.

75. Barboza, David, "Iridium, Bankrupt, Is Planning a Fiery Ending for Its 88 Satellites," *The New York Times*, April 11, 2000.

76. Cooper, Kenneth J., "Coal vs. Goals: India's Dilemma," *The Washington Post*, October 16, 1997, p. A21.

77. Rao, N. Vasuki, "Infrastructure Bottlenecks are Taking Their Toll on India's Future Growth," *The Journal of Commerce*, March 19, 1997, p. 23C. Jensen, Paul, "China in Lights," *Export Today*, April 1997, pp. 56–60.

78. Pearl, Daniel, "Saudis, of all people, Find Industry Hobbled by a Lag in Electricity," *The Wall Street Journal*, August 8, 1996, p. A1.

79. Dugger, Celia W., "India Tries to Plug a Cash Drain: Its Power System," *The New York Times*, February 6, 2000.

80. Tyler, Patrick E., "Power-line Thieves Loot Russia, Often Risking Death or Maiming," *The New York Times*, April 18, 2000.

81. Zachary, G. Pascal, "Water Pressure: Nations Scramble to Defuse Fights Over Supply," *The Wall Street Journal*, December 4, 1997, p. A17.

82. Beaugé, Florence, "L'approvisionnement en Eau: Un Cauchemar pour les Habitants d'Alger," *Le Monde*, May 30, 2002.

83. Swanson, Stevenson, "Urban Repair Bill Hard to Swallow," *The Chicago Tribune*, June 20, 1997.

84. Bangsberg, P. T., "Making a Splash," *The Journal of Commerce*, January 24, 1997, p. 3A.

85. *2002 World Development Indicators* database, World Bank, www.worldbank.org, April 20, 2002.

86. *Ibid*

87. Lelyveld, Michael S., "Iran, Turkey Ready to Build Gas Pipeline," *The Journal of Commerce*, March 6, 1997, p. 1A.

88. Useem, Jerry, "Exxon's African Adventure," *Fortune*, April 15, 2002, pp. 102–114.

89. Gottschalk, Arthur, "Pipeline Deal Nears Completion," *The Journal of Commerce*, February 19, 1997, p. 1A.

Methods of Entry into Foreign Markets

Chapter Four

Source: © 2007 JupiterImages Corporation.

The first venture of most firms in the international arena is usually more the result of serendipity than of careful planning and thoughtful strategic thinking. The first few sales abroad emerge from a chance contact made at a trade show, an unexpected fax sent after a prospect viewed a domestic sales brochure, or a sales inquiry resulting from an ad in a trade magazine. After a few of these haphazard transactions, the firm then realizes that there may be a substantial market—at least large enough to warrant further consideration—for its products outside their original domestic market, and management starts considering selling on a more systematic basis abroad. The pitfalls usually start at this point. Firms rarely assess correctly the market's characteristics, its potential and, particularly, the advantages and disadvantages of a given method of entry, and instead base their entry strategy on a chance encounter at a trade show with a foreign agent or a distributor, or enter a joint venture with a partner met through casual business acquaintances. Unfortunately, some of those decisions end up being inappropriate: Countless headaches can be avoided if the correct strategy is determined early on, using as many pieces of information as possible.

4-1 Entry Strategy Factors

There are many factors that will influence a company's entry strategy into a foreign market. Some of these factors are related to the characteristics of the market that the firm is targeting, and others are related to the characteristics of the product and of the exporter.

Specifically, the exporter should analyze carefully the following determinant factors:

- **The size of the market:** While there is no easy rule, the method of entry is different for a market in which combined sales amount to €10,000,000 (US $12,500,000) per year and a market that exhibits sales in billions of euros.

- **The growth of the market:** A stable market, growing at a moderate rate, will call for a different entry strategy than one in which there is a substantial potential for growth.

- **The potential market share of the exporter:** A market in which the exporter can become a major player will call for a different strategy than one in which the exporter has no chance to be much more than a niche player.

- **The type of product:** Products with technology and a need for after-sale service and parts will require a different entry strategy than a disposable consumer good.

- **The market strategy of the firm:** Although self-evident, a firm whose strategy is to provide a top-of-the-line product will have a different entry strategy than a firm that has chosen to be the lowest cost provider.

- **The willingness of the firm to get involved:** Firms that actively want to develop foreign markets should have a different entry strategy than firms that believe that their domestic market is their primary concern and consider foreign sales as "bothersome."

- **The characteristics of the country considered:** The level of development, the infrastructure of the country, the business sophistication of potential trade partners, the overall climate under which business is conducted, the culture of the market, and the culture of customers should all be considered in the decision of an entry strategy.

- **The time horizon considered:** Products that have a short life cycle, or products that are likely to generate a lot of "me-too" competitors, demand a different entry strategy than products that are patent-protected, or are likely to have a long life cycle or engender a long line of complementary products.

Only after all of these factors are evaluated is it possible for a firm to decide appropriately which market entry strategy to pursue. Overall, great caution should be exercised in decisions regarding entry strategies: Among all the decisions made by marketers regarding the marketing mix, the distribution decision is the one with the longest time horizon, and the least likely to be quickly adjusted. Not that product, promotion, and price can be easily adjusted, but a distribution change can be quite an undertaking, leading to ill feelings and trauma, and therefore the need for a correct initial decision is yet more critical.

The alternative entry strategies available to a casual exporter will be presented first, followed by those alternatives available to an active exporter, and then the strategies available to a company willing to manufacture abroad.

4-2 Indirect Exporting

Some firms are unwilling exporters in that they prefer to concentrate on their domestic markets and handle any foreign inquiry as a "difficult sale." As such, they do not like to handle them. Under this banner of "Indirect Exporting," several alternatives are possible, from the lowest level of involvement to some very moderate interest.

4-2a Export Trading Company (ETC)

In the case where a company is unwilling to undertake any of the activities of marketing abroad, the use of an Export Trading Company is the simplest solution. An Export Trading Company (ETC) is an intermediary that will purchase the goods in the exporting country and resell them to a customer in a foreign country.

The dominant ETCs are very large firms, with local offices in numerous countries. The trading companies operate in the following fashion: They take title to the goods in the exporting country, making this transaction a domestic transaction for the "exporter," and transfer title to the "importer" in the importing country, making that transaction a domestic transaction as well. As far as either of the parties dealing with the trading company is concerned, the product is seemingly handled by a domestic company, its foreign origin is not a concern for the buyer, and its sale abroad is not an issue for the seller.

Trading companies were first created in the Netherlands, France, and Britain for trade with India and Indochina. As these trade routes disappeared, new trading companies were founded in Spain and Portugal for commerce with South America; eventually these trade routes also disappeared in the late nineteenth century. In the twentieth century, trading companies were resurrected in Japan to handle Japan's exporting efforts after World War II. These so-called *sogo shosha* have come to mightily dominate the export trading business: Mitsubishi, Mitsui, Itochu, Marubeni, and Sumitomo. All have sales in the trillions of yen, and trade in all sorts of goods. Mitsui claims to be involved from "noodles to missiles." Because of their presence in all countries of the world, these trading companies have acquired a wealth of information on potential sellers and buyers and they leverage this knowledge into sales. They contact sellers when they are aware of a buyer in some foreign country, and contact buyers when they become aware of a particularly motivated seller. In addition, these trading companies have come to offer a complete "package" of international logistical services; they ship, insure, and finance international trade, and, in some cases, sophisticated traders rely on their services for complex transactions rather than handle them themselves:[1] Their expertise in handling international transactions is unmatched.

Other ETCs are in existence, but they tend to specialize in one geographical area or one product line. However, they still offer the breadth of services that a *sogo shosha* can make available to an exporter; in particular, they take title to the goods in the

African Export Ventures

In a few areas in sub-Saharan Africa, local EMCs, such as Getrade and Fritete African Art Works in Ghana, are spurring the development of an export-led economy. They established contacts with importers in the United States and negotiated large purchases of local African artifacts for such companies as Pier 1 Imports, Cost Plus, and Body Shop International. However, none of the local companies had the capacity to handle such large orders, so the EMCs coordinated the efforts of hundreds of small artisans and, after some initial difficulties, were able to procure most of the orders placed by the U.S. firms. As the artisans realized the profitability of such export sales,

they started accepting orders for artifacts that were non-traditional in their colors or shape, to accommodate the customers' requests, creating a perfect example of international marketing.

In addition, as most small businesses there suffer from a lack of capitalization, the EMCs also brought in the "micro-lenders" or those charitable organizations that will make very small loans (U.S. $500 to $3,000) to help entrepreneurs purchase machinery or obtain working capital. As these loans allow businesses to grow, it is expected that a business infrastructure will grow, allowing greater access to financing and triggering further business development.

exporting country. In the United States, since the passage of the Export Trading Companies Act in 1982, a number of firms have been created, all operating on this smaller scale; however, their number is growing and so is their share of the export volume of the United States.[2]

The use of an ETC makes great sense for the novice exporter or the company unwilling or unable to dabble in the complexities of an occasional international transaction. However, should the company decide to become more involved in the long run, choosing an ETC is a poor strategy as the customers abroad are not the customers of the exporter but of the ETC, and may not be known to the exporter. It is unlikely that the ETC will relinquish this information readily if it is no longer profiting from its efforts at developing the market for the exporter's products; it is equally unlikely that the exporter could benefit from the goodwill created by the ETC with its foreign customers as well.

4-2b Export Management Corporation (EMC)

Despite the similarity in name, an Export Management Corporation (EMC) is an altogether different type of intermediary. An EMC is typically located in the exporting country and is operating as an export-oriented manufacturer's representative (agent) for the exporter (i.e., it does not take title to the goods but earns a commission on the sale).

Most EMCs are small firms, typically with fewer than fifteen employees. The firms rarely have an office abroad, although they do have contacts with a large number of potential importers, and regularly send employees—or, more likely, the owner of the agency—abroad to visit customers and actively attend trade shows and other promotional activities. EMCs tend to restrict their sales efforts to potential customers in one country and often specialize in selling one line of products in that country. Most of them represent more than one manufacturer abroad, usually in complementary lines.

Because an EMC acts as an agent, the exporter is slightly more involved in the foreign sale than with an ETC; for example, the exporter is responsible for shipping the goods, invoicing the importer, and collecting from him. The degree to which the EMC helps the exporter depends on the relationship they have established with each other and the level of sophistication of the exporter. In general, an EMC helps a lot rather than a little: It acts as the export department of the seller, handling every detail of the transaction, from freight forwarding to insurance and from invoicing to collection. The compensation of the EMC therefore varies in function of its involvement: It either earns a higher commission for handling all of the details of the sale or earns a commission on the sale and fixed fees for the remainder of its efforts. The range of alternative arrangements is such that it is difficult to generalize.[3]

The use of an EMC makes great sense for the novice exporter; by working with an EMC, and by at least partially managing its foreign accounts, a firm gains substantial insights, which would become quite valuable should the company decide to become further involved in export sales. In practice, though, because the EMC is a small firm and has valuable contacts abroad, it is often absorbed—at least partially—and transformed into the export department of the exporter. This allows the firm to capitalize on the talent of the personnel of the EMC and the goodwill it generated abroad.

4-2c Piggy-Backing

A third alternative choice exists for a reluctant exporter: it is called "Piggy-Backing" and can refer to one of two possible situations:

1. A customer of a firm enters a foreign market by setting up a manufacturing facility. The customer tells its suppliers that they will need to supply parts for assembly and spare parts for customer service. The suppliers therefore end up selling their product abroad, "piggy-backing" on the strategy of an existing customer. In some cases, the suppliers develop their own independent sales in that market. This piggy-backing also happens with franchised businesses, which require that the equipment of the franchises they establish overseas are equipped with exactly the same machinery and utilize the same supplies worldwide.

2. A successful exporter involves one of its suppliers—or a company that makes a complementary product—in the markets that this exporter has developed. This form of piggy-backing is sometimes referred to as collaborative exporting: Nevertheless, there is certainly an imbalance in the ability of the two partners, with one particularly competent, the other a novice.

Piggy-backing can sometimes be seen as a passive arrangement (triggered by another firm), at which point it is difficult to call it a strategy. Nevertheless, should the opportunity present itself, it makes perfect sense for a company to seize it and acquire some knowledge about selling abroad (see Figure 4-1). If piggy-backing is

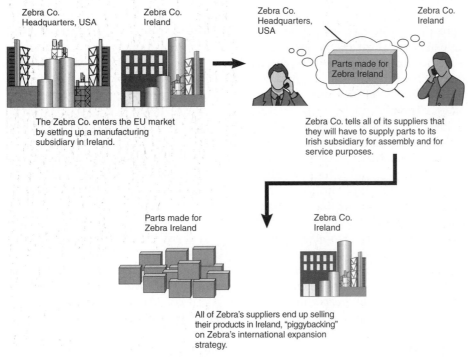

Figure 4-1
Piggy-Backing

initiated by a firm eager to develop its own sales in foreign markets, it is quite an appropriate strategy as the experience gained from the experienced exporter can eventually develop into a solid export strategy with the use of agents, distributors, or even sales subsidiaries.

4-3 Active Exporting

Once a firm realizes that it wants to exploit the possibilities that sales abroad can bring, and decides to become involved in its exporting activities, a number of alternatives open up. Under this banner of "Active Exporting," several alternatives are possible, differing not only in the level of involvement of the exporter, but also in the strategies pursued by the exporter.

4-3a Agent

principal The party represented by an agent in an international agency agreement; the exporter.

An agent is usually a small firm or an individual located in the importing country, which acts as a manufacturer's representative for the exporter. Therefore an agent does not take title to the goods it sells but earns a commission on the sales it makes. In its relationship with an agent, the exporter is also known as the **principal**. An agent often has several principals, and generally sells a group of complementary products rather than products that compete directly with one another. The agent will handle all of the sales functions for the exporter, from the initial prospecting for customers to the close. The agent is usually given varying support by the exporter: Some exporters only provide the bare minimum of a sales brochure and a price list, while the more experienced exporters provide training on the product's characteristics, analysis on the competitors' products, information on the sales and service philosophy of the company, sales support in the form of samples, catalogs (translated or adapted), trade advertising, and financial support to attend trade shows, technical visits by corporate engineers, participation in sales incentive programs, and so on.

Agents, as a whole, like to keep control over their schedule and over their sales approach, but the exporter's support of their efforts is critical to their success and to the extent to which they expend a lot of effort selling the exporter's product. In particular, requests for quotes and *pro-forma* invoices should be handled quite promptly and negotiations on price and delivery done diligently, so as to not delay the agent's sales efforts; time differences sometimes exacerbate the perception of a lack of responsiveness on the part of the exporter.

binding agent An agent who can make decisions that are binding on the principal; the principal must abide by whatever statements the representative has made.

Sometimes, there is the suggestion that, given a set of guidelines, the agent could be trusted to reach decisions and negotiate with the customer on critical aspects of the sale: price, delivery, terms of trade (see Chapter 6), terms of sale (see Chapter 7), and collection. However, it is critical that all such negotiations be handled by the principal, with the agent acting as an intermediary between the exporter and the importer. If the agent is allowed to negotiate directly with the importer, then the agent is considered by a large number of countries' governments as a **binding agent**, and the exporter is considered to have a permanent establishment in the country of import, with significant taxation implications, specifically taxation of the profits realized on sales in that country. After the sale is concluded between the agent and the importer, all of the other aspects of the transaction, from *pro-forma* invoice to the actual collection, are handled directly and solely by the exporter. Finally, the agent does not get paid until after the exporter has been paid by the importer.

The choice of an agent should obviously be made on a large number of criteria: its ability to represent the exporter and its product accurately, its ability to sell, its contacts, its knowledge of the industry that the exporter wants to target, the compatibility of its objectives with those of the exporter, and so on. Moreover, the choice of an agent is a long-term commitment; although the contract is often based on one-year increments, the effective duration of a relationship between an exporter and its agents is much longer.

There are several alternative routes to "finding" agents in foreign countries; among the most commonly used methods are trade shows, trade missions, the commercial attachés of the exporter's country's consulates, and contacts with other successful exporters.

The use of an agent is generally driven by several factors,[4] one or more of which can be enough to trigger this strategic decision:

1. When the firm estimates that its potential sales in that market are small (perhaps no more than 5 or 10 percent of its domestic sales), with moderate or no growth potential

2. When the product is not a stock item, but a product specifically designed and made for a particular customer

3. When the product is a very expensive item, such as operating machinery

4. When the company expects a short product life cycle

5. When the product does not require frequent after-sale service

6. When the exporter is unlikely to ever become one of the dominant players in the market and will remain a niche player

7. When the company is reasonably well equipped to handle export sales

8. When the company is not pursuing a "top-of-the-line" strategy, and does not attempt to collect premium prices

9. When the company wants to keep a reasonable amount of control over its prices and delivery policies.

4-3b Distributor

A distributor is usually a firm located in the importing country—or, rarely, in a neighboring country—that buys the goods from the exporter. A distributor therefore takes title to the goods it sells and earns a profit on the sales it makes. What characterizes a relationship with a distributor is that there are two sets of invoices: one set of international invoices between the exporter and the distributor, who is also the importer; and a set of domestic invoices between the distributor and its customers, who see these transactions as domestic sales of a foreign product. A distributor is therefore carrying inventory of the exporter's goods, and it also often carries inventory of spare parts and provides after-sale service. A distributor will carry complementary products but also may carry products that compete directly with those of the exporter.

A distributor is taking much more risk in its relationship with the exporter than does an agent and experiences much higher costs. The distributor carries the traditional risks associated with inventory and invests a considerable sum of money in the inventory; should the goods not sell well, the distributor is saddled with the unsold or obsolete goods. In addition, it is traditional for a distributor to participate in the costs of advertising, trade show attendance, and so on. In exchange, the distributor has much more freedom in setting prices, negotiating terms with customers and in managing all matters not directly related to the exporter's trademarks or copyrights. However, there is a large number of exporting firms that attempt to limit these freedoms, specifically on price, in order to maintain as standard a strategy as possible from country to country, and to eliminate or reduce "parallel imports" (see Section 4-5).

A distributor should also be considered a long-term partner. Because it makes a substantial investment in inventory and in the training of its employees, the distributor considers itself involved for a long period of time, and great care should be taken in finding the right partner. The choice of a distributor should be made on a large number of criteria: its ability to represent the exporter and its product accurately, its ability to invest in the exporter's products, to sell them, and to provide after-sale service, as well as its employees, their contacts, its knowledge of the industry, the compatibility of its objectives with those of the exporter, and so on.

There are several alternative routes to "finding" distributors in foreign countries; among the most commonly used methods are trade shows, trade missions, the commercial attachés of the exporter's country's consulates, and contacts with other successful exporters.

The use of a distributor is generally driven by several factors,[5] one or more of which can be enough to trigger this strategic decision:

1. When the firm estimates that the market is substantial (perhaps 20 or 25 percent of its domestic sales) or when it estimates that there is substantial growth potential

2. When the product is a stock item, and generally not tailored to the needs of a specific customer

3. When the product is a rather moderately priced item

4. When the company expects a fairly long product life cycle

5. When the product requires (frequent) after-sale service and/or maintenance parts

6. When the company estimates it will not become much more than a minor player in the market

7. When the company prefers to handle export sales with only one customer

8. When the company is not pursuing a prestige pricing strategy with premium prices and service

9. When the company is comfortable relinquishing control of its price and delivery terms.

4-3c Additional Issues in the Agent-Distributorship Decision

There are two other issues to consider when determining whether an agent or a distributor would be the most appropriate strategy: Both of them are legal in nature. First, some countries will not allow agents at all, or will not allow agents to represent foreign manufacturers, or will mandate a physical after-sale service presence on the country's soil, all requirements that mandate the use of a distributor.

The second issue is more complicated: Most governments make a substantive differentiation in the way agents and distributors are considered by their judicial system. Most often, because agents tend to be individuals or very small firms, many countries have decided to place them under the protection of labor law, the code of laws that deals with the relationships between employers and employees (see Section 5-3a). In many countries, notably European countries, labor law tends to be very restrictive in terms of what an employer can and cannot impose on an employee and, in those countries in which labor law applies to agents, what an exporter can and cannot require of an agent. For example, even though the principal-agent contract may call for a termination notice of thirty days and no compensation, labor law can call for a six-month notice and six-month loss-of-income compensation and the terms of the contract are overruled. There are similar restrictions on the number of hours worked, the payment of taxes, the legal requirements of certifications, licenses, and so on.

In contrast, distributors, because they tend to be larger and are assumed to be more sophisticated, are covered in almost all countries by contract law. Contract law is much less restrictive and courts tend to render judgments based upon the terms of the contract; the only restrictions are limited to contracts that are obviously biased or coerced, a situation very unlikely to be observed if one of the International Chamber of Commerce model contracts or an equivalent is used.

4-3d Marketing Subsidiary

Finally, a firm may decide, rather than to employ an agent or a distributor (over neither of which it has much control), to create its own sales or marketing subsidiary in a foreign country. A marketing subsidiary is a foreign office, staffed by employees of the exporting firm, who will sell its goods in the foreign market. A subsidiary is incorporated in the foreign market, so it is the importer of record as far as the foreign government is concerned, and the "export" takes place between two legal entities that are part of the same company, at a transfer price. Although transfer prices can sometimes create problems in the process of clearing Customs, the process is very smooth altogether, as the traditional concerns of payment, terms of sale, and terms of trade are eliminated. All sales made by the foreign subsidiary to its customers are domestic sales and therefore are simpler to manage.

The costs of a marketing subsidiary are higher, and a good portion of them are fixed: A building must be rented, an inventory built, and employees hired and trained before measurable sales can offset these expenses. This is in stark contrast with sales through an agent, which are essentially variable cost sales (the commission is only paid if the agent sells) or sales through a distributor, where that distributor is the one bearing the costs of establishing the business in the foreign market. These investments obviously also require a long-term commitment on the part of the exporting firm (see Table 4-1).

The choice of a sales or marketing subsidiary is made when the company wants to retain control over its sales in that country, usually when the company is faced with one or more of the following situations:

1. When the firm estimates that the market potential is considerable (more than 25 percent of its domestic sales) or when it estimates that there is very substantial growth potential or very substantial profits to be made
2. When the product is technologically driven, with substantial intellectual property content
3. When the product is a rather complicated product to sell
4. When the company expects to be involved for the long run, with additional products introduced later on
5. When the product requires sophisticated after-sale service and/or maintenance parts
6. When the company expects to become one of the major players in the market
7. When the company is exacting premium prices from customers
8. When the company is uncomfortable relinquishing control of its products and prices.

4-3e Coordinating Direct Export Strategies

It should now seem self-evident that there are two types of factors included in the entry decision for an exporter: those factors that are market-driven and those that are company- or product-driven. Consequently, some firms elect to have a policy to always follow a strategy driven by their product line, and always use a sales subsidiary, or a distributor or an agent. However, some firms decide on a country-by-country basis which strategy is the most appropriate and juggle a combination of agents, distributors, and marketing subsidiaries. Each of these overall strategies have advantages and disadvantages.

TABLE 4-1	What is the Correct Entry Strategy?

Match the description of these responsibilities to an agent, distributor, or marketing subsidiary.

Description	
When the company expects a short product life cycle	
When the product is not a stock item, but a product specifically designed and made for a particular customer	
When the company is not pursuing a "top-of-the-line" strategy, and does not attempt to collect premium prices	
When the firm estimates that sales in the potential market are small, with moderate or no growth potential	
When the product is a rather moderately priced item	
When the company prefers to handle export sales with only one customer	
When the product requires frequent after-sales service and/or maintenance parts	
When the product is technology-driven, with substantial intellectual property content	
When the company expects to become one of the major players in the market	
When the company is exacting premium prices from customers	

When a company chooses to have the same entry strategy in all its export markets, it certainly simplifies the management of its exports and presents a unified front to its customers on all aspects of its marketing. In particular, if the firm uses agents or sales subsidiaries in all countries, its prices are bound to be well coordinated and its after-sale policies clearly controlled. If there are any discrepancies, they are known to the firm and can be clearly managed and understood. A firm choosing to use distributors in all of its markets can exercise the same level of control by using contracts that specify clearly which prices distributors are allowed to charge—a practice that is generally legal or, at least, tolerated—and which after-sale service they must provide. However, there are problems with this "fit-all" strategy, as inappropriate strategies may lead to a poor match with the market: A potentially very lucrative market may be given away to an agent, or a sales subsidiary may have to be established in a small market. Moreover, a firm may have to postpone entry in a lucrative market because of a lack of resources if it adheres to a strategy where it will only build subsidiaries.

When a firm chooses to have different entry strategies in different countries, or when it decides to sell through a series of independent distributors, the coordination of prices and after-sale service is more difficult to achieve, and the possibility of parallel imports (see Section 4-5) looms. However, the most appropriate strategy is chosen for each country, and, generally, the greatest profits can be extracted from the foreign markets.

For a firm, the decision to have a coordinated entry strategy is based on criteria that can be interpreted differently by different management teams. However, there is one significant issue to consider once a choice has been made: The costs of changing from one entry strategy where an exporter uses agents or distributors to a strategy based upon sales subsidiaries can exact a significant toll on all involved parties. The agents and distributors have generally invested a considerable amount of time, money, and talent into building a significant market for the exporter's products, for which they are rightfully compensated according to the terms of the original contract. If they are very successful, the exporter is often tempted to recover these "expenses" (the commissions paid to the agents or the profit opportunities given to the distributor) by establishing a sales subsidiary. This change of strategy should be avoided as much as possible, as it is traumatic for all involved parties and often results in reduced sales and profits for several years: The customers' loyalties usually lie more with the agent or the distributor than with the exporter, and regaining these customers' confidence can take considerable efforts. The slighted distributor can also be strongly tempted to counterattack, in court or otherwise: Some companies can suffer greatly from this change of heart in strategy if the courts are sympathetic to the plight of the local firm;[6] they often are.

4-3f Foreign Sales Corporation (FSC)

Foreign sales corporations (FSCs) were created in the United States as a tax break for exporters. It is not a method of entry at all, but rather a way for a United States-based corporation to lower its income tax. The only conditions are that the corporation must export products that have a 50 percent U.S. content and it must incorporate a subsidiary in one of several pre-approved foreign locations, such as the U.S. Virgin Islands, Barbados, or Jamaica. By channeling its export sales through the FSC, the corporation is eligible for a reduction in its tax rate on profits earned on export sales of fifteen percentage points, from 45 percent to 30 percent.[7] It is essentially a tax incentive available to exporters, regardless of the method used for export, with the exception of sales though an ETC, because those sales are domestic in nature (see Section 4-2a).

The European Union brought a complaint to the World Trade Organization (WTO) that the FSC concept was a subsidy to exports, a practice that was prohibited by the agreement, and the WTO ruled against the United States in August 1999. The United States had lost and exhausted all of its appeals by March 2006. Nevertheless, the concept of a tax break to exporters is likely to stay, as the U.S. Congress has shown that it was loathe to eliminate it: In 1984, the Domestic International Sales Corporations (DISCs) were found to be violating the General Agreement on Tariffs and Trade, and Congress created the FSCs in their place. Similarly, before the United States had exhausted its appeals to the WTO regarding FSCs, the U.S. Congress passed the American Job Creation Act of 2004, which created special tax deductions for manufacturing activities that take place in the United States for the purpose of export.[8] If that effort is found to be against WTO rules—and it likely will be—the United States could "move to a territorial tax system, and not tax companies' foreign operations, which would be much more beneficial to export[er]s than the current system of taxing worldwide operations."[9] Such a change in the Tax Code would meet WTO requirements.

4-4 Production Abroad

Another alternative to exporting is for a company to start operations abroad; this strategy can be followed, for example, when the manufacturing costs are lower abroad, or when the shipping costs are prohibitive, or when domestic manufacturing capacity is reached, or when the product has a significant intangible content, such as in services. Here again, the order in which the alternatives are introduced represents an increasing level of involvement for the company interested in penetrating a foreign market.

4-4a Subcontracting/Contract Manufacturing

The first alternative is subcontracting—also called contract manufacturing—which occurs when a company enters an agreement with a producer in the foreign market to manufacture its goods. For example, a publishing firm may contract with a printing facility to publish its books rather than ship them from its home printing plant. Another example would be a cement manufacturer contracting with local producers to make and package cement under its brand. Yet another would be a supplier to an automobile manufacturer (often called an Original Equipment

The "Pet Shop" Bags

Firms frequently contract abroad to have a product manufactured and re-imported in their home country, taking advantage of lower production costs than at home. Nothing is particularly special about this. However, the case of the Scottish Pet Shop bags illustrates the possible unintended consequences of such an arrangement.

Back in 1990, the "Pet Shop" in Glasgow, Scotland, decided to have its plastic bags printed in China. In many ways, the bags were very traditional, with the name of the store and its address appearing on them; however, they were also adorned with a drawing of a red parrot. For some unknown reason, the printing plant where the pet store owner had had the bags printed decided to print millions more, and these additional bags found their way throughout Central Asia. They have been found by tourists and diplomats in Pakistan, China, Uzbekistan, Russia, and Kyrgyzstan. Curious about the provenance of the bags, they sometimes contact the pet store in Glasgow to inquire about the mystery. The shop owner is as baffled as they are.

Eventually, "knock-offs" of the Pet Shop bags started emerging in these countries as well, some with two parrots, some with nonexistent names, or some with the peculiar English found on counterfeit goods all over China, to which my Chinese students refer colloquially as *Chenglish*: "The Plastic Bag Shop. Welcome Patronage."

While it is difficult to argue that there was much intellectual property in the design of a simple shopping bag, and that the pet store actually lost much in the process—actually, this notoriety probably increased its sales—this example makes it evident that it is difficult to control what a contract manufacturer will do when the initial order is completed.

Manufacturer or an OEM) that contracts with a company to provide subassemblies for that OEM's plant in a foreign country.

Contract manufacturing is not truly a method of entry: It is a way to get the product manufactured in a foreign country, and the marketing and distribution of the product remains to be organized. This distribution can be achieved either through a distributor or a marketing subsidiary, or, very occasionally, through the marketing channels used by the local contractor.

Contract manufacturing is often sought as a strategy to enter a market in which there are significant barriers to entry, such as high tariffs and quotas, but there is always great difficulty to find a suitable manufacturing facility in such a country: If it has a protectionist streak, it is unlikely to have domestic firms that are operating at world standards.

4-4b Licensing

Licensing is the granting of rights to **intellectual property** owned by a company to another company for a fee. The intellectual property is either a patent on a specific technology, process, design, or product; a trademark; a brand; a copyright; a trade secret; or other know-how, and it remains the property of the **licensor**—the firm granting the license. The company using the intellectual property—the **licensee**—only has the right to use the property, and for every use, it has to pay a fee called a **royalty**. Licensing is quite common in manufacturing, where companies license processes they have developed to other firms, or products such as chemical compounds or molecules.

In an international environment, the licensor is the "exporting" company and the licensee is the foreign company, and the range of intellectual property commonly licensed increases; several companies license their more visible intellectual property—trademarks, copyrights, or designs—to foreign firms. This strategy is followed when the access to the market is limited by high tariffs or nontariff barriers, when the shipping costs are prohibitive, or when the licensor is uninterested in actively pursuing the market.

Licensing, as a strategy, can be quite beneficial to a firm; it does not have to lay out any capital and can generate worldwide income from its intellectual property fairly rapidly. The down side is that intellectual property is not always well protected in some countries, that piracy is rampant in several, and that these risks can be

---

licensing A process by which a firm possessing some intellectual property item grants another company the right to use the intellectual property item in exchange for a royalty.

intellectual property A type of intangible good that an individual or a firm can own; it is either a copyright, a patent, a trademark, or a trade secret.

licensor The owner of an intellectual property item that grants another firm (the licensee) the right to use that intellectual property in exchange for the payment of a royalty.

licensee The party that is granted the right to use an intellectual property item owned by another party, the licensor, in exchange for payment of a royalty.

royalty The amount of money paid by the licensee to the licensor for the right to use the licensor's intellectual property.

perceived as major deterrents for the owners of intellectual property. However, this is a danger associated more with the ownership of intellectual property than with the strategy of licensing. Should an individual decide to violate a patent or infringe a copyright, s/he certainly does not need a licensing agreement to start: Patent information is available from all patent offices as a matter of course—the U.S. Patent Office has most of its six million patents available online—and copyrights are by definition protecting publicly available products, such as this book and software. To a certain extent, it is probably better to have a local firm enforce its license of a copyright than to attempt to enforce the copyright from abroad.

4-4c Franchising

Franchising is, in concept, quite similar to licensing, except that the **franchisor** is granting the rights to a large number of intellectual property items, all bundled in a business package, to a **franchisee** who pays royalties for using this business model. The business model is comprised of trademarks, copyrights, and patents, as well as know-how, training, and methods of operation. Most franchises tend to be retail establishments, because consumers tend to value a uniform product and service and like to find retail names with which they are familiar. Similarly, entrepreneurs abroad like to invest in a business concept with a proven track record, which most franchised businesses have. Finally, franchisors have the opportunity to gain market share without having to invest any capital. It has proven to be a fairly popular means of expansion both domestically and abroad.

Franchising is usually a very good option for a number of businesses seeking expansion abroad, but it certainly is inappropriate for most. The ones who can enter a market successfully are retail operations that involve a service requiring a fairly low level of employee skills, such as fast food restaurants, car repair shops, hotels, and car rental outlets. It is inappropriate for high-skill consulting or advertising services, and nearly impossible for manufactured goods.

One of the consequences of franchising is that this strategy generates a substantial amount of "piggy-backing": As the franchisors demand that the franchisees use exactly the same equipment worldwide, the suppliers of those pieces of equipment end up selling worldwide as well. This is also true for items such as signage, furniture, and, in some cases, for consumables: In 1997, for every dollar earned by franchisors in foreign franchising fees, $15 were spent on U.S. products by the franchisees to set up and run their franchised operations.[10]

4-4d Joint Venture

With a joint venture (JV), the exporter invests in a facility abroad, but finds one or more partners with which to share the costs of the venture. A joint venture is characterized by the creation of a new corporation in the foreign country, jointly owned by the joint venture partners in any combination of ownership percentages; most joint ventures involving two partners are owned 50 percent–50 percent or 51 percent–49 percent, but they can be held 97 percent–3 percent. Some joint ventures include three or more partners, but they are less frequent.

Entry strategies using joint ventures are generally created for one of several reasons:

1. The firm feels compelled to minimize its exposure in a foreign investment (i.e., the amount of money it has at stake in a foreign country), and it achieves this objective by lowering the investment costs by half or by two-thirds.

2. The firm finds a partner with a complementary line of products to offer to the same market. Both partners feel that a joint effort, with a complete line, is the appropriate strategy, and neither of them is ready to enter the market alone.

franchising A process by which a firm possessing an array of several intellectual property items grants another company the right to use these intellectual property items in exchange for royalties.

franchisor The owner of an array of several intellectual property items that grants another firm the rights to use that group of intellectual property items in exchange for the payment of royalties.

franchisee The party granted the right to use an array of intellectual property items owned by another party in exchange for the payment of royalties.

McDonald's Franchising

McDonald's is a corporation that has used franchising as its main method of expansion in the United States and abroad. As of 2005, McDonald's had a total of 13,727 restaurants in the United States, about 57 percent of which were franchised restaurants owned by about 2,400 independent franchisees.

Abroad, the company has followed the same development policy: There are currently more than 18,159 McDonald's restaurants in 119 countries, with several countries having more than 1,000 restaurants (Canada, Japan, the United Kingdom, and Germany). More than 80 percent of these restaurants are franchised and the company is intent on expanding this percentage, as it believes that franchisees are best at gauging their local markets. This foreign growth was not without some hitches; for example, in 1967, McDonald's Corporation divided Canada into two franchising "territories," which it licensed to two individuals, George Tidball (Western Canada) and George Cohon (Eastern Canada). Realizing that this large market's potential could not be controlled by only two franchisees, McDonald's Corporation purchased these franchises back in 1970 and 1971.

Nevertheless, the franchises have been the greatest strength of McDonald's development: Several of the company's best-selling sandwiches were developed by franchisees, notably the Big Mac (1968) and the Egg McMuffin (1973). The same was true internationally. The former franchisee in Canada, George Cohon, now head of the corporate McDonald's Restaurants of Canada, opened the first restaurant in Moscow, on Pushkin Square, in January 1990. After selling more than 30,000 meals on its first day of operations, this restaurant was still the busiest McDonald's in the world ten years later. As of July 2006, there were 103 restaurants in all of Russia.

In Japan, McDonald's used a slightly different strategy early on; it formed a 50-50 joint venture with Den Fujita in 1970, and it soon opened its first restaurant on the glamorous Ginza in Tokyo. Most of Japan's 2,800 restaurants are owned by the venture, but eventually McDonald's started to add franchised operations, and today 22 percent of the restaurants are franchises.

Systemwide, McDonald's restaurants' sales are roughly U.S. $40 billion, 55 percent of which are generated by outlets in foreign countries. Each of these restaurants grosses an average of approximately U.S. $1,500,000 in sales every year, the franchised restaurants being the most profitable of the lot.

3. The firm wants a minority local partner to teach it the local ways of business and help smooth out the many obstacles that a firm is bound to experience in a foreign venture.

4. The firm is legally required to find a local partner by the host government. This requirement was "popular" until the mid-1990s and it has become less of an issue recently. Generally, the local partner was a politically connected individual rather than a partner who brought in additional capital.

The strategy of joint venture was quite popular until the early 1990s for several reasons. First and foremost, this strategy lowered the exposure of firms to the political risk presented by some countries. As early as the 1950s, some developing countries' governments decided that a good way to obtain means of production and create investment capital would be to "nationalize" plants owned by foreign investors. This policy also looked attractive politically, because the local perception was that the natural resources of a country should be managed and owned by its people. Libya, Egypt, Venezuela, and numerous others decided to just seize, without compensation to their actual owners, all of the petroleum production facilities within their borders. Several other countries followed the same policy, nationalizing any type of foreign-owned facility, until the late 1970s; some did it with some form of compensation, most without. The end result of these expropriation policies was clear: Not only did the countries have difficulties in running plants without the expatriate technicians of the nationalized firm, but they also scared away new foreign investors for decades. A joint venture with another firm was therefore a strategy developed to minimize the impact of a possible nationalization. In addition, a joint venture with a politically well-connected local partner was a good strategy for those firms who sought to minimize the probability of nationalization.

Countries who still wanted to create local ownership of capital and had not practiced nationalization found another effective strategy: Their governments asked foreign enterprises who wanted to invest in their country to take on a local businessman as a joint venture partner. These local businessmen were always very well connected but often largely undercapitalized and therefore did not bring anything but their contacts to the venture. In effect, the requirement was a partial nationalization of sorts, as the 100 percent investment that the foreign corporation made was quickly diluted to a 50 percent ownership of the JV. Some of these partnerships ended up being extreme examples of nepotism, such as in Indonesia, where Suharto's relatives were the only possible JV partners.[11] Obviously, the change in government and the prosecution of Suharto could have substantial consequences for these joint ventures. In other cases, the political partners were more of a hindrance than a help, even in dealing with the government, because they had been chosen more for their contacts than their business acumen and some ended up being dishonest; such were the cases for the respective partners in China of Kimberly-Clark, Borg-Warner, BASF, Potain, and countless others, unfortunately.[12]

However, the greatest problem with joint ventures, and the main reason a large majority of them are unsuccessful, is that they are akin to a marriage in which the spouses change over time. When the joint venture is first created, there is a good fit between all the partners' goals and strategies, and most JVs start well. However, as time goes on, the original management on both sides changes. Some managers might retire or change positions within the firm, one of the original partners may be purchased by a conglomerate, corporate strategies can change, and gradually, the perfect strategic match that created the JV in the first place is gone and partners squabble over the JV's objectives. Eventually, they accuse each other of all ills. The JV between Ford and Volkswagen in Argentina—named Autolatina—failed because the partners' objectives changed as the venture progressed.[13]

Because of all these problems, the strategy of creating joint ventures has become less and less attractive to foreign investors. Some countries have actually retreated and no longer require foreign investors to create a joint venture with a local partner, at least partly because the existence of these policies detracted some highly sought investors from entering their market; for example, Pepsico in India and 3M in China. These countries now routinely allow 100 percent ownership by a foreign entity.

4-4e Subsidiary

A subsidiary, also called a Wholly Owned Foreign Enterprise—or a Wholly Owned Foreign Enterprise (WOFE), pronounced "Woofie"—is an investment of 100 percent in a foreign venture by a firm. This strategy is followed by firms who want total control of an investment and are willing to take the risk of such a venture. A WOFE is either a green-field operation, where a foreign firm builds a brand new facility, or an acquisition of an existing firm, which is the preferred method of entry in most European markets, where it represents 56 percent of all foreign investments.[14] There is another alternative, which is still limited in scope but growing, particularly in the developing countries' markets: A firm will relocate an entire plant to a foreign location, usually to use cheaper labor and forgo the higher costs of a brand-new facility. The technology may not be the latest available, but the cost savings may be numerous, especially if the old plant no longer meets the environmental regulations of the exporting country. As the United States does not track export sales of used equipment—the Shipper's Export Declarations (see Section 9-3c in Chapter 9) do not distinguish between old and new equipment—the extent of this practice is not fully known, but anecdotal evidence abounds.[15]

The WOFE strategy allows the firm to retain complete control over its investment, which has become the main reason for a firm to choose this form of entry. The firm does not have to share its trade secrets, its know-how, and no one is privy to any of its

Kraft Foods Australia

Kraft Foods is one of the world's largest food and beverage companies with sales in more than 145 countries. Kraft was acquired in 1988 by Philip Morris Companies, which also had purchased Miller Brewing in 1985 and Nabisco Holdings in 2000. Philip Morris changed its name to Altria Group in 2003 to reflect its more diversified business ventures.

In 2002, Kraft Foods Australia acquired a manufacturing plant in Broadmeadows, Australia, as a wholly owned subsidiary to manufacture its cookies. The Australian facility, which had been built in 1964, employed 151 people. Kraft then embarked on a strategy to improve the performance of the facility, reduce costs, and maintain quality; however, the cost reductions were not sufficient and the older plant did not have the capacity to support an expanding market. On March 31, 2006, Kraft Foods Australia closed the cookie manufacturing facility and moved the manufacturing of cookies to a regional facility in Suzhou, China. Later in the year, Kraft Foods Australia announced that it would close its distribution center in Port Melbourne and a dairy plant in Strathmerton that manufactured cheese and Vegemite, an exclusively Australian product. All the product lines continue to be sold in Australia with a third-party logistics provider taking responsibility for the distribution of these products in Australia.

The employment contracts that Kraft had negotiated with its unions and the laws of Australia required the company to provide substantial support to its laid-off workers in both locations: They had to be paid a severance package that included four-weeks pay for each year worked at the plant (a benefit called an "entitlement") and given access to outplacement services for a minimum period of eight weeks (called a "redundancy package").[16]

Kraft Foods Vice President and Area Director for Australia/New Zealand Chris Bell said, "Kraft is especially mindful of the impact this decision will have on our employees, as we greatly value the support that all our employees give to Kraft Foods Australia. We will ensure that all affected [. . .] employees are given access to every support during this difficult period, and they are guaranteed to be paid their appropriate entitlements, including a redundancy package. Employees will also have access to comprehensive career transition support services."[17]

When it purchased the Broadmeadows plant in 2002 as a wholly owned Australian subsidiary, Kraft had undoubtedly anticipated the additional costs of its legal obligations to its new workforce, and it had considered the employees when it decided to close the plant. Not all companies who invest abroad do take those factors into consideration.

strategies or policies. The firm does not have to share its profits with anyone else, does not have to rely on anyone else for information on its customers, is free to pull out from a given market if the prospective sales do not become concrete, and so forth.

The WOFE strategy is also often very beneficial to the host country—it creates jobs, for one—and many countries offer substantial incentives to foreign companies willing to establish a facility within their borders: free land, tax abatements of all sorts, training programs, infrastructure improvements, and, if the foreign firm considering the investment is willing to establish itself in a rural or economically depressed area, the incentives can make a WOFE extremely attractive. For example, Ireland put in place an extensive panoply of tax incentives in the 1980s and achieved unprecedented growth and employment in the following decade. Today, Ireland is no longer perceived as an essentially rural country, but as a booming, economically prosperous country with access to the entire European market; its incentive program convinced dozens of firms to invest there.

The drawbacks of a subsidiary strategy are that there is a high cost of setting a facility abroad, and all of it is borne by a single firm. However, the firm can use this facility to manufacture goods to be shipped back to the home country or to other markets; for example, having a facility within the European Union gives a firm duty-free access to the entire Western European market and more favorable duty rates in Eastern Europe than a facility in the United States. The costs can therefore be recovered fairly quickly. Similarly, a Japanese firm can get duty-free access to the United States and Canada by setting up a facility in Mexico, which also enjoys low labor costs.

TABLE 4-2	Production Abroad

Methods of Production Abroad

Licensing	Licensing is the granting of rights to intellectual property owned by a company to another company for a fee. Licensing is quite common in manufacturing, where companies license processes they have developed to other firms, or products such as chemical compounds or molecules.
Joint Venture	With a joint venture, the exporter invests in a facility abroad, but finds one or more partners with which to share the costs of the venture.
Contract Manufacturing	Contract manufacturing occurs when a company enters an agreement with a producer in the foreign market to manufacture its goods. For example, a publishing firm may contract with a printing facility to publish its books rather than ship them from its home printing plant.
Franchising	Franchising is, in concept, quite similar to licensing, except that the franchisor is granting the rights to a large number of intellectual property items, all bundled in a business package, to a franchisee who pays royalties for using this business model. Most franchises tend to be retail establishments, like restaurants or bookshops.
Subsidiary	A subsidiary is an investment of 100 percent in a foreign venture by a firm. This strategy is followed by firms who want total control of an investment and are willing to take the risk of such a venture.

A wholly owned subsidiary subjects the firm to a high exposure to the risks of investments, although it is evident that the risks that make a management team worry about its investments abroad are in decline: Political risks are becoming less prominent, with yet a greater number of countries solidly in the democratic camp, and the economic risks are in decline as well. Except for countries in which there is no real market for many products, the prospects for a stable economy, a stable government, or, at least, a stable transition to a new government are very good.

A WOFE also faces the relocation costs if a decision is made to move the production facility to another country. Cost may include significant compensation to employees who will be laid off during the location process. The expenses vary by country and must be considered in the relocation analysis. In 2006, Kraft Foods decided to move its subsidiary from Australia to China, and this decision resulted in several substantial costs.

Finally, a WOFE presents the disadvantage of having to manage in a foreign country without a very good understanding of local customs and regulations. As a firm invests in a foreign country, it oftentimes chooses to have an expatriate manager at its helm; this manager often runs into difficulties that s/he may have avoided, had the firm elected to have a local partner. For example, the European countries have countless customs that sound peculiar or even counterproductive to any foreigner, but which local managers support heavily: thirty-five-hour workweeks in France, *Mitbestimmung* (co-determination) in Germany, late-night work hours in Spain, and so on. These drawbacks can easily be overcome by hiring a competent local general manager.

All of these methods of producing products abroad are summarized in Table 4-2.

4-5 Parallel Imports

One of the greatest problems faced by a firm involved in several markets is the risk of parallel imports, which is particularly acute if the firm has relinquished some control over its goods' prices; for example, by using distributors.

Parallel imports—or **gray market** goods—are goods that are sold outside the regular distribution channels of a company, usually because there is a discrepancy

gray market A process by which unauthorized intermediaries buy the products of a company in country A, export them to country B, and resell them to retailers and other intermediaries in country B.

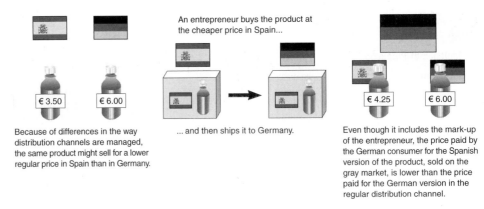

An entrepreneur buys the product at the cheaper price in Spain...

... and then ships it to Germany.

Because of differences in the way distribution channels are managed, the same product might sell for a lower regular price in Spain than in Germany.

Even though it includes the mark-up of the entrepreneur, the price paid by the German consumer for the Spanish version of the product, sold on the gray market, is lower than the price paid for the German version in the regular distribution channel.

Figure 4-2
The Gray Market

between the price charged in one country and the price charged in another. Gray market goods are not counterfeit or shoddy goods: They are the legitimate items, but are sold outside the channel chosen by the company (see Figure 4-2). For example, an item such as shampoo may sell at different prices in Germany and in Spain: For whatever reason, the Spanish version of a brand is significantly cheaper. An entrepreneur buys some shampoo in Spain, ships it to Germany, and sells it through a discount store. The price paid by a consumer in Germany for the Spanish version of the product ends up being lower than the price of the German version; because the sale is "outside" of the regular channel of distribution, it is considered a parallel import. The legitimate retailer in Germany is not happy to be undersold and the shampoo manufacturer has lost some control over the marketing of its products.

Parallel imports occur in all sorts of product lines, from shampoo to cars to spare parts; however, it is a particularly sensitive issue in luxury goods, such as watches, electronics, and high-end automobiles. While there are ways to combat parallel imports, which can be found in any good textbook in international marketing, the best strategy is to avoid having discrepancies in prices from one country to another, which usually means that the firm must have a coherent entry strategy.

On a final note, there is no legal recourse possible, as the product is a legitimate product, manufactured by an authorized plant. The Supreme Court of the United States affirmed this point recently: Once a firm has sold a product, it has no right to keep on controlling it. In Justice John Paul Stephens' words: "The whole point [...] is that once the copyright owner places a copyrighted material in the stream of commerce by selling it, it has exhausted its exclusive statutory right to control its distribution."[18] The U.S. Customs Service will not stop gray market goods unless they are different from the goods sold by the traditional distribution channel in the United States; for example, products with a different chemical composition under the same brand name to satisfy foreign requirements or consumer tastes abroad.[19] Other countries have taken similar stances.

4-6 Counterfeit Goods

counterfeit goods Goods that appear to have been produced by the legitimate manufacturer, but were actually produced by another company intent on deceiving customers and imitating the genuine goods.

One other significant issue when a firm starts to expand abroad is that it increases the probability that unscrupulous competitors—and sometimes partners—will manufacture and distribute counterfeit goods that mimic the original products. **Counterfeit goods** are copies of the original products, sold under the same (or a very similar) brand name, are generally of lower quality, and are sold at much lower prices than the original. Most of the time, the purchasers are well aware that they are not purchasing the genuine product, but do not feel that they are doing anything wrong:

They are intent on saving money or are interested in obtaining the status that the brand conveys, but without paying for it.

Counterfeiting activities generally happen when there is a substantial discrepancy between the variable cost of manufacturing the product and the price at which it sells. Counterfeits are therefore abundant in the software and in the entertainment industries; a DVD of a movie or a CD of a software program can be reproduced for a few pennies, but sell for much more.[20] Counterfeit activities are also common in luxury goods (handbags, watches, clothing),[21] pharmaceutical drugs,[22] and cigarettes,[23] all of which exhibit the same characteristics: low manufacturing costs and high selling prices. The probability increases further if the product is physically small and light enough that it can be sold easily and "discreetly" on the streets: Sidewalk peddlers constitute the most common "distribution channel" for counterfeit goods.

The existence of such counterfeiting activity is not dependent on the method of entry chosen. Whether a firm enters a foreign market through licensing, contract manufacturing, or a wholly owned subsidiary does not matter. Counterfeit manufacturing is generally present in countries in which government authorities have other priorities than defending the intellectual property rights of (foreign) firms. The countries of China and India are often the countries that are most commonly accused of ignoring counterfeiting activities, but they are just the more visible targets. Counterfeiting happens in just about any country in the world.

Since about 2003, many countries have started to crack down seriously on counterfeiting; there are several reasons for that policy. The governments of those countries have realized that counterfeiting is not a crime that just affects the profits of foreign firms, it also affects the health of their citizens, such as when they purchase counterfeit and dangerous pharmaceutical products,[24] it hurts their legitimate entrepreneurs who have intellectual property to protect,[25] and it sometimes hurt the interests of the state itself. China, for example, is cracking down on manufacturers of goods that use a counterfeit 2008 Beijing Olympics logo.[26] However, the task remains daunting; counterfeiting is difficult to prosecute and most consumers—as well as local law enforcement officials who are also consumers—see counterfeiting as a crime that benefits them[27] and only hurts the large foreign corporations with which they do not empathize.

4-7 Other Issues in Methods of Entry

4-7a Foreign Trade Zones (FTZ)

Foreign Trade Zones (FTZs) are areas of a country that have acquired a special Customs status, with the specific purpose of encouraging foreign investments and exports. Effectively, a Foreign Trade Zone—sometimes also called a Free Trade Zone—is an area of a country that is, for Customs purposes, still "outside" of the country; goods can be shipped to the FTZ without being subject to duty and quotas. Once in the FTZ, the goods can be transformed, assembled, repackaged, and so on. If the goods are re-exported, they never pay duty in the host country in which the FTZ is located; if they are sold in the host country, it is only after leaving the FTZ that they have to pay duty.

FTZs exist in one form or another in just about every country. Some countries use them aggressively to encourage foreign investments by allowing just about any economic activity within the zone, including manufacturing; goods come in the trade zone duty-free; are transformed in the zone into a final product, creating jobs in the host country; and the product is then re-exported abroad or in the host country. In China, for example, there were 11,900 foreign firms and 5,900 Chinese firms in FTZs in 1996, and they represented a substantial proportion of the total Chinese export activity.[28]

FTZs are particularly attractive to a manufacturer if the host country has a so-called "inverted tariff structure" (i.e., the tariffs charged on parts are higher than the tariffs charged on the final product).[29] FTZs can also be quite advantageous to hold a good in inventory until sold, or to wait for a numerical quota to open. However, in view of the progress made in the last few years by the WTO to lead countries to lower tariffs and increase trade, FTZs may have a limited future because their advantages are dwindling. Nevertheless, they remain attractive and should be considered as a possible alternative site for a foreign investment, whether a sales subsidiary, a joint venture, or a WOFE.

4-7b Maquiladoras

Maquiladoras are companies in the country of Mexico with a Customs status similar to the status of an FTZ located both in Mexico and in the United States. They can import goods from the United States duty-free, transform these goods by assembling them into products, and then re-export them to the United States, where the goods are only assessed duty on the value added in Mexico. Originally, maquiladora status could only be obtained in a geographic band located just south of Mexico's border with the United States, but it was expanded to the remainder of the country in the late 1980s. Today, with the completion of the North American Free Trade Agreement (NAFTA), maquiladoras have limited attractiveness to a foreign investor, but this alternative is still available.

4-7c Foreign Corrupt Practices Act

One of the last aspects of significant concern in the creation of a method of entry in a foreign country is the fact that business practices in some countries tend to include corruption and bribery. The Organization for Economic Cooperation and Development (OECD) has tried to ban such practices by developing its Anti-Bribery Convention (ABC), which thirty-six countries had ratified by June 2006. One aspect of the Convention is that it asks the developed countries' governments to cease the practice of letting firms deduct bribery as a business expense; as of July 2006, all but one OECD country prohibited the tax deduction of bribes to foreign officials. However, the United States is one of the few countries to have passed a punitive Foreign Corrupt Practices Act (FCPA), which heavily fines companies that are caught using bribery to gain access to some contracts. Several countries have incorporated in their legislation anti-bribery laws that extend beyond the prohibition of bribes directed at foreign government officials.[30]

The FCPA is far-reaching and prohibits "all officers and employees and anyone else acting on behalf of the firm and its subsidiaries [from] offer[ing] any payments, direct or indirect, or through a third party, to government officials in return for getting or keeping business."[31] This includes payments made by an agent to a foreign official, or "special incentives" given to a well-connected partner in exchange for having won a contract: Anything that is not contractual is suspect. The U.S. government prosecutes any firm in the United States that it thinks has violated the law, whether it knew of the practice or not, and fines can run in the millions of U.S. dollars.

The FCPA and the ABC are attempts by the developed countries' governments to "clean up" business practices abroad and prevent firms from being subject to extortion by corrupt foreign government officials. So far, there seems to be minimal evidence that these efforts have been effective, but they have taught foreign officials that it was useless to attempt to request bribes from developed countries' companies, and, in that respect, these efforts have worked. There is substantial grumbling, though, in the export community that the FCPA and the ABC have cost developed countries' exporters billions of dollars in lost business to foreign competitors that are unimpeded by these laws and can deduct bribes as a business expense.[32]

From a practical standpoint, for any exporter, the rules are fairly simple: Business abroad must be conducted above board and remain within the boundaries set in the original agency or distributorship contracts. The only things that the FCPA and the ABC will tolerate is "facilitating payments for routine government actions," such as obtaining permits, speeding up telephone installation, and clearing Customs.[33]

Key Terms

binding agent (p. 60)

counterfeit goods (p. 72)

franchisee (p. 67)

franchising (p. 67)

franchisor (p. 67)

gray market (p. 71)

intellectual property (p. 66)

licensee (p. 66)

licensing (p. 66)

licensor (p. 66)

principal (p. 60)

royalty (p. 66)

Review and Discussion Questions

1. What are the principal differences between an agent and a distributor?

2. What are the different methods of entry regrouped under the term "Indirect Export"?

3. Using a product of your choice and a country of your choice, determine what would be the best method of entry for an exporter interested in that market. Justify your decision using the guidelines provided in the chapter.

4. Why would a company decide to franchise abroad?

5. What advantages would a foreign trade zone represent for an importer/exporter?

6. What are the advantages and disadvantages of using a subsidiary rather than a joint venture for a firm interested in manufacturing abroad?

Endnotes

1. Barovick, Richard, "Sogo Shosha Traders Finance U.S. Exports," *The Journal of Commerce*, April 8, 1998, p. 5A.

2. Selz, Michael, "More Small Firms are Turning to Trade Intermediaries," *The Wall Street Journal*, February 2, 1993, p. B2.

3. Root, Franklin R., *Entry Strategies for International Markets*, Revised and Expanded Edition, Lexington Books, 1994.

4. Bello, Daniel C., and Ritu Lohtia, "Export Channel Design: The Use of Foreign Distributors and Agents," *Journal of the Academy of Marketing Science*, Spring 1995, pp. 83–93.
   —Root, Franklin R., *Entry Strategies for International Markets*, Revised and Expanded Edition, Lexington Books, 1994.
   —Rosenbloom, Bert, and G. Behrens Ulrich, *Marketing Channels: A Management View*, Sixth Edition, The Dryden Press, 1998.

5. *Ibid*

6. Shirouzu, Norihiko, "In Japan, Breaking Up Can Be Hard to Do," *The Wall Street Journal*, December 31, 1997, p. A7.

7. Tirschwell, Peter, "The ABCs of FSCs," *The Journal of Commerce*, November 29, 1997, p. 1C.

8. Olin, Jeffery, "Manufacturers Can Profit from Changes in International Tax Law," *World Trade*, May 2005, p. 8.

9. Platt, Gordon, "U.S. Tax Breaks Are Still Available," *The Journal of Commerce*, October 18, 1999, p. 8.

10. Martin, Josh, "Profitable Supply Chain," *The Journal of Commerce*, March 11, 1998, p. 1C.

11. Engardio, Pete, and Michael Shari, "The Suharto Empire," *Business Week*, August 19, 1996, pp. 46–50.

12. Roberts, Dexter, Christopher Power, and Stephanie Anderson-Forest, "Cheated in China?" *Business Week*, October 6, 1997.
    —Smith, Craig, "Foreign Investors Break Loose from Chinese Partners," *The Wall Street Journal*, June 6, 1998, p. A17.

13. Bradsher, Keith, "After Latin Venture Fails, Volkswagen Succeeds and Ford Scrambles," *The New York Times*, May 16, 1997.

14. Rykken, Rolf, "Buying into Europe," *Export Today*, September 1997, pp. 22–27.

15. Gottschalk, Arthur, "Hand-me-down Factories Fill Niche in Emerging Markets," *The Journal of Commerce*, April 8, 1997, p. 1A.

16. Ross, Emily, "Sack with Care," *Business Management, Compak 2006 Supplement*, http://www.vcta.asn.au/files/2006%20files/compak06/May/BM206_2.pdf, June 6, 2006.

17. "Kraft Foods Cuts Australian Jobs, Moves to China," *China SCR: News & Views on Corporate Social Responsibility in China*, January 12, 2006, http://www.chinacsr.com/2006/01/12/kraft-foods-cuts-australian-jobs-moves-to-china, June 6, 2006.

18. Greenhouse, Linda, "Court Ruling Helps 'Gray Market' in U.S. Goods," *The New York Times*, March 10, 1998.

19. Lucentini, Jack, "Where Can Exports Be Imports?" *The Journal of Commerce*, December 15, 1999, p. 9.

20. Meredith, Robyn, "(Microsoft's) Long March," *Forbes*, February 17, 2003, pp. 78–86. Slater, Joanna, "Author Fights Copycat Tactics of 'Bollywood,'" *The Wall Street Journal*, June 16, 2003, p. B1.

21. White, Erin, and Cecilie Rohwedder, "Tan, Black and Red: All Over?", *The Wall Street Journal*, May 7, 2003, p. B1.

22. Abbod, Leila, Anna Wilde Mathews, and Heather Won Tesoriero, "Fakes in the Medicine Chest," *The Wall Street Journal*, September 22, 2003, p. B1.

23. Wright, Tom, "Indonesia Turns to Trademark Piracy," *The Wall Street Journal*, September 9, 2003, p. A20.

24. Yardley, Jim, "Infants in Chinese City Starve on Protein-Short Formula," *The New York Times*, May 5, 2004.

25. Balfour, Frederik, "Fakes: The Global Counterfeiting Business is Out of Control, Targeting Everything from Computer Chips to Life-Saving Medicines. It's So Bad That Even China May Need to Crack Down," *Business Week*, February 7, 2005, pp. 54–64.

26. Fowler, Geoffrey A., "China's Logo Crackdown," *The Wall Street Journal*, November 4, 2005, p. B1.

27. Fishman, Ted C., "Manufaketure," *The New York Times*, January 9, 2005.

28. Linn, Gene, "China's Bonded Free-Trade Zones May Be Sleeping Economic Giants," *The Journal of Commerce*, March 12, 1997, p. 16C.

29. Schwartz, Beth, "The ABCs of FTZs," *Transportation and Distribution*, November 1998, pp. 79–82.

30. "Country Descriptions of Tax Legislation on the Tax Treatment of Bribes," Organization for Economic Co-operation and Development, June 2006, http://www.oecd.org/dataoecd/42/43/37116153.pdf, July 31, 2006.

31. Gersten, Alan, "Ignorance Is Not Excused," *The Journal of Commerce*, January 15, 1997, p. 1C.

32. Gesteland, Richard R., "Avoiding the Bribery Trap," *Export Today*, February 1996, p. 18.

33. "Foreign Corrupt Practices Act Antibribery Provisions," United States Department of Justice—Fraud Division, and United States Department of Commerce—Office of the Chief Counsel for International Commerce, http://www.usdoj.gov/criminal/fraud/fcpa/dojdocb.htm, October 10, 2000.
    —Finch, Michael J. and Peter J. Pettibone, "Beyond Backsheesh," *Export Today*, February 1996, p. 14.

International Contracts

Chapter **Five**

Source: © 2007 JupiterImages Corporation.

Whenever a firm gets involved in international business, it enters into a substantial number of contracts, either written or implied, with a number of partners, some of which are located abroad. Examples of such contracts would be:

- The contract of sale between the exporter and the importer
- The contract of insurance between the exporter or the importer (depending on the terms of sale, which will be covered in Chapter 6) and an insurance company
- The contract of carriage between the exporter or the importer and the shipping line
- The contract between an exporter and its agent or distributor
- The contract between an exporter or an importer and its bank, regarding payment arrangements such as documentary collection or letters of credit (concepts that will be covered in Chapter 7)
- and so on.

All of these contracts are formed under the precepts of a multitude of traditions, local laws, multilateral governmental agreements, and international treaties that are sometimes not ratified or only partially ratified by some countries. Frequently, these contracts are further complicated by a profoundly different understanding of what a contract represents. Nevertheless, international traders and logistics managers learn to operate within this complex framework.

5-1 *Lex Mercatoria*

Lex Mercatoria The sum total of all the international agreements, international conventions, and other international trade customs that complement the domestic laws of any given country, and to which all international trade transactions are subject.

Whenever a contract is established between two parties in the same country, the law governing the execution of this contract is clearly determined by that country's legal system. In the United States, for example, it is the Uniform Commercial Code, and there is ample jurisprudence and expertise to determine how this contract should be executed. However, when the contract is between two parties in different countries, there is no specific law governing this contract, except what is called *Lex Mercatoria*—trade law—a multitude of international agreements and international trade customs, all of which complement domestic laws.

Lex Mercatoria is complex because it includes a multitude of different sources of law and jurisprudence. There are United Nations treaties and other decisions; international agreements, such as the General Agreement on Tariffs and Trade (GATT), which has given rise to the World Trade Organization (WTO) with its own rules and Court system; multilateral agreements on specific industry issues, such as the Warsaw Convention on international air transport or the textile Multi-Fiber Agreement; regional agreements, such as the European Union or the North American Free Trade Agreement (NAFTA); bilateral agreements, such as the "Open Skies" agreement between the United States and the Netherlands (see Chapter 12) or the special status granted to Hong Kong by the People's Republic of China; International Chamber of Commerce rules, such as the Incoterms for terms of trade (see Chapter 6) or the UCP-500 for bank documentary credits (see Chapter 7); arbitration decisions and jurisprudence, established by the International Chamber of Commerce Arbitration Court or private arbitrators, and so on. In addition, many countries pick and choose which treaties they will ratify and, on occasion, which articles of the treaties they will ratify. They can also choose to become "signatories" to a treaty, which means they do not make a full commitment to a treaty, while others decide to abide by the terms of the treaty, but do not ratify them. Finally, things get even more "interesting" when courts decide that some domestic principle cannot be violated by an international convention or custom. This chapter does not attempt to cover *Lex Mercatoria* in depth; only an overview of three of its major

Web Exercise

For more information on the WTO and trade agreements, check out these websites. Many people oppose the activities of the WTO, and American voters were split over the issue of NAFTA. Take a look at the information and think about how these organizations and treaties would affect a small business owner and a large business owner. Visit the sites on Hong Kong as well, and look in the news for stories on its economic condition. How is its status as a special region of China affecting business? Is this the outcome that was predicted at its handover in 1997?

- World Trade Organization (http://www.wto.org) The official site of the WTO, explaining its goals and

accomplishments, and providing information on meeting dates, members, and more.

- GATT-guide (http://www.ciesin.org/TG/PI/TRADE/gatt.html) A guide to GATT including text of the agreement and related links.

- NAFTA (http://www.nafta-sec-alena.org/english/index.htm) Complete text of the North American Free Trade Agreement and links to NAFTA-related issues and other documents.

- Hong Kong Special Administrative Region (http://www.china-un.org/eng/5295.html)From the Chinese mission to the UN.

- (http://www.uni-wuerzburg.de/law/hk00000_.html) The Hong Kong constitution.

aspects is presented here. The first part covers the issues regarding the contract of sale between an exporter and an importer, which, for most countries, are covered by the United Nations Convention on Contracts for the International Sale of Goods (CISG). The second part of the chapter covers the issues regarding contracts between exporters and agents and contracts between exporters and distributors, as well as the resolution of eventual disputes through the arbitration system.

The specific aspects of contracts as they pertain to the terms of sale—the International Commerce Terms (Incoterms) of the International Chamber of Commerce (ICC)—will be covered in Chapter 6. Contracts relating to banking and payments will be covered in Chapter 7, insurance contracts will be covered in Chapter 10, and contracts of carriage between shippers and carriers will be covered in Chapters 11 and 12.

5-2 International Sales Contracts and the CISG

Whether or not a sales contract is "international" is not always self-evident. Courts will generally look at two criteria to decide whether a contract is international: the economic criterion, that is, whether there was a transaction that involved a transfer of merchandise from one country to another, and its mirror image of a transfer of funds; and the judicial criterion, which is based on whether the transaction has "links" to the laws of different states.[1] For example, a sale of office supplies to a French company's subsidiary in Germany by a German supplier is not considered "international"; however, the same sale to the company's headquarters, located just across the border, would be international. Whenever there is a sales contract between two parties in two different countries, then the domestic laws no longer apply, and it is governed by the Vienna Convention.[2]

The Vienna Convention, or the United Nations Convention on Contracts for the International Sale of Goods (CISG), was born in 1980 of two other conventions, the Uniform Law for the International Sale of Goods (ULIS) and the Uniform Law on the Formation of Contracts for the International Sale of Goods (ULF). Both had been written in the Hague in 1964, but were ratified by only a few countries because they were somewhat deficient.[3] In contrast, the CISG has been ratified by more than sixty countries,[4] whose export and import activities represent more than 80 percent of all world trade. As often is the case, though, several countries, including the United States, have not ratified all of the convention, and left out some provisions, some of which may have conflicted with domestic law. However, the CISG has become the Law of International Contracts, as traders will often elect to have their contracts governed by the laws of a contracting state (e.g., the United States) and therefore the CISG will apply.

The CISG is substantially different from the Uniform Commercial Code (UCC)—the Commercial Law of the United States—in a few of its aspects, notably the contract formation and remedies in the case of nonconforming goods or late delivery. It is likely to be different from a number of other countries' domestic laws as well, as evidenced by the number of countries that have not ratified specific articles of the CISG. Although these exclusions may make good political fodder, they may not be acceptable to the Courts who will have to handle disputes between traders located in countries that have adopted different versions of the CISG, or have amended it to include some other interpretation.[5]

5-2a Contract Formation

The CISG does not consider that a contract has been accepted until both parties agree to all of its terms: It is customary for a seller to make an **offer**. The buyer may respond positively, but indicate that it wants a different schedule of delivery or term of payment, or some other aspect of the transaction to be handled differently. Under the UCC, such a response is construed as an **acceptance** of the offer. Under the CISG, it is understood as a **rejection** of the offer made by the seller and as a **counteroffer** by the buyer, unless the terms suggested do not materially affect the contract. The CISG specifies that changes to "price, payment, quality, and quantity of the goods, place, and time of delivery, extent of one party's liability to the other (most likely to be understood as Incoterms) or the settlement of disputes are considered to alter the terms of the offer materially" and therefore that no acceptance is made in those cases.

Another area of difference between UCC and CISG regarding offer and acceptance of a sales contract is what is referred to by U.S. lawyers as the "Battle of the Forms." For most businesses, an offer or an acceptance is made on some standard business form, with a number of "small print" statements preprinted on it, designed to protect the interests of the party writing the offer (or the acceptance). In most instances, these preprinted clauses do not match. Under the UCC, the Courts have determined that the differences do not matter in the formation of a contract, unless they significantly affect the terms of the contract, and regard these different terms as additions to the terms of the contract, to be sorted by the Court in the case of conflict. Under the CISG, the requirement of a "mirror image" may signify a return to what, for Americans, would be the pre-UCC rules, where the terms of the contract are determined by the form of the party "firing the last shot," or it may signify that there is no contract until all terms match, with little tolerance for differences.[6] There is little evidence that the second interpretation is likely to prevail, especially if both parties thought there was a contract and acted in consequence.

5-2b Creation of the Contract

The CISG treats the length of time during which the offer is considered outstanding in a significantly different manner than the UCC does. Most offers contain a clause stating that the offer is open until a certain date; under the UCC, however, the offer can be withdrawn at any time, without prejudice, for almost any reason. Under the CISG, the offer cannot be withdrawn by the seller (or the buyer) before its expiration date, and the other party can accept it at any time until that time. It is considered an irrevocable offer.

The CISG does not dictate that contracts of sale have to be written: Any agreement between a seller and a buyer can form a contract. Obviously, the issues of the

---

offer The initial step in the formation of a contract. When one of the parties to a potential sale contacts the other party, it does so with an offer to enter into a contract. Offers are treated differently under CISG and UCC.

acceptance The second step in the formation of a contract. After an offer has been made by one of the parties, the contract is formed if the other party accepts the terms of the offer. Acceptance is determined differently under CISG and UCC.

rejection An intermediary step in the formation of a contract. After an offer has been made by one of the parties, the other party may not agree with all of the terms of the offer, reject the original offer, and make a counteroffer.

counteroffer An intermediary step in the formation of a contract. After an offer has been made by one of the parties, the other party may not agree with all of the terms of the offer, and may want to modify them. Counteroffers are treated differently under CISG and UCC.

proof of the existence of a contract and of the terms of the contract then become quite thorny unless there are witnesses to the discussion between seller and buyer. Even in the event where a contract of sale is signed, the written terms of the contract can be superseded by an oral exchange between the two parties, as long as there is evidence that it was the intent of both parties. In one of the jurisprudence cases contained in the United Nations Commission on International Trade Law (UNCI-TRAL) database—called CLOUT, for the Case Law on UNCITRAL texts—two witnesses corroborated that the written terms of the contract had been modified orally by the seller and buyer, and the modifications were used by the Court in determining the case.[7] In contrast, the UCC requires that any sales agreement above U.S. $500 must be in writing.

5-2c Breach of Contract

Finally, the CISG treats nonconforming goods and delays in shipments much differently than does the UCC. Whereas the UCC applies the "perfect tender" principle (i.e., the goods must exactly conform to the goods contracted and be delivered within the framework specified in the contract), the CISG grants the seller more latitude. For example, the buyer cannot refuse delivery or cancel unless the nonconformity or the delay "substantially deprives the buyer of what it was entitled to expect under the contract and, even then, only if the seller foresaw, or a party in its position would have foreseen, such a result."[8] In other words, the buyer cannot avoid the contract unless the seller performs a fundamental **breach** of the contract. Therefore, those firms operating on a just-in-time basis should specifically notify their suppliers that they are following such a manufacturing policy, so that their suppliers can then "foresee" the problem that a delay in shipment would cause.

breach In the event that one of the parties to a contract does not meet its obligation, that party can be found to have broken the terms of the contract, or to be in breach of the contract.

In counterbalance, the CISG allows the buyer to unilaterally apply a price reduction to the amount agreed upon in the contract for nonconforming goods. Such a price reduction should be proportional to the loss of value of the goods (percentage that are nonconforming) or to the loss of market incurred by the buyer, in the event of a delay. However, the burden placed on the buyer to notify the seller in a timely manner and to explain which remedy it will seek has a very high threshold. The notification must be made as soon as possible; it has to be clear and painstakingly detailed in the description of the problem and it has to be extremely clear and specific in the remedies sought. Several cases in CLOUT show that the burden placed on the buyer by the Courts seems unduly harsh: several examples given by McMahon[9] seem that way, anyhow. In addition, this issue is somewhat moot for a buyer paying on a Letter of Credit (see Chapter 7), because it is committed to pay for the full amount in all cases. Finally, the notification by the buyer to the seller that a price reduction will unilaterally be applied must be made within two years; such a long upper limit is also of concern, because the statute of limitations for claims against a carrier may be shorter than that in some countries, preventing the seller from recovering damages caused by a carrier.[10]

5-3 Agency versus Distributorship Legal Issues

The second type of contracts of interest are the contracts between an exporter and its representatives in foreign markets; either an agent or a distributor. To briefly repeat ground covered in Chapter 4, an agent is a representative located abroad and earning a commission on the sales it makes on behalf of the exporter. An agent cannot negotiate prices, delivery, or other sales terms with the buyer, but only represents the decisions made by the exporter. A distributor is also located abroad, but it purchases goods from the exporter, with the idea of reselling them in its country, earning a profit in the process. The distributor is setting its own prices and has an inventory of goods to sell: It is most often responsible for after-sale service as well.

It is difficult to generalize about agency and distributorship agreements: There is no international agreement on the way each of these relationships is governed. In most cases, the country of residence of the agent or of the distributor considers that it has jurisdiction over the agreement, and in many cases, despite the fact that the agreement may specify that the laws of another country apply to the contract (see Section 5-4h and Section 5-4i for specific information regarding the Choice of Law and the Choice of Forum in an international distribution contract). Because each country has its own laws and regulations regarding these agreements and because the jurisprudence of each country may differ even on similar statutes, it is very difficult to be specific without getting into tedious listings of countries. Therefore, only broader issues will be covered, to understand which aspects of a distribution contract should be examined.

5-3a Contract Law versus Labor Law

distribution contract An agreement between an exporter and an intermediary; it can take the form of either an agency or a distributorship agreement.

contract law A set of a country's laws that governs relationships and disputes between the parties who signed a contract. Contract Law essentially dictates that the Courts must settle the dispute by using the terms of the contract.

In the absence of specifics, agreements between an exporter and an agent and agreements between an exporter and a distributor will be called **distribution contracts**. One of the greatest differences among countries is whether they consider such distribution agreements as "contracts between equals" or as "contracts between unequal partners."

In the first case, Courts will consider the terms of the contract when dealing in a dispute: this approach is referred to as **contract law** or case law, where the question is resolved by trying to interpret the meaning of the contract between the two parties. Both parties are considered to have equal sophistication in dealing with legal matters, and therefore none of the parties would have entered a contract without understanding it. Most countries, but certainly not all, consider that agreements between an exporter and a distributor fall into this category: The contract between the two parties is the framework that Courts will consider in dealing with a dispute between the two parties. When the contract is silent about the point in contention, then the Courts will use jurisprudence and what other contracts of the same type have established.

labor law A set of a country's laws that governs relationships and disputes between employers and employees; it assumes that one of the parties (employee) needs to be protected from the other (employer).

In other cases, though, countries will equate an international distribution agreement as something akin to an "employment contract," where the parties are considered unequal in their ability to interpret and understand a legal contract, and therefore where the "weaker party" has to be protected. This point of view calls for the application of **labor law** or for the application of special statutes, dealing specifically with the relationship between an exporter and an agent, or an exporter and a distributor. Such statutes cannot be overruled by the terms of the contract in any way. Therefore, the Courts, in ruling in a dispute between the two contract parties, will ignore the terms of the contract and use the laws of the country in which the agent or distributor is located. Most countries that follow such an interpretation will tend to protect agents rather than distributors—Belgium being the lone country protecting its distributors but not its agents[11]—but several protect both. In addition, this point of view is often independent of the fact that the agent or the distributor is an individual or a corporation, and labor law has been used to supersede contracts between an exporter and an incorporated agent.

5-3b Home Government Restrictions

The main reason some countries use specific statutes to regulate international distribution agreements is that they feel that they need to protect agents and/or distributors against contracts that may not be fair or equitable. Specifically, they want to protect agents or distributors against wrongful or abusive termination (more specific information on this aspect of International Distribution Contracts can be found in Section 5-5).

In addition, those governments can also construct much more complicated systems to manage agents and distributors operating within their borders. They can require the agents and distributors to **register** with the government, which is a system not unlike a professional association, but that often doubles as a tax. They can require that the agents and distributors be nationals of the country in which they represent the exporter; such is the case of most Middle-Eastern countries. They can also mandate that the terms of the contracts be inspected by their administration, in order to monitor the commissions paid to agents, for example, which they sometimes limit with a floor or a ceiling. Other governments will only allow exclusive agents or distributors—a single agent or distributor within a specific geographic area, usually the country itself—as do most South American countries. Finally, some governments will simply not allow agents at all—they mandate a distributor—or not allow any third-party representation, coercing exporters to establish a subsidiary, which they can then tax on income. Unfortunately, it is difficult to generalize about all of these different requirements, as they are very country-specific—they even vary from one region of a country to another, as shown in the laws of the state of Louisiana, which are in contrast with the laws of just about any other area in the United States, or of the laws of the Alsace-Lorraine region, which are significantly different from the remainder of France—and can change at any time. Specific legal expertise and advice is therefore necessary before writing a distribution contract in any country.

register A process whereby an agent or a distributor has to notify the government of the importing country that it has entered into an agency agreement or a distributorship agreement with a foreign manufacturer.

5-4 Elements of an Agency or Distributor Contract

There are a number of points that must be covered in any contract, regardless of the country of the world in which it will be used. This section explores a number of these mandatory contract elements. Some country-specific requirements can obviously still influence each one of them.

5-4a Contract Language

Because distribution agreements are usually entered into by two parties who do not share a common language, it is often necessary to have these contracts written in two languages. However, as any speaker of a foreign language can attest, it is utterly impossible to translate accurately and precisely contract terminology from one language to another. It is therefore critical to include a clause that specifies that the contract written in Language A is the original contract and that the contract written in Language B is a translation, and that in case of dispute or problems of interpretation, the original contract should prevail.

There are exceptions to this practical rule, however. Most international agreements between countries, such as the UN Convention on Contracts for the International Sales of Goods (CISG) or the International Chamber of Commerce's Incoterms, are written in several languages, *all of which* are given the same legal status; they are all "originals," which can sometimes present problems when translations cannot precisely duplicate the meaning of the framers of the agreement. These problems could be avoided by having one original and the others translations, but it would create political uneasiness, so it is not done.

5-4b Good Faith

Another mandatory clause in a distribution agreement is a clause stating that both parties enter into the agreement in **good faith**. A contract is entered in good faith

good faith The assumption that both parties signing an agreement want to enter that agreement and have no ulterior motives.

when neither of the parties has any other ulterior motive about the agreement. It's probably best to understand good faith as the prerequisite for a contract to be formed: Both parties must want to fulfill the terms of the contract rather than pursue some other idea, using the contract agreement to dupe the other party into providing them some necessary material toward that goal.

The same interpretation of good faith applies to the terms of the contract as well; both parties agree that they will adhere to the terms of the contract in good faith (i.e., interpret them without trying to distort them to their advantage). Both parties agree to deal fairly with each other, and not try to dupe the other by attempting to find "loopholes" in the terms of the contract.

5-4c *Force Majeure*

force majeure An event beyond the control of any of the parties in an agreement that prevents one of the parties from fulfilling its commitment.

All contracts contain some sort of a *force majeure* clause. This is a French expression that translates loosely as "overwhelming power," but which refers to any event that cannot be avoided and for which no one is responsible, at least none of the two parties entering the contract. Contracts may also contain phrases such as "Acts of God" or "Powers of Princes" to address acts beyond the control of the parties. Examples of such events would be a major storm that sinks the ship carrying products to the distributor, or a fire that prevents a firm from producing the goods on time, civil unrest, or a lengthy strike at a port that delays the delivery of the goods. Contracts always contain a clause that absolves either party from not fulfilling their responsibilities in case of *force majeure*, or a cause of non-performance beyond their control. Generally, there is also some statement that qualifies such exemption of liability to perform: "as long as the affected party resumes the performance of this agreement" after the *force majeure*.

5-4d Scope of Appointment

The scope of appointment clause principally defines the function that the representative will perform; it is the clause that spells out whether it will be an agent or a distributor and it is generally the first clause in the contract.

It also indicates the products to which both parties agree the contract applies, to define the minimum product line that the agent or distributor is expected to sell, and at the same time to limit the product line the representative is allowed to sell. There is often language to the effect that the representative cannot "cherry pick" the most profitable products and ignore the remainder of the line; this latter requirement may be expressed in quantitative terms. In addition, a list of the products that are to be sold by the representative is often placed in an Appendix and made part of the contract.

The scope of appointment clause also refers to the territory of the agreement and to corporate accounts, both of which are defined later in the agreement.

5-4e Territory

The territory clause defines the geographical limits within which the agent or distributor is authorized (expected) to sell. It is generally the entire country in which the representative is located, with some possible exceptions. In very large countries, there may be a regional appointment, and for countries with limited sales potential, there may be several countries included. The clause also spells out whether the agreement makes the agent or distributor an **exclusive representative** in that territory, which essentially grants a monopoly to the representative.

exclusive representative An agent or a distributor that has been granted the right of being the sole representative of the exporter in a given territory.

There are many problems associated with the definition of an exclusive territory, specifically in the European Union: While it is possible to write a contract limiting a representative to a single country's territory, the EU considers that a firm operating in one EU country can also legally sell in any other. It is therefore difficult for the exporter to limit the activities of a representative to a single country—it is contrary to the laws of the EU, and has been construed as an antitrust violation[12]—and it is difficult to grant exclusive rights to a territory when neighboring representatives have the right to sell there as well.

In many South American countries, the issue is different: Unless an international representation agreement specifically spells out that it is non-exclusive, then it is always interpreted as an exclusive agreement in that territory.[13]

5-4f Corporate Accounts

Some agreements will specify which customers remain corporate accounts, or customers to which the representative is not allowed to sell, for whatever reason. Generally, corporate accounts are very large customers who have negotiated terms that will apply to all their purchases worldwide. The agreement always includes some provisions under which the list of corporate accounts can be amended.

It is important for an exporter to pay close attention to the number of corporate accounts that are included in a representation agreement, because too many of them may discourage the representative. An example of such a counterproductive agreement would be one that specifies that all accounts above a certain level of sales automatically become corporate accounts; consequently, a successful agent, after having developed an account and reached that critical level of sales, would see it removed from its commission basis, and, therefore, from its income. This is certainly not the way to reward a good representative intent on excelling and is likely to limit the sales of the exporter, as such a policy encourages the representative to limit its efforts to stay "just below" the critical threshold.

5-4g Term of Appointment

This clause determines the duration of the appointment of the representative. It must always be a definite period, with the possibility of renewal if certain performance criteria are met.

It is critical to determine the original duration of the contract appropriately; finding the balance between a sufficiently long appointment period, so that the representative has enough time to develop the market to the point where it is a sustainable venture, and a sufficiently short period, so that an ineffective representative may be removed and replaced without too much of an opportunity cost to the exporter, is a very delicate task. Most of the time, such an initial appointment period is dictated by the market conditions and by the type of product sold. If the representative is expected to do so-called "pioneer sales," in which it has to sell a new product with little brand awareness and unique characteristics, a longer period is necessary than for a standard product with multiple competitors and a well-known brand. If the market is characterized by personal contacts and long-term relationships between customers and suppliers, then a longer period is necessary than in a market that is more competitive and fluid.

The clause also specifies, once the initial appointment period is completed, the renewal period, and, very importantly, the conditions under which the contract will be renewed for that duration. Renewal periods can be similar in duration to the initial appointment period, or can be shorter; there are no specific recommendations either way. What is important is to specify clearly the performance criteria for renewal: level of sales reached, market share obtained, number of customers contacted, amount spent on advertising, number of sales calls made, and so forth. The issue is to make sure that the contract is not renewed as a matter of course.

Should the representative not meet the criteria for renewal set in the contract at the end of the initial appointment period, then the principal has two alternatives. It certainly can terminate the contract, which is often a bad solution, unless the representative has done particularly poorly, as the exporter is now confronted with the task of finding another representative. This decision also creates ill will: The slighted representative can always retaliate and create problems for the next appointed representative and alienate existing customers by giving them the impression that the firm is not committed to that market.

The other alternative is to renew the contract anyhow: The representative may have been unable to achieve the objectives set in the original agreement because of circumstances beyond its control, or because the difficulties of entering the market had been underestimated, or because the market potential had been overestimated. In any case, what is important is to renew the contract but to make clear to the representative, in a carefully worded communication, that the terms of the renewal had not been met, but that the exporter was willing to renew because of the circumstances.

Should such a communication be omitted and the contract be renewed anyhow, it could then be construed by a Court as an **evergreen contract**; that is, a contract with no determined duration, and a contract that can no longer be terminated for non-performance as there was a precedent of non-performance and simultaneous renewal. Although generally a couple of instances are necessary before such a conclusion is reached, some overprotective Court may not see it that way.

evergreen contract A contract that, by design or by default, does not have a specific term of appointment.

5-4h Choice of Law

Because an international contract is a contract that has links to the laws of two different countries, some different interpretations of specific clauses are quite possible. To avoid these problems of interpretation, every contract includes a clause that determines which of the two sets of laws should be used by a Court or by an arbitration panel when a conflict arises between the parties. In general, the Choice of Law is made by the exporter rather than the agent or distributor; however, this does not preclude a possible resolution in the Courts of the importing country, which may assume jurisdiction over the contract because of their country's statutes regarding agents or distributors, despite the clause.

In a well-publicized case, individual American investors in Lloyd's of London insurance syndicates tried to sue the company in U.S. Courts, to circumvent an exemption from liability from negligence that the company enjoys in the United Kingdom. However, because the contract between the investors and Lloyd's clearly stated that the laws of the United Kingdom would prevail in case of dispute—the Choice of Law—the Supreme Court ruled that the U.S. Courts had no jurisdiction over the dispute,[14] even though such an exemption is contrary to generally accepted principles of law in the United States. The peculiarities of Lloyd's insurance market and its functioning, as well as its problems with investors, will be covered in Chapter 10.

The International Chamber of Commerce (ICC) Model Contracts for Agency[15] and for Distributorship[16] approach the issue of Choice of Law innovatively, by giving the contract writer two possibilities: The first is the traditional choice of a specific country's laws, the second being the "principles of law generally recognized in international trade as applicable to international agency [distribution] contracts,"[17] or those principles that constitute the *Lex Mercatoria* mentioned earlier in this chapter. As more and more arbitration jurisprudence accumulates, this alternative may become the preferred way of wording Choice of Law clauses as it shields both parties from unexpected outcomes.

5-4i Choice of Forum or Venue

Strongly linked to the Choice of Law is the Choice of Forum or Venue clause. In it, both parties agree on the location of the Court that will rule on an eventual dispute, using the laws chosen in the Choice of Law clause. In most instances, the Choice of Law somewhat dictates the Choice of Forum, as it makes logical sense to link both, and benefit from a Court experienced in the jurisprudence of the laws governing the contract.

5-4j Arbitration Clause

An increasing number of contracts include a clause, which does not call for a Court to settle disputes, but for an **arbitration panel**. Either the arbitration panel is decided upon at the outset of the contract, or a mention is made of the "Rules of Conciliation and Arbitration of the International Chamber of Commerce" to outline how the panel should be chosen. Generally speaking, the panel is made up of three arbitrators, with each of the parties choosing one and the third chosen by the arbitration organization, such as the ICC. In many instances, the clause states that the dispute will be "finally settled"[18] by the panel (i.e., that the panel's decision is binding on both parties). If the country in which the **arbitration** takes place is one of the 130 signatory countries to the New York Convention on the Enforcement of Foreign Arbitral Awards, then the ruling can be enforced just about anywhere;[19] unfortunately, China, although a signatory, has stood out as the only country where arbitration awards have not been enforced.[20] There are several specific advantages to settling a dispute through arbitration, most of which are outlined in Section 5-6.

arbitration panel A group of (generally) three arbitrators who are empowered by the parties involved in a contract dispute to reach a decision on the facts of the dispute, and whose decision is binding on all parties.

arbitration A process by which the parties to a contract can settle a dispute, involving a panel of arbitrators who will render a decision in a much shorter period of time.

5-4k Mediation Clause

In some contracts, the possibility of **mediation** or conciliation is encouraged before arbitration or **litigation** is undertaken: A mediator is an individual who will encourage and facilitate the communication between both parties in a dispute so that they can reach a compromise satisfactory to both. A mediator will not reach a decision for the parties; she or he will only lead the parties toward a compromise. Mediation is not binding, which means that the decision cannot be enforced and has to be agreed upon by both parties. Because mediation is also done in private, there are no public records of mediation, and it is an appropriate alternative to settling disputes when one of the parties is concerned about "saving face."[21] Mediation is sometimes initiated by the arbitration panel or the Court for resolutions of disputes where both parties seem open to conciliation. (The advantages of mediation over arbitration and litigation are outlined in Section 5-7.)

mediation A process by which the parties to a contract can attempt to settle a dispute, generally involving a third, independent party who can suggest a compromise solution, acceptable to all concerned parties.

litigation A process by which the parties to a contract can settle a dispute, involving the Courts of the country chosen in the "Choice of Forum" clause of an international contract.

5-4l Profitability or Commission

This clause is worded quite differently if it spells out the amount of commission that the agent will earn or, reciprocally, the price at which the distributor is expected to sell the product, or the margin that it is expected to add to its costs.

For agency agreements, the exporter spells out the commission that the agent will earn for sales in its territory. It may vary from product to product, so that the agent is given a financial incentive to sell a specific product, but it generally is around 5 percent of the selling price of the products, but obviously depends on the type of industry in which the agreement takes place. A savvy exporter sometimes adds the possibility of negotiating the commission with its agent, in order to win a contract for which the price is critical. Agents usually go along with such reduced commissions, on the philosophy that "a lower commission is better than no commission at all," if the sale is not successful. For sales outside of the territory that the agent may generate accidentally—for example, by attending a trade show and meeting some prospect from a different country—the contract will often call for a lower commission.

Finally, the exporter will also spell out when the commission will be paid to the agent. As a matter of course, the commission is never paid until after the customer has paid the exporter to which the agent sold the product. Commissions can then be paid as they are earned, or monthly, quarterly, even semi-annually or annually.

For distributorship agreements, the issue of price can be thorny; if the distributor is completely free to set its own prices, then there is always the possibility of having substantially different prices for the same product in different countries, therefore creating the possibility of parallel imports (see Section 4-5) and risking the aggravation of customers and distributors alike.

However, if an exporter is attempting to limit the probability of parallel imports, for example by trying to control the price at which the distributor sells the product or the margin—markup—that the distributor can add to the product, then there is always the possibility that such a clause will be construed as "price fixing" and therefore an attempt at reducing competition. Nevertheless, several versions of such clauses exist: Some companies bluntly set exactly the same price worldwide, and argue that they do not want their distributors to compete on price, but rather on such other attributes as service, assortment, and repair facilities. Others make advertising support and other sales help conditional upon the distributor keeping the price in line with the exporter's guidelines. Some others do not contractually state anything but make explicit "threats" of possible delays in delivery for those distributors who do not respect guidelines. Obviously, all of these attempts can be struck by Courts as collusion, but such agreements evidently exist worldwide. Advice from an experienced lawyer in drafting such clauses would be money well spent.

5-4m Miscellaneous Other Clauses

There are evidently many more clauses in a foreign distribution contract, whether with an agent or a distributor, most of which are more "managerial" in nature, and become much more specific to the industry, the strategy of the exporter, and its representatives than can be generalized upon.

facilities and activities In a contract between a principal and an agent or distributor, a clause that spells out what specific facilities each will maintain and what specific activities each will engage in.

For example, the **facilities and activities** clause spells out what the exporter and the agent or distributor have agreed with respect to the type of establishment that the representative will maintain; the size of retail establishments, the size of inventory they will carry, the type of training that employees will receive, and the expectations of managerial policies toward customer complaints, all of which are specific to an industry or a corporate strategy. McDonald's has much more stringent requirements in that respect than does an exporter of agricultural by-products.

advertising A marketing term that includes all of the techniques that a firm uses to promote its products by using communication media, such as television, radio, and print.

The same is true regarding the **advertising** clause, which spells out the obligations of both parties regarding promotional activities such as advertising, trade show attendance, ownership of ideas for advertising campaigns and sales promotion items, and, very importantly, how the costs of such promotional activities will be paid for. For many consumer products, advertising costs are shared by the exporter and the representative in some varying percentages, but for industrial products, the spectrum can go from "entirely the responsibility of the exporter" to "entirely the responsibility of the representative." This may also vary as a function of the country in which the representative operates. A word of caution, though: If there are large discrepancies among the cost burden of distributors in different countries, the sale price may be affected and parallel imports triggered, which is something that an exporter should attempt to avoid.

competing lines In a contract between a principal and an agent or distributor, competing lines are products manufactured by a company other than the principal that compete with the products manufactured by the principal.

The clause regarding **competing lines** spells out how an agent or distributor will be allowed to handle products manufactured by competitors. In most instances, an agent is not allowed to represent firms that are competing with the exporter's products, but a distributor is allowed to do so. Both are encouraged to carry products that complement the product line of the exporter, with the understanding that they would increase the attractiveness of the agent or the distributor's assortment. Some exporters, though, prefer that the agent or the distributor sell their products at the exclusion of all others, to ensure that the representative is concentrating its efforts on their products. Such decisions are made generally in function of the bargaining strength of the parties: A Japanese *sogo shosha* will carry whatever it pleases, whereas a small dealer involved in distributing products manufactured by a large firm, such as Caterpillar, will have to abide by whatever its principal dictates.

TABLE 5-1	Contract Checklist

Michigan Marmalades, Inc. contract negotiations with a distributor, Confitures de France

Contract Language	Because the two parties in the contract speak different languages, MMI drafted the contract in English and had it translated into French. They included a clause stating that the English contract was the original and the French one a translation, in case of a dispute.
Good Faith	MMI and Confitures agreed to do business fairly and honorably with one another.
Force Majeure	This standard clause covers any unforeseen and unpreventable incidents that might disrupt the normal course of business. For instance, if a shipment of MMI Lemon Spread sinks during a storm, MMI can't be held responsible by Confitures.
Scope of Appointment	The scope of appointment specifies which products Confitures must sell and what other responsibilities Confitures has as a distributor.
Territory	The territory clause defines the geographical areas in which Confitures is to work as the distributor for MMI. MMI and Confitures decide that Confitures will be responsible for the entire area of France and Belgium.
Corporate Accounts	This clause states that Confitures cannot sell to certain customers, who will remain corporate accounts. These customers are the two supermarket chains who buy directly from MMI: Carrefour and Auchan.
Term of Appointment	The term of appointment is the definite length of time Confitures will serve as distributor for MMI. MMI and Confitures agree to an initial term of three years. After three years, MMI will renew its contract for another year if it is satisfied with Confitures' performance. The contract will be renewed yearly thereafter.
Choice of Law	Usually, the exporter makes the Choice of Law decision: In the event of a dispute, MMI decides that all legal issues will be settled in the United States. Confitures de France agrees.
Choice of Forum, Mediation and Arbitration	MMI and Confitures de France agree that they want to avoid going to court in case of a dispute. Therefore, they include in the contract a chosen mediator whom they will involve to work out disagreements. The clause in the contract also specifies an arbitration panel that will be used in the event mediation fails.
Profitability and Commission	If Confitures were acting as an agent for MMI, this part of the contract would spell out the price at which Confitures is expected to sell MMI's products, and what commission it would earn by doing so. Because Confitures is used as a distributor, MMI has less control over pricing; however, MMI includes the minimum and maximum prices at which Confitures must sell the jellies in order to avoid parallel import problems.
Miscellaneous Other Clauses	The facilities and activities clause states that Confitures will maintain a specific level of inventory of MMI's products, and clarifies how the employees will be trained, and how Confitures will handle customer service. The advertising clause specifies how Confitures will promote MMI's spreads, how the costs of promotion will be shared, and what public relations activities Confitures will undertake. In the competition clause, MMI and Confitures agree that Confitures may carry other products that will enhance sales of MMI's products. Confitures also is granted the right to carry products that compete with MMI's marmalades. The trademarks, patents, and copyrights clause specifies how Confitures can use MMI's logo and other protected information, and the confidentiality clause allows Confitures' access to MMI's production secrets. Finally, the ownership of customer lists clause resolves that Confitures will share its customer list with MMI.

trademark An intangible good (intellectual property) that an individual or a firm can own. A trademark represents the rights to a commercial name or slogan.

patent An intangible good (intellectual property) that an individual or a firm can own. A patent is the term used to refer to the rights to a process, a material, or a design.

copyright An intangible good (intellectual property) that an individual or a firm can own. A copyright is the term used to refer to the rights to a work of art, a musical piece, or a written article.

confidentiality In a contract between two parties, the promise by each of the parties to not divulge what it has learned about the other party's customers, manufacturing processes, and business practices.

ownership of the customers' list The list of the customers of a particular company is considered a business asset.

Exporters who benefit from substantial advantages due to intellectual properties will also want to specify the handling of **trademarks**, **patents**, and **copyrights** particularly carefully, as well as spell out in a **confidentiality** clause how trade secrets and other strategic advantages are handled. Generally, improvements to existing products made by the agent or the distributor become the property of the exporter, with some sort of compensation.

Finally, the issue of the **ownership of the customers' list** has to be resolved for distributors: Because they sell for their own account, the exporter is usually not privy to the identity of these customers. In some cases, the exporter may find out who the distributor's customers are when they are requested to fill out some sort of warranty registration form, but in general, they are unknown to the exporter. Some exporters demand that the distributor report the names of its customers, while others prefer to leave this issue alone. Except for warranty issues, the only reasons an exporter would want to know the names of the distributor's customers are in expectation of poor performance of the distributor or in expectation of the creation of a sales subsidiary in the future, neither of which represent a good basis on which to start a contract. As far as agents are concerned, because the exporter is shipping and billing directly to the customers to whom the agent sold, the exporter is aware of the customers' identity, and therefore the issue is of much lesser significance.

Table 5-1 illustrates what a company, Michigan Marmalades, Inc. (MMI), must review before entering into contract negotiations with a distributor, Confitures de France. Here is the checklist of decisions and issues Michigan Marmalades must cover in its contract with Confitures.

5-5 Termination

Most definitely, the most sensitive issue in an international distribution contract is the issue of termination, or the act of ending the relationship between the exporter and the agent or the exporter and the distributor. All contracts will spell out a termination clause, which will include:

- A pre-termination notice, which spells out how many days the exporter must give to the agent or the distributor before the termination becomes effective: This duration usually is shorter for agents than it is for distributors, but country statutes can extend it far beyond the contractual agreement. Some contracts call for no pre-termination notice—the contract is cancelled immediately upon notice[22]—and some go as high as a year.

- A termination compensation, often called a "goodwill compensation," which would be equivalent to the amount of income the agent or distributor would have earned for a certain period. This compensation can be as low as none, and as high as two years' worth of income. Again, this provision of the contract may also be rendered null by the importing country's statutes, which may mandate a specific compensation.

Both of these issues are quite dependent upon the reason behind the termination of the contract, and it can be terminated for either of two reasons.

5-5a Just Cause

termination for "just cause" The unilateral decision, by one of the parties to a contract, to end a contract before its term of appointment expires, because the other party has not met some of the terms of the contract that it had agreed to perform.

A **termination for "just cause"** is triggered when either of the parties (exporter, agent, or distributor) is not honoring the terms of the contract. Generally, the representative is not doing something that it is contractually obligated to do, such as meet the sales performance objectives, spend a certain percentage of sales on advertising, or maintain the type of establishment spelled out in the contract; or the representative is doing something that it is contractually not allowed to do: for example, selling competitors' products, applying for patent protection on the improvements it has made to the products, or keeping the list of customers a secret. Only in a few cases is the exporter not performing its obligations, such as not providing the agent with prompt *pro-forma* invoices—quotes—or not shipping diligently: Most terminations for just cause are triggered by a problem with the representative's performance.

In any case, it is relatively easy to terminate a contract for just cause, as there is a reason to terminate it. In most instances, the party "guilty" of not fulfilling its part of the agreement is not entitled to compensation and little or no notice. Nevertheless, statutes may still supersede the agreement in such cases, and mandate a minimum notice period and a minimum compensation, even though there is breach of the contract.

5-5b Convenience

A **termination for "convenience"** is a termination for any other reason than non-performance: It can be triggered by any of the parties, but generally, it is the exporter that is seeking to terminate the contract. One of the most egregious—but unfortunately very common—reasons is that the representative is very successful and that the exporter realizes that it is earning "too much," and wants to replace it with a sales subsidiary. Another cause for termination is a change in the exporter's strategy that modifies how the exporter intends to penetrate foreign markets, or, worse, necessitates a complete retrenchment on the domestic market. In any case, the problem is that the termination is not linked to the contract—or the lack of fulfillment of the contract—but due to some extraneous reason.

A termination for convenience should be handled with the greatest care as the potential for damages to the spurned party can be substantial; in those cases, a lengthy termination notice, as well as a generous goodwill compensation package, is the only way to ensure no litigation and a smoother termination. In particular, if there are issues to resolve, such as inventories of unsold merchandise or outstanding orders, every effort should be made by the exporter to compensate the distributor or the agent. If it is not done, the representatives can very easily ask Courts to intervene: In most instances, Courts look upon terminations for convenience very harshly, sometimes assimilating distributors to agents so as to give them the advantages that the statutes of their country give agents.[23] These statutes usually mandate long notice periods and generous compensation packages. Belgium courts granted three months of income to a distributor in compensation for a contract that lasted only four months, and *three years* of profits in compensation to a distributor who was associated with a manufacturer for twenty-two years, but had been fairly unsuccessful, with yearly sales of BFr. 1,400,000 or roughly U.S. $28,000 at that time.[24]

Unfortunately, going to Court may even be perceived as one of the best case scenarios, as several injured representatives took upon themselves to sabotage the efforts of the exporter later on, through all sorts of means: from mentioning to all of their customers the callous treatment they suffered in the hands of the exporter to attracting new competitors in the market.

termination for "convenience" The unilateral decision, by one of the parties to a contract, to end a contract before its term of appointment expires, for reasons unrelated to the performance of the contract by the other party(ies).

5-6 Arbitration

Arbitration is fast becoming the preferred way of resolving disputes between international partners. In 1960, the International Chamber of Commerce (ICC) received about fifty requests for arbitration; in 1999, it received 529 requests. In order to accommodate such growth, the ICC developed its "Rules of Conciliation and Arbitration," as did the United Nations Conference on International Trade Law (UNCITRAL), both of which are the most commonly used frameworks under which arbitration takes place.[25] However, there are many alternative venues for arbitration: the London Court of International Arbitration, the Stockholm Chamber of Commerce, the World Intellectual Property Organization, the American Arbitration Association, and countless individual law firms that specialize in this function, a number of which are located in Switzerland.[26]

The advantages presented by arbitration over litigation in court are many:

- Arbitration tends to be perceived as fair; arbitration panels are not a Court in either of the parties' countries and therefore are perceived as being more independent and even-handed. This is, of course, only a perception, because Courts in any developed country using a modern commercial code are fair, but it is often a perception of importance in dealing with sensitive litigants.

- Arbitration tends to be much more expeditious than litigation. Arbitration panels are numerous and do not have the same backlog as traditional Courts, which are generally understaffed and overworked. In some countries, commercial disputes can drag on for years: In India, probably one of the worst cases, there are more than three million backlogged civil cases—by the government's own admission—12 percent of which have gone on for more than ten years![27]

- Arbitration tends to be much more efficient: Because arbitration panels do not have to follow the same rules of evidence as Courts, proceedings go much faster, and testimony can be given much more efficiently. Because other procedures are also simplified—there is no pretrial discovery—an arbitration meeting generally lasts a few days, whereas a lawsuit can take weeks.

- Arbitration tends to be much more "creative": Arbitrators seek to resolve the dispute to the satisfaction of both parties, and can find compromises that are impossible in a formal Court, where one of the parties has to win, while the other loses. There is also the possibility of iterative negotiations between the parties and the arbitration panel, a process that can lead to an acceptable compromise. Courts do not have this freedom.

- Arbitration tends to be more effective: Arbitrators generally have a wealth of experience in international business matters and can very quickly understand the issues at stake, draw on their experience and knowledge of arbitration jurisprudence, and settle the dispute to the satisfaction of both parties more effectively than can a Court with limited experience in international business matters.

- Arbitration is not open to the public: Whereas court decision are generallypublished and available to all, arbitration decisions are private and only the parties involved in the dispute know what steps were taken to resolve the dispute.

- Probably most importantly, arbitration is cheaper: All of the advantages previously presented tend to lower the costs of the litigation. In addition, these lower costs are generally shared by the parties in dispute, whereas Court costs are usually borne by the loser, a custom called "European rules"; in the United States, both parties pay their own costs.

The only step to ensure arbitration in the case of disputes between the exporter and its representatives abroad is to include a clause directing that "any dispute [...] shall be finally settled in accordance with the Rules of Conciliation and Arbitration of the International Chamber of Commerce."[28]

5-7 Mediation

Mediation is a process by which a mediator will attempt to find a middle ground between the parties who are having a dispute. The mediator will often "shuttle" between the two companies and seek to find a commonly acceptable solution to both parties. Most mediators are people with a legal background or people who have knowledge of the particulars of an industry; they can be found through referrals and within the trade associations of most industries.

Mediation presents several advantages over litigation or arbitration in several cases:

- Mediation is less formal: The parties in a dispute are often concerned about arbitration because it is a fairly formal process, taking place over a few days, involving meetings in a neutral venue and restricted to a few individual managers. Litigation is even more formal. Mediation is often achieved over a longer period of time and each party has the opportunity to meet with the mediator in its own corporate environment, and the mediator can meet with many different people in both organizations, in order to get a better idea of the issue.

- Mediation is nonbinding: It can be the first step in resolving a dispute and can help both parties assess how their positions are perceived by unrelated parties. In other words, it is an indicator for both litigants of the strength of their respective positions, and of their probabilities of winning an arbitration hearing or a court case.

- Mediation is more practical for smaller disputes or when parties are interested in keeping a business relationship: Unfortunately, arbitration is commonly perceived as resulting in the formal severing of all commercial relationships between both parties. Mediation allows both parties to resolve a dispute without affecting the remainder of their business.

- Mediation is often best for disputes that have arisen from misunderstandings: Both parties are unable to reach a compromise because they do not understand what the other was trying to accomplish and the mediator can help them reach that middle ground.

Mediation is often the best approach when there is a genuine interest on the part of both parties to resolve the dispute in a manner that is fair to both parties and when both parties are interested in resuming normal business relationships as quickly as possible.

Key Terms

acceptance (p. 80)

advertising (p. 88)

arbitration (p. 87)

arbitration panel (p. 87)

breach (p. 81)

competing lines (p. 88)

confidentiality (p. 90)

contract law (p. 82)

copyrights (p. 90)

counteroffer (p. 80)

distribution contracts (p. 82)

evergreen contract (p. 86)

exclusive representative (p. 84)

facilities and activities (p. 88)

force majeure (p. 84)

good faith (p. 83)

labor law (p. 82)

Lex Mercatoria (p. 78)

litigation (p. 87)

mediation (p. 87)

offer (p. 80)

ownership of the customers' list (p. 90)

patents (p. 90)

register (p. 83)

rejection (p. 80)

termination for "convenience" (p. 91)

termination for "just cause" (p. 90)

trademark, patent, and copyright (p. 90)

Review and Discussion Questions

1. What are the general provisions of the United Nations' Convention on Contracts for the International Sale of Goods?

2. What are the issues brought about by the concept of "labor law" in an international distribution agreement?

3. Describe three of the elements generally found in an agency or distributorship agreement.

4. What are the differences between the "Choice of Law" and "Choice of Forum" clauses? How are they related?

5. What two possible forms of termination are there? How differently will they be handled by a Court of Law?

6. What are the differences between mediation and arbitration? How different are they from a proceeding in a Court of Law?

Endnotes

1. Gourion, Pierre-Alain, and Georges Peyrard, *Droit du Commerce International*, 1997, Librairie Générale de Droit et de Jurisprudence, 14, rue Pierre et Marie Curie, 75005 Paris, France.

2. JBC International, "Think You Understand the Vienna Convention? Then read this Sad Tale," *The Journal of Commerce*, June 24, 1998, p. 12C.

3. Lookofsky, Joseph M., *Understanding the CIGS in the USA: A Compact Guide to the 1980 United Nations Convention on Contracts for the International Sale of Goods*, 1995, Klumer Law International, Boston, The Hague, London.

4. Kritzer, Albert, "CISG: Table of Contracting States," Pace Law School Institute of International Commercial Law, http://www.cisg.law.pace.edu/cisg/countries/cntries.html, November 26, 2000.

5. Ziegler, Jacob, "Canada Prepares to Adopt the International Sales Convention," *Canadian Business Law Journal*, Vol. 18, Issue 3, Fall 1991.

6. Gellman, Gila E., "Forming International Sales Pacts," *Marketing Management*, Winter 1994, pp. 60–62.

7. Kritzer, Albert, "CISG: Table of Contracting States," Pace Law School Institute of International Commercial Law, http://www.cisg.law.pace.edu/cisg/countries/cntries.html, November 26, 2000.

8. McMahon, John P., "Applying the CISG: Guide for Business Managers and Counsels," Pace Law School Institute of International Law, http://www.cisg. law.pace.edu/cisg/guides.html, November 26, 2000.

9. *Ibid*

10. Gellman, Gila E., "Forming International Sales Pacts," *Marketing Management*, Winter 1994, pp. 60–62.

11. Heron, Karl G., and David D. Knoll, "Negotiating and Drafting International Distribution, Agency, and Representative Agreements: The United States Exporter's Perspective," *The International Lawyer*, Fall 1987, pp. 939–983.

12. *Ibid*

13. Dubberly, David E., "When Giving Your Rep the Boot: In Latin America, Labor Laws May Prove Surprisingly Costly, Unless You Plan Ahead," *Export Today*, May 1998, p. 26.

14. "Lloyd's Revamp Won't Be Challenged," Associated Press News Release, June 23, 1997.

15. *The ICC Model Commercial Agency Contract*, 1991, publication No. 496 of the International Chamber of Commerce, ICC Publishing, 156 Fifth Avenue, New York, NY 10010, USA and ICC Publishing SA, 38, Cours Albert 1er, 75008 Paris, France.

16. *The ICC Model Distributorship Contract*, 1993, publication No. 518 of the International Chamber of Commerce, ICC Publishing, 156 Fifth Avenue, New York, NY 10010, USA and ICC Publishing SA, 38, Cours Albert 1er, 75008 Paris, France.

17. *The ICC Model Commercial Agency Contract, op. cit.*

18. *The ICC Model Commercial Agency Contract, op. cit.*

19. Ulmer, Nicolas C., "Bullet-proofing Your International Arbitration: Part 2 of 2," *World Trade*, August 2000, p. 68.

20. Connors, Kathleen, "Arbitration Taking Hold in Asia with Help of International Chamber," *The Journal of Commerce*, April 2, 1997, p. 8A. Zirin, James D., "Confucian Confusion," *Forbes*, February 24, 1997, p. 136.

21. Mullins, Ronald Gift, "Mediation Gains in Maritime Cases," *The Journal of Commerce*, April 3, 2000, p. 10.

22. *The ICC Model Commercial Agency Contract, op. cit.*

23. Puelinckx, A. H., and H. A. Tielemans, "The Termination of Agency and Distributorship Agreements: A Comparative Survey," *Northwestern Journal of International Law and Business*, Fall 1981, Vol. 3: Issue 452, pp. 452–495.

24. *Ibid*

25. Ulmer, Nicolas C., "Bullet-proofing Your International Arbitration: Part 2 of 2," *World Trade*, August 2000, p. 68.

26. Ulmer, Nicolas C., "Bullet-proofing Your International Arbitration; Part 1 of 2," *World Trade*, July 2000, p. 70.

27. Karp, Jonathan, "India's Laws a Mixed Blessing for Investors," *The Wall Street Journal*, July 11, 1997, p. A10.

28. *The ICC Model Distributorship Contract, op. cit.*

Terms of Trade or Incoterms

Chapter Six

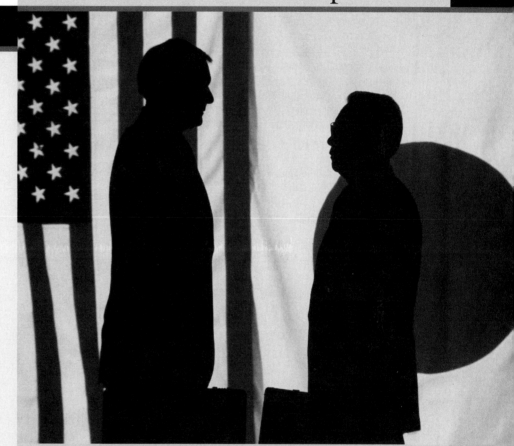

Source: © 2007 JupiterImages Corporation.

Whenever an exporter sells goods to a foreign company, whether through an intermediary such as an agent or a distributor or directly to an importer, there is a large number of steps involved in getting the goods to the customer:

- clearing the goods for export
- organizing the transport of the goods between the exporter and the importer, often using several means of transportation
- clearing Customs in the importing country.

The Terms of Trade used in the contract of sale determines which of these steps are the responsibility of the exporter and which are the responsibility of the importer. Often, the number of issues involved in an international shipment is substantial, and specifically dividing all of these tasks between the exporter and the importer for each shipment would be a daunting task. In addition, it would be virtually impossible to anticipate everything that could go "wrong" during transit and determine at the time of the contract which of the parties should be responsible for each incident.[1]

6-1 International Commerce Terms

Fortunately, a set of standardized Terms of Trade was created in 1936 by the International Chamber of Commerce: They have evolved into thirteen International Commerce Terms, from which the acronym **Incoterms** is derived. These Incoterms were revised in 1953, 1967, 1976, 1980, and most recently in 1990 and 2000, the latter revision bringing only moderate changes to a few terms.[2] It is of significant benefit to both parties to use one of these Incoterms, because ample information is available for each and substantial jurisprudence has accumulated for each through the International Chamber of Commerce arbitration system. For example, a *pro-forma* invoice would read: "FCA Milwaukee, Wisconsin, USA" to indicate which tasks the exporter would be willing to perform and which tasks would remain the responsibility of the importer[3] If a standard contract is used, the same clarification should be made.

Incoterm An International Commerce Term, or a formalized international Term of Trade, which specifies the responsibilities of the exporter and the responsibilities of the importer in an international transaction.

6-2 Understanding Incoterms

The Terms of Trade or Incoterms that the exporter and the importer agree to use in a given transaction defines several aspects of an international sale:

- Which tasks will be performed by the exporter
- Which tasks will be performed by the importer
- Which activities will be paid by the exporter
- Which activities will be paid by the importer
- When the transfer of responsibility for the goods will take place.

This last point is complicated: It is conceptually difficult to make the distinction between (1) the transfer of responsibility for the goods between the exporter and the importer and (2) the transfer of title between the exporter and the importer. The transfer of responsibility (transfer of risk) is dictated by the choice of the Incoterm. The transfer of title (transfer of ownership) is usually done when the importer has either paid the exporter (and obtained the original bill of lading), accepted to sign a draft (see Chapter 7), or performed some other event specifically outlined in the contract of sale between both parties. The transfer of responsibility happens at the delivery of the goods, a point that is clearly outlined in each of the Incoterms, and in most cases, a point that occurs chronologically much earlier than the transfer of title.

The transfer of responsibility of the exporter never extends beyond the services for which that company has paid. There are several Incoterms, however, where the exporter is obligated to pre-pay a portion of the transportation costs, even though it is no longer responsible for the goods. Such is the case for the so-called C-terms, the ones whose acronyms start with the letter C.

6-3 Incoterm Strategy

The proper choice of an Incoterm is therefore contingent upon the strategy followed by the exporting firm, but is also somewhat constrained by the following parameters:

- The type of product sold: Several industries (commodities in particular) prefer using some specific Terms of Trade rather than others.
- The method of shipment: Goods shipped by ocean or barge will be sold under different Incoterms than containerized goods using several transportation modes.
- The ability of either of the parties to perform the tasks involved in the shipment.
- The amount of trust placed by either of the parties toward the other.

Nevertheless, the greatest criterion to be used is the willingness of both parties to perform and pay for some of the tasks involved in the shipment. In some cases, a strategic advantage can be gained by an exporter willing to facilitate the sale of its products by assisting the importer in the shipment. In others, a price advantage may be obtained by an importer willing to perform all or most of the tasks involved in the shipment. A company generally does not determine which Incoterm to use on a case-by-case basis, but will determine which strategy it would like to pursue and determine which Term of Trade should be used regularly, given its product line, its customers' expectations, and its trade volume.

Another issue to understand clearly in this decision is that, regardless of the Incoterm chosen, the importer is always paying for the transportation and other costs of shipping internationally. The fact that the exporter is pre-paying and arranging for certain aspects of the shipment is reflected in the invoice price; therefore, the importer ends up paying for it. In addition, it is likely, although not always the case, that the exporter's invoice is going to include a charge that is higher than the actual cost of the service. Some exporters add a premium to these costs to reflect the fact that it took some time and effort for the exporter to arrange for those services.

Nevertheless, the choice of Incoterm is often the exporter's decision: It is difficult for an exporter to "adapt" its Incoterm strategy to accommodate the requirements of an importer, as it may require the exporter to be responsible for tasks that it has decided it would rather not perform. Should the importer feel that the exporter is not providing a service that is adequate, it can always purchase from another source. However, should the importer want to perform more tasks than what the exporter prefers, it is certainly possible for the exporter to do *less* than what it expected, and use a different Incoterm on that transaction, one for which it is responsible for less.

Finally, the choice of the proper Incoterm is a critical decision for a firm, as it is an integral part of its export strategy and linked to the level of customer service it is aiming to provide.[4] The thirteen Incoterms are reviewed in a progressive order of service provided by the exporter (see Table 6-1).

6-4 Ex-Works (EXW)

The EXW Incoterm can be used for any merchandise and for any means of transportation. It should be used with the following syntax:

EXW Poughkeepsie, New York, USA

where Poughkeepsie is the town in which the exporter will hold the merchandise available to the importer. It is usually located in the exporting country.

Ex-Works is the "easiest" of the Incoterms for the exporter, and the most difficult for the importer. In an Ex-Works transaction, the exporter only has the obligation to "place the goods at the disposal of the buyer" and "render every assistance [...] in obtaining [...] any export license or other official authorization necessary for the export of the goods."[5] In addition, the exporter has to package the goods for export, but the exporter does not even have to load the goods onto the importer's prearranged vehicle. It should be evident that this is not an advantageous Incoterm from the importer's perspective: Arranging to pick up goods in a foreign country is not easy, and neither is providing domestic transportation nor clearing goods for export in a foreign country.

In the case where the exporter and the importer agree that the expense and responsibility of loading the goods should fall on the exporter, it is possible to amend the Incoterm to include this condition, usually by what ICC refers to as a **variant** of an Incoterm. This is usually accomplished by including "EXW loaded" to

variant A modification to one of the Incoterms codified by the International Chamber of Commerce. Variants are generally used to further clarify the responsibilities of the exporter and of the importer in a given transaction.

TABLE 6-1	Incoterms Summary

The responsibilities of the exporter are denoted with an "X," those of the importer with an "I." Whenever there is no obligation on either party, or whenever there is ambiguity as to whether the activity is the responsibility of the exporter or the importer, the spot is left blank. Please refer back to the appropriate section for further details.

Task	EXW	FCA	FAS	FOB	CFR	CIF	CPT	CIP	DES	DEQ	DAF	DDU	DDP
Export Packing	X	X	X	X	X	X	X	X	X	X	X	X	X
Inland Freight	I		X	X	X	X	X	X	X	X	X	X	X
Export Clearance	I	X	X	X	X	X	X	X	X	X	X	X	X
Arrange Carrier	I	I	I	I	X	X	X	X	X	X	X	X	X
Load onto Carrier	I	I	I	X	X	X	X	X	X	X	X	X	X
Pay Carrier	I	I	I	I	X	X	X	X	X	X	X	X	X
Unload Carrier	I	I	I	I			I	I	I	X	I	X	X
Pay Insurance						X		X					
Import Clearance	I	I	I	I	I	I	I	I	I	I	I	I	X
Pay Duty	I	I	I	I	I	I	I	I	I	I	I	I	X
Pay Inland Freight	I	I	I	I	I	I	I	I	I	I	I	X	X

The possible alternative Incoterms for a given means of transportation are marked with a "YES." Those that would be improper or likely to present problems are clearly marked as such.

Mode of Transport	EXW	FCA	FAS	FOB	CFR	CIF	CPT	CIP	DES	DEQ	DAF	DDU	DDP
Break-Bulk Ocean Cargo	YES	NO	YES	YES	YES	YES	NO	NO	YES	YES	NO	YES	YES
Bulk Ocean Cargo	YES	NO	YES	YES	YES	YES	NO	NO	YES	YES	NO	YES	YES
Roll-On/Roll-Off	YES	YES	NO	NO	NO	NO	YES	YES	NO	NO	YES	YES	YES
Multi-modal (FCL)	YES	YES	NO	NO	NO	NO	YES	YES	NO	NO	YES	YES	YES
Multi-modal (LCL)	YES	YES	NO	NO	NO	NO	YES	YES	NO	NO	YES	YES	YES
Rail	YES	YES	NO	NO	NO	NO	YES	YES	NO	NO	YES	YES	YES
Road	YES	YES	NO	NO	NO	NO	YES	YES	NO	NO	YES	YES	YES
Air	YES	YES	NO	NO	NO	NO	YES	YES	NO	NO	YES	YES	YES

the *pro-forma* invoice. Because variants of Incoterms are not defined by the International Chamber of Commerce, the correct syntax for such a modification should be:

EXW Poughkeepsie, New York, USA, loaded

The choice of an EXW Incoterm should only be made when the exporter knows that the importer is extremely savvy; otherwise, there is a strong possibility that the quote will not be turned into a sale, as the exporter's competitors are likely to offer better (more importer-friendly) Terms of Trade.

6-4a Delivery under EXW

There is nothing specified in this Incoterm regarding delivery. It occurs at the time that the importer (or the importer's agent) picks up the goods at the exporter's plant. This delivery has to take place at a mutually convenient time. The exporter has the obligation to notify the importer that the goods are available for pickup and the importer has the obligation to notify the exporter of the time at which the goods will be picked up.

There is no specific transportation document corresponding to the delivery of the goods under this Incoterm, although, if a transportation company is picking up the goods, the exporter will generally be given a copy of the bill of lading or some form of receipt for the goods.

6-4b Exporter's and Importer's Responsibilities under EXW

The exporter's responsibilities are limited to the most basic functions: make the goods available to the buyer, package the goods for export shipment, assist in the export clearance procedures, and provide the documents to the importer so that the goods can clear Customs in the importing country or be insured. None of these requirements are trivial, though.

The exporter has to package the goods in such a way that the goods are protected during their international voyage. That requirement means that the exporter should find out what the means of transportation will be and make sure that the goods are adequately packaged to make sure that they are not damaged. If the goods are damaged in transit due to "improper packaging," the exporter is responsible and the insurance coverage contracted by the importer will not cover the costs of the damage.

The exporter also has to provide all of the documents necessary for the importer to clear Customs in the importing country; this means that the invoice has to be a good international invoice and include product description, Harmonized System numbers, weights, volume measures, unit price, total price, and so on (see Chapter 9 for further details and examples), that the other documents be prepared carefully and accurately (certificate of origin, packing list, and so on), and that the correct number of originals and copies be included. Because the importer is also the one in charge of exporting the products, the exporter should provide the documents necessary to clear the exporting requirements of the exporting country.

As far as the documents necessary for export are concerned, the United States has recently made a change in the Shipper's Export Declaration (SED) (an export document explained in Chapter 9), specifically to record correctly who the exporter was in the case of a sale under an EXW Incoterm: Until very recently, the exporter of record was the importer (or the importer's freight forwarder). Under rules put in place on July 10, 2000, the importer is no longer listed as the exporter of record, and the seller-exporter is listed as the "U.S. principal party in interest." This terminology was specifically created to allow the U.S. Census to record who was the exporter of specific merchandise under an EXW sale, rather than record the importer of the goods: The term "exporter" has been stricken from the SED. Because of this requirement, the United States government has placed the responsibility of providing the correct Export Commodity Classification Number (ECCN) and any information that could affect an export license on the exporter in the case of an EXW transaction.[6]

The importer is responsible for all other aspects of the shipment in an EXW transaction: It has to clear the goods for exports, arrange for transportation, clear Customs in the importing country, purchase insurance, and provide domestic transportation in the importing country.

6-5 Free Carrier (FCA)

The FCA Incoterm can be used for any merchandise and for any means of transportation, but it was specifically created for goods shipped through multi-modal transportation (i.e., merchandise that is shipped through multiple means of transportation without being "handled" because it is containerized). This Incoterm can be used for shipments of either full-container loads (FCL) or less-than-container loads (LCL). FCA is expected to become one of the most popular Incoterms as the number of multi-modal shipments increases. This Incoterm should be used with the following syntax:

FCA Castres, France

where Castres is the city in which delivery takes place. It is usually located in the exporting country or in a neighboring country.

In an FCA transaction, the exporter delivers the goods to a carrier selected by the importer. Because FCA is a fairly recent Incoterm—it was created in 1990—great care has been taken to define specifically what responsibilities are borne by the exporter, and which are borne by the importer. There are no known variants to this Incoterm.

The FCA Incoterm replaced three other Incoterms, which were abandoned in 1990: Free on Rail (FOR), Free on Truck (FOT), and Free on Board-Airport (FOB-Airport).

6-5a Delivery under FCA

Under FCA, the delivery takes place when either of two conditions is met:

- If the named point in the Incoterm refers to the exporter's plant, then delivery takes place when the goods are loaded, by the exporter and at its expense, onto the carrier's truck.

- If the named point in the Incoterm refers to the carrier's premises, then delivery takes place when the goods are made available to the carrier (i.e., when the goods have arrived at the carrier's dock). The goods are unloaded from the exporter's truck by the carrier and at the carrier's expense (i.e., at the importer's expense).

The document that corresponds clearly to the transfer of responsibility for an FCA shipment is the receipt given by the carrier to the exporter; it can be a bill of lading, a sea waybill, an air waybill, or a multi-modal bill of lading (see Chapter 9 for an explanation of each of these terms).

6-5b Exporter's and Importer's Responsibilities under FCA

The exporter is still in charge of packing the merchandise for export, as it was under EXW. However, its responsibilities increase to include loading the merchandise into a container provided by the carrier, loading the container on the carrier's truck, or delivering the merchandise to the carrier's facilities. In addition, the exporter is responsible for clearing the merchandise for export, and has to provide whatever information is needed by the importer to clear Customs in the importing country and to obtain insurance. In the United States, the exporter fills out the Shipper's Export Declaration and is the "U.S. principal party in interest." In countries where export authorities require a Pre-Shipment Inspection (see Chapter 15), the exporter has to pay for it.

The importer is responsible for arranging the contract of carriage (i.e., finding a carrier between the exporter's town and the final destination) and communicating to the exporter which carrier it is. The importer is also responsible for arranging for insurance and for clearing Customs in the importing country. If the importing country requires a Pre-Shipment Inspection, the importer has to pay for it.

6-6 Free Alongside Ship (FAS)

Although the FAS Incoterm can be used for any merchandise, it is specifically designed for ocean transportation, and is not meant for any other means of transportation or for merchandise that is not destined to be handed to an ocean shipping line at the port of departure. This Incoterm should be used with the following syntax:

> FAS Santos, Brazil

where Santos is the port in which the delivery takes place. This port is usually located in the exporting country or a neighboring country.

In a Free Alongside Ship transaction, the exporter is responsible to bring the goods to the port, "alongside" a ship designated by the importer, at which time the responsibility shifts to the importer. One major change was made in the 2000 version of the FAS Incoterm; the exporter is now responsible to clear the merchandise for export, leaving EXW as the only Incoterm for which the importer has to perform this task.

6-6a Delivery under FAS

The delivery officially takes place when the exporter has delivered the goods "along-side" a ship designated by the importer. The problem with this Incoterm is that ports rarely keep merchandise "alongside" a ship, or keep merchandise on a quay waiting for a ship. There is always delivery to a holding area, then cartage (transportation within the port area) from the holding area to the ship before the **stevedoring** (loading onto the ship) takes place. When and where the delivery does take place is sometimes difficult to determine.

stevedore A company or a person whose responsibility is to load and unload ships in a port.

Compounding this difficulty is the fact that there is no transport document that clearly corresponds to a delivery to a holding area or to the quay alongside the ship. The suggestion by the ICC that the exporter must obtain "a transport document (for example, a negotiable bill of lading, a non-negotiable sea waybill")[7] is contradicted by the fact that no ocean carrier will issue a bill of lading until the goods have been received in good condition on board the vessel. ICC further comments that the seller "may not always receive a receipt or a transport document from the carrier"[8] and adds that the exporter must then "provide some other document to prove that the goods have been delivered"[9] but does not suggest what it may be. A dock receipt from the port authorities may be sufficient; however, this lack of clear physical evidence of delivery could be a substantial deterrent to the use of the FAS Incoterm. However, the use of Electronic Data Interchange (EDI) by the parties involved can remedy this problem: The exporter can notify the importer that the delivery has been made in the port of departure and the terminal operator can also do the same. However, as of June 2006, there was no evidence that the ICC considers such notices proof of delivery.

6-6b Exporter's and Importer's Responsibilities under FAS

The exporter is responsible for packing the goods for export, transporting them to the port, and unloading them onto the quay or holding area in the port. With the advent of the 2000 version of Incoterms, another duty was added to the responsibilities of the exporter under an FAS transaction. The exporter is responsible for clearing the goods for export, providing whatever documents and assistance the importer may need to clear Customs in the importing country and to obtain insurance. In the United States, the exporter fills out the Shipper's Export Declaration and is the "U.S. principal party in interest" or the exporter of record. In countries where export authorities require a Pre-Shipment Inspection, the exporter has to pay for it.

The importer is responsible for the shipment starting from the point of delivery. Therefore the importer is responsible for port handling charges, stevedoring (loading the goods in the vessel), and for ocean transportation costs, as well as insurance, unloading in the port of arrival, and Customs duties in the importing country. If the importing country requires a Pre-Shipment Inspection, the importer has to pay for it.

6-7 Free on Board (FOB) Port of Departure

Although the FOB Incoterm can be used for any merchandise, it is specifically designed for ocean transportation, and is not meant for any other means of transportation or for merchandise that is not destined to then be handed to an ocean shipping line at the port of departure. This Incoterm should be used with the following syntax:

FOB Cape Town, South Africa

where Cape Town is the port in which the delivery takes place. This port is generally located in the exporting country or a neighboring country.

The Free On Board term, sometimes called Freight On Board, is one of the oldest maritime Terms of Trade. The exporter is responsible for the goods until they are placed on the ship. The importer is responsible for them after that.

Unfortunately, because FOB is such an old Term of Trade, its meaning is somewhat dependent on the practices of the port in which the goods are loaded. These differences matter specifically in the way the loading costs are billed: Some ports have the tradition to include loading, stowing, and securing the goods in the hold of the ship as part of the stevedoring costs. Some other ports will customarily bill for these services as part of the ocean cargo costs. The shipping line contracted by the importer obviously would be able to communicate what the practice is at a given port of departure. However, these differences in practices have triggered the need for a variant to the FOB Incoterm to reflect which of the trade partners is responsible for handling costs on the ship; either "FOB stowed" or "FOB stowed, trimmed, and secured"[10] can be used to denote that the exporter is responsible for those specific costs. Here again, because the International Chamber of Commerce does not regulate Incoterm variants, the correct syntax should be:

> FOB Cape Town, South Africa, stowed

6-7a Delivery under FOB

In an FOB transaction, the point of delivery is extremely clear and has been governed by centuries of maritime tradition. The "FOB point," the point at which the responsibility shifts from the exporter to the importer, is the **ship's rail**. Until the merchandise has cleared the ship's rail, it is the responsibility of the exporter. After that, it is the responsibility of the importer. What happens if the merchandise falls and is damaged as it crosses the ship's rail depends on whether it remains on the ship or falls back toward the quay.[11]

ship's rail An imaginary rail that circles the entire hull of a ship.

The document associated with the FOB term is also quite clear: The proof of delivery is an ocean bill of lading or a sea waybill. Only after receiving the goods will the shipping line issue this document, giving a copy to the exporter.

EXW Ex-Works	FCA Free Carrier	FAS Free Alongside Ship	FOB Free on Board
ANY	MULTI-MODAL	OCEAN	OCEAN
The exporter only has the obligation to place the goods at the disposal of the buyer.	The exporter delivers the goods to a carrier selected by the importer.	The exporter is responsible for bringing the goods to the port, "alongside" a ship designated by the importer, at which time the responsibility shifts to the importer.	The exporter is responsible for the goods until they are placed on the ship. The importer is responsible for them after that.

Figure 6-1
Incoterms

6-7b Exporter's and Importer's Responsibilities under FOB

The exporter is responsible for packaging the goods for export, shipping them to the port of departure, and loading them onto the ship. The exporter is responsible for clearing the goods for export, and has the obligation of providing whatever documents and assistance the importer may need to clear Customs in the importing country and to obtain insurance. In the United States, the exporter fills out the Shipper's Export Declaration and is the "U.S. principal party in interest" or the exporter of record. In countries where export authorities require a Pre-Shipment Inspection, the exporter has to pay for it.

The importer is responsible for arranging and paying for ocean transportation from the port of departure to the goods' destination, Customs' clearance in the importing country, and eventually arranging and paying for insurance. If the importing country requires a Pre-Shipment Inspection, the importer has to pay for it.

Figure 6-1 provides a summary for the EXW, FCA, FAS, and FOB Incoterms.

6-8 Cost and Freight (CFR)

Although the CFR Incoterm can be used for any merchandise, it is specifically designed for ocean transportation, and is not meant for any other means of transportation or for merchandise that is not destined to then be handed to an ocean shipping line at the port of departure. This Incoterm should be used with the following syntax:

> CFR Lagos, Nigeria

where Lagos is the port of destination in which the importer takes physical control of the goods. This port is usually located in the importing country or in a neighboring country. In a CFR transaction, the delivery (the transfer or responsibility or the transfer of risk) does not take place in the port of destination, but in the port of departure.

The Cost and Freight term is also one of the oldest maritime Terms of Trade, and it was known until the 1990 Incoterms as C&F or C+F, abbreviations that are now obsolete. The exporter is responsible for the goods until they are placed on the ship and the importer is responsible for them after that, but the exporter pre-pays the ocean freight.

Unfortunately, because CFR is such an old Term of Trade, its meaning is somewhat dependent on the practices of the port in which the goods are unloaded. These differences matter specifically in the way the unloading costs are billed: Some ports have the tradition to bill separately for the unloading of the goods as stevedoring costs, and others will ask shipping lines to bill for these services as part of the ocean cargo costs. The shipping line contracted by the exporter obviously would be able to communicate what the practice is at a given port of discharge. Nevertheless, in order to account for these differences in practices, variants to the CFR Incoterm were created to reflect which of the trade partners was responsible for unloading costs. "CFR landed" explicitly states that the costs of unloading are borne by the exporter, and "CFR undischarged" notes unloading costs are borne by the importer.[12] In these cases, the correct syntax should be:

> CFR Lagos, Nigeria, landed

6-8a Delivery under CFR

In a CFR transaction, the point of delivery is the "FOB point," the point at which the responsibility shifts from the exporter to the importer, the ship's rail. Until the merchandise has cleared the ship's rail, it is the responsibility of the exporter; after that, the responsibility shifts to the importer.

The document associated with the CFR term is also quite clear: The proof of delivery is an ocean bill of lading or a sea waybill. Only after receiving the goods will the shipping line issue this document, giving one of the originals to the exporter.

6-8b Exporter's and Importer's Responsibilities under CFR

The exporter is responsible to package the goods, ship them to the port of departure, load them onto a ship "of the type normally used for the transport of goods of the contract description,"[13] and pre-pay for the shipment. Depending on the practices at the port of destination, this pre-paid contract of carriage may include the costs of unloading the goods. If it does not, then the importer has to pay for unloading the ship. The exporter is also responsible to clear the goods for export, assist the importer in providing the documentation necessary to clear Customs in the importing country, and obtain insurance. In the United States, the exporter fills out the Shipper's Export Declaration and is the "U.S. principal party in interest" or the exporter of record. In countries where export authorities require a Pre-Shipment Inspection, the exporter has to pay for it.

The importer takes responsibility for the goods at the delivery point (i.e., at the ship's rail in the port of departure), even though the exporter is the one who contracts for the ocean shipping of the goods. Depending on the practice at the port of destination, and the possible Incoterm variant used, the importer may also have to pay for the unloading costs. It is also responsible for clearing Customs in the importing country and for inland transportation after that. If the importing country requires a Pre-Shipment Inspection, the importer has to pay for it.

6-9 Cost, Insurance, and Freight (CIF)

Although the CIF Incoterm can be used for any merchandise, it is specifically designed for ocean transportation, and is not meant for any other means of transportation or for merchandise that is not destined to then be handed to an ocean shipping line at the port of departure. This Incoterm should be used with the following syntax:

> CIF Kobe, Japan

where Kobe is the port of destination in the importing country in which the importer takes control of the goods. In a Cost, Insurance, and Freight transaction, the delivery does not take place in the port of destination, but in the port of departure.

The CIF Incoterm is quite similar to the CFR term, with the exception that the exporter has the additional responsibility to pre-pay for Marine Cargo Insurance until the port of destination. Unfortunately, the mandate of the International Chamber of Commerce is for "minimum cover," that is, the so-called Coverage C of the Institute Cargo Clauses (see Section 10-8d), resulting in yet another Incoterm variant.[14] CIF maximum cover—mandating Coverage A of the Institute Cargo Clauses—exists in addition to the predictable CIF undischarged and CIF landed, which are mirrors of their CFR equivalents. The syntax again must accommodate the fact that Incoterm variants are not regulated by the International Chamber of Commerce and should read:

> CIF Kobe, Japan, maximum cover, landed

Finally, under the CIF Incoterm, the amount insured must be at least 110 percent of the value of the goods, a custom that dates back to 1906, when Great Britain instituted the Marine Insurance Act.[15]

One aspect of CIF is also unusual: Certain countries (see Table 6-2) do not allow their importers to purchase insurance abroad, and therefore prevent any import on a CIF basis. This restriction is in place to conserve foreign currency—it obligates importers to purchase insurance locally in local currency—and to subsidize the national insurance industry; all of the countries practicing this restriction are relatively small traders.

TABLE 6-2	Countries' Restrictions on Incoterms

The following countries place restrictions on the Incoterms that can be used by their exporters or importers: These restrictions are current as of March 2006.*

Country	A	B	C	Country	A	B	C
Algeria		X	X	Kenya		X	X
Angola		X		Liberia	X		
Bangladesh		X	X	Libya		X	
Benin		X	X	Mali		X	X
Bolivia	X	X	X	Mauritania	X	X	X
Brazil		X	X	Morocco		X	X
Burkina Faso		X	X	Nicaragua		X	X
Burundi	X	X	X	Niger		X	X
Cambodia		X	X	Nigeria		X	X
Cameroon		X	X	Oman	X	X	X
Cape Verde	X	X	X	Pakistan		X	X
Central African Republic		X	X	Rwanda	X	X	X
Chad		X	X	Senegal		X	X
Congo (Brazzaville)		X	X	Seychelles	X	X	X
Congo (Kinshasa)	X	X	X	Sierra Leone		X	X
Djibouti		X	X	Solomon Islands		X	X
Dominican Republic		X	X	Somalia		X	X
Ecuador		X	X	Sudan		X	X
Ethiopia		X	X	Syria		X	X
Gabon		X	X	Tanzania		X	X
Ghana		X	X	Togo		X	X
Guinea		X	X	Tunisia		X	X
Indonesia		X	X	Uganda	X	X	X
Iran		X	X	Yemen		X	X
Jordan		X	X				

The definitions of these restrictions are summarized as follows:

Restriction A: An exporter from that country is not allowed to purchase insurance abroad (it is therefore possibly more difficult for an exporter from that country to offer CIP, CIF, DDU, and DDP as it limits the exporter's access to some insurance providers).

Restriction B: An importer in that country is not allowed to purchase insurance abroad (it is therefore presumably impossible to sell to an importer in that country on CIP or CIF terms).

Restriction C: An importer in that country is not allowed to import on a CIF basis (it is therefore presumably illegal to offer CIP, and possibly DOU, and DDP terms to an importer in that country as well).

Most of the countries in this list tend to be fairly small trade partners: If further information is specifically necessary for any of them, the commercial attaché of any embassy to this country would be the best source of information on the exact implementations of these restrictions.

*"Restrictive Laws and Regulations," International Union of Marine Insurance, as quoted by the American Institute of Marine Underwriters, http://www.aimu.org/brochures.html, March 7, 2006.

6-9a Delivery under CIF

In a CIF transaction, the point of delivery is again the "FOB point," the point at which the responsibility shifts from the exporter to the importer, the ship's rail. Until the merchandise has cleared the ship's rail, it is the responsibility of the exporter; after that, the responsibility shifts to the importer.

The document associated with the CIF term is also quite clear: The proof of delivery is an ocean bill of lading or a sea waybill. Only after receiving the goods will the shipping line issue this document, giving one of the originals to the exporter.

6-9b Exporter's and Importer's Responsibilities under CIF

The exporter has to package the goods for export, and has to pay for shipping costs and minimum insurance costs to the port of destination. It is also responsible for clearing the goods for export. In the United States, the exporter fills out the Shipper's Export Declaration and is the "U.S. principal party in interest" or the exporter of record. In countries where export authorities require a Pre-Shipment Inspection, the exporter has to pay for it.

The importer is taking responsibility for the goods at the ship's rail in the port of departure, even though the contract of carriage is between the seller and the ocean shipping line. The importer is responsible for clearing Customs in the importing country and for inland transportation after that. If the importing country requires a Pre-Shipment Inspection, the importer has to pay for it.

6-10 Carriage Paid To (CPT)

Conceptually, the CPT Incoterm is the same as the CFR Incoterm, except that it applies to goods shipped by means other than ocean transport, or shipped by sea without being handed over the ship's rail (i.e., in the case of roll-on/roll-off cargo), or containerized cargo using multiple modes of transportation, including ocean transport as one of the modes. This Incoterm should be used with the following syntax:

CPT Köln, Germany

where Köln is the city of destination in which the importer takes control of the goods. This city is generally located in the importing country or a neighboring country.

In a Carriage Paid To transaction, the delivery does not take place in the city of destination, but in the city where the exporter delivers the goods to the carrier. The exporter pre-pays shipping charges until the city of destination. Unless unusual circumstances prevail, shipping charges do not include the unloading of the merchandise in the destination city.

6-10a Delivery under CPT

Delivery takes place when the exporter hands over the goods to the carrier in the exporting country and the exporter is given a bill of lading or equivalent document (air waybill, sea waybill, multi-modal bill of lading), which acts as the proof of delivery.

6-10b Exporter's and Importer's Responsibilities under CPT

The exporter is responsible for packaging the goods for export, shipping them to the carrier, and pre-paying the shipping costs to the city of destination. In the United States, the exporter fills out the Shipper's Export Declaration and is the "U.S. principal party in interest" or the exporter of record. In countries where export authorities require a Pre-Shipment Inspection, the exporter has to pay for it.

The importer assumes responsibility for the goods at the time the seller delivers them to the carrier. The importer is responsible for unloading the goods from the carrier's truck, clearing Customs, and for paying inland transportation (if any) beyond the city of destination. If the importing country requires a Pre-Shipment Inspection, the importer has to pay for it.

6-11 Carriage and Insurance Paid To (CIP)

Conceptually, the CIP Incoterm is the same as the CIF Incoterm, except it applies to goods shipped by means other than ocean transport, or shipped by sea without being handed over the ship's rail (i.e., in the case of roll-on/roll-off cargo), or containerized cargo using multiple modes of transportation, including ocean transport as one of the modes. This Incoterm should be used with the following syntax:

CIP Sofia, Bulgaria

where Sofia is the city of destination in which the importer takes control of the goods. This city is located in the importing country or a neighboring country.

In a Carriage and Insurance Paid To transaction, the delivery does not take place in the city of destination, but in the city where the exporter delivers the goods to the carrier. Unlike the CPT Incoterm, the exporter has the added responsibility of pre-paying for minimum-cover insurance (coverage C of Institute Cargo Clauses) until the city of destination. Therefore, an additional variant of the CIP Incoterm has emerged, CIP maximum cover, to request that the exporter take on the responsibility to provide coverage A of the Institute Cargo Clauses. The syntax again must accommodate the fact that Incoterm variants are not regulated by the International Chamber of Commerce and should read:

CIP Sofia, Bulgaria, maximum cover

Finally, under the CIP Incoterm, the amount insured must be at least 110 percent of the value of the goods, a custom that dates back to 1906, when Great Britain instituted the Marine Insurance Act.[16]

6-11a Delivery under CIP

Delivery takes place when the exporter hands over the goods to the carrier in the exporting country and the exporter is given a bill of lading or equivalent document (air waybill, sea waybill, multi-modal bill of lading), which acts as the proof of delivery.

6-11b Exporter's and Importer's Responsibilities under CIP

The exporter is responsible for export packing, transportation costs to the city of destination, and for minimum insurance costs. In addition, the exporter is responsible for clearing the goods for export. In the United States, the exporter fills out the Shipper's Export Declaration and is the "U.S. principal party in interest" or the exporter of record. In countries where export authorities require a Pre-Shipment Inspection, the exporter has to pay for it.

The importer's responsibility starts when the exporter delivers the goods to the carrier, even though the exporter is the party that contracted with the carrier to get the goods delivered. The importer is responsible for unloading the carrier's truck, clearing Customs in the importing country, and for transportation costs beyond the city of destination. If the importing country requires a Pre-Shipment Inspection, the importer has to pay for it.

Figure 6-2 provides a summary for the CFR, CIF, CPT, and CIP Incoterms.

6-12 Delivered Ex-Ship (DES)

Although the DES Incoterm can be used for any merchandise, it is specifically designed for ocean transportation, and is not meant for any other means of

CFR Cost and Freight	CIF Cost, Insurance, and Freight	CPT Carriage Paid To	CIP Carriage and Insurance Paid To
OCEAN	OCEAN	MULTI-MODAL	MULTI-MODAL
The exporter is responsible for the goods until they are placed on the ship and the importer is responsible for them after that, but the exporter prepays the ocean freight.	Until the merchandise has cleared the ship's rail, it is the responsibility of the exporter; after that, the responsibility shifts to the importer.	The importer assumes responsibility for the goods at the time the seller delivers them to the carrier.	The importer's responsibility starts when the exporter delivers the goods to the carrier, even though the exporter is the party that contracted with the carrier to get the goods delivered.

Figure 6-2
Incoterms

transportation or for merchandise that is not destined to be delivered by an ocean shipping line at the port of destination. In practice, the DES Incoterm is mostly used for bulk shipments of commodities where the parties wish to have the importer pay for the unloading of the ship. This Incoterm should be used with the following syntax:

> DES Istanbul, Turkey

where Istanbul is the port of destination in which the importer takes responsibility for the goods. That port is usually located in the importing country or in a neighboring country.

In a Delivered Ex-Ship transaction, the exporter is responsible for the goods until they are placed at the disposal of the importer in the port of destination.

6-12a Delivery under DES

The delivery takes place in the port of destination, once the ship has reached port and makes the merchandise available to the importer.

There is no specific document that conveys the transfer of responsibility between the exporter and the importer at the point of delivery. It is common practice to have the exporter provide the ocean bill of lading as evidence of delivery in the port of destination, although it is only proof of delivery in the port of departure. Should something happen to the goods during the ocean voyage, while under the responsibility of the exporter, the bill of lading is unaffected, even though delivery has certainly not been made, because the goods have not been made available to the importer. Nevertheless, this is not as major an issue as with the EXW or FAS Incoterms, as the importer is often represented in the port of destination and delivery problems can easily be uncovered.

6-12b Exporter's and Importer's Responsibilities under DES

The responsibilities of the exporter include the handling of the goods until their arrival in the port of destination; however, the exporter does not handle (or pay for) unloading the ship. In addition, the exporter must clear the goods for export. In the United States, the exporter fills out the Shipper's Export Declaration and is the

"U.S. principal party in interest" or the exporter of record. In countries where export authorities require a Pre-Shipment Inspection, the exporter has to pay for it.

The importer is responsible for unloading the ship, clearing Customs in the importing country, and paying for whatever shipment costs there may be beyond the port of destination. If the importing country mandates a Pre-Shipment Inspection, the importer has to pay for it.

6-13 Delivered Ex-Quay (DEQ)

Although the DEQ Incoterm can be used for any merchandise, it is specifically designed for ocean transportation, and is not meant for any other means of transportation or for merchandise that is not destined to then be handed to an ocean shipping line at the port of departure. In practice, the DEQ Incoterm is mostly used for bulk shipments of commodities where the parties wish to have the exporter pay for the unloading of the ship. This Incoterm should be used with the following syntax:

DEQ Santiago, Chile

where Santiago is the port of destination in which the importer takes control of the goods. This port is generally located in the importing country or in a neighboring country.

In a Delivered Ex-Quay transaction, the exporter is responsible for the goods until they are unloaded from the ship in the port of destination. The only difference between the DES and DEQ Incoterms is that the unloading costs are borne by the exporter in the DEQ transaction.

6-13a Delivery under DEQ

The delivery for a DEQ shipment takes place when the goods are placed, once they have been unloaded ("landed"), at the disposal of the importer. There is no specific document that conveys the transfer of responsibility between the exporter and the importer at the point of delivery. It is common practice to have the exporter provide the ocean bill of lading as evidence of delivery in the port of destination.

6-13b Exporter's and Importer's Responsibilities under DEQ

Under a DEQ shipment, the exporter has the same responsibility as in a DES shipment, with the following exception: The exporter has to pay for the unloading of the ship in the port of destination.

6-14 Delivered at Frontier (DAF)

The DAF Incoterm can be used for any merchandise, but it is specifically designed for land transportation, and should not be used for ocean transportation, where the DES or DEQ Incoterms fulfill the same function. This Incoterm should be used with the following syntax:

DAF Nogales, Arizona, USA

where Nogales is the border city in which the importer takes physical control of the goods. This city is usually located at the border between the exporting country and the importing country or a neighboring country.

In a Delivered at Frontier transaction, the delivery (the transfer or responsibility or the transfer of risk) takes place in the city named in the Incoterm, but with the merchandise still loaded on the vehicle or the railroad car on which it arrived in that city. Common practice calls for the merchandise to remain on the truck or the railroad car until its final destination, but the responsibility of getting it there shifts to the importer who must contract for carriage. When carriage is done by railroad, it is not unusual for the term to read "DAF Poland-Belarus border," and for the goods to remain on the same train until their destination with no exact location mentioned; the final crossing point is left to the discretion of the railroad company. In trade within NAFTA, this Incoterm is very commonly used between the United States (or Canada) and Mexico, and usually specifies a town; there is still some political uneasiness about letting Mexican trucks and trailers on U.S. and Canadian highways, but it should subside.

The DAF Incoterm was almost eliminated from the 2000 Incoterm revisions for several reasons: It is rarely used, it can be easily replaced with a DDU (see Section 6-15) or possibly a DDP (see Section 6-16), and no specific documents mark the transfer of responsibility between the exporter and the importer.[17] Nevertheless, with the advent of Electronic Data Interchange (EDI), it is possible for the carrier to notify both the exporter and the importer that the goods are at the border and that they have been delivered by the carrier to the importer. However, as of June 2006, there is no evidence that the International Chamber of Commerce accepts such notices as evidence of delivery.

6-14a Delivery under DAF

In a DAF transaction, the delivery takes place when the merchandise, still on the truck or the railroad car, is placed at the disposal of the importer at the border city.

There is no specific transportation document that conveys the transfer of responsibility between the exporter and the importer, but some carriers provide a "through document of transport" that fulfills that role.[18]

6-14b Exporter's and Importer's Responsibilities under DAF

In a DAF shipment, the exporter is responsible for packing the goods for export and paying for transportation until the border city. The exporter is responsible for clearing the goods for export and providing information to the importer so that the merchandise can be insured and can clear Customs in the importing country. In the United States, the exporter fills out the Shipper's Export

Declaration and is the "U.S. principal party in interest" or the exporter of record. In countries where export authorities require a Pre-Shipment Inspection, the exporter has to pay for it.

The importer is responsible for the costs of transportation from the border city to the final destination and for the costs of clearing Customs. If the importing country requires a Pre-Shipment Inspection, the importer has to pay for it.

6-15 Delivered Duty Unpaid (DDU)

The DDU Incoterm can be used for any merchandise, and can be used for any means of transportation, including goods that are meant to be carried by ocean. However, this Incoterm is not meant for ocean goods to be delivered to a port of destination, for which the DES and DEQ Incoterms were specifically designed. The DDU Incoterm is meant to be used when the exporter is willing to perform most of the tasks involved in a shipment, up to the city named in the Incoterm, with the exclusion of Customs clearance and duty payment. This Incoterm should be used with the following syntax:

DDU Xi'An, China

where Xi'An is the city of destination in which the importer takes control of the goods. This city is generally the place of business of the importer, but can be any city located in the importing country or in a neighboring country.

In a Delivered Duty Unpaid transaction, the exporter is responsible for the goods until they arrive, still loaded on a truck or a railroad car, in the city of destination. The unloading costs are borne by the importer.

In most cases, the DDU Incoterm is used in those cases where the exporter wants to offer the greatest level of customer service, but when it is impossible for a foreign company to be the importer of record; it may be illegal for a foreign company to apply for an import license, the Customs official may only want to deal with local firms, or some other compelling reason exists to prevent the exporter from providing a Delivered Duty Paid (DDP) shipment.

6-15a Delivery under DDU

Under the DDU Incoterm, the delivery takes place when the exporter places the goods at the disposal of the importer in the city of delivery mentioned in the Incoterm. The goods are delivered unloaded (i.e., it is the responsibility of the importer to arrange and pay for unloading the goods). However, this is often a very minor point, as the point of delivery is often the importer's plant, which obviously has the ability to unload a truck.

Although there is no transportation document that corresponds to this delivery, it is common for the exporter to provide the bill of lading at the time of delivery.

6-15b Exporter's and Importer's Responsibilities under DDU

The exporter is responsible for arranging and paying for all shipping issues until the goods are delivered to the importer, with the exception of paying duty and clearing Customs. The exporter is therefore responsible for export packing, export clearance, domestic transportation in the exporting country, international transportation, domestic transportation in the importing country, and insurance. In the United States, the exporter fills out the Shipper's Export Declaration and is the "U.S. principal party in interest" or the exporter of record. In countries where export authorities require a Pre-Shipment Inspection, the exporter has to pay for it.

The importer is responsible for Customs clearance and for paying duty. If the importing country mandates a Pre-Shipment Inspection, the importer is responsible for that cost.

6-16 Delivered Duty Paid (DDP)

The DDP Incoterm can be used for any merchandise and for any means of transportation. However, if the goods are carried by ocean and delivered in the port of destination, then the correct Incoterms to use are DES and DEQ. This Incoterm should be used with the following syntax:

DDP Karlsruhe, Germany

where Karlsruhe is the city of destination in which the importer takes control of the goods. This city is generally the place of business of the importer, but can be any city located in the importing country or in a neighboring country.

Choosing the DDP Incoterm is the ultimate in customer service on the part of the exporter. The exporter handles everything for the importer, including shipment to the customer's plant and Customs clearance. For the importer, this type of transaction is exactly equivalent to receiving a domestic shipment from a domestic supplier: The only thing left to the importer's care is the unloading of the merchandise, something that is usually its responsibility under a domestic shipment.

In some cases, it may be advantageous for pragmatic reasons to use a variant of the DDP Incoterm: In a number of countries, the Customs authorities collect not only duty on the goods imported but also Value Added Tax (VAT) on the value of the goods. Because of the peculiarities of VAT accounting, it is often much more convenient for the importer to pay for the VAT than it is for the exporter. In those circumstances, the DDP VAT unpaid Incoterm variant may be used. The syntax should be:

DDP Karlsruhe, Germany, VAT unpaid

to reflect the fact that the variant is not officially sanctioned by the International Chamber of Commerce.

6-16a Delivery under DDP

Under the DDP Incoterm, the delivery takes place when the exporter places the goods at the disposal of the importer in the city of delivery mentioned in the Incoterm. The goods are delivered unloaded (i.e., it is the responsibility of the importer to arrange and pay for unloading the goods). However, this is often a very minor point, as the destination of the delivery is often the importer's plant, which obviously has the ability to unload a truck.

Although there is no transportation document that corresponds to this delivery, a commonly used alternative is for the exporter to provide the bill of lading at the time of delivery.

6-16b Exporter's and Importer's Responsibilities under DDP

The exporter assumes all responsibilities in a DDP shipment: clearing the goods for export, transporting them to the importer's facilities, and clearing Customs in the importing country. All costs and responsibilities are for the exporter.

The importer only has the responsibility to receive the goods at delivery and unload them. Figure 6-3 provides a summary for the DES, DEQ, DAF, DDU, and DDP Incoterms.

6-17 Electronic Data Interchange

Electronic Data Interchange (see Chapter 9) has somewhat changed one of the main issues in Incoterms: the documentation of the delivery.

For a number of Incoterms, there is no transport document that is issued at the point where the responsibility shifts from the exporter to the importer (i.e., when the delivery takes place). For example, in an EXW transaction, the delivery takes place when the merchandise is placed "at the importer's disposal," and a similar situation is present with the use of the FAS Incoterm, and, to a lesser degree, of the DES, DEQ, DAF, DDU, and DDP Incoterms as well.

EDI has, to a considerable extent, solved this problem: Whenever there is no transport document possible, the exporter can still send an EDI "notice" to the importer, which acts as a document for both parties. The exporter has a record of the notification sent, and the importer knows unambiguously when the goods were delivered to the quay (FAS shipment) or when they arrived in port (DES and DEQ shipments). Therefore, one of the problems associated with the use of Incoterms is likely to abate substantially over the next few years, as the use of EDI increases. Unfortunately, EDI usage is still fairly new and limited to developed countries.

DES
Delivery Ex-Ship

OCEAN

The responsibilities of the exporter include the handling of the goods until their arrival in the port of destination; the importer is responsible for unloading the ship, clearing Customs in the importing country, and paying for whatever shipment costs there may be beyond the port of destination.

DEQ
Delivered Ex-Quay

OCEAN

The exporter has the same responsibility as in a DES shipment, with the following exception: the exporter has to pay for the unloading of the ship in the port of destination.

DAF
Delivered at Frontier

LAND

The exporter is responsible for packing the goods for export and paying for transportation until the border city.

DDU
Delivered Duty Unpaid

ANY

The exporter is responsible for arranging and paying for all shipping issues until the goods are delivered to the importer, with the exception of paying duty and clearing Customs.

DDP
Delivered Duty Paid

ANY

The exporter assumes all responsibilities in a DDP shipment: clearing the goods for export, transporting them to the importer's facilities and clearing Customs in the importing country.

Figure 6-3
Incoterms

6-18 Common Errors in Incoterm Usage

6-18a Incoterms Confusion with Domestic Terms

Probably the most commonly made errors in international Terms of Trade is the substitution of domestic Terms of Trade for international Terms of Trade: An inexperienced exporter will use "FOB factory" rather than the correct corresponding Ex-Works (EXW) Incoterm; similarly, rather than the correct Delivered Duty Paid (DDP) Incoterm, the same inexperienced exporter would use "FOB destination."

"FOB factory" (also known as "FOB origin") is a term of trade used in the United States for domestic sales that limits the responsibility of the seller to the loading of the merchandise onto a vehicle owned or hired by the buyer. At the time at which the merchandise is loaded onto the vehicle, the title of the merchandise transfers to the buyer. There are therefore several differences between the "FOB factory" concept and its closest Incoterm equivalent, which is Ex-Works (EXW). Firstly, it shows a transfer of title, which none of the Incoterms do, rather than a transfer of responsibility, the only concept to which the Incoterms refer. Secondly, it specifically includes the loading of merchandise onto the vehicle provided by the buyer, which EXW does not explicitly do, except in a variant called EXW-loaded. Thirdly, "FOB factory" does not make reference to any form of documentation, which is critical to the international buyer, because these documents are needed to clear Customs. Fourthly, it applies to any form of transportation, and not only to ocean transportation, as the FOB Incoterm does. Finally, "FOB factory" does not have any specific requirements regarding packaging, whereas EXW clearly requires packaging sufficient to withstand the international voyage.

"FOB destination" (also known as "FOB delivered") is also a term used in the United States for domestic sales that extends the responsibility of the seller to the delivery point, at the buyer's place of business; the seller pays for the carriage cost to the point of delivery. At the time at which the merchandise is unloaded from the vehicle, the title transfers to the buyer. The "FOB destination" term of sale is not equivalent to the DDP Incoterm. For one, it also refers to the transfer of title, whereas the DDP Incoterm does not. Second, it makes no reference to Customs clearance, which DDP requires.

Other terms that are also used incorrectly in international trade are "Freight Pre-Paid" and "Freight Collect," which are generally used for small packages (Less than Truckload or LTL) and refer to the fact that the seller either includes the cost of shipment in the invoice or excludes it. Both of these terms do not work in an international environment for essentially the same reasons that "FOB factory" and "FOB destination" do not.

On occasion, there are some other terms used in international trade that have their roots in domestic trade, although they have become obsolete. For example, some invoices will reflect a "franco" price, which is conceptually equivalent to the "FOB factory" term; however, it does not specifically require the loading of the merchandise onto the vehicle provided by the buyer. There are no reasons to use this term of trade domestically, and a multitude of reasons not to use it internationally.

6-18b Incoterms Confusion with Older Incoterm Versions

The International Chamber of Commerce modified the Incoterms in 1980, 1990, and 2000. It eliminated some Incoterms, modified others, and created some new ones. For a number of reasons, several exporters have failed to adapt to these changes.

Older ICC versions included several Incoterms that eventually disappeared: FOB rail (which eventually changed to FOR, "Free on Rail" in 1980, and eventually was abandoned altogether in 1990), FOB truck (which became FOT, "Free on Truck" in 1980, and which was also abandoned in 1990), and FOB airport (eliminated in 1990). On occasion, though, such older Incoterms are still used on invoices. Although this is a practice that is allowed under ICC rules, it is most likely that the use of such obsolete Incoterms is more due to carelessness than to a deliberate attempt at using an Incoterm that has advantages over the current version. It is therefore preferable to use the 1990 creation of Free Carrier (FCA) instead of the previous similar Incoterms, as fewer and fewer people are familiar with the specific requirements of the former Incoterms.

Less of a problem is the use of C&F or C+F rather than CFR to communicate that an ocean shipment is made under a Cost and Freight Incoterm, because only the abbreviation changed. However, it should be avoided: Because the CFR acronym was created in the 1990 version of Incoterms, it is possible that the use of another abbreviation could confuse the importer and present challenges, should the shipment experience a mishap.

Another obsolete term is "Free Domicile," although there is no evidence that such a term was ever part of the recognized Incoterms. This pricing term is used when the exporter pays all the applicable duties, all the transportation and other charges until the shipment is delivered to the importer's premises. Because this term is not recognized by the International Chamber of Commerce Arbitration Panel, it should be replaced by the Incoterm Delivered Duty Paid (DDP).

6-18c Improper Use of Correct Incoterms

Another cause of possible problems is the misuse of correct Incoterms. Probably the most frequent misuse occurrence is when FOB is used with an air shipment, when FOB is only designed to be used with an ocean shipment term. The correct Incoterm to use for an air shipment should be Free Carrier (FCA), to clearly outline the responsibilities of the exporter and of the importer.

6-19 Incoterms as a Marketing Tool

As mentioned earlier, the greatest criterion to be used in the choice of a particular Incoterm is the willingness of both parties to perform and pay for some of the tasks involved in the shipment. In some cases, a strategic advantage can be gained by an exporter willing to facilitate the sale of its products by assisting a novice importer in the handling of a shipment. In other cases, a price advantage may be obtained by an experienced importer willing to perform all or most of the tasks involved in the shipment.

Generally speaking, an exporter does not determine which Incoterm to use on a case-by-case basis. It adopts a "policy" to include in international quotes those services that it feels competent providing. It is difficult for an exporter to adapt its Incoterm strategy to accommodate the requirements of an importer, as it may require the exporter to be responsible for tasks that it has decided it would rather not perform. However, should the importer want to perform more tasks than what the exporter prefers, it is certainly possible for the exporter to do *less* than what it expected, and use a different Incoterm on that transaction that allows the importer to do more.

The choice of the proper Incoterm is a critical decision for a firm: It is an integral part of its export strategy and linked to the level of customer service it is aiming to provide. From this perspective, therefore, it makes most sense for an exporter to become as well-versed as possible in international logistics and be prepared to include as many of the transportation functions as possible in its quote.

An exporter intent on increasing its sales should therefore offer to provide the importer with the most customer-friendly Incoterm quotes (either DDU or DDP), if only by using the services of a competent freight forwarder. Should the importer want to shoulder more responsibilities, it is always possible for the exporter to reduce its involvement and quote FCA or even EXW. The best type of quote would be one in which the exporter lists different prices for different Incoterms, leaving the importer with the decision to choose which is best for its specific case.

For example, a quote could read:

- EXW Cleveland, Ohio: $10,000
- FCA Cincinnati Airport: Covington, Kentucky: $11,000
- CIP Paris, France: $15,500
- DDU Clermont-Ferrand, France: $16,500
- DDP Clermont-Ferrand, France: $17,800

and leave the customer to decide which of the Incoterms it would like to choose.

Key Terms

Incoterm (p. 99)

ship's rail (p. 105)

stevedoring (p. 104)

variant (p. 101)

Review and Discussion Questions

1. Describe two Incoterms of your choice.

2. What is the Incoterm that is most importer-friendly? Least importer-friendly? Justify your answer.

3. Which of the Incoterms include a requirement of "insurance" by the exporter?

4. The "Delivered" Incoterms (DEQ, DES, DDP, and DDU) do not include insurance. Why not?

5. Using a product of your choice as well as an importer and an exporter of your choice, determine what would be the ideal Incoterm for a transaction. Make

as many assumptions as necessary to justify your decision.

6. Explain why a developing country would want to prevent its importers from purchasing CIF or CIP and instead require CFR or CPT shipments.

7. A certain *sogo shosha* (a Japanese Trading Company) always requests its suppliers to provide an EXW quote. Knowing what you know about trading companies, why do you think this is the case?

Endnotes

1. Debattista, Charles, Editor, *Incoterms in Practice*, 1995, International Chamber of Commerce Publication No. 505(E), ICC Publishing S.A., 38 Cours Albert 1er, 75008 Paris, France and ICC Publishing, Inc., 156 Fifth Avenue, Suite 417, New York, NY 10010, USA (refers to 1990 Incoterms).

2. Gooley, Toby B., "Incoterms 2000: What the Changes Mean to You," *Logistics Management Distribution Report*, January 31, 2000, p. 49.

3. Reynolds, Frank, "Implications of Incoterms 2000," *Journal of Commerce*, September 15, 1999, p. 10.

4. Freudmann, Aviva, "Traders get a Brand-new Bible," *Journal of Commerce*, September 9, 1999, p. 1.

5. *Incoterms 2000*, 1999, International Chamber of Commerce Publication No. 560, ICC Publishing S.A., 38 Cours Albert 1er, 75008 Paris, France and ICC Publishing, Inc., 156 Fifth Avenue, Suite 417, New York, NY 10010, USA.

6. Biederman, David, "New Rules for Exports," *JoC Week*, July 24–30, 2000, pp.10–12.

7. *Incoterms 2000*, 1999, International Chamber of Commerce Publication No. 560, ICC Publishing S.A., 38 Cours Albert 1er, 75008 Paris, France and ICC Publishing, Inc., 156 Fifth Avenue, Suite 417, New York, NY 10010, USA.

8. Ramberg, Jan, *ICC Guide to Incoterms 2000*, 1999, International Chamber of Commerce Publication No. 620, ICC Publishing S.A., 38 Cours Albert 1er, 75008 Paris, France and ICC Publishing, Inc., 156 Fifth Avenue, Suite 417, New York, NY 10010, USA.

9. *Ibid*

10. Raty, Asko, "Variants on Incoterms (Part 2)," in Debattista, Charles, Editor, *Incoterms in Practice*, 1995.

11. Reynolds, Frank, "Tale of a Rail and Other Nuances of the Marine Cargo Insurance Experience," *Journal of Commerce*, November 18, 1998, p. 10A.

12. Raty, Asko, "Variants on Incoterms (Part 2)," in Debattista, Charles, Editor, *Incoterms in Practice*, 1995.

13. *Incoterms 2000*, 1999, International Chamber of Commerce Publication No. 560, ICC Publishing S.A., 38 Cours Albert 1er, 75008 Paris, France and ICC Publishing, Inc., 156 Fifth Avenue, Suite 417, New York, NY 10010, USA.

14. Mikkola, Kainu, "Variants on Incoterms (Part 1)," in Debattista, Charles, Editor, *Incoterms in Practice*, 1995.

15. Reynolds, Frank, "Seminar in Paris Yields Answers to Widely Asked Questions on Incoterms," *Journal of Commerce*, April 22, 1998, p. 2C.

16. *Ibid*

17. Reynolds, Frank, *Incoterms for Americans*, 1999, published by International Projects, Inc., P.O. 352650, Toledo, Ohio 43635-2650, USA.

18. Ramberg, Jan, *ICC Guide to Incoterms 2000*, 1999, International Chamber of Commerce Publication No. 620, ICC Publishing S.A., 38 Cours Albert 1er, 75008 Paris, France and ICC Publishing, Inc., 156 Fifth Avenue, Suite 417, New York, NY 10010, USA.

Terms of Payment

Chapter Seven

Source: © 2007 JupiterImages Corporation.

One of the greatest concerns an exporting company has is to make sure that it will be able to collect payment from its foreign customers. Although this is also a legitimate concern domestically, an international transaction is generally perceived to involve a much greater non-payment risk than a strictly domestic sale for many reasons.

There are a number of ways in which an exporting company can ensure it will get paid and be paid on time; a company can always tailor its international terms of payment to the characteristics of its customers, the countries in which it does business, and its own tolerance for risk. Although these methods are more complex than the open account arrangements found in all domestic sales, they are universally accepted and there is ample jurisprudence to buttress them. It is therefore relatively simple to arrive at a choice of international terms of trade that will secure the interests of the exporter.

What is difficult in choosing an international term of trade is managing the delicate balance between protecting the interests of the exporter and offering good marketing practices that will engender good customer relations.

7-1 Characteristics of International Payment Issues

Exporters tend to prefer conservative measures in handling their foreign receivables. They tend to err on the side of caution for several reasons:

- **Credit Information** There is generally much less information available on the creditworthiness of a creditor in a foreign market than there is for a domestic customer. Although a few credit reporting agencies, accounting firms, and factoring houses do keep information, it is not always readily obtainable or is not always in existence for a specific customer, especially if the customer is a recently created firm, or if the customer is in a developing country. Some improvements have been made recently, though, with the creation of centralized credit information portals, which offer links to access foreign countries' credit agencies. The task, though, is usually much more complicated for a foreign customer than for a domestic one, if only because the identity of a domestic firm is usually easier to establish. The paucity of information about certain countries is often coupled with an unfamiliarity with the diverse business organizations (different types of partnership and corporations) of a foreign country's legal system and with an inability to decipher businesses' names.

- **Lack of Personal Contact** International transactions tend to be conducted in a more impersonal fashion (through fax, telex) than are domestic transactions, which tend to be conducted at least initially with some sort of personal contact (in person or over the phone). This lack of contact tends to lead to a climate in which the exporter has no way to evaluate the "character" of the importer, and where the possibility of a greater risk is often assumed. Where there is personal contact, it is often between people who are not always well versed in intercultural communication and can substantially misunderstand each other. This can foster the perception of a greater risk and encourages a more cautious approach.

- **Collections Are Difficult and Expensive** Should a foreign customer renege on a payment, the collection of such a past-due account can be particularly difficult. Although there is a generally well-structured system on the domestic side, there are few firms that have the capability of offering international collection services. Those that do, tend to offer the service at a very high price.[1] In some cases, relying on a foreign collection agency can lead a company to unwillingly employ some pretty unsavory characters, a situation that can eventually taint the image of the exporter, as Citibank discovered to its detriment when it used a "strong-armed" collection company in India.[2]

- **No Easy Legal Recourse** Unlike in a domestic setting, in which there is often a commercial code (of laws) and abundant jurisprudence, there is little of either in international trade. In addition, there is no Court with jurisdiction over international disputes and therefore a ruling by a Court in the exporter's country cannot be easily enforced in the importer's country. The reciprocal is also true.

  The creation of the United Nations Convention on Contracts for the International Sale of Goods (CISG) and its implementation in 1980 have helped establish a body of legal principles for the sale of goods between companies located in two different sovereign countries. As of 2006, sixty-eight countries had ratified this treaty, representing about 80 percent of the world's trade, but some countries, such as the United States, have ratified only part of it,[3] presumably those articles that did not conflict with their own Code Law (Uniform Commercial Code for the United States). The United Kingdom has yet to ratify this convention at all. The enforcement of the convention is left to the domestic courts' interpretation and, although there is some jurisprudence in this area, it is still fairly scant (all of the available jurisprudence is made accessible through a database created by the United Nations Commission on International Trade Law [UNCITRAL] called CLOUT, for "Case Law on UNCITRAL texts"). There are always concerns on the part of exporters that conflicts of law between domestic laws and the CISG and differences in interpretation by the courts make the prospect of a court battle much more daunting. Section 5-2 outlined several of the differences between the CISG and the United States' UCC.

  It is a common misconception that there is some sort of an international court of justice; although the International Court in the Hague (the Netherlands) arbitrates disputes between governments and between governments and multinational corporations, it never interferes in disputes between corporations. In addition, its rulings are non-binding, as the Court does not have the executive authority to enforce them.

- **Higher Litigation Costs** The costs of international litigation, arbitration, or mediation are generally much greater than those of domestic litigation. Seeking a ruling against an importer in the importer's country is time-consuming, can involve several trips abroad, and necessitates the hiring of foreign law specialists, a process that involves greater expenses than domestic disputes. In some countries, the backlog of civil and commercial cases in the court system is such as to render impossible the probability of a swift decision. In India, for example, a judgment is generally not rendered for at least ten years, with cases meandering through the system for much longer periods than that. Other countries, such as China, Russia, Indonesia, or the Ukraine, are not much different.[4]

  Suing a foreign customer for non-payment in the courts of the exporter's country could be perceived as a means to speed this process up and eventually lower its costs; however, it is only followed by the prospect of having to file suit in the importing country's courts as well, just to enforce the judgment rendered against the importer. Most exporters perceive that litigation should be an absolute last resort.

- **Mistrust** Finally, there is the perception that the importing company is well aware of all these factors and knows that the exporter is unlikely to aggressively pursue an uncollected foreign receivable. This creates a climate of distrust on the part of the exporter who could assume the worst intentions on the part of the importer.

7-2 Alternative Terms of Payment

There are essentially four "traditional" methods to handle the issue of payment in foreign transactions, all involving a different level of risk: Cash in Advance, Open Account, Documentary Collection, and Letters of Credit. Although there are variations in each of these methods, each designed to mitigate one or another aspect of the risks involved in the transaction, they have not changed much in the past thirty years. However, in the past ten years, an interesting fifth alternative has emerged, called "TradeCard," and it promises to become a particularly effective means of securing payment from a customer abroad without involving as many fees or intermediaries as some of the more secure traditional alternatives.

Each of these five general alternatives presents advantages and disadvantages, and can be generally seen as a trade-off between the risk of non-payment and risk of losing the business to a more aggressive competitor who is willing to accept a greater risk and therefore present the customer with a "simpler" alternative form of payment. Table 7-1 gives an example of the most common perceptions in terms of this trade-off.[5]

Nevertheless, Table 7-1 is an overly simplified summary of the different alternatives. The ultimate choice of a term of sale should be carefully determined as a function of several objective and subjective factors, and each variant of the preferred method given careful consideration. Unfortunately, if only for the obvious reason of simplification of the process of selling, several exporting firms do not have the inclination—nor do they have the time and personnel—to tailor terms of payment to specific customers or countries, and these firms have designed a "foreign sales policy" to deal with all orders from importers, regardless of where these customers are located, or of who they are. Such a lack of flexibility tends to lead to exceedingly conservative policies. One exporter confessed to the author that it only considered "Cash in Advance" sales orders; undoubtedly this conservative stance never got its author into trouble, but it very likely yielded much lower sales than a slightly more aggressive approach. Ideally, the terms of sale of a particular transaction should be evaluated according to the risks attached to the transaction.

7-3 Risks in International Trade

commercial risk The probability of not getting paid by a certain creditor, because this creditor does not have the funds to pay the debt or because the creditor refuses to pay the debt.

country risk or political risk The probability of not getting paid by a certain creditor, because the creditor's country does not have the funds to pay the debt (insufficient foreign exchange reserves) or because the creditor is not legally allowed to pay the debt (political embargo).

There are three sources of risks in international trade that need to be considered. First is obviously the **commercial risk**, which is also encountered in domestic transactions, and that relates to the ability of the importer to pay the invoice in time. However, there is also the **country risk** that encompasses all of the issues related to the country to which an exporter is shipping and that may affect payment, regardless of the creditworthiness of the

TABLE 7-1	Advantages and Disadvantages of Several Terms of Payment	
Term of Payment	**Probability of Losing the Probability of Loss due to Business Because of the Non-Payment Choice of Method of Payment**	
Cash in Advance	High	Nil
Letter of Credit	Fairly High	Almost Nil
Documentary Collection	Low	Low
Open Account	Nil	Relatively High
TradeCard	Low	Almost Nil

importer. Finally, exporters also associate risk with **exposure,** which is the potential financial impact of non-payment or reduced payment on the exporter's business.

7-3a Country Risk

Country risk is made up of an aggregate of different issues, some political, and some strictly economical.

On the political side, the government's stability should be considered; for example, the possibility that a government may be changed (with a new election) may influence import policies, which, in turn, could mean that goods cannot clear Customs as easily, or that tariffs increase, or that other policies are changed to such an extent that the importer will refuse delivery. In a country in which such a **political risk** is perceived, the exporter would prefer a term of payment that is more secure. Similarly, a government that is in a weak position could also see its policies challenged by a strong public opposition, a situation that can lead to strong political unrest, as was seen in France in late 1995 when the country was essentially paralyzed by strikes for several weeks.

Port personnel or other personnel critical to the timeliness of a shipment—such as Customs officers—strike often in some countries, and this fact should be factored in the decision of the terms of payment. Japan, for example, has an almost yearly strike in its ports. Finally, in some cases, the government chooses to delay payment of international obligations, including trade obligations, whenever it is found to make sense politically. However, although a few governments have reneged on their public debt, there has been no recent evidence of governments reneging on their commercial (trade) debt.

Secondly, the overall health of the economy should also be considered. If there is high unemployment, policies against "job-stealing imports" could be implemented. If there is high inflation, price controls may be initiated. Moreover, the balance of payments of the importing country may also be relevant: If it is badly in a deficit position, imports of "non-essential" goods could be curtailed. Such would be the case when the "import cover," or the amount of foreign currency that the country has to cover its imports, starts to become low; generally, the import cover is expressed in months (i.e., foreign currency reserves can cover the next X months of imports).

Finally, a quick survey of the social system of the country could be conducted. Some countries' societies foster a climate where fraud is commonplace, sometimes prevalent (e.g., Nigeria),[6] a situation that is conducive to much caution on the part of an exporter. The fairness of the legal system should also be considered. An importer located in a country in which claims are handled professionally should be offered more lenient terms of payment than one located in a country where the justice system is notoriously biased, inadequate, or agonizingly slow.

The magazine *World Trade*, in each of its issues, provides a summary report of a region of the world and of the situation in each country of that region. It also provides recommended terms of payment and credit terms generally expected in that country. The data is consolidated from several reliable sources: Dun & Bradstreet and *The Economist*'s Intelligence Unit. Table 7-2 is an excerpt of the information

exposure The relative consequences of a particular risk for an exporter; the risk of a $50,000 loss would represent a greater exposure for a small exporter than for a large exporter.

country risk or political risk The probability of not getting paid by a certain creditor, because the creditor's country does not have the funds to pay the debt (insufficient foreign exchange reserves) or because the creditor is not legally allowed to pay the debt (political embargo).

TABLE 7-2	Recommended Credit Terms and Terms of Payment (August 2006)	
Country	**Credit Terms**	**Recommended Terms of Payment**
Finland	14–30 days	Open Account
Bolivia	60–90 days	Confirmed Letter of Credit
Japan	30–60 days	Sight Draft (Documentary Collection)
Czech Republic	14–30 days	Letter of Credit
Singapore	30–60 days	Open Account
Nigeria	30–60 days	Confirmed Letter of Credit
United Kingdom	30–60 days	Open Account

TABLE 7-3	Several Credit Reporting Services	
Company	**U.S. Phone Number**	**Web Address**
COFACE	213-503-6739	http://www.cofacerating.com
Latin American Business Credit Reporting Association		http://www.alaic.com
Creditworthy.com	503-694-5897	http://www.creditworthy.com
Dun & Bradstreet	800-519-3111	http://www.dnb.com
FCIB-NACM	410-423-1840	http://www.fcibglobal.com
Graydon International (UK)	44-20-8515-1406	http://www.graydonamerica.com
Kreller Business Information	513-723-8900	http://www.kreller.com
Owens Online	813-877-2008	http://www.owens.com

published in Dun & Bradstreet's *Exporters' Encyclopaedia*.[7] Note that expectations of currency fluctuations do not affect the choice of the term of payment, but will affect the choice of the currency of quote (see Chapter 8).

7-3b Commercial Risk

This is the area in which it is more difficult to obtain accurate and reliable information. If the potential customer is a distributor who does business with other exporting firms, it is often possible to obtain firsthand information from these other exporters. Actually, it is considered good commercial practice in the United States to share information on the creditworthiness of a common customer—and in some cases to monitor this customer's payments—with other suppliers.

Commercial risk can also be evaluated from private sources, including credit report companies, factoring houses, some accounting firms, insurance companies, and banks. However, these are usually fee-based services and tend to be focused on larger established firms in developed countries. These sources are reliable and unbiased, though they tend to be conservative in their evaluations.

Table 7-3 lists several companies offering foreign credit reports on overseas customers. Each of these firms usually issues a report on a foreign customer for about U.S. $125.[8]

7-3c Exposure

The risk of non-payment is the *probability* of not getting paid or of being paid late, and it therefore dictates the terms of payment chosen by the exporter.

However, another issue to be considered is the consequence of that loss on a company, or the exposure of a company. At equal probabilities of loss, a small business would be much more careful in handling a U.S. $50,000 export transaction than a large company would be. The amount is a much greater percentage of its business, and the loss of this amount could be very significant. The greater the exposure, the more secure the terms of payment should be.

7-4 Cash in Advance

7-4a Definition

In a Cash in Advance transaction, the exporter requests that the customer provide payment in advance, before shipment of the goods can take place. Payment is usually made with an electronic SWIFT (Society for Worldwide Interbank Financial Tele-communication) fund transfer from the customer's bank to the exporter's bank.

This is the ultimate "risk-free" alternative for the exporter. The importer has to pay before the goods are released; therefore, there are no collection worries, no foreign exchange fluctuation exposure, no cash-flow problem, and only nominal fees to pay to banks.

In a Cash in Advance transaction, the risk is completely transferred to the importer. It sends cash to the exporter with the expectation that the exporter will ship the goods that were requested, in the quantity that was ordered, in due time, and with the documents necessary to clear Customs in the importing country. In addition, this takes place in an atmosphere in which the exporter just demonstrated that it has no trust whatsoever in the importer because it is requesting "Cash in Advance."

7-4b Applicability

Cash in Advance is a recommended way of conducting international transactions in countries in which fraud is rampant, in countries in which there is a substantial risk of political instability or the possibility of foreign exchange "freezes," and in countries that do not have a convertible currency. Transactions conducted in the Republics of the former Soviet Union and Eastern Europe, with the possible exclusions of Hungary and the Czech Republic, would probably best be conducted on a Cash in Advance basis.

However, this method is unsound for business conducted in developed countries and in countries in which there is a significant level of sophistication in international business. In these countries, the probability that an importer will place a Cash in Advance purchase is infinitesimally small if there are other comparable suppliers available, and insisting on this method of payment is likely to create resentment on the part of the importer rather than initiate an amicable business relationship. It should be avoided at all costs.

7-5 Open Account

7-5a Definition

In an Open Account transaction, the exporter conducts international business in a manner similar to the way it conducts business domestically. The exporter just sends an invoice to the importer along with the shipment and trusts the customer to pay within a reasonable amount of time, commensurate with the credit usually granted in the country in which the importer operates, usually thirty to ninety days. It is essentially the conceptual opposite of Cash in Advance, as the exporter shows complete trust in the importer and ships the merchandise without any guarantee that it will be paid. The only recourse in case of non-payment is legal action in the importing country, a time-consuming and expensive process that exporters rarely undertake.

7-5b Applicability

This term of payment should be reserved to established customers, or customers with whom the exporter expects to have an ongoing relationship. It could possibly be extended to new orders from large companies and/or companies for which commercial credit data is available, and whose credit rating is excellent. At least, that's theoretically the way that this term of payment should be used.

In practice, however, this term of sale has become almost necessary in some markets if the exporter is to expect any sales. For example, in the European Union, it has become very difficult to conduct business on any other basis. It is to be expected that the trend will continue and expand to other markets as well: For example, European Union companies offer Open Account terms of payment to 80 percent of their customers[9] outside of the EU. The main reason is that, historically, European exporters have often benefited from their government's support, and were often offered free (or substantially discounted) commercial insurance on their foreign receivables. Until 1994, for example, a French exporter could obtain insurance from the COFACE—the *Compagnie Française d'Assurance pour le Commerce Extérieur*, a government-run insurance company—at a greatly reduced cost; its risk of non-payment had therefore essentially been assumed by the government. Today, COFACE and other European-based companies constitute the largest providers of international commercial **credit insurance** and are present in many different countries,[10] a position reached through many consolidations.

credit insurance An insurance policy under which commercial risk is covered; in exchange for a premium paid by the exporter, the insurance company will bear the risk of nonpayment by the importer, deducting a slight percentage of the receivable.

7-5c Commercial Insurance

In order to compete in those markets in which Open Account has become the rule, companies must offer this term of payment in their quotes to new customers. However, the risks associated with an Open Account transaction should entice an exporter to acquire credit insurance on those sales.

Therefore a commercial policy covering credit risks should be contracted, either on a "blanket" basis (i.e., covering all export transactions, up to a certain overall amount) or on a per-sale basis (i.e., each individual transaction is covered by a separate commercial insurance contract). Section 10-12 gives more detailed information on these types of coverage.

7-5d Factoring

international factoring A means of financing international receivable accounts, by which a firm can ask a factoring company to advance funds on a receivable account.

In those cases where the importer wants credit terms that are beyond what the exporter is comfortable giving—for example, a ninety-day credit is requested when the exporter can only afford a thirty-day credit—there is the possibility of using **international factoring** as a means to extend this credit. In an international transaction, factoring is much more complicated than in a domestic sale: The exporter would contact a factoring firm in the exporting country who would in turn contact a factoring firm in the importing country. Once both factoring parties agree to the transaction, the sale is completed on an Open Account basis. The exporter, once the invoice is sent, sells the receivable to the factoring house and collects its face value, from which are deducted the fees and interest charges covering the period of time during which credit is extended.[11]

The transaction is generally without recourse (i.e., the factoring house is responsible for collecting the receivable and cannot turn to the exporter if it is unable to collect). This is the main reason why factoring houses often involve a second factoring company located in the importing country; its responsibility is to check the creditworthiness of the importer, and, in some cases, to act as a collection agent for the factoring company in the exporting country.

7-6 Letter of Credit

7-6a Definition

A Letter of Credit is a document in which the importer's bank essentially promises to pay the exporter if the importer does not pay. The creditworthiness of the bank is substituted for the creditworthiness of the importer. However, the concept is substantially more complex than this. The promise is not made upon the exporter meeting certain conditions (or the importer not meeting certain conditions), but it is made on the *documents* of the transaction: This is the reason why a Letter of Credit is often called a Documentary Letter of Credit. The bank is under no obligation to pay even though delivery has been made and the importer has obtained control of the merchandise; similarly, the bank has to pay even though the merchandise may be shoddy or not fit for sale. The bank is obligated to pay only if the documents are in order. The Letter of Credit is therefore a contractual agreement between the **Issuing Bank** and the **beneficiary**, independent of the underlying relationship between the exporter and the importer; only the *documents* relating to the exporter-importer transaction matter. This obviously means that extreme care must be taken in handling the documents related to a Letter of Credit; otherwise, it triggers a very time-consuming and expensive process of amendments and corrections to the Letter of Credit.

A transaction conducted on a Letter of Credit basis is almost as good as one made on a Cash in Advance basis in that the exporter will be paid, but it involves going through a lot more steps and paying a lot more banking fees. Figures 7-1 through 7-3 explain the process followed by a Letter of Credit transaction from issuance to payment.

7-6b Process

Issuance

- The first step in the process (see Figure 7-1) is the negotiation, which takes place between the exporter and the importer, in which it is agreed that the terms of payment will be by Letter of Credit. The exporter then sends a *pro-forma* invoice to the importer, which estimates the terms of the transaction as closely as possible (see Section 9-2b for further details on the elements of a *pro-forma* invoice).

- The second step takes place when the importer (the **applicant**) requests its bank (the Issuing Bank) to open a Letter of Credit on the importer's behalf, naming the exporter as the beneficiary. Because it is promising that it will pay if the importer

Issuing Bank The bank providing the Letter of Credit to the importer. It is that bank that, should the importer be unable to pay, and should the exporter provide all the necessary documents, has the contractual obligation to pay the beneficiary.

beneficiary The firm named in a Letter of Credit as the firm to whom the bank is insuring payment if the importer does not pay. Usually, the beneficiary of a Letter of Credit is the exporter.

applicant The firm asking the Issuing Bank for a Letter of Credit. Usually, the applicant is the importer.

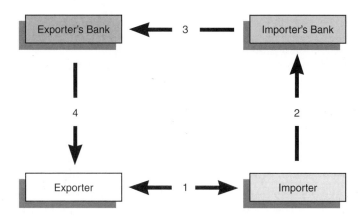

1. The Exporter and the Importer agree on a sale under "Letter of Credit" terms. The Exporter sends a *pro-forma* invoice to the Importer.

2. The Importer takes the *pro-forma* invoice to its Bank and requests a Letter of Credit.

3. The Importer's Bank issues a Letter of Credit and sends it to the Exporter's Bank.

4. The Exporter's Bank advises the Letter of Credit and notifies the Exporter that it is OK to ship the merchandise to the Importer.

Figure 7-1
Issuance of a Letter of Credit

does not pay, the bank may request that the importer "freeze" a certain percentage (from 0 to 100 percent) of the amount of the Letter of Credit in an account or on a line of credit, essentially ensuring that the importer will pay the bank by obtaining the funds before the letter of credit is issued. This constraint on cash flow is one of the reasons why importers prefer other terms of payment to a Letter of Credit. Another is the fact that the Issuing Bank will request a fee that will vary between 0.5 and 3 percent of the amount of the Letter of Credit, although most of them request about 1.5 percent.

Advising Bank The bank that determines whether the Issuing Bank is a legitimate bank, and whether the terms of the Letter of Credit offered by the issuing bank on behalf of the importer are appropriate.

- In the third step, the Issuing Bank sends the Letter of Credit (either electronically [using the SWIFT network], by fax, or by mail) to the exporter's bank, which acts as the **Advising Bank** (in this simplified example). The Advising Bank checks a number of things: first, that the Letter of Credit is drawn on a legitimate bank and that its content meets the requirements of the exporter. It also wants to make sure that the Letter of Credit is irrevocable: An irrevocable Letter of Credit cannot be modified without the express consent of both the issuer and the beneficiary. All Letters of Credit issued under the Universal Customs and Practice for Documentary Credit of the International Chamber of Commerce (UCP 500) are irrevocable unless specifically marked as "revocable." The Advising Bank finally wants to confirm that the Letter of Credit's information matches the *pro-forma* invoice exactly and that the expiration date is appropriate for the transaction.

- The Advising Bank then notifies the beneficiary that the Letter of Credit is acceptable. By doing so, the bank is not engaging its responsibility; it is only acting as an adviser to the exporter and will not have to pay if the Issuing Bank does not honor its commitment.

Shipment

- The fifth step in the process of a Letter of Credit takes place when the exporter ships the merchandise to the importer. In this process, the exporter generates a lot of paperwork (an invoice, a certificate of origin, an export license, a packing list, a Shipper's Export Declaration [U.S.], and so on) and collects a lot of paperwork,

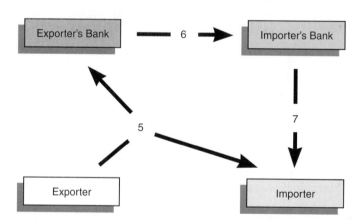

5. The Exporter sends the merchandise to the Importer, but gathers all documents and sends them to the Exporter's Bank.

6. The Exporter's Bank checks that the documents match the requirements of the Letter of Credit, and sends them to the Importer's Bank.

7. The Importer's Bank verifies that the documents match the requirements of the Letter of Credit and notifies the Importer that everything is in order.

Figure 7-2
Shipment under a Letter of Credit

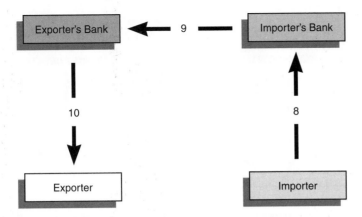

8. The Importer pays the Importer's Bank in order to be able to collect the documents that it will need to collect the merchandise and clear Customs.

9. The Importer's Bank sends the Importer's payment to the Exporter's Bank.

10. The Exporter's Bank notifies the Exporter that it has been paid.

Figure 7-3
Payment under a Letter of Credit

such as a bill of lading or an air waybill from the shipping company and miscellaneous certificates (insurance, inspection, and so on) from different suppliers (for more information on all of these terms, please see Chapter 9). Extreme care must be given to make sure that the paperwork matches precisely the requirements of the Letter of Credit, as the Issuing Bank's promise to pay is contingent upon presenting the proper documents.

• After these documents are collected, the exporter will send them to its bank (the Advising Bank), which will check them against the terms of the Letter of Credit. If the documents conform, the bank will then send the documents (sixth step) to the importer's bank (the Issuing Bank). In some cases, depending on the working relationship between the Issuing Bank and the Advising Bank, the Advising Bank could issue a credit (payment) to the exporter at that point. However, this payment is not final and is dependent on the Issuing Bank honoring the Letter of Credit. The simplest example illustrated in Figure 7-2 does not presume such a relationship and assumes that the Advising Bank will wait until it is actually paid by the Issuing Bank before it credits the exporter's bank account.

• After receiving them, the Issuing Bank will check the documents sent by the exporter's bank and determine whether they conform to the requirements of the Letter of Credit. If the documents conform, the issuing bank notifies the importer that the documents are in order and it exchanges them (concentrating on the bill of lading or the air waybill, which act as the certificate of title to the goods) against payment by the importer. The importer can then clear Customs in the importing country.

Payment
• The payment of a Letter of Credit is a fairly simple process: Payment is first made by the importer to its bank, then the importing bank wires the payment to the exporter's bank, and finally the exporter's account is credited (see Figure 7-3).

The entire process of a Letter of Credit is shown in Figure 7-4. The reason the process is labeled "simplified" is because a number of additional parties can get involved in the process.

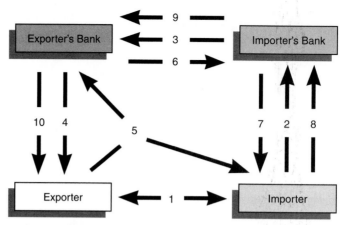

Figure 7-4
Entire (Simplified) Process of a Letter of Credit

7-6c Additional Information

Irrevocable Letter of Credit

Irrevocable Letter of Credit
A Letter of Credit is a document whereby a bank promises that it will pay the beneficiary (the exporter) a predetermined amount of money, should the beneficiary present a certain set of documents to the bank.

An **Irrevocable Letter of Credit** is one that cannot be canceled by the Issuing Bank for any reason, unless the beneficiary agrees to it. A Revocable Letter of Credit is one that can be changed by the importer (or the Issuing Bank) without prior approval of the beneficiary. In very few cases does it make sense for a beneficiary to accept a Revocable Letter of Credit. The overwhelming majority of Letters of Credit are Irrevocable Letters of Credit.

A Letter of Credit issued under the Universal Customs and Practice for Documentary Credit (UCP 500)—and almost all of them are—is assumed to be irrevocable unless otherwise specified. Under the previous guidelines (UCP 400), the opposite was true; a Letter of Credit was not irrevocable unless it specifically stated so. Even though the UCP 500 replaced the UCP 400 in 1993, there seems to still be some confusion regarding this important distinction.

Confirming Bank

Confirmed Letter of Credit
A payment alternative in which the exporter asks a bank to provide an additional level of payment security to a Letter of Credit: Should the importer not pay and should the Issuing Bank not pay, the Confirming Bank will pay.

Confirming Bank The bank providing an additional level of payment security to the beneficiary of a Letter of Credit; the Confirming Bank certifies that it will pay the Letter of Credit if the importer and the Issuing Bank do not pay.

In some cases, the exporting company may not be comfortable doing business with the Issuing Bank, which, after all, is an unknown foreign entity. It may not know the bank's creditworthiness, feel that the risk of relying on a foreign bank is too high, or simply be quite risk averse or new to the export business. In any case, the exporter can ask its Advising Bank to confirm the Letter of Credit; it then becomes a **Confirmed Letter of Credit**. In the event the Issuing Bank does not honor its Letter of Credit, then the **Confirming Bank** will pay the exporter, as long as the documents submitted conform to the terms of the Letter of Credit. It is a way to substitute the creditworthiness of the domestic bank for that of the Issuing Bank. Because the Confirming Bank is often also the Advising Bank, the practice is that the Confirming Bank will issue a credit to the exporter upon presentation of the documents at the time of shipment. It therefore speeds up the process of collection by a week or so.

In most cases, confirming a Letter of Credit is not a wise choice, as banks tend to be creditworthy. In addition, confirming a Letter of Credit is expensive, costing 0.5 to 1.5 percent of the amount of the Letter of Credit, a substantial cost considering that foreign banks rarely fail. Some U.S. companies have a policy of always confirming Letters of Credit, generally because they prefer dealing with a U.S. bank should there be difficulties in collection; nevertheless, this leads companies to confirm Letters of Credit drawn on extraordinarily solid banks, such as Crédit Suisse, with less-than-stellar U.S. banks. Then again, venerable banks have been known to fail; Barings did in 1995.

TABLE 7-4	Leading Causes of Discrepancies in Letters of Credit [as a percentage of all discrepancies]	
Inconsistent data		25.1%
Absence of documents		8.4%
Late presentation		7.9%
Carrier not named		8.8%
Incorrect goods description		4.1%
Incorrect data		7.1%
Incorrect BOL Endorsement		3.8%
Incorrect Insurance Cover		1.8%

Correspondent Bank

In some cases, a third bank can get involved in the process. Quite a few banks enter agreements in which they act as **Correspondent Banks** for each other. The purpose of these agreements is for each bank to have a "representation" in a foreign market. The consequence of these agreements is that the banks tend to favor their Correspondent Banks, and in some cases will funnel all the business they conduct in the Correspondent Bank's country to that bank.

For the sake of example, let's pretend that Bank A in Germany has an agreement with Bank Z in Thailand in which they are each other's Correspondent Bank. An exporter in Germany, doing business with Bank B, requests a Letter of Credit from its Thai customer who himself has an account with Bank Z. It is quite likely for Bank A to be part of the transaction and act as the "courier" between Bank Z and Bank B, or even for Bank Z to request that Bank A become the Advising Bank. In most cases, it would be advantageous for the German exporter to have Bank A involved as Bank A may release the funds *on behalf of* the Issuing Bank Z (see Section 7-6f). Payment would then be collected earlier.

Correspondent Bank
A foreign bank with which a domestic bank has a preferred business relationship.

Amendments

In the unfortunately fairly frequent case in which the Letter of Credit and the documents do not match perfectly, it is the role of the Advising Bank to request an amendment to the Letter of Credit from the Issuing Bank. (Although this method is in no way mandated by international conventions, it is the preferred method, as the Advising Bank is seen as a more impartial and neutral party than the exporter.) Such discrepancies can be on shipping dates, changes in the number of packages, changes in part numbers, suppliers' costs (insurance, shipping charges), and so on (see Table 7-4[12]). It is estimated that around 50 percent of all Letters of Credit have some sort of **discrepancy**.[13]

An **amendment** is a change that must be authorized by both parties; the beneficiary and the importer (through the Issuing Bank) must agree to it. There is usually a fee attached to an amendment, and in some cases it can be difficult to obtain because the importing country's government gets involved (the import license may have to be changed) or because the change is not to the advantage of the importer (a delay in shipping date, for example). In the overwhelming majority of the cases, though, the problem can be solved to the satisfaction of both parties; one personal banking acquaintance could only recall of one "deal gone bad" in twenty years of Letters of Credit management.

Given these potential problems, it should be evident that it is crucial for the exporter to pay close attention to the terms of the Letter of Credit, and attempt to adhere to them as closely as possible. In a related manner, great care should be given to the preparation of the *pro-forma* invoice, as this is the document upon which the Issuing Bank relies to issue the Letter of Credit. In those few cases in which the

discrepancy A difference between the documents required by the Letter of Credit and the documents provided by the exporter.

amendment A change to a Letter of Credit to which all parties to a Letter of Credit agree: the exporter, the importer, the Issuing Bank, and the Advising Bank.

Letter of Credit does not reflect exactly the *pro-forma* invoice (misspellings, for example), it is wiser to issue an invoice that matches the Letter of Credit rather than attempt to obtain an amendment. This is obviously difficult to do on an automated invoice processing system, but can quickly become an issue. Actually, many bankers have "horror stories" of Issuing Banks refusing payment on a Letter of Credit because there is a typo on the Letter of Credit—an error on their part as they miscopied the *pro-forma* invoice—which obviously does not appear on the commercial invoice.[14] This can be construed as a ploy to generate additional amendment fees from a "hostage" exporter, but it is unfortunately prevalent at some banks.[15] To their defense, though, a Letter of Credit issued by a bank in a third-world country may have been typed by a clerk with no knowledge whatsoever of the exporter's language.

UCP 500

The UCP 500[16] is the *Universal Customs and Practice for Documentary Credit*, 1993 Revision, Publication 500 of the International Chamber of Commerce. It is a publication that details the responsibilities of the banks involved in Letters of Credit, as well as the responsibilities of the applicant and of the beneficiary. It also attempts to address most of the areas in which there could be misunderstandings between the Issuing Bank, the Advising Bank, the applicant, and the beneficiary. Because of the jurisprudence that has accumulated with the almost universal usage of UCP 500, it is greatly preferable to always follow its guidelines, and request that the Letter of Credit be issued "subject to" the UCP 500.[17]

Whenever a Letter of Credit is issued through the SWIFT network, it is by convention issued under UCP 500 guidelines unless otherwise noted. Because most banks belong to the SWIFT network, almost all Letters of Credit are therefore issued under UCP 500.

Yet More Complications

Things can get a lot more complicated in a Letter of Credit transaction as yet more parties can get involved; for example, the exporter's bank may feel that it is unqualified to advise the Letter of Credit and will request that another, larger or more experienced bank become the Advising Bank. In some cases, the Advising Bank and the Confirming Bank are in different countries, leading to the possible situation where there are two Correspondent Banks involved. The worst-case scenario is probably much more horrid than that, and it can quickly become quite confusing.

Drafts

It is possible to add a draft (see Section 7-7) to a Letter of Credit. The draft is an instrument that legally binds the importer to pay within a certain period of time. This allows the exporter to grant commercial credit to the importer whenever it is deemed necessary. If no draft is attached to a Letter of Credit, the assumption is that the importer is not granted any credit (i.e., that the Letter of Credit is payable at sight; in other words, immediately). The different types of drafts are presented in Sections 7-7b, 7-7c, and Sections 7-7d.

Electronic Letters of Credit

Toward the end of 1999, the Society for Worldwide Interbank Financial Telecommunication (SWIFT) and Imperial Bank created an electronic version of the Letter of Credit for Imperial Bank's customers, which allows online applications, online tracking, and online dissemination of Letters of Credit to the beneficiary by the applicant.[18] However, such a system was likely to be trumped by a system that combines the advantages of an electronic Letter of Credit as well as electronic transfer of documents, such as the TradeCard electronic system (see Section 7-9). Therefore, in mid-2006, SWIFT launched a product called SwiftNet Trade Services Utility (TSU) that encompasses both financial information and trade documents.

7-6d Stand-By Letters of Credit

A Stand-By Letter of Credit is similar to a "simple" Letter of Credit, with a few exceptions. First, it generally has a much longer validity period, sometimes longer than a year. Second, it usually applies to more than one shipment from the exporter to the importer; under such a system, the exporter will make shipments on an Open Account basis, and will "call" on the Letter of Credit only if the importer is not meeting its obligations;[19] for example, if it is not paying on time. These qualities make Stand-By Letters of Credit a tool of choice for handling business with a distributor, for example, or making a series of shipments to a customer.

The Stand-By Letter of Credit is an instrument that was created by United States banks as a substitute for bank guarantees, because U.S. banks are prohibited from offering them.[20] Therefore, Stand-By Letters of Credit are often also used to secure the obligations of the seller/exporter (as in a performance bond) (see Section 7-10). The sums secured by Stand-by Letters of Credit total $700 billion, an amount roughly four times as large as the amount secured by traditional Letters of Credit.[21]

The rules for Stand-By Letters of Credit are regulated by the International Stand-By Practices ISP98, a series of eighty-nine rules governing the language, documentation, and practices of these Letters of Credit.[22]

7-6e Applicability

A Letter of Credit used to be the instrument of choice in international transactions, especially in those cases in which the exporter had no pre-existing business relationship with the importer, or when the importer was located in a country that was considered to be risky. It still is an outstanding means of making sure that the exporter will be paid, and is recommended in situations in which the exporter is risk-averse, new to the business of exporting, has substantial exposure in the transaction in question, or in those cases in which there is some uneasiness regarding the creditworthiness of the importer.

However, it is often a disadvantage to request a Letter of Credit because of the costs (and the cumbersome process) associated with a Letter of Credit. It is also unwise to demand payment on such restrictive terms when other competitors can offer Open Account terms. Therefore, it may be a more sensible alternative, especially in Western Europe, to offer terms that are more favorable to the importer and use commercial insurance to cover the commercial risk.

7-6f URR 525

The International Chamber of Commerce also has published a document entitled *Uniform Rules for Bank-to-Bank Reimbursements under Documentary Credits.*[23]

These rules outline the responsibilities of the banks involved in an international transaction conducted under the UCP 500, and in which payment to the exporter is made directly by the Advising Bank (or by the Correspondent Bank of the Issuing Bank). The paying bank is then reimbursed by the Issuing Bank. This practice is becoming more and more common as a means to expedite the process of a Letter of Credit. The International Chamber of Commerce felt that Uniform Rules were necessary in this matter. Although these rules apply to banks rather than exporters, it might be advisable to refer to them before requesting payment from the Advising or the Correspondent Bank of the Issuing Bank.

7-7 Documentary Collection

7-7a Definition

Documentary Collection is a process by which an exporter asks a bank to "safe-guard" its interests in the foreign country by not releasing the documents (specifically the bill of lading, which is the certificate of title to the goods [see Chapter 9]) until the importer satisfies certain requirements, most often paying the exporter or signing a financial document (called a draft or a **bill of exchange**) promising that it will pay the exporter within a given amount of time. This allows the exporter, should the importer decide not to take delivery of the goods, to have them shipped back to the exporting country and to lose only the costs of shipment rather than the total value of the goods. Another possibility is to find another customer for these goods.

The exporter can set up a Documentary Collection through its own bank, who then acts as the **Remitting Bank** by collecting the documents from the exporter and sending them to a bank in the importing country (the **Presenting Bank**) along with an instruction letter (see Section 7-7e).

7-7b Sight Draft

One alternative is for the exporter to request a bank in the importing country (the Presenting Bank) to deliver the documents to the importer (also called the **drawee**) only after it has collected payment. This is often called either a "Documents against Payment" (D/P) or a sight draft transaction, with the latter meaning that the draft (a promissory note) is payable "at sight" (i.e., immediately). In this case, the exporter retains the title to the goods, embodied in the bill of lading or air waybill, until payment is made and the bill of lading or air waybill is given to the importer.

7-7c Time Draft

In some cases, the exporter may want to grant some credit terms to the importer but still want some means to ensure it will be paid. In that case, it can request that the bank exchange the documents against a **time draft**: The importer has to sign (endorse) a document promising it will pay within a certain time (generally a multiple of thirty days: 30, 60, 90, or 180 days are the most common credit terms) after the draft is endorsed. The Presenting Bank should specifically be instructed to remit the documents when the draft is signed ("Documents against Acceptance" [D/A]), or to remit them against payment (D/P), in which case the importer will not take title to the goods until after payment is made, a requirement that mostly defeats the purpose of granting credit. Specifically because of problems associated with D/P and **date drafts** (specifically the custody of the goods between their arrival in the importing country and the time they become the property of the importer), the International Chamber of Commerce advises that "Collections should not contain bill of exchange payable at a future date with instructions that commercial documents are to be delivered against payment."[24]

A draft (or a bill of exchange) is a legal document in the importing country in which the importer officially recognizes a commercial debt toward the exporter. This makes it easier to collect payment if the importer decides not to honor its commitment, as the default is now a *domestic* issue rather than an international one, a dispute over which a domestic Court would have no problem ruling. Specifically, in the instructions to the Presenting Bank, it is possible to request a **protest** in case of a non-payment on a draft, which is a legal process that can have serious consequences for an importer; it may be difficult (if not impossible) for the importer to obtain credit after it has been recorded that it does not honor its debt. In some countries,

bill of exchange In a Documentary Collection transaction, another term for a draft.

Remitting Bank In a Documentary Collection transaction, the bank that interacts with the exporter and with the Presenting Bank in the importing country. The Remitting Bank is the one that receives the documents from the exporter and then sends them to the Presenting Bank.

Presenting Bank In a Documentary Collection transaction, the bank that interacts with the importer on behalf of the exporter. The Presenting Bank is the one receiving the documents from the exporter or from the Remitting Bank and that holds them until the importer either signs a draft or pays the exporter.

drawee In a Documentary Collection transaction, another term for the importer who signs the draft.

time draft In a Documentary Collection transaction, a time draft is a promissory note that the importer has to pay a number of days (thirty, sixty, ninety, or 180 days) after it accepts the draft by signing it.

protest In a Documentary Collection transaction, if the drawee (importer) does not pay a draft that it has signed, the Presenting Bank will file a protest, a legal document that notifies other parties that the drawee is not honoring its debts.

such defaults are published prominently in the local business press, tarnishing the reputation of a business.

7-7d Date Draft

Another type of draft is a date draft, which is another way of granting credit to the importer. The difference is that the credit is extended to the importer for thirty, sixty, or ninety days from the *shipment date* rather than from the endorsement of the draft. The shipment date is determined by the main contract of carriage, generally the date at which the ocean bill of lading or the air waybill is issued.[25] The advantage of the date draft over the time draft is that the exporter has control over the date at which shipment is initiated (and therefore over the date at which the payment is due), whereas it has no control over the date at which the importer will endorse the draft.

A date draft transaction therefore alleviates one of the problems of Documentary Collection in general, which is the date at which the importer will endorse the draft. Under the *Uniform Rules for Collection*,[26] the bank must notify the importer as soon as it receives the documents. However, the importer has no incentive to come to the bank to collect them—if the draft is a sight or time draft—because delaying endorsement delays payment as well.

7-7e Instruction Letter

In addition to the "normal" documents (invoice, bill of lading, certificates, licenses, and such) and to the draft, each Documentary Collection should include an **instruction letter** in which the exporter—through the Remitting Bank—tells the Presenting Bank what it is expected to accomplish.

The instruction letter is a document in which the Remitting Bank instructs the Presenting Bank on the procedures it should follow in its dealings with the importer; for example, whether the documents should be exchanged against payment (D/P) or against an acceptance of the draft (D/A), but also what the procedures should be if the importer refuses to sign the draft, if the importer refuses to pay for the fees (if any), or if the importer does not honor its signature: The Presenting Bank could be asked to file a protest, for example.

This instruction letter is the only document that the Presenting Bank will follow in a Documentary Collection: The bank does not need to find its instructions among the other documents that accompany the Documentary Collection; the International Chamber of Commerce is quite clear about this issue in its new *Uniform Rules for Collections* (URC 522) (see Section 7-7h). It is also preferable to mention in the instruction letter that the collection is subject to URC 522.

7-7f Trade Acceptance

The responsibilities of the Presenting Bank in the importing country generally stop at notifying the importer that the documents have arrived and at requesting that the importer endorse the draft (D/A) or at requesting payment (D/P) before releasing the documents. This process is called **trade acceptance**—sometimes "trader's acceptance"—as the importer has control over the decision to accept or reject the draft and over the timing of the endorsement.

This could be somewhat inconvenient for the exporter, as the importer could delay acceptance of the draft for an inordinate amount of time—a problem that can be solved with a date draft—or even refuse to sign the draft. In such a case, the exporter still has title, but over merchandise that is warehoused in a foreign country. The costs associated with warehousing goods in an unknown location, as well as the risks of pilferage and the exporter's difficulties in arranging for such storage can lead unscrupulous importers to take advantage of the situation by extorting better terms

---

date draft In a Documentary Collection transaction, a date draft is a promissory note that the importer has to pay a number of days (thirty, sixty, ninety, or 180 days) after the exporter ships the goods.

instruction letter A document sent by the exporter to the Presenting Bank where it spells out its instructions regarding how it expects the bank to handle the documents and how it expects the bank to handle an importer who does not accept the draft sent.

trade acceptance In a Documentary Collection transaction, the alternative where the exporter expects the importer to readily accept signing a draft after being notified by the Presenting Bank that the documents have arrived.

from the exporter (e.g., a discounted price, given the costs of repatriating the goods) before signing the draft.

7-7g Banker's Acceptance and Aval

The problems presented by a trade acceptance can be solved by requesting a **banker's acceptance**. In this case, it is the Presenting Bank that endorses the draft on behalf of the importer. The bank will usually endorse the draft immediately upon receipt of the documents, and the endorsement of the bank engages the responsibility of the importer: It signs on behalf of the importer. The Presenting Bank is unlikely to offer a banker's acceptance unless it feels in a position to "aval" the draft.

An **aval** is a promise by the Presenting Bank that the importer will honor the draft, and that, should the importer default, the bank will make the payment. The bank therefore acts as a "co-signor" of the draft.

Although an aval is theoretically independent and different from a banker's acceptance, in practice the latter is often used as a substitute for "aval." Therefore the Remitting Bank will often offer credit to an exporter based upon a "banker's acceptance" as it understands that the credit risk is now based upon the creditworthiness of the Presenting Bank, which is a situation almost as good as a Letter of Credit.

7-7h URC 522

The International Chamber of Commerce also publishes guidelines for Documentary Collections in a document called *Uniform Rules for Collections* (URC 522).[27]

The main benefit of these rules is that they outline specifically the responsibilities of the Remitting Bank and the responsibilities of the Presenting Bank, as well as the limits to their responsibilities: For example, the Presenting Bank has to make sure that it promptly notifies the importer to come in to sign the draft (D/A), is responsible to make sure that the draft is signed properly (according to local laws), but has no obligation to determine that the person has the authority to sign. All of these obligations (and limitations) are very well described and explained in the *Commentary on URC 522*.[28]

One issue that is quite clear (and a change from the previous *Uniform Rules for Collections* [URC 322]) is the inclusion of an obligatory instruction letter to the Presenting Bank, which clarifies what the Presenting Bank has to do with the documents. Because the URC 522 is becoming the international standard for Documentary Collection—although it has not reached the universal nature of the UCP 500—it is advisable to always state in the letter of instruction that the collection is subject to the Uniform Rules for Collections (URC 522) of the International Chamber of Commerce.

7-7i Applicability

Documentary Collections are a good way to conduct international sales because they are clearly less cumbersome (and less expensive) than Letters of Credit and provide a good amount of safety. The title remains in the hands of the exporter until the importer accepts the draft (D/A) or makes payment (D/P). This risk is further reduced if a banker's acceptance is requested.

However, Documentary Collections represent more risk for the exporter than a Letter of Credit, because payment is dependent upon the primary transaction (the contract of sale); the importer could refuse to sign the draft (invoking poor quality merchandise, for example) or delay signing the draft (until it has resold the merchandise), in which cases the exporter retains title, but does not get paid. A Letter of

Credit, however, is not dependent on the primary transaction, but only on the documents; it will ensure payment as long as documents are in the proper form.

A Documentary Collection could be used for customers in which there is a fair amount of trust, but for which an Open Account transaction is out of the question for whatever reason. A banker's acceptance could be used for customers who refuse to conduct business on a Letter of Credit basis and about whose creditworthiness the exporter is uncertain.

7-7j Forfaiting

In those cases where the importer wants credit terms that are beyond what the exporter is comfortable giving—for example, a five-year term is requested on a piece of machinery when the exporter can only extend a 180-day credit—there is the possibility of using **international forfaiting** as a means to extend this credit. In an international transaction, forfaiting is generally achieved with the help of a series of drafts from the importer, which have been given an aval by the importer's bank.[29] Forfaiting is used for longer credit terms than factoring, which tends to be used for credit terms for up to 180 days: In contrast, forfaiting can be used for terms as long as seven years.

The exporter, once it has obtained an agreement from the forfaiting firm, will obtain this series of drafts, all with different due dates from the importer. It will then sell this series of drafts to the forfaiting firm at a discount. The forfaiting firm purchases them without recourse, which means it cannot hold the exporter responsible for non-payment by the importer. Forfaiting is an arrangement that usually satisfies the credit requirements of the importer at no risk—and at a fairly moderate cost—to the exporter.[30]

international forfaiting
A means of financing an international transaction in which an exporter collects a series of drafts from the importer and sells them to a forfaiting firm who buys them without recourse.

7-8 Procurement Cards

A number of banks have started offering a system of credit cards for their corporate accounts;[31] The product originates from the observation that companies purchase myriad small items, from office supplies to small maintenance parts. In most instances, the traditional process to purchase these parts is through a centralized Purchasing Department that issues a purchase order, processes a significant amount of paperwork, and then pays an invoice. The idea of a procurement card is to allow a department to make certain purchases directly from a vendor, which is a much more expedient process. The procurement card is similar in concept to a consumer's credit card; it has a certain credit limit, it is billed directly to the department (or at least can provide an itemized billing statement showing which department is responsible for a specific purchase), and most importantly, it allows transactions to be conducted extremely rapidly. Moreover, the supplier is paid immediately—minus a certain transaction percentage, in the neighborhood of 2 percent—and the customer is billed at the end of the month.

There are several advantages for using a procurement card for international purchases: The first is that the exporter is essentially paid "in advance," because it is paid almost immediately after the goods have been shipped. The second is that the exchange rate on the transaction is essentially the best one can get: Because the banks process many transactions on the same date worth millions of dollars, the exchange rate is the one that such large transactions can earn. Finally, the importer has some sort of recourse (in a way similar to a consumer using a Visa or American Express card) if the merchandise is defective. It should be expected that this type of transaction will increasingly take place in international business, particularly for small items (maintenance parts) and will facilitate the handling of rush orders, which will increase the level of customer service a company can offer from its home country.[32]

This product seems to present only advantages and the number of banks currently offering such a service is increasing rapidly. However, one issue that has recently affected negatively the use of procurement cards is the way that banks have modified their foreign exchange procedures: In 2005, many of the banks that offer procurement cards changed their policies on currency exchange and added a fee on foreign currency transactions that can vary from 1 to 3 percent of the value of the transaction. This additional cost negates the advantageous exchange rates that procurement cards can offer. Another slight disadvantage is that the exchange rate in effect on the processing date may differ from the rate on the date used for the transaction, resulting in a slightly different currency exchange rate than was initially anticipated.

7-9 TradeCard

Created by the World Trade Centers Association in 1994, TradeCard is a proprietary electronic system that is gaining greater acceptance in the trade community and is an alternative that combines the advantages of Letters of Credit and those of procurement cards:

- No payment is made until all the documents are in order and there are no discrepancies.
- The buyer is obligated to pay if the documents are in order.
- The system is expedient (payment is received quickly).

TradeCard also has two advantages over both of these methods of payment in that it is extremely inexpensive, charging only $150 for a transaction up to $100,000, in contrast to 1 to 3 percent for Letters of Credit and 2 to 3 percent for procurement cards, and that it combines document handling as well as payments, which gives it an edge over the electronic system of the Imperial Bank, which handles only financial information, and the Bolero system of the Society for Worldwide Interbank Financial Telecommunication, which handles only documents (see Section 9-6b). The introduction of SwiftNet Trade Services Utility (TSU) in 2006 is its first direct competitor.

TradeCard encompasses several electronic tools: First, it does have a secure system for the transmission of documents, from the *pro-forma* invoice to the bill of lading, packing list, and other transportation documents.[33] It also has a system that checks the creditworthiness of the customer and, should the importer be deemed creditworthy, guarantees payment to the exporter if the documents conform. This service is offered through a partnership with the *Compagnie Française d'Assurance pour le Commerce Extérieur* (COFACE).[34] Finally, TradeCard has a system that automatically settles invoices once the documents have been found to be in order and without discrepancies.[35]

Unfortunately, TradeCard has still not achieved "critical mass" (a significant enough number of customers), and therefore, as of 2006, despite its gains, it remains an unusual form of payment in international trade, far behind Letters of Credit, Documentary Collections, and Open Accounts. When an exporter suggests a payment on TradeCard, it is unlikely that the importer already has an account with TradeCard, and therefore it is unlikely that the transaction will be completed under this term of sale. The reciprocal is also true; a savvy importer may have a TradeCard account, but the exporter may not have one. Add to this issue the fact that importers and exporters often ask their bankers for advice in such matters, and that the latter are generally quite conservative in their recommendations, and it becomes clear why this method of payment has not gained as much momentum as was originally anticipated. Nevertheless, TradeCard presents such advantages over the other forms of international payment that it should be expected to become the dominant method of payment in the 2010s.

It is quite possible, but speculative, that SwiftNet (TSU) may gain greater acceptance in the trade community because most banks are quite familiar with SWIFT and already have business relationships with that firm.

7-10 Bank Guarantees

7-10a Definition

A **bank guarantee** is another instrument used in international trade, but is used in different situations: A bank guarantee is usually requested to secure the performance of the seller (exporter), rather than to ensure that payment will be made by the buyer (importer). This requirement happens in cases in which the exporter is a company contracting to build a plant, establish a drilling platform, or install a sewer system; for example, companies like Bechtel and Bouygues. A bank guarantee is applicable to all long-term contracts in which the importer wants to ensure that the work will be brought to completion. Frequently, the bank guarantee is offered by a group of banks rather than a single bank, because of the amounts involved. Finally, a bank guarantee is usually for an amount that is only a fraction of the total amount of the contract.

As in a Letter of Credit, a bank guarantee is an independent contract between the bank giving the guarantee (**guarantor**) and the beneficiary.

7-10b Guarantee Payable on First Demand (at First Request)

A bank guarantee payable at first request is one in which the beneficiary does not have to provide any evidence that the terms of the underlying contract between the **contractor** and the beneficiary have not been met; the Issuing Bank has to pay at the first request of the beneficiary, solely upon the presentation of a request for payment, sometimes accompanied by a statement from the beneficiary stating that the contractor is not meeting its obligations. No other proof is necessary. This type of bank guarantee is the most common one.

7-10c Guarantees based upon Documents—Cautions

In some cases, a guarantee can be made conditional upon presentation of certain documents rather than "on first demand." The beneficiary must present documents that demonstrate that the contractor is not meeting its obligations; such a document may be a ruling by a Court, or some other evidence as agreed upon in the terms of the guarantee.

The International Chamber of Commerce has issued a series of conventions regarding Documentary Bank Guarantees in publication No. 325, *Uniform Rules for Contract Guarantees*. These rules are not widely used,[36] primarily because documentary guarantees are rarely used.

7-10d Stand-By Letters of Credit

Because United States law prohibits bank guarantees, American banks instead offer the same type of financial instrument through their **Stand-By Letters of Credit**. The only difference between a Stand-By Letter of Credit and a bank guarantee is that the Stand-By Letter of Credit is *documentary* (i.e., the Beneficiary must present a document before collecting from the bank). A simple statement that the contractor is not performing is usually considered sufficient.[37]

bank guarantee A contract from a bank where the bank guarantees that an exporter will perform as required by its contract with the importer. If the exporter does not perform, the bank pays a compensation to the importer. Bank guarantees are illegal in the United States.

guarantor The bank that provides a bank guarantee. If the party to which it provides a guarantee does not perform, the bank pays a compensation to the injured party.

contractor When used in the context of a bank guarantee, a company fulfilling a large construction contract, usually the construction of a substantial infrastructure work or a major project.

Stand-By Letter of Credit A type of Letter of Credit that covers more than one shipment; a Stand-By Letter of Credit allows for multiple bills of lading, issued on different dates.

7-10e Types of Bank Guarantees

Several types of bank guarantees—or Stand-By Letters of Credit—are available:

- The tender guarantee or bid guarantee is one that is requested by a beneficiary to ensure that the contractor is bidding in good faith and will enter the contract if awarded.

- The performance guarantee is the most commonly used type of guarantee, and is used to ensure that the contractor finishes the project.

- The maintenance guarantee is used to ensure that the contractor performs the services necessitated by the contract after the completion of the project (i.e., maintenance and after-sale service).

- The advance payment guarantee or repayment guarantee is used to ensure that payments made by the beneficiary in advance of the work (to enable the contractor to purchase supplies or machinery) would be reimbursed if the contractor fails to start the project.

- The payment guarantee is used in a very different context. It covers the obligations of the buyer (often a distributor) toward the exporter, and is presented in Section 7-6d.

7-11 Terms of Payment as a Marketing Tool

An exporter has several alternatives from which to choose in negotiating terms of payment with the importer. Although most certainly, the choice of the term of sale is dependent on the level of experience of both the exporter and the importer and on the level of confidence that the exporter has in the ability of the importer to make the payment, there are some alternatives that are definitely preferable and will increase an exporter's probability to clinch the sale.

An importer, in most situations, is getting several possible quotes from several exporters located in different countries. For example, a Brazilian newspaper looking to replace a printing press will seek bids from a number of suppliers, who could very well be located in the United States, Germany, Japan, Switzerland, Taiwan, and Canada. Although the alternative bids are likely to be evaluated on a large combination of criteria (price, specific capabilities, after-sale service, delivery terms, credit terms, financing, and so on), one of the issues will be the ease with which the purchase transaction will take place. From the importer's perspective, the easiest alternative—and the one that does not demand that cash flow be affected—is to purchase on an Open Account basis. It is likely that at least one of the potential suppliers will offer such terms, and that others will ask for a Letter of Credit. Therefore, the supplier offering an Open Account transaction has an advantage over the others, and, if it has purchased credit insurance, has not affected its probability of getting paid.

A quick review of Table 7-5[38] shows that, even if there are some regions of the world in which Letters of Credit are still playing a significant role, in just about all cases, more than half of all transactions and more than 90 percent of the transactions in which the importer is located in the fifteen original European Union countries or North America are conducted using some other means of payment. Although no specific information is known, it is likely that the rank order of the other methods of payment are:

1. Open Account (with or without credit insurance)
2. Documentary Collection
3. Procurement cards (for smaller purchases)
4. TradeCard (for larger purchases)
5. Cash in Advance

TABLE 7-5	Percentage of Transactions Conducted on a Letter of Credit (given the location of the importer)
European Union [15]	9%
Rest of Europe	20%
North America	11%
Latin America	27%
Middle East	52%
Asia-Pacific	43%
Africa	49%
Asia	46%
Australia-New Zealand	17%

An exporter intent on increasing its sales should choose to display that it is confident in the ability of the importer to pay for the goods by using an Open Account: After all, this is the way its domestic sales are conducted, and generally how many other competing exporters are intent on selling. If it is unsure about the ability of the importer to pay, it should consider purchasing a credit insurance policy.

Key Terms

Advising Bank (p. 130)
amendment (p. 133)
applicant (p. 129)
aval (p. 138)
bank guarantee (p. 141)
banker's acceptance (p. 138)
beneficiary (p. 129)
bill of exchange (p. 136)
commercial risk (p. 124)
Confirmed Letter of Credit (p. 132)
Confirming Bank (p. 132)

contractor (p. 141)
Correspondent Bank (p. 133)
country risk (p. 124)
credit insurance (p. 128)
date draft (p. 136)
discrepancy (p. 133)
drawee (p. 136)
exposure (p. 125)
guarantor (p. 141)
instruction letter (p. 137)
international factoring (p. 128)

international forfaiting (p. 139)
Irrevocable Letter of Credit (p. 132)
Issuing Bank (p. 129)
political risk (p. 125)
Presenting Bank (p. 136)
protest (p. 136)
Remitting Bank (p. 136)
Stand-By Letters of Credit (p. 141)
time draft (p. 136)
trade acceptance (p. 137)

Review and Discussion Questions

1. Why is it more difficult and riskier to collect receivables from a foreign purchaser?

2. What are the differences between political risks and commercial risks of non-payment?

3. Describe the concept of "Cash in Advance."

4. Describe the process of "Documentary Collection."

5. Describe the mechanism of a "Letter of Credit," from the exchange of *pro-forma* information to final payment.

6. What is credit insurance? Why is it associated with "open account" transactions?

7. Several people claim that Letters of Credit will eventually—soon—be replaced by the concept of "Trade-Card." What is this product, and why do those people think it has such a bright future?

8. Describe the concept of bank guarantees. What are the different types of bank guarantees?

Endnotes

1. Platt, Gordon, "International Collection Services Use Local Presence to Get Results," *The Journal of Commerce*, April 1, 1998, p. 9C.

2. Stecklow, Steve and Jonathan Karp, "Citibank in India Used Collectors Accused of Strong-Arm Tactics," *The Wall Street Journal*, May 5, 1999, p. A1.

3. CISG Table of Contracting States. Institute of International Law, Pace Law Library, Pace University, http://www.cisg.law.pace.edu/cisg/countries/cntries.html, July 31, 2006.

4. Freedman, Michael, "Judgment Day: U.S. Companies Complain They Can't Get a Fair Shake from America's Plaintiff-Friendly Juries. Try Resolving a Dispute in Russia, Indonesia, or [the] Ukraine," *Forbes*, June 7, 2004, pp. 97–98. Dolven, Ben, "Foreign Investors Find that China's Legal System Resolves Few Disputes," *The Wall Street Journal*, April 7, 2003, p. A14.

5. "Getting Paid or 'What's a Transaction For?'," *World Trade*, September 1999, pp. 42–52.

6. Reynolds, Frank, "Nigerian Scam Fails to Pull the $25 Million Carpet Over this Importer's Eyes," *The Journal of Commerce*, August 12, 1998, p. 2C.

7. *Exporters' Encyclopaedia*, Dun & Bradstreet, August 2005.

8. Barovick, Richard, "Exporters Rely More on Credit Reports," *The Journal of Commerce*, March 4, 1998, p. 1C.

9. Banham, Russ, "Credit Clout: Export Credit Insurance Offers Low-Cost Insurance that Protects Shippers from Non-Payment," *International Business*, March 1997, pp. 8–44.

10. Barovick, Richard, "Export Credit Power," *The Journal of Commerce*, March 25, 1998, p. 1C.

11. Pereira, Ray, "International Factoring: The Viable Financing Alternative," *World Trade*, December 1999, pp. 68–69.

12. Adapted from "Report on the Use of Export Letters of Credit 2001/2002," dated April 11, 2003, Sitpro, Simplifying International Trade, http://sitpro.org.uk/reports/lettcredr, June 1, 2006.

13. Maulella, Vincent, "Payment Pitfalls for the Unwary," *World Trade*, April 1999, pp. 76–79.

14. Biederman, David, "A Tale of Letters of Credit," *JoC Week*, February 12–18, 2001, p. 25.

15. Mehta, Ravi and R. Singh, "Freak and Faulty L/C's from Third World and Eastern Europe," *The Exporter*, September 1997, pp. 15–17.

16. *Uniform Customs and Practice for Documentary Credits: 1993 Revision [UCP 500]*, 1993, publication No. 500 of the International Chamber of Commerce, ICC Publishing S.A., 38 Cours Albert 1er, 75008 Paris, France and ICC Publishing, 156 Fifth Avenue, New York, NY 10010.

17. Wunnicke, Brooke and Diane B. Wunnicke, *UCP 500 and Stand-By Letters of Credit*, 1994, John Wiley and Sons, New York, New York.

18. Simpson, Paul, "What's Ahead for Top Trade Banks?" *World Trade*, June 2000, pp. 78–81.

19. Tyler, Joseph W. "Financing Exports," in *Export Practice: Customs and International Trade Law*, Terence P. Stewart, editor, 1994, Practicing Law Institute, New York, New York.

20. Bertrams, R.I.V.F., *Bank Guarantees in International Trade*, Kluwer Law and Taxation Publishers, Deventer, The Netherlands, 1990.

21. Platt, Gordon, "Rules for Standby Letters of Credit Will Be Implemented January 1, 1999," *The Journal of Commerce*, September 16, 1998, p. 9C.

22. *International Standby Practices, ISP98*, Institute of International Banking Law and Practice, Inc., publication No. 590 of the International Chamber of Commerce, ICC Publishing S.A., 38 Cours Albert 1er, 75008 Paris, France and ICC Publishing, 156 Fifth Avenue, New York, NY 10010.

23. *Uniform Rules for Bank-to-Bank Reimbursements under Documentary Credits [URR 525]*, 1995, publication No. 525 of the International Chamber of Commerce, ICC Publishing S.A., 38 Cours Albert 1er, 75008 Paris, France and ICC Publishing, 156 Fifth Avenue, New York, NY 10010.

24. *Uniform Rules for Collection [URC 522]*, 1995, publication No. 522 of the International Chamber of Commerce, ICC Publishing S.A., 38 Cours Albert 1er, 75008 Paris, France and ICC Publishing, 156 Fifth Avenue, New York, NY 10010.

25. Reynolds, Frank, "Use Caution with Semi-Secured Terms," *The Journal of Commerce*, October 20, 1999, p. 10.

26. *Uniform Rules for Collections, op. cit.*

27. *Ibid*

28. *Commentary on the ICC Uniform Rules for Collections*, 1995, publication No. 550 of the International Chamber of Commerce, ICC Publishing S.A., 38 Cours Albert 1er, 75008 Paris, France and ICC Publishing, 156 Fifth Avenue, New York, NY 10010.

29. Levine, Daniel, "Forfaiting; An Alternative Financing Tool," *World Trade*, December 1998, p. 55.

30. Platt, Gordon, "Forfaiting Helps Exporters to Remove Risks Involved in Selling Overseas," *The Journal of Commerce*, April 9, 1997, p. 9C.

31. Block, Valerie, "National City to Use Processing Clout for a Procurement Card," *American Banker*, May 19, 1995.

32. Brevetti, Francine, "Trading Plastic," *Global Sales Force*, date unknown, p. 12.

33. Platt, Gordon, "TradeCard Automates International Transactions," *The Journal of Commerce*, November 23, 1998, p. 7A.

34. Biederman, David, "TradeCard Gears for Growth," *JoC Week*, October 16–22, 2000, p. 29.

35. Atkinson, Helen, "New options from TradeCard," *JoC Week*, March 26–April 1, 2001, p. 32.

36. Bertrams, R.I.V.F., *Bank Guarantees in International Trade*, Kluwer Law and Taxation Publishers, Deventer, The Netherlands, 1990.

37. *Ibid*

38. "Ninth Survey of International Services Provided to Exporters," commissioned by the Institute of Exporters, and reproduced in the "Report on the Use of Export Letters of Credit 2001/2002," dated April 11, 2003, Sitpro, Simplifying International Trade, http://sitpro.org.uk/reports/lettcredr, June 1, 2006.

Currency of Payment (Managing Transaction Risks)

Chapter **Eight**

Source: © 2007 JupiterImages Corporation.

term of trade An element in a contract of sale that specifies the responsibilities of the exporter and the responsibilities of the importer.

term of sale An element in a contract of sale that specifies the method of payment to which an exporter and an importer have agreed.

currency The monetary unit used in a particular country for economic transactions.

The previous chapters have shown that, for each international sale, the exporter and the importer must agree on two particular points:

- The **terms of trade** under which the sale is conducted (i.e., the costs the exporter should pay, the costs the importer should pay, and the point at which the responsibility for the cargo shifts from one to the other). These responsibilities are determined by the Incoterm chosen.
- The **terms of sale** under which the transaction is performed (i.e., at what point in the transaction the exporter wants to be paid, and what its level of confidence is in the ability of the importer to pay). The exporter and the importer can choose any number of alternatives, from Cash in Advance to an Open Account transaction to a TradeCard.

However, there is still one more issue for the exporter and the importer to consider: the **currency** under which this transaction is undertaken. There are three alternatives possible: the exporter's country's currency, the importer's country's currency, or a third country's currency.

8-1 Sales Contract's Currency of Quote

In the choice of a currency for a given transaction, two factors should be considered:

- The risk of currency fluctuation: This is a speculative risk, that is, one for which there is the possibility of a gain or of a loss, depending on which "way" the exchange rate fluctuates, and depending on who (the exporter or the importer) is holding the currency risk. If the transaction is conducted in the exporter's currency, then the importer is the one who is carrying the exchange rate risk. If the transaction is conducted in the importer's currency, it is the exporter who is assuming the exchange rate risk. The two vignettes illustrate this point.

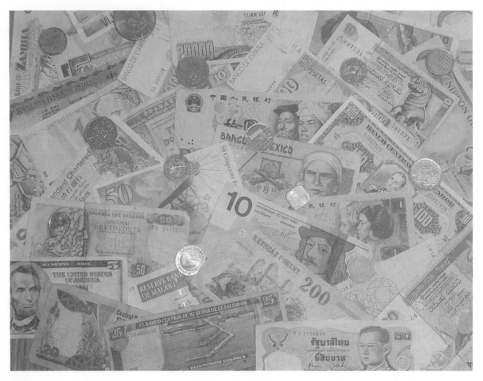

Figure 8-1
Banknotes of the World

Choice of Currency: When the Exporter Carries the Exchange Rate Fluctuation Risk

The choice of a currency is a fundamental aspect of the sale: It can substantially affect the profitability of a sale for an exporter. Take for example a sale for U.S. $1,000,000 on which an exporter was expecting to generate a 10 percent profit margin; its total costs are therefore U.S. $900,000 and its expected profits are $100,000.

Suppose that the exporter and the importer agree to conduct this transaction in European euro, and therefore the exporter will be the one assuming the exchange rate fluctuation risk. Assuming that the exchange rate at the time of the sale is $1.2761/€; the exporter bills the importer for €783,637.65.

Assume now that the exchange rate between the two currencies changes 2 percent by the time the actual payment is made, about a month later, and that the exchange rate at that time is $1.2506/€ (the value of the euro went down 2 percent relative to the value of the U.S. dollar during that period). When the customer pays the invoice for €783,637.65, the U.S. exporter converts that amount of money into U.S. dollars, and collects $980,017.24, assuming, for the sake of this example, that there are no banking fees collected. The importer pays exactly what had been agreed, and carries no currency fluctuation risk whatsoever.

However, the profit that the exporter was anticipating was $100,000, but it actually only earns a profit of [$980,017.24 – 900,000], or $80,017.24, which is about 20 percent less than what it had anticipated.

The reverse can also happen: The profitability of the exporter can be drastically affected by an increase in the value of the currency that it uses to pay for its merchandise. For example, if the exchange rate had changed the "other way," and the euro had gone up in value by 2 percent, the new exchange rate would have been $1.3016, which means that the U.S. exporter, after collecting his €783,637.65, would have been able to convert the currency into $1,019,982.77, an increase of roughly 20 percent in its profits.

- The convertibility of the currency (i.e., the degree to which a currency can be converted into other currencies): Major countries' currencies are fully convertible—they are called **hard currencies**—and these currencies can be freely exchanged, at a moment's notice: They are also called **convertible currencies**.

hard currency A currency that can easily be converted into another currency.

convertible currency A currency that can be converted into another currency.

However, some developing countries' currencies are not readily convertible into hard currencies, because the country has few exports and its government controls which imports get paid first. The ability to convert a currency into hard currency is generally measured in "months of foreign exchange cover" or an approximation of the size of the hard currency stock a given country has, expressed in months of import activities this stock can cover. In most cases, the lack of convertibility of the currency just delays the date at which it can be exchanged for hard currency. All currencies that are difficult to convert into hard currencies are called **soft currencies**.

In some rare cases, the currency is not convertible at all (i.e., the currency cannot be exchanged for any other currency, at any time), or more commonly, the currency has a different exchange rate for purchases and for sales. Finally, some currencies can be purchased, but not sold. All of these currencies are collectively called **inconvertible currencies**.

soft currency A currency that cannot be easily converted into another currency.

inconvertible currency A currency that cannot be converted into another currency.

The three alternative currency possibilities for an international transaction—exporter, importer, and third-country currency—are summarized in the following sections.

8-1a Exporter's Currency

In this first case, the exporter and the importer agree that the currency of the transaction will be the currency of the exporter's country. For example, if the exporter is located in Germany and the importer is located in Colombia, then the transaction takes place in euros, the currency of (most of) the European Union.

In this case, the exchange rate fluctuation risk is nil for the exporter; all of the risks are borne by the importer, and it has to determine how it will handle its transaction

Choice of Currency: When the Importer Carries the Exchange Rate Fluctuation Risk

The first textbox was an example of a sale for which the exporter assumed the currency fluctuation risk. Assume now instead that the exporter and the importer agree that the transaction will take place in U.S. dollars and therefore the importer assumes the currency fluctuation risk.

For the sake of simplification, take the same sale on which the exporter is expecting to generate a 10 percent profit margin; its selling price is $1,000,000, its total costs are $900,000 and its expected profits are $100,000.

Suppose also that the exchange rate at the time of the sale is $1.2761/€, the same as it was in the previous example: The exporter bills the importer for $1,000,000, and the importer equates this amount to a payment of €783,637.65.

Assume now that the exchange rate between the two currencies changes 2 percent by the time the actual payment is made, about a month later, and that the exchange rate at that time is $1.2506/€ (where the value of the euro went down 2 percent relative to the value of the U.S. dollar during that period). When the customer pays the invoice for $1,000,000, the U.S. exporter collects exactly what he had anticipated, but the importer needs to supply its bank with €799,616.18, assuming, for the sake of this example, that there are no banking fees collected.

The cost to the importer for these goods was anticipated at €783,637.65, but it actually has to pay €799,616.18, which is about 2 percent more.

The reverse can also happen: The cost for the importer can be lower if the value of the currency that it uses to pay for its merchandise increases. For example, if the exchange rate had changed the "other way," and the euro had gone up in value by 2 percent, the new exchange rate would have been $1.3016, which means that the importer, in order to pay the $1,000,000 that it owes the exporter, would need to convert only €768,285.19, a 2 percent decrease.

Figure 8-2a
The Euro Currency

Source: Photo © European Central Bank. Used with permission.

risks. In addition, the possible convertibility problems of the currency are to be resolved by the importer. In this particular case, because the Colombian peso is fully convertible, this is not an issue.

8-1b Importer's Currency

In this case, the exporter and the importer determine that the currency of the transaction will be the currency of the importer's country. For example, if the exporter is located in Jordan and the importer is located in the United States, then the transaction takes place in U.S. dollars, the currency of the United States.

In this case, the exchange risk fluctuation risk is nil for the importer; all of the risks are borne by the exporter, and it has to determine how it will handle its transaction risks. It is also ultimately responsible for converting the currency so any convertibility problem will have to be resolved by the exporter. In this particular case, there is no issue as the Jordanian dinar is fully convertible.

8-1c Third Country's Currency

Finally, the exporter and the importer can agree that the currency of the transaction will be a third country's currency. For example, if the exporter is located in Thailand and the importer is located in India, they may decide to use the U.S. dollar as the currency of the transaction.

This alternative presents several advantages for both the exporter and the importer: For example, they each bear the risks of currency fluctuation of their respective country's currency against the currency of the transaction. In this example, the exporter is responsible for the fluctuations of the baht against the dollar, and the importer is responsible for the fluctuations of the rupee against the dollar.

TABLE 8-1	Value of the Euro to Previous National Eurozone Currencies on January 1, 2002

On January 1, 2002, 1 Euro =

Belgium (franc)	40.3399 BEF
Germany (mark)	1.95583 DEM
Spain (peseta)	166.386 ESP
France (franc)	6.55957 FRF
Ireland (punt)	0.787564 IEP
Italy (lira)	1936.27 ITL
Luxembourg (franc)	40.3399 LUF
The Netherlands (guilder)	2.20371 NLG
Austria (schilling)	13.7603 ATS
Portugal (escudo)	200.482 PTE
Finland (markka)	5.94573 FIM
Greece (drachma)	340.750 GRD

In some cases, the exporter and the importer choose an artificial currency (a non-circulating currency) for a transaction, such as the **Special Drawing Right (SDR)** of the International Monetary Fund, which is sometimes used for international contracts; such is the case of the Liability Conventions of the ocean shipping industry (see Section 11-6).

All three of these alternatives present challenges and call for some form of management of the risks presented by exchange rates.

8-1d The Special Status of the Euro

The **euro** was first created as an artificial currency; in its early years, when it was known as the European Currency Unit (ECU), its value was determined by the value of a basket consisting of the various currencies of the European Union. When it was officially unveiled as the euro in 1999, its value was fixed in terms of each of the eleven (later twelve) currencies of the participating EU countries. Only in January 2002 did it become a circulating currency, losing its status as an artificial currency.

The euro is a unique case as a truly international currency; not only has it become the official domestic currency of twelve of the European Union countries, but it is also used for all of the intra-European trade in the Eurozone and is therefore a currency used extensively to settle international debts. The stated goal of the European Union is to eventually transform the euro as a challenger to the U.S. dollar as the preferred third-country currency.

Table 8-1 lists the rate at which the legacy currencies of the European Union countries were converted to the dollar and Table 8-2[1] lists the status of the conversion for the thirteen countries of the European Union that have not yet adopted the euro.

8-2 The System of Currency Exchange Rates

In order to manage the risks presented by currency exchange rate fluctuations, it is necessary to have a good understanding of the functioning of the system of exchange rates. Unfortunately, this section can only be a cursory review of the current knowledge in this area; the reader interested in obtaining a greater understanding of the field of international corporate finance should refer to any number of excellent textbooks in this field.[2]

Special Drawing Right (SDR) An artificial currency of the International Monetary Fund. Its value is determined by the value of a basket of four currencies: the euro, the Japanese yen, the U.S. dollar, and the British pound.

euro The common currency of twelve of the twenty-five countries of the European Union, developed in the late 1990s and placed in circulation on January 1, 2002.

Figure 8-2b
The Euro Currency

Source: Photo © European Central Bank. Used with permission.

TABLE 8-2	European Countries That Have Not Yet Adopted the Euro

Country (currency)	Status
Cyprus (pound)	Cyprus will adopt the euro in 2008, probably at the same time as Malta.
Czech Republic (koruna)	The Czech Republic will probably adopt the euro in 2010.
Denmark (markka)	Denmark rejected the euro by referendum on September 28, 2002.
Estonia (kroon)	Estonia will adopt the euro on January 1, 2007. The kroon is pegged to the euro.
Hungary (forint)	Hungary will adopt the euro on January 1, 2010. The forint is pegged to the euro.
Latvia (latvian)	Latvia will adopt the euro on January 1, 2008.
Lithuania (litas)	Lithuania will adopt the euro on January 1, 2007. The litas was pegged to the U.S. dollar and is now pegged to the euro.
Malta (lira)	Malta will adopt the euro in 2008, probably at the same time as Cyprus.
Poland (zloty)	Poland had no plans to introduce the euro as of June 2006.
Slovakia (koruna)	Slovakia will adopt the euro on January 1, 2008.
Slovenia (tolar)	Slovenia will adopt the euro on January 1, 2007.
Sweden (krona)	Sweden rejected the euro by referendum on September 13, 2003.
United Kingdom (pound)	The United Kingdom is officially in favor of adopting the euro, but there are five economic tests that the UK economy must meet before the UK government decides on a change-over date.

8-2a Types of Exchange Rates

The exchange rate of two currencies is the value of one currency expressed in units of the second. For example, on June 7, 2006, the exchange rate for the euro against the U.S. dollar was $1.2791/euro (i.e., one euro was worth U.S. $1.2791).[3] As the *Wall Street Journal* quotes it, the exchange rate is the midpoint between the bid and offer rates for exchanges of a value greater than $1,000,000 between banks. The *Financial Times* published the midpoint, as well as the bid-offer spread.[4] The actual exchange rate offered to a company seeking to purchase euros would be different: It would have to pay more, say $1.295, for every euro purchased. Reciprocally, the exchange rate offered to a company seeking to sell euros would be lower: It would collect less, say $1.26, for every euro sold.

Traders in foreign exchange consider two ways to quote a currency:

direct quote The value of a foreign currency expressed in units of the domestic currency.

- The first way to value a currency is the **direct quote**, in which the value of the foreign currency is expressed in units of the domestic currency. For example, the direct quote for the U.S. dollar and the euro would be $1.2791/€, as of June 7, 2006. This is the preferred way of quoting the euro, the British pound, the Australian dollar, and the New Zealand dollar.

indirect quote The value of the domestic currency expressed in units of the foreign currency.

- The second way to value a currency is the **indirect quote**, in which the value of the domestic currency is expressed in units of foreign currency. For example, the indirect quote for the yen and the U.S. dollar would be ¥113.47/$ as of June 7, 2006. Many currencies are traditionally expressed as indirect quotes: the Canadian dollar, the Swiss franc, and the Japanese yen, for example.

It should be self-evident that there is an inverse relationship between the two ways of quoting a currency exchange rate between two currencies:

$$\text{Direct quote} = \frac{1}{\text{Indirect quote}}$$

Spot Exchange Rate

spot exchange rate The exchange rate of a foreign currency for immediate delivery (within forty-eight hours).

The first type of exchange rate is the **spot exchange rate**, or the exchange rate for a foreign currency for immediate delivery. This "immediate delivery" is somewhat subject to interpretations that vary from country to country and, within one country, from one currency to another; however, it is (roughly) the price of a foreign currency to be delivered within forty-eight hours.

		U.S. $ Equivalent (Direct Quote)	Currency per U.S. $ (Indirect Quote)
Country	**Currency**		
Argentina	Peso	0.3245	3.0817
Australia	Dollar	0.7405	1.3504
Brazil	Real	0.44429	2.2578
Canada	Dollar	0.8981	1.1135
Chile	Peso	0.001848	541.13
China	Renminbi/Yuan	0.1247	8.0170
Czech Republic	Koruna	0.04540	22.026
Denmark	Krone	0.1715	5.8309
Hong Kong	Dollar	0.1288	7.7619
Hungary	Forint	0.004888	204.58
India	Rupee	0.02180	45.872
Indonesia	Rupiah	0.00010666	9381.0
Israel	Shekel	0.2239	4.4663
Japan	Yen	0.008813	113.47
Jordan	Dinar	1.4106	0.7089
Kuwait	Dinar	3.4570	0.2893
Lebanon	Pound	0.0006651	1503.53
Malaysia	Ringgit	0.2734	3.6576
Mexico	Peso	0.0882	11.3443
New Zealand	Dollar	0.6257	1.5982
Norway	Krone	0.1637	6.1087
Pakistan	Rupee	0.01664	60.096
Peru	New Sol	0.3067	3.2605
Philippines	Peso	0.01890	52.910
Russia	Ruble	0.03725	26.846
Saudi Arabia	Riyal	0.2666	3.7509
Singapore	Dollar	0.6310	1.5848
South Africa	Rand	0.1487	6.7249
South Korea	Won	0.0010547	948.14
Sweden	Krona	0.1389	7.1994
Switzerland	Franc	0.8189	1.2212
Taiwan	Dollar	0.03104	32.217
Thailand	Bhat	0.02613	38.270
Turkey	New Lira	0.6590	1.5175
United Kingdom	Pound	1.8560	0.5388
Venezuela	Bolivar	0.000466	2145.92
Special Drawing Right	SDR	1.4879	0.6721
European Union	Euro	1.2791	0.7818

TABLE 8-3 Selected Spot Rates for Foreign Currencies, June 7, 2006

This is the exchange rate with which most international travelers are familiar: It is the one used by foreign exchange kiosks and banks all over the world (see Table 8-3[5]). Comprehensive spot currency exchange rates are published daily in *The Wall Street Journal* and many dailies; however, the *Financial Times* is the most comprehensive of all periodicals in that respect and it quotes daily the spot currency exchange rates for more than 150 currencies against the U.S. dollar, the British pound, the European euro, and the Japanese yen.[6] These quotes are available for free.

Forward Exchange Rates

The second type of exchange rate is the **forward exchange rate**, or the exchange rate for a foreign currency to be delivered 30, 90, 180 days, or one year from the date of

forward exchange rate The exchange rate of a foreign currency for delivery in thirty, ninety, or 180 days from the date of the quote.

| TABLE 8-4 | Selected Forward Exchange Rates for Foreign Currency, June 7, 2006 |

Country	Currency	Delivery	U.S. $ Equivalent (Direct Quote)	Currency per U.S. $ (Indirect Quote)
Canada	Dollar	Spot	0.8981	1.1135
		Forward 30 Days	0.8988	1.1126
		Forward 90 Days	0.9003	1.1107
		Forward 180 Days	0.9027	1.1078
Japan	Yen	Spot	0.008813	113.47
		Forward 30 Days	0.008851	112.98
		Forward 90 Days	0.008927	112.02
		Forward 180 Days	0.009037	110.66
Switzerland	Franc	Spot	0.8189	1.2212
		Forward 30 Days	0.8215	1.2173
		Forward 90 Days	0.8270	1.2092
		Forward 180 Days	0.8346	1.1982
United Kingdom	Pound	Spot	1.8560	0.5388
		Forward 30 Days	1.8569	0.5385
		Forward 90 Days	1.8591	0.5379
		Forward 180 Days	1.8622	0.5370
European Union	Euro	Spot	1.2791	0.7818
		Forward 30 Days	1.2800	0.7812
		Forward 90 Days	1.2852	0.7781
		Forward 180 Days	1.2938	0.7729

outright rate The exchange rate of a foreign currency for delivery in thirty, ninety, or 180 days from the date of the quote. The outright rate is the rate at which a commercial customer would purchase the currency.

swap rate The exchange rate of a foreign currency for delivery in thirty, ninety, or 180 days from the date of the quote. The swap rate is the difference between the current spot rate and the rate at which a commercial customer would purchase the currency. It is expressed in points that must be subtracted or added to the spot rate.

points In a forward exchange rate, the difference between the outright rate and the swap rate. Points are not fixed units; their value depends on the way a currency is expressed, but is the smallest decimal value in which that currency is traded.

the quote. The parties entering into a forward currency contract are committing to purchasing (and supplying) a foreign currency at a certain price on a certain date. The exchange rates given are the mid-points for transactions of U.S. $1,000,000 or more that take place between banks; the actual exchange rate obtainable by a company involved in international trade would be less favorable.

In the United States, *The Wall Street Journal* only publishes the forward rates for four currencies: the British pound, the Japanese yen, the Swiss franc, and the Canadian dollar. Surprisingly, as of June 2006, it was still not publishing forward rates for the European euro. However, there is a forward market for just about any currency, and most are published in the *Financial Times*, which covers the forward exchange rates for the Czech krona as well as the Indian rupee and the Thai baht. Another difference between these two periodicals is that *The Wall Street Journal* publishes rates for 30, 90, and 180 days, but does not publish a one-year forward rate, and that the *Financial Times* publishes 30 and 90 days and one-year rates, but not a 180-day rate (see Table 8-4[7]).

The **outright rate** is the rate at which a commercial customer purchases or sells a foreign currency forward. However, in the interbank market, forward rates are quoted as a premium on—or a discount from—the spot rate. Such a forward rate is called the **swap rate** and is expressed in **points** that must be subtracted or added to the spot rate in order to arrive at the forward exchange rate. A point is the unit of the last digit quoted: For example, if the spot exchange rate for the Japanese yen was $0.008813/¥ on a given date, and the forward swap rate for 180 days was expressed at an eighty-five points premium on the same day, then the 180-day forward exchange rate would be $0.008813 plus 0.000085, for an actual forward exchange rate of $0.008898/¥ for a delivery 180 days from that date.

The reason behind such a swap rate is the practice of "swapping," or the simultaneous purchase of one currency on the spot market and the sale of the same currency on the forward market, a method used to minimize a company's foreign exchange exposure.[8]

Currency Futures

Finally, some currencies are also traded in the **currency futures'** market as commodities: In the United States, futures for six currencies are traded on the Chicago Mercantile Exchange.

A futures' contract is an agreement between two parties: the seller (called the "short") who promises to deliver the currency on a certain date, and the buyer (called the "long") who agrees to buy the currency at a price that is agreed upon ahead of time.

Futures' contracts were first created for commodities other than currencies (such as corn or wheat) and fulfill very different purposes for the parties that use them. Generally, the contract takes place between a party that wants to limit its risk and a party that is speculating. For example, a farmer knows that he will be able to harvest a certain amount of corn; in order to limit his uncertainty regarding the price at which he will be able to sell this commodity, he enters into a futures contract, which obligates him to deliver a specified amount of corn on a certain date, at a set price. The other party in the contract is a speculator who is not interested in the corn at all, but is intent on reselling it immediately to another party and speculates that the corn, on that date, will fetch a higher price than what he has paid the farmer.

Similarly, a company that uses wheat for a particular purpose may enter into a futures' contract to make sure it can purchase a certain amount of that commodity on that date at a set price. The other party in the futures' contract is a speculator who thinks that he can obtain the wheat on that date for less than what he can sell it to the company.

In the first case, the farmer is intent on minimizing his risk (for example, a bumper crop lowers the value of his corn), and in the second case, the company is looking to minimize its uncertainty regarding the price of one of its raw materials. In both cases, the speculator is taking the risk; if the corn supply is lower than what the market anticipated, he will be able to take delivery from the farmer at a price lower than the spot price and make money. In the second case, he makes money if the supply of wheat is larger than what the market anticipated, and he will make money. If he is incorrect, he loses money, but must make good on his promise to purchase the corn or sell the wheat.

There are two major differences between a forward contract and a futures' contract as they apply to currency exchange rates:

1. The amount of the foreign currency for which a company can purchase futures is fixed; in the United States, they are only available in increments of 100,000 Australian dollars, 62,500 British pounds, 100,000 Canadian dollars, 125,000 euros, 12.5 million Japanese yen, and 500,000 Mexican pesos. This is in contrast with the forward market, in which any given amount can be purchased or sold.

2. The date at which the future has to be settled (purchased or sold) is fixed: In the United States, it is always the third Wednesday of the month. This is in contrast with the forward market, in which any given date can be chosen in advance.

Because of this lack of flexibility, futures' contracts for currencies are not used as frequently as forward contracts.

Currency Options

In addition to the futures market, there is also a **currency options'** market, which takes place, in the United States, at the Philadelphia Stock Exchange's United Currency Options Market.

An option contract is quite different from a futures' contract. In a futures' contract, both parties are obligated to deliver (or buy) the currency on the date at which the futures' contract is settled. In contrast, in the options' market, the buyer of the option is purchasing the right (the option) to buy or sell a particular currency at a predetermined

currency futures A method used to trade currencies; the value of a fixed quantity of foreign currency for delivery at a fixed point in the future is determined by market forces.

currency options A method used to speculate on the value of a currency in the future. A firm can purchase options to buy (called call options) or options to sell (called put options) a particular currency at a particular price, called the strike price, on a given date.

How Does the Options Market Work?

Call Options:

A U.S. firm purchases a call option—the right to buy—British pounds on November 1, for a predetermined exchange rate of £1.00/U.S. $1.88; that price is called the strike price. The firm has to pay U.S. $4,000 for that option.

On November 1, it can exercise its call option and tell the seller of the option that it wants delivery of the currency, and the seller of the option has to comply. The buyer of the option only does that if the spot exchange rate of that currency on November 1 were higher that the agreed-upon strike price, say £1.00/U.S. $1.90, because buying British pounds on the spot market on that date would be more expensive than exercising the option. If the spot exchange rate were lower, say £1.00/U.S. $1.84, the buyer of the option would not exercise its option and purchase the currency on the spot market instead; it would willingly forego what it had paid for the option or U.S. $4,000.

Put Options:

A German firm purchases a put option—the right to sell—European euros on December 1, for a predetermined exchange rate of €1.00/U.S. $1.26; that price is called the strike price. The firm has to pay €3,000 for that option.

On December 1, it can exercise its put option and tell the seller of the option that it wants the money for the currency, and the seller of the option has to comply (buy the currency from the German firm). The buyer of the option only does that if the spot exchange rate of that currency on December 1 were lower that the agreed-upon strike price, say €1.00/U.S. $1.24, because selling the euros on the spot market on that date would be more attractive than exercising the option. If the spot exchange rate were higher—say €1.00/U.S. $1.30, the buyer of the option would not exercise its option and sell the currency on the spot market instead; it would willingly forego what it had paid for the option, or €3,000.

price. However, the buyer of the option does not have the obligation to exercise that option; it can decline to purchase or sell at that price. If the buyer of the option elects to exercise the option, however, the seller of the option is obligated to comply.

There are two types of options: **call options** and **put options**. A call option is the right to buy—but not the obligation to buy—a predetermined amount of foreign currency at a predetermined price (called the **strike price**) on a predetermined date. A put option is the right to sell—but not the obligation to sell—the same. If the buyer of the option decides not to exercise its option, it only loses the amount that it paid for that option. The seller of the option keeps the amount that it charged for the option, regardless of what the buyer decides to do.

To add to the complexity, there are two styles of options: The U.S.-style option gives a company the right to exercise its option at any time until the expiration date, while a European-style option only allows it to exercise that option on that date.

An option is priced by the "market" between companies wanting to purchase options and speculators and other companies who are selling options. Several mathematical models can be used in determining the pricing of options, but their complexity is beyond the scope of this textbook.

8-2b Types of Currencies

In determining the exchange rate risks carried by a specific transaction, it is helpful to determine the type of currency with which the exporter (or importer) is dealing. There are three types of currencies.

Floating Currencies

Floating currencies are foreign currencies whose value changes (or *can* change) daily against other currencies. For example, the U.S. dollar changes in value all the time as it is traded between companies having dollars and companies wanting dollars; only the market determines its value. Figure 8-3 illustrates the exchange rate between the U.S. dollar and the European euro since its creation in January 1999.[9] The countries representing the greatest percentage of world trade all have floating currencies.

call options A currency option in which a firm agrees to buy a particular currency at a particular price, called the strike price, on a given date.

put options A currency option in which a firm agrees to sell a particular currency at a particular price, called the strike price, on a given date.

strike price The price at which a currency option is exercised.

floating currency A currency whose value is determined by market forces. The exchange rate of a floating currency varies frequently.

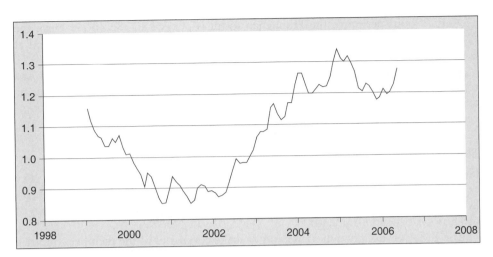

Figure 8-3

The U.S./Euro Foreign Exchange Rate (U.S. Dollars to One Euro), January 1999 to June 2006
Source: Board of Governors of the Federal Reserve System.

The fact that a currency is floating does not always represent unpredictability for a company involved in international trade; most currencies are relatively stable in their values in the short term. However, those currencies that are considered "volatile" (i.e., currencies that can experience a great deal of variation in their exchange rates from one day to the next) can present significant risk. Even though the euro has fluctuated substantially against the U.S. dollar—from a low of €1.00/ U.S. $0.8270 on October 25, 2000, to a high of €1.00/U.S. $1.3625 on December 27, 2004[10]—in the seven years since its inception, neither the euro nor the U.S. dollar are considered volatile currencies.

In order to squelch some of this volatility, currencies are sometimes "assisted" by their country's government, which intervenes in the foreign exchange markets in order to sustain the value of a currency. Such policies can be quite onerous for countries: In order to support the value of a currency, the government must purchase it in the market, and that is only achieved by selling foreign exchange, or the proceeds of export sales. George Soros made a fortune (more than U.S. $1 billion) by betting against the British pound in September 1992, at a time when the British government was intent on shoring up its value.

Most of the developed countries have currencies that are stable, that is, currencies for which it is reasonable to expect a predictable exchange rate. It's only under those conditions that an international firm will accept payment—or agree to pay—in that country's currency.

Pegged Currencies

A number of countries have been plagued with very volatile currencies. There are several reasons for this situation, most notably the lack of a sustained level of trade, giving rise to substantially varying demands on the currency from one month to the next. Because it was too complicated—and expensive—for the governments of these countries to intervene in the foreign exchange markets, they decided to "peg" their currency to another, more stable currency.

Pegging a currency makes it worth a fixed exchange rate relative to another, stronger currency. The exchange rate is therefore entirely predictable at any time. In most instances, the currency chosen is that of the greatest trading partner, and therefore it is often the United States dollar; such was the case of the Argentinean peso, which, until February 2002, was pegged to the U.S. dollar. It is now a floating currency. Some of the ten countries that recently joined the European Union have pegged their currencies to the European euro: The Estonian kroon is pegged at

pegged currency A currency whose value is determined by a fixed exchange rate with another, more widely traded currency.

15.6465 kroons per euro, the Hungarian forint is pegged at 282.36 per euro, the Cypriot pound is pegged at 0.58 per euro, and the Lithuanian litas is pegged at 3.4528 per euro.

In some rare cases, the country can elect to completely eliminate its currency and replace it with the currency of another country altogether. This occurred in Panama and Ecuador, which both have adopted the U.S. dollar as their currency, a phenomenon dubbed the **dollarization** of these economies.

dollarization A phenomenon where other countries decide to adopt the U.S. dollar as their circulating currency.

Floating Currency Blocks—European Monetary System

Finally, there is the case of countries that trade so much with each other that they decide to create a **currency block**. Such was the case of the European Monetary System (EMS), which eventually gave rise to the creation of the common currency of the European Union, the euro.

currency block A group of currencies whose values fluctuate in parallel fashion. The currencies within the group have a fixed exchange rate, but their exchange rates with currencies outside of the group float.

The EMS was designed in such a way that the currencies of the member countries would have to stay within a few percentage points of each other's value, a policy that was called the Exchange Rate Mechanism (ERM). In the beginning of this experiment, the maximum percentage variation allowed was 5 percent, and toward the end of the system, it was as low as 1 percent. Such variations were continuously controlled by the governments of the European countries, which intervened routinely in the foreign exchange markets. Such a system allowed the EMS currencies to float as a "bloc" against other non-EMS currencies, while maintaining a very stable foreign exchange environment within the European Union, a situation that greatly promoted trade among the Union members.

artificial currency A currency that is not in circulation. After the euro was changed into a circulating currency on January 1, 2002, the only artificial currency left was the Special Drawing Rights of the International Monetary Fund.

Eventually such a bloc can evolve into a fixed exchange rate between all the internal currencies. In Europe, the fixed exchange rates were established in terms of an **artificial currency**, the European Currency Unit (ECU), which was created in January 1999, and whose value was determined by the values of a basket of the internal currencies. The European Currency Unit was named the euro soon thereafter. Finally, on January 1, 2002, all internal currencies were eliminated and the European euro became the only circulating currency for twelve of the European countries (see Table 8-1). When the European Union was expanded on June 1, 2004, the EMS was resurrected and many of these countries' currencies will eventually be replaced by the euro (see Table 8-2).

8-3 Theories of Exchange Rate Determinations

In order for a company to determine what its risks are in an international currency transaction, it is imperative to understand how exchange rates are determined. Once a company's management understands the theories behind the exchange rate fluctuations, it can then forecast them, and therefore determine what would be its best strategy for a specific transaction.

There are a total of five different, complementary theories that help explain the variations between two countries' exchange rates. After each one is presented, Section 8-3e and Figure 8-8 will summarize how these theories interact and influence the change in the spot exchange rate of two currencies.

8-3a Purchasing Power Parity

Purchasing Power Parity An economic theory that holds that exchange rates should reflect the price differences of each and every product between countries.

In its absolute form, the **Purchasing Power Parity** theory holds that exchange rates should reflect the price differences of each and every product between countries. The idea is that exchange rates should fluctuate in such a way as to "equalize" the price differences of similar products between countries, so that a set amount of currency would purchase the same goods in any country of the world.

TABLE 8-5	The Big Mac Index

In this famous study from *The Economist*, the Purchasing Power Parity of worldwide currencies is exemplified by the cost of a McDonald's Big Mac. These prices were in effect in May 2006.

Country	In Local Currency	In U.S. Dollars	As % of U.S. price
United States	$2.49	2.49	100
Argentina	Peso 7.00	2.28	92
Australia	A$3.25	2.49	100
Brazil	Real 6.40	2.92	117
Bulgaria	Lev 2.99	1.95	78
Canada	C$3.52	3.11	125
Chile	Peso 1,560	2.88	116
China	Yuan 10.50	**1.32**	**53**
Czech Republic	Koruna 59.05	2.66	107
Denmark	DKr 27.75	4.77	192
Eurozone	€2.94	3.77	151
Hong Kong	HK$12.00	1.54	62
Hungary	Forint 560	2.61	105
Iceland	Kronur 459	6.39	257
Indonesia	Rupiah 14,600	1.61	65
Japan	¥250	2.18	88
Latvia	Lats 1.35	2.48	100
Malaysia	Ringgit 5.50	1.50	60
Mexico	Peso 29.00	2.63	106
New Zealand	NZ$4.45	2.76	179
Norway	Kroner 43.00	**7.00**	**281**
Pakistan	Rupee 130	2.16	87
Peru	New Sol 9.50	2.93	118
The Philippines	Peso 85.00	1.65	66
Poland	Zloty 6.50	2.12	85
Russia	Rouble 48.00	1.79	72
Singapore	S$3.60	2.28	92
South Africa	Rand 13.95	2.01	81
Sweden	SKr 33.00	4.60	185
Switzerland	SFr 6.30	5.14	206
Taiwan	NT$75.00	2.29	92
Thailand	Bhat 60.00	1.58	63
Turkey	Lira 4.20	3.85	155
United Kingdom	£1.94	3.63	146
Venezuela	Bolivar 5,701	2.66	107

However, this is essentially impossible to achieve (and measure), given the disparity of goods and services that are purchased worldwide: Even for a perfectly uniform good, there are wide discrepancies in its price from one country to the next. This inconsistency is illustrated very well with the Big Mac Index, published by *The Economist* (see Table 8-5[11]), which observes that the price of one of McDonald's Big Mac sandwiches can vary from 53 percent (in China) to 281 percent (in Norway) of the U.S. price. In effect, the price of a Big Mac is 5.3 *times* as much in Norway as it is in China.

Practically speaking, the absolute Purchasing Power Parity is determined by using a "basket of goods" and calculating how much domestic currency an average person would have to spend to purchase it. The World Bank uses this version of the Purchasing Power Parity to determine the GDP *per capita* (PPP adjusted) of all the nations of the world.

In its relative form, as used in international finance as a determinant of changes in exchange rates, the Purchasing Power Parity is calculated using inflation rates, which is only a slightly different methodology, because in each country, inflation rates are determined by taking the level of prices of a basket of goods. Therefore, the only differences between the Purchasing Power Parity determined by the World Bank and Purchasing Power Parity determined through inflation rates is that the basket of goods of the World Bank attempts to be identical in each country, whereas the inflation rate is calculated using different baskets of goods in most countries, and that the basket of goods used for inflation determination tends to include a wider number of items.

Purchasing Power Parity theory holds that exchange rates should reflect the differences in inflation rates between countries. In other words, if the inflation rate is higher in one country, then its currency should decrease in value relative to other currencies. This can be illustrated mathematically as:[12]

$$\frac{\text{Spot value of Currency F at time } t \text{ in Country D}}{\text{Spot value of Currency F at time 0 in Country D}} = \frac{(1 + \text{inflation rate in Country D})^t}{(1 + \text{inflation rate in Country F})^t}$$

or

$$\frac{S(e_t)}{S(e_0)} = \frac{(1 + inf_D)^t}{(1 + inf_F)^t}$$

and schematically as shown in Figure 8-4.

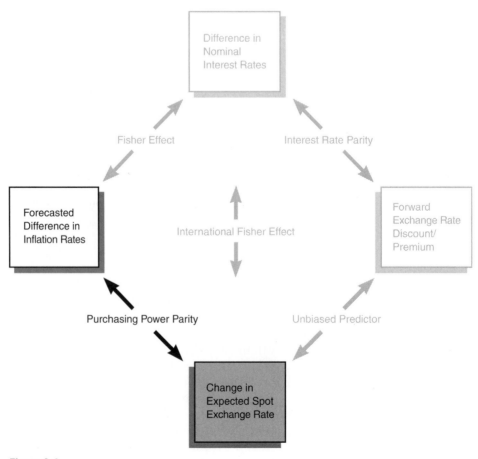

Figure 8-4
Purchasing Power Parity

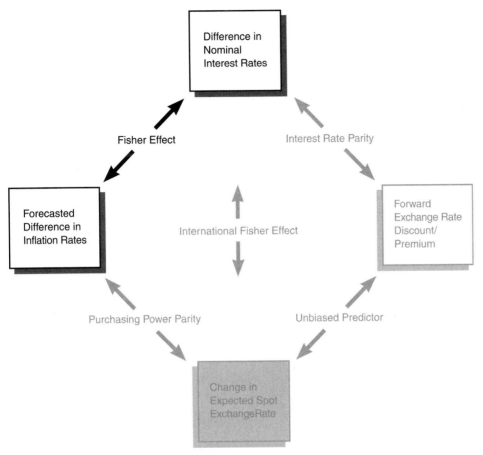

Figure 8-5
The Fisher Effect

8-3b Fisher Effect

The **Fisher Effect** is the observation that a country's nominal interest rate (what a borrower actually has to pay for a loan) comprises both the inflation rate in that country and the real interest rate that borrowers are paying. This real interest rate is expected to be "uniform" throughout the world. In other words, the theory holds that people expect to pay the same real interest rate in every country, at all points in time. Therefore, countries with high inflation rates should be expected to have high nominal interest rates. The mathematical representation of this phenomenon is:

$$(1 + \text{real interest rate}) \times (1 + \text{inflation rate}) = 1 + \text{nominal interest rate}$$

or

$$(1 + \text{rir})(1 + \text{inf}) = 1 + \text{nir} \quad \text{or} \quad \text{nir} = \text{inf} + \text{rir} + (\text{inf} \times \text{rir}) \approx \text{inf} + \text{rir}$$

and schematically as shown in Figure 8-5.

8-3c International Fisher Effect

The **International Fisher Effect** is the observation that exchange rates reflect the differences between nominal interest rates in different countries. It posits that, if nominal interest rates are higher in country F than in country D, then country F's currency should be expected to decrease in value relative to country D's currency.

Fisher Effect An economic theory that holds that the interest rates that businesses and individuals should pay to borrow money should be uniform throughout the world and that the nominal interest rates that they actually pay in a given country are composed of this common interest rate and the inflation rate of that country.

International Fisher Effect An economic theory that holds that the spot exchange rates between two countries' currencies should change in function of the differences between these two countries' nominal interest rates.

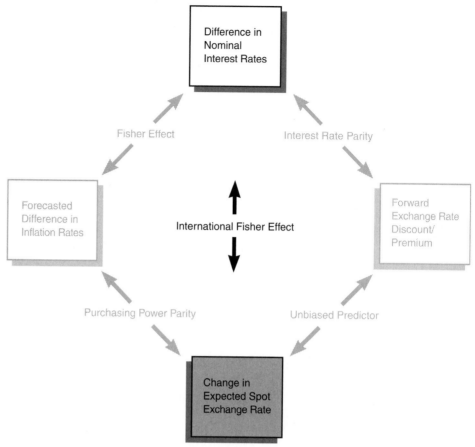

Figure 8-6
The International Fisher Effect

Conceptually, the expected spot rate reflects the fact that an investor would get the same yield on an investment, whether it is made in country D or country F. Mathematically, this can be described as:

$$\frac{\text{Spot value of Currency F at time } (t+1) \text{ in Country D}}{\text{Spot value of Currency F at time } t \text{ in Country D}} = \frac{(1 + \text{nominal interest rate in country D})}{(1 + \text{nominal interest rate in Country F})}$$

or

$$\frac{S(e_{t+1})}{S(e_t)} = \frac{(1 + \text{nir}_D)}{(1 + \text{nir}_F)}$$

and schematically as shown in Figure 8-6.

8-3d Interest Rate Parity

Interest Rate Parity An economic theory that holds that the forward exchange rate between two currencies should reflect the differences in the interest rates in those two countries.

The **Interest Rate Parity** theory links the forward exchange rate of a foreign currency to its spot rate, using the differences in nominal interest rates between the foreign country and the domestic country. The principle is that the forward exchange rate should be expressed as a discount if the foreign country is experiencing higher nominal interest rates than the domestic country, and should reflect a premium if the foreign nominal interest rates are lower.

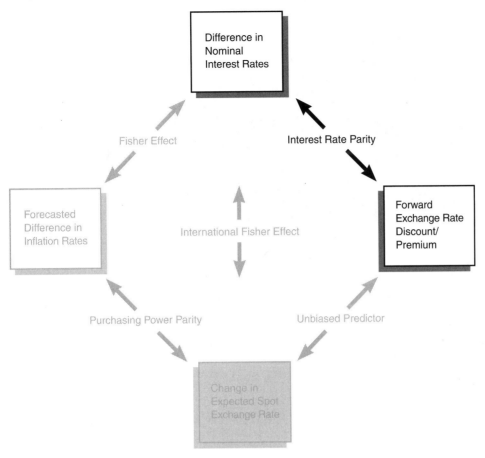

Figure 8-7
Interest Rate Parity

In other words, at time t, the forward exchange rate $F \{t + 1\}(e_t)$ for delivering currency F n days from t—that is, at time $t + 1$—reflects the difference between the nominal interest rate in country D and the nominal interest rate in country F, adjusted for the length of n days.

This relationship translates mathematically as:

$$\frac{F_n(e_t) - S(e_t)}{S(e_t)} \times \frac{360}{n} = nir_D - nir_F$$

and schematically as shown in Figure 8-7.

8-3e Forward Rate as Unbiased Predictor of Spot Rate

This theory holds that forward exchange rates for currencies are good predictors of the future spot exchange rates of that currency. In other words, if the forward rate for a currency shows a discount of 2 percent for a maturity date of n days, then the spot rate in n days should be 2 percent lower than it is today.

Conceptually, the relationship is that the forward exchange rate of currency F at time t in country D for delivery at time $t+1$ is the expected (average) spot value of currency F at time $t+1$ in country D.

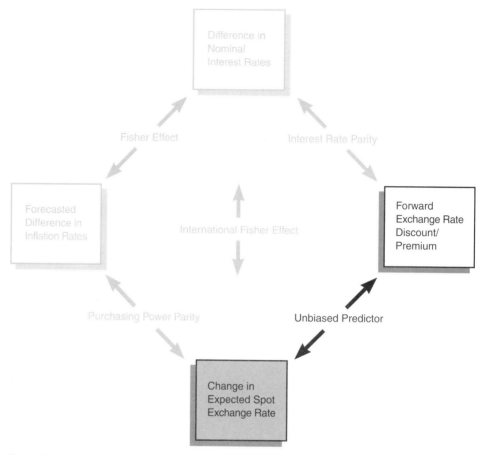

Figure 8-8
Forward Rates as Predictors of Spot Rates

This can be expressed mathematically as:

$$F_{t+1}(e_t) = S(e_{t+1})$$

and schematically as shown in Figure 8-8.

8-3f Entire Predictive Model

The five relationships can be combined to understand how each can be used to forecast expected spot exchange rates, as shown in Figure 8-9.[13]

8-4 Exchange Rate Forecasting

It should now be evident that forecasting exchange rates is difficult. In addition to the five theories mentioned in the preceding section, there are always political changes, unpredictable economic variations, and the occasional natural catastrophe that influence the exchange rate of a given currency. Figure 8-10 illustrates the exchange rate of the Japanese yen with the U.S. dollar over the past thirty-five years;[14] it has been altogether very unpredictable, although reasonably stable in the short run. Historical exchange rates can easily be obtained, for any currency, from the Bank of Canada[15] and from the Pacific Exchange Rate Service at the University of British Columbia.[16]

There are three general methods that can be utilized for forecasting exchange rates, and, again, the reader should refer to textbooks dealing with forecasting

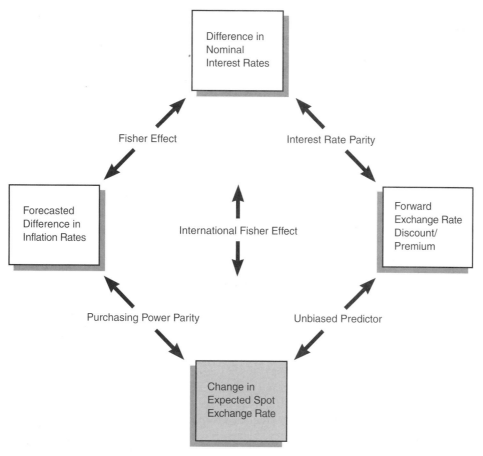

Figure 8-9
Understanding How Exchange Rates Change

specifically in order to understand these techniques better. Only a cursory review is made here.

8-4a Technical Forecasting

The so-called technical forecasting methods are essentially all based upon time-series analysis, from simple moving averages (something that can be done easily on a spreadsheet) to sophisticated ARIMA (Auto-Regressive Integrated Moving Average)—also called Box-Jenkins—methods and neural-network models that require dedicated software packages and pretty powerful computers. Several possible sources on technical forecasting exist.[17]

Technical forecasting is based on the premise that future movements in the value of a currency are "mathematically" linked to its past movements, and use techniques that extract patterns in the historical data. These patterns are then duplicated with very recent data to forecast the future exchange rates of the currency.

Such technical forecasts are valuable in determining the possible variations of a currency's exchange rate in the short run. In the long run, they tend to accumulate errors fairly quickly, as they ignore the economic fundamentals of exchange rate determination.

8-4b Fundamental Forecasting

The idea behind fundamental forecasting is to integrate all of the theories presented in Section 8-4 into a mathematical, causal model that would use the exchange rate of a specific currency as the dependent variable and the expected inflation rates, nominal

Figure 8-10
The Japan/U.S. Foreign Exchange Rate (Japanese Yen to One U.S. Dollar), February 1971 to June 2006
Source: Board of Governors of the Federal Reserve System.

interest rates, forward interest rates, and real interest rates as the independent variables. Fundamental forecasting is "just" the use of a large multiple linear regression and of ANOVA—Analysis of Variance—techniques, and it can be done with any good spreadsheet program. However, there are several pitfalls with causal models, and a good survey of such models should be undertaken before they are used. A good source of information on causal models is the text by Neter, Wasserman, and Kutner, entitled *Applied Linear Statistical Models.*[18]

The problem with causal models in general, and especially in the case of foreign exchange forecasting, is the difficulty in accounting for all of the possible influences on a given currency's exchange rate—it is impossible to isolate its movements to a single pair of currencies—and, at the same time, limit the inevitable collinearity of the independent variables. Novices tend to increase the number of independent variables, as it increases the coefficient of determination (R^2), but often overlook the problem of collinearity that this strategy brings along.

8-4c Market-Based Forecasting

Market-based forecasting is based on the premise that "the market knows best" and that, therefore, the forward exchange rate of a given currency is the best unbiased predictor of the future spot rate of a particular currency.

Because it is very likely that speculators have conducted their own analytical and mathematical forecasts for a given currency, it is quite logical to conclude that the forward exchange rate includes the entire wisdom of the market, and that, therefore, it is the best predictor of the future value of a currency. This observation is called the Efficient Market Hypothesis.

However, this assumption may be incorrect, as forward rates often reflect the futures' contract rates, which are set by speculators who may include people motivated by entirely different motives than the actual purchase and delivery of a currency. Such was the case with George Soros in 1992 when he decided to "bet" against the British pound, driving the government of the United Kingdom to spend a large amount of foreign currency to sustain its value, and eventually forcing the pound out of the Exchange Rate Mechanism (ERM) of the European Union.[19]

Moreover, the forward rates do not account for government interventions, which can wreak havoc on the actual spot rates of currencies. For example, in the spring of 2002, the Japanese government consistently kept the value of the yen down, in order to boost the Japanese economy through undervalued exports. The forward rates also do not reflect the possibility of an unexpected change or a currency crisis; such was the case when the Argentinean peso, which was pegged to the U.S. dollar at the rate of $1.00 per peso, suddenly was allowed to float on January 6, 2002, and reached $0.25 on March 25, 2002. By July 15, 2006, it stood at U.S. $0.32. The Chinese currency, the renminbi (also known as the RMB or the yuan), was also artificially kept at a pegged rate against the U.S. dollar at the rate of RMB8.28/$ from 1994 until July 2005, when it was changed to "better reflect market conditions" and appreciated to RMB8.11/$. From July 2005 until June 2006, the yuan slowly appreciated to RMB8.01/$. Nevertheless, the yuan is still quite undervalued, helping Chinese exports and making imports to China more expensive.

8-5 Managing Transaction Exposure

Whenever a company is engaged in an international transaction and agrees to use a foreign currency to conduct this transaction, it is then exposed to a certain amount of risk, due to possible fluctuations in currency exchange rates. Such risk is called **transaction exposure** and can be handled in one of two ways: It can be retained by the firm, or it can be "hedged," or reduced, by using one of three possible techniques, which will be presented in Sections 8-5b, 8-5c, and 8-5d.

Under these general guidelines, firms can pursue one of two strategies:

1. Determine what its decision should be on an invoice-by-invoice basis, depending on the currency at stake, the amount of the invoice, and its forecast of the currency's exchange rate.
2. Set a policy that the firm follows for all of its foreign currency receivables and payables.

In either case, the choice of the strategy should be dependent on the forecast that the company makes of the exchange rate at stake; it also depends on the size of the firm, the firm's ability to weather a currency risk, the size of the invoice relative to the firm's total sales (what is called the exposure), and the company's degree of sophistication in terms of international finance. In general terms, it is almost always better for a firm to hedge its foreign exchange risks, with only a few exceptions; however, certain firms choose to retain their currency fluctuation risks instead.

> **transaction exposure** The risk represented by the fluctuation in exchange rates between the time at which two companies enter in an international contract and the time at which that contract is paid.

8-5a Risk Retention

The strategy of **risk retention** is fairly simple: The company decides that it is best to retain the risk of currency fluctuation. There are three different types of companies that will decide to systematically retain their currency risks:

- Very large traders—importers and exporters, often in the same currency—that simultaneously carry risks on the "up" side (they can earn additional income because of a favorable exchange rate change) and on the "down" side (they can lose money for exactly the same reason). Overall, for these firms, transaction exchange rate risks are a zero-sum game, and it is not necessary to hedge, as the positions they hold offset each other. Nevertheless, those firms tend to be very sophisticated in international finance, and they would actually hedge their positions, and even speculate in the currency markets.

> **risk retention** A risk management strategy in which a company elects to retain a certain type of risk and decided not to insure that risk.

- Exporters or importers that have little exposure (i.e., which are shipping or buying goods of relatively small value, in fairly small shipments, and therefore for which a currency loss would not have substantial financial consequences). Often, for these firms, the costs of hedging, or of determining whether they should hedge, exceed the benefits that they would accrue.

- Firms that do not evaluate the international currency transaction risks clearly; they are not following a specific policy; they just have no policy, or have a management that is not well versed in the intricacies of international trade. Those firms are also often the ones that cannot afford not to hedge, as they tend to be smaller, and therefore more susceptible to a partial loss due to exchange rate fluctuations.

8-5b Forward Market Hedges

forward market hedge
A financial technique designed to reduce exchange rate fluctuation risks in which a business agrees to purchase (or sell) a particular currency at a predetermined exchange rate at some future time (generally thirty, sixty, ninety, 180, or 360 days later).

The first of the strategies that a company can follow to protect itself from currency fluctuations is a **forward market hedge**. This strategy involves selling forward a future receivable in a foreign currency, or purchasing forward the currency necessary to cover a foreign payable. This strategy varies in its implementation for each situation.

Two examples will make this strategy much clearer:

- A U.S.-based company is selling a product to an Italian firm on March 1, 2006; the invoice is payable in euros on June 1, 2006 (ninety-day credit). The amount that the firm would like to collect is U.S. $200,000. If it used the spot exchange rate—U.S. $1.2822/€—the firm could then bill the customer for €155,982.00.[20] However, as of March 1, 2006, the ninety-day forward exchange rate for the euro is U.S. $1.2730/€, indicating that the market is expecting a decrease in the value of the euro against the U.S. dollar. The firm therefore decides to invoice its customer for $200,000/1.2730 = €157,109.00. A forward market hedge, in this case, would consist of the U.S. firm entering a forward contract with a bank, in which it would promise to sell €157,109.00 to the bank on June 1, 2006, at the predetermined (forward) exchange rate of U.S. $1.2730/€. On that date, the U.S. company presents €157,109.00 to the bank and collects the U.S. $200,000 it wanted to collect. The U.S. firm is unconcerned about the spot exchange rate of the euro on June 1, 2006.

- A German firm is purchasing a product from a British firm for £250,000.00. The machine is delivered on May 31, 2006, and payment is expected (in pounds) on August 31, 2006. On May 31, 2006, this amount was equivalent to €364,910.00 because the spot exchange rate between the UK pound and the euro was €1.4596/£.[21] The German firm can use a forward market hedge by entering into a contract with a bank in which it promises to purchase £250,000 on August 31, 2006, at a predetermined (forward) exchange rate of €1.4415/£. On that date, the German firm hands €360,375 to the bank and obtains in exchange the £250,000 that it needs to pay its British supplier. The German firm ends up paying exactly what it had expected to pay for the machine and is unconcerned about the spot exchange rate of the British pound on August 31, 2006.

In either of these cases, the firm has eliminated its currency fluctuation risk by using a forward market hedge; it knew, with total certainty, at the time it entered the forward contract with the bank how much it would collect (U.S. firm) or how much it would have to pay (German firm).

8-5c Money Market Hedges

money market hedge
A financial technique designed to reduce exchange rate fluctuation risks in which a business invests funds in an interest-bearing account abroad or borrows funds from a bank abroad.

A **money market hedge** consists of using the banking system of the country of the currency in which the receivable or the payable is going to be paid. The firm hedging its exposure either borrows from a bank in the foreign country or deposits money in a bank in the foreign country.

This can again be explained best with two illustrations:

- A firm located in Switzerland sells a piece of machinery to a firm located in Japan, for the equivalent of SwF 150,000.00; it will bill in Japanese yen, though. The transaction takes place on October 5, 2005, with a payment date of December 5, 2005. The transaction amount is expressed in Japanese yen, for a total of ¥13,199,310.00 because the exchange rate on October 5 is ¥87.9954/SwF.[22] To protect itself from currency fluctuations, the Swiss firm can use a money market hedge, by borrowing from a Japanese bank the present value (as of October 5, 2005) of ¥13,199,310.00 on December 5, 2005. Supposing that the commercial lending rate in Japan on October 5, 2005, was 3 percent *per annum*, the amount the Swiss firm would borrow would be ¥ $(1-0.005) \times 13,199,310.00 = 13,133,313.45$; it will pay the bank back on December 5, 2005, using the payment of ¥13,199,310.00 made by its customer. On October 5, 2005, the Swiss firm would exchange the proceeds from the loan for SwF 149,250.00, and get an amount roughly equal to the payment of SwF 150,000.00 it had expected, although decreased by the cost of getting the money two months earlier. The Swiss firm is unconcerned about the spot exchange rate of the yen on December 5, 2006.

- On June 28, 2006, a firm located in Denmark purchases raw materials from a firm located in Australia, which insists on being paid in Australian dollars. The amount of the invoice is A$20,000,000, payable on December 28, 2006. The Danish firm can use a money market hedge by investing a sum in an Australian bank that will mature to A$20,000,000 on December 28, 2006. Assuming an annual interest rate of 4 percent paid on deposits in Australia, the Danish firm would have to invest A$20,000,000/$(1 + 0.02) = 19,607,845$ to have enough to cover its obligation on December 28, 2006. On June 28, 2006, the Danish firm then converts DKr 86,730,268.86[23] into Australian dollars. The Danish firm is unconcerned about the spot exchange rate of the Australian dollar on December 28, 2006, and it has paid exactly what it intended to pay for the machine.

The money market hedging strategy is effective because it allows the firm to use the exchange rate as of the date of the transaction rather than speculate on the value of the exchange rate at the date of payment. In that respect, it is a strategy that eliminates the risks of currency fluctuations; the only cost to the Swiss firm is the interest it has to pay to the Japanese bank, in addition to the fees that will be charged for the foreign exchange transactions. However, the amount of interest it pays should be the same as what it would have paid by borrowing the same amount in Switzerland, at least if the Interest Rate Parity holds. Similarly, the only cost to the Danish firm—in addition to the fees—is the opportunity cost of the investment, from which the interest earned in Australia must be deducted. Both of these should offset each other approximately as well.

8-5d Options Market Hedges

It is also possible to hedge a foreign currency fluctuation risk with options. An **options market hedge** is yet a more sophisticated alternative, because it amounts to remaining unhedged—retaining the risk—if the exchange rate fluctuations turn favorable and to purchasing an insurance policy to protect against unfavorable exchange rate fluctuations. If the exchange rate turns unfavorable, the firm can exercise its option—its insurance policy—and is covered. If the exchange rate turns favorable, the firm can still benefit from this situation by not exercising its option, even though it will lose the cost of the option.

This strategy involves purchasing put or call options, or the option to sell or purchase certain currencies at a certain exchange rate on (European-style options) or

options market hedge
A financial technique designed to reduce exchange rate fluctuation risks in which a business purchases (or sells) options in a particular currency.

before (U.S.-style options) a certain date. This agreed-upon exchange rate is called the strike price. Here again, two examples will illustrate the concepts better than an abstract description:

- A company located in the United States sells a large piece of equipment to a firm located in the United Kingdom, and agrees to be paid in pounds. The invoice, for £1,000,000, was issued on December 10, 2005, but is not payable until March 10, 2006. The exporting firm can minimize its currency fluctuation risk by using an option hedge; it will purchase a put option—the right to sell £1,000,000—at an exchange rate of U.S. $1.7140/£. If the spot exchange rate on March 10, 2006, is lower than U.S. $1.7140/£, then the American firm will exercise its option and sell the currency at that price. If the spot rate is higher than that, then the firm will let its option lapse and will sell the currency it received at the spot market rate. Because the exchange rate was U.S. $1.7255/£ on March 10, 2006,[24] the firm sold its pounds without using its option. The firm still incurred the cost of the option, which was approximately 1.25 percent of the contract amount, or about U.S. $17,562.50; however, this cost is offset by the fact that it sold its pounds for U.S. $11,500 more than it had anticipated. The net cost of this "insurance policy" was U.S. $6,562.50.

- A company located in Spain purchases a plant located in Canada. The contract is signed on August 1, 2005, and the firm has agreed to pay in three installments of Can$1,000,000 each on November 1, 2005, February 1, 2006, and August 1, 2006. In order to minimize its currency risks, the Spanish firm can use an option hedge by purchasing call options—the right to buy Can $1,000,000— at exchange rates of Can$1.3522/€ for November 1, 2005, Can$1.4141/€ for February 1, 2006, and Can$1.4452/€ for August 1, 2006. Because the spot exchange rate for the Canadian dollar was Can$1.4117/€ on November 1, 2005,[25] the Spanish firm did not exercise its option, purchased the Canadian dollars on the spot market, and sent them to the Canadian supplier. On February 1, 2006, the spot market was Can$1.3786/€,[26] and therefore the Spanish firm exercised its option and purchased the Canadian dollars at Can$1.4141/€ (the strike price of its option), because it was a more favorable exchange rate than the spot market. As for its future August 1, 2006, payment, the firm still has the possibility of saving money if the spot rate is lower than its option rate; if not, it will exercise its option. The cost of these successive options for the Spanish firm was approximately 1 percent, 1.5 percent, and 2.5 percent of the contract amounts for November, February, and August, respectively, for a total of €150,000.00. However, the costs were reduced by the fact that the firm saved € 31,170.00 in November by not having to spend as many euros as it had anticipated.

The main problem with option hedging is that options are very expensive, which is somewhat understandable as they are only covering the "down side." The second issue is that options are only commonly traded for a limited number of currencies, and that the amounts are not as flexible as in forward markets. Nevertheless, some banks will write options that are tailored to their customers' needs. For the sophisticated firm involved in international trade, this strategy has great potential.

For further information on this hedging strategy, the other hedging strategies described in this section, as well as additional strategies, the reader is referred to a number of textbooks in international finance[27] or to textbooks on options and futures.[28]

8-6 International Banking Institutions

There are several institutions that are involved in international banking; however, only a few of these have a function that is linked to international payments. A brief synopsis of each of these institutions is given in this section. The reader interested in gaining more information on these institutions should consult a textbook in international economics or international banking.[29]

8-6a Central National Banks

In every country in the world, there is a Central Bank, or some institution that acts as a Central Bank: Great Britain has its Bank of England, the European Union has its European Central Bank (ECB), and the United States has the Federal Reserve System that, although not technically a Central Bank, fulfills the role of one. Each of the countries of the European Union has also retained its Central Bank, because only the control of the monetary supply is in the hands of the ECB; France has its Banque de France and Germany has its cherished Bundes Bank.

Central Banks provide several services to the domestic banks of their respective countries. Their first role is the creation and control of the monetary supply, through market operations and the control of currency. This role can be one of maintenance or a more active role, such as executing monetary policy operations. Their second role is their function as a check clearinghouse where accounts regarding checks written on different domestic banks' accounts are settled. In some countries, they also "manage"—if conceivable—the exchange rate of the national currency and the national foreign exchange reserves.

8-6b International Monetary Fund

The International Monetary Fund (IMF) was created in 1944 at the Bretton-Woods Conference; it was designed to oversee the fixed exchange rate system that the Conference had started. When exchange rates started to float in 1971—the end of the gold standard—the IMF changed its focus to helping countries manage their balance of payments. In particular, the IMF lends money to countries that experience difficulties with their balance of payments. These loans are usually accompanied by a number of conditions to which the country has to agree; inflation control and money supply growth are often on the list. The funds necessary for those loans are collected from the countries that become members of the IMF; they are assessed a "quota" that is determined by the country's economic size.[30]

The IMF is also the curator of an artificial currency called the "Special Drawing Rights" (SDR), which was designed to supplement the U.S. dollar in its role as the international currency. The SDR's value is determined by a basket of four currencies (U.S. dollar, European euro, British pound, and Japanese yen). Although the SDR is not often used by businesses, it is often used by governments to settle their debts with each other. It is also used in the settlement of disputes under the liability conventions of ocean cargo shipping (see Section 11-6).

8-6c Bank for International Settlements

The Bank for International Settlements was created after World War I to manage Germany's war reparation payments. Since then it has evolved into a major international institution, providing support to Central Banks—which constitute its membership—and particularly recently providing guidance to the new Central Banks of the former Eastern Bloc Countries.[31] Although membership was originally limited to European Central Banks, the United States' Federal Reserve System joined in 1994.

8-6d International Bank for Reconstruction and Development— World Bank

The International Bank for Reconstruction and Development—known as the World Bank—was created in 1945 after the Bretton-Woods Conference. Its purpose was to help countries rebuild their infrastructure after World War II, and it has slowly changed to become the bank in charge of financing large infrastructure projects. The government borrowing the funds must be a member of the IMF and the loan is usually repaid as a long-term loan.

8-6e Ex-Im Bank

The Export-Import Bank (Ex-Im Bank) is a federal agency of the United States' government. Its purpose is to provide assistance to U.S. exporters in the form of loans (only available to large exporters), loan guarantees (available to banks who finance exporters), or in the form of political risk insurance policies available through the Foreign Credit Insurance Association (FCIA). See Section 10-12c for further details.

8-6f Society for Worldwide Interbank Financial Telecommunication (SWIFT)

The Society for Worldwide Interbank Financial Telecommunication (SWIFT) is a corporation supporting an Electronic Data Interchange network that was created by banks to obtain a secure and reliable means of transferring financial information internationally. In particular, it allows the communication of Letters of Credit and miscellaneous fund transfers. Because of the high level of security that the network enjoys, documents transferred through the network have the same value as original paper documents.

8-7 Currency of Payment as a Marketing Tool

In an international transaction, the choice of the currency exposes the exporter (or the importer) to the risk of currency exchange rate fluctuation. Rather than consider this risk to be a drawback in an international sale, a good exporter should consider it an opportunity.

There are four main tactics that the exporter can pursue to eliminate this foreign exchange risk:

- Elect to quote in the exporter's currency. Although this is the easiest of the alternatives for the exporter, it only shifts the risk onto the importer, who is just as likely to consider this risk to be a burden. In addition, if the exporter's quote is being evaluated against other quotes, including some domestic proposals, a quote that is presented in a foreign currency is going to be less attractive to the importer.

- Elect to quote in the importer's currency and minimize the risk of exchange rate fluctuation with a forward market hedge. In that case, the importer has no currency fluctuation risk and the exporter knows exactly what its foreign exchange "cost" is going to be at the time of the transaction. The only drawback is that the exporter may not have easy access to the forward market of some currencies that are not commonly traded in the forward markets (a currency other than the European euro, the Japanese yen, the British pound, or the Canadian dollar). Nevertheless, these other currencies are traded in the forward market in London and, with some help from a savvy international banker, an exporter can hedge just about any receivable in any currency.

- Elect to quote in the importer's currency and minimize the risk of exchange rate fluctuation with a money market hedge. In that case, the importer has no currency fluctuation risk; the exporter also knows exactly what its foreign exchange cost is going to be, although it requires knowing what the interest rates are in the importing country. However, the exporter has to be quite experienced—and have an international presence—to be able to borrow from a bank in a foreign market; only a few companies have this option available, although a savvy international banker can provide substantial help in this regard.

- Elect to quote in the importer's currency and minimize the risk of exchange rate fluctuation with an options market hedge. In that case, the importer has no currency fluctuation risk and the exporter benefits in two ways. If the exchange rate fluctuation is favorable, the exporter benefits from it. If the exchange rate fluctuation is unfavorable, the exporter has minimized its risk. The main issue with options market hedges is the same as with the forward market hedges: Not all currencies are readily available in the home country of the exporter, and the help of a savvy international banker may be required to purchase options on the London market, for example.

Because of the intense competition that an exporter faces in international markets, it is very likely that a significant percentage of its competitors will offer quotes in the importer's currency. Because it is easier for the importer to handle a purchase in its own currency, it would place an exporter at a strategic disadvantage not to quote in that currency.

An exporter intent on increasing its sales abroad should therefore consider very seriously offering quotes in the importer's currency and discuss with its banker which of the three hedging tactics would be most appropriate.

Key Terms

artificial currency (p. 158)
call options (p. 156)
convertible currencies (p. 149)
currency (p. 148)
currency block (p. 158)
currency futures (p. 155)
currency options (p. 155)
direct quote (p. 152)
dollarization (p. 158)
euro (p. 151)
Fisher Effect (p. 161)
floating currencies (p. 156)

forward exchange rate (p. 153)
forward market hedge (p. 168)
hard currencies (p. 149)
inconvertible currencies (p. 149)
indirect quote (p. 152)
Interest Rate Parity (p. 162)
International Fisher Effect (p. 161)
money market hedge (p. 168)
options market hedge (p. 169)
outright rate (p. 154)
pegged currency (p. 158)
points (p. 154)

Purchasing Power Parity (p. 158)
put options (p. 156)
risk retention (p. 167)
soft currency (p. 149)
Special Drawing Right (SDR) (p. 151)
spot exchange rate (p. 152)
strike price (p. 156)
swap rate (p. 154)
terms of sale (p. 148)
terms of trade (p. 148)
transaction exposure (p. 167)

Review and Discussion Questions

1. What are three of the possible choices that an exporter can make (in terms of currency) for a specific transaction?

2. Explain the three different types of exchange rates. Find the three exchange rates for a currency of your choice and explain the values you find.

3. Explain the three different types of currencies. Give an example of each.

4. Choose two of the theories of exchange rate determination and explain them.

5. What does it mean for a firm to retain its currency fluctuation risk in a transaction?

6. There are three types of hedges that a firm can use to protect itself against transaction exposure. Choose one of them and explain it.

Endnotes

1. "Second Report on the Practical Preparations for the Future Enlargement of the Euro Area," Commission of the European Community, April 11, 2005, http://ec.europa.eu/economy_finance/euro/documents/comm2005_545annex_en.pdf, June 8, 2006. "The U.K. Government's Policy on Economic and Monetary Union [EMU]," Her Majesty's Treasury, http://www.hm-treasury.gov.uk./documents/international_issues/the_euro/euro_index_index.cfm, June 8, 2006.

2. Baker, James C., *International Finance: Management, Markets, and Institutions*, 1998, Prentice-Hall, Upper Saddle River, New Jersey. Eiteman, David K., Arthur I. Stonehill, and Michael H. Moffett, *Multinational Business Finance*, 2004, Tenth Edition, Pearson-Addison-Wesley Publishing Company, Reading, Massachusetts. Madura, Jeff, *International Financial Management*, 1998, South-Western Publishing, Cincinnati, Ohio. Shapiro, Alan C., *Multinational Financial Management*, 1996, Fifth Edition, Prentice-Hall, Upper Saddle River, New Jersey.

3. "Currency Trading," *The Wall Street Journal*, June 8, 2006, C9.

4. "Currencies and Interest Rates," *Financial Times*, U.S. Edition, June 8, 2006, 27.

5. "Foreign Exchange Rates," *The Wall Street Journal*, June 8, 2006, C9.

6. World Currencies, Financial Times Currency Information, "http://news.ft.com/markets/currencies, June 8, 2006.

7. "Foreign Exchange Rates," *The Wall Street Journal*, June 8, 2006, C9 and *The Financial Times*, June 8, 2006.

8. Eiteman, David K., Arthur I. Stonehill, and Michael H. Moffett, *Multinational Business Finance*, 2004, Tenth Edition, Pearson-Addison-Wesley Publishing Company, Reading, Massachusetts.

9. Board of Governors of the Federal Reserve System, http://research.stlouisfed.org/fred2/series/EXUSEU/downloaddata, June 8, 2006.

10. "U.S./Euro Exchange Rate," Economic Research, Federal Reserve Bank of St. Louis, http://research.stlouisfed.org/fred2/series/DEXUSEU/15, June 8, 2006.

11. Adapted from"Mac Currencies: Happy 20th Birthday to our Big Mac Index," *The Economist*, May 25, 2006, p. 33.

12. Shapiro, Alan C., *Multinational Financial Management*, 1996, Fifth Edition, Prentice-Hall, Upper Saddle River, New Jersey.

13. Peck, Earl, "Prices, Interest Rates, and Exchange Rates in Equilibrium," unpublished research paper, Baldwin-Wallace College, Berea, Ohio.

14. Board of Governors of the Federal Reserve System, http://research.stlouisfed.org/fred2/data/EXJPUS.txt, June 8, 2006.

15. "10-Year Currency Converter," Bank of Canada, http://www.bankofcanada.ca/en/rates/exchform.html, July 31, 2006.

16. Antweiler, Werner, "Pacific Exchange Rate Service," http://pacific.commerce.ubc.ca/xr/, March 23, 2002.

17. Bowerman, Bruce L., and Richard L. O'Connell, *Time Series Forecasting*, 1987, Second Edition, Duxbury Press, Boston, Massachusetts. Box, George E., Gwilym M. Jenkins, and Gregory C. Reinsel, *Time Series Analysis: Forecasting and Control*, 1994, Third Edition, Prentice-Hall, Englewood Cliffs, New Jersey. Makridakis, Spyros, Steven C. Wheelwright, and Victor E. McGee, *Forecasting: Methods and Applications*, 1983, Second Edition, John Wiley and Sons, Inc., New York, New York. Masters, Timothy, *Neural, Novel and Hybrid Algorithms for Time Series Predictions*, 1995, John Wiley and Sons, Inc. New York, New York.

18. Neter, John, William Wasserman, and Michael H. Kutner, *Applied Linear Statistical Models*, 1985, Second Edition, Irwin, Homewood, Illinois.

19. Weiss, Gary, "George Soros, All Warm and Cuddly," *Business Week*, March 4, 2002, p. 68, reporting on Michael T. Kaufmann's *Soros: The Life and Times of a Messianic Billionaire*, 2002, Alfred A. Knopf, New York.

20. "10-Year Currency Converter" Bank of Canada, http://www.bankofcanada.ca/en/rates/exchform.html, July 31, 2006.

21. *Ibid*

22. *Ibid*

23. *Ibid*

24. *Ibid*

25. *Ibid*

26. *Ibid*

27. Baker, James C., *International Finance: Management, Markets, and Institutions*, 1998, Prentice-Hall, Upper Saddle River, New Jersey. Eiteman, David K., Arthur I. Stonehill, and Michael H. Moffett, *Multinational Business Finance*, 2004, Tenth Edition, Pearson-Addison-Wesley Publishing Company, Reading, Massachusetts. Madura, Jeff, *International Financial Management*, 1998, South-Western Publishing, Cincinnati, Ohio. Shapiro, Alan C., *Multinational Financial Management*, 1996, Fifth Edition, Prentice-Hall, Upper Saddle River, New Jersey.

28. Edwards, Franklin R., and Cindy W. Ma, *Futures and Options*, 1992, McGraw-Hill, Inc., New York, New York.

29. Caves, Richard E., Jeffrey A. Frankel, and Ronald W. Jones, *World Trade and Payments: An Introduction*, 1996, Seventh Edition, Harper Collins College Publishers. Kim, Taeho, *International Money and Banking*, 1993, Routledge Publishers, London and New York, New York.

30. Daniels, John D., and Lee H. Radebaugh, *International Business: Environments and Operations*, 1992, Sixth Edition, Addison-Wesley Publishing, Reading, Massachusetts.

31. Siegman, Charles J., "The Bank for International Settlement and the Federal Reserve," *Federal Reserve Bulletin*, October 1994, 900–906.

International Commercial Documents

Source: © 2007 JupiterImages Corporation.

A very large number of documents is involved in international transactions, many more than in a purely domestic exchange. Some of these documents are required by the exporting country, some by the importing country, some by the banks involved (especially if the shipment is made under a Letter of Credit), some by the shipping (transportation) company, and some by the importer of the goods.

Under each of the Incoterms outlined in Chapter 6, the exporter is responsible for generating and collecting all—or almost all—of the documents linked to an international transaction. Any error or omission in the creation of these documents can create difficulties for both the exporter and the importer, as the goods will be detained by Customs in the importing country, the bank will request amendments in order to process payment, or the carrier will load the goods improperly.

It is therefore imperative for international logistics managers to exert special care and follow "best practices" in generating the documents linked to every international transaction.

9-1 Documentation Requirements

Most international trade transactions require numerous documents and each of these documents must be filled in a very specific fashion, depending on the country of destination for the goods, the type of goods, the method of transportation, the method of payment chosen by the exporter and importer, the bank(s) involved, and so on. Each of these documents must also contain very detailed information and specific statements, and must often be filed in a certain time frame with a specific administration. Such are the difficulties of generating these documents that a multitude of software packages exist to help the international logistics manager complete the task. Most of them promise that they can help an exporter complete an entire set in "as little as two hours."

In addition, it is a common requirement to issue more than one *original* for some of these documents, as well as a multitude of copies—one for just about every possible intermediary involved. For some transactions, the number of originals and copies can be staggering: A particularly egregious case was a Letter of Credit from Ethiopia for $1,067 that called for "15 original invoices, five of them certified by a chamber of commerce."[1] In most cases, therefore, the thickness of the export documentation necessary for an international transaction reaches more than 1.5 cm (0.5 inch), even for a simple export.

Finally, most countries still require all of these documents to be issued on paper. Although there has been a recent increase in the number of countries that *accept* electronic submissions of paperwork, most still prefer paper. For many of them, it is required to file everything on paper; for others, only documents that are in paper form have legal status. This is the case in countries that have a legal system based on the old Napoleonic Code and have not updated their laws. Italy, for example, only formally gave an equivalent legal status to electronic documents in February 2002.[2]

9-2 Invoices

One of the documents common to both international and domestic transactions is the bill (invoice) that the exporter sends to the importer. However, the content of an international invoice is more complex and should be prepared substantially differently for a foreign customer than for a domestic one.

9-2a Commercial Invoice

The invoice that accompanies the shipment is called the **commercial invoice**. Depending on the Terms of Payment to which the exporter and the importer agreed (see Chapter 7), the commercial invoice may be sent directly to the importer (with the merchandise) or indirectly, through the banking channels.

This invoice should present precisely what the importer is being billed for. This seems obvious, but it is a much greater challenge to fulfill this requirement for an international transaction than it is for a domestic transaction. Several areas of the invoice must be very carefully written in order to avoid problems later on (see Figure 9-1):

- A very precise description of the product should be given. In domestic marketing, it is common to just print a part number, a number of units, a per-piece price, and a total. This is highly insufficient in international trade, as the invoice is one of the documents that will be used by the importer (or the exporter, depending on the Terms of Trade or Incoterm; see Chapter 6) to clear Customs in the importing country. Because the tariff paid is a function of the classification (type) of the product imported (see Section 15-1), a clear and accurate description of the product should be written on the invoice, including the Harmonized System Number. In addition, because tariff rates are determined using a multiplicity of criteria—the number of units in the shipment, their dimensions, weight, and total value—such information should also be included. It is not possible to assume that tariffs will be calculated on the same basis everywhere; Switzerland, for example, uses weight to calculate duty for a number of products, including computers.

- The Terms of Trade (or Incoterms) should be made quite clear and should indicate that the seller intends to follow the guidelines proposed by the International Chamber of Commerce (see Chapter 6). This information is crucial to clarify whether the exporter or the importer is responsible for the payment of a number of ancillary services and fees: shipping, stevedoring, insurance, dock fees, duty, and so on. A misunderstanding in this area can cause countless problems and cost a substantial amount of money. The use of nontraditional Terms of Trade or the use of domestic Terms of Trade in an international transaction, which no one understands, should be avoided at all costs.

- A detailed list of the items that the exporter has prepaid for the importer should be noted; for example, the amount paid by the exporter for international insurance should be clearly indicated in the case of a CIF or CIP shipment, as some importing countries—such as the United States—will exclude this amount from the amount on which duty is calculated. Stevedoring charges in the port of departure should be spelled out for the same reason. There are probably countries for which it would make sense to spell out what amounts were prepaid for domestic transportation in the exporting country as well.

- The Terms of Payment (see Chapter 7) should also be clearly detailed; they are the conditions under which the invoice should be paid. The invoice may be

commercial invoice The invoice sent by the seller to the buyer, detailing the goods purchased and the amount due. A bill. In international trade, a commercial invoice should be quite detailed and include all of the pertinent information.

EBERT PIPE ORGANS, INC.

INVOICE: 072306-001   **Date:** July 23, 2006

Sold By: **Shipped By:**
Ebert Pipe Organs, Inc.   Ebert Inc. Warehouse
1234 Carnegie Avenue   7200 Industrial Parkway
Cleveland, OH 44111   Cleveland, OH 44111
USA   USA

Sold To: **Shipped To:**
Australian Importers   St. John's Methodist Church
4/2 Wilson Avenue   76 Ewing Road
Brunswick, Victoria 3089   Brunswick, Victoria 3095
Australia   Australia

Crates: 3   **Weight:** 57.55 kg net each   **Volume:** 1.2 x 0.6 x 0.4 m each
                          65.00 kg gross each   0.288 m³ each
                          195.00 kg total   0.864 m³ total

Purchase Order: 062083

Quantity	Description	Unit Price	Total
3	Catalog Item # 095673. Pipe organ blower. HS 8414.59.1000	USD 975.00	USD 2,925.00
	Insurance paid to Brunswick, Australia	USD 128.70	
	Airfreight Costs to Brunswick, Australia	USD 585.00	
	US Domestic Transportation Costs	USD 87.00	
	Total:		USD 3,725.70

Shipped via: Trans-Air   CIP Brunswick, Australia, Incoterms 2000

Country of Origin: USA

Terms: 1.5% 10 days / net 30 days

Figure 9-1
A Good Example of an International Invoice
Source: Courtesy of Jamie Serenko.

accompanied by a Letter of Credit or a bank draft. It could also indicate that the merchandise has already been paid for (as in a "Cash in Advance" or a "procurement card" or TradeCard purchase) or just show a due date (as in the case of a sale conducted on an "Open Account" basis).

- The currency in which the payment is to be made should be clear. The issues regarding the choice of the currency and ways to manage the risk of currency fluctuations are presented in Chapter 8.

- The shipping information should also be presented; it includes the ports of departure and destination, the name of the shipping company(ies), the dates of the shipment, the number of boxes or containers, their weight (gross and net), and their size.

- Finally, the customary information should be provided: the name of the seller-exporter, the name of the buyer-importer, the persons to be contacted, addresses, and so forth. The telephone access codes should be eliminated, so as to not confuse the foreign customer.*

9-2b *Pro-forma* Invoice

A *pro-forma* invoice is a very common international document; despite its name, it is not an invoice at all, but a quote.

An international transaction includes so many variables that it is sometimes difficult for an importer to have a good grasp of what its final costs will be; for example, the cost of the goods is increased by the costs of shipping, insurance, and so forth. In order to determine these costs, the importer may request a *pro-forma* invoice, literally an invoice "as a matter of form" (i.e., an invoice in advance—an accurate and precise preview of what the actual invoice would be like if the transaction were to take place). The importer can then compare this invoice to the other quotes it receives.

In those cases in which the exporter requests payment on a Letter of Credit basis, the information contained on the *pro-forma* invoice is used by the Issuing Bank to open the Letter of Credit. Because the Letter of Credit dictates that the documents submitted for payment must match exactly those outlined in the Letter of Credit, it is therefore against the information contained in the *pro-forma* invoice that the actual documents will be reviewed. Extreme care should therefore be given to the writing of a *pro-forma* invoice, as the final commercial invoice should not vary from it. If it does, it is likely that this situation will be considered a discrepancy between the Letter of Credit and the actual documents, and amendments will have to be made, not to mention paid for. It is therefore imperative for the exporter to have a very accurate *pro-forma* invoice, including exactly the same type of information as the final commercial invoice would have, in the same amount, with exact quotes from the other suppliers involved (shipping, insurance, and the like).

It also should include an expiration date, or the date after which the quote is no longer valid. The expiration date in an international transaction is treated very differently than in a domestic transaction. Whereas under the Uniform Commercial Code of the United States (UCC) and under the domestic laws of many other countries, where the offer can be withdrawn at any time, without prejudice, for almost whatever reason, it is not the case in an international transaction conducted under the United Nations' Convention on the International Sales of Goods (CISG). Under the CISG, the offer cannot be withdrawn by the seller (or the buyer) before its expiration date, and the other party can accept it at any time until that time; it is an irrevocable offer. Most countries have now adopted this convention for international sales contracts (see Section 5-2 for further details).

Casual handling of a *pro-forma* invoice may cause countless problems later on. As *A Basic Guide to Exporting* wisely points out, "problems [...] are more easily avoided than rectified after they occur."[3]

9-2c Consular Invoice

For exports to some countries—specifically a decreasing number of Latin American countries—a **Consular invoice** may be necessary. A Consular invoice is nothing more than a regular commercial invoice, but printed on stationery (paper) provided by the

pro-forma invoice A quote provided by the exporter to the importer for the purpose of the importer obtaining a Letter of Credit.

consular invoice A commercial invoice that is printed on stationery provided by the Consulate of the country in which the goods will be imported.

---

* In the United States, it is necessary to dial a one before making a phone call to another state. In France, it is necessary to dial a zero before making a domestic call. These access digits should be omitted from the letterhead.

importing country's Consulate, and *visa*-ed (stamped, embossed, or whatever other procedure) by the Consulate before the invoice can be sent to the importer. The process of obtaining a Consular invoice is often time-consuming as it involves at least one exchange (by mail or in person) with the Consulate. Because Consulates for most countries are rarely located in a city convenient to the exporter, there are a number of messenger service companies that provide a courier who will pick up the invoice, wait in line at the Consulate, have it *visa*-ed, and return it to the exporting company.

This process is usually favored by countries that want to accurately forecast their needs for foreign currency. From these Consular invoices, they can determine their foreign currency outflows and therefore accurately manage their needs for foreign currency. However, this process also has the added "benefit" of generating additional revenues, as the stationery sold by the Consulate and the **visa** procedure are usually quite expensive. All of these fees are also obviously generated in "hard currency," another added benefit.

Fortunately, this type of requirement is slowly disappearing as it is often viewed as a nontrade barrier by exporters. As of May 2006, Consular invoices were still required in a dozen countries.

> **visa** A process by which the Consulate of the country in which the goods will be imported reviews and approves the Consular invoice for a fee. A visa shows on the Consular invoice as a rubber stamp or a seal.

9-2d Specialized Commercial Invoices

Some countries require that all commercial invoices be printed on a standard form, which is usually easily available at a low cost from specialized printers of international stationery, such as Unz & Co. These countries include Canada, Mexico, New Zealand, Brazil, and Israel.[4] In general, these requirements are not considered trade barriers and it is understood that their purpose is to simplify the work of Customs' employees.

9-3 Export Documents

A country's government may require a number of documents before a product can be exported. These requirements are primarily motivated by the desire to keep accurate data on what is exported from that country—such is the case for the **Shipper's Export Declaration** in the United States, for example. In some cases, though, the government also wants to control the outflow of certain types of merchandise, or does not want to trade with certain countries for political reasons (embargos). In those cases, the country will require the exporter to obtain an export license.

> **Shipper's Export Declaration** A document collected by U.S. Customs designed to keep track of the type of goods exported from the United States, as well as their destination and their value.

9-3a Export Licenses

An export license is an express authorization by a given country's government to export a specific product before it is shipped. There are many reasons for a government to require an export license, but they are usually triggered by one of the following two viewpoints:

- The government is attempting to control the export of national treasures or antiques. This is the case in India, which prohibits the export of any object older than 100 years old[5] with Britain and with France, which both control the export of antiques and works of art,[6] and with Turkey, which was recently involved in a high-stake fight over a trove of antique coins that were discovered in 1984 and were eventually smuggled to the United States.[7] Some states have been successful in repatriating such artifacts: Italy convinced the Metropolitan Museum of Art in New York City to return some fifteen objects.[8] Greece is in the process of pursuing the same outcome with the Getty Museum in Los Angeles.

- The government is trying to exert some control over foreign trade for political or military reasons: This is mostly the way the United States government manages its export licensing program; the process it follows is described further in the next section. Some other countries also pursue similar objectives: China seized and prohibited from export a book published by an American firm but printed in China, as it depicted opinions with which the Chinese government was at odds.[9] The European Union prohibits the export of personal data gathered on customers or consumers.[10]

9-3b U.S. Export Controls

The United States' government's policy regarding export controls is anchored in several milestones: the existence of a (once secret) agreement between Western countries to deny access to certain military technologies (nicknamed CoCom), which ceased to exist in 1994;[11] the Export Administration Act, which controlled the type of goods that could be exported to certain "unfriendly" countries, but that lapsed in 1992; the Fenwick Anti-Terrorist Amendment of the Export Administration Act, written to prevent exports to nations supportive of international terrorism; and the Comprehensive Anti-Apartheid Act, which created a number of regulations for exports to the country of South Africa. These documents brought into existence the current **Commodity Control List**, which details which products can and cannot be shipped to certain countries. The list is updated regularly, and published in the *U.S. Export Administration Regulations* (EAR).[12] In 1996, the EAR was completely revised to reflect a major shift from a policy of "everything that is not explicitly authorized needs an export license" to a policy of "everything is authorized unless it is specifically prohibited." Finally, in April of 2002, the Bureau of Export Administration, which was in charge of administering the Export Administration Regulations, changed its name to the Bureau of Industry and Security.

Commodity Control List
A list, maintained by the Bureau of Industry and Security, which details which products cannot be exported from the United States without the express authorization of the U.S. government.

For some products, therefore, the United States' government wants to ascertain that the goods are purchased for a legitimate commercial purpose (and not a military one) and that there is no risk of diversion (sale to another, unfriendly company or country). This is particularly true of products that have a dual-use (i.e., that can be used for several purposes, one of which is commercial, the other military in nature). For example, Polaroid employees need to use night-vision goggles to assemble some instant cameras. When sales of the product surged in Japan, the company tried to expand its manufacturing facility in Mexico, and attempted to ship more night-vision goggles there, but was rebuffed by the Bureau of Export Administration (BXA), the predecessor of the Bureau of Industry and Security, because these instruments have a dual use.[13]

The United States export control policies are focusing on three elements: the product considered for export, the entity abroad that is buying the product or an intermediary (abroad or in the United States) involved in the sale of the product, and finally, the ultimate country of destination for the product.

The Product Exported

To determine which products fall under the possible control of the Export Administration Regulations (EAR), the BIS publishes a Commodity Control List (CCL) on which it lists all products for which the BIS has deemed that exports should be of concern to the United States. Each product on the CCL is given an Export Control Classification Number (ECCN)—which is different from the Harmonized System Number used by Customs—and determines whether it will necessitate an export license. All of the products that do not fall on the CCL list are given the classification "EAR99" by the Bureau of Industry and Security. However, a few of the EAR99 products can still require an export license, if they fall under the jurisdiction of another government entity that controls export. For example, the Drug Enforcement

Internet Business and Security

The Internet is a growing area of interest for companies who expect to be able to conduct business by using this international network. However, conducting business transactions through a computer network necessitates a means to keep certain data, such as credit card information, confidential.

It is quite possible to keep data secure with encryption software, a type of computer program that scrambles data in such a way that it cannot be read intelligibly by anyone but the intended recipient equipped with the same software. However, the United States' government has long regarded encryption technology as "sensitive"—it could be used for military purposes—and therefore has kept it on its Commodity Control List.[14] For years, it steadfastly refused to allow companies to use encryption software on the Internet, as it considered its use to be an export because the network is essentially borderless. Only banks, subsidiaries of U.S. firms, health and medical facilities, and online merchants were allowed to have access to U.S. encryption technology abroad.

It is only recently that the Bureau of Industry and Security (BIS) has allowed "low level" encryption to be sold freely abroad. However, only software products containing up to 64-bit encryption and 512-bit key management products are exempt from licensing requirements;[15] anything else requires the express authorization of the BIS.

Administration controls the export of pharmaceuticals under the authority of the Controlled Substances Act and can require an export license for some products.

For all products listed on the Commodity Control List, the BIS gives the reason for their inclusion: items are listed for reasons of national security, anti-terrorism, crime control, chemical and biological weapons control, nuclear non-proliferation, regional stability, encryption, short supply, United Nations embargo, or "significant item."

Depending on the reason for which they were listed, ECCN commodities do not require a license for some countries, but do for others. The BIS maintains a Product/Country License Determination Matrix to help the exporter in determining its obligations.[16]

The Purchaser of the Product

In those cases where the ECCN classification does not require a license, or when the product is classified as EAR99, the exporter is still required to determine whether the importer or an intermediary involved in the sale is on one of several lists:

- The "Entity List," which is a list that identifies people, companies, and organizations engaged in weapon proliferation, drug smuggling, or terrorism, and to which the United States government wants to control exports. Sales to persons or organizations on the "Entities List" require an export license. That list is maintained by the BIS.

- The "Unverified List" of individuals, companies, and organizations, which are suspected of engaging in activities that the BIS considers illegal. Before making a sale to a person on that list, the exporter is required to inquire with the BIS about possible issues. That list is also maintained by the BIS. In addition, the exporter is required to report a suspect transaction when the transaction has elements that the BIS considers "red flags," such as when a cash sale is made for a product that is generally purchased on credit terms, or when a product is sold to a company that does not appear to be in the exporter's main line of business.

- The "List of Specially Designated Nationals and Blocked Persons List," or persons located abroad with whom exporters are expressly warned not to do business. These persons have been deemed to represent countries to which the United States does not want to export, or they represent companies or organizations engaged in terrorism or trafficking. That list is maintained by the Department of the Treasury.

- The "Denied Persons List," which identifies U.S. persons, companies, or organizations "whose export privileges have been revoked:" Some of these companies are located in the United States. That list is maintained by the BIS. An exporter is expressly prohibited to sell to a person on that list, and a company that is contacted (for a domestic sale) by one of these companies must notify the Bureau of Industry and Security.

The Country of Import

The Commodity Control List determines whether a given product, for which an ECCN exists, can be sold to a specific country. There are substantial differences in an exporter's ability to export to countries that the United States considers "friendly" and to countries that are considered "unfriendly."

In addition, though, the United States has embargoes on sales of certain products to several countries: Exporters cannot sell any of these products and will never be able to obtain an export license.[17] Finally, the United States has a total embargo with six countries; no products whatsoever can be exported to the countries of Cuba, Iran, Libya, North Korea, Sudan, and Syria.

In any of the cases in which a license is deemed necessary, the U.S. government requires an exporter to obtain an **Individual Validated Export License**, or an express authorization to ship that particular product to a particular country, as well as to write a **Destination Control Statement** on the commercial invoice and the Shipper's Export Declaration: *This merchandise licensed by U.S. for ultimate destination [country]. Diversion contrary to U.S. Law prohibited.* A Validated Export License is generally granted with very specific terms and conditions to which the exporter is required to adhere. Heavy fines can result if the importer diverts the goods to another country, even if the exporter has little or no control over such activity.[18]

A product not on the CCL or whose ECCN does not call for an export license is classified as "EAR99," a classification that needs to be included on the Shipper's Export Declaration.

9-3c Shipper's Export Declaration

The Shipper's Export Declaration (SED) is a data-collection document required by the U.S. government for all exports valued at more than $2,500 per item category, as determined by the Harmonized System Number ($500 for parcels sent through the postal system), and for all shipments that require an Individual Validated Export License. The SED is not required for exports to Canada, and it is required for shipments to Puerto Rico, the U.S. Virgin Islands, and Guam, even though those shipments are not exports. The SED must be sent to the U.S. Customs Service.

This form (see Figure 9-2) allows the U.S. government to tabulate what products are exported from the United States, and to determine where these products are sold. The data are available for all commodities and for all countries in the National Trade Data Bank, available on the Internet at www.stat-usa.gov with a subscription. However, this procedure does not ensure that all exports are accounted for. As late as 1998, it was estimated that up to 50 percent of the SEDs had defective entries, from the value of the goods to their classification.[19] In addition, many SEDs were filed very late and several shipments that would have been inspected or seized had already left the United States. The results were fines for the shipping lines that accepted such shipments.[20] For that reason, the SED must now be in the hands of Customs before the shipment is allowed to leave the United States.

In 1999, the Census Bureau, the entity that eventually collects all of this information through Customs, decided to strongly entice exporters to use a new electronic system for filing SEDs, one that would no longer allow errors or incomplete entries as the old system did. This Automated Export System (AES) became the only efficient way with which an exporter could submit an SED in August 2000, when the Census Bureau also prohibited faxed SEDs, which were often riddled with errors or illegible. In July 2003, it became mandatory for SEDs for goods that required a Validated Export License to be filed through the AES. The paper option is still available for other goods, but cumbersome: The Census Bureau is considering making AES mandatory for all goods.

Individual Validated Export License The express authorization, granted by the government of the exporting country, to export a particular product, or to export to a particular country or particular individual.

Destination Control Statement A formal statement, which an exporter has to print on its invoice and on the Shipper's Export Declaration if the goods shipped are subject to a validated export license: "This merchandise licensed by U.S. for ultimate destination [country]; diversion contrary to U.S. law prohibited."

U.S. DEPARTMENT OF COMMERCE – U.S. CENSUS BUREAU – Economics and Statistics Administration – BUREAU OF EXPORT ADMINISTRATION

FORM 7525-V (7-25-2000)   **SHIPPER'S EXPORT DECLARATION**   OMB No. 0607-0152

1a. U.S. PRINCIPAL PARTY IN INTEREST (USPPI) (Complete name and address)

ZIP CODE | **2.** DATE OF EXPORTAION | **3.** TRANSPORTATION REFERENCE NO.

b. USPII EIN (IRS) OR ID NO. | **c.** PARTIES TO TRANSACTION

___Related   ___Non-related

4a. ULTIMATE CONSIGNEE (Complete name and address)

b. INTERMEDIATE CONSIGNEE (Complete name and address)

5. FORWARDING AGENT (Complete name and address)

6. POINT (STATE) OF ORIGIN OR FTZ NO. | **7.** COUNTRY OF ULTIMATE DESTINATION

8. LOADING PIER (Vessel only) | **9.** METHOD OF TRANSPORTATION (Specify) | **14.** CARRIER IDENTIFICATION CODE | **15.** SHIPMENT REFERENCE NO.

10. EXPORTING CARRIER | **11.** PORT OF EXPORT | **16.** ENTRY NUMBER | **17.** HAZARDOUS MATERIALS

_____YES   _____NO

12. PORT OF UNLOADING (Vessel and air only) | **13.** CONTAINERIZED (Vessel only)

_____YES   _____NO | **18.** IN BOND CODE | **19.** ROUTED EXPORT TRANSACTION

_____YES   _____NO

20. SCHEDULE B DESCRIPTION OF COMMODITIES (Use columns 22–24)

D?F or M (21)	SCHEDULE B NUMBER (22)	QUANTITY – SCHEDULE B UNIT(S) (23)	SHIPPING WEIGHT (Kilograms) (24)	VIN/PRODUCT NUMBER/ VEHICLE TITLE NUMBER (25)	VALUE (U.S. dollars, omit cents) (Selling price of cost if not sold) (26)

27. LICENSE NO./LICENSE EXCEPTION SYMBOL/AUTHORIZATION | **28.** ECCN (When required)

29. Duly authorized | The USPPI authorizes the forwarder named above to act as forwarding agent for export control and customs purposes.

30. I certify that all statement made and all information contained herein are true and correct and that I have read and understand the instructions for preparation of this document, set forth in the **"CORRECT WAY TO FILL OUT THE SHIPPER'S EXPORT DECLARATION."** I understand that civil and criminal penalties, including forfeiture and sale, may be imposed for making false or fraudulent statements herein, failing to provide the requested information or for violation of U.S. laws on exportation (13 U.S.C. Sec. 305; 22 U.S.C. Sec. 401; 18 U.S.C. Sec. 1001; 50 U.S.C. App. 2410)

Signature | **Confidential –** For use solely for official purposes authorized by the Secretary of Commerce (13 U.S.C. 301(g)).

Title | Export shipments are subject to inspection by U.S. Customs Service and/or Office of Export Enforcement.

Date | **31.** AUTHENTICATION (When required)

Telephone No. (Include Area Code) | E-mail address

This form may be printed by private parties provided it conforms to the official form. For sale by the Superintendent of Documents, Government Pricing Office, Washington, DC 20402, and local Customs District Directors. The **"Correct Way to Fill Out the Shipper's Export Declaration"** is available from the U.S. Census Bureau, Washington, DC 20233.

Figure 9-2
The U.S. Shipper's Export Declaration

The Missing Money

In a fairly old *Fortune* article, Vivian Browstein reported that some economists added up all the world's trade and payments accounts—a sum that essentially should have been zero because one country's exports are another's imports—and found $100 billion (1982) "missing."[21] In 1999, the situation had improved, but the discrepancy still amounted to $80 billion.[22]

Some illegal trades (drugs, for example) were obviously not accounted for in this computation and could account for some of the deficit; however, these trades are just as unlikely to be counted as an export as they are to be counted as an import. In other words, these hidden trades do not influence that global "deficit."

Other likely reasons for the discrepancy between the sum-total of the exports and the sum-total of the imports include the fact that exports are usually based on FOB or FCA value and that imports are generally evaluated on CIF or CIP. On occasion, exporting companies also misrepresent the value of the exported goods on their invoice, in order to give their customer a savings on duty and tariffs,[23] thereby underreporting the exporting country's exports.

Nevertheless, the main reason for such a discrepancy resides in the difference between the extreme care with which countries keep records of imports (through their Customs service) and how poorly they seem to keep track of exports. For example, a country is quite likely to keep an excellent record of how many students are studying abroad, because it monitors foreign currency cash outflows, but the country in which these students are registered does not have a formal way of counting them, even though the education "sold" to these students is rightfully an "export" and should be counted as such. Companies dealing in small packages also are generally exempt from export reporting requirements, but these shipments are still counted as imports and may account for a substantial proportion of this discrepancy. Amazon.com is suspected of shipping millions of dollars worth of books abroad, none of which appear on the United States' export statistics.[24]

A cursory analysis of this data shows that most countries underestimate their exports by between 3 and 10 percent, which would indicate that a balance of payment is in deficit only if exports represent significantly less than 95 percent of imports, a rule of thumb that is prevalent in some European countries (see Figure 9-3[25]).

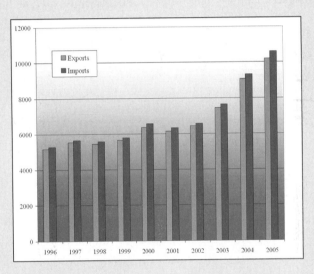

Figure 9-3
World Total Exports and World Total Imports

Several other recent changes in the Shipper's Export Declaration include the definition of the "exporter" it uses. Because errors in classifications can sometimes be attributable to a lack of understanding of the products being shipped, the exporter of record—now called euphemistically "U.S. principal party in interest"—is now always the manufacturer of the goods, even on an EXW shipment, where the exporter is actually the importer, or, more accurately, its agent in the United States. With this move, the Census Bureau has effectively increased the responsibility of the seller to provide accurate and timely information to the importer's agent, who is still responsible for filling and filing the Shipper's Export Declaration. Both of these policy changes are likely to increase the reliability of the export statistics of the United States.

9-3d Certificates of End-Use

In some cases, and in particular for shipments of military equipment, an importer will be required to provide the exporter with a **Certificate of End-Use**, or a document that certifies that the product is going to be used for a legitimate purpose—such as military training—and that the product will not be diverted to another, less

Certificate of End-Use
A document required by some export governments in the case of sensitive exports, such as ammunition, to ensure that the product is used for acceptable (to the exporting country's government) purposes.

acceptable task—such as police ammunition against a civil unrest. Most of these certificates are provided by the governments of the importing country.

9-3e Export Taxes

Several countries require exporters to pay an export tax on certain commodities. While this appears at first sight to be quite counterproductive—discouraging exports prevents a country from earning foreign currency with which it could import other products, and is likely to affect negatively its balance of trade—it can make sense in the case where the goods are minerals in short supply, or when the product has been heavily subsidized by the government. This was the case for the European Union, when it decided to tax the export of wheat in 1996.[26]

9-3f Export Quotas

export quota A limit, set by the exporting country's government, on the quantity of a specific commodity that can be exported in a given year.

In the same spirit, several countries have **export quotas**, which physically limit the amount of a certain category of goods that can be exported from the country. This strategy can be followed in an attempt to control scarce resources, but it also is used to attempt to control the prices of a commodity for which the country has a monopoly. Such is the case with Russia, which imposes strict export quotas on platinum (22 tons), palladium (100 tons), rhodium (2 tons), and ruthenium (1 ton), commodities for which it is one of the very few world suppliers.[27]

9-4 Import Documents

A very large number of documents are required by countries in which goods are imported. There are several reasons for these requirements. These documents:

- ensure that no shoddy quality goods are imported
- help determine the appropriate tariff classification
- help determine the correct value of imported goods
- protect importers from fraudulent exporters
- limit (or eliminate) imports of products that the government finds inappropriate for whatever reason

However, there is also the possibility that the country is trying—not so subtly—to hinder imports and therefore adopt a protectionist stance. In India, for example, it takes an average of twenty-four days to clear Customs at the Delhi airport, and shipments into Bombay require fifty-four documents before clearance is given.[28]

9-4a Certificate of Origin

Certificate of Origin A document provided by the exporter's Chamber of Commerce that attests that the goods originated from the country in which the exporter is located.

The most common type of required document is a **Certificate of Origin**, which the exporter must have signed by its Chamber of Commerce (see Figure 9-4). It is a statement that the goods *originated* from a particular country; it is important to note that the Certificate of Origin does not attest to the location where the product was manufactured, but only that the goods were shipped from a specific locale. This situation sometimes leads to abuses (fraud), in which merchandise is shipped from a different country than the one in which it was manufactured, often to avoid numerical quotas or higher tariffs. In order to prevent these practices, the Certificate of Manufacture was instituted (see Section 9-4b).

The Certificate of Origin is often used by importing countries to determine the tariff applied to the goods, as most countries apply a multi-column tariff system—

Certificate of Origin

The undersigned _____ Robert E. Ebert _____
(Owner or Agent)

for _____ Ebert Pipe Organs, Inc. _____ **declares**
(Shipper's Name and Address)

the following listed goods shipped on _____ Trans-Air _____
(Name of Carrier)

on ____ July 25, 2006 ____ **consigned to** ____ Australian Importers, ____
(Shipment Date)

Brunswick, Australia _____ **are the products of the United States of America.**

Marks and Numbers	No. of Pkgs Boxes or Cases	Weight in Kilos Full		Description of Item
		Gross	Net	
095673	3	195	173	Pipe Organ Blowers

State of _____ Ohio _____

Country of _____ United States of America _____

Sworn to me _____ Ronald Ehresman _____

This __25th__ **day of** ____ July ____ **2006** _____
(Signature of Owner or Agent)

The Greater Cleveland Partnership, a recognized Chamber of Commerce under the laws of the State of Ohio, has examined the manufacturer's invoice or shipper's affidavit concerning the origin of the merchandise and, according to the best of its knowledge and belief, finds the products named originated in the United States of America.

Secretary_____

Figure 9-4
A U.S. Certificate of Origin
Source: Courtesy of Jamie Serenko.

different groups of countries pay different tariffs (see Chapter 15)—and to compile trade statistics. As in the case of commercial invoices, some countries require a specialized Certificate of Origin; for example, there is a specific NAFTA Certificate of Origin (see Figure 9-5).

In most countries, more than one original copy of the Certificate of Origin must be provided; in the countries that were formerly part of the Soviet Union, three copies are required, but, in addition, all of these copies must be notarized—embossed—and signed.[29]

9-4b Certificate of Manufacture

A **Certificate of Manufacture** is quite similar to a Certificate of Origin, except that it attests to the location of manufacture of the exporting products. The

Certificate of Manufacture
A document provided by the exporter's Chamber of Commerce that attests that the goods were manufactured in the country in which the exporter is located.

Figure 9-5
A NAFTA Certificate of Origin, U.S. Version

Certificate of Manufacture must also be signed by the Chamber of Commerce of the exporter.

9-4c Certificate of Inspection

Certificate of Inspection
A document provided by an independent inspection company that attests that the goods conform to the description contained in the invoice provided by the exporter.

In some cases, an importer will request a **Certificate of Inspection**, which is a document signed by an independent company—a third party—which attests to the authenticity and accuracy of the shipment. The company determines that the product being shipped is actually the product shown on the invoice, that the quantity shipped is actually the one for which the importer is invoiced, that the product is in the same condition as the importer expects (new rather than used, for example), and so forth (see Figure 9-6).

CSI

Control Services, Inc.

Certificate of Inspection

1234 Broadway Avenue
New York, N.Y. 10004
Tel: (212) 555-4500
Fax: (212) 555-4501

July 29, 2006

MATEXIM COMPANY
HOANG QUOC VIET STR.,CAU GIAY DIST.,
HA NOI CITY, VIETNAM

REFERENCE: invoice 987654

INSPECTION, TESTWEIGHING AND SAMPLING CARRIED OUT AT:

Warehouse No. 1, City Docks, Hai Phong City, Vietnam

ON: July 23, 2006

ON A SHIPMENT OF:

30,000 cartons of roasted peanuts marked "Roasted Peanuts with coconut oil", each carton containing 50 cellophane packages of 500g each.

PACKING: In cellophane bags and corrugated cardboard cartons in good condition, loaded on plastic pallets, in 30 containers. All containers clean and dry.

WEIGHT: Testweighing of 600 cartons (or 2%), selected at random, and test taring of 5 empty cartons indicated:

Average per carton	26 kg gross
	1 kg tare
	25 kg net

On this basis 30,000 cartons would weigh:

780.000 kg gross
30.000 kg tare
750.000 kg net

SAMPLING & ANALYSIS: Representative sampling of 600 cartons (or 2%) selected at random yielded 10 kilos, a composite of which was analyzed by our Laboratory with these results, which meet contract specifications:

(18% Moisture Basis)
Protein   27.84%
Ash   0.46%
Moisture   16.30%

LOADING: Shipment loaded aboard MV "Shining Star," in 30 containers, Lower Hold and Tweendeck No. 1, July 23, 2006 under our supervision.

ALL INSPECTIONS ARE CARRIED OUT TO THE BEST OF OUR KNOWLEDGE AND ABILITY
AND OUR RESPONSIBILITY IS LIMITED TO THE EXERCISE OF REASONABLE CARE

Figure 9-6
A Certificate of Inspection

Source: Courtesy of Jamie Serenko.

A Certificate of Inspection is useful to the importer in several situations; for example, in a purchase conducted on the basis of Documentary Collection, or with a Letter of Credit, the documents are the only items that the bank will inspect before making payment on behalf of the importer, or before committing the importer to pay (see Chapter 7). There is no possible way of withdrawing payment if there is a problem with the merchandise, and often no way to inspect the merchandise without first taking delivery. A Certificate of Inspection provides evidence that there are no problems with the merchandise.

TABLE 9-1	Countries for Which PSIs Are Mandatory

Angola	Liberia
Bangladesh	Madagascar
Benin	Malawi
Burkina Faso	Mali (under review as of 06/2006)
Burundi	Mauritania
Cambodia	Mexico (a few non-NAFTA products)
Cameroon	Moldova (under review as of 06/2006)
Central African Republic	Mozambique
Comoros	Niger
Republic of Congo	Nigeria
Democratic Republic of Congo	Peru
Cote d'Ivoire	Rwanda
Ecuador	Saudi Arabia (a few products)
Ethiopia	Senegal
Guinea	Sierra Leone
India (steel products)	Togo
Indonesia (steel and waste products)	Uzbekistan
Iran	Venezuela
Kenya (under review as of 06/2006)	Zanzibar
Kuwait (a few products)	

Pre-Shipment Inspection (PSI) An inspection conducted by an independent inspection company before the goods are shipped internationally. A Pre-Shipment Inspection generates a Certificate of Inspection.

There are several companies that provide what is referred to as **Pre-Shipment Inspection (PSI)** services (see Table 9-1[30]), and the largest—with an estimated 60 to 70 percent of the world's business—is the firm *Société Générale de Surveillance* (SGS) from Switzerland.[31] In some cases, the SGS has an agreement with a country that all shipments made to that country must have a Certificate of Inspection signed by SGS (this is the case, for example, for Indonesia).

PSIs are often considered by exporters as a major hindrance, because inspection companies delve into information that exporters feel should not be divulged to a third party. In addition, because the inspection companies have the responsibility to make sure that the shipment is valued correctly, they can—and sometimes do—recommend a change in the value of the merchandise on the invoice. This generally infuriates sellers, justifiably, especially when they feel that the inspection company inflates the value of the goods to increase tariff revenues in the importing country.[32] Nevertheless, the inspection companies provide a valuable service to the importer; had Daewoo used their services, it would have discovered that its Chinese supplier shipped fifteen containers of cement blocks rather than the expected plastic videocassette holders. Because the shipment was made on a Letter of Credit and because the documents were in perfect order, Daewoo had to pay for the shipment.[33]

9-4d Certificate of Certification

A number of countries have industrial standards that define quite clearly the technical characteristics that a part or product must possess before being allowed for sale in that country. For example, Germany has the *Deutsche Industrie Normen* (DIN), Japan has the *Japanese Industrial Standards* (JIS), and France has the *Normes Françaises* (NF). The United States has several of its own as well, such as the *American National Standards Institute* (ANSI).

An importer may require a Certificate of Certification in order to ascertain that the product purchased meets the requirements of the standard, and that the product can "pass" whatever certification procedures are required by the standard. In some countries, this certificate is called a **Certificate of Conformity**.

Although there are no well-defined procedures for a **Certificate of Certification**, it is often assumed that it is written by an independent company or by a trade association's representative. However, there are some cases in which the exporter writes and signs the certificate and has it countersigned by its Chamber of Commerce, in a way similar to the manner a Certificate of Origin is obtained.

9-4e Phyto-Sanitary Certificate

In the cases of transactions involving agricultural products and foodstuffs, the importing country often requires a **Phyto-Sanitary Certificate** along with the paperwork (see Figure 9-7). Such a certificate is used to ensure that the product being shipped is free of (certain) diseases, that it is fit for human (or animal) consumption, that it is free of pests, and so forth.

This certificate is often written by the governmental agency in charge of Agricultural and Food Services in the exporting country (such as the United States' Department of Agriculture or the Food and Drug Administration), but it also can be obtained from a commercial third party.

9-4f Certificate of Analysis

A **Certificate of Analysis** is a document attesting to the composition of certain products; for example, it is used to determine the purity of certain chemicals (for example, the exact percentage of alcohol in a "pure alcohol" shipment, which always has some amount of water) or the exact composition of certain mixtures (cement, steel alloys, plastic polymers).

A Certificate of Analysis is usually provided by an independent laboratory or another independent inspection company, such as SGS.

9-4g Certificate of Free Sale

A **Certificate of Free Sale** attests that the product sold by the exporter can be sold legally in the country of export. Such a certificate is usually written and signed by the exporter and is countersigned by the local chamber of commerce or the regulatory agency that is responsible for this type of product. In the United States, that could be the U.S. Department of Agriculture or the Food and Drug Administration.

A government or an importer concerned that the exporter might attempt to send some "defective" or "second-rate" products that it could not sell in its home country might require a certificate of free sale to protect itself from this possibility. Neither the importing government nor the importer wants to be perceived as possible dumping grounds for products that are not legally sellable in the exporting country. This is a common fear if the requirements of the importing country are in some way less stringent than the ones of the exporting country.

This type of certificate has become relatively common in pharmaceutical imports. Because of stringent regulations, medical supplies have a relatively short shelf life in most developed countries and some pharmaceutical firms sell or donate expired or soon-to-expire drugs to relief agencies in order to generate tax write-offs and generate goodwill.[34] While some may perceive this behavior as unethical, the companies argue that most drugs are equally useful beyond their artificially determined expiration dates. Nevertheless, the governments of countries where

Certificate of Conformity
Another term for a Certificate of Certification.

Certificate of Certification
A document provided by an independent inspection company that attests that the goods conform to the manufacturing standards of the importing country.

Phyto-Sanitary Certificate
A document provided by an independent inspection company, or by the Agricultural Department of the exporting country's government, that attests that the goods conform to the agricultural standards of the importing country.

Certificate of Analysis
A document provided by an independent inspection company that attests that the goods conform to the chemical description and purity levels contained in the invoice provided by the exporter.

Certificate of Free Sale
A certificate that attests that the product that is exported conforms to all of the regulations in place in the exporting country and that it can be sold freely in the exporting country.

Figure 9-7
A Phyto-Sanitary Certificate

Source: Courtesy of Jeff Halaparda.

these products are sold are requiring Certificates of Free Sale with increasing frequency.

In commercial transactions, a possible example of the use of a Certificate of Free Sale would have been when Coca-Cola introduced its Dasani purified water in the United Kingdom. By adding calcium to its purified water, the company also inadvertently added bromates, at a level that exceeded the standards of the United Kingdom, but not those of the remainder of the European Union and of the United

States.[35] A concerned importer may have wanted to get a Certificate of Free Sale to make sure that it was not sold these "sub-standard" products.

9-4h Import License

Some countries, notably developing countries, will require the importer to obtain an **import license**, or an express authorization to import a given product or commodity. Often, this requirement is instituted to prevent the import of items considered luxurious or nonessential, especially in countries in which there is a short supply of foreign currency, which the government would rather spend on imports that enhance the country's economic position.

import license The express authorization, granted by the government of the importing country, to import a particular product in a given quantity.

The process by which an importer obtains an import license varies from country to country, but it is often assumed that it is the responsibility of the importer. In that regard, the importer will probably need a *pro-forma* invoice before requesting an import license.

9-4i Consular Invoice

In some cases, an importing country can require the exporter to provide a Consular invoice. A Consular invoice is a regular commercial invoice, but printed on stationery provided by the country of import and *visa*-ed by its Consulate in the exporter's country. For more details, please see Section 9-2.

9-4j Certificate of Insurance

Depending on the Terms of Trade of a specific shipment—and particularly on whether contracting insurance for the shipment is the responsibility of the exporter or of the importer, a responsibility determined by the Incoterm chosen—the importer or the importing country can require a **Certificate of Insurance** with the shipment. This certificate is easily obtainable from the insurance company that insures the cargo. For further details on the content of insurance policies in international shipments, please see Section 10-7.

Certificate of Insurance A document provided by the insurance company of the exporter that attests that the goods are insured during their international voyage.

9-5 Transportation Documents

9-5a Bill of Lading

A **bill of lading** is a fundamental international shipping document used in ocean transportation: It is also referred to as the **ocean bill of lading**; its (almost) equivalent for shipments by air is called the **air waybill** (see Section 9-5d). A bill of lading (see Figure 9-8) is the contract of carriage used for the shipment of containers, automobiles, crates, and any form of cargo that does not requisition the capacity of the entire ship; when a shipment requires the use of the entire capacity of a ship—generally a bulk shipment of oil or other commodities, another document, called a "charter party" is used (see Section 9-5i).

bill of lading A generic term used to describe the contract of carriage issued by the carrier to the shipper.

ocean bill of lading A bill of lading used in international transportation of goods on oceangoing vessels.

The bill of lading is extremely important because it fulfills three roles in an international transaction:

1. *It is a Contract.* The shipping company agrees with the **shipper**—either the exporter or the importer, depending on the Terms of Trade (or Incoterms), see Chapter 6—to transport the merchandise from one port to another for a given amount of money; it is a contract of carriage.

2. *It is a Receipt for the Goods.* When the shipping company signs the bill of lading, it is acknowledging that it has received the goods in good condition and

air waybill A bill of lading used in the transportation of goods by air, domestically or internationally.

shipper The party to an international transaction that is responsible for arranging the transportation of the goods.

Shipper MATEXIM COMPANY HOANG QUOC VIET STR., CAU GIAY DIST., HA NOI CITY, VIETNAM	Document No. VN/ 02459	Bill of Lading No. **SHINING LINES** VN 919242
	Export references Shipper's Ref. 987654	
Consignee (not negotiable unless consigned to order) OOO "KORVET TEKHKOR" LIT. A 10 BLDG, GONCHARNAYA STR. 193036 SAINT PETERSBURG RUSSIAN FEDERATION	Forwarding agent - references (complete names and addresses) Shining Ocean Lines 345 Strumond Street Hong Kong	
Notify party (see Clause 19) OOO "KORVET TEKHKOR" LIT. A 10 BLDG, GONCHARNAYA STR. 193036 SAINT PETERSBURG RUSSIAN FEDERATION	Unless marked "NON NEGOTIABLE/EXPRESS BILL", one original BILL of Lading must be surrendered endorsed in exchange in for the goods or delivery order. For the release of goods apply to: Shining Ocean Lines Warehouse Complex No. 3 Port of Saint Petersburg 193036 Saint Petersburg Russian Federation Tel. : 00132 628990 Fax : 00132 628991	

Pre-carriage by	Place of receipt by pre-carrier Hai Phong Vietnam	
Vessel/Voy. No. V.90 MV Shining Star	Port of loading Hai Phong	On carriage to
Port of discharge Saint Petersburg	Place of delivery by on-carrier Saint Petersburg	

Marks and Numbers	**Number of Container(s) or pkgs**	**Kind of packages - description of goods**	**Gross weight (kilos)**	**Measurement (cubic metres)**
See attached list	30	Containers	26,000 net each 27,000 gross 810,000 total	72.5 each 2175 total

Total number of Container(s) or Pkgs 30	Freight payable by Origin	**Excess Value Declaration: Refer to Clause 13 and 14 on reverse side.** N/A		

Freight and charges		Quantity based on	Rate	Per	Prepaid	Collect
USD 25,500 Stevedoring		30	850	Cont.	X	
USD 6,000 Document Prep.		30	200	Cont.	X	
USD 350 Storage Fees						
USD 2,000						
TOTAL: USD 33,850						

RECEIVED by the carrier from the shipper in apparent good order and condition (unless otherwise noted herein) the total number or quantity of containers or other packages or units indicated stated by the shipper to comprise the goods specified for carriage subject to all the terms hereof (INCLUDING THE TERMS ON PAGE 1 HEREOF AND THE TERMS OF THE CARRIER'S APPLICATION TARIFF) from the place of receipt or the port of loading, whichever is applicable to the port of discharge or the place of the delivery, whichever is applicable. In accepting the Bill of Lading the merchant expressly accepts and agrees to all its terms, conditions and exceptions whether printed, stamped or written, or otherwise incorporated, notwithstanding the non-signing of this Bill of Lading by the merchant	IN WITNESS whereof the number of the original Bills of Lading stated below all of this tenor and date has been signed, one of which being accomplished, the other(s) to stand void. Number of original B(S)/L These commodities, technology or software were exported from the U.S in Accordance with the Export Administration Regulations. Diversion contrary to U.S. law Prohibited.	Place of B(S)/L issue DATE Cleveland 06/30/07 **SHINING OCEAN SERVICES** As Agents for the Carrier **SHINING OCEAN LINES** COPY Not Negotiable

Figure 9-8
A Bill of Lading

Source: Courtesy of Jeff Halaparda.

that everything seems in proper order. The document acts as a receipt for the goods; the shipping company accepts responsibility for the goods until their port of destination. However, in some cases, the shipping company finds that something is "wrong" with the merchandise it is picking up (for example, the drums in which the merchandise is contained are rusty, or there are some damaged crates, or the merchandise was loaded when it was raining, or the merchandise was packaged in crates that are too weak to sustain an ocean voyage) and it does not want to assume responsibility for that condition. In those cases, the shipping company will make a note about the issue or write an exception on the bill of lading of what it has observed. The bill of lading then becomes a **soiled bill of lading** or a **foul bill of lading**. In the opposite situation (i.e., when the shipping company finds everything in proper order at the time of loading and does not record any reservations at the receipt of the goods), the bill of lading is considered clean. In general, Letters of Credit and Documentary Collection transactions require a **clean bill of lading;** should the bill of lading be soiled, it would require an amendment to the Letter of Credit. Carriers may not accept goods for transportation if loading them would result in a soiled bill of lading.

3. *It is a Certificate of Title.* The document that the shipping company will need to see to authorize the release of the goods in the port of destination will also be the bill of lading. It is commonly considered that the company who has the *original* of the bill of lading is the one to which the goods belong, or that the bill of lading is a Certificate of Title.[36] There are two types of bills of lading in this respect; the **straight bill of lading** is one on which the name of the **consignee** (the person or company who will pick up the goods at the port of destination) is specified. The **to order bill of lading** is one in which the name of the consignee is left blank or the term "to order" is written. This means that the bill of lading is **negotiable**; in other words, it allows the sale of the cargo while it is at sea. This is a common occurrence in certain industries, notably in the oil business, in which it is not unusual to see a specific cargo change hands several times during a given voyage. In some cases, the cargo is sold to a company that wants the cargo delivered in a different port, and the shipping company is asked to arrange for that alternative.

9-5b Uniform Bill of Lading

The **uniform bill of lading** is a document that fulfills the same functions as an ocean bill of lading, but is used either for inland transportation between the exporter's place of business and the port of departure, or for land transportation (rail or road) between the exporter and a foreign customer. In the immense majority of cases, the uniform bill of lading is a straight bill of lading. The uniform bill of lading also acts as a receipt for the goods and as a contract between the shipper and the carrier.

9-5c Intermodal Bill of Lading

The **intermodal bill of lading** is a fairly recent document that has emerged because of the substantial increase in the number of international shipments in which the exporter delivers the goods to a **carrier** who will arrange for the transportation and delivery of the shipment until its final destination. Because the shipment is likely to take more than one mode of transportation, it is called an "**intermodal shipment**." Intermodal bills of lading, therefore, cover several legs of an international shipment. They are straight bills of lading in the majority of cases. Intermodal bills of lading are also receipts for the goods and evidence of a contract of carriage between the shipper and the carrier.

9-5d Air Waybill

An air waybill is a document that fulfills the same function as an ocean bill of lading, but applies only to airfreight. An air waybill is always a straight air waybill and is therefore non-negotiable (see Figure 9-9). This can be easily understood because, in most cases, the documents and the merchandise arrive approximately at the same time in the country of destination and there is literally no time to sell the cargo while it is in shipment. As the other bills of lading, it is also a receipt for the goods and a contract between the shipper and the air carrier.

soiled bill of lading A bill of lading that reflects the fact that the carrier received the goods in anything other than good condition.

foul bill of lading Another term for a *soiled bill of lading,* which is a bill of lading reflecting the fact that the carrier received the goods in anything other than good condition.

clean bill of lading A bill of lading that reflects the fact that the carrier received the goods in good condition.

straight bill of lading A bill of lading on which the name of the consignee has been entered.

consignee The party named on a bill of lading as the owner of the goods, or, at least, as the party to whom the goods should be surrendered at their destination.

to order bill of lading A bill of lading on which the name of the consignee has been left blank, or where the words "to order" have been entered.

negotiable bill of lading A bill of lading on which the name of the consignee has been left blank, or where the words "to order" have been entered.

uniform bill of lading A bill of lading used in the transportation of goods on trucks and trains, either domestically or internationally.

intermodal bill of lading A bill of lading used in the intermodal transportation, domestic or international, of goods.

carrier The transportation company that will provide transportation services to the shipper.

intermodal shipment An international shipment that will use several means of transportation under a single bill of lading.

Doc No.	Destination Airport Code MEL (Melbourne)	Flight 5698	Date 2006-07-24	**AIR WAYBILL** NON-NEGOTIABLE

Consignee Account No. MEL 341	Consignee Order No.		**TRANS-AIR, INC.**

Consignee Name and Address Australian Importers 4/2 Wilson Avenue Brunswick, Victoria 3089, Australia	Carrier / Agent TRANS-AIR, Inc., Cleveland
	The shipper certifies that the particulars on the face hereof are correct, agrees to the Conditions on Reverse hereof, accepts that carrier's liability is limited as stated, and accepts such value unless a higher value for carriage is declared.

Shipper Account No.	Shipper's Reference No. 072306-001	

Shipper Name and Address Ebert Pipe Organs, Inc. 1234 Carnegie Avenue Cleveland, OH 44111, USA	These commodities, technologies or software were exported from the United States in accordance with the Export Administration regulations. Diversion contrary to U.S. Law prohibited.

No of pieces or packages	Dimensions			Weight		Carrier certifies goods described herein were received for carriage subject to the conditions on the reverse thereof, the goods then being in apparent good order and condition except as noted hereon.
	Length	Width	Height	lbs	kg	Quantity, Description and Marks
3	1.2 m	0.6 m	0.4 m	429.00	195.00	Pipe organ blowers (3) Boxes marked "Ebert Pipe Organs, Inc" FRAGILE Each crate sealed with seals No: 158062, 158063 and 158064.

Total Pieces 3	Cubic Content 86,400 cm³	Total Dimensional Weight 14.4 kg	
	Shipper's Declared Value USD 2,925.00	Total Gross Weight 195.00 kg	

Total Freight Charge USD 585.00		Chargeable Weight 195	Commodity No. 8414	Rate 3/kg	Air Carriage To MEL Qantas To LAX United

Inbound Freight Advance	

Origin Handling Fees USD 57.00	Detail of all origin and handling fees
	FSH USD 22.80 SSF USD 43.20

USD 128.70	Shipper's Requested Insurance Fee	Amount USD 3,217.50	Rate USD 0.04	If the shipper has requested insurance as provided for, shipment is insured in the amount specified by the shipper, recovery being limited to actual loss.

USD 30.00	Pickup Charge	Remit to: TRANS-AIR, Inc. 3450 United Avenue St Louis, MO 63011
USD 800.70	TOTAL DUE CARRIER	
		Carrier's Air Waybill No. CLE 23012003-0007

1. SHIPPER (ORIGINAL). THIS COPY FOR YOUR FILES. THIS IS NOT AN INVOICE.

Figure 9-9
An Air Waybill

9-5e Charter Parties

Whenever it is shipping bulk commodities (oil, ores, grains, polymers, sand, cement, sugar, and so on), an exporter does so in such large quantities that an entire ship is often necessary to accommodate the goods. In those cases, the ocean bill of lading is not the document used as the contract of carriage; the contract between the carrier and the shipper is called a **charter party**.

Charter parties are fairly complex, as they can be negotiated for a single shipment (a voyage charter party) or for a period of time (a time charter party); charter parties that cover more than one voyage but do not demand the exclusive use of the ship for a specific period of time (for example, one shipment every other month) are called contracts of affreightment. Moreover, some shippers negotiate charter parties that only include the use of the ship, exclusive of the boat's crew, as

charter party A type of contract of carriage between a carrier and a shipper, in which the shipper uses all or most of the carrying capacity of the ship to transport commodities.

the shipper provides the captain and the crew (a bareboat charter party). Finally, because there are different requirements for different commodities, most charter parties are industry specific (oil, grain, gas, and so forth).

Similarly, the owner of a freight aircraft can lease its equipment under three types of charter agreements, whether for a single voyage or for a duration of time. A **wet lease** agreement is one under which the owner of the aircraft provides the airplane, insurance, maintenance services, and a flight crew to the lessor, who has to cover all of the other variable costs: fuel and airport fees, for example. A **dry lease** is one under which the owner only provides the aircraft, and the lessor has to secure a crew, insurance, and has to provide maintenance. A **damp lease** is yet another type of agreement under which the owner provides fewer services than in a wet lease, but more than in a dry lease. For example, a damp lease could include the aircraft, maintenance, and insurance, but not the crew, which would need to be hired by the lessee.

9-5f Packing List

A **packing list** always accompanies the shipment. It is a detailed document provided by the exporter that spells out how many containers there are in the shipment and which merchandise is packaged in each container. Because of the recent emphasis placed by the International Maritime Organization and world governments on security, packing lists have become more precise; while at one time it was acceptable to mention "freight all kinds," often abbreviated FAK, it is now necessary to clearly list all items in a shipment, in as detailed a manner as possible. Whenever authorities determine that a shipment presents some risks and should be inspected, a detailed packing list can prevent the inspection and avoid further delays. Some shippers combine the packing list and the invoice in one document, providing such level of detail on the invoice that it can substitute as a packing list. Such is the case with one of the largest industrial fair organizers in the world, the Bremen Messe (see Figure 9-10).[37]

9-5g Shipper's Letter of Instruction

A **Shipper's Letter of Instruction** is delivered to the shipping company when the shipper—again, either the exporter or the importer, depending on the Terms of Trade or Incoterms—wants specific steps taken during the transport of the merchandise. For example, the shipper may request that the cargo be stowed below deck (if there's a problem if the cargo became wet), or stowed at the "water line" (i.e., the location in the ship that experiences the least movement), or even above deck (if the cargo is dangerous). When the cargo is livestock, the Shipper's Letter of Instruction explains what to do in most situations.

9-5h Shipments of Dangerous Goods

International shipments of dangerous goods are regulated by either the International Maritime Organization's *International Maritime Dangerous Goods Code*,[38] by the International Air Transport Association's *Dangerous Goods Regulations*,[39] by the International Civil Aviation Organization's *Technical Instructions for the Safe Transport of Dangerous Goods by Air* or by local shipment codes, such as the United States' Code of Federal Regulations, Title 49 (abbreviated 49CFR).[40]

There are such an extensive number of regulations that can affect a shipment of hazardous goods, that it is always best to entrust a specialized shipper to handle the

wet lease An agreement under which the owner of the aircraft provides the airplane, insurance, maintenance services, and a flight crew to the lessor, who has to cover all of the other variable costs: fuel and airport fees, for example.

dry lease A dry lease is an agreement between the owner (lessor) of an aircraft and a lessor, in which the owner provides only the aircraft and no other services.

damp lease A damp lease is an agreement between the owner (lessor) of an aircraft and the lessee, under which the owner provides some services in addition to the aircraft itself.

packing list A detailed list of what is contained in a shipment.

Shipper's Letter of Instruction A document in which the shipper spells out how it wants the carrier to handle the goods while they are in transit.

COMBINED COMMERCIAL INVOICE & PACKING LIST

SENDER:	CONSIGNEE:	EXHIBITION:

TOTAL PIECES: _____ TOTAL WEIGHT (KGS): _____ TOTAL CBM: _____ TOTAL VALUE: _____ CURRENCY: _____

CASE NO	DIMENSIONS L×W×H (IN CMS)	WEIGHT (IN KGS)		DESCRIPTION OF GOODS (IN ENGLISH)	BTN	QTY	CURRENCY:_____		STATUS*			
		GROSS	NET				UNIT VALUE (CIF)	TTL. VALUE (CIF)	A	B	C	D

The invoiced goods are of _____ origin and are intended for display only at the exhibition site. We certify that the information given above is true and correct.

SIGNATURE / DATE: _____ COMPANY STAMP/NAME & TITLE OF SIGNATORY : _____

*__STATUS__   A: RE-EXPORT AFTER EXHIBITION   B: DISPOSED OF / CONSUMED   C: GIVEN AWAY   D: SOLD

PAGE_____ OUT OF _____

Figure 9-10
Combined Commercial Invoice and Packing List
Source: Bremen Messe. Used with permission.

A Whale of a Shipment

The business of shipping live animals is quite substantial: The value of such shipments reached more than $900 million in 2005.[41] It is also the part of international shipping in which the Shipper's Letter of Instruction is critical, as every shipment is somewhat different because every animal has its own requirements regarding temperature, humidity, and its tolerance for shipment delays.

As he related it in a lengthy article,[42] Barry Lopez spent days accompanying airfreight cargo pilots on forty flights, totaling 110,000 nautical miles, to report on this part of international lore. In some legs of his journey, the cargo included Vietnamese potbelly pigs, a killer whale, racehorses, and ostriches. In these situations, the shipper can ask for very specific considerations. Lopez reports that on his flight from Chicago to Tokyo, during which he traveled with sixteen horses, "[t]he pilot made a shallow climb out of Chicago to lessen the strain on the horses' back legs." (It has since become common practice to ship horses facing the rear of the plane to lessen the strain on their necks and front legs.) When the plane hit some turbulence, the pilot changed altitude and a handler went in the cargo hold to soothe the animals.

Shipments of live animals cannot be mixed with shipments of frozen goods kept in dry ice, because dry ice is carbon dioxide and the gas would kill the animals.[43] Cattle require handlers to feed them and clean their stalls, especially on long ocean voyages.[44] However, it is "exotic animals," such as elephants, rhinoceroses, and the like, that place the greatest number of constraints on the shipper, with numerous instructions, including climate control in the airports. Consider that a firm shipping salmon embryos from Alaska to Chile managed to lower its mortality rate by 66 percent by improving the way the airlines handled the fish.[45]

paperwork associated with such a shipment—this statement is also true for the packing and the labeling of the goods. There are often very specific forms to be filled; in the case of an air shipment, a Shipper's Declaration for Dangerous Goods must be provided and a specific mention must be made on the air waybill that the shipment contains dangerous goods. In some cases, the air waybill must also specify that the cargo cannot be shipped on a passenger airplane, but only on a cargo airplane. Similar restrictions must also be observed for ocean, road, and railroad cargos.

The complexity of the rules is such that in an audit conducted by the Canadian Coast Guard in 1995, 66 percent of hazardous shipments inspected were found to have some rule violation: 41 percent did not have the correct markings, 31 percent did not have the correct documentation, 19 percent were incorrectly stowed (secured in the containers or on the ship), and so on.[46]

9-5i Manifest

The **manifest** is a shipping document that is quite dissimilar to the documents seen so far in this chapter. The manifest is a document created by the shipping company (the operator of the ship or the aircraft) that lists the exact makeup of the cargo, its ownership, its port of origin and its port of destination, whether there are specific handling instructions, and so forth. Although officially an internal document of the shipping company, it is often used by public authorities to verify that rules and regulations are respected. The following example may clarify this point.

A number of Middle-Eastern countries—Jordan, Saudi Arabia, United Arab Emirates, Syria, Kuwait, Iraq, Iran, and Libya—engage in what is referred to as the Arab embargo of Israel; no ship that delivers goods to these Arab nations can have stopped (or be planning to stop) in any Israeli port, or have cargo coming from or going to Israel. The manifest is used by authorities in those countries to determine whether the ship or its cargo has had any "unlawful" contact with Israel.[47] American firms dealing in that region are prohibited from honoring this embargo, a situation that makes for complicated arrangements, which both Israel and its neighbors conveniently chose to ignore—business is business, after all.

manifest A document, internal to the shipping company (the carrier), which lists all cargo onboard the transportation vehicle.

Worlds of Paperwork

Invoices:
Commercial,
Pro-Forma,
Consular,
Specialized

Export Documents:
Export Licenses,
Shipper's Export Declaration,
Certificates of End-Use

Electronic Data:
EDI and SWIFT's
Bolero System

Import Documents:
Certificates of Origin,
Manufacture, Inspection,
Certification, Analysis,
Insurance, Import License,
Consular Invoice,
Phyto-Sanitary Certificate

Transportation Documents:
Ocean Bill of Lading,
Uniform Bill of Lading,
Intermodal Bill of Lading,
Air Waybill, Packing List,
Shipper's Letter of Instruction,
Manifest

Figure 9-11
Tons of Paperwork

9-6 Electronic Data Interchange

9-6a Proprietary Commercial Electronic Data Interchange

Electronic Data Interchange (EDI) A method to send documents (invoice, certificates, packing list, and so on) from one company to another, using electronic means.

The alternative way to send documents overseas is through **Electronic Data Interchange (EDI)** rather than by airmail. The best way to define EDI is to determine what it is not: first, it is not a fax, which only transmits a reproduction of a paper document. A fax is essentially a copy machine where the original is in one location and the copy is in another location. Second, EDI is not e-mail (electronic mail). E-mail is only the electronic transmission of text, as in a letter or a memo: There is no need to have a specified format ahead of time.

EDI is an electronic exchange of documents, from computer to computer, following a format to which both the sending and the receiving parties have agreed. There are two areas in which the agreement to a common format is crucial:

- First, the sender and the recipient have to agree to a *technical* EDI understanding; for example, the choice of a computer protocol, the determination of a standard outline—which electronic field corresponds to which information on the document (sender, consignee, product description, purchase order number, invoice number, and so forth)—and the possible use of a third-party intermediary to "translate" one electronic format into another or archive the transmissions between the parties. Such translating service providers are called "Value-Added Networks (VAN)." They also archive whatever transmission takes place between the two parties.

- Currently, there are only a few international agreements on EDI formats; they tend to be company, industry, or country specific. The most likely to prevail internationally is the standard developed by the United Nations' Working Party on the Facilitation of International Trade Procedures of the Committee on Trade of the Economic Commission for Europe (nicknamed WP 4, for short), called the United Nations' Electronic Data Interchange for Administration, Commerce, and Transport (UN-EDIFACT), which has been accepted by a significant number of countries, including the United States. Actually some U.S. firms have adopted EDIFACT for all of their EDI communications with their suppliers. General Motors is one of them.[48]

- The second issue is the existence of a *legal* agreement between the parties; not only the definition of responsibilities (acknowledgement of an EDI transmission, procedure to follow when there is a "garbled" transmission, confidentiality of the data) should be specified, but also the timing of the contract formation, liabilities for errors in the communication, the "evidentiary value" of messages—whether they can be introduced in a Court proceeding—and other legal issues have to be addressed.

To this date, there have been several efforts made to create a universal EDI agreement; the International Chamber of Commerce has a *Uniform Rules of Conduct for Interchange of Trade Data by Teletransmission* (UNCID), and several EDI associations have created their own versions.[49] Nevertheless, there is yet no agreement that has international acceptance and Courts tend to be relying on laws designed for written documents whenever there are problems.

9-6b Network Electronic Data Interchange: SWIFT's Bolero System

Another well-developed EDI system is the one that was developed by the Society for Worldwide Interbank Financial Telecommunication (SWIFT) to facilitate the exchange of banking documents such as Letters of Credit. As banks become members of the SWIFT system, they can exchange secure messages with each other. Because of a large number of safeguards in the network,[50] banks can rely on the data transmitted over the network, and a Letter of Credit transmitted by SWIFT is considered genuine (as good as a paper original). In addition, the SWIFT network adds new services regularly, such as Interbank File Transfers (in free form: database files, graphs, spreadsheets) over a secure network, a requirement that is of paramount importance to the banks. The security and reliability of the network is ascertained by the protocols that the computers in the network must follow. Each login is recorded and must be cleared, messages must first be stored before they are sent, there must be positive confirmation of each message by the recipient, there are redundant links, there is a double backup of each file, and so forth.

Because of the reliability of its system—and its experience in that area—the Society for Worldwide Financial Telecommunication created the Bolero network. Bolero is similar to the SWIFT banking network, but it allows the transmission of all sorts of documents (specifically logistics documents) such as invoices, bills of lading, certificates, and so on; however, Bolero does not support payment through the network. Bolero became active in September 1999.

Such an EDI network is "shared" by several hundreds of customers worldwide, which makes it very different from proprietary EDI systems because communications between member parties are authenticated and there is a common standard. Therefore, both of the issues of proprietary EDI are overcome: It is a much more efficient way of exchanging information.

Bolero is currently competing with TradeCard on many points; Bolero has the distinct advantage that it is supported by a company with which bankers have dealt for a long time and trust. TradeCard has the advantage of offering payment options through its network; time will tell whether both of these systems will remain or whether one will start dominating the business. One thing is certain, though; paper documents are in jeopardy, and they will undoubtedly disappear by 2015.

9-7 Document Preparation as a Marketing Tool

It should be relatively clear by now that accurate and timely documents are an essential part of international logistics and of the smooth transfer of goods from an exporter to an importer:

- The *pro-forma* invoice must be a perfect preview of the actual invoice. Otherwise, payment through the Letter of Credit can be affected—i.e., the actual invoice does not match the requirements of the LOC and both parties have to pay for amendments—or Customs clearance can be delayed because the actual invoice does not match the import license.

- The commercial invoice must be clear, detailed, and precise. It must include all the information (description, Harmonized System number, weight, size, number of packages, domestic transportation costs, insurance costs, stevedoring charges, international transportation costs, and so on) that is necessary for the importer to clear Customs and minimize the duty that it has to pay. It also minimizes the probability of an inspection.

- Certificates of many kinds have to be provided. They have to be properly prepared, signed, and occasionally stamped and notarized to facilitate the goods' Customs clearance in the importing country.

- The correct number of originals and copies of a multitude of documents must be prepared (invoices, certificates, and so on) or collected (bill of lading). A discrepancy in the number of originals can delay Customs clearance until another original is mailed to the importer.

- The packing list must be prepared carefully and precisely. An incomplete or imprecise packing list increases the probability of a Customs inspection.

- The export paperwork must be prepared and filed correctly and in a timely manner. Several countries, including the United States, will not allow goods to be loaded if there are issues with the export paperwork (SED).

Any failure to provide these documents or failure to provide complete and accurate documents in a timely manner is likely to delay a shipment, generate additional costs by requiring last-minute mailings of critical documents or create "headaches" for one or more of the parties involved in the transaction. Unfortunately, problems with documents are common, although they are clearly avoidable in most instances.

Because the responsibility of proper document preparation falls mostly on the exporter, regardless of the Incoterm used in a transaction, an exporter can turn its ability to do a good and thorough job in this aspect of international logistics into a marketing advantage.

An exporter intent on increasing its sales should therefore be thorough and meticulous in the way it prepares the documents that it provides to the importer. This should be reflected in the first contact, the *pro-forma* invoice, and be communicated to the importer by emphasizing the experience of the company at providing accurate and thorough documents.

Key Terms

air waybill (p. 195)

bill of lading (p. 195)

carrier (p. 197)

Certificate of Analysis (p. 193)

Certificate of Certification (p. 193)

Certificate of Conformity (p. 193)

Certificate of End-Use (p. 187)

Certificate of Free Sale (p. 193)

Certificate of Inspection (p. 190)

Certificate of Insurance (p. 195)

Certificate of Manufacture (p. 189)

Certificate of Origin (p. 188)

charter party (p. 198)

clean bill of lading (p. 197)

commercial invoice (p. 179)

Commodity Control List (p. 183)

consignee (p. 197)

consular invoice (p. 181)

damp lease (p. 199)

Destination Control Statement (p. 185)

dry lease (p. 199)

Electronic Data Interchange (EDI) (p. 202)

export quota (p. 188)

foul bill of lading (p. 197)

import license (p. 195)

Individual Validated Export License (p. 185)

intermodal bill of lading (p. 197)

intermodal shipment (p. 197)

manifest (p. 201)

ocean bill of lading (p. 195)

packing list (p. 199)

Phyto-Sanitary Certificate (p. 193)

Pre-Shipment Inspection (PSI) (p. 192)

pro-forma invoice (p. 181)

shipper (p. 195)

Shipper's Export Declaration (p. 182)

Shipper's Letter of Instruction (p. 199)

soiled bill of lading (p. 197)

straight bill of lading (p. 197)

to order bill of lading (p. 197)

uniform bill of lading (p. 197)

visa (p. 182)

wet lease (p. 199)

Review and Discussion Questions

1. There are three types of "invoices" mentioned in this chapter. Explain each one of them and tell which is truly an "invoice" and which is not.

2. Explain why a country could consider having no deficit in its balance of trade even though the value of its exports only represents 98% of the value of its imports.

3. What documents are necessary for exporting from the United States?

4. There are many different types of certificates that can be requested by the importing country or the importer. Describe three of them.

5. A Pre-Shipment Inspection Certificate can be requested by the importing country or by the importer. Why would a country request one? Why would an importer request one?

6. The ocean bill of lading has three general functions: Explain each one in detail and tell what alternative "types" of ocean bills of lading there are.

7. What are the advantages of conducting international trade using electronic document transmissions, such as EDI, Bolero, or TradeCard?

Endnotes

1. Mehta, Ravi R. Singh, "Freak and Faulty L/C's from Third World and Eastern Europe," *The Exporter*, September 1997, pp. 15–17.

2. Scannicchio, Tommaso, "Important Decision of the Italian Supreme Court of Cassazione in the Matter of Electronic Documents," *Electronic Law Journals*, JILT 2002, http://www2.warwick.ac.uk/fac/soc/law/elj/jilt/2002_2/scannicchio/#a3, August 1, 2006.

3. *A Basic Guide to Exporting*, U.S. Department of Commerce, Government Printing Office, Washington, DC 20402.

4. *The UNZ & Co. Sourcebook: A How-to Guide for Exporters and Importers*, Unz & Co., 190 Baldwin Avenue, P.O. Box 308, Jersey City, NJ 07303.

5. "India Fights Pillaging of Art," *Associated Press News Release*, April 9, 1997, published in *The New York Times*, April 9, 1997.

6. Vogel, Carol, "New York: A Thriving Market for Old Masters," *The New York Times*, January 31, 2000.

7. Meier, Barry, "The Costly, Bitter Case of the Coins of Elmali," *The New York Times*, September 24, 1998.

8. Eakin, Hugh and Elizabetta Povoledo, "Ceding Art to Italy, Met Avoids Showdown," *The New York Times*, February 21, 2006.

9. Kirkpatrick, David, "China Seizure Halts Delivery of U.S. Book," *The New York Times*, August 28, 2000.

10. Clayton, Gary E., "Eurocrats Try to Stop Data at Border," *The Wall Street Journal*, November 2, 1998, p. A34.

11. Litman, Gary V., and John M. Breen "Overview of Federal Export Restriction Programs," in *Export Practice: Customs and International Trade Law*, Terence P. Stewart, editor, Practicing Law Institute, New York, New York.

12. *U.S. Export Administration Regulations*, Bureau of Export Administration, Government Printing Office, Washington, DC 20402.

13. Klein, Alec, "The Techies Grumbled, but Polaroid's Pocket Turned into a Huge Hit," *The Wall Street Journal*, May 2, 2000, p. A1.

14. Adams, Susan, "The Code Breakers," *Forbes*, February 26, 1996, p. 100.

15. "Category 5: Telecommunications and 'Information Security,'" Commerce Control List, Supplement No. 1 to Part 774, Bureau of Industry and Security, http://www.access.gpo.gov/bis/ear/pdf/ccl5-pt2.pdf, June 5, 2006.

16. Biederman, David, "Screening Exports for Problems," *JoC Week*, August 7–13, 2000, p. 24. "Introduction to Commerce Department Export Controls," Bureau of Industry and Security, http://www.bis.doc.gov/licensing/exportingbasics.htm, June 5, 2006.

17. "Embargo Reference Chart," Directorate of Defense Trade Controls, U.S. State Department, http://pmdtc.org/country.htm, June 5, 2006.

18. Biederman, David, "Liability for Export Licenses," *JoC Week*, July 24–30, 2000, p. 31.

19. Lelyveld, Michael S., "Electronic Export Filings Triple, Boosting Census," *The Journal of Commerce*, April 20, 1998, p. 6A.

20. Tirschwell, Peter, "The New Cost of Exporting," *JoC Week*, August 14–20, 2000, p. 4.

21. Brownstein, Vivian, "The World's Missing Billions," *Fortune*, August 22, 1983, pp. 154–155.

22. *1999 Annual Report of the IMF Committee on Balance of Payment Statistics*, IMF Committee on Balance of Payment Statistics, International Monetary Fund, 700 19th Street, N.W., Washington, DC 20431, June 2000.

23. Lucentini, Jack, "Company Agrees to Pay $48,000 Fine," *The Journal of Commerce*, September 23, 1999, p. 15.

24. "The Trade Gap May Be Inflated," *Business Week*, July 3, 2000, p. 32.

25. International Financial Statistics, International Monetary Fund, http://www.imf.org/external/pubs/cat/longres.cfm, June 5, 2006.

26. Kilman, Scott, "High Grain Prices Lift Farmers, but Will They Overexpand as Before?" *The Wall Street Journal*, March 21, 1996, p. A1.

27. Helmer, John, "Shipment Delays Blamed on Quotas," *The Journal of Commerce*, January 21, 1998, p. 8A

28. Rao, N. Vasuki, "Indian Customs System Stuck in Miles of Thick, Red Tape," *The Journal of Commerce*, January 7, 1998, p. 4A.

29. Feller, Gordon, "CIS Customs: The Limits of Automation," *Export Today*, October 1996, p. 76.

30. "When Is Pre-Shipment Inspection Required?," http://www.export.gov/logistics/exp_inspections.asp, June 5, 2006.

31. Freudmann, Aviva, "Top Provider Alters Its Approach," *The Journal of Commerce*, April 7, 2000, p. 1.

32. Green, Paula, "U.S. Exporters Slam Inspection Companies," *The Journal of Commerce*, December 31, 1997, p. 1A.

33. Mottley, Robert, "Shippers' Case Law: Consignee, Nvos Clash Over Sealed Shipments," *American Shipper*, April 2000, p. 69.

34. Russell, Timothy E., "The Humanitarian Relief Supply Chain: Analysis of the 2004 South-East Asia Earthquake and Tsunami," Master's of Engineering in Logistics thesis, Massachusetts Institute of Technology, June 2005, http://ctl.mit.edu, August 1, 2006.

35. Jones, Chris, "Coke Admits Defeat in Dasani Rollout," *Food and Drink Europe*, March 26, 2003, http://www.foodanddrinkeurope.com/news/ng.asp?id=50947-coke-admits-defeat. "Dasani UK Delay Cans Europe Sales," BBC News, March 24, 2004, http://news.bbc.co.uk/1/hi/business/3566233.stm.

36. Reynolds, Frank, "Debating the Rights (and Wrongs) of Consignees of Various Bills of Lading," *The Journal of Commerce*, December 24, 1997, p. 2C.

37. Combined Commercial Invoice and Packing List, Bremen Messe, http://www.messe-bremen.de/robocup_pdf/RC_Commercial_invoice.pdf, June 5, 2006.

38. *International Maritime Dangerous Goods Code*, 1994, Consolidated Edition, International Maritime Organization, 4 Albert Embankment, London SE1 7SR, United Kingdom, www.imo.org.

39. *Dangerous Goods Regulations*, 1996, 37th Edition, International Air Transport Association, 33 Route de l'Aéroport, Case Postale 672, CH-1215 Genève 15 Aéroport, Switzerland and 2000 Peel Street, Montréal, Québec, Canada H3A 2R4.

40. *Code of Federal Regulations, Title 49*, 1995, Government Printing Office, Washington, DC 20402.

41. *First Quarter 2006 Newsletter*, Animal Air Transportation Association, http://www.aata-animaltransport.org/publications.htm#AATA%20Newsletters.

42. Lopez, Barry, "On the Wings of Commerce," *Harper's*, October 1995, pp. 39–54.

43. Putzger, Ian, "Live Seafood Takes to the Skies as Northeast Cargo Market Evolves," *The Journal of Commerce*, February 2, 1999, p. 6A.

44. Tower, Courtney, "Canned Cattle," *The Journal of Commerce*, September 2, 1997, p. 1A.

45. Banham, Russ, "Fish Embryos Take to the Sky like Ducks to Water," *The Journal of Commerce*, June 6, 1997, p. 8C.

46. Compton, Mike, "Saying and Doing," *Cargo Systems*, March 1996, pp. 77–78.

47. Lelyveld, Michael S., "Peace Dividend: Easing in Arab Boycott of Israel," *The Journal of Commerce*, February 17, 1997.

48. Zuckerman, Amy, "Edifact Gaining in Acceptance," *The Journal of Commerce*, November 10, 1999, p. 16.

49. Boss, Amelia H., and Jeffrey B. Ritter, *Electronic Data Interchange Agreements*, 1993, International Chamber of Commerce, ICC Publishing, 156 Fifth Avenue, New York, NY 10010.

50. Isobe, Asahiko, Kevin J. Kerney, and Shirley Kearney-Stevens, editors, *Payment Systems: Strategic Choices for the Future*, 1993, Hitachi Research Institute, Institute of Advanced Business Systems Hitachi, Ltd., published by F.I.A. Financial Publishing Co.

International Insurance

Chapter **Ten**

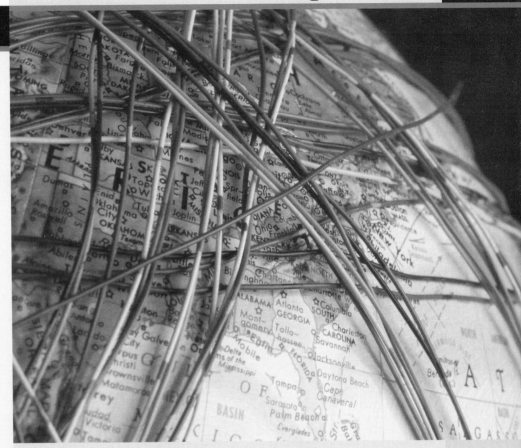

Source: © 2007 JupiterImages Corporation.

One of the most complex issues in international logistics is the field of international insurance. Not only is the topic difficult to understand, but it also involves a plethora of vocabulary exclusively used in the marine cargo insurance field and nowhere else, such as "jettison," "barratry," and "Inchmaree." In addition, in an international insurance contract, the term "Average" denotes something else entirely than the arithmetic mean. The difficulty is compounded by the fact that there are centuries-old traditions and concepts, some of which have essentially not changed for that long, and that can be interpreted either the British way or the United States way.

Nevertheless, the topic is of utmost importance: Shipping goods abroad is fraught with perils. A company has to knowingly accept these risks or transfer them onto an insurance company. This chapter will first present some of the terms used in international insurance, then explain the risks associated with shipping goods internationally by ocean and by air and introduce possible strategies for dealing with those risks, and finally conclude with more details on the elements of a marine cargo insurance policy, which is the name used for this type of policy, whether the goods actually travel by ocean or by air.

Eventually, another form of insurance will be presented: commercial credit insurance, which is one of the alternatives available to cover one of the other great risks of international trade: the possibility that the importer will default on an "Open Account" transaction. For details on this and other terms of payment, see Chapter 7.

10-1 Pitfalls of International Insurance

One of the greatest concerns in international insurance is to make sure that the coverage of the shipment is the coverage that the exporting firm prefers. All too often, the fact that the firm is improperly insured is only discovered after a loss. This is due to several reasons:

- The complexity of the field is substantial. Not only is there a minimum of six different standard insurance policies, but there are also countless variations in the specific clauses that can be included or excluded. Section 10-8 explains these different policies in detail.
- Many of the risks are misunderstood. Historically, international shippers were located in ports or near ports, and had a good understanding of the risks of the sea. Today's international shippers are located inland, and have a hard time comprehending the damage that a "bad storm" can inflict on cargo. Sections 10-3 and Section 10-4 present some of the many risks an international shipment faces.
- The Incoterms are somewhat misleading. Although both CIF (Cost, Insurance, and Freight) and CIP (Carriage and Insurance Paid) both mention insurance, they refer to the most basic coverage available, which can be inadequate for many goods (see Section 10-8).
- The carriers offer very limited coverage. Under the various international liability conventions, carriers offer very basic coverage, with very low limits, and are exempt of liability in many cases. Section 11-6 covers that aspect.

The international logistics manager should therefore become familiar with all of the peculiarities of this field in order to reach the best decisions.

10-2 Insurance Glossary

Insurance uses a precise terminology linked to risks and it makes sense to understand this terminology before using it to develop risk management strategy.

Average: A loss incurred on an ocean voyage by a cargo owner. It can be further qualified as a General Average or as a Particular Average.

　General Average: A loss incurred on an ocean voyage that is "general," in the sense that it involves all of the cargo owners on board. A general average can occur when the captain of the ship takes an action that will jeopardize some of the cargo in order to save the ship, the crew, and the remainder of the cargo; for example, the captain decides to ground the ship to prevent a total loss. The owners of the cargo that was saved by this action are indebted to the owners of the cargo that was lost and to the owners of the damaged ship. This complex concept is explained in Section 10-3h.

　Particular Average: A partial loss incurred by a cargo owner on an ocean voyage; the cargo may have become wet from seawater or may have been damaged by rough seas. Unlike a general average, the costs of a particular average fall exclusively on the owner of the cargo or its insurance company.

Barratry: An act of disobedience or willful misconduct by the captain or the crew of a ship that causes damage to the ship or the cargo.

Hazard: A situation that increases the probability of a peril and therefore of a loss. For example, a hazard would be a storm, which increases the probability of the peril of water damage, or a poorly trained crew, which increases the probability of improper stowing.

Jettison: The act of throwing overboard part of the cargo of a ship (or the fuel of an airplane) in an attempt to lighten the ship. The purpose of such an action is to save the ship, the remainder of the cargo, and the crew.

Peril: The event that brings about a loss. For example, a fire, a collision, and a flood are perils.

Risk: The chance or the probability of a loss. There are different types of risks:

Speculative Risk: The chance or probability of a loss or a gain (i.e., an investment in the stock market).

Pure Risk: The chance or the probability of a loss only. Pure risks can be insured against (i.e., transferred to an insurance company).

Objective Risk: The chance of a loss that can be accurately calculated, because ample empirical data are available (probability of a fire causing a total loss on a residence) or because a good mathematical model has been developed.

Subjective Risk: The perceived risk of a loss by an individual or company. Whether this perception is correct can only be settled by calculating the objective risk.

10-3 Perils of the Sea

A shipment by ocean is subject to a large number of risks, most of which are only vaguely familiar to a land-based exporter accustomed to shipping by truck or rail to its domestic customers. However, these risks are frequent, with losses in the billions of U.S. dollars every year. The trade magazine *Marine Digest and Transportation News* lists incidents occurring every month in the territorial waters of the United States, and it is rare that there are fewer than fifteen reports per month of fires, groundings, or capsizings. Because the United States has pretty stringent policies for safety and seaworthiness, it is not an exaggeration to estimate that it experiences fewer incidents than the rest of the world. Assuming a 5 percent "market share" of incidents worldwide, there are conservatively 300 maritime losses every month. Each of these involves cargo.

The perils of transporting cargo by ocean—and to a lesser extent by road, rail, and air—evidently have implications on insurance coverage. However, they also influence the way a company packages its products for export and the way it packs them in containers. Chapter 14 will specifically address the packing choices available to a shipper.

10-3a Cargo Movements

A shipment by ocean is subjected to numerous cargo movements, many more than during a strictly land-based domestic shipment. In the case of containerized cargo, the goods are placed in the container at the exporter's facility and loaded onto a truck. Generally, this is done carefully as the employees of the exporter are aware of the contents and of their value. However, once it has left the exporter's shipping dock, the goods are in the care of less scrupulous hands. The goods are unloaded in the port, placed in a holding area, handled a couple of times, then loaded onto the ship by a stevedore in a hurry, handled again several times in the same manner in the port of arrival, then loaded onto a truck for final delivery. A typical container will be handled four to six times in each of the ports of departure and destination.[1] In some cases, the

Web Exercise

There are several sources that detail some of the incidents that happen at sea and even include photographs. There are two websites in particular that list accidents at sea and provide photographs when they are available.

• http://www.cargolaw.com

• http://www.containershipping.nl

This website provides a comprehensive list of all the incidents that occur at sea worldwide.

• http://www.wkwebster.com/general/recent0.asp

Figure 10-1
Container Damaged During Loading Operations in the Port of Departure and Awaiting Unloading in the Port of Rotterdam
Source: Photo © Danny Cornelissen. Used with permission.

goods are loaded onto another ocean shipment as the container is transited though a port before being sent, by ocean, to its final destination. In some cases, the container is damaged in these multiple handlings and the cargo can be damaged (see Figure 10-1).

However, it is on the ship that the cargo is subjected to the greatest number of shocks and movements. A ship moves in six directions at once, often in an irregular fashion, and repetitively, even during a voyage with good weather. If the weather is stormy, the cargo is shaken in often inconceivable ways: "boxes [containers] stowed on the outside, on either side of the bows, endure sixty-foot elevator drops. Plus, they are tossed in an arc, up and over, as the ship tilts to starboard. Up and down, over and back, side to side," relates Tom Baldwin, a respected journalist, when he visited a containership in a near gale.[2] The different types of movement are shown in Figure 10-2 and can cause severe damage to all but the most carefully packed cargo.

10-3b Water Damage

Obviously, bad weather also affects the cargo in another way. As the ship tosses and shakes in a stormy sea, waves wash overboard and can slowly infiltrate the cargo containers or the break-bulk cargo on board. Pacific Ocean storms produce seventy-foot swells several times a year, which submerge the decks of many containerships. At times, the ship can avoid such storms, but at other times, because they are on tight schedules, they choose not to, or because the storm is moving too fast, they cannot.[3] The end results are that there is a strong possibility of water damage to the cargo on those ships unless the cargo is very well packed and protected. In some instances, the pounding of the waves is such that it deforms the container walls and crushes the cargo inside (see Figure 10-3).

While it is traditional for a shipper of higher value merchandise to request that the cargo be stored "under deck" (i.e., inside the ship) rather than "on deck" (outside, exposed to the elements), the way a container or cargo is actually stowed is mostly

Figure 10-2
Cargo Movements on Ships
Source: USCG photo by Petty Officer Kevin Martin. Used with permission.

Figure 10-3
Containers Damaged by Wave Action During a Storm
Source: Photo © Danny Cornelissen. Used with permission.

out of the control of the shipper. In addition, on very modern containerships equipped with stack bars (see Figure 11-5), the concept of deck has disappeared, making the distinction moot and increasing the possibility that a cargo will be exposed to serious quantities of sea- and rainwater.

Another possibility is that the storm will cause cargo to shift on board and to damage the ship to the point where water seeps in the hull: "At some point in the storm, a bulldozer fell off its carriage [a flat container, called a half-rack], and punched a hole in a fuel tank ... [and] split a seam in the hull. Some 15 feet [4.5 meters] of water and fuel oil subsequently flooded a container-laden hold."[4]

Yet another peril is water damage from the rain, as well as water damage caused by having a container sit in a low area in a port that floods during a rainstorm. During Hurricane Katrina in August 2005, several ports reported substantial flooding: All of the ports in the states of Mississippi and Louisiana were extensively flooded, particularly in the container staging areas (see Figure 3-3).

Finally, cargo can be damaged by container "sweat": most containers are pretty tightly closed, and no air circulation takes place. If some of the cargo inside the container has a high moisture content (agricultural or forestry products, for example), or if the cargo was loaded in a hot and humid area, then the humidity can condense on the inside walls of the container and damage the remainder of the cargo. A similar problem can happen for break-bulk merchandise placed in a tight cargo hold, as the ship "sweats" as well. These humidity problems can be solved by proper packaging and the use of desiccants. Figure 10-4 shows the variations in temperature and humidity for a container shipped from Houjie, near Guangzhou [Canton] in the province of Guangdong in the south of China, to Glenwillow, a suburb of Cleveland, in the state of Ohio, in the Midwest of the United States. For a shipment that traveled in March of 2006, the temperatures ranged from a high of 122° Fahrenheit (50° Celsius) to a low of 9°F (–13°C), and humidity levels ranged from a high of 91 percent to a low of 13 percent.

Figure 10-4

Variations in Temperature and Relative Humidity in a Container Shipment

Source: Diagram courtesy of Royal Appliance Manufacturing Co. Used with permission.

Legendary Container Losses

Although a major loss for any company whose container falls into the sea, a few container spills in the trade lanes of the North Pacific have allowed geo-scientists to develop better models of currents in the North Pacific.

The way geo-scientists traditionally trace currents is by releasing drift bottles at certain points in the ocean and noting where these bottles land on beaches. Generally, these releases are small in number: for example, the Project North Pacific released 34,000 bottles between 1956 and 1959 in increments of 500 to 1,000 bottles.

A container spill in May 1990 included 80,000 Nike shoes, most of which were eventually recovered by beachcombers on the North West Coast of the United States and West Coast of Canada. Scientists asked beachcombers—who were holding swap meets to find matching pairs—to report where they had found these shoes. From these data, and using models of the North Pacific, scientists were able to improve their knowledge of ocean currents in that region of the world.

However, the most notorious of all spills used for scientific purposes was the loss of twelve containers, one of which was owned by a company shipping plastic bathtub animals, or "rubber duckies." Some 29,000 toys spilled in the ocean in January 1992, and some ten months later, they landed on the beaches of Alaska. Scientists were able to develop a model to simulate the currents that brought these toys back to shore so some good came out of this loss. There also were quite a few grins about the methodology, including an article in the *Journal of Irreproducible Results*.

10-3c Overboard Losses

Another common problem for cargo is the fact that it can be lost overboard in a storm; it is not uncommon for ships to lose containers overboard: actually, worldwide, it is a daily occurrence.[5] The containers placed on top of the ship's deck are lashed down with bars holding them to the deck and to each other (see Figure 11-4). However, the cargo inside a container can shift, causing the container's balance to change; the container can also be improperly tied down, or the cleats holding the container can be damaged, and therefore the lash bars break or become loose, allowing some containers to fall overboard. The remainder of the container stack usually collapses as well, a situation that leads to crushed and damaged cargo. During the month of October 1998, four of the world's largest containerships experienced a deckstow collapse and lost some containers overboard.[6] (Visit the websites in the Web Exercise for photographs of such deckstow collapses.)

Sometimes, the containers that fall overboard float for weeks on end, and end up being hazards to other ships; such "flotsam" (the term applies to cargo that accidentally falls overboard) and "jetsam" (the term refers to cargo that was deliberately jettisoned, or thrown overboard by the crew, an action described in Section 10-3e) can still be the responsibility of the carrier if they cause damage. If they present a risk of environmental damage because they contain hazardous cargo, the carrier is often obligated to retrieve them, especially in United States or European waters.[7] Most eventually sink or wash up on some shore.

10-3d Jettison

In some cases, a container lost overboard is not an accident: The captain of a ship is allowed, if s/he thinks that this action will save the ship and the remainder of the cargo, to toss containers or cargo overboard to lighten the ship, to remove a container that may have become dangerous because it became loose, or to throw overboard some cargo to free a stranded ship. Such acts are called jettison or jettisoning and they are a fairly common occurrence. When this is the case, an old maritime tradition, called "General Average," dictates how the owners of the jettisoned cargo are compensated (see Section 10-3h); all parties on board pay for this loss.

10-3e Fire

Fire is also a fairly significant peril of shipping by ocean cargo containers. Because all dangerous cargo can only legally travel internationally by ocean—and not by air—such cargo is often present on board; fireworks, explosives, compressed gases, ammunition, and chemicals of all sorts are crowded on deck. If these items happen to be poorly stowed, or are damaged in a storm, they can leak and mix with one another, resulting in fires or explosions. According to John Waite, Chief Surveyor of the Salvage Association, the most pressing issue for container vessels is fire, because "there is no effective measure by which crews can fight a deck fire on a modern container ship." Moreover, he notes that almost all cargo carried above deck is flammable, and that chemical products account for 10 to 25 percent of it.[8]

For example, the containership *Harmony* was the victim of an explosion on November 16, 1998, which triggered a fire that was not extinguished until four days later. The ship lost 85 to 90 percent of its cargo in this fire, or approximately 1,100 containers.[9] The shipping line declared a "General Average," which is to say that this incident's costs will be borne by the owners of all of the cargo on board.

In March of 2006, the containership *Hyundai Fortune* (built in 1996) suffered a major explosion and massive fire in stacks of containers that were stowed on-deck while in the Gulf of Aden (see Figure 10-5). The entire aft end (rear part) of the ship was completely engulfed in fire. Multiple explosions ensued, as the ship was carrying fireworks. Containers were blown over the side, and the area around the vessel was covered with flotsam. The crew abandoned ship. It is estimated that 500 containers were lost. On April 17, 2006, the ship was safely towed into Port Salalah, Oman, where the remaining 2,249 containers were discharged. General Average was declared for the vessel and cargo losses. Marine cargo experts at insurance broking group Aon estimate that total losses will amount to at least U.S. $300 million.[10]

Figure 10-5
Fire Aboard the Containership *Hyundai Fortune*
Source: Photo © Royal Netherland Navy. Used with permission.

10-3f Sinking

One of the other consequences of bad weather is the possibility of sinking: While not common for modern containerships, the possibility of sinking is always present. While most of the ships lost every year to sinking are older bulk ships flying third-world countries' flags (i.e., not always very well maintained), even the most modern ships can fall prey to a rogue wave and be lost or seriously damaged at sea. The newly formed International Underwriting Association (formerly the Institute of London Underwriters) reports on the number of ships lost at sea as well as the human casualties. In 1999, there were 175 ships lost at sea, with 500 crew members dead or missing.[13]

10-3g Stranding

Another peril facing cargo is the possibility of stranding, which also happens fairly frequently. Mechanical breakdown, stormy weather, and sometimes incompetent crews are responsible for a significant number of grounded ships every year. The improvements made on navigational technologies, such as the Global Positioning System, have improved the precision with which ships operate. However, they cannot rely on precise maps: Only about 35% of the world's oceans have been accurately mapped and many charts rely on data that were collected—somewhat inaccurately—some fifty to 100 years ago. In addition, currents, coastal rivers, and strong storms modify the relief of coastal areas frequently; this is why many ports employ pilots to guide ships in their approach to port.

For example, a combination of bad luck and a partially inaccurate map caused the stranding of the *Queen Elizabeth 2* ocean liner in August 1992 in Martha's Vineyard Sound, off the coast of Massachusetts. It shows that strandings can still occur in well-traveled shipping lanes and with exceptional crews. She damaged part of her hull, passengers had to be evacuated, and Cunard Lines had to put the ship in dry dock for repairs.[14] The cruise ship *Royal Caribbean Monarch of the Seas*, a four-year-old ship equipped with the most modern of technologies, struck a reef in Saint Maarten in December 1998 and had to be beached to avoid sinking.[15]

Direct damage to the cargo is not very likely when a ship is stranded. Nevertheless, because stranded vessels can take days or weeks to be freed, the cargo on board can

The MSC *Carla*'s Christmas Cargo Loss

On November 24, 1997, the containership MSC *Carla*, designed to hold approximately 3,300 containers, was traveling from Le Havre, France, to Boston. About 300 kilometers (200 miles) north of the Azores Islands, the ship was caught in a storm and hit with a very large wave, called a "rogue" wave, estimated to be 30 meters (100 feet) high, which split the ship's hull in half. The bow section of the ship, while it stayed afloat for a few days, finally sank with 1,000 containers on board. The stern, after being heroically kept afloat by its crew, was eventually towed by a high-sea tugboat to the Canary Islands, a few weeks later. Fortunately, there was no loss of life.[11]

The cargo losses included a lot of goods destined for American consumers for Christmas: in particular, several hundred cases of rare wines, old Cognacs, and irreplaceable Armagnac bottles, some of them valued at $700 per bottle. Unfortunately, the goods sank in such deep waters (3,000 meters or 10,000 feet) that they could not be rescued. Even for those goods that were "safe" in the Canaries, a lot of them were damaged and unsellable: frozen foods had thawed—all the electrical power on board had been used to operate the pumps—and other cargo was heavily water damaged. "High-quality slabs of architectural stone were reduced to a 'pile of shattered granite and small lumps of marble.'"

The task of sorting out the responsibilities and settling the insurance claims is a job that took more than three years (it was settled in 2001) because the Mediterranean Shipping Company had declared a "General Average," which meant that the U.S. $17 million cost of the accident was shared by all the cargo owners on the ship. The final dispute between the insurers and the builders of the ship was finally settled by the United States Court of Appeals in 2005.[12]

Figure 10-6

The Stranded *APL Panama* being Unloaded After a Temporary Jetee was Built

Source: Photo © Charlie Neuman, *San Diego Union-Tribune.* Used with permission.

be damaged while it waits; it is obviously the case for refrigerated or produce cargo. In addition, when the ship is freed, cargo is often "lightered" onto another ship, with all the perils associated with a transfer of cargo in less-than-ideal conditions. If the ship's hull is damaged, there can also be significant water infiltration and the cargo can be flooded. In other cases, part of the cargo is simply jettisoned to lighten the ship. This is more often the case with bulk cargo of low value rather than with cargo of higher value or containerized cargo.

On December 25, 2005, the *APL Panama* (built in 2001) grounded itself on sand while inbound to the port of Ensenada, Mexico. The vessel had 1,805 containers aboard when it became stranded. It wasn't until after seventy-five days that salvors were able to get it afloat after discharging approximately 1,300 containers using helicopters and a shore crane operating from a makeshift jetee, and removing sand from around the hull with dredging equipment (see Figure 10-6). General Average was declared. After being refloated the vessel was towed to a shipyard due to the damage to its propeller.[16]

10-3h General Average

The concept of General Average is exclusively used in marine insurance. It predates the concept of insurance, and was the idea that, when there is an "Average"—a term derived from the French word *avarie*, which means "damage to a ship or its cargo"—or a major loss on a ship, all cargo owners and the ship owner share in the loss. In other words, a General Average is a general loss, or a loss affecting all the parties involved in an ocean voyage. It is based on the principle that the owner of the ship and the cargo owners all share the goal of a successful completion of the voyage and that therefore all share in the risks and the costs of the venture.

The concept is applied in a very unusual fashion; when a portion of the cargo is lost in bad weather, or when there is a major fire on board (see the case of the *Hyundai Fortune* in Section 10-3e), or when a portion of the cargo is jettisoned to save the ship, all of the owners of the cargo and the owner of the ship (or their insurers) pay for the lost cargo if a "General Average" is declared by the ship owner.

It's probably best to explain how this works with a specific example; assume a bulk cargo ship, valued at $1,070,000 loses power to its rudder and becomes stranded in shallow waters. It is carrying a shipment of iron ore in its fore holds (front of the ship) valued at $100,000, and a shipment of coal in its aft holds, valued at $80,000. In order to free the ship, the captain calls on a tug, and the decision is made that a portion of the ore will have to be jettisoned to allow the bow of the ship to get free. The ship is then towed to a port where several repairs are made to make the ship seaworthy again. After this adventure, the owner of the ship declares a General Average and an adjuster is called to settle the claims.

First, the adjuster calculates the market value of the jettisoned cargo; in this case, the ore that was jettisoned would have been sold for $10,000. Second, the cost of the salvage operation, including the damage done to the ship while freeing it, is added up: The tug charged $45,000, and damage to the hull, engine, and propeller shaft ended up costing $20,000. Finally, the ratio of the losses to the combined value of the cargo and the ship is calculated:

$$\frac{(10,000 + 45,000 + 20,000)}{(1,070,000 + 100,000 + 80,000)} = \frac{75,000}{1,250,000} = 0.06 = 6 \text{ percent}$$

The adjuster then uses this ratio to calculate the liabilities of the cargo owners and of the ship owner:

- The company shipping the iron ore cargo has a liability of $100,000 × 6 percent = $6,000. However, because it had a loss of $10,000 for the jettisoned cargo, it collects the difference of $10,000 – $6,000 = $4,000 from the adjuster. Realistically, if the cargo owner is insured, it will collect $10,000 from its insurer and, eventually, the latter will collect $4,000 from the adjuster.
- The company shipping the coal has a liability of $80,000 × 6 percent = $4,800, which it (or its insurance company) pays to the adjuster.
- The company owning the ship has a liability of $1,070,000 × 6 percent = $64,200. Once the direct costs are deducted, though, it ends up collecting $65,000 – $64,200 = $800. Most likely, its hull insurance coverage would have covered the remainder.

For at least a portion of the owners of cargo on board, General Average means that the owners of the goods that arrive safely have a liability toward the owners of the goods that did not arrive. Companies that had sufficient insurance have only their goods to worry about; companies with no insurance will have to place a cash deposit with the adjuster of roughly one-third of the value of the goods on the ship.[17] Because of its complexity—imagine a ship such as the *Carla* with 3,000 containers aboard, most likely owned by a similar number of different owners—the settlement of a General Average situation can take years to complete. Every year, there are approximately three situations in which a shipping company declares a General Average involving cargo from United States shippers.[18]

10-3i Theft

Cargo theft is yet another concern for companies shipping by ocean: While the risks are much greater on shore, or specifically in transit to the port of departure and from the port of arrival, it is becoming a major concern of exporters and importers of cargo that is easy to resell, such as athletic shoes, cellular telephones, or computer equipment. The total value of cargo thefts is difficult to pinpoint, as the police often tally these data together with other types of thefts, but it is estimated to be at least U.S. $10 billion per year in the United States and U.S. $30 billion worldwide.[19]

Cargo theft can be classified in three basic ways:

- **Pilferage** occurs where individuals steal cargo when they see an opportunity; such crimes are not planned and usually happen at random. They are more

pilferage Theft of part of a cargo shipment due to "opportunity." The thief did not plan the crime; the circumstances were such that it was possible to commit it.

frequent for cargo that can be identified by its markings or packaging, because it makes a more tempting target. Containerization has reduced pilferage because it makes the cargo much more difficult to identify and more difficult to steal in small quantity.

- **Organized theft** refers to carefully planned operations that are directed at the entire container. Organized theft usually targets high value cargo and often includes a group of individuals, some of whom can be "insiders" in the supply chain and provide information about the content of the container.

- **System's theft** uses the information system of the supply chain to change paperwork, substitute paperwork, or delete files so that cargo can be removed without immediate detection. This type of theft requires either inside accomplices or the ability to gain access to a company's computer system.

Depending on a company's operating profitability, it can take from $10 to $15 in increased revenues to make up for every dollar lost through theft. Corporations should be guided by a strong preventive security and loss prevention program. An effective security and loss prevention program is therefore money well spent for most companies whose cargo can be tempting to thieves. There are several texts and classes that international logisticians can use to assist in preparing a comprehensive, yet broad-based transportation security program.[20]

To protect itself from theft, a company can take several measures. First, it should try very hard to ship through unmarked containers and unmarked pallets and use seals and other methods that show evidence of tampering. It should make sure that the carriers it uses screen the employees who have access to the cargo, and restrict to an absolute minimum the number of people who have access to the documents related to the cargo (bill of lading, packing list, manifest). Two other measures that are useful in preventing cargo theft are a reward program that includes incentives for reporting suspect activities and a systematic collaborative effort with law enforcement authorities.

A few companies adopt original methods: New Balance Athletic Shoes, Inc. of Boston claims that it separately ships left and right shoes to Brazil and Argentina for its top-of-the-line models.[21] Although this is an ongoing rumor, the logistical nightmare and costs of reuniting shoes in the country of destination seem too high for it to be justified. In addition, at one point in the country of destination, the shoes are once again reunited before transiting in pairs to the retail establishments, negating some of the benefits of such an approach. Finally, should a container of left shoes be stolen—worthless to the thieves—it instantly renders its complementary container of right shoes equally worthless for the manufacturer. This strategy nevertheless could be effective because it could act as a deterrent.

Finally, the leg of the trip during which the cargo is most at risk is its inland portion: Several firms, after having suffered substantial losses on their shipments to Mexico because of truck hijackings, have taken the unusual step of transporting their goods by armored tractor-trailers. It is estimated that there were approximately 1,000 armored tractor-trailers in Mexico as of October 2000.[22]

10-3j Piracy

Piracy is the last of the major risks associated with shipping by ocean; although the mention of this term always raises a chuckle in any audience, it is a serious risk in several parts of the world: Consider that the International Chamber of Commerce reported a total of 469 attacks for 2000, the worst year since accurate records have been kept. Figure 10-7 shows the number of attacks and armed robbery against ships from 1994 to 2005.[23] The problem is so significant that the ICC created the Piracy Reporting Centre in Kuala Lumpur, Malaysia, in October 1992, which issues a weekly piracy report.[24]

organized theft Theft of a cargo shipment (or part of a cargo shipment) that is due to organized criminal activity, in which one or more individuals plan and eventually commit the theft.

system's theft Theft that is perpetrated by someone who also gains access to a computer in the information system of the supply chain and deletes the files related to that shipment to make the theft undetectable.

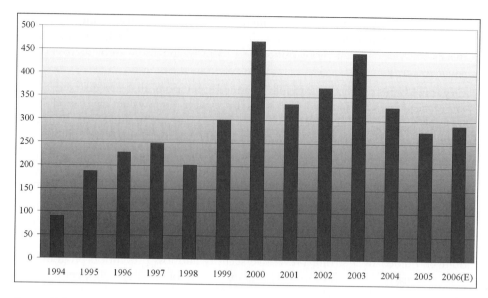

Figure 10-7
Number of Piracy and Armed Robbery Attacks Against Ships

The areas of the world in which piracy is most active are the Indonesian archipelago, Bangladesh, Somalia, Nigeria, and the Gulf of Aden. The greatest number of ships that are attacked are bulk or tanker ships carrying commodities that can be relatively easily sold in some loosely policed countries; these two categories combined represented 40 percent of all ships attacked. However, general merchandise ships and container ships represented about 15 percent of all victims, respectively.

Most of the piracy incidents involve thugs attacking a ship and stealing the crew's possessions. However, on a number of occasions, the ship's crew is transferred to a small boat and left adrift, while the pirates take the ship and its cargo.[25] Still at sea, the ship is renamed, all evidence of its former identity is destroyed, a complete makeover is executed— including a new paint job—and a new set of paperwork is created. Although it may sound impossible to "pull this off," the reality is that it is a strong possibility, especially for bulk cargo shipped on relatively small ships; there are roughly 40,000 such ships, none of which are particularly distinct from one another, and who change legal ownership fairly frequently. In addition, in those parts of the world where most of these attacks occur, the police are either too busy with other pressing matters or cannot be bothered. Despite those odds, the Piracy Reporting Centre has helped recover many of the hijacked ships that were reported.[26]

The number of piracy attacks has prompted several shipping lines to train their crew in anti-piracy techniques, specifically by increasing the number of crewmembers on watch in sensitive geographic areas. It also prompted ship owners to invest in satellite tracking systems and other security measures. One company even offers the services of former British Commandos (Gurkhas) as on-board ship escorts,[27] while another has a "rapid response team" that it can fly by corporate jet to any area of the world to recover a hijacked ship.[28]

10-3k Other Risks

Numerous other risks exist in shipping by sea:

- The risk of collision at sea is not substantial, but is still present. Collisions usually happen in crowded shipping lanes, such as the Channel or the Strait of Gibraltar. Thanks to radar equipment, this risk has been minimized, but it still happens. In

August 1999, the *Ever Decent*, a modern containership, collided in the English Channel with the *Norwegian Dream*, a newly built cruise ship.[29] One of the possible reasons for the collision was the poor training of the crews of both ships; both ships were flying convenience flags, one Panamanian, one Bahamian, and these countries are much more lax on crew training requirements (see Section 11-4).

- There is also the risk of collision with non-vessels; floating or sunk containers or debris are present in shipping lanes as well, and represent some degree of risk for ships, but little for cargo. Oddly enough, there is still the possibility of collision with icebergs, including very large ones from Antarctica. Iceberg A22A, has been drifting in the Antarctic Ocean since October 1986 and this mass of ice 50 km by 67 km (27 by 36 nautical miles) was still floating near the shipping lanes of the South Atlantic in June 2006. Its progress, and that of other very large Antarctic icebergs, is monitored by the National Ice Center.[30]

- Other collisions can happen as well: In May 1980, a freighter hit the Skyway Bridge in Tampa, Florida, United States, and caused the collapse of a 420-meter (1,400-foot) span of the bridge,[31] damaging part of the ship and its cargo. In February 1997, in the port of San Francisco, an indisposed pilot left the bridge of the *Orion* for a few minutes and the ship ended up crashing into the pier, causing U.S. $250,000 worth of damage to a gantry crane.[32]

- The risk of having a cargo contaminated or affected by other cargo is also present. It is always possible for a cargo to be contaminated by residues of the cargo that was previously in the same container or in the same ship, particularly foodstuffs contaminated by chemical products. A shipper importing rice found that it was unsellable due to the smell it acquired in the cargo hold of the ship.[33] Another found that its cargo of 2,500 tons of vinyl pellets was contaminated by a few pounds of styrene left in the hold. Refining costs amounted to U.S. $188,000.[34]

- In some cases, other cargo on board can be a hindrance to a shipper: For example, a ship was recently carrying a cargo of wheat to the Dominican Republic and stopped in Dakar, Senegal, to pick up an additional load of groundnuts. The nuts eventually proved to be infested with khapra beetles. After the beetles were discovered in the port of destination, the ship was fumigated twice, which nonetheless failed to rid the cargo of the pests. The ship was then ordered to dump all of its cargo— including the wheat—in the sea.[35] The owners of the wheat cargo had done nothing improper; they just happened to have loaded it on the "wrong" ship.

- For some ships sailing out of impoverished countries, another increasing problem is stowaways: Young men sneak in the cargo holds, or in containers, and hide until they are discovered at sea. In most cases, the stowaways only are a problem at the port of destination where police and immigration officials fine the ship and question the crew. In 1999, there were 200 stowaways found in the Pacific Coast ports of the United States and Canada.[36] Many more were not discovered; the U.S. Citizenship and Immigration Services estimate that about 3,000 stowaways enter the United States every year.[37] In most countries, the responsibility to repatriate the discovered stowaways falls on the carrier that brought them in the country. The expense of repatriating stowaways, who frequently are in small groups of two or three, and who have no identifying papers, runs in the thousands of dollars. In a few instances, the fear of these delays, expenses, and fines leads the crew to get involved in criminal behaviors, such as killing the stowaways or sending them adrift at sea on a makeshift raft.[38]

    The consequences for the cargo beyond the delay are many; most of the time, the cargo is damaged by the stowaways while they are living with the merchandise from a few days to a few weeks. Approximately 2 percent of all vehicles going from Mexico to the United States by rail are damaged by stowaways who sleep, eat, and defecate in the cars.[39] Sometimes, the stowaways hide in cargo holds that are closed and where the cargo is often laden with toxic chemicals or fumigated with insecticides. The stowaways die and the cargo is then considered unfit for consumption and destroyed in the country of destination.[40] There are unfortunately no practical ways to prevent this type of occurrence.

- In some cases, and for whatever reason, a government may decide to arrest a ship (i.e., keep it in port rather than let it sail away). Such was the case for five Yugoslav ships that were held in United States ports for more than five years, when the U.S. government seized all Yugoslav assets during the Bosnian civil war.[41] The cargo destined for the United States had been unloaded, but the cargo loaded for the return trip was on board for the entire duration of the ordeal.

- In other cases, the owners of a ship declare bankruptcy while the ship is away, or they just decide to abandon the ship and its crew for economic reasons. In 1998, there were a substantial number of ships, most of them from the former Soviet Union, the "East Bloc," or flying convenience flags, which had been abandoned by their owners. The crew of the *Delta Pride* was abandoned by its Karachi owners in the waters of Mexico; fourteen months later, the men finally made it to the United States and were flown home after a Pakistani charity got involved and the ship and its cargo were sold at auction.[42] The *Oituz*, one of twenty-two Romanian ships abandoned by its owners, waited with its cargo of 14,000 tons of sugar for nine months off the coast of Mexico.[43] The current whereabouts of the ship, its crew, and its cargo are unknown. There were a total of 3,500 seafarers abandoned by ship owners between 1995 and 1998, according to the International Transport Workers Federation.[44]

- In ports where the equipment is inadequate, or in ports where equipment is in short supply, some of the cargo may be unloaded from the ship by taking apart the crates and the merchandise, and reconstructing the goods and the crate on the quay. This can be quite damaging to the cargo. In Chapter 3, this issue, as it relates to packaging and packing the goods, will be discussed. Cigna, the insurance corporation, publishes a guide to the equipment in place in all the ports worldwide, called *Ports of the World*,[45] so that a firm may plan the size of its shipment accordingly.

- Some ports have a history of social unrest, and are shut down for several days by strikes or other civil disturbances. During the summer of 2000, French fishermen and French truckers blockaded the ports and then the refineries of the country to protest high diesel fuel prices. The government eventually lowered taxes on that fuel. Soon, their counterparts in Spain, Britain, Italy, and Germany followed suit and, for about a month, all cargo traffic in Europe was affected. Time-sensitive cargo was delayed, and transportation costs increased. Strikes in the ports of Japan occur almost annually to force negotiations of higher wages for dockworkers.[46] All of these actions affect cargo movements in many ways; even if cargo going from Cairo to Bombay is not specifically caught in an Italian strike, it is delayed because the containership on which it was supposed to sail is delayed.

The possible perils that cargo can encounter at sea and on its way to and from a seaport are many; this list illustrates the point that many of the risks that are associated with a sea voyage may be easily underestimated by an exporter or an importer arranging for ocean cargo services. The importer or the exporter, whichever is responsible for the cargo, must be quite alert in its management of these risks.

10-4 Perils Associated with Air Shipments

Compared to what can happen to an ocean shipment, the perils to which an air shipment is exposed are minimal, a situation mostly due to the fact that air transport is, by nature, less perilous than ocean transportation. In addition, the airline industry is still dominated by companies located in, and therefore regulated by, developed countries' governments, which tend to have stringent rules regarding safety, pilot training, and maintenance. Despite the large number of aircrafts in operation—in 2004, there were approximately 14,000 commercial airplanes in the world, including 1,757 freighters[47]—and the correspondingly high number of voyages, the number of accidents per year is very small, reflecting the emphasis on safety of the entire industry.

The risks of fire and explosion are greatly diminished, mostly because countries routinely prohibit shipments of dangerous goods by air. The risks of total loss to cargo due to aircraft crashes is essentially nil, as are the risks of losses while the aircraft is aloft. The three biggest concerns for shippers should be:

Cargo movements: While in the aircraft, the cargo is subjected to rough weather and sudden and quick accelerations and decelerations. Because freighter airplanes do not have to worry about passenger comfort, their pilots do not fly around turbulences the way passenger airline pilots do, and the cargo on board can be subjected to sudden and fairly violent "bumps." In a similar fashion, the aircrafts will brake faster on landing, bank at a wider angle on approach, and altogether be less gentle than with passengers on board. However, it is still a minute problem, as a good percentage of cargo moves in passenger airplanes, which do not experience such conditions. In addition, the greatest hazards are still in the shipping and handling that precedes the flight: in the truck on the way to the airport, in the warehouse, and in their counterpart activities in the transit airport and the airport of arrival (forklift truck damage, for example).

Theft and pilferage: While airports tend to have a fairly good handle on controlling theft while the goods are on the airport premises, it is not often the case in the vicinity of the airports, where problems abound in warehouses, truck terminals, and other satellite locations. Because most cargo sent by air has a high value, it is interesting to thieves, and because it tends to be packaged in cardboard boxes and not palletized, it is somewhat more easily pilfered and stolen. The key to controlling losses in these instances is to make sure that the cargo documents are handled by as few people as possible and that the boxes are not marked in any way to indicate their content.

Exposure to inclement weather: Although it seems counterintuitive, goods in transit from a warm place to another warm place may be subjected to very cold weather; for example, the third largest freight airport in the world is Anchorage in the northern U.S. state of Alaska (after Memphis and Hong Kong), where the average high temperature is below freezing from mid-October to early April. Reciprocally, cargo moving from a cold climate to another cold climate may stop at a tropical airport; such was the case of salmon fry shipped from Alaska to southern Chile, which routinely stopped in Miami. Cargo is commonly left on the tarmac for a couple of hours between aircrafts, and the shipper should anticipate that the cargo will be exposed to extreme atmospheric conditions.

There are a number of other risks associated with air shipment, particularly the cold and the changes in air pressure that can be found in some freighters. Cargo tends to be kept at lower temperatures and operated at lower air pressure during the flight than what is practiced in passenger airplanes, for obvious reasons of cost. For most cargo, these slight differences may not be significant but, for some cargo, it can be a problem. Because, by definition, sensitive cargo moves by air, care should be exerted in making sure that perishable cargo is not kept at temperatures than it cannot handle or that live cargo and sensitive mechanical instruments are not subjected to air pressures that are too low. Again, though, the greatest risk is usually not while the airfreighter is in flight, but while the cargo is on the tarmac, waiting to be loaded, or already loaded and waiting to take off; it can be exposed to extreme temperatures.

10-5 Insurable Interest

There are several parties interested in the safe arrival of an international cargo shipment. The first, obviously, is the owner of the goods. Whether the owner is the exporter or the importer is dependent on a number of factors, principally the "Terms of Payment" of the transaction (see Chapter 7). However, there are many cases in which non-owners are interested in making sure that the goods arrive safely to their destination. The Terms of Trade or Incoterms used in the transaction between the exporter and the importer (see Chapter 6) determine the cases in which the exporter is responsible for the goods before the title transfers to the importer. However, even if the importer is not responsible for the goods while they are in transit, it still has an interest in making sure that the goods arrive safely to their destination.

All of these situations illustrate the concept of "insurable interest":

> An insurance contract is legally binding only if the insured has an interest in the subject matter of the insurance and this interest is in fact *insurable*. In most instances, an insurable interest exists only if the insured [were to] suffer a financial loss in the event of damage to, or destruction of, the subject matter of the insurance.[48]

The use of Incoterms helps the exporter and the importer determine where their respective responsibilities start and end. It should therefore follow that the insurable interest of the exporter ends when possession shifts to the importer, at which time the importer is the party with an insurable interest; unfortunately, while this is correct, it is not that simple.

The issue is, once again, muddied by several factors. Several examples can be used to illustrate them:

Foreign exchange exposure: An exporter in a developing country sells to an importer in a developed country on a CIF basis: Responsibility transfers once the merchandise crosses the ship's rail (see Section 6-9), but the exporter is responsible to provide minimum cover insurance (i.e., Coverage C of the Institute Marine Cargo Clauses—see Section 10-8d). Assuming that the importer is in agreement with such minimum coverage, there is still the problem that, should there be a loss, the importer would have to file a claim with the insurer in the developing country, or, at least, an insurer not chosen by the importer. It is possible that the claim processing will take a few months, leaving the importer with the risk of foreign exchange devaluation. Because the terms are CIF, the exporter delivers the goods as agreed—when the goods cross the ship's rail—and therefore the invoice has to be paid by the importer, causing a cash-flow problem as well. In this case, the importer has an insurable interest and can obtain coverage in its country to minimize its foreign exchange risk exposure. A similar situation can arise in a CIP shipment.

Trust: An exporter may sell FCA to an importer in a country that mandates that the importer buy insurance in the importing country. The exporter usually ships without evidence of coverage, and correctly so, because the responsibility shifts to the importer as soon as the goods are in the carrier's care. However, should they be damaged in transit, the importer may refuse payment, despite the fact that the accident happened under its responsibility. The exporter has therefore an insurable interest in the completion of the trip: Note that the problem would be avoided if the exporter sold on a Letter of Credit basis, as the *documents* for the shipment, including the intermodal bill of lading, would be in order, and the Issuing Bank would have to pay (see Section 7-6a). The same situation would arise in FAS, FOB, CFR, CPT, and DAF shipments; it could also happen in an EXW transaction.

Insufficient coverage: An exporter agrees to sell to an importer on a CIF basis. The importer requests that the terms be modified to "CIF maximum cover" (i.e., Coverage A of the Institute Marine Cargo Clauses—see Section 10-8a) but, because it is an Open Account shipment, it does not obtain evidence of this coverage. The goods are slightly damaged in transit by condensation, and the importer seeks to collect compensation under the terms of the insurance policy provided by the exporter. However, the claim is turned down because the exporter did not contract for Coverage A, but for Coverage B or C, which do not allow claims for such damage. Clearly, the importer has an insurable interest in this cargo and can obtain coverage in its country to protect itself from such losses.

While the owner of the goods has a clear insurable interest in the merchandise while it is in transit, non-owners, such as the buyer in the first and third example above, have an insurable interest that is less direct; it is usually qualified as a "contingent" insurable interest.[49]

10-6 Risk Management

There are three ways in which a company can manage its risks, whether they are international cargo insurance or any other type of risk: It can retain the risk, it can transfer the risk, or it can take a mixed approach and retain some risks and transfer others.[50] This section will concentrate on the management of international logistics risks, mainly the risks associated with transporting goods from one country to another.

10-6a Risk Retention

The strategy of risk retention is fairly clear; the company decides that it is more economical to not purchase insurance for those risks. In general, there are four reasons for which a company will decide to retain its international logistics risks:

1. Very large international traders—importers or exporters—are likely to follow this strategy as they already act somewhat as an insurance company in some respect: They have a lot of merchandise in transit, and therefore would have to pay large insurance premiums, but would only occasionally collect on a loss. Therefore, the many savings incurred by not paying premiums end up covering the few losses they experience. Those firms have decided to "self-insure," which is the euphemism for not contracting with an insurance company and for deciding to pay all risks with current cash flow.

2. Exporters or importers that have little exposure. They are shipping or buying goods of fairly small value, in fairly small shipments, and therefore, a loss would not have substantial financial or cash-flow consequences for those companies.

3. Exporters or importers that have little relative exposure because international transactions represent such a small percentage of their business. The individual amount may be large, but relative to the size of their domestic sales, it is not significant.

4. Firms that did not evaluate the international transaction risks clearly. They are not insuring because they do not insure their domestic transactions or, for whatever reasons, think that the risks of shipping internationally are not very high. Generally, the firms that are choosing to retain these risks by ignorance are also the ones that are more likely to incur losses because of improper packing or improper security measures for the same reasons. Relying upon the liability coverage provided by the shipping line is also imprudent; the current liability for shipping lines under U.S. law—the Carriage of Goods by Sea Act (COGSA)—provides a maximum coverage of U.S. $500 per package, which is often interpreted as a "container," and the shipping lines have seventeen specified defenses they can invoke, essentially shielding them from liability except in the most egregious cases.

10-6b Risk Transfer

The strategy of risk transfer is also fairly clear: The firm decides to transfer all of its risks to an insurance company. In exchange for paying a premium for an insurance policy, the firm is certain to be covered against losses experienced during international shipments. This strategy is followed for three reasons:

1. Firms may have a lot of exposure. The value of the goods they ship or import is high, and the loss of some or all of these shipments would be a substantial financial blow to their operations. In those cases where goods are expensive, though, the insurance companies often request, in cooperation with the firms, to restrict the total amount at risk on any single shipment. Usually this is achieved by having the shipment split over several carriers.

2. Firms may have a relatively high exposure. Even though the amount may be small, it ends up being relatively high for the firms. A perfect example of such a situation is found in personal effects shipments, which generally are worth fairly small sums, but are relatively quite valuable to their owners.

3. Firms that lack experience in international trade will insure because they are uncomfortable with the risks involved or because they are unable to properly assess their exposure.

10-6c Mixed Approach

The mixed approach is one where the firm decides to retain some of the risk and transfer the rest. This strategy can be achieved in two different ways:

1. The decision is made based upon the maximum amount of exposure that a firm is willing to risk: This objective is traditionally achieved with the use of a deductible. A deductible can be managed on a per-claim basis—the insurance company is responsible for the portion of a given loss that is greater than the deductible and the firm is responsible for the amount of the deductible, as well as all losses that have a value lower than the deductible. It can also be a cumulative deductible, where the firm pays for losses until the cumulative deductible amount is reached, and the insurance company pays for the losses incurred beyond the amount of the deductible.

2. The decision is made based on the types of risks that the firm is willing to take, and those that it would rather transfer to an insurance company. For example, a firm may choose to insure using Coverage B of the Institute Marine Cargo Clauses (see Section 10-8c) and retain the risks not covered by this policy, among which are condensation, pilferage, leakage, and breakage.

Either of these strategies can be followed for a number of reasons as well; however, while the choice of a monetary deductible is essentially based upon the maximum amount of exposure that a firm is willing to bear, the strategy of splitting risks between the firm and an insurance company is a much more difficult strategy to implement, as it involves identifying risks, determining whether they are significant enough to transfer, and negotiating with an insurance company a specific contract of insurance, taking advantage of the fact that "customized cargo policies are limited only by the imagination of the carriers offering them."[51]

10-7 Marine Insurance Policies

An international trading firm—exporter or importer—intent on transferring all or part of its international shipping risks is generally only interested in purchasing Marine Cargo Insurance, because it just needs to protect itself from damage to the cargo as well as from its liability toward the ship owners and the rest of the cargo in a

General Average case. However, there are a couple of additional insurance coverages available in international shipping that should be mentioned: They pertain mainly to vessel or aircraft owners, but, on rare occasions, those policies matter to an exporter or importer chartering an entire ship for a bulk shipment.

10-7a Marine Cargo Insurance

Marine Cargo Insurance can be purchased either under an open ocean cargo policy or under a special cargo policy.

Open Policy

An open policy is an insurance contract with which a firm insures every international shipment it makes for a fixed period of time. Such a policy is formally known as an Open Ocean Cargo Policy and it automatically covers all the shipments of the insured, as long as the firm reports every shipment to the insurance company. This reporting is done using a set of declaration forms, either every time an export shipment is made—or an import shipment is received—or on a monthly basis. There is a presumption of goodwill on the part of the firm in that the insurance company will cover damage to an undeclared shipment, as long as the firm intended to notify the insurance company.[52] Because the premiums are based upon the value of the shipments made under such a policy, it presents one great advantage: The firm knows the costs of its insurance coverage and can easily incorporate it in its *pro-forma* invoices without having to request a quote for each shipment.

Special Cargo Policy

The second alternative is for the exporter or importer to purchase an individual policy, called a Special Cargo Policy, for each of its shipments. This alternative allows a firm to specifically purchase coverage that pertains best to a shipment. However, it tends to be cumbersome to enter a contract every time the firm gets involved in an international transaction, and this method is not very commonly used.

Obtaining Insurance Certificates

On a large number of occasions, the exporter is requested to provide a Certificate of Insurance to the importer and its bank, often because this Certificate is required by the Letter of Credit. This requirement is usually not a problem under a Special Cargo Policy, because there is evidence from the insurance company that a specific shipment is insured.

Under an Open Ocean Cargo Policy, however, this requirement used to present some difficulties until recently. The practice used to be that the insurance company would provide the exporter with a Certificate of Open Insurance; however, this certificate did not specifically address the insurance status of a given shipment, and some (few) banks did not accept evidence of an open policy as a proof of insurance for a specific shipment as required in the terms of the Letter of Credit.[53] Therefore, the practice is now for the insurance company to give the insured a supply of blank Special Cargo Policy forms, which are then filled by the exporter to show that a specific shipment is covered. These forms appear—to the Issuing Bank—as if a special Cargo Policy has been contracted for the shipment, even though it is covered under an open policy.[54]

Purchasing Marine Cargo Insurance

Marine Cargo Insurance can be purchased from two sources:

1. An insurance agent, who can assist the firm in obtaining the most appropriate coverage, given its product mix and its risk management strategy; as such, agents sell most open ocean cargo policies.

2. A freight forwarder, who can provide "generic" coverage for a given shipment almost immediately; as such, freight forwarders sell a lot of special cargo policies.

10-7b Hull Insurance

Hull insurance is contracted by the ship owners to cover the risk of damage to their ship when it is involved in a peril, such as grounding or fire. It also covers the owner in case of a complete loss, such as a sinking. This policy also covers the owners' liability toward the cargo owners in the case of a General Average and its damages in the event of a collision with another ship. An equivalent hull insurance is available to owners of aircrafts.

Hull insurance rates are dependent on the seaworthiness of a ship, the way it is maintained, and the equipment it has on board, all three of which are appraised by **Classification Societies**. Ships are placed in different classes and hull insurance rates are dependent on the class of a ship. The Lloyd's Register of Ships—in its 236th year, and now available on CD-ROM[55]—keeps information on almost all ships in the world and their classification. Hull insurance is effectively paid indirectly by the cargo owners, as the cost of the insurance is included in the freight rates quoted.

Classification Society
A company that is responsible for determining the seaworthiness of a particular vessel. It places a ship in a specific "class" as a function of its age, maintenance records, and the availability of on-board equipment.

10-7c Protection and Indemnity

Protection and Indemnity is yet another form of insurance for a ship owner; it is a protection against liability to other parties when a ship sinks or is damaged. In the last few decades, it has meant liability for oil spills—specifically cargo spills, but also ship fuel spills—on beaches, and their extensive clean-up costs. However, it also includes the ship owners' liability toward the crew (injury, death) or in repatriating stowaways.

Protection and Indemnity insurance is not a traditional insurance, as it is a mutual **P&I Club** to which ship owners contribute, and which absorbs the costs of one of the owners' mishaps. The liability of a single P&I Club is limited to an amount of U.S. $5,000,000; for claims that are higher than that, the fourteen P&I Clubs form an alliance and mutually insure each other, up to a limit of approximately U.S. $78,000,000.[56] Claims beyond this amount usually involve a cargo of crude oil and are covered by an international fund, called the International Fund for Oil Pollution Compensation.[57] If it is not a claim involving oil cargo, the P&I Clubs are reinsured through Lloyd's for the remainder of the claim.

Protection and Indemnity Club (P&I) A group of ship owners who agree to mutually share the costs of a member's liabilities to other parties; for example, the club members would be individually responsible for the costs of a single member's liability in the event of an oil spill.

10-8 Coverages under a Marine Cargo Insurance Policy

There are two major groups of policies that can be purchased in order to protect cargo during an ocean or air shipment. The first group is governed by British Law and was completely rewritten in 1982. This group of insurance policies seems to have become the standard for other countries as well. They are known as the Institute Marine Cargo Clauses, Coverage A, B, or C.

The second group is older, with some antiquated clauses and more modern ones, and is mostly written by U.S.-based insurance companies, although some of the coverage can be written using older British clauses. These traditional policies are known as "All Risks," "General Average," and "Free of Particular Average."

To make things more interesting, these six general policies can be modified to add coverage that is not included in the original contract, such as the risks of strikes and civil unrest. However, none of the policies will cover five specific risks, against which it is impossible to find insurance:

Improper packing: The goods must be adequately packed for an ocean voyage and be well protected against shocks and water damage, as well as well secured in the container or the crate. Chapter 14 discusses this issue in depth.

Inherent vice: The goods shipped have a natural propensity to be affected in a certain way; for example, steel will exhibit surface rust after being exposed for some time to air and moisture, agricultural product shipments will foster insects and rodents, and wood will warp and split. None of these "inherent vices" are insurable.

Ordinary leakage: Also known as "ordinary loss in weight and volume" and "ordinary wear and tear," this states that several products, when shipped, will leak or lose weight; for example, any agricultural product, such as wool, will lose some weight as its moisture content decreases; petroleum oil transported in bulk will partially evaporate; and an automobile carried on a roll-on/roll-off ship will show additional mileage. Again, none of these risks are insurable.

Unseaworthy vessel: This exclusion is not a problem for goods shipped by regularly scheduled container or break-bulk ships; however, it puts a burden of care on the shipper in the case of a shipment going by bulk ship, as the shipper must make certain that the ship is classified by a Classification Society as seaworthy. In addition, a vessel can depart for a voyage in seaworthy condition and then become unseaworthy due to the perils it encounters. When a ship becomes unseaworthy during a voyage, most policies include a statement that "an unreasonable delay in repairing the ship exonerates the insurer from liability on any loss arising from the defect."

Nuclear war: This risk is always specifically excluded from policies. Note that the risk not covered is the direct result of nuclear war, such as irradiation or destruction. However, should a shipment be damaged by a fire caused by nuclear war, the shipment is covered—if the risk of fire is covered in the policy—because the fire was the peril that caused the loss.

10-8a Institute Marine Cargo Clauses—Coverage A

The first general policy is referred to as Coverage A of the Institute Marine Cargo Clauses. Coverage A is quite similar to a traditional "All Risks" policy (see Section 10-8b), in that it covers "all risks of loss or damage to the subject-matter insured,"[58] yet it is not identical to one. For one, it is written in plain English, which makes it much simpler to decipher. Moreover, unlike traditional "All Risks" policies, which can be written with U.S. or British clauses—and the different interpretations they imply—a policy written with Coverage A of the Institute Marine Cargo Clauses is identical in all countries.

Despite its name, a Coverage A policy—and an All Risks policy—is not truly an All Risks policy, as it covers all perils except the ones mentioned earlier (improper packing, inherent vice, ordinary leakage, unseaworthy vessel, and nuclear war), as well as a number of risks for which specific additional coverage must be purchased separately as endorsements to the main policy: strikes and other civil disturbances (see the Strikes, Riots, and Civil Commotions clause in Section 10-8g) and acts of war and seizure by a government (see the Free of Seizure and Capture clause in Section 10-8h).

Nevertheless, Coverage A of the Institute Marine Cargo Clauses is the maximum coverage that an exporter or an importer would need to purchase in the case of a shipment for most trade lanes in the world, specifically from a developed country to another, as long as the route does not cross a particularly hot spot of the world.

10-8b All Risks Coverage

An "All Risks" policy is an older—but still very commonly used, particularly in the United States—-type of policy. Because an All Risks policy can be written as an American contract or as a British contract, it will contain different wordings of the clauses and other relatively minor changes, which will make an American policy different from a British policy on a few points; therefore, careful reading of such policies should always be done to ensure that there is a proper match between the risks that the shipper—exporter or importer—is willing to assume and the ones that the policy excludes.

For a United States All Risks policy, the goods have to be shipped "under deck," which means that the goods must be stowed inside the ship, for the obvious reason that goods inside a ship are exposed to fewer perils than goods stowed "on deck." However, this presents a practical problem because the shipper usually is unaware of the way the goods are stowed in a ship, and because some containerships no longer have a deck and are instead equipped with stack bars. The problem is solved by requesting that the insurance company cover the goods based upon the Shipper's Letter of Instruction, which requests that the goods be shipped under deck, and not based upon the way the goods are actually stowed by the steamship line. Such coverage can be obtained as an endorsement to the main policy, usually at no additional charge.[59] Once this endorsement has been granted, the All Risks policy is even more similar to a Coverage A policy, and therefore an All Risk policy is also quite appropriate for shipments of any nature between two developed countries.

10-8c Institute Marine Cargo Clauses—Coverage B

Another general policy is referred to as Coverage B of the Institute Marine Cargo Clauses. It is also called a "named perils" policy, as it lists specifically the risks that it will cover. The list of covered perils includes fire, stranding, sinking, collision, jettison, washing overboard, water damages, and *total* losses during loading and unloading; however, losses due to bad weather are not covered, and neither are partial losses happening during loading and unloading of the ship. For a complete list, please refer to Table 10-1, where a comparison is given for all six standard coverages.

Coverage B of the Institute Marine Cargo Clauses is appropriate for goods that have a good tolerance for bad weather, such as bulk raw materials including coal, iron ore, polymer pellets, and lumber. It would not be appropriate for machinery, paper, and any type of finished goods, unless they were particularly resilient.

10-8d Institute Marine Cargo Clauses—Coverage C

The last of the general Institute Marine Cargo Clauses is Coverage C. It is also a "named perils" policy, as it lists specifically the risks that it will cover. The list of covered perils is limited to fire, stranding, sinking, collision, and jettison; it does not include washing overboard, rough weather damages, or water damages and losses during loading and unloading. For a complete list, please refer to Table 10-1, where a comparison is given for all six standard coverages.

Coverage C is the minimum coverage required by the Incoterms CIF and CIP. It is minimal enough as to be inappropriate for most goods, and companies doing business on CIF or CIP terms should definitely extend this coverage to "maximum cover" (i.e., Coverage A of the Institute Marine Cargo Clauses), or, if they are importing on those Incoterms, purchase Difference in Condition Insurance (see Section 10-8j).

Coverage C is generally insufficient for most containerized goods, with the possible exception of goods that are unlikely to be affected by an international voyage in any way, and, if lost overboard, would not be a major loss. There are few cargos that fit this description, with the possible exception of scrap merchandise, such as scrap metal or recyclable paper. Coverage C is appropriate for bulk cargo, as it is unlikely to experience a loss unless there is major damage to the ship.[60]

TABLE 10-1	Marine Insurance Coverage Summary					
Perils Covered Against	**A**	**B**	**C**	**AR**	**WA**	**FPA**
Fire	X	X	X	X	X	X
Explosion	X	X	X	X	X	X
Stranding	X	X	X	X	X	X
Sinking	X	X	X	X	X	X
Collision	X	X	X	X	X	X
General Average	X	X	X	X	X	X
Jettison	X	X	X	X	X	(*)
Loss Overboard	X	X		X	X	(*)
Seawater Damage	X	X		X	X	(*)
Lightening	X	X		X	X	(*)
Condensation	X			X		
Improper Stowage by Carrier	X			X		
Theft	X			X		
Pilferage	X			X		
Leakage	X			X		
Breakage	X			X		
Damage while Loading/Unloading	X	X		X	X	
Damage on land before Loading	X	X	X	X	X	X

(*) Under an FPA policy, any partial loss incurred would not be covered unless it is due to a ship sinking, burning, becoming stranded, or being involved in a collision; a total loss would be covered.
A Coverage A of the Institute Marine Cargo Clauses
B Coverage B of the Institute Marine Cargo Clauses
C Coverage C of the Institute Marine Cargo Clauses
AR All Risks Coverage
WA With Average (Typical Coverage)
FPA Free of Particular Average (Typical Coverage)

NOTE: Because so many different types of WA and FPA policies exist, the table is only indicative. Please refer to the actual policy for definitive coverage.

10-8e With Average Coverage

The "With Average" policy is generally written to include coverage in between an "All Risks" policy and a policy with Coverage B of the Institute Marine Cargo Clauses. A With Average policy is also named a "named perils" policy, as it lists specifically the risks that it will cover. Again, because a With Average policy can also be written as an American contract or as a British contract, care should be given to ensure that the shipper is not unwillingly accepting a risk that it does not want to retain.

A With Average policy covers risks such as fire, explosion, stranding, collision, and so on (see Table 10-1), but covers damage to cargo from heavy weather, as well as partial losses while loading and unloading the vessel, and the bursting of boilers, none of which Coverage B provides.

The way a With Average policy insures partial losses is through the use of a **franchise**, which is to say that for partial damage below a certain percentage—say 3 percent—of the value of the merchandise, the goods are not covered. For partial losses greater than this franchise, the entire loss to the insured is covered. A franchise is therefore different from a deductible, which would consider that, if a loss of 10 percent of the value of the merchandise occurred, the insured would be responsible for the first 3 percent and the insurance company would be responsible for the remaining 7 percent. In a With Average policy with a franchise of 3 percent, the insurance would cover the entire 10 percent.

franchise The portion of a loss, expressed as a percentage, below which a "With Average" insurance policy will not cover a partial loss. If the amount of the partial loss exceeds the franchise, then the entire costs of the partial loss are covered.

A standard With Average policy is appropriate for some percentage of the merchandise shipped internationally; however, because some other coverages such as fresh water damage, condensation, or breakage and pilferage are often added,[61] it seems that shippers use a With Average policy to tailor their coverage to include those perils to which the merchandise they export or import is sensitive.

10-8f Free of Particular Average Coverage

The last general policy is referred to as a "Free of Particular Average" policy, which is also a "named perils" policy. A "Free of Particular Average" policy covers total losses, but only covers partial losses in some circumstances. The major issue is whether the policy is a "Free of Particular Average—English Conditions" policy or a "Free of Particular Average—American Conditions" policy. Under an American Conditions policy, partial losses are covered only if they result *directly* from a fire, a stranding, a sinking, or a collision. Under an English Conditions policy, the partial losses are covered if they occur on the same voyage that a fire, a stranding, a sinking, or a collision occurs, without these perils having directly caused the loss.

A "Free of Particular Average" policy is even more restrictive than Coverage C of the Institute Marine Cargo Clauses. It does not cover many of the risks associated with an international shipment and it is rarely sufficient or appropriate for an international shipment of containerized or break-bulk cargo, unless the cargo considered is particularly inexpensive and a loss would be no substantial problem for the shipper. It would be appropriate (with some reservation, because no partial losses are covered) for some bulk cargo of minimal value.

Finally, a "Free of Particular Average" policy would not be enough to cover the minimum insurance requirements of a CIF or CIP shipment, which both require the "minimum cover" of Coverage C of the Institute Marine Cargo Clauses.[62]

10-8g Strikes Coverage

All the previous standard policies include a clause, called the "Strikes, Riots, and Civil Commotions" (S.R. & C.C.) clause in the American policies and the "Strikes Exclusion" clause in the Institute Marine Cargo policies, which excludes coverage of damage to cargo due to strikes and other civil disturbances.

Should a shipper be concerned about the possibility of such problems in a specific port or during a specific period, a possible amendment to include such coverage can always be added, generally called an S.R. & C.C. Endorsement. However, the coverage would include only direct physical damage to the goods or the additional costs incurred in storing the goods during the strike, but would not include incidental damage caused by delay to market, nor the financial losses that accompany a delay in the sale of a cargo.

10-8h War and Seizure Coverage

All the previous standard policies also include a clause, called the "Free of Capture and Seizure" (F.C. & S.) clause in the American policies and the "War Exclusion" clause in the Institute Marine Cargo policies, which excludes coverage of damage to cargo due to war and warlike situations, such as the seizure of a ship by a foreign government or the accidental collision of a ship with a mine.

It is possible for a shipper to insure its cargo against war damages, but it is through an additional policy, called the "War Risks Only" policy, which would cover hostile acts by a foreign government or by an organized power. For obvious reasons, a War Risks policy is cancelable by the insurance company with forty-eight hours' notice; however, it cannot be canceled for cargo that is in transit (i.e., that has already left the port of departure), which is really the coverage that any shipper would want. Most open cargo policies are accompanied by a separate War Risks policy, according to Cigna Insurance Companies.[63] In times of naval warfare against merchant ships, war risk insurance may only be obtainable through a government-backed policy. This was the case for most Allied vessels and cargoes during World War II.

10-8i Warehouse-to-Warehouse Coverage

Another common additional coverage to an open cargo policy is the "Warehouse-to-Warehouse" coverage, which covers the goods from the time they leave the exporter's warehouse until the time they arrive at the importer's warehouse, or fifteen days after they arrive in the port of destination, whichever occurs first.

The Warehouse-to-Warehouse coverage grew from the demands of shippers who were tired of only finding coverage for the ocean portion of the voyage. First, the All Risks and With Average insurance policies added a "Shore Perils" endorsement to include the perils occurring while loading and unloading ships; this clause was also made part of the Institute Marine Cargo Clauses. Finally, a true "Warehouse-to-Warehouse" clause was added to most open cargo policies. In addition, in some policies, there is also a "Marine Extension Clause," which essentially expands the Warehouse-to-Warehouse coverage to ensure unforeseen changes in the voyage and unexpected transshipments. Such a clause was developed during World War II to account for unusual and unknown transshipments, because all shipping data was classified.[64] It fulfills few practical purposes today.

The "Warehouse-to-Warehouse" coverage is an extension to the traditional All Risks, With Average, and Free of Particular Average policies, but it is an integral part of the Institute Marine Cargo Clauses policies, for Coverages A, B, and C, in which it is called a "transit clause."

10-8j Difference in Conditions

Another addition of significance to open cargo policies would be "Difference in Conditions" coverage. Difference in Conditions coverage is designed to fill the gap between what an importer would like to have covered under its open cargo policy and what is covered under its supplier's CIF or CIP coverage.

Because the International Chamber of Commerce only requires Coverage C of the Institute Marine Cargo Clauses for a CIF or CIP shipment, it can be difficult to ensure that a supplier will actually cover the shipment more fully, even though the importer may request maximum cover. In those cases, it is simpler for the importer to purchase a Difference in Conditions endorsement and not have to worry about what the supplier will provide.

10-8k Other Clauses of a Marine Insurance Policy

There are many other clauses in a marine insurance policy, either as a part of the general policy or as an endorsement to the general policy. This section will give a brief overview of some of them.

General Average Clause
All insurance policies contain a "General Average" clause, which specifies that the insurer will cover the General Average responsibilities of a shipper.

Constructive Total Loss Coverage Clause
All insurance policies contain a "Constructive Total Loss Coverage" clause, which essentially specifies that the insurer will reimburse the shipper for goods that have been abandoned after a stranding or a sinking, as long as the costs of recovering the

goods and making them marketable is greater than their value. If it is possible to recover the goods at a cost lower than their value, then the insurance company pays for these costs.

Sue and Labor

All traditional insurance policies—All Risks, With Average, and Free of Particular Average—have a clause called "Sue and Labor" (policies written under the Institute Marine Cargo Clauses have similar wording but do not use this clause name), which direct the shipper to act in the best interest of the insurance company when a loss occurs. The principle is that, after a loss, the insured should protect the cargo from further damage, as it would if it had not been insured, in order to keep the loss to a minimum.

Inchmaree Clause

One of the quaint vestiges of the old marine insurance policies is the "Inchmaree" clause, so named after a lawsuit between the owners of the *Inchmaree*, a vessel, and the insurers of its cargo, which determined that damage caused by a burst boiler (steamship engine) was not covered by the traditional marine insurance policy of the time. Insurers quickly added this coverage to their policy and it has remained to this date in the All Risks, With Average, and Free of Particular Average policies. The Inchmaree clause also covers cargo owners in the event that the ship owner is guilty of errors in navigation and seamanship.

Coverages A through C of the Institute Marine Cargo Clauses do not include the Inchmaree clause and do not mention coverage of poor navigation. An analysis of the American Carriage of Goods by Sea Act, in Section 11-6, will cover this issue of seamanship further.

10-9 Elements of an Airfreight Policy

Fortunately, airfreight policies tend to be much less complicated than ocean marine cargo insurance policies: They are all written as "All Risks" policies, with the exclusions already described in Section 10-8:

Improper packing: The goods must be adequately packed for an air shipment and be reasonably protected against shocks and rainwater damage, as well as well secured in the container or the crate. The standards for airfreight packing are much less stringent than for an ocean shipment.

Inherent vice: This problem is essentially moot in an air shipment as the goods are in transit a much shorter period of time. Nevertheless the risk is specifically excluded from coverage.

Ordinary leakage: Also known as "ordinary loss in weight and volume," and "ordinary wear and tear," this is also much less of a concern for air shipments as transit times are much shorter.

Unairworthy aircraft: This exclusion is not a problem for goods shipped by air; governments do extend much greater efforts to the oversight of aircrafts than they do for ships. The absence of "flags of convenience" is also a positive factor.

Nuclear war: This is a traditional exclusion.

In addition, policies will also exclude war coverage and S.R. & C.C. coverage, as they are for an ocean cargo policy, as well as two risks inherent to air travel: damage caused by cold and changes in atmospheric pressure. All of these risks can be covered, however, by purchasing additional coverage.

Practically speaking, most air cargo policies are included as a clause in the open cargo policy of a firm, which allows the firm to manage its shipping risks with a single document, whether its goods are moving by ocean or by air.

10-10 Filing an Insurance Claim

Unfortunately, any company that engages in international business faces the prospect of cargo loss or damage, and with that occurrence follows the need to file an insurance claim. Proper handling of an insurance claim is paramount to making sure that the company recovers its loss. There are several steps that must be taken by the insured.

10-10a Notification

The first and most important step is to promptly notify both the carrier and the insurance company of the loss. The best practice is to notify the carrier or the carrier's agent and the insurance company immediately if the damage is visible at the time the goods are discharged: if the packaging shows signs of damage, the container seal show signs of tampering, or the shipment shows some other outward sign of damage are some examples. If there is no apparent exterior damage, there are different requirements for the timely notification and eventual filing of a claim, depending on the mode of transportation. If the cargo was transported by ocean, the carrier should be notified within three days. For international air shipments, the carrier must be notified within seven days. For international and domestic land transportation, and for domestic shipments, the notification requirements vary, and are spelled out in the air waybill or the (intermodal) bill of lading; however, such a notification will likely be within, at most, seven days as well.

It is therefore quite important to inspect cargo as quickly as possible after it has been received, even if it shows no sign of damage or pilferage, so that, should the cargo be damaged, a notification and eventual claim can be filed within the contractual time limits.

This notification has to be made in writing in all cases; it should include a description of the damage and a record of the seal number and of its condition. The notification should be sent to the insurance company, to the insurance agent, and to the carriers involved in the shipment, even if they are "agents" of the main carrier, if they are known; for example, the trucking company hired by the shipping line to make the final delivery should be notified. Notification should be made by certified mail, with return receipt requested, to provide evidence of a timely notification. Even in cases where the damage is apparent, it is not sufficient, although it is definitely necessary, to make an annotation on the delivery receipt for the goods. In addition, the more precise the annotation on the delivery receipt, the greater the level of protection for the insured.

Once damage is discovered, the insured should hire a **surveyor**, an independent company that is not affiliated with the insurance company and whose responsibility is to evaluate and assess the damage to the cargo. The insured may use any surveyor who is approved by Lloyd's of London or the American Institute of Marine Underwriters. In most cases, the insurance company can recommend a surveyor. The surveyor is directly paid by the insurance company in most cases, although in some cases, the insured pays the surveyor, and is then reimbursed by the insurance company. A surveyor may not be necessary if the damage is minor.

surveyor An individual or company whose responsibility it is to determine the extent and the circumstances of a marine cargo loss.

10-10b Protection of the Damaged Cargo

Once an insured has identified that the cargo has been damaged, it has several responsibilities. As much as possible, it should stop unloading the goods from the container and leave the cargo as it was found; if that is not possible, an extensive number of photographs should be taken to document the problem thoroughly. In all cases, the insured should segregate the damaged cargo from other cargo, appropriately mark the damaged cargo so that it is not inadvertently mixed with other shipments, and protect it so that there will be no further damage. There are several reasons for those recommendations.

The first reason, one of the important tenets of insurance, is that the insured must protect the property "as if it were not insured" as the insured has an "onus of good faith" and must protect the interests of the insurance company. For example, further damage, resulting from lack of care after the goods have been damaged, is not covered: If a shipment of cement arrives with several torn bags, the insured must make sure that the cement is protected from rain, even if the torn bags are no longer usable. The damage to the cement bags that occurred during the voyage (torn bags) would likely be paid by the insurance company as long as it falls within the coverage of the policy, but the water damage after the shipment arrived would not be covered, because it was due to the negligence of the insured. Actually, in cases where the insured has to incur additional costs in order to prevent further loss, the insurance company will cover such costs under the "sue and labor" clause of the ocean cargo policy.

The second reason is to make sure that the cause of the damage is correctly determined. Such procedures facilitate the work of the surveyor who is responsible for inspecting the cargo and determining the party responsible for the damage. For example, the surveyor may want to determine the type of bracing that was used in the container. Because improper packing is neither the responsibility of the carrier nor of the insurance company, but that of the exporter, the surveyor will want to see how the cargo was stowed in the container. If that evidence is no longer there, it affects its ability to assess responsibility accurately. Finally, following these guidelines will also allow the carrier(s) to inspect the goods and protect its interests.

10-10c Filing of a Claim

Two fundamental requirements drive the system in properly filing a claim for recovery of losses. The first requirement is the timeliness of the filing of the claim, and the second is the submission of proper documentation for the claim. The logistics manager should review the insurance policy to see that all requirements in the event of a claim are met.

As mentioned earlier, there are very strict time limits for notifying carriers and insurance companies of the filing of a claim: three days for ocean cargo, seven days for international air transport, and an estimated seven days for other forms of transportation. The formal filing of the claim may take somewhat longer, so that the documents required to complete the claim can be collected. The filing of a claim should also be made by certified mail, with return receipt requested.

The claim must be in writing and follow a format that is acceptable to the insurance company. For example, claims filed electronically (by e-mail or internet) may not be acceptable to some carriers and in some jurisdictions. The claim must contain information to identify the shipment, must assert liability against the carrier, and must be for a specific or determinable amount.

Filing an insurance claim also necessitates collecting and copying a large number of documents, most of which should be submitted with the claim; however, the specific documents should be determined from the contractual language on the back of the bills of lading, on the insurance certificate, and in consultation with the insurance company. Generally speaking, the following documents should be included:

- Insurance Policy or Certificate of Insurance
- All Bills of Lading from origin to final destination
- All invoices (from the exporter, all carriers and service providers)
- Cargo surveyor's report
- Complete packing lists and manifests
- Seal Numbers and Reports

- Any and all documents generated during the voyage of the cargo; depending on the type of shipment, the country of origin and the country of destination, and the mode of transportation, a shipment can generate a very large number of possible reports, all of which should be included with the claim. Such reports include pre-shipment inspection reports, monitoring tapes and logs (especially for refrigerated cargo), delivery receipts, transportation interchange reports, equipment interchange reports, exception reports, dock receipts, warehouse and container freight station receipts, survey requests, loading surveys, mate's receipts, vessel stowage plan, ship's bridge log, deck reefer log, bilge and engineer's log, vessel hatch survey, discharge survey, and so on.

- Product destroyed or thrown away (such as perishable products) will need a certificate of destruction filed with the claim.

- Cargo that can be salvaged at a cost should include salvage bids and receipts.

10-10d Carrier Liability Limits

A shipment that is not insured by a specific marine cargo insurance policy can still be covered by the insurance policy of the carrier. However, carriers, as noted earlier in this chapter and explained in greater depth in Chapters 11 and 12, have limits on their liability. When a claim is filed against a marine cargo insurance, it becomes the responsibility of the insurance company to pursue its own claim against the carrier.

To that effect, the controlling law noted in the Bill of Lading must be reviewed: usually it is the Carriage of Goods by Sea Act (COGSA), or the so-called Hague, Hague-Visby, or Hamburg Rules for ocean shipments, and the Warsaw convention for international air shipments. However the bill of lading may cite different laws that are applicable. Therefore, the contractual portion of the bill of lading should be reviewed in terms of the stated damage limit and the controlling law; that contractual language is usually found on the reverse of the Bill of Lading.

In the case of an intermodal shipment, because a through or combined bill of lading was issued, the company needs to determine which carrier is "principal" and which carrier is "agent."[65] When filing a claim for an intermodal shipment, the principal carrier should be notified; however, as noted earlier, notifying agent carriers at the same time is a prudent course.

Freight forwarders, Nonvessel Operating Common Carriers, and other third-party logistics providers (called 3PLs in the United States and in the United Kingdom) frequently limit their liability and also set their own statute of limitations on the submission of a claim.[66] The 3PL may obtain insurance coverage only on specific instructions from the shipper. The 3PLs will normally accept claims only for damages from their own actions, not those of carriers even though the 3PL may have issued a combined or intermodal bill of lading. The 3PLs may be required by regulatory bodies to have a bond for insurance purposes and there may be additional regulations regarding filing claim against the bond.[67]

Unfortunately, even though a claim may have been filed with all the proper documentation and in a timely manner, there is no guarantee that the claim will be honored; there is also the possibility that the insurance company will only partially cover the losses. In those cases, it may become necessary for the shipper to file a lawsuit against the carrier; this action should be undertaken by an attorney who practices cargo law and, if appropriate, admiralty law and is licensed to practice in the court that has jurisdiction.

10-11 Lloyd's

Lloyd's of London is the oldest insurance *market* in the history of shipping, having started in Edward Lloyd's coffee house as early as 1688. Although it is commonly perceived as an insurance company, that perception is incorrect. Since its humble beginnings in Lloyd's coffee shop, the company has acted as an intermediary between people who wanted insurance and those willing to provide it. Lloyd's does not provide insurance coverage; when one hears of an athlete whose legs are insured "by Lloyd's of London," it is an inaccurate statement: The athlete's legs are insured *through* Lloyd's.

10-11a Principles

Before explaining how the functioning of Lloyd's is different from the functioning of an insurance company, it seems relevant to explain how the latter works. An insurance company attempts to strike a balance between the collection of a large number of premiums, each of a moderate monetary amount, and the payment of a few claims, each of a large monetary amount. The correct calculation of a premium relies upon the determination of the expected monetary value of claims (their probability multiplied by their expected costs) divided by the number of policyholders. Over time, the law of averages—arithmetic averages—allows an insurance company to be profitable. In order to determine the probability of a loss, insurance companies rely on **actuarial tables** that are tables of statistical data collected over a significant period of time.

In contrast, Lloyd's of London acts as a market through which unusual risks are insured; unusual risks are those that a traditional insurance company would not consider covering because there is no way to collect a large number of premiums and therefore the law of averages does not apply. For example, consider a firm that would like to insure the launching of its communication satellite. Although there may be as many as fifty satellite launches worldwide every year, the number of companies launching a satellite—the possible number of premiums to collect—is too small to spread the high expected monetary value of a single loss. Therefore the firm would be faced with a series of years in which it would collect premiums without a loss, and then would have one or two losses in a single year, which would have a substantial adverse effect on its income.

Lloyd's of London is the place where companies and people wanting to have such risks insured find a group of "members" willing to assume (insure) this risk. These members are either individual persons, who are called **Bespoke Names** in Lloyd's particular vernacular, or corporations, which are called Corporate Members. All members are organized in a **Syndicate**. Each member is actually "wagering" that the loss will not happen, and collects a portion of the premium that the member shares with the remainder of the Syndicate. This share of the premium is therefore income to the member. Should a loss occur, the member is then asked to pay its share of the loss, along with every other member in the remainder of the Syndicate. This payment comes out of the member's income or assets. The members, organized in a Syndicate, are the **Underwriters** of the insurance.

Historically, all members of Lloyd's were "Names," and very wealthy individuals; this is still the case for current Names. For Names, participation in a Syndicate can be quite a profitable venture. It is not truly an investment, because the Name only collects premiums (additional income) while a portion of his or her assets can continue to be invested in other vehicles on which he or she collects market rates. However, because each Name has unlimited liability on his or her personal assets, this can also be an extremely risky venture. Because of this risk, each Name must have substantial personal assets—as of June 2006, the required net wealth was £350,000 (U.S. $650,000), only 50 percent of which have to be invested with Lloyd's—in order to be allowed to participate in a Syndicate. A Name cannot ever "retire" from Lloyd's; they can stop underwriting new risks, but they have to remain in the syndicate until all of their liabilities have been settled.

In 1994, Lloyd's decided to allow Corporate Members. These corporate members were given the advantage of having limited liability and joined syndicates in which individual Names retained unlimited liability. This decision, which allowed the

actuarial tables Tables used by insurance companies that illustrate the exact probability, based upon historical data, of a particular peril.

Bespoke Names In the Lloyd's of London vernacular, the individuals who take on the risks insured by syndicates, and who have unlimited liability for those risks on their personal assets.

Syndicate Under the Lloyd's concept of an insurance market, a group of Names who agree to insure a certain type of loss. The risks are shared by all the members of the Syndicate.

Underwriter The company, Syndicate, or Name that assumes the risk of a loss for another party, in exchange for a premium.

syndicates to have more capitalization, also created some friction, as individual Names resented the creation of two classes of members and responsibilities. Today, most of Lloyd's underwriting capability is provided by corporations. In 2006, the number of individual unlimited liability Names had dropped to 1,497, with 714 corporate members.[68]

Over the years, the type of insurance coverage provided through Lloyd's has increased to include more traditional risks, such as automobile and home insurance. However, most of the Lloyd's Syndicates will cover risks that a traditional insurance company will not consider. As of 2006, there were sixty-two underwriting Syndicates.[69]

Some of the risks that Lloyd's Syndicates covered in the last few decades included the risk of asbestos product liability: Such was the extent of the liability, though, that many Names were brought to personal bankruptcy, despite efforts by Lloyd's to spread the risk to more Syndicates than had originally been involved. The number of Names soared from 14,000 in 1978 to 34,000 by the end of the 1980s. Some of the Names who joined in the 1980s claim to not have been informed of the extent of the liabilities that Lloyd's Syndicates faced, and filed lawsuits alleging fraud.[70] In November 2000, Lloyd's was found not guilty of fraud by the British courts, but the language used by the judge in its decision was quite strong, calling Lloyd's "grossly negligent."[71] Some criminal lawsuits against Lloyd's are still pending as of June 2006.

10-11b Lloyd's in International Logistics

From the perspective of an exporter or importer, the Lloyd's market would only be used for some of what is referred to as "project cargo," or cargo of exceptional dimensions that would not fit in a traditional container or would need special arrangements with the shipping line. An example of such extraordinary project cargo would be a firm shipping several large pieces of equipment to a customer or a subsidiary overseas. Because such cargo may not be insurable by a traditional insurance company, it could be insured through Lloyd's.

Lloyd's is also used substantially by carriers in insuring their transportation assets, such as ships, aircrafts, and pipelines.

10-12 Commercial Credit Insurance

Another area where a firm involved in international matters can transfer some of its risks is in the commercial credit area.

Increasingly, competitive pressures are pushing firms to sell on an "Open Account" basis, as customers try to acquire the best possible payment alternatives. Several countries used to offer subsidized terms on export insurance to their exporters and, although these practices have officially ended with the creation of the World Trade Organization (WTO), which prohibits export subsidies, the mindset was established. In France, for example, nearly 25 percent of all export sales are insured by the *Compagnie Française d'Assurance pour le Commerce Extérieur* (COFACE), which was privatized in May 1994, but was still heavily subsidized by the French government, to the tune of FFr. 2.5 billion—U.S. $500 million—in 1996.[72]

A firm may have to cover several types of transactions for which it feels uncomfortable:

- A sale to a foreign customer on an "Open Account" basis, where the firm is concerned about its exposure, or the amount of money it has at stake in the sale.

- A sale to a foreign customer on credit terms: The customer has requested that payments be extended over a period of several months. The terms are also "Open

Account" because the sellers' competitors have offered this alternative to the customer. The exporter is concerned about its exposure to this stream of payment.

- A construction firm retained by a foreign customer to build a plant; however, in order to earn the contract, it must post a number of performance bank guarantees (or performance bonds). It is concerned about its exposure in the case of unexpected delays, such as if the customer calls on the bank guarantee. For more information on bank guarantees, please refer to Section 7-10.

10-12a Risks Involved

In each of these transactions, there are two components to the risk of non-payment:

Political risk: This is the risk presented by the country in which the transaction takes place. This risk can take many forms. The country's government can decide to increase tariffs on certain imports while the customer refuses delivery, the country's government can decide to freeze accounts held in foreign currencies while the customer cannot pay, the country's government can decide to prohibit the sale of a particular product, the country's government can commit a political *faux pas* and an embargo is declared by the remainder of the world, which means that no payments can be forwarded by the customer, and so on.

Commercial risk: This is the risk presented by the customer defaulting on its obligation to pay, for whatever reason. Generally, the customer encounters financial difficulties or the customer has a complaint about the product that it cannot resolve any other way—in its management's mind, at least—than by withholding payment to the exporter.

10-12b Risk Management Alternatives

As in the case of international cargo insurance, the firm exposed to these risks has three alternatives available to manage them: It can decide to retain the risk, it can decide to transfer the risk to an insurance company, or it can follow a mixed strategy of retaining some of the risks and transferring others.

There are many different reasons for choosing one strategy or another, most of which were covered in Section 10-7, so they will not be repeated here.

10-12c Insurance Policies Available

Should a company decide to cover its receivable risks with insurance coverage, there are many alternatives available, which can be obtained from a large number of insurance companies and governmental or quasi-governmental agencies. Most of these sources have multiple programs, presenting a dizzying array of possible contracts. Most companies interested in such programs should contact an insurance agency specializing in these types of policies, as well as contact their banks or governmental export support agencies in their country for further and more specific information.

A quick summary of the programs available in the United States gives an example of what is possible.

Government Programs
There are three government-related organizations in the United States that provide exporters with commercial and political insurance coverage:

The Ex-Im Bank: The Export-Import Bank was created as an independent government agency in 1934. Its mission is to help create jobs in the United

States by supporting export sales. It has a very large number of programs, from political and commercial credit insurance to loan guarantees (for banks lending money to an exporter) and loans extended to foreign purchasers of American products. For years, the Ex-Im Bank was the only provider of political risk insurance in the United States.

There are two difficulties in dealing with the Ex-Im Bank. The first is the lengthy delays that usually accompany an application—which means that an exporter involved in a negotiation with a foreign customer should attempt to secure coverage very early. The second is that it is an arm of the U.S. government and therefore subject to political pressures, such as abrupt cancellation of coverage for certain countries of the world. In addition, the product sold abroad must have at least 50 percent American content. Nevertheless, the Ex-Im Bank provides programs that are extremely popular with exporters and their bankers, such as the Ex-Im Bank Guarantee, which covers loan repayments by foreign purchasers. The complete program of the Ex-Im Bank is available at its website (www.exim.gov).

OPIC: The Overseas Private Investment Corporation is also a governmental agency, created in 1971 with the purpose of encouraging private investments in developing countries. Its purpose is quite political, as it seeks to further U.S. values overseas, but it offers several programs of loans, political insurance, and private equity investment funds, all quite advantageous to corporations interested in investing in developing countries. As of October 2002, there were more than 140 countries eligible for its programs, details of which can be found at its website (www.opic.gov).

Unfortunately, OPIC presents the same challenge as the Ex-Im Bank—long processing times—but, because the products it offers cover long-term investments owned by U.S. firms, these delays are less critical.

SBA: The Small Business Administration has created a few programs designed to help exporters finance their sales abroad: working capital loans and long-term loans for capital investments. However, the SBA does not provide insurance of any sort for exporters.

All of these programs, even if not used, present substantial value to an exporter. For example, the U.S. Export-Import (Ex-Im) Bank has established exposure fees for medium- and long-term loans. Its cost of guarantees and insurance vary, among other factors, according to the political and commercial risks of non-repayment in a given country and for a particular creditor. The Ex-Im Bank assigns exposure fee levels and transaction risk increments to transactions on the basis of this risk, and calculates them relying upon:[73]

- Credit ratings and market spreads
- Credit agency and bank references
- Historical financial statements
- Ex-Im Bank's credit experience with the borrower/guarantor and its industry.

Because banks involved in foreign trade often use a process similar to the Ex-Im Bank's process as their model for establishing transaction risk, it would be useful to an exporter to assess quickly a risk with which it may be unfamiliar.

Private Insurance Companies

There has recently been a substantial increase in the number of programs offered by private insurance companies in the United States, but it still is a business restricted to a few players. The practice of insuring a company's foreign receivables is still not as well established in that country as it is in many European countries. In the United States, there are few insurance agencies specializing in this field, with approximately twenty of them underwriting most of the business.[74]

The insurance companies that dominate the market are:

FCIA: The Foreign Credit Insurance Association was created in 1961, primarily to offer products that combined the Ex-Im Bank's political insurance coverage and commercial credit insurance products. Today, many of the Ex-Im Bank products that contain credit insurance are using the FCIA for that portion of the coverage. The FCIA, though, is not a government agency, but is owned by Great American Insurance Company, a conglomerate of insurance companies. The FCIA products are mostly commercial credit insurance products, ranging from short-term to medium-term coverage for receivables. More information on the company's products can be found on its website (www.fcia.com).

Euler-ACI: American Credit Indemnity is the other large player in the field, offering a similar array of commercial credit insurance products. It was recently purchased by the Euler Group, a French insurance conglomerate. More information on ACI's products can be found on its website (www.aciins.com).

American International Group: American International Group (AIG) is the largest U.S.-based provider of commercial credit insurance, a product it calls Trade Credit Insurance; more information is available on its website (www.aig.com).

Lloyd's: Certain Lloyd's Syndicates have added coverage of political risks to their underwriting portfolio and present the advantage of offering insurance for countries for which the United States' government will not provide any, such as Afghanistan, Albania, or Belarus. Although the United States government allows trade with any of these countries, it will not provide political insurance coverage; however, a Lloyd's Syndicate will.

Key Terms

actuarial tables (p. 238)
average (p. 209)
barratry (p. 209)
Bespoke Names (p. 238)
Classification Society (p. 228)
franchise (p. 231)
general average (p. 209)
hazard (p. 209)

jettison (p. 209)
objective risk (p. 210)
organized theft (p. 219)
particular average (p. 209)
peril (p. 209)
pilferage (p. 218)
Protection and Indemnity Club (P&I) (p. 228)

pure risk (p. 210)
risk (p. 209)
speculative risk (p. 210)
subjective risk (p. 210)
surveyor (p. 235)
syndicate (p. 238)
system's theft (p. 219)
Underwriter (p. 238)

Review and Discussion Questions

1. Describe some of the risks that an ocean shipment faces.

2. Describe some of the risks that an air shipment faces.

3. Explain the concept of General Average, and explain, with a numerical example, how it is utilized.

4. Explain the concept of "insurable interest." Explain who has an insurable interest in three different transactions conducted under three different Incoterms.

5. What possible risk management strategies can an exporter/importer follow? Explain each strategy's advantages and disadvantages from the perspective of a small exporter.

6. What insurance coverage is required under CIF or CIP Incoterms? Explain which risks are not covered, and how an importer can still protect itself against them.

7. Choose three possible Marine Insurance clauses and describe their usefulness.

8. Explain the concept of International Credit Insurance and explain how it is possible to contract a policy covering commercial and political risks.

Endnotes

1. Mongelluzzo, Bill, "Ports Looking Inland for Success," *The Journal of Commerce*, March 17, 1998, p. 1B.

2. Baldwin, Tom, "It's Time to Inspect the Containers… (Don't Attempt this One at Home, Folks)," *The Journal of Commerce*, November 13, 1997, p. 2B.

3. Baldwin, Tom, "Container Industry Braces for Lawsuits," *The Journal of Commerce*, November 12, 1998, p. 1A.

4. *Ibid*

5. Baldwin, Tom, "Storm-tossed Boxship Splits: Crew Rescued," *The Journal of Commerce*, November 26, 1997, p. 12A.

6. Cottrill, Ken, "A Poseidon Adventure," *Traffic World*, January 20, 1999.

7. "Toxic Containers Recovered from North Sea," Hazcheck Systems, 9th February 2004. http://www.hazcheck.com/general.asp?np=news_89, June 20, 2006.

8. Journal of Commerce Staff, "Complexity, Speed of Modern Ships Increases Risks," *The Journal of Commerce*, November 19, 1999, p. 9.

9. Baldwin, Tom, "Ship Hit by Fire and Explosion Has Lost 85% to 90% of its Cargo," *The Journal of Commerce*, November 25, 1998, p. 16A.

10. "Impact on Insurance Market of M/V Hyundai Fortune," *Lloyd's Press*, March 31, 2006.

11. Baldwin, Tom, "Salvors Struggle to Stabilize the Carla in Stormy Atlantic," *The Journal of Commerce*, December 2, 1997. Baldwin, Tom, "Storm-tossed Boxship Splits: Crew Rescued," *The Journal of Commerce*, November 26, 1997.

12. Rible, Stephen, *Rationis Enterprises, Inc. of Panama, vs. Hyundai Mipo Dockyard Co., Ltd*, 2005, U.S. App. Lexis 22323 (2nd Cir. 2005), http://www.usaverageadjusters.org/Rationis.pdf, August 2, 2006.

13. Jowit, Juliette, "Inspection Plan Ordered for Tankers," *The Financial Times*, May 5, 2000, p. 8. International Underwriting Association, http://www.iua.co.uk.

14. Baldwin, Tom, "The Case of the Reappearing Rock, and Other Unchartered Navigational Hazards," *The Journal of Commerce*, April 30, 1998, p. 2B.

15. Associated Press News Release, "Cruise Ship Hits Caribbean Reef," December 15, 1998.

16. Dibble, Sandra, "German Container Ship Sticks Around for Easter," *San Diego Union-Tribune*, April 12, 2006.

17. Hastings, Warren, *Marine Insurance Compendium*, 1999, General Management Services, Inc., Publisher, 76 Mamaroneck Avenue, Suite 6, White Plains, NY 10601, USA.

18. Fabey, Michael, "Remember the Titanic? Your Business Does Not Have to Sink, Even If Your Cargo Does," *World Trade*, January 1998, p. 54.

19. Barth, Steve, and Michael D. White, "Hazardous Cargo," *World Trade*, November 1998, pp. 46–48.

20. Tyska, Louis A., and Lawrence J. Fennelly, *Cargo Theft Prevention: A Handbook for Logistics Security*, American Society for Industrial Security; 2001.

21. Barnett, Chris, "Taking Steps to Trip Cargo Thieves," *The Journal of Commerce*, April 3, 1998, p. 1A.

22. McCosh, Daniel J., "Theft Drives Firms to Armor Trucks," *The Journal of Commerce*, August 30, 1999, p. 1.

23. *Piracy and Armed Robbery Against Ships: Report for the Period 1 January–31 March, 2006*, ICC International Maritime Bureau, dated April 2006.

24. "Weekly Piracy Report," International Chamber of Commerce—International Maritime Bureau, Piracy Reporting Centre, http://www.iccwbo.org/ccs/imb_piracy/weekly_piracy_report.asp, October 8, 2000.

25. Bangsberg, P. T., "Crew Rescued, Ship Missing in Latest Attack," *The Journal of Commerce*, November 12, 1999, p. 15.

26. "Piracy Reporting Centre Foils Another Hijack on the High Seas," Press Release of the Piracy Reporting Centre, June 16, 2000, http://www.iccwbo.org/ccs/news_archives, October 5, 2000.

27. Bangsberg, P. T., "Gurkhas Offered for On-Board Protection," *The Journal of Commerce*, February 28, 2000, p. 19.

28. Mullins, Ronald Gift, "Now There's a Lojack for Ships," *The Journal of Commerce*, July 13, 1998, p. 1B.

29. Richardson, Paul, "A Marine Accident just Waiting to Happen," *The Journal of Commerce*, August 30, 1999.

30. Kaser, Tom, "Iceberg Ahead! Mariners Alerted," *The Journal of Commerce*, October 2, 1998, p. 1B.

31. Associated Press News Release, "Skyway Disaster Lives Remembered," May 8, 2000.

32. Tirschwell, Peter, "Pilot's Trip to Restroom Leads to Expensive Damage to Crane," *The Journal of Commerce*, February 19, 1997, p. 3B.

33. Motley, Robert, "Shippers' Case Law," *American Shipper*, February 1999, p. 36.

34. Motley, Robert, "Shippers' Case Law," *American Shipper*, March 2000, p. 46.

35. Motley, Robert, "Shippers' Case Law," *American Shipper*, June 1998, p. 40.

36. Mongelluzzo, Bill, "Lines Face Higher Costs, Possible Delays," *The Journal of Commerce*, January 14, 2000, p. 1.

37. "Non-immigrants Admitted by Class of Admission: Selected Fiscal Years 1981–2003," U.S. Citizenship and Immigration Services, http://www.uscis.gov/graphics/shared/aboutus/statistics/temp03yrbk/tempexcel/table 24d.xls, June 20, 2006.

38. Malcomson, Scott L., "The Unquiet Ship," *The New Yorker*, January 20, 1997, pp. 72–81.

39. Hall, Kevin G., "Free Rides Have Big Price Tags," *The Journal of Commerce*, March 11, 1997, p. 1A.

40. Bunce, Matthew, "Stowaway Deaths Haunt Ship Industry in Africa," *The Journal of Commerce*, March 13, 1997, p. 3B.

41. Associated Press, "Yugoslav Ship May Be Set Free," *The Journal of Commerce*, March 31, 1997, p. 4B.

42. Scherer, Ron, "Abandon Ship: New Law of Sea," *The Christian Science Monitor*, December 29, 1998, p. 2.

43. Associated Press News Release, "Romanian Sailors Abandoned on Decaying Ship," April 8, 1998.

44. Associated Press News Release, "Abandoned Crews Victims of Politics," June 22, 2000.

45. *Ports of the World*, Fifteenth Edition, Cigna Insurance Corporation, available from Publisher, *Ports of the World*, Cigna Companies, P.O. Box 7716, Philadelphia, Pennsylvania 19192, USA.

46. Kutoba, Coco, and Bill Mongelluzzo, "Japanese Dock Strike Disrupt Carriers," *The Journal of Commerce*, March 12, 1997, p. 1A.

47. Crabtree, Tom, Tom Hoang, and Jim Edgar, *The World Air Cargo Forecast*, Boeing Corporation, http://www.boeing.com/commercial/cargo/WACF_2004-2005, June 16, 2006.

48. Vaughan, Emmett J., and Therese M. Vaughan, *Fundamentals of Risk and Insurance*, Eighth Edition, John Wiley and Sons, New York, New York, USA, 1999.

49. *Marine Insurance: Notes and Comments on Ocean Cargo Insurance*, Cigna Property and Casualty Specialty Insurance, P.O. Box 7716, Philadelphia, Pennsylvania 19192, USA.

50. Vaughan, Emmett J., and Therese M. Vaughan, *Fundamentals of Risk and Insurance*, Eighth Edition, John Wiley and Sons, New York, New York, USA, 1999.

51. Banham, Russ, "They've Got Them Covered," *The Journal of Commerce*, February 23, 1998, p. 6A.

52. *Marine Insurance: Notes and Comments on Ocean Cargo Insurance*, Cigna Property and Casualty Specialty Insurance, P.O. Box 7716, Philadelphia, Pennsylvania 19192, USA.

53. *Ibid*

54. *Ocean Cargo Handbook*, Chubb Group of Insurance Companies, Warren, New Jersey 07059, USA.

55. *The Register of Ships on CD ROM*, Lloyd's Register, available at http://www.fairplay-publications.co.uk/archway/services/CDRom/RoSCDROM.htm.

56. Santi, Pascale, "Bien Assuré, Totalfina Ne Devrait Théoriquement Rien Payer," *Le Monde*, December 25, 1999.

57. "Explanatory Note Prepared by the 1992 Fund Secretariat," International Oil Pollution Compensation Fund, http://www.iopcfund.org/gennote.htm, October 13, 2000.

58. "Institute Marine Cargo Clauses–A," found at http://www.jus.uio.no/lm/institute.marine.cargo.clauses.a.1982/doc.html, October 13, 2000.

59. "Risk Management and Audit Techniques: Ocean Cargo," excerpted from *Risk Management and Audit Techniques*, Revised Edition, Standard Publishing Corp., Boston, Massachusetts, USA, and reprinted at http://www.poulton.com/carginf2.htm, October 2, 2000.

60. Ramberg, Jan, *ICC Guide to Incoterms 2000*, 1999, International Chamber of Commerce Publication No. 620, ICC Publishing S.A., 38 Cours Albert 1er, 75008 Paris, France and ICC Publishing, Inc., 156 Fifth Avenue, Suite 417, New York, NY 10010, USA.

61. *Marine Insurance: Notes and Comments on Ocean Cargo Insurance*, Cigna Property and Casualty Specialty Insurance, P.O. Box 7716, Philadelphia, Pennsylvania 19192, USA.

62. Ramberg, Jan, *ICC Guide to Incoterms 2000*, 1999, International Chamber of Commerce Publication No. 620, ICC Publishing S.A., 38 Cours Albert 1er, 75008 Paris, France and ICC Publishing, Inc., 156 Fifth Avenue, Suite 417, New York, NY 10010, USA.

63. *Marine Insurance: Notes and Comments on Ocean Cargo Insurance*, Cigna Property and Casualty Specialty Insurance, P.O. Box 7716, Philadelphia, Pennsylvania 19192, USA.

64. *Ocean Cargo Handbook*, Chubb Group of Insurance Companies, Warren, New Jersey 07059, USA.

65. Faber, Diana, et al., *Multimodal Transport: Avoiding Legal Problems*, LLP, London, UK, 1997.

66. Clark Worldwide Transport, Inc. Terms and Conditions of Service, http://www.clarkworldwide.com/terms.jsp, April 30, 2006.

67. U.S. Federal Maritime Commission, Subchapter B—Regulations Affecting Ocean Shipping in Foreign Commerce Part 515—Licensing, Financial Responsibility Requirements, and General Duties for Ocean Transportation Intermediaries, April 30, 2006, http://www.fmc.gov/home/515Licensingandsuretyrequirementsforoceantransportationintermediaries.asp.

68. "Members," Lloyd's Market, http://www.lloyds.com/Lloyds_Market/Capacity/Members.htm, June 20, 2006.

69. *Ibid*

70. McClintick, David, "The Decline and Fall of Lloyd's of London," *Time*, European Edition, February 21, 2000.

71. Redman, Christopher, "For Whom the Bell Tolls," *Time*, European Edition, November 13, 2000, p. 42.

72. Laurent, "COFACE: Les Outils pour Équilibrer vos Risques," *Le MOCI [Moniteur du Commerce International]*, September 28, 1995, pp. 116–125.

73. "Exposure Fee Table and Calculator," Export-Import Bank of the United States, http://www.exim.gov/tools/fee_calc.html, March 15, 2006.

74. Barovick, Richard, "Brokers Sit in Catbird Seat," *The Journal of Commerce*, September 24, 1997, p. 1C.

International Ocean Transportation

Chapter Eleven

Source: © 2007 JupiterImages Corporation.

In order to manage international logistics, it is fundamental to have a good understanding of the transportation alternatives open to an international shipper. The next three chapters provide an overview of the many options given to an exporter or an importer interested in making transportation arrangements for a given shipment.

The first chapter (Chapter 11) deals with the alternatives available in ocean transportation and the complexities of the international framework of rules that enable shipping lines to operate. The second chapter (Chapter 12) deals with air transportation and its rules and regulations. The third chapter (Chapter 13) deals with land transportation—rail and road—but also covers multi-modal transportation, which is not really a mode of transportation, but a shipping alternative that simplifies the work of the shipper—exporter or importer—by allowing it to send its freight with only one shipping company (carrier). It also covers pipelines and several other unusual modes of transportation, mostly used in very limited domestic markets.

The world's merchant fleet is registered in over 150 nations, and manned by over a million seafarers of virtually every nationality. The international shipping industry is responsible for the carriage of 90 percent of world trade (by weight). Shipping is key to the global economy. Without shipping, the transport of raw materials and the import/export of affordable food and manufactured goods would be impossible. Modern ships are technically sophisticated, high-value assets: Large ships have a capital cost of well over U.S. $100 million. Merchant ship operations generate an estimated annual revenue of over U.S. $380 billion in freight within the global economy.[1]

11-1 Types of Service

liner A ship that operates on a regular schedule, traveling from a group of ports to another group of ports.

tramp A ship that does not operate on a regular schedule and is available to be chartered for any voyage, from any port to any port.

The first differentiation to be made is the one between **liner** and **tramp** ships.

Liner ships travel on a regular voyage, following a pre-established schedule, and with determined ports of call. A scheduled voyage may include only two ports (Santos, Brazil, to Miami, USA, and back) or, more commonly, a series of ports in one region of the world (for example, Bremerhaven, Germany; Rotterdam, The Netherlands; Felixtowe, Great Britain) to another (for example, Boston, USA: Baltimore, USA; Nassau, Bahamas). Quite a few liners follow "round the world" (RTW) schedules, either eastbound or westbound, passing through the Panama Canal and the Suez Canal. There are many types of liner ships, a large number of which are adapted to specific routes, their size and equipment dependent on the ports of call they visit, and on the specific types of cargo that their trade route entails. Liners are common carriers in that they offer their services to any company that will pay the freight rate.[2]

Unlike liners, tramp ships operate wherever the market dictates. They do not operate on a regular schedule but travel wherever the company that has contracted (chartered) the vessel wants the cargo delivered. Because of the way they operate, tramp ships usually carry only one type of cargo at a time, for one exporter or importer. Most tramp ships therefore are designed for one type of cargo exclusively, even if they carry several "dry" cargoes or several grades of petroleum products. A possible analogy is that a tramp vessel is a taxicab, whereas a liner ship is a public bus.

11-2 Size of Vessels

The second principal differentiation to be made is the size of the vessel. Vessel size dictates trade routes, economies of scale, and ports of entry.

Ships are often categorized by their size, which is expressed in tons. Unfortunately, there are several ways of evaluating the tonnage of a vessel, and the "tonnage" of a vessel can be used for very different purposes. All of this leads to some differentiations that are pretty difficult to comprehend.

11-2a Dead-Weight Tonnage and Cubic Capacity

The **dead-weight tonnage (dwt)** is the total capacity of the ship (i.e., the maximum weight of the cargo that a vessel can carry) expressed in long tons (2,240 lbs) or in metric tons (2204.6 lbs). It is the measurement used by companies interested in shipping cargo, and is often just called "tonnage." It is measured using the weight of the difference in water displacement when the ship is empty and when it is fully loaded to its maximum. The dead-weight tonnage of a ship includes the fuel that the ship needs to travel—called **bunker**—and the supplies that it needs to function—called **stores**—and any ballast that the vessel may carry, therefore, it is the theoretical capacity of the ship more than its actual capacity. Vessels also have volumetric capacity for cargo that is called **grain** or **bale** cubic capacity. The grain cubic capacity is the cargo space available for loading a flowing cargo such as grain. The bale cubic capacity represents the total volume of space available for loading solid cargoes such as bales or boxes. The grain cubic capacity is always a larger figure. A vessel, when loaded with a very dense material—such as iron ore—can utilize its weight capacity before it reaches its cubic (volume) capacity; conversely, it can reach its volume capacity before it reaches its weight capacity if it is loaded with a light but voluminous cargo, such as timber or corn. A vessel that uses all of its cubic capacity and is also loaded down to its maximum draft is said to be "full and down."

11-2b Gross and Net Tonnage

The **gross tonnage** is the total *volume* capacity of the ship, expressed in hundreds of cubic feet (2.83 cubic meters). It only measures the capacity of the ship below its deck, so this measurement is not appropriate for determining the cargo-carrying capacity of a ship because a good number of vessels also carry cargo above deck. This measurement is used to determine how much a ship owner will have to pay in taxes to the country in which the ship is registered, or tolls to the authorities of the ports it visits or the canals it uses; that measure is also used for regulatory purposes. In that case, gross tonnage is referred to as Gross Registered Tonnage (GRT), which takes into account the specific way a canal authority (such as Suez or Panama) determines gross tonnage. Once the volume occupied by the engine room, the crew, and other space necessary for the good operation of the ship is removed, the **net tonnage** is obtained.

Gross tonnage is commonly used when assessing the size of fleets for statistical purposes. Because different organizations set the cutoff for ship size at different gross tonnage levels (for example, in increments of 300 or 1,000 gross tons), this difference in base line often is the principal cause of fleet size discrepancy between reports.

11-2c Displacement

The **displacement tonnage** is the total weight of the ship, when fully loaded, measured by the weight of the volume of water it displaces. The **light tonnage** is the weight of the ship, measured the same way, but when the vessel is empty, which means that it is the displacement of the vessel after it was built but before any ballast, cargo, fuel, or supplies were put aboard. Both are generally measured in long tons, and are used for naval architecture purposes in order to determine the vessel's stability, the stress it endures, and other engineering issues.

11-2d Plimsoll Mark and Load Lines

One more difficulty arises when one understands that ships are considered "fully loaded" at different drafts (how deep they sit in the water) in function of the season in which they are operating, of the latitudes under which it plies its trade, and of the density of the water. The deepest draft a ship can sit in is called the "tropical line" (T), followed by the "summer line" (S), the "winter line" (W), and the

dead-weight tonnage (dwt) The maximum weight that a ship can carry.

bunker The amount of fuel that a ship carries on board and that it needs to travel.

stores All the supplies that a ship carries and that it needs to function.

grain An agricultural commodity, such as corn, wheat, oats, or soybeans.

bale The end result of a packaging technique that consists of taking a commodity and unitizing it by compressing it and placing it into a bag or encircling it with string, metal, or plastic bands.

gross tonnage The total volume of a ship's carrying capacity, measured as the space available below deck, and expressed in hundreds of cubic feet.

net tonnage Obtained by subtracting the volume occupied by the engine room and the spaces necessary for the operation of the ship (crew quarters, bridge) from the gross tonnage.

displacement tonnage The total weight of the ship, when fully loaded, measured by using the weight of the water being displaced.

light tonnage The total weight of the ship, when empty, measured by using the weight of the water being displaced.

Vessel Tonnage

The relationship between vessel tonnages can be expressed mathematically and the following is an example of an actual 35,000 dwt (dead-weight tonnage) ton Handysize Bulk vessel ready for a 3,500 Nautical Mile voyage:

Length Over All (LOA)	611'03"
Beam (width)	93'02"
Summer draft (amount of water needed to float)	35'02.5"
Freeboard (distance between the water line and deck)	15'.75"
Winter draft	34'05.5"
Fresh Water draft	35'11.5"
Net Tonnage (NT)	19,513
Gross Tonnage (GT)	24,384
Suez Gross Registered Tonnage (GRT)	24,596

Displacement	44,122 LT
Light Ship Displacement	7,646 LT
Dead-Weight Tonnage (dwt) at Summer loadline	36,476 LT
Bunker Capacity (varies with voyage length)	600 LT
Potable Drinking water (varies with voyage length)	240 LT
Constant (allowance for crew and consumable stores)	150 LT
Ballast (carried for trim if needed)	100 LT
Cargo Deadweight (deadweight available for cargo)	35,386 LT

"Winter North Atlantic" (WNA) line. A "fresh water" (F) line is also present, as fresh water density is lower—a ship will sit lower in fresh water than it would in saltwater with the same quantity of cargo. At the same height as the vessel's summer dead-weight draft, there is another diagram called the Plimsoll Mark: a circle bisected by a horizontal line, which identifies the Classification Society that determined the vessel's load lines. Figure 11-1 shows the Plimsoll Mark and load lines for a ship classified by Lloyd's Register. The Plimsoll Mark and load lines are located on the hull of a ship, amidships (halfway between the bow and the stern), and are marked with a bead welded onto the hull and painted.

The dead-weight tonnage is generally determined at the summer line or at the line that represents accurately the conditions under which a ship is used. For example, a

LR: Lloyd's Register
TF: Tropical Fresh Water
F: Fresh Water
T: Tropical Seas
S: Summer Seas
W: Winter Seas
WNA: Winter North Atlantic

Figure 11-1
The Plimsoll Mark and Load Lines
Source: Diagram courtesy of Natalie David. Used with permission.

Figure 11-2
A Panamax Containership in the Miraflores Locks

Source: Photo © Thorwald Westmaas, www.ilisa.com. *Used with permission.*

vessel used consistently in the Caribbean would have its dead-weight tonnage calculated with the tropical load line. The load lines correspond to geographical regions of the globe and a vessel must be at the appropriate load line when it arrives in the geographical region. For instance, a vessel that loads in Matadi, Congo, in January and sails for Antwerp will load to the tropical load line (T) but must consume enough fuel to be at the Winter North Atlantic (WNA) load line when the vessel arrives in that geographic region. A vessel that exceeds appropriate load lines is subject to heavy fines and may also be considered to be in an unseaworthy state.

11-2e Size Categories

One of the biggest distinctions made on ships' sizes is the one made between the ships that can travel through the locks of the Panama Canal and the ones that cannot. A ship of the maximum size that can possibly fit through these locks is called a **Panamax** ship; such a ship can have up to 75,000 tons of dead-weight tonnage and its outside dimensions allow it to barely fit within the locks, with only a few inches of clearance between the locks' walls and the ship (see Figure 11-2). The locks are 1,000 feet long and 110 feet wide. The longest ship to cross the Panama Canal is the *Marcona Prospector*, which is 973 feet long and 106 feet wide. The widest is the USS *New Jersey*, which is 108 feet wide.[3] All ships built that are larger than this size are called **post-Panamax** ships. Other terminologies used are:

- **Handysize ship:** A term commonly used in the dry-bulk trade and which refers to ships in the 10,000 to 50,000 dead-weight ton range.[4] Such ships tend to be used for tramp service.

- **Suez-Max ships:** This term is used to describe ships sized at roughly 150,000 dead-weight tons and which are of the maximum size that can fit through the Suez Canal (about 285 meters long, thirty-five meters wide, and twenty-three meters of draft). In 1996, the Suez Canal was deepened and widened, so the Suez-Max terminology is losing some of its validity.[5]

Panamax A ship of the maximum size that can enter the locks of the Panama Canal.

post-Panamax A ship whose size is too large to enter the locks of the Panama Canal.

- **Capesize ships:** This term is used to describe large dry-bulk carriers of a capacity greater than 80,000 dead-weight tons.[6]
- **Very large crude carrier:** This term is used to describe an oil tanker of up to 300,000 dead-weight tonnage, which is about 350 meters long, fifty-five meters wide, and has twenty-eight meters of draft.[7] That's 1,150 feet long, 180 feet wide, and ninety-two feet of draft.
- **Ultra large crude carrier:** This term describes an oil tanker of more than 300,000 dead-weight tonnage. One of the largest ULCCs built, the *Sea Giant*, is of 555,000 dead-weight tonnage, is 415 meters long, sixty-three meters wide, and has a draft of thirty-five meters.[8] That represents a surface of 2.5 hectares, which translates to 1,360 feet long, 207 feet wide, a draft of 115 feet, and an area of 6.5 acres. Such ships generally are unable to go into traditional ports and remain in deep sea at all times: Their cargo is removed using a process called "lightering" (see Section 11-3f).

For comparison purposes, one of the largest containerships, the *Regina Maersk*, is 302 meters long, forty-three meters wide, has a draft of twelve meters, and has a dead-weight tonnage of 65,600 tons.[9]

11-3 Types of Vessels

The third principal differentiation to be made is based on the type of cargo carried by the vessels, and those cargoes are used to classify merchant ships into many different categories (see Figure 11-3).[10] First, a distinction is made between cargo ships that carry **wet-bulk (liquid) cargoes** and those vessels that carry **dry-bulk cargoes**. Second, wet and dry cargoes can either be shipped in bulk or unitized (shipped in units that are unloaded one at a time, such as boxes, crates, or containers).

There are more than 46,000 commercial ships worldwide of a capacity over 500 gross registered tonnes, with a combined tonnage of 597,709,000 gross registered tonnes (see Figures 11-4[11] and 11-5).[12] Almost every single one of these ships is designed differently: It is therefore difficult to classify them much better than in broad-based groups, with many ships not fitting neatly into one category.

wet-bulk (liquid bulk) cargo Liquid cargo that is loaded directly into the hold of a ship, without any form of unitization.

dry-bulk cargo Dry cargo that is loaded directly into the hold of a ship, without any form of unitization. Although dry, the cargo exhibits the properties of a liquid, in that it takes the shape of the hold.

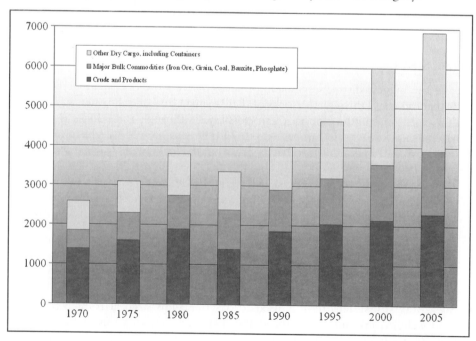

Figure 11-3
Ocean Worldwide Trade by Type of Cargo (in millions of tons)

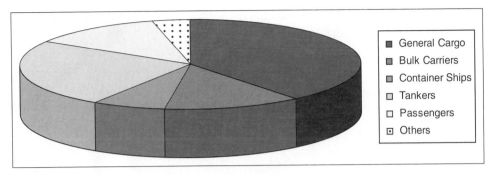

Figure 11-4
Worldwide Number of Vessels in Each Category (2005)

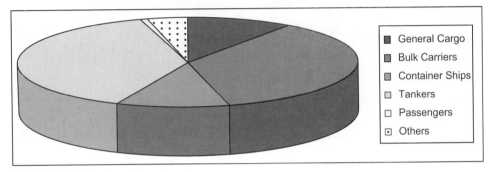

Figure 11-5
Worldwide Tonnage (dwt) of Vessels in Each Category (2005)

11-3a Containerships

The containerized trade is growing rapidly: Approximately 60 percent of the world trade is containerized (most manufactured products are shipped in containers), and container transportation volume is growing by 9 percent per year. Even in trade lanes where containers are solidly implanted, such as Asia-North America or Europe-North America, the growth in the volume of shipment is estimated at 6 to 8 percent.[13] Given the fact that goods that traditionally traveled in bulk are now shipped using containers—for example, forestry products or grain—and given the fact that inter-modal transportation is responding well to customer needs, it seems that the container, which was created in 1956, will dominate international trade yet further.

Containerships, also known as "box ships," carry containerized cargo on a scheduled voyage. Vessels dedicated to the container trade can carry up to 10,000 TEUs—twenty-foot equivalent unit, or the space equivalent of a twenty-foot container—but there is a large number of mixed-cargo ships that can also carry containers, sometimes as few as 100 TEUs. Most containerships rely upon the port cranes to unload their cargo, but some do have cranes on board. All containerships used to be capable of going through the Panama Canal and carried around 3,000 TEUs. When the first post-Panamax containerships were delivered, they carried upward of 4,500 TEUs and forced some substantial changes in ports. For example, they were so wide and so high (see Figure 11-6) that some ports had to upgrade their crane equipment. Moreover, some ports became entirely inaccessible; some of the post-Panamax ships cannot enter some of the ports on the East Coast of the United States, as they do not "fit" under the bridges or the channels are not deep enough (for example, Port Elizabeth of the Port of New York-New Jersey).

As there are plans to build yet larger ships, as big as 18,000 TEUs,[14] there will be additional demands made on port infrastructure, and it will certainly reduce the number of ports in which these giant ships can berth to a handful worldwide. The

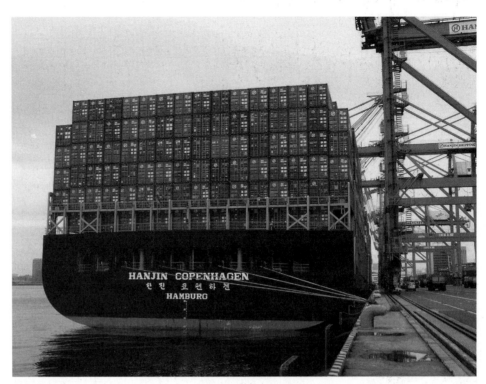

Figure 11-6
A Post-Panamax Containership
Source: Photo © Jun Takahashi. Used with permission.

trend in the industry is therefore seen as the creation of a system of large "hubs,"[15] to and from which the mega-ships would travel, coupled with a number of smaller ships, called "feeder ships," which would travel between these giant hub ports and smaller ports. Those feeder ships would essentially be the existing fleet of traditional containerships. Although this would cause transshipments to occur, it is estimated that it would lower transportation costs.[16]

Traditional containerships hold containers "under deck" as well as "on deck." Some containers are first loaded in the holds of the ship, then the hatch covers (the deck) are put in place, and the remainder of the containers are placed on top of that. Containers placed under deck are usually held in place by vertical guides, along which the crane operator slides them. On-deck containers are usually stacked on top of each other, and latched to each other with metal bars and twistlocks (see Figure 11-7). Since the early 1990s, several shipping lines have tried to speed up the process of loading containers by equipping their ships with vertical guides for on-deck containers as well, and some have eliminated the deck hatches altogether (see Figure 11-8), simply choosing to equip the vessel with much larger bilge pumps (the pumps that remove the water from the inside of a ship). Eventually, it is conceivable that the concept of "deck" will no longer exist in the container trade.[17]

Another possible change in the container industry would be the creation of fast ships, or ships capable of crossing the Atlantic Ocean in three and a half days, a project pursued by a company aptly named FastShip. Those ships would carry 1,500 TEUs and travel between two specifically equipped ports—Philadelphia, USA, and Cherbourg, France—reducing the transit time from supplier to customer to seven days, or somewhat similar to the six days that an airline can achieve. While the costs of shipping would be 60 percent higher than for a traditional trans-Atlantic crossing, the founders of the venture estimate that some time-sensitive cargo could benefit from their service.[18] Skeptics abound, but there is certainly a trend toward faster transportation and reduced inventory costs. In addition, it is likely that such competition will reduce the costs of airfreight, so most shippers should benefit.

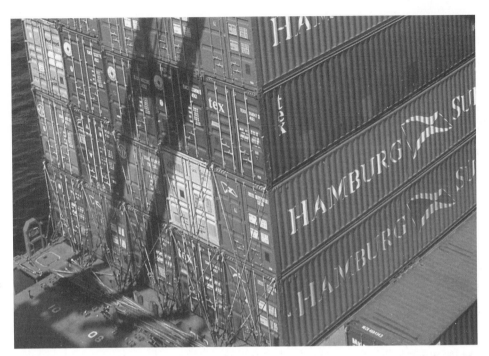

Figure 11-7
Containers Lashed on the Deck of a Containership
Source: Photo © Hamburg Süd. Used with permission.

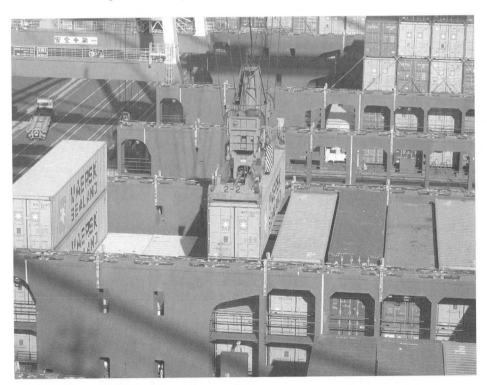

Figure 11-8
Containers on a Hatchless Containership
Source: Photo © Jun Takahashi. Used with permission.

The principal problem for such a service will be to make high-speed, low-drag hull forms and fuel-efficient propulsion systems cost effective enough for a business model to work. A 2003 RAND study pointed out that today's "fast ships are not generally considered to be commercially viable because of their very high operating costs."[19].

However, as fuel costs increase, fast ships are becoming increasingly more attractive, as they consume 60 percent less fuel (per ton of cargo transported) than air freighters.

11-3b Roll-On/Roll-Off Ships

Roll-on/roll-off (RORO) ships were created to accommodate cargo that was self-propelled, such as automobiles or trucks, or cargo that could be wheeled into a ship, such as railroad cars. They are essentially floating parking garages (see Figure 11-9).

The concept is fairly straightforward. Because it takes a long time to load such vehicles "over the rail" (i.e., by using a crane), it is preferable to load them by rolling them onto the ship. RORO ships therefore have a portion of their hull that opens up and acts as a ramp on which the vehicles are driven before being parked on the many decks of the ship and secured with chains. The hull opening is either on the side of the ship or on its stern (rear).

RORO ships have an advantage in that specialized lifting equipment is not required, even for the heaviest of loads, because the cargo rolls under its own power or is pulled by a tractor. It therefore only needs some docking space and a substantial number of dock workers to load or unload its cargo. There are distinctions between a pure car-carrier (PCC) ship, which loads only cars and has decks with only five feet of overhead clearance,[20] and other, more versatile, "true" RORO ships that can accommodate larger cargo. Many RORO ships are equipped with adjustable decks, which allow them to transport any sort of rolling cargo.[21]

As the number of cars manufactured worldwide increases, it seems that the future of the RORO concept is secure. However, there are several companies that are selling specialized containers that can handle six automobiles (on two levels) at once, containers that can be collapsed and placed into a regular containership for the return trip.[22] This concept is attractive as it overcomes two drawbacks of the RORO ships: First, there is no need to hire expensive stevedore labor to drive the vehicles onto the ship—it is replaced with cheaper "inland" labor to load and unload the containers—and, second, it eliminates the cost of modifying the configuration of the decks so that regular bulk cargo can be loaded in the now-empty RORO ship on the return trip. The latter issue is significant for trades with countries that import a lot of vehicles but export fewer, such as the United States.

The concept of RORO has been expanded to another variation, designed for the transport of livestock, which are led aboard the ship rather than hoisted over its rail. Therefore, the ships are given the moniker of **trot-on/trot-off** ships.

trot-on/trot-off A ship designed to carry livestock. It possesses a ramp that the animals can use to walk on board and exit the vessel.

Figure 11-9
A Roll-On/Roll-Off Ship in Port
Source: Photo © Höegh Autoliners. Used with permission.

11-3c Break-Bulk or General Merchandise Ships

Break-bulk ships (also called general-merchandise ships) constitute the least-homogenous category of vessels. There are all sorts of break-bulk ships, which were often created for a specialized trade or a given shipping lane. Altogether, though, break-bulk cargo ships are multipurpose ships that can transport shipments of unusual sizes, unitized on pallets, in bags, or in crates (see Figure 11-10). Because of the increase in the percentage of international cargo shipments that are containerized, including the "containerization" of some goods that are larger than what can "normally" fit in a regular container (see Section 13-3a), and because of the increasing role of RORO ships, break-bulk ships' share of international trade is decreasing but is still the single largest fleet in number of ships.

The main problem with general-merchandise ships stems from their labor-intensive loading and unloading; each unitized piece must be handled separately, with several stevedores in the hull of the ship and several stevedores on the quay, in addition to the crane operators. In addition, because the cargo is of different sizes, each piece may require different equipment (a different number of hooks, shorter or longer slings, and so on), and in some cases, demand "problem solving," which may involve a few attempts before it is loaded or unloaded successfully (see Figure 14-5). In addition, the securing of the loads on the decks is just as labor intensive, because pieces of cargo have odd sizes. Consequently, break-bulk ships stay in ports much longer, especially because they cannot load or unload in the rain,[23] and their schedules can be erratic.

The advantage of break-bulk ships is that they can call at just about any port to pick up different kinds of cargo loads, giving them a flexibility that containerships do not yet have. In addition, a large percentage of break-bulk ships are equipped with an on-board crane, which allows them to load and unload without relying on port equipment. Although decreasing in percentage, the break-bulk trade has a significant future in that it will always carry odd-sized shipments and always carry heavy cargoes that cannot be containerized.

Nevertheless, it is likely that there will be fewer general-merchandise ships in the future—almost no new break-bulk ships have been built in the last fifteen years—although it is likely that there will be a corresponding increase in the number of "combination ships," which will carry break-bulk cargo, but also some bulk, some RORO, and a few containers.[24]

Figure 11-10
A Break-Bulk Ship

Source: Photo © Silvio Roberto Smera. Used with permission.

11-3d Combination Ships

The ultimate multipurpose ships are combination ships, which are designed to carry all sorts of different loads in a single voyage. A typical combination ship has several holds in which bulk cargo, such as timber or grain, can be placed. Those holds can also be used for break-bulk cargo, especially oversized and heavy cargo, such as machinery, and sometimes containers. It also has a **tweendeck**, or a deck below the main deck, which accommodates smaller break-bulk cargo, as well as vehicles that are loaded through a RORO access door. On its main deck, the typical combination ship can carry several containers as well. Finally, a combination ship has one or more on-board cranes, to increase its versatility and allow it to unload its cargo in any port (see Figure 11-11).

Combination ships thrive in shipping lanes that have a low volume of trade, such as the trade between developed countries and developing countries, or the trade to and from small island nations, such as those in the South Pacific or the Caribbean.

11-3e LASH Ships

Lighter-aboard-ship (LASH) ships represent yet another type of ship that is quite versatile. The concept is similar to a containership, in that the LASH ship carries standardized units of cargo, but with the difference that the units of cargo are much larger, each with a capacity of 385 metric tons of dead-weight tonnage. Because these units can also float, they are called **LASH barges**. Their dimensions are eighteen meters long, nine meters wide, and three meters deep (translating to fifty-nine feet, thirty feet, and ten feet, respectively). Each barge is covered with a hatch cover and is watertight.[25] The capacity of the average LASH ship, also called the **LASH mothership**, is about eighty barges. The concept of LASH was created in 1969 to carry forest products from the United States to Northern Europe,[26] and this trade is still one of the concept's mainstays (see Figure 11-12).

Just like containers, LASH barges present the advantage of allowing the shipper to pack and unpack the barge independently of the ship's schedule, and it allows for a very fast loading and unloading of the vessel carrying the LASH barges. In addition, the LASH system also has an advantage in that the barges can be floated to the mothership, then loaded on board using the crane of the vessel. This allows the ship to call on ports that have very little lifting equipment or call on ports that are very shallow. It actually allows the LASH vessel to load and unload at anchor (i.e., without having to be docked). Many project cargo barges can then be delivered to remote areas of the world, either in coastal areas or at the mouths of rivers, or to

tweendeck In a combination ship, a deck located below the main deck that is used to carry smaller size break-bulk cargo, such as vehicles.

Lighter Aboard Ship (LASH) Barge A floating container measuring eighteen meters by nine meters by three meters that can be loaded and unloaded from a LASH mothership and can be tugged to its destination in a port or to an area without port facilities.

Lighter Aboard Ship (LASH) Mothership A ship equipped with cranes that is designed to carry around eighty LASH barges and can load and unload them at anchor (i.e., without having to be in a port).

Figure 11-11
A Combination Ship
Source: Photo © Losinjska Plovidba. Used with permission.

Figure 11-12
LASH Barges and their LASH Mothership
Source: Photo © Donn Young, Port of New Orleans. Used with permission.

areas where ocean-going ships cannot go, such as inland ports. The barges can then be unpacked after the mothership has unloaded them.

11-3f Product, Chemical, and Crude Carriers

Petroleum products transported in bulk by ships are broken down into three principal trades: product, chemical, and crude.

Product vessels transport refined products such as gasoline, diesel oil, or other refined products. These products need to be carefully segregated and kept from contamination. The vessels range in size from small coastal vessels (about 1,000 dead-weight tonnage [dwt]) to large product carriers, roughly 60,000 dwt in size. The vessels may carry up to six different products if the vessel's tank and piping system allow segregation.

Chemical Carriers are specially designed ships in the 1,000 to 40,000 dwt range that carry chemicals (see Figure 11-13). Some may transport as many as forty different chemicals and are referred to as "drugstore" ships. The hazardous nature of some chemicals, such as benzene, and the handling requirements of other chemicals that require special tanks, dedicated piping systems, and complex safeguards limit the vessels to the chemical trade.

Crude carriers are the bulk ships dedicated to the transport of unrefined (crude) oil. The largest ships in the world are crude carriers; there is a distinction made between crude carriers up to 80,000 dwt, which are called AfraMax, and very large crude carriers (VLCC), up to 300,000 dwt, and ultra large crude carriers (ULCC) beyond this tonnage. There were approximately 450 VLCCs and ULCCs in 1997, a figure that is unlikely to have changed in 2006, even though the international oil trade is growing; the only change being that older ships are replaced with more

Figure 11-13
A Chemical Carrier

Source: Photo © Silvio Roberto Smera. Used with permission.

modern ships, equipped with double hulls, which makes them less likely to spill their cargo when they accidentally run aground.

VLCCs and ULCCs are such large ships that they can call on only a few ports in the world; because their draft, when loaded, can reach thirty-five meters (115 feet) they need very deep ports and, because they are so long and wide, a very large docking area. In a number of cases, the VLCCs and ULCCs do not enter a port but stay at anchor outside of the port in deep waters. The oil cargo of the large crude carrier is then transferred into smaller crude carriers that then transport it and unload it into the port (see Figure 11-14). This process is called **lightering** and is also occasionally used for traditional break-bulk or dry-bulk ships. On other occasions, the VLCCs and ULCCs are connected to an artificial island, or a "floating island," which is a pipeline terminal in deep waters. Some countries have transformed natural islands into deep-water oil terminals for such ships, such as in the case of Kharg Island in Iran.

After the oil spill from the VLCC *Exxon Valdez* into Alaskan waters in March 1989, the United States enacted the Oil Pollution Act of 1990. This unilateral act impacted all tankers worldwide, because most will eventually travel to the United States, as it is the highest oil-consuming nation. This act requires a phase-in of double hulled tankers, and its first phase was completed in 2005; some more recent tankers can wait until 2015. The double hulls are believed to provide some protection in the case of certain types of groundings but the design reduces the carrying

lightering The process by which a large vessel's cargo is unloaded offshore into smaller vessels that then take the cargo to nearby ports.

Figure 11-14
A Very Large Crude Carrier Being Lightered by a Smaller Tanker

Source: Photo © Skaugen PetroTrans, Inc. Used with permission.

Becoming a "Master Unlimited"

Maneuvering an ultra large crude carrier (ULCC) is a job that few people can handle, but it is the daily responsibility of captains who have reached the prestigious title of "Master Unlimited"—there are only about 3,000 of them worldwide and they are the only ones accredited to command ships of more than 5,000 tons GRT.[27] It can be quite a hair-raising experience. Consider that a ULCC can be as long as four football fields, and that, at cruising speed and fully loaded, it stops in a mere six miles if its engine is stopped. If put in full reverse, the distance "shrinks" to two miles.[28]

In order to learn how to pilot these behemoths, captains either practice on computer simulations or travel to the unusual training camp of Port Revel in the foothills of the Alps in France, where they are placed in models of large ships. A similar model training program is operated by the Massachusetts Maritime Academy in Buzzards Bay, Massachusetts, in the United States. Like their real-life equivalent, these model ships are extremely underpowered: A ship of this size is "like a large lorry [truck] with a moped engine and no brakes" says an instructor at Port Revel, noting that the forty-foot-long model *Europe*, weighing 41,000 lbs, has a motor of less than one horsepower with which the skipper has to maneuver it.[29] After a few days on the pond at Port Revel, these gifted sailors are capable of maneuvering these ships so well that they can squeeze a 700-foot behemoth in the 750-foot space left between two other ships in port without the help of a tug. In other words, simple parallel parking.

capacity of vessels by as much as 15 percent, and adds to the cost of construction and maintenance.

11-3g Dry-Bulk Carriers

Dry-bulk carriers operate on the same basis as oil tankers in that they are chartered for a whole voyage. Dry-bulk ships (see Figure 11-15) have several holds in their hull, in which non-unitized cargo is placed. There are many types of dry-bulk ships, and because of the trade in which they are engaged—the type of merchandise that they carry and the ports on which they call—dry-bulk ships can have specialized configurations or equipment. Generally speaking, dry-bulk ships carry agricultural products, such as cereals, as well as coal, ores, scrap iron, dry chemicals, and other bulk commodities. Some of those ships, because of the versatility of the cargo that they can carry, are called Oil-Bulk-Ore (O-B-O) carriers, as they can transport oil during one leg of the voyage and then on the next leg, after cleaning the tanks/holds, carry dry-bulk products.

In terms of size, dry-bulk ships are generally classified into three types: Cape size, which are ships that are too large to fit through the Suez Canal and must go around the Cape of Good Hope on the southern tip of Africa; Panamax ships, which are small enough to fit through the Panama Canal; and the Handysize bulkers, which are from 10,000 to 45,000 dead-weight tons. Many of these Handysize tramp bulkers are somewhat older vessels.

A good portion of the trade in commodities in the world transits through a myriad of these Handysize vessels, carrying cargoes of sugar, rice, and other staples from small ports to other small ports. These ships are chartered primary through the Baltic Exchange, which is a meeting place for brokers representing the ship owners and the cargo owners to meet and conduct business. The business is initially done verbally and the word of the brokers is their bond.[30]

As seen in Section 9-5e, three types of charters are typically used for bulk vessels. The first is a **voyage charter** that hires the ship with all functions provided such as crew, management, and fuel by the ship owner to deliver cargo between one or more ports in the world. A **time charter** is when the vessel is hired to deliver cargo, with the ship owner providing all services over a fixed period of time that may vary from a few months to several years in duration. A **bareboat or demise charter** is one where the vessel is hired and run by another party. The ship owner provides a

voyage charter A lease agreement between the owner (lessor) of a bulk cargo ship and a lessee, in which the owner provides the lessee with the ship, the crew, and all other services or supplies, for a single voyage.

time charter A lease agreement between the owner (lessor) of a bulk cargo ship and a lessee in which the owner provides the lessee with the ship, the crew, and all other services or supplies, for an agreed-upon period of time.

bareboat or demise charter A lease agreement between the owner (lessor) of a bulk cargo ship and a lessee, in which the owner provides the lessee with only the ship, and no other services or supplies.

Figure 11-15
A Dry-Bulk Carrier Being Unloaded

Source: Photo © Alcan Primary metals. Used with permission.

laker A cargo ship designed for the Great Lakes of the United States and Canada. Their maximum size is dictated by the size of the locks through which they travel.

vessel that is bare of crew and supplies. The vessel charterer operates the vessel in all respects and returns the bareboat to the ship owner after the end of the demise charter, which can last months or years. Both dry and wet trade vessels are chartered.

There is a specific group of dry-bulk carriers that serve the ports of the Great Lakes, between the United States and Canada, called **lakers**. Their characteristics are determined by the size of the canal locks of the Welland Canal, which gives them long and narrow hulls. Lakers trade mostly in three commodities: iron ore and iron ore pellets, coal, and finished steel. They are not "ocean-going vessels," but they fit the general description of dry-bulk carriers. These vessels have self-unloading gear that allows for the rapid (10,000 tons per hour) unloading of bulk cargoes. The design of the self-unloading booms allows the vessels to place cargo up to 150 feet off the side of the vessel (see Figure 11-16). A number of the self-unloading lakers are over 1,000 feet in length and can trade only in four of the five Great Lakes as they cannot fit through the Welland Canal into Lake Ontario.

Although not altogether the same as dry-bulk carriers, there is also a large number of ships that carry specialized cargoes that can be considered as dry bulk. Examples are refrigerated ships—also called "reefer ships"—that are slowly being replaced by refrigerated containers aboard containerships, with the possible exception of specialized refrigerated ships called banana ships; liquid food carriers, which therefore carry liquid bulk cargoes such as molasses, orange juice, and vegetable oils; lumber carriers; and cement carriers.

Figure 11-16
A Canadian Laker Using Self-Unloading Gear to Discharge Limesone
Source: Photo © Ken Newhams, Duluth Shipping News. Used with permission.

11-3h Gas Carriers

Another important bulk trade is the transportation of liquefied natural gas (LNG) and of liquefied petroleum gas (LPG). These types of carriers have a very distinctive shape. These ships hold several spheres of compressed gasses, only part of which are visible above their main deck (see Figure 11-17). The LNG and LPG trades tend to be slightly different than the average bulk transport, as they are used in a particular trade for long periods of time, on long-term contracts—called time charter parties (see Section 9-5e)—and therefore nearly have a sailing schedule, not unlike liner ships. They only carry cargo on half of their voyage and return empty.

Figure 11-17
A Liquefied Natural Gas Carrier
Source: Photo © Corel Corporation. Used with permission.

The End of the Shipping Line

Most ships, after a mere twenty to twenty-five years at sea, end up so damaged by the sea and the elements that they are no longer economically viable vessels (it costs too much to maintain them). In addition, as the size of ships increases, shipping lines have a surplus of capacity that they are loathe to sell, as they do not want to encourage new competitors.[31]

Where do all of these old ships end their lives?

Many of them end up on the beaches of Pakistan, Bangladesh, or India, where they are dismantled, by hand, into sellable chunks of scrap steel and other metals. At the present time, 90 percent of older ships end their lives in these three countries, and half of them die in Alang, a beach in the Indian State of Gujarat where 600 or so scrap businesses dismantle 400 ships every year.[32] These are dangerous and poorly paid jobs, but it is estimated that they provide direct and indirect employment for at least 200,000 workers.

Despite governmental protests about the impact of this business on India's image and its workers' health, more and more ships are dismantled in this area of the world, and, as the world fleet ages and is replaced with more modern and technologically advanced ships, this trend shows no sign of abating.[33]

11-4 Flag

By international convention, each vessel engaged in international trade must be registered in a specific country, and therefore "flies" a specific country's flag. In many ways, the vessel is an extension of the territory of this country, and all its laws and regulations apply on board the ship. In exchange, the naval forces of the flag of registry will protect those flagged merchant ships in time of conflict. In addition, the vessel must pay the taxes that this country imposes. There is one significant caveat to this situation: With very few exceptions, a ship owner can *choose* the country in which its ship is registered, or choose the flag that it flies.

The flags of developed countries tend to impose very substantial regulations on the way a ship is operated in such areas as the composition of the crew on board, its minimum training requirement, its nationality (because it is a country's extension of its territory, its immigration rules apply), the work rules on board (such as the number of hours worked per day and week, before overtime pay is earned), the vacation time earned by the crew, and so on. In addition, taxation can be significantly higher. However, regulations and taxes for some developing countries are minimal. It is estimated that flying an American flag rather than a developing country's flag can add at least 30 percent[34] to the operating costs of a vessel. A 1997 Maritime Administration study showed that a break-bulk ship flying the U.S. flag required a crew of thirty-four and cost U.S. $13,300 per day, whereas the same ship flying a developing country's flag would require a crew of twenty-four and cost U.S. $1,400 per day.[35]

A small number of countries have created what is called an **open registry**, which means that any ship owner can choose to have its vessel fly this flag. There are no requirements regarding the citizenship of the owners of the ship. Because these countries tend to have minimal on-board requirements and taxes, many ship owners decide to fly such countries' flags, which have been derisively called **flags of convenience**. Most of these open registries emanate from developing countries, but, fairly recently, some developed countries established their own versions of open registries, which are called **secondary registries**, with much less stringent requirements than their "normal" registries in order to prevent their merchant fleet from being entirely registered with flags of convenience. Norway, Denmark, and France are three notorious examples. Table 11-1 shows the six largest open registry fleets in the world[36] and Table 11-2[37] shows the true nationality of the ships flying these open registries, as well as the percentages of the largest fleets in the world that are registered under a flag of convenience.

It should be noted that the choice of a flag regulates the qualifications of the crew, its compensation, and the amount of taxes that the ship owners pay. It does not influence the seaworthiness of the vessel, which is evaluated by Classification Societies and determines

open registry A country that allows vessels owned by companies having no business relations in its territory to be registered in that country and carry its flag.

flag of convenience A country with an open registry that has lower taxes and more lenient on-board regulations than other countries with open registries. A derogatory term.

secondary registry A response by developed countries to the threat of open registries and flags of convenience: They created a secondary registry with lower on-board standards and taxes to entice ship owners to carry their flag and not defect to flag of convenience countries.

TABLE 11-1	Tonnage and Number of Ships in the Top Six Open-Registry Fleets (2005)

Country	Number of Ships	Tonnage (000s of DWT)
Panama	4,266	177,866
Liberia	1,328	76,322
Bahamas	999	41,835
Malta	913	30,971
Cyprus	867	31,585
Bermuda	95	6,206

TABLE 11-2	True Nationality of Ships Registered in the Top Six Open Registries, by Decreasing Fleet Size (2005)

	Panama	Liberia	Bahamas	Malta	Cyprus	Bermuda	Percentage of National Fleet in Foreign Registries	Percentage in Own Registry
Japan	45.3	6.0	3.9	0.1	1.0	0.0	89.3	10.7
Greece	11.5	13.3	19.0	66.1	54.4	0.2	67.1	32.8
Germany	0.8	22.4	1.7	3.0	18.1	0.3	84.4	15.6
United States	1.1	5.2	21.4	0.1	4.1	4.4	77.8	22.2
China	5.7	3.5	0.5	0.6	0.5	0.0	52.3	46.7
Norway	0.8	5.8	15.8	1.7	1.1	0.9	67.4	32.6
Hong Kong	4.8	2.1	2.0	0.1	0.1	10.0	57.9	42.1
Taiwan	4.9	5.4	0.0	0.1	0.0	0.0	77.3	22.7
Korea	8.0	0.0	0.0	0.2	0.2	0.0	61.9	30.1
United Kingdom	0.4	3.0	2.4	0.6	3.0	45.2	58.0	42.0
Switzerland	3.5	0.4	2.2	2.0	0.3	8.1	93.1	6.9
Singapore	1.0	4.5	0.6	0.0	0.2	0.0	44.4	55.6
Others	12.2	28.4	30.5	25.5	17.0	30.9		
	100%	100%	100%	100%	100%	100%		

the insurance premiums (hull insurance and P&I insurance) that the vessel owners have to pay (see Section 10-7). A competent crew and a seaworthy vessel are guaranteed if the vessel is registered in a developed country, if it is operated by a reputable shipping company, or if it is classed with one of the major classification societies; however, problems are more likely to arise with vessels registered under a flag of convenience.

Countries attempt to influence, as much as possible, the flags of the ships that enter their ports. Although they cannot outright ban certain nationalities, they can prevent ships not registered in their country from carrying certain freight. For example, the Cargo Preference Act of the United States requires that at least 50 percent of U.S. government cargo be carried by U.S.-flagged ships. The Jones Act requires that cargo transported from one port in the United States to another port in the United States—a trade called **cabotage** (from the French verb *caboter*, which means "sail along the coast")—must be carried exclusively on U.S.-flagged ships.[38] This is the case for cargo going from the West Coast to Hawaii, for example. Finally, all cargo in trades supported by the Ex-Im Bank must be shipped through U.S.-flagged ships.[39] A study by the Maritime Administration of the United States found that over fifty maritime countries had some form of cabotage or flag protection laws of one form or another.[40]

The United States' situation is yet more complicated. It compensates select ship owners who elect to flag their vessels with the stars-and-stripes to the tune of $2.1 million per year per vessel,[47] but not just because it is more expensive to run a

cabotage An ocean trade consisting of shipping between ports located in the same country.

Flying the Flag

The choice of a flag has many consequences beyond the crew's training and the taxes that the ship owners have to pay:

- Cabotage rules require that American flags and crews be used for ships traveling from one port in the United States to another port in the United States. Cruise ships, not one of which flies the U.S. flag, therefore cannot travel between two U.S. ports. Cruise ships destined for Alaska leave from Vancouver, Canada, and cruise ships destined for Hawaii leave from Ensenada, Mexico.[41]

- Most of the cruise ships fly flags of convenience, such as the Bahamas, or secondary registries, such as that of Norway. Because those registries do not exert much oversight over working conditions on their vessels, working cruise ship crews are generally employed for substandard wages and in miserable jobs. Very low wages are commonplace, and so are twelve- to fifteen-hour days. Passengers are usually oblivious to the discrepancies between their lifestyle on board and that of the crew around them.[42] Recent U.S. court decisions have determined that because these cruise vessels are homeported in U.S. ports, select U.S.

labor laws apply.[43] There may be a growing trend to extending port state control over labor issues aboard vessels.

- When Hong Kong rejoined the People's Republic of China in July 1997, a flag issue surfaced. Because it is common courtesy to fly a host port's flag on a ship, it meant that Evergreen's (a Taiwanese shipping company) ships would have had to fly the PRC's flag when they called on the port of Hong Kong, and that Hong Kong ships would have had to fly the Taiwanese flag when they were in Taipei. Neither alternative was welcome; the issue was finally resolved when both sides decided not to fly any flag in each other's ports.[44]

- During the conflict between Iran and Iraq in the Persian Gulf, several Kuwaiti ships were temporarily placed under the U.S. flag so that they could gain the protection of the U.S. Navy, a protection it refused to extend to U.S. owners of tankers flying flags of convenience.[45] The U.S. Navy finally relented, and all crude carriers were temporarily re-flagged as American while they were in the Persian Gulf.[46]

U.S.-flagged ship. The reason is purely military. Because of its geographic situation, the United States would need a lot of ship transport capacity to ship troops and military materials abroad in the case of a conflict such as the 1990 Persian Gulf War, and the current program was developed in response to military sealift issues.[48] In that eventuality, the U.S. government can then requisition all merchant ships registered with the U.S. flag that are under the subsidy program. In order to ensure that it does have some ships to requisition, the U.S. government subsidizes ship owners who choose this alternative. In 1997, two large shipping companies re-flagged some of their ships with the U.S. flag—Maersk[49] and APL[50]—because of this incentive.

11-5 Conferences

conference A group of shipping companies (carriers) that operate vessels competing in the same trade lanes, and that have legally agreed to not compete on price and charge the same amount for the same type of cargo and the same voyage.

tariff The price that conference members have agreed to charge for a specific commodity going from one specific port to another.

One of the unusual characteristics of international liners is that they often (used to) operate within the confines of a **conference**, or a legal cartel within which all shipping line members of the conference operate. Conferences are organized on trade routes, usually a series of ports in one country and another in another country; for example, a conference will cover the trade between United States' Atlantic ports and European ports. Within the conference, the prices charged by the shipping lines are identical by commodity, for the same volume and the same weight.[51] All of these rates are called **tariffs** and are published. The complexity of such arrangements is extraordinary: there are some auditing firms whose sole job is to make sure that the shipping lines charged the proper amount for a given shipment. Shipping lines, on the other hand, try to fight the purposeful misidentification of cargo by shippers who try to get a lower rate.[52]

Additional enforcement of such standardized prices falls on some government agency; in the United States, it is the responsibility of the Federal Maritime Commission.[53] It may seem paradoxical that the United States' government has an agency in charge of preventing cartels and collusions (the Federal Trade Commission) while at the same time it has one in charge of enforcing some, but this is nevertheless the case.

The reason behind the existence of conferences is that the liner trade is extremely capital intensive, and that most costs for a liner ship are fixed costs. It is estimated that they can amount to 80 percent of the costs of a shipping company, leaving only 20 percent of the costs dependent on the weight of the cargo. The existence of regulated conferences prevent shipping lines from competing on price, potentially a very detrimental behavior, as was observed in the 1980s in the U.S. domestic airline industry after its deregulation. From the perspective of a government that would want its economy to have access to reliable ocean transportation, there are other reasons for the existence of conferences: It is also a way to "move" cargo expeditiously from a given port and free it from clutter. Because all rates paid on conference ships are the same, no shipper will wait for the next cheaper ship, and this will increase the probability that the cargo will just take the next available ship to that destination.

On May 1, 1999, the Ocean Shipping Reform Act (OSRA) took effect in the United States, and it brought many changes to the conference system. Although conferences are not eliminated, and although shipping lines retain their antitrust immunity, the creation of private, confidential price agreements between large shippers and shipping lines is now authorized. Since this date, several shipping lines have left conferences and negotiated private, confidential contracts with their customers. At the date of this writing, the future of the conference system in the United States is in doubt,[54] although the concept is still alive and well in other countries—China instituted one in 2001.[55]

The impact of OSRA is not yet fully known, although it seems to have had a similar impact on the market as deregulation: tremendous uncertainty in an industry that was used to "business as usual" for a number of years. Undoubtedly, OSRA has had a positive impact for large shippers and, specifically, for companies making a lot of multi-modal shipments.[56] It may also have lessened the competitiveness of smaller shippers, which are not large enough to negotiate rates below the ones published by the shipping lines. OSRA has also triggered a call for reform—or abolition—of the antitrust immunity of shipping lines in the United States and the rest of the world.[57]

11-6 Liability Conventions

The Ocean Shipping Reform Act also seems to have had one significant impact: It brought yet one more level of complexity to the conventions regulating the liability of shipping lines by allowing private, confidential contracts between shippers and shipping lines, where traditional liability constraints are replaced by negotiated ones.[58] But, first, a review of the complex array of alternatives is necessary.

In 1924, an "International Convention for the Unification of Certain Rules of Law relating to Bills of Lading" was adopted by twenty-six participating countries. This convention, known as the **Hague Rules**, limits the liability of a ship owner toward the cargo owners to U.S. $500 per package "or customary freight unit," and it allows ship owners to escape liability in seventeen specified cases—called the seventeen "defenses"—including the infamous **nautical fault**, or errors of the crew of the ship in its management or navigation.[59] In 1936, the United States adopted the Hague Rules by incorporating them in the Carriage of Goods by Sea Act (COGSA).

The U.S. $500 limit per package became a problem with the advent of containers, when shipping lines began claiming that they were "freight units" and attempting to limit their liability to U.S. $500 per container. The Hague Rules were therefore revised in 1968 to clarify the definition of "package" to the units listed on the bill of lading. It also increased the liability of the carrier to U.S. $666.67 or U.S. $2 per

Hague Rules An international liability convention for ocean-going carriers that limits their liability to $500 per package. The liability convention followed by United States' carriers.

nautical fault An error in navigation made by the crew of a ship.

Hague-Visby Rules An international liability convention for ocean-going carriers that limits their liability to SDR 667 per package or SDR 2 per kilogram, whichever is higher. This liability convention is the most commonly used in the world; however, the United States has not ratified this convention and therefore still abides by the Hague Rules.

Hamburg Rules An international liability convention for ocean-going carriers that limits their liability to SDR 835 per package or SDR 2.50 per kilogram, whichever is higher and eliminates most of the "defenses" a carrier could use to discharge itself of liability. The Hamburg Rules have not been ratified by many countries.

kilogram, whichever was higher.[60] These revised rules are known as **Hague-Visby Rules**. The United States has not ratified this treaty, although it has been ratified by all of its major trading partners. In 1979, the Hague-Visby Rules were amended to reflect the declining value of the U.S. dollar, and the liability limits were expressed in Special Drawing Rights (SDR), the artificial currency of the International Monetary Fund (IMF), and set at SDR 666.67 per package or SDR 2 per kilogram, whichever was highest.[61]

The advent of better navigational equipment and the annoyance of shippers at the continuous existence of the nautical fault defense triggered yet another round of international negotiations led by the United Nations Commission on International Trade Law (UNCITRAL), which abolished the seventeen defenses of the Hague and Hague-Visby Rules and replaced them with only three: (1) damage the carrier took all reasonable steps to avoid, (2) damage by fire, and (3) damage due to an attempt by the carrier to save life or property at sea. It also increased liability limits to SDR 835 per package and SDR 2.5 per kilogram. These rules are known as the **Hamburg Rules** and have only been ratified by a small number of countries, only a handful of which are significant international traders. A complete list of which countries have adopted which rules is available on the Internet.[62]

Because the United States has not ratified either the Hague-Visby Rules or the Hamburg Rules, the COGSA is still in effect, even though it is grossly outdated with its limit of U.S. $500.[63] Several efforts have been made to attempt to revise COGSA, but none of them has been successful to date. However, with the advent of OSRA and of private contracts between shippers and shipping lines, it seems that the liability limit has been lifted in many contracts, and that all but a handful of defenses have been eliminated.[64] Therefore, the revision of COGSA may become moot in the near future.

There is still a problem with liability in intermodal freight; that is, freight that is shipped through several means of transportation using only one bill of lading. The liability limits are different for domestic transport in the exporting country, international transport by ocean (and they depend further on the nationality of the carrier), and domestic transport in the importing country. When cargo is damaged in transit without the possibility of tracing where specifically in the voyage the peril occurred, which liability limit is applicable? This is a question that the United Nations Conference on Trade and Development (UNCTAD) answered in 1980, in a treaty that was proposed but never ratified. These rules, though, form the basis for the guidelines developed by the International Chamber of Commerce. In June 2000, the United Nations Commission on International Trade Law (UNCITRAL) started the process of creating a formal multi-modal liability framework.[65]

Not only are these issues of interest to insurance companies, but they also are of interest to any shipper who decides to retain its shipping risks and decline insurance coverage. As the liability of the carrier is very difficult to engage, even in the case of navigational errors or negligence, it may make more sense to purchase insurance coverage (see Section 10-6).

11-7 Non-Vessel-Operating Common Carriers

Non-vessel-operating common carriers (NVOCC) make up another type of shipping company, but with the caveat that they do not own and operate ships. Nevertheless, NVOCCs are regulated by the Federal Maritime Commission (FMC). The way an NVOCC operates is by purchasing space on a ship on a given voyage and by selling this space to companies that need to ship cargo. The shipping line gets paid for the space—and weight—whether or not the NVOCC fills its allocation. The NVOCC only makes money by reselling the space at a higher rate than the one at which it purchased it. In most instances, an NVOCC also acts as a freight consolidator and aggregates less-than-container-load (LCL) freight from several customers into a full container. This allows

Freight Charges

Shipping lines will charge for container shipping either by following published tariff rates or by negotiating contract rates with large volume shippers. All tariff rates can be negotiated and shipping lines will negotiate rates for as few as twelve containers shipped at once. Rates are determined per package or by weight, including cargo shipped in containers on a less-than-container-load (LCL) basis. In addition to the freight rate, there are additional charges of which the international logistics professional must be aware:[66]

ARB—Arbitrary charge. This charge is for added expenses, such as for transshipment in an intermediary port, ice-breaking, cleaning of returned containers that are not ready for the next cargo, electrical power to refrigerated containers, and monitoring of refrigerated containers.

BAF or **FAF**—Bunker adjustment factor, also known as fuel adjustment factor or surcharge. This is an extra charge applied by shipping lines, or set by liner conferences on behalf of their members, to reflect fluctuations in the cost of bunker fuel. This surcharge is expressed either as an amount per freight ton or as a percentage of the freight charge.

CAF—Currency adjustment factor. This is a surcharge applied to freight rates by shipping lines or set by liner conferences on behalf of their members. It is to ensure that the revenue of the shipping lines is unaffected by movements in the currencies in which transactions are carried out by the lines in relation to the freight rate currency. It is normally expressed as a percentage of the freight and may be negative as well as positive.

CY/CY—Container yard to container yard movement of cargo. This is a charge added to the freight rate to reflect the cost of moving cargo from one yard in the port to another yard, a function that is fulfilled by a cartage company.

CFS/CY—Container freight stations to container yard movement of cargo. This is a charge added to the freight rate to reflect the cost of moving cargo from outside of the port to a yard inside the port, a function that is fulfilled by a cartage company.

Chassis charge—This is a charge imposed by container shipping lines for providing customers with a truck chassis at the harbor terminals. A chassis is a truck trailer on which the container will be placed before it is loaded onto the ship or after it is unloaded from the ship.

THC—Terminal handling charge, also known as container yard charge. This is a charge payable to a shipping line either for receiving a full container load at the container terminal, storing it, and delivering it to the ship at the load port or for receiving it from the ship at the discharge port, storing it, and delivering it to the consignee.

Determining the correct charge for a container can be challenging and can amount to much more than the published or negotiated freight rate: Here is an example of the calculation of the cost of a full container shipment from Oakland, California, to Singapore. The container is filled with paper products.

Base container rate	U.S. $2,000
Additional charges:	
CAF - Currency adjustment factor	5%
THC - Terminal handling charge	U.S. $125
BAF - Bunker adjust factor	15%
ARB - Arbitrary charge: cleaning fee	U.S. $40
Total container freight cost:	

container rate + [container rate x (CAF)] + THC + [container rate × BAF} + ARB =
$2,000 + [$2,000 × .05} + $125 + {$2,000 × .15} + $40 =
$2,000 + $100 + $125 + $300 + $40 = **$2,565**

Note: Container-based rates may at times be calculated by weight or by package, especially if the shipment is less-than-container load (LCL).

small shippers to benefit from the protection of a container and allows them to ship without the extra packing protection that break-bulk demands.

The NVOCC system was the basis for the model followed by consolidators in the air passenger business. These consolidators purchase a block of seats on an airplane and resell them to individuals, generally through discount travel agencies.

11-8 Security Requirements

After the terrorist attacks in New York on September 11, 2001, a number of measures were taken worldwide to limit the probability of terrorist attacks. The countries that felt that they could be targets reasoned that an "easy" way for a terrorist organization to smuggle a dangerous weapon was to bring it in using the traditional import channels, either mixed with traditional ocean cargo, or by truck or train. Several initiatives to limit the probability of a terrorist attack through ocean imports were started within a few years, most by the United States, but several others by other countries and the International Maritime Organization. In 2006, only a few of these initiatives were fully operational, and only a portion of the investments necessary had been made.[67]

11-8a United States' Security Requirements

The United States has always had a program under which it inspects cargo when it arrives in the U.S. port of destination. Depending on the port, between 1 and 5 percent of all shipments entering the United States are inspected upon arrival. Such inspections were traditionally conducted to prevent fraud (the import of products that were not correctly identified on the import documentation), but such inspections are now much more focused on terrorism prevention. In addition, the United States has implemented at least four new programs to lower the probability of terrorist shipments into the United States.

The **twenty-four-hour rule** is a program that is administered by the United States Customs and Border Protection Agency (CBP) of the Department of Homeland Security. That rule requires that all importers (and carriers) provide a copy of the manifest of an ocean shipment bound for the United States, including shipments that are just transiting through a United States port and are bound for another country, twenty-four hours before that shipment is loaded onto the vessel bound for the United States. A similar rule is in place for shipments made by truck and train, except that notification must be made two hours before the shipment crosses the United States border.

The purpose of this rule is for the CBP to be able to inspect the paperwork, and eventually warn the carrier that something may be inappropriate with the shipment. When a shipment is identified as problematic, the shipment is not loaded, and is inspected in the port of departure before it is loaded on the next available ship. In some cases, the inspection is conducted by CBP inspectors assigned to the foreign port.

The **Custom-Trade Partnership Against Terrorism (C-TPAT)** is an initiative where the CBP entices importers to voluntarily enhance the security of their supply chains and that of their suppliers abroad. Importers vouch for the fact that their foreign warehouses are fenced, that the premises are under camera surveillance, that their personnel is screened and trained appropriately, that procedures are in place to minimize the number of people who have access to cargo paperwork and cargo, that there are conveyance procedures that emphasize security, and so on. Importers also have to ensure that their suppliers have similar measures. In exchange for evidence of such enhanced security, CBP guarantees that the shipments for those importers that participate are not to be delayed for inspection in the port of departure or the U.S. port of destination, a process that is nicknamed "green lane."

C-TPAT was originally designed as a voluntary program, but it has slowly evolved into a quasi-mandatory program; there is much uneasiness among importers in the United States about this program, as they see little evidence that the "green lane" process is working. They mostly feel that they are expected to participate, bear the costs of the program, and get few benefits in return.[68]

The **Container Security Initiative** is a program of CBP through which CBP inspectors are temporarily assigned to foreign ports where they inspect containers bound for the United States. Such containers are either pulled at random or are flagged as suspicious by CBP when these containers' contents are reviewed under the twenty-four-hour rule program.

The **Foreign Port Program** is a CBP initiative under which ports abroad that agree to purchase container-scanning equipment and agree to inspect cargo that the CBP considers suspicious also get preferential treatment in the United States when cargo having originated in those ports arrives in the United States. There are about twenty ports that are participating in this effort.[69]

---

twenty-four-hour rule A rule first instituted by the U.S. Customs and Border Protection Agency, which requires that carriers send Customs the manifest of all cargo destined for the United States twenty-four hours prior to the cargo being loaded in the port of departure.

Custom-Trade Partnership Against Terrorism (C-TPAT) A program instituted by the U.S. Customs and Border Protection Agency, through which Customs gives preferential treatment to companies that have implemented a number of security measures in their supply chains.

Container Security Initiative A program instituted by the U.S. Customs and Border Protection Agency, through which Customs agents are sent to the port of departure to inspect containers bound for the United States.

Foreign Port Program A U.S. Customs and Border Protection initiative under which ports abroad purchase container-scanning equipment and agree to inspect cargo that the CBP considers suspicious.

11-8b Other Countries' Security Requirements

Following the example of the United States, several countries have implemented a twenty-four-hour rule, and called it an "advanced cargo declaration system for maritime overseas containers": the European Union's Parliament voted for implementation in February 2005,[70] but no date of actual implementation was known as of July 2006. Canada implemented a twenty-four-hour rule in April 2005.[71]

Sixty governments signed the Proliferation Security Initiative in September 2003, targeting the movements of technologies that could be used to make weapons of mass destruction. In August 2004, those countries also agreed in principle to the creation of a worldwide twenty-four-hour rule, but with no specific implementation date. As of July 2006, only a handful had adopted such measures, but it is expected that many will eventually follow.[72]

11-8c International Ship and Port Security (ISPS)

The International Maritime Organization created the International Ship and Port Security (ISPS) program to address the problems of terrorism and cargo security worldwide. It was implemented worldwide in July 2004 and is a prescriptive program, mandating ship owners and port operators to follow certain procedures.[73]

Ship owners must adhere to standards for procedures dealing with the security of the cargo, such as conduct background checks before the hiring of crew members, ensure the security of paperwork on board, train employees, and so on. Similarly, port terminals and ports have to fence their facilities, monitor them electronically, and keep video records of the activity in the port and the loading yards, conduct background checks on their employees, verify the identity of all people entering the port facilities (including truck drivers making deliveries), isolate suspicious containers, and so on.

11-8d Commercial Efforts

In addition to governmental efforts, there are several efforts made by traders to enhance the security of the supply chain. They participate in the ISPS and C-TPAT programs, but also are attempting to work on other concepts. For example, shippers are worried about possible infiltration of containers by terrorists. To that effect, they have been working on using better seals, on designing so-called "smart containers" that would have recording devices that note when and whether a container's doors are open, or whether the container's contents were disturbed by monitoring when light entered the container.[74]

However, the most effective way to prevent issues with shipments is to make sure that the shipment is always "moving" through the supply chain as quickly as possible. The longer a shipment is idled in a port, on the side of a road, or in a warehouse, the greater the probability that it will be tampered.

11-8e Effectiveness of Security Measures

The effectiveness of all of these measures is challenged by many people, for sometimes quite divergent reasons.

Politicians intent on showing that they are "tough on terrorism" advocate inspecting all cargo entering a country. Such inspection would be a disaster: There is no possible way to inspect the millions of containers entering any country without generating enormous bottlenecks in the ports, which are not equipped to hold containers for any length of time. In addition, the manpower needed to inspect all containers would be colossal: A ship discharges 100 to 200 containers an hour, and sometimes unloads 3,000 containers continuously. Assuming five man-hours to inspect a container thoroughly (unloading it completely, reloading it completely, checking the paperwork), that represents a minimum of 1,800 inspectors working an eight-hour shift for each ship. Although the current system may not be very effective, inspecting all (or more) shipments is certainly not the answer.

Importers are often bothered by the C-TPAT and CSI programs and have seen few benefits by participating: Their containers can be delayed in the port of departure because another container is suspicious, and the entire voyage is delayed until that container is identified and unloaded. Shipments can be delayed at sea as well; in 2004, the containership *RioPuelo* was prevented for several days from entering the United States because a shipment of five containers of lemons was considered suspicious by CBP.[75] Yet, importers have to bear the majority of the costs of the C-TPAT program. They are also worried that some confidential commercial information could be compromised by reporting them to CBP.[76] In addition, despite the "green lane" concept, a fair percentage of containers imported by C-TPAT participants are still inspected.

Security specialists rile about programs that are giving only "lip service" to security. When CBP did an inventory of what was needed in U.S. ports to secure them against terrorism, it determined that it would need U.S. $7.3 billion. The budget of the U.S. government for port security enhancement was a paltry U.S. $46 million in 2005.[77] That is 0.6 percent of what its own administration says is needed. The number of sensitive points in the international supply chain is enormous; there is just no way to secure all of them. These efforts are not worthless, but they are unlikely to prevent a well-organized terrorist act.

Key Terms

bale (p. 249)

bareboat or demise charter (p. 261)

bunker (p. 249)

cabotage (p. 265)

conference (p. 266)

Container Security Initiative (p. 270)

Custom-Trade Partnership Against Terrorism (C-TPAT) (p. 270)

dead-weight tonnage (dwt) (p. 249)

displacement tonnage (p. 249)

dry-bulk cargo (p. 252)

flag of convenience (p. 264)

Foreign Port Program (p. 270)

grain (p. 249)

gross tonnage (p. 249)

Hague Rules (p. 267)

Hague-Visby Rules (p. 268)

Hamburg Rules (p. 268)

laker (p. 262)

LASH barges (p. 258)

LASH mothership (p. 258)

light tonnage (p. 249)

lightering (p. 260)

liner (p. 248)

nautical fault (p. 267)

net tonnage (p. 249)

open registry (p. 264)

Panamax (p. 251)

post-Panamax (p. 251)

secondary registry (p. 264)

stores (p. 249)

tariff (p. 266)

time charter (p. 261)

tramp (p. 248)

trot-on/trot-off (p. 256)

tweendeck (p. 258)

twenty-four-hour rule (p. 270)

voyage charter (p. 261)

wet-bulk (liquid bulk) cargo (p. 252)

Review and Discussion Questions

1. What two different types of ocean cargo services are there?

2. Describe three different types of ships used in international ocean transportation. What type of cargos are they used for?

3. Explain the concept of a "flag." Why does a ship need a flag? Why would an owner choose to fly a "flag of convenience"?

4. What is a Conference? Why would it make sense for shipping lines to join a Conference? Why are they disappearing?

5. What are the differences among the "Hague rules," the "Hague-Visby rules," and the "Hamburg rules"?

6. What are the major initiatives of the U.S. government and of the International Maritime Organization in terms of cargo security?

Endnotes

1. Shipping Key Facts: http://www.marisec.org/shipp ingfacts/keyfacts.htm, Maritime International Secretariat Services, 2005.

2. Abrahamsson, Bernhard J. *International Ocean Shipping: Current Concepts and Principles*, Westview Press, Boulder, Colorado, 1980.

3. *The Panama Canal*, November 1987, a publication of the Panama Canal Commission Office of Public Affairs, APO Miami 34011-5000.

4. Kendall, Lane, and Buckley, James, *The Business of Shipping*, 7th Edition, Cornell Maritime Press, Maryland, 2001.

5. Marcus, Amy Dockser, "Egypt Fights to Pump Up Suez Revenue," *The Wall Street Journal*, July 25, 1996, p. A19.

6. "Glossary of Shipping Terms," FrontLine Limited, Bermuda, http://www.frontmgt.no/org/glossary. html, November 8, 2000.

7. "The Various Types of Tankers," Elf Corporation, http://www.elf.fr/odyssee/us/trans/703.htm, November 7, 2000.

8. "Standard Tanker Voyage Chartering Questionnaire," 1988, http://www.frontmgt.no/pdf/Sea_ Giant.pdf, November 7, 2000.

9. "Great Ships: Regina Maersk," www.marinelink. com/dec96/gships/regina.html, November 7, 2000.

10. *Review of Maritime Transport 2005*, United Nations Conference on Trade and Development, United Nations, http://www.unctad.org/en/docs/rmt2005_en.pdf, July 20, 2006.

11. *Lloyd's Register Fairplay January 2005*.

12. *Review of Maritime Transport 2005*, United Nations Conference on Trade and Development, United Nations, http://www.unctad.org/en/docs/rmt2005_en.pdf, July 20, 2006.

13. Tower, Courtney, "Mega-ships Drive Freight's Future," *The Journal of Commerce*, October 22, 1998, p. 1B.

14. Freudmann, Aviva, "Big Ships, New Problems," *JoC Weekly*, June 5–11, 2000, p. 22.

15. Machalaba, Daniel, "Maersk is Ready to Start on Giant Port," *The Wall Street Journal*, June 5, 2000, p. A4.

16. Richardson, Paul, "The 18,000-TEU Ship," *JoC Weekly*, June 5–11, 2000, p. 19.

17. *Ibid*

18. Lucentini, Jack, "FastShip Makes Progress, but Who Can Afford It?" *The Journal of Commerce*, August 7, 1998, p. 1A.

19. John Gordon, and David Orletsky, *Chap. 9, Moving Rapidly to the Fight*, The U.S. Army and the New National Security Strategy, RAND Corporation, 2003.

20. Rapoport, Carla, "Hyundai's Car Carrier Unit Aims for Bigger Cargo," *The Journal of Commerce*, May 6, 1998, p. 1B.

21. Porter, Janet, "Can One Size Really Fit All?" *The Journal of Commerce*, July 14, 1997, p. 1C.

22. Hensel, Bill, Jr., "Cars in a Box," *JoC Weekly*, July 31–August 6, 2000, p. 36.

23. Journal of Commerce Staff, "Specialty Carriers Thrive in Midst of Container Age," *The Journal of Commerce*, September 22, 1997, p. 5C.

24. *Ibid*

25. "LASH Barges," Forest Lines, International Ship holding Corporation, http://www.forest-lines.com/ FLI_LASHbarge.htm, November 7, 2000.

26. Plume, Janet, "LASH Vessels Still Providing Snappy Service," *The Journal of Commerce*, September 22, 1997, p. 7C.

27. Sullivan, Allanna, "A 700-ft Tanker Just Does Not Handle Quite Like a Honda," *The Wall Street Journal*, April 14, 1989, p. 1.

28. Wells, Ken, "Captain's Course: Life on a Supertanker Mixes Tedium, Stress for Kenneth Campbell," *The Wall Street Journal*, September 11, 1986, p. 1.

29. McPhee, John, "The Ships of Port Revel," *The Atlantic Monthly*, October 1998, pp. 67–80.

30. Alderton, Patrick, M., *Reeds Sea Transport: Operations and Economics*, 5th Edition, Adlard Coles Nautical, London, 2004.

31. Knee, Richard, "Many Owners of Aging Vessels Would Rather Scrap than Sell," *The Journal of Commerce*, May 7, 1998, p. 13A.

32. LangeWiesche, William, "The Shipbreakers," *The Atlantic Monthly*, August 2000, pp. 31–49.

33. "India Bars Dismantling of U.S. Ships that Held Hazardous Materials," *The Journal of Commerce*, Reuters News Release, August 7, 1997, p. 2B.

34. Mongelluzzo, Bill, "Boxships Buck Currents," *The Journal of Commerce*, December 15, 1997, p. 1B.

35. Lesher, Dave, "Sailing Through the School of Experience," *Los Angeles Times*, July 30, 1997.

36. *Review of Maritime Transport 2005*, United Nations Conference on Trade and Development, United Nations, http://www.unctad.org/en/docs/rmt2005_en.pdf, July 20, 2006.

37. *Ibid*

38. Roberts, Michael G., "Don't Touch the Jones Act," *The Journal of Commerce*, February 7, 1997, p. 6A.

39. Sansbury, Tim, "Exporters Assail U.S. Cargo Policy," *The Journal of Commerce*, October 23, 1998, p. 1A.

40. MARAD publication, *By the Capes Around the World: A Summary of World Cabotage Practices*, U.S. Maritime Administration, 1995.

41. Sneider, Daniel, "A Cruise from Seattle to Alaska via Congress," *The Christian Science Monitor*, May 21, 1997, p. 4.

42. Prager, Joshua Harris, "For Cruise Workers, Life is No 'Love Boat,'" *The Wall Street Journal*, July 3, 1997, p. B1.

43. *Dahingo v. Royal Caribbean Cruises, Ltd, 99 CIV 12774, 312 F. Supp. 2d 440 442 S.D.N.Y. 2004 United States District Court Southern District of New York.*

44. Bangsberg, P. T., "Shipowners Tackle Asia Flag Question," *The Journal of Commerce*, May 29, 1997, p. 8B.

45. Carrington, Tim, "U.S. Owners of Foreign-Registry Ships Want Navy to Rally Round the Flag their Vessels Don't Fly," *The Wall Street Journal*, December 29, 1987, p. 44.

46. O'Rourke, Ronald, "Gulf Ops," *Proceedings, U.S. Naval Institute*, May 1989, pp. 42–43.

47. Mongelluzzo, Bill, "Boxships Buck Currents," *The Journal of Commerce*, December 15, 1997, p. 1B.

48. David G. Harris, and Richard D. Stewart, "U.S. Surge Sealift Capabilities: A Question of Sufficiency," *Parameters U.S. Army War College Quarterly*, Spring 1998.

49. Baldwin, Tom, "Maersk Reflags Four More Ships," *The Journal of Commerce*, February 11, 1997, p. 1A.

50. Mongelluzzo, Bill, "Boxships Buck Currents," *The Journal of Commerce*, December 15, 1997, p. 1B.

51. Brennan, Terry, "TWRA Signs Contracts for Chilled Beef to Head Off Non-Conference Diversion," *Traffic World*, February 5, 1996.

52. Tirschwell, Peter, "Lines Plan Crackdown on Cargo Tricksters," *The Journal of Commerce*, December 24, 1996, p. 1A.

53. Mathews, Anna Wilde, "Five Members of Shipping Cartel Are Focus of Space-Sharing Probe," *The Wall Street Journal*, May 6, 1997, p. B8.

54. Beargie, Tony, "Re-inventing Conferences," *American Shipper*, December 1998, p. 12.

55. Beargie, Tony, "Re-regulation," *American Shipper*, February 1999, p. 8.

56. Damas, Philip, "Great Expectations," *American Shipper*, May 2000, p. 23.

57. "One Small Step for OECD: Will Nations Leap at Antitrust Reform?" *American Shipper*, July 2000, pp. 8–15.

58. Mottley, Robert, "OSRA and Admiralty Law," *American Shipper*, May 2000, p. 40.

59. Freudmann, Aviva, "Plumbing the Depths of 'Nautical Fault,'" *The Journal of Commerce*, May 19, 1998, p. 7A.

60. Mandelbaum, Samuel Robert, "International Ocean Shipping and Risk Allocation for Cargo Loss, Damage, and Delay: A U.S. Approach to COGSA, Hague-Visby, Hamburg and the Multimodal Rules," *Journal of Transnational Law and Policy*, 1996, Vol. 5, Issue 1.

61. *Ibid*

62. "International Conventions Membership List," *InforMARE*, www.informare.it/dbase/convuk.htm, November 14, 2000.

63. Augello, William J., "Ocean Cargo Liability Law to be Revised," *Logistics Management*, March 1998, p. 37.

64. Mottley, Robert, "OSRA and Admiralty Law," *American Shipper*, May 2000, p. 40.

65. Freudmann, Aviva, "No Easy Answer," *JoC Weekly*, June 12–18, 2000, p. 16.

66. Brodie, P., *Dictionary of Shipping Terms*. Lloyd's of London Press, Ltd. 1994.

67. Kulish, Eric, "Homeland Insecurity," *American Shipper*, September 2004, pp. 8–20.

68. Edmonson, R. G. "C-TPAT's New Look," *The Journal of Commerce*, April 4, 2005, pp. 10–11.

69. Lipton, Eric, "U.S. Effort to Secure Foreign Ports is Faulted," *The New York Times*, May 25, 2005.

70. Stares, Justin, "Europe One Step Closer to U.S.-Style 24-Hour Rule," *Financial Times*, February 25, 2005.

71. Wallis, Keith, "Canada to Apply 24-Hour Rule," *The Financial Times*, April 15, 2003.

72. Stares, Justin, "Worldwide Accord on 24-Hour Box Rule," *The Financial Times*, August 6, 2004.

73. "IMO Adopts Comprehensive Maritime Security Measures," Conference of Contracting Governments to the International Convention for the Safety of Life at Sea, International Maritime Organization, http://www.imo.org/Newsroom/mainframe.asp?topic_id=583&doc_id=2689, July 20, 2006.

74. Eisenberg, Anne, "Cargo Containers' Electronic Sensor Says 'Do not Disturb,'" *The New York Times*, January 20, 2005.

75. "Coast Guard Holds Shipment of Lemons To Ensure Safety," United States Coast Guard Press Release, August 6, 2004, http://www.uscg.mil/d1/staff/m/rrt/incidents/Rio%20Puelo%20PR%20final.pdf, July 20, 2006.

76. Edmonson, R. G., "Customs Opens a Pandora's Box," *The Journal of Commerce*, January 20–26, 2003, pp. 16–17.

77. Buckman, Rebecca, "Maritime Security Measures Begin," *The Wall Street Journal*, July 1, 2004, p. A12.

International Air Transportation

Chapter Twelve

Source: © 2007 JupiterImages Corporation.

Air transport has grown rapidly in the last three decades, primarily through the advent of "time-defined" deliveries, a concept created by Federal Express in the United States market in 1981, which has been adopted by just about all cargo airlines in the international arena. Federal Express (now called FedEx) is the largest airfreight company in the world, having carried a total of 14.6 billion FTKs* in 2004, 5.6 billion of which were international. The top spot for international cargo volume is Korean Air with 8.2 billion FTKs (see Table 12-1).[1]

The total amount of freight carried by air grew from just over seventy-five billion FTKs in 1994 to 120 billion FTKs in 2002 and it reached 145 billion FTKs in 2005, a compounded rate of growth in excess of 5.5 percent *per annum*.[2] The volume of international air cargo is expected to continue to grow in the foreseeable future at a similar pace (see Figure 12-1).[3]

TABLE 12-1	Top Ten International Cargo Airlines
Airline	**FTKs Millions***
Korean Air	8,164
Lufthansa	8,028
Singapore Airlines	7,143
Cathay Pacific Airways	5,876
China Airlines	5,642
FedEx	5,595
Eva Airways	5,477
Air France	5,384
British Airways	4,771
Cargolux	4,670

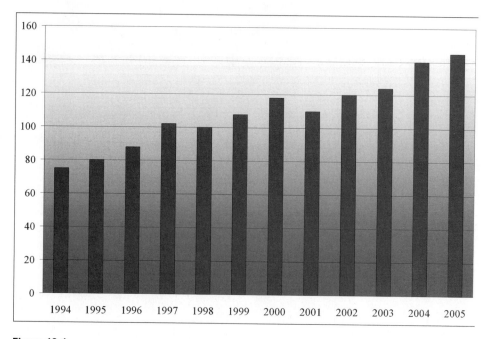

Figure 12-1
Annual Freight Traffic (in billions of FTKs)

---

*FTKs, freight tonne kilometers, are the number of metric tons of freight carried multiplied by the distance they were carried, expressed in kilometers.

12-1 Types of Service

In ocean shipping, there are two main types of cargo services offered; for air shipments, that is the case as well, but it is slightly different.

While **airlines** offer liner services, which are regularly scheduled voyages between two airports, they also provide two types of air cargo services with their liner aircrafts. The first is provided on passenger airplanes, in which, in addition to the luggage and personal effects of the passengers, the "belly" of the aircraft or, in some cases, part of the main deck of the aircraft, carries cargo (see Figure 12-2).

The other is also a regularly scheduled air service, but it utilizes an all-freight cargo aircraft that does not include any room for passengers. In an **airfreighter**, both the main deck and the belly of the aircraft carry cargo. This service is generally provided at hours that are not "convenient" to passenger traffic, and both types of services complement each other: Airlines can offer to their customers a "next flight out" service that will either place the shipment in the next available passenger or freighter flight.

Cargo airlines also provide **charter airplane** services for large air shipments between two points. These large shipments can be made using traditional freighter aircrafts, such as when there is an increase in seasonal traffic (cherries from the Northwest of the United States to Japan in July, for example, or roses from Colombia to the United States in February) or when there is an increase in volume on a particular route due to a large increase in the volume of a single new product (a product launch, for example, or the arrival of *Beaujolais Nouveau* from France to the United States and Japan in November), and additional capacity needs to be made available on certain routes.

However, it is also possible that the shipper needs to ship a product that does not "fit" in a traditional cargo aircraft, or it has to be shipped to a smaller airport that cannot accommodate a traditional cargo aircraft, and therefore an aircraft with non-traditional characteristics will handle the shipment; an aircraft with a large fuselage,

airline A company that provides regularly scheduled air transportation services for passengers or freight.

airfreighter An aircraft entirely dedicated to the transport of cargo.

charter airplane An aircraft that is leased for a single voyage (or a limited number of voyages) under a wet lease.

Figure 12-2
A Container Placed in the Belly of a Passenger Aircraft
Source: Photo © Japan Air System. Used with permission.

such as the Airbus A-300 Beluga (see Figure 12-7), or an aircraft with a large fuselage able to land on a short runway, such as the Antonov-124 Ruslan (see Figure 12-6) or the largest freighter in the world, the Antonov-225 Mriya. Smaller aircrafts, such as refurbished corporate jets also fall into this category, because they can quickly connect two smaller airports.

12-2 Types of Aircrafts

A variety of aircrafts are used to ship cargo, and this variety reflects the service that they provide. A first differentiation is made between passenger airplanes that happen to carry cargo on board and pure cargo planes that only carry freight. A second differentiation also needs to be made between planes used in cargo services that are regularly scheduled (passenger and cargo airlines alike) and planes used by cargo services that are contracted on a single voyage basis, as a charter. Their equipment tends to be different.

12-2a Passenger Airplanes

passenger airplane A type of airplane that is designed to carry passengers on the main deck of the plane; it can also carry cargo below the main deck, in its "belly," but the size and type of cargo are restricted.

Just about every **passenger airplane** transports cargo in addition to the passengers carried on its main deck. The "belly" of the aircraft is designed to accommodate the passengers' luggage and additional airfreight. Some of this airfreight cargo is "loose" (i.e., not palletized) and is shipped piece by piece; the packages are not secured onto the aircraft, and are shipped in a manner that is similar to passenger luggage. In larger, so-called "wide-body" aircrafts, the freight is palletized and secured onto the aircraft. International cargo services on passenger airplanes are somewhat unreliable as airlines sometimes "bump" freight, creating more capacity to carry additional passengers and their luggage.[4] Therefore, only the most urgent of cargo makes it on passenger aircrafts: Oftentimes, it is made up of machine or computer parts, necessary for the repair of a critical piece of equipment, or small shipments of fresh produce, such as fish.[5]

The biggest constraint on a shipper regarding the use of passenger airplanes for shipping freight is the maximum size that the shipment can be. The main issues are the size of the hold—which varies depending on the airplane used, obviously—on the weight capacity of the floor of the cargo hold, and on the size of the door to access that hold. Most freight forwarders have a good grasp of the maximum sizes of packages that can be shipped in passenger airplanes and are quite helpful in determining whether or not the cargo will be allowed on a passenger flight. The second constraint is that there are many items that are not allowed in passenger planes, even if they are acceptable for air transport. These items have to be shipped in airfreighters.

on-board courier (OBC) A passenger on a regularly scheduled flight who relinquishes his or her baggage allocation, allowing companies to ship extremely urgent cargo.

Another alternative way of using passenger airplanes for cargo is to use an **on-board courier (OBC)** service. A courier is often a student or a retiree who will fly to a city and take cargo as his or her luggage. This is often the fastest way for cargo to get anywhere and is a service used for delivery of critical parts and documents. It also presents the advantage of the cargo always "making" the plane, as passengers' luggage has priority over all other freight. The OBC business is substantial, but unfortunately there are no aggregate statistics for this activity. One OBC company in San Francisco shipped 2,000 tons of freight in 1996.[6] That's a lot of document pouches.

12-2b Combis

combi airplane A type of airplane that is designed to carry both passengers and cargo on the main deck of the plane.

Combi airplanes are passenger airplanes that are designed so that freight is carried on the main deck as well as in the belly hold. The main deck is therefore "split" at some point in the middle of the aircraft, with the fore (front) portion of the plane reserved for passengers and the aft portion reserved for freight. Some aircrafts are designed in such a way that this partition is somewhat mobile, depending on the demand for passenger seats (a decision usually made upon seasonal fluctuations).

Most of the combis are large airplanes (Boeing 747 or DC-10) that are necessary for nonstop passenger travel to remote areas of the world, such as the islands of the South Pacific[7] (from anywhere) or the Caribbean (from Europe), but that cannot be expected to fill to capacity because the number of passengers is not sufficient. The airlines therefore split this capacity between passenger and cargo service.

For shippers, combis present an advantage in that the size limitations of passenger aircrafts are essentially gone. The main deck has a greater weight capacity, a much larger door, and can accommodate palletized and containerized cargo. Moreover, the cargo can be secured onto the plane with slings to prevent damage caused by movement within the plane. However, the restrictions on what can be shipped with passengers aboard remain.

12-2c Freighters

Most airfreighters are "liners" (i.e., they operate on a regular schedule) traveling between two airports, one of which is usually a "hub," the location at which the cargo will be transferred to another flight. The types of airplanes used in this trade are usually the same as in passenger service (see Figure 12-3), with the exception that the freighter is equipped with a roller deck (see Figure 12-4). A **"roller deck"** is a main deck equipped with rollers that allow the palletized or containerized cargo to be pushed in the aircraft, either through an oversize side door or through the nose of the airplane, which can be lifted (see Figure 12-5). The cargo is then secured to the aircraft floor and walls using hooks and slings. Airfreighters can be purchased new from the aircraft manufacturer as cargo carriers, but most often, they are passenger airplanes that are retrofitted to cargo service by specialized firms.[8] Most of the cargo airplanes are older and noisier than the ones used for passenger service: There are still about 1,500 DC-3 airplanes in operation around the world, even though they were designed and built in the 1930s and 1940s. These very old airplanes are not just flown in developing countries; they are heavily used in the United States as well,[9] although mostly as charter planes. The same is true for older jet-powered planes.

Because these older airfreighters operate at the airports' off-hours, often at night, their noise can create problems with airport neighbors. Some airports have considered banning night flights altogether. Brussels, Belgium,[10] and the

roller deck The configuration of the deck of an aircraft when it is designed to accept cargo shipments; the deck is equipped with rollers and bearings that allow cargo to be moved in any direction without much friction.

Figure 12-3
A Large Cargo Airliner: The Boeing 747-400F

Source: Photo © M. Radzi Desa, courtesy of www.airliners.net. Used with permission.

Figure 12-4
The "Roller Deck" of a Freighter Aircraft
Source: Photo © Miguel Snoep, courtesy of www.airliners.net. Used with permission.

Figure 12-5
A Freighter Can Be Loaded through Its Nose
Source: Photo © Edward Lai, courtesy of www.airliners.net. Used with permission.

European Union have enacted some very stringent noise regulations, mostly aimed at older airfreighters.[11] The future is likely to hold yet more regulations for other heavily used metropolitan airports, leaving room for the creation of other hubs in less urbanized centers, such as Prestwick in Scotland, Hahn in Germany, and Chateauroux in France.[12] To some extent, this development mirrors that of the Memphis airport, which has become the largest cargo airport in the world, with 2.4 million tons of freight in 1999,[13] even though it is not located in a large metropolitan center.

Airfreighters present the advantage for shippers of offering a regular service on which palletized or containerized cargo can be loaded (see Section 13-3d for information on the different airplane containers available). As of 2000, the largest airline freighter is the Boeing 747-400, but the development of the Airbus A-380, scheduled to fly in 2007, will jeopardize this standing. The newer two-deck design will allow more cargo to be shipped using the same number of landing slots, which is a serious advantage, especially because the airport infrastructure does not need to be updated. The landing gear of the A-380 spreads the weight over more wheels so that it can use the same runways as current aircrafts, despite being 150 tons heavier than the 747.[14] FedEx and UPS have each ordered ten of these A-380 freighters.

12-2d Charters

The last category of cargo airplanes serve chartered transportation (i.e., they serve shippers on a single voyage basis under one of three conditions):

1. The goods need to be there as soon as possible, and using a regularly scheduled airline flight would delay the shipment to an unacceptable level. Examples of such extremely urgent shipments abound in the Just-in-Time manufacturing environment, in which a delay for a part may cost the company thousands of dollars (for example, an assembly line may sit idle until the part arrives). Such shipments are transported by small aircrafts—former corporate jets transformed into freighters as well as the DC-3s mentioned earlier—or by helicopters. It is not uncommon for U.S. automobile assembly plants to use such services.

2. The goods to be shipped do not fit into the airplanes regularly scheduled on the route; either they are too heavy or too large. In those cases, the shipper will charter a heavylift cargo airplane to accommodate the shipment. Such specialized cargoes are usually handled by specialized aircrafts such as the Antonov-124 (see Figure 12-6), an aircraft capable of carrying 150 tons,[15] or the Airbus "Beluga," designed for large volume cargoes. It can carry 1,400 m³—49,000 cubic feet—but a maximum of forty-seven metric tons (see Figure 12-7). In one exceptional case, NASA decided to ship its space shuttle on the "back" of a Boeing 747 freighter.

3. The goods need to be delivered to a location where regularly scheduled airfreight service is not available. On occasion, the location is near an airport whose runway is not up to world standards, and aircrafts capable of landing on such runways have to be utilized. The DC-3 is a common choice for those assignments because of its ability to land on just about any terrain.

12-3 International Regulations

In terms of regulations, the international airfreight business is dominated by the International Air Transport Association (IATA) and by the International Civil Aviation Organization (ICAO). However, a large number of bilateral agreements have

Figure 12-6
Project Cargo Being Loaded on an Antonov-124
Source: Photo © Air America Fuel and Services, Inc. by Larry Godden, CEO. Used with permission.

open skies agreement An agreement between two or more countries where air carriers from one of the countries are allowed to serve any of the other countries' airports.

been signed recently to circumvent some of the restrictions placed by IATA and ICAO, and have led to so-called **open skies agreements**.

International regulation of air traffic started with the Paris Convention of 1919, which established the concept of sovereignty of a country over its airspace. In 1929, the Warsaw Convention was signed, limiting the liability of international airlines in case of accidents toward their passengers and toward the freight they carried. Both liability limits were eventually increased in 1955 with The Hague Protocol, in 1966 with the Montréal Agreement, in 1971 with the Guatemala City Protocol, and finally with the IATA Intercarrier Agreement on Passenger Liability and the Montréal Protocol n°4. In 2000, the liability limits stand at SDR 100,000 (Special Drawing Rights) for death and SDR seventeen per kilogram for cargo. However, because a number of countries, including the

Figure 12-7
A Large Capacity Airfreighter: The A 300-600 ST "Beluga"

Source: Photo © Airbus Industrie. Used with permission.

United States, have not ratified anything beyond the Warsaw Convention of 1929, these limits are not often used for flights originating or terminating in the United States. Unilaterally, several international airlines have therefore decided to not abide by these liability limits, because courts have routinely ignored them,[20] and because the Montréal Protocol n°4 was encouraging their elimination,[21] allowing unlimited liability.

Under IATA and ICAO rules, a country can restrict the number of airline flights in and out of its airspace. Generally, the limit is set to favor national airline companies; however, in 1992, the United States and the Netherlands agreed to set

Cherries and Carnations

In 1999, U.S. $870 million worth of cut flowers entered the United States through the Miami Airport, 70 percent of which came from Colombia.[16] All of this trade was done with airfreighters, and a good portion of it was the domain of Aeroflora, a Colombian business specializing in that freight. Aeroflora sends an average of fifteen airfreighters every week to the United States, filled with only one cargo: cut flowers,[17] mostly roses and carnations.

However, it is the week preceding the Valentine's Day holiday that this business becomes crazy. In 1999, Aeroflora sent a total of eighteen Boeing 747s packed with flowers in the forty-eight hours preceding the holiday. Every year, Federal Express dedicates two or three of its DC-10s for that purpose. Packed to the gills, a 747 can hold 3.6 million roses.[18]

Cut flowers are not the only unusually large business handled by airfreighters, though. From late May until late June, it is "cherry season" on the West Coast of the United States. More than 1.1 million cartons (cardboard boxes of 18 lbs—8.2 kg) of cherries leave the United States for the Japanese market. That is more than 9,000 metric tons of cherries, all traveling by airfreighters or in the bellies of passenger flights, at sometimes prohibitive rates because all West-bound capacity at that time is taken by these fruits (U.S. $1.95 per kg, whereas cargo normally fetches no more than U.S. $1.00 per kg on that route). It is the most profitable period of the year for the airlines involved in that trade,[19] because Narita Airport operates at full capacity and cannot accommodate any more flights.

no limit to the number of flights that each other's airlines could fly into the other's territory—an "open-skies" agreement. In the last five years, many more of these agreements were signed, and this trend is likely to continue; as of August 2006, there were about 100 open skies agreements.[22] Nevertheless, the number of flights in and out of a specific airport is still restricted to the number of "landing slots" available at that airport. Specifically, despite such an agreement between Japan and the United States, Narita Airport still cannot accommodate any more flights than it already handles.[23]

12-4 Freight Tariffs

The tariff structure of international air cargo is not nearly as complicated as that of the ocean cargo industry, with its innumerable categories. Airfreight is priced as a function of two things: its weight and its volume.

In order to arrive at the freight cost of a particular shipment, airlines will calculate two alternatives; the first will be based on the actual weight of the shipment and the other will be its **volume-weight**, a computation based upon the volume of the cargo. The volume-weight of a shipment is also called its dimensional weight. The airline will then charge the higher of the volume-weight or the actual weight of the cargo. On international shipments, the volume-weight conversion traditionally uses 6,000 cm^3 per kilogram—or 166 cubic inches per pound—although some airlines may calculate this ratio slightly differently.[24]

The difficulty for a shipper using airfreight for lightweight products—products for which the volume-weight of the shipment exceeds their actual weight—is to make sure that it does not pay too much for shipping by using packaging that is too voluminous. The trade-off is relatively simple. The shipper must decide between using packaging that protects the product well for the trip but reduces the overall dimensions of the cargo and therefore reduces its volume-weight, and using more traditional packaging, which is likely to be less expensive, but increases the freight costs by increasing the volume weight. The decision to simply decrease the packaging should never be made; improper packaging is always one of the reasons for an insurance company to deny a claim.

volume-weight A weight, calculated based upon the dimensions of a shipment, used by airlines to determine the tariff to be charged to a shipper, when a shipment is not very dense.

Key Terms

airfreighter (p. 279)

airline (p. 279)

charter airplane (p. 279)

Combi airplanes (p. 280)

on-board courier (OBC) (p. 280)

open skies agreements (p. 285)

passenger airplane (p. 280)

roller deck (p. 281)

volume-weight (p. 286)

Review and Discussion Questions

1. What different types of air cargo services are there?
2. How would an airline determine how much a shipment will cost, based on the highest of actual weight or volume weight? What can a shipper do to reduce the costs of shipping a light but voluminous package?
3. What are the different types of aircrafts that are used to ship cargo?

Endnotes

1. "The World's Top Cargo Airlines," *Air Cargo World*, http://www.aircargoworld.com/features/0905_1.htm, July 4, 2006.

2. "Cargo," International Air Transport Association, http://www.iata.org/whatwedo/cargo, July 4, 2006.

3. Adapted from "Air Cargo; The Bottom Line," *Air Cargo World*, July 2006, p. 54, based on International Civil Aviation Organization data.

4. Putzger, Ian, "Air Cargo Capacity to Area Limited," *The Journal of Commerce*, February 3, 1997, p. 9B.

5. Aeppel, Timothy, "Weird Amazon Fish Hook Trendy Chefs," *The Wall Street Journal*, June 18, 1996, p. B1.

6. Kayal, Michele, "Couriers on Board: Crucial Links between You and Your Packages," *The Journal of Commerce*, November 3, 1997, p. 1A.

7. McCartney, Scott, "This Puddle-Jumper Has One Big Puddle: The Pacific Ocean," *The Wall Street Journal*, October 24, 1996, p. A1.

8. Davies, John, "Boeing Creates Unit for Jet Conversion," *The Journal of Commerce*, November 17, 1998.

9. Barnett, Chris, "Workhorse DC-3s Live On," *The Journal of Commerce*, January 18, 2000, p. 11.

10. Barnard, Bruce, "Night Flights to Be Banned in Brussels," *The Journal of Commerce*, January 5, 2000, p. 3.

11. *Ibid*

12. Conway, Peter, "Taking the High Road," *Air Cargo World*, January 2000, pp. 62–67.

13. "Air Cargo: The Bottom Line," *Air Cargo World*, May 2000, p. 78.

14. Cole, Jeff, "Flight of Fancy: Airbus Prepares to 'Bet the Company' as It Builds a Huge New Jet," *The Wall Street Journal*, November 3, 1999, p. A1.

15. Barnard, Bruce, "Antonov 124: Ukraine's High Flyer," *The Journal of Commerce*, November 23, 1999, p. 8.

16. Forsyth, Gordon, "Flying Flowers," *American Shipper*, June 20, 2000, pp. 52–56.

17. Krause, Kristin S., "Lay Low, Fly High," *Traffic World*, December 1997.

18. Sharpe, Rochelle, "Hearts of Gold: All Romance Aside, Valentine's Day Can Be Frantic—and Lucrative," *The Wall Street Journal*, February 15, 1996, p. A1.

19. Barnett, Chris, "Race for the Gold," *JoC Weekly*, June 5–11, 2000, p. 36.

20. Wilkison, David, "KAL Crash Jury Awards $2.1 Million," *Washington Post*, March 20, 1997.

21. Kayal, Michele, "Accord to Aid Cargo Flow," *The Journal of Commerce*, February 25, 1997, p. 8B.

22. Goldsmith, Charles, "Open-skies Pacts Lift U.S., European Carriers," *The Wall Street Journal*, September 24, 1997, p. A15. "U.S. Reaches 'Open Skies' Agreement," *Associated Press News Release*, November 15, 2000.

23. Wald, Matthew L., "U.S., Japan to Remove Air-Traffic Restrictions," *The New York Times*, January 31, 1998.

24. Putzger, Ian, "Cargo Spaces Out," *Air Cargo World*, August 1999, pp. 42–45.

International Land and Multi-Modal Transportation

Source: © 2007 JupiterImages Corporation.

This chapter is the last of a series of three covering the means of transportation available to an international shipper. The preceding two chapters covered ocean and air transportation. This chapter presents the remaining alternatives.

First, it will present the two main land-based shipping methods available to an international shipper: road and rail transportation. Both are much more frequently used in Europe for international freight, where they represent approximately 95 percent of the total intra-European freight traffic,[1] than they are in Asia and North America. However, practices differ and a savvy international logistics manager should be familiar with the issues presented by road and rail transportation.

In its second part, the chapter will cover the specifics of international intermodal transportation, which is not a transportation alternative properly speaking, but is the practice of shipping a product under a single bill of lading that covers more than one mode of transportation. For many shippers, that practice is often associated with container shipping.

Finally, two additional alternative methods of transportation are covered: inland waterway barges and pipelines. Although both represent a large percentage of the volume of the international shipments of some specific commodities (agricultural raw materials and crude oil), they are quite limited in their capabilities.

13-1 Truck Transportation

Trucking, from a North-American perspective, is primarily a domestic means of transportation, with the exception of the significant amount of trade between Canada and the United States, and some limited trade between the United States and Mexico. However, the latter is still mostly trade to and from the U.S.-Mexico border, as a large percentage of the trade is done on a DAF (Delivered at Frontier) basis (see Chapter 6) and because Mexican trucks are, for all intents and purposes, not yet authorized on American highways.

For the rest of the world, though, trucking is a vital way of shipping goods internationally. More than 80 percent of merchandise shipped internationally within the European Union is shipped by road,[2] and this share is increasing.[3]

Worldwide, trucking is still dominated by a patchwork of domestic rules and regulations, which greatly influence the way the industry is organized. There are limits on the number of axles a truck may have, on the weight it can carry per axle, on its total weight, on its length and width, as well as requirements regarding its mandatory equipment, the training of its driver, and the number of consecutive hours that s/he can drive. All of these constraints generate fleets of trucks that are slightly different from country to country. Altogether, though, trucks carrying international cargo tend to be semi-trucks (i.e., they are made up of two distinct units: a **tractor** pulling a **trailer**, both of which take on characteristics that are country-specific) (see Figures 13-1 and 13-2).

The biggest challenge in shipping goods internationally by trucks is to abide by all these rules and regulations, the complexity of which should not be underestimated. Case in point: European countries, even the smallest ones, like Luxemburg, have driving bans on certain days—generally Sundays—but none of these bans are coordinated or harmonized. There are forty-eight different driving bans in Western Europe alone,[4] which can create havoc on a company's ability to ship goods Just-in-Time, or for a shipper to reach a port before a sailing. Poland, for example, prohibits trucks from driving when temperatures reach 30° Celsius (86° Fahrenheit) and Switzerland prohibits trucks weighing more that twenty-eight tons from going further into Switzerland than ten km (six miles), relegating all large trucks crossing the country to "**piggy-back**" on railroad cars (see Figure 13-3).[5]

Such constraints often have the effect of creating giant "parking lots" of trucks at the entry points into a country and at highway exits. The enforcement of this myriad

tractor The part of an articulated semi-truck that is in the front and whose engine pulls the trailer.

trailer The part of an articulated semi-truck that is in the rear and is pulled by the tractor.

piggy-back A technique, developed by railroad and trucking companies, that consists of placing truck trailers on specially designed railroad cars, so that the trailers can be carried over long distances more economically.

Figure 13-1
A Typical European Semi-Truck . . .
Source: Photo © Timothy Jennings. Used with Permission.

Figure 13-2
. . . And Its North-American Counterpart
Source: Photo © Judy Baxter. Used with Permission.

of rules and regulations also creates delays. Although there are officially no longer any border controls for trucks within the European Union, police routinely stop truckers in order to enforce rules regarding driving times, speed limits, and so on, none of which are the same from one country to the next.

Figure 13-3
The Swiss "Rolling Highway"
Source: Photo © Hupac Intermodal. Used with permission.

The second challenge regarding shipping by truck is the state of the infrastructure: Load limits, height limits, and speed limits (road conditions) hinder the smooth transportation of goods and have an impact on packing. For example, the E-30 highway, one of the key links between Western Europe (Berlin) and Russia, is so crowded and in such a state of disrepair that traffic runs very slow, making it one of the most dangerous highways in the world. Such is the state of this road, that many shippers have made the decision to ship through Finland and St. Petersburg, and on to Moscow, despite the increased distance of such a trip. With only two lanes and thousands of trucks shuttling between Western and Eastern Europe, its replacement is long overdue, but unlikely to appear in the near future.[6]

But that is not all: The prohibitive taxation of diesel fuel in some countries influences the power of trucks, the size of the trailers, and the speeds at which cargo moves. The high tolls of some European highways lure truckers into driving on secondary roads that are not as cargo-friendly. Some companies are "flagging out" their trucks—registering them in other countries—to take advantage of lower taxation and regulations,[7] bringing the same kind of concerns that "flags of convenience" have triggered for the marine industry. Another factor is the "cultural" aspect of the industry. While **overloaded** trucks are rare in North America and Europe, they are strikingly commonplace in Africa and in some parts of Asia, where, seemingly, a truck is not full until one more piece of cargo will fit (see Figure 13-4).

Finally, the complementary infrastructure of railroads influences the way that some goods are shipped. In North America, for example, a large fleet of railroad cars capable of carrying truck trailers enables trucking companies to load trailers onto trains rather than drive them across the country. In Australia, however, the seemingly complete lack of railroads has pushed trucking companies to develop "**road-trains**," which are tractors pulling three to five full-size semi-trailers (see Figure 13-5).

The last challenge regarding trucking, specifically in Europe, is the fact that road transport is often delayed by social unrest. In the first six months of 2006, there were no fewer than ten instances during which some group or another blocked truck traffic somewhere in the European Union. Farmers protesting high gas prices, truckers protesting low wages, ecologists worried about pollution—just about every pretext was used to block entrances to highways, harbors, refineries, Alpine routes, or whatever else, causing lengthy (up to seven days) delays for truck shipments. Because governments routinely cave in to these demands, it is unlikely that the number of such protests will diminish in the future.

overloaded A mode of transportation that is carrying cargo of a greater weight or greater volume than it is designed to carry.

road-trains An Australian trucking technique, consisting of having one tractor pulling multiple trailers. Road-trains are the conceptual equivalent of trains, but operating on a road.

Figure 13-4
An Overloaded Truck in India
Source: Photo © Dhruv Dhindsa. Used with permission.

Figure 13-5
An Australian Road Train
Source: Photo © Volvo Truck Corporation. Used with permission.

13-2 Rail Transportation

Another contrast between North America and the rest of the world is the extent railroads are used for freight movements. In the United States, for example, 1.72 trillion ton-miles were shipped by rail in 2004, or a "market share" of more than 40 percent of all ton-miles shipped long-distance in the country.[8] The growth of intermodal freight accounted for more than one-third of the total number of carloads transported, a total of 9.96 million trailers or containers. Although there are no figures available for international freight in North America, it is likely that the percentages are similar. In contrast, about 16 percent of international shipments within the European Community were by rail in 2006 (see Figure 13-6), an increase from about 12 percent in 2001; however, that figure is somewhat distorted by the fact that the EU has added ten new countries, in which rail transport has a 36 percent market share.[9] Only a small percentage of those were intermodal, where the railcars carried a container (see Figure 13-7). The railroad infrastructure in Europe is still mostly focused on passenger traffic, and freight traffic is mostly neglected, with almost no investments in railroad cars and facilities designed to facilitate intermodal cargo.

Figure 13-6
A Traditional European Freight Train with Bulk and Box Cars
Source: Photo © Alain D. Boillat, SBB. Used with permission.

Figure 13-7
A European Single-Stack Container Train
Source: Photo © Alain D. Boillat, SBB. Used with permission.

In the last few years, the European Community has introduced the idea of "freight corridors" that would carry freight from Northern Europe's major ports (Antwerp, Belgium, and Amsterdam, the Netherlands) to the cities of Milan, Italy, and Vienna, Austria—and eventually to other cities as well—bypassing the requirements to change to a national locomotive and a national crew at every border crossing.[10]

Nevertheless, as these "rail freight freeways" are going to utilize currently existing lines, and because passenger trains have priority over all other traffic, there are widespread doubts about the feasibility of this politically motivated initiative.[11] Two of these corridors had been implemented. The Société Nationale des Chemins de Fer Français (SNCF), the French national railroad company, boasts on its website that Belgium can be linked to Northern Italy in a mere thirty-three hours, or at an average of thirty-five km/h or less than twenty-five mph. Combine that with the fact that there were only two departures per day, except Saturdays, Sundays, and holidays, when there are none, and the conclusion is that rail transportation in Europe is far from being a viable alternative for all but the least time-sensitive cargo.

To date, a single rail project involving a new rail corridor has been built, from the port of Rotterdam to the Netherlands-Germany border: It is called the Betuweroute. It carries only freight trains, and has a capacity of ten trains in either direction every hour. It connects to the network of the Dutch and German railways, and relieves congestion in the port.

In contrast, in the United States railroads have traditionally had three business activities:

1. Bulk freight, not only grain, coal, lumber, steel, ores, chemicals, and oil, but also molasses, vegetable oils, and other heavy items. Each of these bulk cargoes tends to have its own type of railroad car.

2. Break-bulk freight placed in boxcars, either palletized or simply in its packaging.

3. Automobiles, placed on specialized car carriers.

In the last two decades, the advent of intermodal transportation has radically changed this mix and dramatically altered the railroad business. Railroads are now carrying an increasing number of containers placed on container carriers (see Figure 13-8) and of truck trailers on piggy-back cars (see Figure 13-9).

First these container carriers were designed to be only one container high, but then double-stacks were introduced, which eventually doubled the capacity of each train, but forced railroads to update their infrastructure—tunnels in particular—so that these cars would "fit." In 2005, the United States railroads carried a total of 11.7 million trailers or containers,[12] an estimated 25 percent of which were transiting on a "land bridge" between Asia and Europe (see Section 13-3b).

The discrepancy between North American and European railroads is striking. As much as the future of rail transportation in the United States was bleak in the 1970s, it has transformed itself into a customer-oriented vibrant industry—despite some serious disturbances when Union Pacific bought Southern Pacific[13]—with

Figure 13-8
A U.S. Double-Stack Container Train

Source: Photo © Trista Belfoure. Used with permission.

Figure 13-9
A U.S. Piggy-Back Train
Source: Photo © Chuck Donaldson. Used with permission.

substantial expected growth emerging from its traditional cargoes moving to containers, such as grain and automobiles.[14] The European railroads appear to have noticed this trend and are attempting to embrace it; however, the national railroads are such bloated bureaucracies that progress is slow and success is elusive. In November 2000, EU railroad companies passed a resolution that they will open their network to each other's crews and engines; however, as of 2006, that resolution was still only a plan. Moreover, France opposes opening its network despite the agreement, so a large, geographically necessary swath of the network may not be available at all.[15] Add to this information the discrepancies of at least two railroad gauges, five electrical systems, and *sixteen* signaling systems, and the task seems daunting.[16]

Another possible development is the replacement of some ocean trade with rail transportation, notably between the Far East (China, Korea) and Europe; such a possibility would seriously shorten transit times between the two areas, and relieve some of the congestion in Southern China's ports.[17] At this point, though, the traffic on such a lane is very modest, with only about 55,000 containers going from the port of Vostochny on the eastern shore of Russia to Europe for the entire 2000 calendar year.[18]

13-3 Intermodal Transportation

intermodal A shipment that takes several different means of transportation from its point of departure (seller/exporter) to its point of destination (buyer/importer).

Probably the best way to introduce **intermodal** transportation is to define the concept:

> Intermodal describes a shipment that takes several different means of transportation—road, rail, ocean, air—from its point of departure (seller/exporter) to its point of destination (buyer/importer). The meaning has evolved recently to limit the use of this term to freight for which a single bill of lading covering more than one of these alternatives is issued.

multi-modal Another term for intermodal.

Intermodal transportation is therefore not a means of transportation per se, but instead describes the practice of utilizing a single bill of lading to cover several means of transportation for a single shipment. For that reason, it is also called **multi-modal** transportation. To use a recent cliché, the changes in means of transportation are "transparent" to the user, which means that the shipper does not have to worry about them, but only needs to be aware of them, so as to pack accordingly. The responsibility of arranging for all of the means of transportation falls onto the shipping company.[19]

Shipping companies have had to change their perspectives from that of a simple transportation provider to that of a provider of a multiplicity of services, one of which is transportation in their core competency, such as ocean shipping. However, they also have to provide transportation services in other modes, such as trucking or rail. In addition, shipping companies now interact with their customers directly and offer such ancillary services as tracking of shipments online. Most important of all, intermodal service created the possibility for an exporter (or an importer) to have a single interlocutor in a complex international shipment involving more than one mode of transportation. This "one-stop" shopping is probably what has made intermodal transportation so popular with shippers.

Because of the ubiquitous use of the seagoing container in multi-modal shipments, the term "intermodal" has also been strongly associated with this transportation concept. The container idea is fairly recent: It was created in 1956 by Malcom[PD1] McLean in an attempt to eliminate the large number of handlings to which ocean cargo was subjected, and to speed up the loading and unloading of ships. This concept of container has been a smashing success, with more than 8.8 million TEUs—twenty-foot equivalent units—in use worldwide.[20] Certainly, the use of containers allowed the concept of intermodal to develop, but the two concepts are not tied: It is quite possible to have an intermodal shipment that is not packaged in a container, and it is possible to have containerized cargo use only one mode of transportation. Nevertheless, the two are strongly tied together, and probably 95 percent of all intermodal cargo is shipped in a container—they are many different types. In addition, that percentage is growing, as more container types are created to allow nonstandard cargo to be containerized.

13-3a Types of Seagoing Containers

The greatest number of containers in the seagoing trade are the "standard" twenty-foot and forty-foot units (6.1 and 12.2 meters, respectively), called "boxes"; these containers are eight feet wide, eight feet tall (2.44 meters), and fully enclosed in steel. They are equipped with a double door at one end (called the front of the container) and have a wooden floor; some have wooden sides as well. Seagoing containers can be stacked up to nine high, and in some cases, they are stacked higher (under deck, in the holds of the larger containerships).[21] Whenever the capacity of a ship is measured, it is given in TEUs, or the number of twenty-foot equivalent units it can transport.

There are a large number of variants that were designed around this common "platform" of 8 × 8 × 40. Each of these alternatives is called a "special" and its availability may be limited to certain routes and/or certain shipping lines.

- The liquid-bulk container (see Figure 13-11), in which a tank designed to hold liquids is placed inside a frame that has the same outside dimensions as a twenty-foot unit. Containers holding liquid bulk actually have different designs depending on the type of cargo carried and can be made of a variety of materials as well. Nevertheless, the frame is built to ISO standards, and liquid-bulk containers can be stacked with traditional containers.

- The dry-bulk container, which is designed to hold dry-bulk products, such as grain or polymer pellets. This method of shipping dry bulk is becoming more common, as it allows for fewer handlings than when the cargo is strictly bulk, or packaged in drums or bags (see Section 14-3c). Because some bulk cargo is quite heavy (grain, for example), a shorter container was created—about five feet tall— so that three containers can "fit" where two traditional ones normally do. This design greatly facilitates rail transport as three containers fit on a double-stack train. Those containers can also be stacked with traditional ISO boxes as well.

Movable Boxes

International commerce was completely changed by the arrival of the container.[22]

Before containers, the traditional method for loading and unloading a ship was a very time-consuming and labor-intensive process. Goods, in boxes small enough to be handled by humans, were loaded by cranes onto break-bulk ships. Gangs of longshoremen were responsible for stowing them into the ship and making sure that they would not be damaged during the ocean voyage. They had to make sure that heavy goods were lower in the hold than lighter goods, that the weight of the cargo was distributed correctly through the ship, and that every piece of cargo was wedged solidly against the others. It was backbreaking, dangerous work. Because a ship could not be loaded until it had completely been unloaded, it took days to perform both operations. As trade increased, there was evermore gridlock in the ports and ocean shipping was agonizingly slow.

Containers revolutionized this system; containers would be loaded, once, in the plant that manufactured the product, and unloaded, once, in the plant of the customer. There were no intermediary handling, no chance for pilferage, no possible damage from mishandling. The labor costs would be lower, as the laborers loading the containers would be inland, and not part of the strong (and costly) longshoremen's unions.

Containers of different sizes had been proposed several times before, but it was Malcom McLean, the owner of a trucking company, who eventually made the first investment in movable boxes of a size similar to a truck trailer, and shipped them from Newark to Houston in April 1956. It eventually expanded this concept to other U.S. routes: West Coast to Hawaii, Miami to Puerto Rico.

His greatest challenges were with the unions of the ports in which he set up his operations; while West Coast ports' unions embraced the system, the East Coast unions were more difficult to convince. He also had difficulties convincing port authorities to invest in cranes and docks; in particular the Port of New York was unwilling to invest

Figure 13-10
Containers in the Port of Elizabeth, New Jersey
Source: Photo © National Oceanic and Atmospheric Administration. Used with permission.

in docks that were wide enough to allow trucks to come alongside ships. Eventually, the movable container prevailed, as all began to understand the benefits of the concept.

In the late 1950s, containers were everywhere in the United States, except that they were of different sizes; as McLean had expanded its concept, others had copied him, and chosen different standard sizes. The incompatibility of these sizes made for a cumbersome system. It was eventually determined, after long negotiations between truckers, ship owners, railroads, and port authorities, both in the United States and Europe, that containers should be eight feet wide, eight feet high, and either ten, twenty, or forty feet long. This standardization effort took the better part of a decade. Today, seagoing containers are only twenty or forty feet long, so that they can fit in the holds of containerships. A few exceptions to these sizes exist.

As of 2006, there were more than thirteen million containers worldwide (see Table 13-1).[23]

TABLE 13-1	Worldwide Container Fleet (2006)
20-foot boxes	5,583,000
40-foot boxes	2,716,000
40-foot high cubes	3,696,000
Reefers (all sizes)	534,000
Open tops	153,000
Others	454,000

Figure 13-11
A Stacker Moving a Liquid-Bulk Container in the Port of Santos

- The open-top container (see Figure 13-12), which is designed to hold cargo that is too large to fit through the door of a regular container, and therefore must be loaded from the top. Sometimes the container is then covered with a tarpaulin. Open-top containers can also be used to hold cargo that is taller than eight feet, and the cargo then protrudes through the top of the container. Because it is then impossible to stack another container on top of that tall cargo, these containers are always considered "top of stack," whether placed under deck or on deck.

- The extended-length container, which is designed to hold cargo that does not fit in a forty-foot container. These containers, designed so that the cargo "sticks out" of the traditional container, are fairly difficult to pack and load onto the ship, as the center of gravity still has to be within the box itself. They are generally placed on top of stacks, but must have the next stack's slot empty as well, so that the cargo is not damaged. These containers probably represent an extreme utilization of containers for what otherwise would be break-bulk cargo.

- The flat rack (see Figure 13-13) is designed to hold cargo that is less than eight feet wide, but would not fit in a standard container, which has inside dimensions of 92.5 inches (2.35 meters). Sometimes the flat rack has corners or two end walls, giving the flat rack a ⊔ shape that allows a flat rack to be part of a stack. Sometimes it does not, which then forces it to be a top of stack as well. Flat racks are used for shipments of pleasure boats, trucks, and military vehicles.

- The refrigerated container (see Figure 13-14) is designed to hold cargo at a constant temperature during the voyage. These containers need an outside power source (electricity) to function, and must be plugged in during all the legs of their intermodal journey. Most containerships can accommodate a few refrigerated container units. These containers are also called "reefers."

- The high cube container is no more than a container that is 9.5 feet tall, and therefore can hold slightly more cargo. Such containers are designed to hold cargo that "cubes out" before it "weighs out" (i.e., it fills the volume of the container before it reaches the maximum weight limit of a container, which is 52,910 lbs (24 metric tons) for a twenty-foot container and 67,200 lbs (30.5 metric tons) for a forty-foot container.

Figure 13-12
An Open-Top Container

Figure 13-13
A Flat Rack Container

- The hanger container is designed to hold garments "on hanger" (i.e., it is equipped with steel bars on which clothes are hung). The hanger container is a relatively new device, but it seems to fulfill the need for a more convenient way to ship hanging clothes, which may be damaged when they are shipped flat in boxes or may be difficult to fold. Garment containers seem to be all high-cube containers as well.

A myriad of other "specials" are available: Several have been designed to ship automobiles, several to ship livestock, and others to ship ever-different cargo that

Figure 13-14
A Refrigerated Container or "Reefer"

could not otherwise be shipped in a standard ISO box. One aspect of importance in these modifications made to the standard, though, is that they all can accommodate the rigors of ocean shipping and fit within the existing ocean vessel and port infrastructure. In that, they are still all intermodal containers.

One of the difficulties of the development of "specials" is the fact that they are not multi-purpose: While a traditional ISO box that held a cargo of automobile parts from the United States to Malaysia can be used on the way back to ship garments or toys, such is not the case with a livestock container. If it is designed for cattle, it is unlikely that it can be used for anything else but cattle, and will come back empty, forcing its owner to pay for the return trip.

To a much lesser extent, a similar problem exists with all ISO boxes because of the imbalance of trade between ports. For example, much more trade arrives in the ports of Los Angeles and Long Beach in the United States from Asia than leaves the ports for Asian destinations. There is therefore an accumulation of "empties" in the United States while, at the same time, there is a shortage of boxes in most Asian ports.[24] For some trade routes, there is another reason for the shortage of boxes in one direction: A substantial portion of empty containers shipped to some destinations "disappear," as they are used for storage or housing. Such is the case in some of the Republics of the former Soviet Union and some African countries.

Shippers returning empty containers are charged freight for transport. Empty containers entering the United States are considered "Implements of International Trade," and do not require a Customs Entry Processing form. However, U.S. Customs requires that empty containers be manifested and clears them as an entry-exempt item. Empty containers must be completely empty: No blocking, bracing, or securing equipment, materials, or residual products of any kind can be found inside them. Because they can be inspected by U.S. Customs, the shipper is subject to being fined for illegal entry of goods if they are not completely empty.

13-3b Land Bridges

The intermodal environment created several new ways of shipping goods internationally. One of the striking changes made was the concept of "land bridges." A land bridge conveys that cargo traveling on ocean liners can cross a land obstacle by being unloaded in one port, transferred to a train, carried across the land area by rail, and reloaded onto another ship.

land bridge A term coined to describe the practice of shipping goods from Asia to Europe through the United States by using railroads.

The use of a typical **land bridge** would involve cargo going from the Far East to Europe. A few years ago, it would have been break-bulk cargo loaded onto a ship that would have crossed the Pacific, gone through the Panama Canal, and crossed the Atlantic before reaching its destination. (It could also have gone westward, through the Suez Canal, but then it would be a different story). Today, the same cargo would be containerized and could use a land bridge: The cargo is shipped by ocean from the Far East to the West Coast of the United States, after which it is unloaded and placed on a train that takes it to the East Coast of the United States. It is then reloaded onto another ship and sent to its destination in Europe. Using a land bridge is the penultimate in "intermodal shipments"; such changes in modes of transportation are so transparent to the shipper that it generally has no idea that its international cargo traveled through the Arizona desert on its way from Kobe, Japan, to Rotterdam, the Netherlands.

Such land bridges emerged because of several factors. The first is that the time spent by a ship traveling the Panama Canal route was greater than the time necessary to unload the cargo, cross the United States, and reload the cargo. The second is that it was equivalent in costs, or cheaper. The third was that economies of scale could be achieved with larger ships, which would not fit through the Canal. The fourth was the concern, expressed by a few shipping lines, regarding the reliability of the Canal when it became the responsibility of the Panamanian government, a concern that fortunately did not materialize.

There are several possible other locations for land bridges outside of the United States. The African continent is an obvious one, but at this time land bridges do not exist and are not planned. Another is the traffic from the Far East to Eastern Europe, which can transit faster through Russia than by vessel: The port of Vostochny on the eastern shore of Russia was developed in the mid-1970s using Japanese funds to provide such a service. From a height of 143,000 containers in 1983 to 55,000 in 2000, this land bridge is but a speck in the transit from Japan and Korea to Europe.[25] However, the development of a seriously important land bridge is possible if North Korea re-opened its railway system, a move that would allow cargo from South Korea to link with the Russian Trans-Siberian railway and Europe.

A growing problem with land bridge use in the United States is the increasing demand for domestic intermodal service, which competes for capacity with international container service (see Table 13-2).[26] Specially designed fifty-three-foot-long, high-capacity containers have been built and put into use by Schneider National, the largest private trucking company in the United States. The company expects to have 30 percent or more of its trucks going intermodal by 2010. These domestic intermodal movements add strain to a rail system that is already at or near capacity on key corridors, the primary routes for international intermodal cargo. Therefore, the potential for higher freight rates exists.

13-3c Liability Issues

One of the aspects of intermodal shipping that has yet to be resolved is the issue of liability of the carrier toward the shipper when the goods are damaged while in its care. As goods travel from one mode of transportation to another, the legal or regulatory liability limits change: The limits are different for the trucking leg of the trip, the rail leg,

TABLE 13-2	Annual United States Intermodal Volume Figures, 2001–2005				
	2001	**2002**	**2003**	**2004**	**2005**
Containers	7,921,213	8,588,822	9,472,518	10,283,491	11,057,610
Trailers	2,413,933	2,345,508	2,424,407	2,639,545	2,584,262
Total Rail Intermodal Volume	*10,335,146*	*10,934,330*	*11,896,925*	*12,923,036*	*13,641,872*

and the ocean leg. In many cases, they are also different from one carrier to another, if such carrier has negotiated a different limit under the U.S. Ocean Shipping Reform Act (OSRA), or because the flag of the carrier matters. This issue is mostly relevant for shippers who elect to not insure their cargo and for insurance companies. Nevertheless, it is one of the few drawbacks of intermodal transportation. As mentioned in Section 11-6, in June 2000, the United Nations Commission on International Trade Law (UNCITRAL) started the process of creating a formal multi-modal liability framework.[27] As of July 2006, the committee in charge of coordinating this effort had created a draft agreement and was starting the process of soliciting comments.

13-3d Aircraft Containers

The types of containers used in air transport are radically different from the ones used in ocean shipping for several reasons. The major differences in the way they are built and used are:

1. They are used to aggregate small individual packages rather than to form a whole shipment. Freight consolidators and airlines bundle together several different freight packages going to the same destination and unbundle them at the destination airport, sometimes to rebundle them in another container for shipment to their final destination. In that regard, containers are used to speed up the loading and unloading of aircrafts by shifting the task of loading and unloading small packages from the airplane to airport facilities. It also allows airfreight companies to use space more efficiently, for example, by building shelves in the containers, which allow more freight to be carried.

2. Although there have been some standardization attempts, most containers are designed to fit a specific aircraft. There are at least twenty different sizes, all identified by a code such as L-2 or EH, and some variants within the same size can be used as well: L-2 for example, can only be used in the belly of a Boeing 767, but the EH can be used on any aircraft's main deck. Most aircraft containers therefore cannot be conveniently transported from one airplane to the next, and cargo must be decontainerized and recontainerized at airport facilities. This certainly removes the advantage of being able to securely pack a container and leave it undisturbed until it is unpacked by the consignee.

3. Aircraft containers are made of lightweight materials and are not designed to protect the cargo in any significant way. Most containers are made of aluminum, Plexiglas, or sometimes plywood, with "doors" that can be made of the same material, or made of fabric, or even be nonexistent, with the cargo instead being held by a net. These containers offer little protection against the elements and against theft (see Figure 13-15).

4. Aircraft containers are not intermodal in intent: They are only designed to be used in aircraft and, possibly, for very short truck routes. They are rarely used outside of airport facilities.

13-4 Freight Forwarders

This complex array of alternatives is often bewildering to an occasional shipper; in those cases, it makes sense for the shipper to use the services of a **freight forwarder**, or a firm specializing in handling freight, particularly international freight.

A freight forwarder is, in layman's terms, a travel agent for freight: It knows what alternative routes are available, it knows how to determine the cost of shipping goods between two points, and it can arrange all of the paperwork necessary to ship the goods, from the exporting country's requirements to the importing country's Customs clearance.

Freight forwarders are different from Customs brokers, who specialize in clearing Customs for freight, and who have to take, at least in the United States, a rigorous

freight forwarder A company that specializes in shipping cargo on behalf of shippers (exporters or importers).

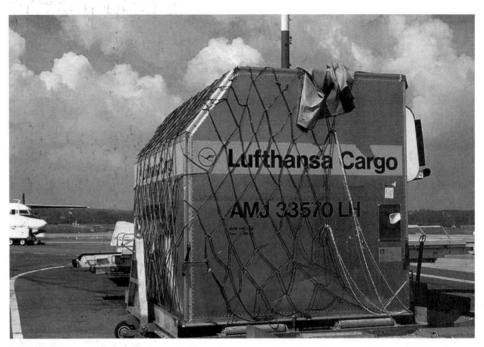

Figure 13-15
An Air Cargo Container
Source: Photo © Willfried Schmid. Used with permission.

examination to be allowed to fulfill this role. Freight forwarders are also different from NVOCCs (Non-Vessel Operating Common Carriers), who buy space on liner ships or airfreighters and resell it to LCL (Less-than-Container-Load) customers, and who are regulated by the FMC. Nevertheless, it is not uncommon for all three functions to be present in the same firm.

The business of freight forwarders is highly fragmented, including a large number of firms. Some are very large, with operations in just about every country. Others are quite small, and to distinguish themselves from others, end up specializing in a specific market, such as moving hazardous cargo, moving live animals, or moving what is known as **project cargo**.

project cargo A type of cargo that requires more advance planning because of its size, weight, or volume.

13-5 Project Cargo

The term "project cargo" is used to characterize cargo that is outside the normal realm of what shipping companies handle, specifically in terms of weight, volume, or destination. Most often, it encompasses all of the pieces of machinery or equipment required by a single project, such as the building of a dam or power plant, but can be an entire plant as well, which is being moved from a developed country, where its technology is outdated, to a developing country, where it will finish its useful life.[28] Project cargo also includes anything that requires some extra planning, such as the shipping of locomotives, railroad cars, large trucks, pleasure boats, large engines, electric generators, and so on.

In general, project cargo needs careful planning in order to reach its destination: The trucks used to transport it to the port need to trace their itineraries very carefully, not only to avoid low bridges and tunnels, but also to make sure that the proper permits can be secured. Port cranes have to be checked to make sure they can handle the load, or else floating cranes have to be rented. The ship carrying the cargo has to be selected carefully, to make sure it can accommodate the cargo—ROROs and LASH barges are the most commonly used means of getting project cargoes to their port of destination. Finally, the final road trip has to be planned thoroughly as well. It is not unusual for such shipments to be planned more than a year in advance and cost several millions of U.S. dollars because of their complexity.[29]

Such project cargo also moves quite slowly; it is difficult to make a 550,000-lb piece of equipment move quickly, especially when it involves using all lanes of a highway at once, or taking down and replacing all overhanging electric, telephone, and other utility wires.[30]

In late 2005, a 1.5-million-pound hydro cracker for Canada's oil-sands project in Long Lake, Alberta, was moved by heavy lift ship to the Port of Duluth Minnesota. From the port, the unusual cargo traveled by rail on the world's largest rail car, the thirty-six-axle German-made Schnabel car. The planning for the transportation of such a massive piece of equipment took two years. Ed Clarke, the logistician in charge of the move, said, "It's all about preplanning. At every step along the way you have to check weights, dimensions, clearances. And you have to know everything about the environment in which the equipment will be handled."[31] On a typical oversize, heavy-lift project, the logistics manager has a long list of items to check: the cargo itself, generally where it is manufactured; the docks and cargo-handling equipment (cranes) in the ports in which the cargo will be handled; the vessel on which the oversize piece will be shipped; the rail cars, the rails, the bridges and tunnels along the trip, and even the rail beds on which the cargo will be hauled.

13-6 Alternative Means of Transportation

Despite the preponderance of the traditional means of transportation of ocean shipping, air freight, trucking, and railroads for moving cargo internationally, a few alternative ways are used on a regular basis.

13-6a Pipelines

Probably the most easily overlooked of the alternative means of transportation are **pipelines**, which carry a substantial percentage of the world's petroleum oil and natural gas. Many of these pipelines are international; for example, Gazprom, the state-owned producer of gas in Russia, ships 525 billion cubic meters (18.5 trillion cubic feet) of gas to Europe in a single pipeline, which meanders through Belarus, the Ukraine, Poland, Slovakia, and the Czech Republic before stopping in Germany, and provides fully 20 percent of the European Union's gas needs.[32] A second pipeline is being planned. Many other pipelines crisscross the Persian Gulf area and the North American continent.

Pipelines can also be used to replace ships for some areas of the world where it is particularly hazardous to navigate: One such planned pipeline would allow oil shipped from the oil fields of southern Russia to bypass the Bosporus, a particularly congested area located in the middle of a very densely populated city, Istanbul.[33] More than 50,000 ships travel its waters every year. The people of Istanbul and their government have been advocating such a pipeline, as they cannot control what goes through the strait—it is considered international waters—and they fear a catastrophic accident. Given the condition of some oil tankers, the treacheries of the currents in the narrow passage, and the fact that dozens of ships run aground or collide in the Bosporus every year,[34] it is not an unfounded fear. An oil and gas pipeline would remove some of this hazardous traffic.

pipelines A mode of transportation consisting of a long series of pipes, connected end-to-end, and used for the transport of some liquid cargo.

Pipelines can be used for transporting coal as well, in the form of "slurry," a mix of water and pulverized coal that is then shipped as a liquid. Such a method can, in some cases, present some economic advantage over traditional railroad and truck transportation.[35]

13-6b Barges

barges Flat-bottomed boats designed to carry cargo on rivers and canals, and that are designed to be pushed or pulled.

River **barges** are also commonly used to carry international cargo, and are often significant sources of transportation services on certain routes and for certain merchandises. For example, 50 percent of all the cargo (by weight) shipped to and from Rotterdam, the largest seaport in the world, travels by barge, with 25 percent traveling by truck, 4 percent traveling by rail—a very small amount, although it is expected to increase with the construction of the Betuweroute—and 21 percent traveling by pipeline.[36] More than one billion tons (mostly commodities such as coal and grain) were carried on U.S. waterways in 1997,[37] mostly on the Mississippi and Ohio River networks. They can easily be delayed, though, by natural variations in the weather: Barges on the Mississippi River are often delayed when the Mississippi is in a flood stage or when there is a drought, as the river is lower than normal. Although they are much slower, river barges offer a more economical alternative to trucks and railroads.

Ocean barges are also commonly used for shipping, although it is unclear how much of this mode of transportation is used for international shipping. Nevertheless, most of the traffic between the continental United States and Puerto Rico is done by barge, and so is some of the traffic with small Alaskan towns.[38]

Key Terms

barges (p. 306)

freight forwarder (p. 303)

intermodal (p. 296)

land bridge (p. 302)

multi-modal (p. 296)

overloaded (p. 292)

piggy-back (p. 290)

pipelines (p. 305)

project cargo (p. 304)

road-trains (p. 292)

tractor (p. 290)

trailer (p. 290)

Review and Discussion Questions

1. How different are the ground transport alternatives in different areas of the world? What constraints does a shipper face when shipping with ground transport?

2. What is the concept of a land bridge? What effect will such a concept have on the frequency of use of containers in shipping cargo?

3. Choose three different types of ocean containers and explain how they are used.

4. In what ways are ocean-going containers and aircraft containers different?

5. Comment on the opinion that "the number of cargo handling points is not diminished with the use of aircraft containers."

Endnotes

1. "Modal Split of Freight Transport," Eurostat, European Statistical Agency, http://epp.eurostat.ec.europa.eu, August 5, 2006.

2. Kaps, Roderick and Christoph Wolff, "The Transformation of European Rail: Deregulation on Track?" *The McKinsey Quarterly*, 1997, Vol. 4, pp. 107–119.

3. Rykken, Rolf, "Gauging Intermodal," *Export Today*, April 1998, pp. 62–67.

4. Carding, Tony, "Truckers Decry Bans," *Traffic World*, August 1997.

5. Koenig, Robert, "Switzerland, EU Reach Tentative Truck Agreement," *The Journal of Commerce*, January 27, 1998, p. 12A.

6. Ford, Peter, "Jammed in a 'Pipeline' of Trucks," *The Christian Science Monitor*, August 4, 1998, p. 1.

7. Koenig, Robert, "Danes Planning to 'Flag Out' Their Trucks," *The Journal of Commerce*, January 10, 2000, p. 3.

8. "Class I Railroad Statistics," Association of American Railroads, Documents/AboutTheIndustry/Statistics. pdf, July 10, 2006.

9. Clark, Nicola, "Putting Europe Back on Track," *International Herald Tribune*, July 1, 2006.

10. Barnard, Bruce, "Europe's First Rail Freight 'Freeway' Could Link Two Northern Ports to Milan by June," *The Journal of Commerce*, April 2, 1997, p. 4B.

11. Barnard, Bruce, and Aviva Freudmann, "EU to Open Cross-Border Rail Freight Corridors," *The Journal of Commerce*, January 15, 1998, p. 1A.

12. "Class I Railroad Statistics," Association of American Railroads, http://www.aar.org/PubCommon/Documents/AboutTheIndustry/Statistics.pdf, July 10, 2006.

13. Machalaba, Daniel, "A Big Railroad Merger Goes Terribly Awry in a Very Short Time," *The Wall Street Journal*, October 2, 1997, p. A1.

14. Lomazzi, Marc, "Le Train Passe la Grande Vitesse," *le MOCI [Moniteur du Commerce International]*, May 28, 1998, p. 31.

15. Barnard, Bruce, "EU Members Agree to Tear Down Rail-Freight Borders," *JoC Online*, November 24, 2000, http://www.joc.com/20001124/sections/logis/w47712.shtml, November 27, 2000.

16. Freudmann, Aviva, "Cross-border Plan Gains Momentum," *The Journal of Commerce*, December 16, 1999, p. 1.

17. French, Howard W., "Railroad Trip to Europe? Koreans Savor the Idea," *The New York Times*, November 7, 2000.

18. Working, Russell, "Port Offers Shippers a Siberian Shortcut," *The New York Times*, December 3, 2000.

19. Mathews, Anna Wilde, "More Firms Rely on 'One-Stop' Shipping," *The Wall Street Journal*, April 29, 1997.

20. *2006 Annual Leased Container Fleet Survey*, Institute of International Container Lessors, http://www.iicl.org/PDF%20Docs/18thcontainer_fleet_survey.pdf, July 10, 2006.

21. Linares, Jean-Louis, former crane operator, Port Autonome de Marseille, personal interview, October 31, 2000.

22. Levinson, Marc, *The Box: How the Shipping Container Made the World Smaller and the World Economy Bigger*, Princeton University Press, Princeton, New Jersey, 2006.

23. Calculated from: *2006 Annual Leased Container Fleet Survey*, Institute of International Container Lessors, Press Release, March 10, 2006. "Providing an Extensive, High Quality Network," World Shipping Council, http://www.worldshipping.org/ind_2.html, July 20, 2006.

24. Knee, Richard, "Container Pileup," *The Journal of Commerce*, June 26, 1997, p. 4C.

25. Working, Russell, "Port Offers Shippers a Siberian Shortcut," *The New York Times*, December 3, 2000.

26. *Intermodal Market Trends and Statistics Report*, Intermodal Association of North America (IANA), http://www.intermodal.org/fact.html.

27. Freudmann, Aviva, "No Easy Answer," *JoC Weekly*, June 12–18, 2000, p. 16.

28. Baldwin, Tom, "Carriers Move the Immovable," *The Journal of Commerce*, October 26, 1998, p. 1C.

29. *Ibid*

30. Mathews, Anna Wilde, "Hauling Super Freight Takes Ingenuity and a Huge Rig," *The Wall Street Journal*, April 13, 1998, p. B1.

31. Marciniak, Lisa, "Making the Big Jobs Look Easy" *North Star Port*, Duluth Seaway Port Authority, Winter 2005–2006 Issue.

32. Gubert, Romain, "Querelle de Gazoduc," *Le Point*, November 3, 2000, p. 25.

33. Chelminsky, Rudolph, "The Bosporus: A Disaster Waiting to Happen," *Smithsonian*, November 1998, pp. 110–123.

34. Moore, Molly, "Is the Bosporus Taking on More Than It Can Handle?" *International Herald Tribune*, November 17, 2000, p. 2.

35. Wall Street Journal Editorial Staff, "Coal-Slurry Spigot," *The Wall Street Journal*, September 16, 1983.

36. Barnard, Bruce, "Inland Shipping Leaves Trucks, Rails in Its Wake on Rhine," *The Journal of Commerce*, January 29, 1999, p. 1B.

37. "Freight Carried on Major U.S. Waterways," *Statistical Abstract of the United States—1993*, p. 669.

38. Mathews, Anna Wilde, "Jet-age Anomalies, Slowpoke Barges Do Brisk Business," *The Wall Street Journal*, May 15, 1998, p. B1.

Packaging for Export

Chapter Fourteen

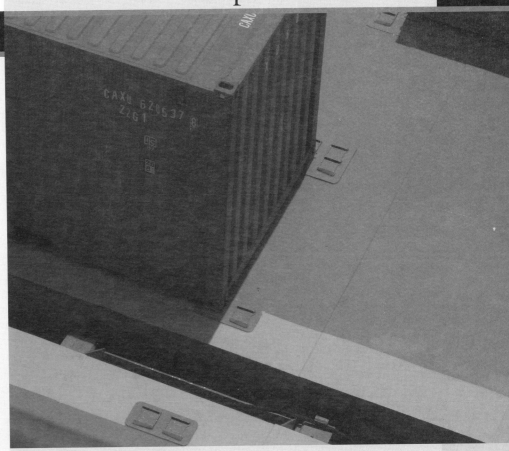

Source: © 2007 JupiterImages Corporation.

One of the challenging practical areas of international logistics is the packaging of goods for international shipments. This is a responsibility that always falls on the exporter, regardless of the Terms of Trade, or Incoterms, chosen (see Chapter 6). Unfortunately, it is a function that is oftentimes just left to the shipping department, with few guidelines other than to make sure it gets to the customers without problems, and quite often with pressures to control costs; there is rarely a strategy developed for packaging, even though it is an area that certainly has strategic implications.

This chapter makes a distinction between primary, secondary, and tertiary packaging, as seen in Figure 14-1. Primary packaging is consumer packaging, or what consumers see when they purchase and handle the product. It is part of the marketing function of the firm and is traditionally covered in marketing management textbooks as part of the promotional efforts of the firm; primary packaging is only occasionally mentioned in this chapter. Secondary packaging is the packaging that usually groups several of the consumer goods into one unit, usually a thin cardboard box or a shrink-wrap. This is what the retailer sees and handles before the goods are placed on the shelves. In discount retail stores, this packaging may be seen by the consumer. Tertiary packaging, or transportation packaging, includes all of the activities designed to ensure "safe and efficient delivery of the goods in sound condition"[1] to their foreign purchaser. Tertiary packaging for consumer goods is therefore the packaging placed around the secondary retail packaging units. For industrial goods, because there is generally no primary or secondary packaging of the products, the tertiary packaging encompasses all the packaging activities aimed at protecting the goods during shipment.

14-1 Packaging Functions

The first function of correct packaging for export is obviously the protection of the goods from the hazards of international shipping by ocean or by air. Proper packaging has direct cost implications. On the one hand, it is certain that the costs of packaging generally increase as the protection of the goods increases; however, on the other hand, the costs of losing part of the cargo to **improper packaging** are generally much higher,[2] cannot be insured against (see Section 10-8 for further details), and no real trade-off exists. It is generally in the best interest of the exporter to ensure that goods are properly packaged so that they arrive undamaged at their destination. This chapter will expand on this aspect of packaging, explaining the alternatives available and their advantages and disadvantages.

The second function of correct packaging is to facilitate the handling of goods while they are in transit; a well-designed package will allow the stevedores, the shipping line, and the trucking companies to handle it without difficulties, but mostly without having to improvise an inappropriate handling method. The capabilities of the equipment likely

improper packaging The lack of appropriate packaging materials for an international shipment. The decision is oftentimes reached by an insurance company when it refuses to pay a damage claim that it considers avoidable had proper packaging procedures been followed.

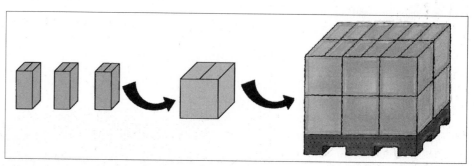

Figure 14-1
Primary, Secondary, and Tertiary Packaging
Source: Diagram courtesy of Jeff Post and Bob Iben. Used with permission.

to be used in the handling of the goods must be respected (i.e., the dimensional constraints and weight constraints they place on the package, as well as the different standards and regulations used in the countries through which the goods will travel). Finally, all the handling and care instructions must be clearly marked on the package.

The third function of correct packaging, and one that is often overlooked, is that it is part of the customer service strategy of the firm. While a customer expects to receive the goods in sellable or usable condition in all cases, it also expects to be able to quickly unpack the goods and not spend considerable time and money preparing them to be used or sold. This objective is often much more difficult to achieve than just protecting the goods for transport and facilitating their handling while in transit. The packaging has to be simple enough to be opened without using specialized tools or exerting much effort, but most of all, it has to be designed so that it can be opened without damaging the goods. To a great extent, the packaging used by a firm should also reflect the image it is trying to project to its customers. A well-conceived and well-constructed package is a positive reflection on the ability of a company to manufacture quality products. Similarly, more and more customers are sensitive to a packaging alternative that is easily reused or placed in the waste stream. In some cases, it is legally mandatory.

14-2 Packaging Objectives

Three of the objectives of proper packaging are to make sure that goods are protected from the three major losses that can occur in an international transit:

1. Protecting the goods in transit from mechanical damage: breakage, crushes, nicks, and dents (these perils represent roughly 43 percent of all claims made by shippers to their insurance companies).[3]

2. Protecting the goods from water damage: sea water, rain, floods, and container sweat (15 percent of claims made).

3. Protecting the goods from theft and pilferage (21 percent of claims made).

The remaining 21 percent of the claims were linked to fire, strandings, sinkings, collision, overboard losses, and jettison.

Each of these perils can be prevented to a great extent by the proper use of packaging techniques and by the correct design of the protective systems around the cargo.

However, that's not all: Another objective of packaging is to provide good customer service to the recipient of the goods. This is achieved by paying attention to the smaller details of the packaging process and designing a "smarter" package. While it is difficult to give specific guidance, a few examples may illustrate the concept better:

- Instead of gluing—and then nailing—the plywood panels onto a crate, a customer-focused exporter would just nail them or, even better, screw them, so that they can be more easily taken apart by the receiving department of the importer. The boards can then be reused internally by the importer or by its employees rather than discarded. An exporter shipping to countries where packaging materials may end up as housing materials would be even more responsive if it considered using a slightly better grade of boards and plywood, and making sure that they have been heat-treated rather than fumigated with chemicals.

- Another way of displaying customer focus would be to include a packaging list in the recipient's language and to clearly mark all of the packages within a shipment—for example, by color-coding or letter-coding each pallet and its corresponding manifest.

- Yet another way of showing customer concern is to utilize unitized packages that match the size of the ones used by the customer, so that goods can be placed directly in its warehouse, without having to be reloaded onto the proper pallet size.

While it only takes a few extra minutes (and only a bit more money) to pack a shipment "smarter," the importer will appreciate the attention; it may actually become a strategic advantage over a competitor, whose shipping department is inattentive to details. In addition, it helps prevent claims of shortages when the customer cannot locate items within a shipment.

Finally, packaging should reflect the increasing sensitivity to recycling and energy conservation present in many countries. The focus in this case should be for the exporter to use recyclable and reusable materials rather than disposable materials; for example, it should use starch "peanuts" (packaging pellets) or recycled paper cubes rather than Styrofoam,[4] inflatable dunnage rather than scrap pallets, or load the goods on pallets of the same size used by the customer.

14-3 Ocean Cargo

Ocean cargo can be shipped using a large number of alternative packaging alternatives. Because an increasing percentage of cargo shipped by ocean is now containerized, this particular mode will be covered first, followed by break-bulk cargo and its packaging alternatives.

14-3a Full-Container-Load (FCL) Cargo

Full-Container-Load (FCL)
A shipment whose volume and weight are close to the volume and weight limits of a container or for which the shipper requests that it be the only cargo in a container.

container A large metal box used in international shipments that can be loaded directly onto a truck, a railroad car, or an oceangoing vessel.

While it is true that containers protect the cargo well against most damages, the choice of the proper container is important when shipping a **Full-Container-Load (FCL)** shipment. An FCL shipment is one that utilizes the entire capacity of a container, whether it is by weight or by volume.

Choice of Container

After having determined the correct type of **container** (see Section 13-3a) in which the cargo will be shipped, the exporter should, as much as possible, inspect the container used for a particular shipment. It is particularly important if the cargo to be placed inside it will not be unitized on pallets or in crates, but will simply be placed in corrugated cardboard boxes or in their retail packaging.

The container should first be inspected from the outside for possible structural damage: A structurally unsound container could collapse under the weight of the several containers that will eventually be placed on top of it. Containers are designed to withstand the weight of up to eight other containers; a slight structural problem could weaken it enough to collapse under this kind of weight and a heavy sea. Hundreds of them do every year. The frame should look straight, the fittings used for lifting it and securing it on the ship or on a truck should be in place and not damaged, the doors should close properly, the repairs—if any—should appear to have been done competently, and there should be no visible structural rust. Surface rust is not pretty, but it usually does not affect the cargo carried; nevertheless, it may be a sign that the container is not very carefully maintained.

The container should also be inspected from the inside, with the doors closed, for possible light "leakage," which would indicate a water infiltration risk during shipment. Sometimes, such leakage also indicates a structural problem as well. The container should also have a wooden floor (plywood sheathing) and ideally wooden sides as well, so as to prevent condensation damage inside the container (container "sweat") and protect the cargo from direct contact with the metal sides. The container should also have all of its inside hardware in place (tie-down rings and cleats), to allow for good securing of the cargo. The container should also be inspected for foul and persistent odors: Several cargoes have been damaged by the content of a preceding shipment. Protruding nails or other fasteners should be removed to prevent an accidental puncture to the cargo. Finally, the container should be clean of grease, dirt, and other foreign material so as to keep the cargo clean.[5]

Palletization

Most of the time, it is better for the shipment to be unitized (placed on **pallets**) within the container rather than left in its **corrugated cardboard boxes**. The fact that the goods are placed on pallets and shrink-wrapped protects them better from water infiltration and from condensation in the container. It also facilitates handling and protects the goods once they have arrived at the customer's warehouse; the lower the probability that the goods are manipulated by hand, the greater the probability that they will be unloaded in good condition. Unitizing mostly prevents the primary package from being crushed, and therefore allows the goods to be immediately sellable; in those cases where the boxes have cosmetic damages, it is costly to repackage the goods into a new box. It is generally much cheaper to properly unitize them.

Another advantage of a palletized unit is that the secondary packaging may then be sufficient to protect the goods, as long as the pallets are protected on the corners, as seen in Figure 14-2, and are properly stacked by adding a rigid support between the lower and upper pallets. This support could be heavy corrugated cardboard or plywood.

When unitizing the boxes onto pallets, there is another issue to take into consideration: Most pallets are built by alternating the boxes so that they constitute a "brick" pattern, as such patterns are generally believed to be stronger (see Figure 14-2). However, the stronger parts of the boxes are their corners, and therefore corners should

pallet An item made out of wood or plastic on which the goods are placed. The pallet allows the use of mechanical equipment to move the merchandise as a unit. Goods shipped on pallets are also called unitized packages. The pallet prevents some of the problems presented by manual handling of the goods. Pallets also offer an additional level of protection by insulating the goods from water standing on the ground.

corrugated cardboard box A type of box made of paper fibers in which two flat sheets are glued to both sides of a "wall" made of a sinusoidally shaped sheet.

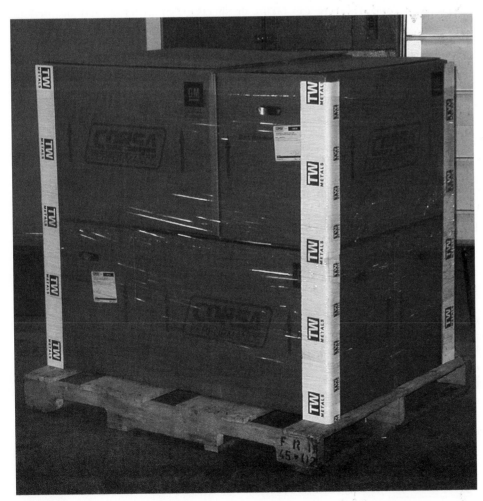

Figure 14-2
A Unitized, Shrink-wrapped Pallet with Its Four Corners Protected

support most of the weight of the boxes on top of them. By alternating corners, as in a brick pattern, the weaker part of the box supports the greatest weight. Such a pattern results in a greater likelihood of crushed boxes and therefore should be avoided. It is generally better to build pallets in columns, where boxes fit directly on top of one another, as such a practice results in fewer crushed or damaged boxes (see Figure 14-3).*

Although unitized cargo is preferable, it can also present challenges. For one, the standardized size of pallets in Europe has been 80 cm × 120 cm (31.5 inches × 47.25 inches) since 1959. Pallet sizes in the United States are, for all intents and purposes, not standardized, even though a great percentage of them are 36 in × 48 in (91.5 cm × 122 cm). This presents difficulties, as pallets of one standard do not fit neatly in containers designed for the other. In addition, there are problems when boxes that were designed to "cover" a pallet's footprint do not conveniently fill another size; for example, a European exporter may have boxes that have a base of 40 cm × 40 cm, and while such boxes fit nicely on a European pallet, they leave a good portion of a U.S. 36-inch pallet unused. Unfortunately, a dimension that is compatible with both standards is a difficult compromise.

Non-unitized Cargo

If the goods inside the container are not unitized, for whatever reason, it is preferable that they be somewhat protected from crushing and moisture by being packaged in a higher grade of corrugated cardboard, double- or triple-walled; regular secondary packaging is generally insufficient, and its use should be avoided. If the goods are to be stacked, layers of strong cardboard or sheets of plywood should be used in between the layers to protect the lower levels from collapsing and to prevent crushed boxes. If the goods are to be shipped from (or to) a high-humidity area, a layer of plywood on the floor of the container, or a layer of pallets should be considered. In addition, cardboard should be avoided as much as possible, as it loses up to 60 percent of its strength under those humid conditions.[6] Figure 10-4 illustrated the differences in relative humidity levels for an ocean container shipment from China to the United States.

Blocking Materials

When loading a container, it would be ideal if the goods could fill out the space as completely as possible, leaving no room for the cargo to shift. Unfortunately, that is generally unrealistic. Therefore, a number of blocking materials have been developed, collectively called **dunnage**.

dunnage Packaging material designed to prevent the cargo from moving while in transit.

The first thing to do, though, is to secure the goods to the container itself, if that is possible. This is normally done with hooks and straps, a system that is particularly good at keeping the cargo from moving inside the container. The second is to insert some sort of "spacer" in between the pallets or the packages. Some companies use old pallets, some use bracing contraptions made with wooden beams (in American measurements, "4 × 4," which measures 3.5 inches by 3.5 inches, or roughly 9 cm by 9 cm), and some use inflatable bags (see Figure 14-4). Before the door of the container is closed, similar bracing material must be inserted between the cargo and the door to prevent shifting. Insurance "claim handlers frequently come across cargo poorly secured in a container, perhaps because void spaces are not filled, or because heavier items are not lashed down."[7] As a reminder, insurance policies do not cover claims for improperly packaged cargo (see Section 10-8).

The critical part is that the entire floor space in the container must be occupied, so that none of the cargo may move. However heavy the cargo may be, it will move and

---

*The authors are indebted to Professor Bud Cohan from Columbus State Community College for this point.

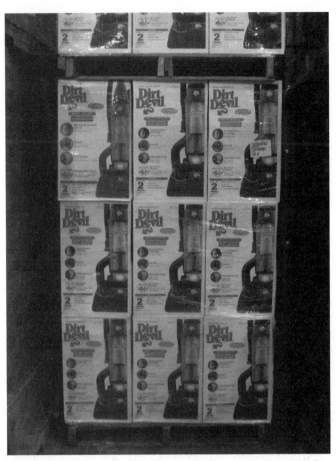

Figure 14-3
A Pallet with Goods Placed in Columns, for Reduced Risk of Damage
Source: Photo © Jamie Serenko. Used with permission.

Figure 14-4
A Container with Inflatable Dunnage in the Center
Source: Photo © International Paper Co. Used with permission.

eventually be damaged if it is not braced securely. The costs of replacing damaged cargo will undoubtedly exceed whatever savings there were in not using proper dunnage.

Loading the Container

If there are different types of goods to be placed in the same container, the heavier ones should always be placed on the bottom to lower the center of gravity of the load. Similarly, great care should be taken to make sure that the center of gravity is somewhat in the center of the container. This is achieved by making sure that the goods are loaded in symmetrical fashion in the container, and that the blocking material is placed in between, as shown in Figure 14-4. Several software packages have been designed to help exporters load a mixed load of cargo in a container in the most efficient manner.[8]

14-3b Less-than-Container-Load (LCL) Cargo

Less-Than-Containerload (LCL) A shipment whose volume and weight are below the capacity of a container and for which the shipper does not request that it be the only cargo in a container.

Single shipments that are too small to be shipped as a full container, called **Less-Than-Containerload (LCL)** shipments, are consolidated by a freight forwarder or a Non-Vessel-Operating Common Carrier (NVOCC) with other freight and then shipped in a full container. Because of the greater number of instances during which the freight is handled, it is mandatory that these goods be unitized on a pallet or placed in a crate or box, as well as extremely well protected from water damage. Because the nature of the freight with which the shipment is placed is never known, the greatest amount of care should be exercised in packaging such goods. In addition to the risks normally associated with a shipment by ocean, there is also the possibility of damage caused by other cargo in the container; a heavy load can inadvertently be placed on top of the pallet or another can be poorly braced in the container and move in heavy seas. An LCL shipment can also be subjected to other cargo's leakage, odors, and other hazards. Although the consolidator is almost always quite good at packaging a container properly, with proper dunnage and protection, the owners of other cargo on board the consolidated container may be not be as careful, and that represents a hazard.

14-3c Break-Bulk Cargo

break-bulk cargo Cargo that is unitized in a box or crate, and that is placed directly into the hold of a ship. It is generally too large or too heavy to be placed in a container.

Break-bulk cargo is cargo that cannot be containerized because it is too large and won't fit in a traditional container or because it exceeds the maximum weight of a containerload. Great efforts have been extended to containerize as much cargo as possible, with the creation of special container sizes (see Section 13-3a). However, a substantial proportion of cargo is still shipped as break-bulk cargo.

Break-bulk cargo is placed directly in the holds of the ship and therefore has to be packaged differently than containerized cargo, which enjoys the "all-around" protection of the metal box. In addition, break-bulk cargo (in its tertiary packaging) is handled more frequently than containerized cargo; for example, it is loaded onto a truck or rail car on its way to the port, then unloaded in the port, loaded onto the ship, unloaded from the ship, and so on. Therefore, break-bulk cargo should be packed in such a way as to be well protected to reflect both the rigors of the journey and the extra handling.

Finally, the company responsible for shipping break-bulk cargo should ensure that the weight and dimensions of the cargo can be handled by all the facilities through which the cargo will travel; if the break-bulk cargo weighs more than the maximum capacity crane in a given port, an alternative route should be found, or arrangements should be made to rent specialized or larger equipment. If the cargo's weight exceeds the port cranes' capacity, there is a great risk that the break-bulk cargo will be taken out of its crate and dismantled so it can be handled by the port's equipment. There is also the risk that the port personnel will try to move the cargo with the existing equipment (using it beyond its rated capacity) and damage the cargo in the process. Cigna Insurance Company publishes a guide to the equipment in place in all the ports worldwide, called *Ports of the World*,[9] so that a firm may plan the size of its shipment accordingly. Very heavy and cumbersome cargo, called "Project Cargo" is usually handled by specialized freight forwarders (see Section 13-5) who have an excellent knowledge of all of these limitations.

Crates and Boxes

Crates and boxes—as shown in Figures 14-5 and 14-6—are very appropriate containers for either break-bulk cargo or for LCL cargo to be handed to a freight consolidator. The crate or box should be built in a size that accommodates the goods without allowing them to shift. It should be very solidly built and be reinforced at those points where the crate is likely to be lifted. If the cargo needs to be kept in an upright position, the best alternative is to mount the box or crate on a pallet or to equip it with hooks or straps that allow the goods to be handled in only one direction.

Boxes and crates are built somewhat differently. While boxes are containers made of wood where the sides are an integral part of the structure of the container (see Figure 14-5), crates are containers built on a wooden frame, and are either open or enclosed with plywood (see Figure 14-6). In general terms, well-built crates are stronger than boxes, because the wood used for the frame of the crate is of a larger size. Well-built crates are constructed with three-way corners (see Figure 14-7), which is the strongest possible corner design. Unfortunately, this technique appears to be an "art" that is disappearing, although it makes a substantial difference in the ability of the crate to resist shocks and crushing. Both crates and boxes should always be reinforced with corner strapping and with metallic bands (see Figure 14-8).

crate A wooden box made especially for a product to be shipped break-bulk because it does not fit into a container, or because the exporter deems that an additional level of protection is necessary.

Figure 14-5
Loading Boxes Containing Parts of the Large Binocular Telescope, the Largest Telescope in the World
Source: Photo © Luciano Miglietta. Used with permission.

Open crates are obviously not appropriate for cargo that is not impervious to water. Boxes and enclosed crates protecting a shipment that is sensitive to water or moisture should be lined with a waterproof material such as polyethylene. Some packaging specialists prefer leaving the bottom of the boxes and crates free of waterproof material, while others prefer placing small holes in it to allow drainage should some water infiltration occur. To further protect crated machinery and metallic parts from water damage, it is common practice to simply spray them with oil.

Figure 14-6
An Open Crate, with Corner Reinforcements, Strapped to a Flat Rack

Figure 14-7
The Three-Way Corner Design
Source: Diagram courtesy of Jeff Post and Bob Iben. Used with permission.

Figure 14-8
Boxes Built for Cable Spools, Reinforced with Metal Bands

Bags

Bags can also be used to transport break-bulk merchandise: The multi-wall shipping bag (which can hold around 25 kg [50 lbs]) is designed to be used with chemicals, plastics, and other powdered materials that are somewhat unaffected by water and unlikely to be pilfered.

The bag is made up of several layers of kraft paper and/or light polymers, and is not very good at withstanding numerous manipulations. It is recommended to add about 3 percent additional empty, slightly larger bags to contain those bags that may be damaged during an international shipment.[10] Shipping bags are quite sensitive to rough handling by dockhands, including damage by accidental contact with mechanical equipment or other cargo with sharp angles such as boxes, crates, or pallets. The integrity of these bags is increased by palletizing and shrink-wrapping them, because mechanical equipment must then be used to handle them.

The second type of bag is a very large size bag called a **Flexible Intermediate Bulk Container (FIBC).** FIBCs are constructed of woven polymer fibers, such as polyethylene or polypropylene (see Figure 14-9). They are usually of a capacity of about one cubic meter and can weigh up to one metric ton, but many different sizes and types exist. They are used for transporting granular cargo, such as plastics, grains, and some chemicals.[11]

Flexible Intermediate Bulk Container (FIBC) A type of large-capacity woven bag designed to unitize goods that would otherwise be carried as dry bulk.

Drums

Drums are used in two forms: metallic drums (steel drums) and fiber drums. Steel drums, shown in Figure 14-10, can be used for wet or dry cargo, and are pretty resilient containers that can withstand a good amount of abuse. They present great resistance to water damage and pilferage and have been used for a long time in ocean shipping. Their main disadvantage is their cost and their individual weight. Fiber drums, however, can only be used for dry cargo, such as plastic pellets or fertilizers, and they are usually lined with a polymer bag.

Fiber drums are slightly more resistant to water damage than bags, and are more resistant to pilferage. However, they are often damaged when port personnel handle them in the same manner as they do steel drums, such as rolling them on their side,

Figure 14-9
Flexible Intermediate Bulk Containers
Source: Photo © Codefine®. Used with permission.

Figure 14-10
A Steel Drum

which they are not designed to do. Fiber drums are also somewhat sensitive to mechanical damage, such as that caused by careless forklift truck drivers or sharp corners.

14-3d Wood Requirements

Since March 2005, all wood products used in packaging or dunnage must conform to the International Phytosanitary Measure 15, a convention that was signed by

144 countries, and which is designed to further prevent the threat of wood pests, specifically the Asian long-horned beetle that attacked hardwood forests in North America and Europe, and the North American pinewood nematode, which attacked softwood forests in Europe and Asia. All wood products used in international trade must be marked with the **International Plant Protection Convention (IPPC)** symbol or face heavy fines. An unwary exporter had to pay U.S. $10,000 when it shipped goods on unmarked pallets to Finland to cover the cost of destroying them.[12]

The IPPC mark identifies the country in which the wood product was treated with the first two letters. Figure 14-11 shows a U.S. example. The marking also identifies the plant at which the process was conducted with a three-digit code. Finally, the process used in treating the product is identified; HT means that the wood was heat-treated, and MB means that the product was treated with methyl bromide. These are the only two allowable treatments to date, and MB is a gas that the United States Environmental Protection Agency will phase out in 2007, although it will continue allowing it for IPPC purposes.[13] Any wood product that has been marked with the IPPC symbol can be reused indefinitely in the international supply chain.

International Plant Protection Convention (IPPC) An international convention, which 144 countries have ratified, that mandates that wood used for packing or dunnage be heat-treated or treated with chemicals to prevent insect infestations.

14-3e Markings

There are two reasons to properly mark the cargo as it is shipped: It has to be protected from poor handling, and it has to be protected from theft and pilferage.

To protect the cargo from poor handling, it is necessary to use as many of the international pictorials for cargo handling as are relevant. A number of these pictorials, as standardized by the International Organization for Standards (ISO), are shown in Figure 14-12. If at all possible, they should be accompanied by their translations in the languages of the ports through which the cargo is expected to transit. Both the net weight (the weight of the cargo alone) and the gross weight (the cargo plus the weight of the packaging) should be clearly displayed in metric units and so-called English units on the outside of the package. The outside dimensions of the goods should also be clearly displayed, both in English and metric units. This is to prevent, as much as possible, inappropriate equipment from handling the goods at any point.

To protect break-bulk or LCL cargo from being lost or shipped to the wrong consignee, it should be clearly marked with the consignee's name—the name of the company that will pick it up at the port of the destination—as well as the shipment number. It is always a good idea to write that information on several of the sides of

Figure 14-11
The International Plant Protection Convention Mark
Source: Diagram courtesy of Natalie David. Used with permission.

Figure 14-12
International Handling Pictorials

the load; that way, the information is never hidden from view. If at all possible, the name of the consignee should not include information that could indicate the brand or the type of the goods in the shipment, for security reasons. Such markings only increase the probability of theft or pilferage.

All the units belonging to the same shipment should be marked as such—that is, as "1 of 4," "2 of 4," and so on. Another useful "trick" is to mark all the units in a given shipment with a particular color—for example, on the corners of the boxes—so that they are clearly designated as parts of one shipment and so that none of them are left behind. The temptation of using a color associated with a particular company should be avoided, however, to prevent jeopardizing the firm's security efforts. For the same reasons, the color should be changed regularly.

There are a number of alternatives meant to determine whether a shipment has been the victim of theft: Some shippers paint the outside of their shipment with a uniform color in order to determine whether a shipment has been tampered with. Some use shipping tape of a specific design—while avoiding using a tape marked with their company logo—and others use a shrink-wrap of a particular color. All of these attempts have the added benefit of keeping the shipment "uniform" and therefore clearly identifiable.

Finally, it should be reiterated that markings that reveal the identity of the shipper and/or the content of the package should be avoided at all costs. "Advertising" to potential thieves the content of the cargo is foolish and can only lead to problems. Many companies use codes rather than brand markings to identify their shipments and change the code on a regular basis, without patterns, in an attempt to avoid security problems.

14-4 Air Transport

Because air transport is, by nature, less hazardous than ocean transport, packaging as a protection against damage is of lesser importance than for ocean shipping. Nevertheless, some perils still exist, such as water condensation and air pressure changes. Still, the biggest problem for air cargo, by far, is theft and pilferage.

14-4a Containers

Containers used in air transport are much different than the ones used in ocean cargo and are not intermodal (i.e., they cannot be used conveniently in other modes of transportation, with the possible exception of one size—a twenty-foot container that can be used in cargo planes and on trucks). The consequence of this situation is that cargo is usually placed (consolidated) in containers at the airport of departure, then manipulated again at the airport of arrival and placed into trucks. This additional handling should be taken into consideration when packaging goods for export by air. It is also likely that the goods will be unloaded from a container and reloaded into another at a connecting airport.

Containers used in air transport are lightweight, made of wood, Plexiglas, or aluminum, and are generally clean. As some containers are not fully enclosed, or are enclosed with netting rather than a solid wall, some damage may occur in the voyage when cargo shifts. Nevertheless, most damage occurs in the handling before and after the flight; for example, while the container waits on the tarmac, the goods in the container could easily become wet from rain or snow. Such exposure should be considered when deciding on a proper package.

14-4b Packaging Materials

While most air cargo tends to be shipped by air in its secondary packaging, it is generally not an appropriate method for two reasons:

- Secondary packaging is not sufficient to protect the goods well from the hazards of manipulation before and after the flight. In many cases, the airline operates on a "hub-and-spoke" model, and the goods are unloaded and manipulated at one or more hub airports. Goods in secondary packaging can be tossed by airport personnel, and boxes can fall from conveyor belts traveling at very high speeds (thirty mph or forty-five km/h).

- Secondary packaging often includes markings including the brand name of the goods, as well as model numbers and/or illustrations, which make them very tempting targets for thieves.

Appropriate shipping packaging would therefore be tertiary in nature and include one additional layer of cardboard, preferably double-walled, and a shrink-wrap. The United Nations established rules in the 1980s regarding the resistance of air packages to drops and crushes; today, these minimum requirements are considered inadequate, but have not been replaced.[14] Nevertheless, a number of shippers still do not follow these rules.

For shipments that are fragile, the best strategy is to use a box within a box; the primary package is placed in a much larger box, which is then filled with packing material around the smaller, fragile product. While this is relatively simple, the cost of packaging in such a way can be substantial, as airlines charge a shipper on the higher of two alternatives: the actual weight of the product or its "volume-weight," which is a weight calculated on the basis of the volume of the shipment. There can therefore be a substantial cost to using a box that is slightly too large.

For cargo sensitive to humidity, a possible way of avoiding condensation damage is to add small packets of desiccant material in the box with the goods, as they are designed to absorb ambient humidity. An additional layer of shrink-wrap is always advisable as well, to protect against other condensation, rain, or leakage caused by other cargo on the plane.

For shipments susceptible to leakage if its primary packaging breaks, such as glass or plastic bottles, the United States Federal Aviation Administration regulations (and the United Nations rules) require that the secondary or tertiary package must be capable of containing an accidental leakage. Most secondary packaging is not designed for such a contingency, so adequate additional absorbent material must be packed with the goods. The shipper of a three fluid ounce (8.9 cl) bottle of perfume was fined U.S. $132,500 when its package broke, leaked in the plane, and "contaminated" other cargoes.[15]

14-4c Markings

Markings in international air shipments should be handled in much the same way as markings on ocean shipments. The use of the pictorials shown in Figure 14-12 is quite appropriate.

14-5 Road and Rail Transport

In the case of international road and rail transportation, a policy of protecting the cargo in much the same way as that used for shipment by ocean container is most appropriate. It is always best to unitize the cargo into pallets so as to facilitate handling at the point where the goods are loaded and unloaded. The cargo pallets should be protected on all four corners, banded with nylon or steel straps, and should be shrink-wrapped for protection against rain and ambient humidity. As much as possible, the cargo should be blocked and braced in the truck trailer and, if applicable, in the railroad car to avoid all damage due to the cargo shifting and sudden accelerations and decelerations.

Domestic shipments in the United States are almost all made by truck or by rail; the cargo is loaded on a trailer that is then either driven to its destination or loaded on a railroad car (piggy-backed) to an intermediary destination and then driven to its final destination. From 1996 to 1999, the costs of goods damaged in transportation rose from U.S. $3.3 billion to U.S. $4 billion, or from 0.75 percent to 0.96 percent of Gross Domestic Sales, according to the Grocery Manufacturers of America. Such costs increased to 1.13 percent in 2004, but decreased to 1.04 percent in 2005. The primary cause of the decrease was attributed to "improvements in packaging." In its 1999 study, the trade group had reported that 44 percent of these losses were due to crushed, dented, or collapsed packages.[16]

Should the cargo be sensitive to theft, it should also be packed in unmarked boxes to prevent the possibility of pilferage.

14-6 Security

The issue of theft and pilferage is becoming an increasing problem for cargo shippers. It is estimated that theft represents losses of at least U.S. $10 billion per year in the United States and U.S. $30 billion worldwide.[17] Many methods have been developed to foil theft attempts against cargo, none of which have proven completely effective, but a combination of several should cover most shippers and prevent theft and pilferage.

As much as possible, the cargo should not bear the name of the shipper, especially if it is a brand that has street appeal; this issue is crucial for goods that are shipped in their secondary packaging and for which the primary packaging and the secondary

Shipping Computers to China

The Chinese market for personal computers has always appeared very attractive to United States' corporations because of the vast potential for sales it represents. However, there have been many difficulties for the companies involved in manufacturing personal computers in China: Compaq found some of its distributors did not honor their debts, and AST found that many of the PC units it exported to Hong Kong were smuggled back into the country.

IBM, meanwhile, faced charges that it was selling used machines when it was actually shipping brand new products. It turns out that the confusion arose over a packaging problem: The computers were wrapped in two layers of plastic and then shipped in cardboard boxes. However, this was not enough to protect them from the pervasive dust that floats around many Chinese cities—Beijing in particular—and the goods arrived dirty in the consumers' hands. An additional layer of shrink-wrap on the cardboard retail package solved the problem.

This problem was in addition to the many problems that packaging has to solve in China: A large percentage of personal computers are delivered to their final destination strapped on the luggage rack of a bicycle (see Figure 14-13), and most deliveries to retailers and wholesalers are made in flatbed trucks, barely protected from the elements by a tarpaulin. As for units shipped to distant cities, they are shipped by railroads: Extremely sturdy packaging should be used in that case, as an IBM manager observed, "the [cargo handlers] virtually throw[ing computer] cartons into trains."[19]

Figure 14-13
Computers Delivered on Bicycles in China
Source: Photo © Hui Lu. Used with permission.

packaging are one and the same, as for electronics or appliances.[18] Such a practice jeopardizes the safety of the cargo. A possible way to prevent this problem would be to ship exclusively in Full Container Loads (FCL) or Full Truck Loads (FTL), so as to hide the cargo from anyone other than the exporter or the importer. Another is to place the goods in an additional blank cardboard box, which would be recommended for goods shipped as Less than Container Load (LCL) or Less than Truck Load (LTL) goods anyhow, to protect them from handling damage.

A plethora of different methods exists to place **seals** on containers, and all present advantages and disadvantages; however, all show whether the container has been opened. One critical aspect of seals is that the seal number should be written on the intermodal bill of lading so that the importer can check, upon arrival, that the seal on the container is the same as the seal with which the container left the exporter's premises.[20]

Upon realizing that container seals invite theft—after all, seals are only placed on valuable merchandise—some companies have created invisible locks that are placed inside the doors of the container or the truck trailer, and are operated with a coded transmitter from the outside. Such positive innovations prevent thieves from opening the doors, but demand that all customers of the exporter be airmailed a transmitter prior to the first shipment, which can be a substantial hassle and expense.

Altogether, though, the aspect that security experts insist is critical when shipping internationally or domestically is the personnel involved.[21] Most thefts

seal A lock especially designed to be applied to containers and truck trailers and that the importer must break in order to get entry into the container or trailer.

Trade in Precious and Valuable Goods and Stones

Trade in precious goods and valuables is an entire branch of logistics that, although not officially calculated separately from other data, is worth millions of U.S. dollars; in the United States alone, it is estimated at U.S. $50 million. The crash of Swissair 111 on September 2, 1998, exposed some of the extent of its international scale: The airplane was carrying fifty kg (110 lbs) of cash, two kg of diamonds, two kg of watches, five kg of jewelry, and an artwork by Picasso entitled "The Painter."[23] Lloyd's of London, through which this cargo was insured, has never disclosed the value of these cargoes, although there are speculations that it exceeded U.S. $300 million.

There is a substantial business in shipping precious stones internationally, such as diamonds and emeralds, because the stones are often produced, cut, set, and sold in different countries. Artwork travels from museum collections to museum exhibits (and back). Antiques and collectibles travel to and from dealers and auction houses. Cash travels to where tourists flock.

Altogether, there are few firms specializing in the shipment of precious and valuable goods, and these firms emphasize discretion; they do not advertise, do not display their names on their vehicles, and operate out of anonymous office buildings and warehouses. The additional security measures they take are many: They do not ship more than a certain amount on a specific airplane or ship, they use ever-changing consignee names, and they have created a whole series of specialized packaging technologies.

Artex is such a firm. It is located in Washington, D.C., and specializes in the business of moving artwork, antiques, and jewelry collections. It employs a crew of seventy-five employees, most of whom are artists or art experts with museum experience. Each piece of work is moved in a crate that is specifically designed for that work of art and fitted with foam to the exact dimensions and shape of the artwork. When Artex was selected to move an African-American burial site from New York City to Howard University, it took the firm's employees three months to pack the 20,000 objects this move represented.[24]

In addition, Artex's warehouse and trucks are equipped with air conditioning to keep humidity to a minimum. Each of its trucks is tracked with satellite transmitters and the Global Positioning System; this way, the firm knows at all times where the art is located. Finally, each of the trucks is driven by a team of at least two drivers equipped with cellular phones and sometimes accompanied by armed guards. Nevertheless, the best security is when no one knows that a move is occurring.

seem to have taken place with some insider involvement.[22] All attempts should therefore be made to limit the number of people who know the content of the shipment by making sure that the bill of lading and packaging lists are given to trusted employees only, by keeping track of non-employees on the premises, by making sure that managers are present during loading and unloading operations, and so on. Some companies keep their docks under constant video surveillance to deter crime.

14-7 Hazardous Cargo

Hazardous cargo can be shipped by ocean and by air, but, generally speaking, most dangerous goods that are flammable, explosive, or toxic are shipped by sea.

The shipment of dangerous goods by sea is regulated by the International Maritime Organization (IMO), which publishes an International Maritime Dangerous Goods Code (IMDG Code) that has undergone many changes over the years, in order to keep up with the rapid expansion of the types of materials created. In May 2000, the IMO's Maritime Safety Committee approved its thirtieth amendment, which is a complete revision and simplification of the existing Code, and which was published in October 2000. This amendment became effective January 1, 2001, with an implementation period of one year. It is a two-volume document—the preceding was four volumes large—and is quite complex. It governs the packaging of hazardous cargo, as well as labeling, handling, and emergency responses.

The shipment of dangerous goods by air is regulated by the International Air Transport Association (IATA) and by the International Civil Aviation Organization

(ICAO), which both adopted new standards on January 1, 1999. The shipment of hazardous cargo by air is no less complicated and cumbersome than by sea.

In addition to these international requirements, a shipper must abide by domestic regulatory agencies as well, as there often are two domestic legs to any international shipment, one in the exporter's country, the other in the importer's country. The complexity of such requirements, and their contradictory statements on occasion, makes it an obligation to contract with a specialized freight forwarder or a specialized consultant before undertaking any international shipment of hazardous goods. Shipments of products containing radioactive components are even more complicated.

14-8 Refrigerated Goods

Goods requiring refrigeration make up another category of cargo that demands particular care and specialized packaging services. It is difficult to generalize about refrigerated goods, as every commodity usually requires very specific handling; therefore, most refrigerated goods travel "alone" (i.e., different refrigerated goods are not mixed with one another, as they require different temperatures and different humidity settings). In addition, some fresh produce simply cannot be mixed together as they emit odors and other gasses that would spoil the rest of the cargo. For example, a load of cucumbers should not be mixed with apples, as cucumbers are sensitive to the ethylene that the apples produce,[25] and for obvious reasons, onions and strawberries do not travel well together.

When goods needing refrigeration travel by ocean, they usually travel in a refrigerated container—also known as a "reefer." Great care should be taken in ensuring that the temperature is kept at its correct setting throughout the voyage, which is achieved with temperature-sensitive indicators. Because containers are not very effective at cooling goods—but are effective at keeping them cool—several shippers are making sure that the goods are well refrigerated before they are loaded to prevent possible damage. It should also be understood that reefers cannot possibly have a completely uniform temperature: Temperatures within the box can vary by as much as five degrees Celsius (ten degrees Fahrenheit) just because air circulation cannot be made uniform. Finally, another common problem with refrigerated cargo coming in or out of the United States is the confusion between Fahrenheit and Celsius temperature settings and the errors this causes.[26]

With refrigerated cargo, the loading of the refrigerated container must allow air circulation around the cargo; this requirement means that the goods must be loaded in the center of the container, with sufficient space in between the walls of the container and the cargo for circulation, and that the goods must be braced with a frame rather than with inflatable dunnage, which would prevent air circulation. In addition, some goods need to travel in controlled atmospheres—mixtures of oxygen and nitrogen in different percentages than ambient air—to prevent spoilage. Some experiments are being conducted to determine whether a controlled atmosphere can also be effective against some pests as well.[27]

Fresh produce must also be kept at humidity levels of 95 to 100 percent to maintain its freshness as well as prevent weight loss due to evaporation. Most produce is made up of at least 80 percent water and is quite sensitive to water loss; for example, grapes will wrinkle and soften, and stems will turn brown, with a weight loss of only 4 percent, making them more difficult to sell.[28] In addition, because produce is sold by weight, a small weight loss can translate into a substantial decrease in revenue for the importer.

For air shipments of refrigerated cargo, the challenges are different, because the cargo is not placed in refrigerated containers but in cargo holds that have different temperature settings. For example, Lufthansa offers five different cargo holds, kept at

Banana Business

In 1996, Chiquita Brands was the largest American importer (measured by the number of containers brought into the United States), with about 79,000 TEUs—twenty-foot equivalent units—surpassing even Wal-Mart, which "only" imported 76,000 TEUs.[30] By 2004, Wal-Mart's imports had grown to 576,000 TEUs, and Chiquita imported 115,000 containers of essentially a single product, bananas.[31]

Bananas are harvested green and hard, and immediately refrigerated. They are then loaded into one of Chiquita's fifteen dedicated banana ships or on a number of other ships that the firm charters. About half of these ships are completely containerized, while the others transport bananas on pallets as break-bulk cargo in refrigerated holds and in containers on deck. During their trip, the bananas are kept in a controlled atmosphere environment. At their arrival, bananas are then placed in a ripening environment where they acquire their yellow color before being shipped to retail stores.

Wilmington, Delaware, is by far the largest port of entry for bananas, and about 1.2 million tons of its traffic is fresh produce.[32] Altogether, imported fresh produce accounts for 35 percent of produce sold in the United States. See the textbox on flowers in Section 12-2d for more information about the United States' reliance on Colombia in the business of cut flowers.

different temperature settings, to keep perishables in their optimum environments.[29] However, because of the possibility that incompatible cargo might be mixed together—such as the onions and strawberries mentioned earlier—great care should be extended to protect sensitive goods from this eventuality by keeping them in solid-wall cardboard boxes and possibly in shrink-wrap, if applicable.

14-9 Domestic Retail Packaging Issues

In dealing with consumer products specifically, several packaging issues are also greatly influenced by primary packaging, or the design of the packaging in which the final consumer purchases the goods, as well as by secondary packaging, or the design of the packaging designed to facilitate handling in the retail environment. Collectively, these constraints tend to be domestic in nature (i.e., they are specific to a single country or possibly a group of countries).

Adapting a firm's strategy to the different market requirements of a particular country adds substantially to the costs of manufacturing, as well as to inventory and logistical expenses. A firm has to determine whether it makes economic sense to adapt its approach to these different markets and incur those additional costs or decide to ignore them at the risk of losing potential sales. This is the same strategic dilemma faced by a firm involved in international marketing: adapt or standardize?

Some of the factors that may affect primary and secondary packaging will now be explored.

14-9a Size

Consumer packages abroad may be of a different size than consumer packages in the domestic market because of consumer preferences: They are generally smaller in those countries in which retail shopping is done frequently, and larger for those in which consumers shop at greater intervals. However, consumer packaging is complicated; consumers may demand smaller or larger packages based on preferences and customs, as well as packages of different shapes and materials. For example, sugar is sold in some countries in paper bags weighing five lbs (2.5 kg), in others in cardboard boxes weighing one kg (two lbs), and yet in others, in tin cans of one lb (0.5 kg). Even products that are held as great examples of "international standardization," such as Coca-Cola soft drinks, are sold in a myriad of sizes and therefore of primary and secondary packaging units.

Consumer packaging may also be seriously influenced by the layout of the shelves in the stores, such as their depth and the linear space allocated, constraining manufacturers to use different retail packaging.

Secondary packaging—the unit that holds several consumer packages—is influenced by the size of the retail stores and their configuration, as well as the size of the delivery trucks; the tertiary packaging unit, such as the pallet; or even the configuration of the storage area. In addition, it is also influenced by the frequency and the volume of sales of the retail units.

14-9b Legal Issues

Consumer packaging may also be influenced by legal requirements; some countries regulate sizes to be a multiple of simple metric units (one kg or one liter), while others do not, allowing packages of any size and weight. However, the greatest requirements are in the legal constraints on handling: Many countries regulate the maximum weight an employee may carry, and that influences the weight of the secondary packaging unit, and consequently, of both consumer packaging and tertiary packaging as well.

The legal constraints placed on the distribution channels can also influence consumer packaging. For example, the United States allows retail sales of some medicines "over-the-counter," which means that consumers buy them in drugstores, most often in a self-service environment. In France, in contrast, all drugs, including drugs not prescribed by a medical doctor, are sold exclusively through specialized stores called *pharmacies.* The primary package in a drugstore is often a blister pack or some variation of that type of package, as the goods are sold hanging from an aisle rack. The primary package from a pharmacy is usually a cardboard box, as the pharmacist keeps them on small shelves or in large-size drawers. In addition, the drugstore may purchase goods in larger quantities than the pharmacies. In any case, the primary packaging is different, and therefore the secondary and tertiary packaging will also be different.

14-9c Storage and Transportation Environment

Finally, there are a number of environmental influences on packaging, such as the dusty conditions under which transportation takes place, mentioned in the textbox about IBM's packaging of personal computers in China (see page 325). There are similar constraints triggered by high humidity, heat, or cold.

There are also constraints placed by the lack of refrigeration resources. The best example is probably the existence of long-conservation milk, which is sold unrefrigerated with "expiration dates" six or seven months after its production in a large number of European countries. Not only does this packaging alternative allow the use of nonrefrigerated shelving in the store, but it also requires no refrigeration at all in the rest of the supply chain, from warehouses to transportation. It can also be transported safely quite far from its production location, including internationally.

All in all, several domestic issues in the importing country will also affect the packaging of goods. Companies should develop appropriate strategies to account for the possible diversity of consumer and retail packaging alternatives present in their export markets.

14-10 Packaging as a Marketing Tool

It should be relatively clear by now that good handling of the packaging requirements by the exporter will help considerably in the smooth transfer of goods from the exporter to the importer.

The most important way of looking at packaging is to prepare for the worst. The exporter should truly imagine the worst-case scenarios and the roughest possible journey in packaging the goods that it ships at export. It is only under this premise that it will adequately serve the needs of the importer to receive goods in sellable and usable conditions.

The exporter should make sure that the goods are protected from physical damage by ensuring that they are packaged in sturdy cartons, that they are loaded correctly on pallets, that the pallets are separated by appropriate dunnage such as plywood and inflatable bags, and that all goods are protected from humidity and rain by protecting them with a plastic film and by outfitting the container with desiccant strips. The container should be cleaned and inspected before it is loaded, and the seals used on the container should be of good quality. The procedures in place should be effective in keeping the paperwork in the hands of appropriate personnel only.

Although such procedures are more expensive than a more casual attitude, the benefits are substantial. Consider a hypothetical case where, from the use of an inexpensive plywood sheet spread over three pallets (a plywood sheet is four foot by eight foot, or 122 cm × 244 cm), several boxes are slightly crushed, and the importer has to repackage the goods to make them saleable. The costs of repackaging these few boxes (labor, new boxes, calling the importer to resolve the issue) far exceed the original cost of the plywood sheet. Identical benefits can be drawn from using good pallets that do not break when the goods are unloaded, making sure that the container is watertight, and so on. In addition, because poor packaging is always a "defense" used by insurance companies, it "pays" to have a track record of stellar packaging.

However, the greatest benefits from such a good packaging policy are the goodwill that it generates with the importer and the marketing benefits that can be derived from it. Because the importer is obviously not interested in having to challenge invoices or having to ask for allowances for goods that were damaged in transit, it welcomes shipments that arrive packaged carefully enough that it does not have to worry about anything. This enhances the relationship between exporter and importer, and builds trust.

Finally, the exporter should also make sure that the packaging is "friendly" to the employees who will unpack the goods, that the packing list is written in their language, that shipments are identified with colors that identify pallets that "belong" together, that the wood dunnage is assembled in a way that it can easily be taken apart, and so on. When shipping to countries in which the dunnage and packaging materials are likely to be recycled as housing materials, an exporter would be even more responsive if it considered using a slightly better grade of boards and plywood, and making sure that they have been heat-treated rather than fumigated with methyl bromide.

Key Terms

break-bulk cargo (p. 316)
container (p. 312)
corrugated cardboard box (p. 313)
crate (p. 317)
dunnage (p. 314)

Flexible Intermediate Bulk Container (FIBC) (p. 319)
Full-Container-Load (FCL) (p. 312)
improper packaging (p. 310)
International Plant Protection Convention (IPPC) (p. 321)

Less-Than-Containerload (LCL) (p. 316)
pallet (p. 313)
seal (p. 325)

Review and Discussion Questions

1. What are the consequences of improper packaging for the exporter? Does your response depend on the Incoterm used? Does it depend on the insurance policy in force?

2. What are the different alternative means of packaging products that are not containerized?

3. What are some of the issues and risks that international packaging face and that are not present in a domestic shipment?

4. Use a product of your choice and ship it from one country to another on a multi-modal shipment. What packaging methods would you use? Why?

Endnotes

1. "General Syllabus for Postgraduate Studies in Packaging Logistics," Lund University, Department of Design Sciences, Lund, Sweden, http://www.pkglog.lth.se, October 20, 2000.

2. Hensel, Bill, Jr., "A Loaded Problem," *JoC Week*, August 14–20, 2000, p. 13.

3. *Ports of the World*, Fifteenth Edition, Cigna Insurance Corporation, available from Publisher, *Ports of the World*, Cigna Companies, P.O. Box 7716, Philadelphia, Pennsylvania 19192, USA.

4. Harps, Leslie Hansen, "Popcorn! Peanuts! Bubble Wrap! Thinking Inside the Box," *Inbound Logistics*, November 2000, pp. 40–46.

5. "Container Matters" and "Any Fool Can Stuff a Container," videos published by the Thomas Miller P&I Ltd, International House, 26 Creechurch Lane, London, EC3A 5BA, United Kingdom.

6. Mottley, Robert, "Chilling out," *American Shipper*, June 2000, pp. 43–51.

7. Porter, Janet, "Insurer Warns of the Dangers of Incorrectly Packed Containers," *The Journal of Commerce*, August 4, 1997, p. 16A.

8. Barrett, Colin, "Mixing and Matching Sizes in Computerized Loads," *Traffic World*, July 3, 1989, p. 40.

9. *Ports of the World*, Fifteenth Edition, Cigna Insurance Corporation, available from Publisher, *Ports of the World*, Cigna Companies, P.O. Box 7716, Philadelphia, Pennsylvania 19192, USA.

10. *Ibid*

11. Zelade, Richard, "It's in the Bag," *International Business*, October 1996, p. 44.

12. Edmonson, R.G., "Look for the No-bug Stamp," *The Journal of Commerce*, February 7, 2005, pp. 30–31.

13. Brindley, Chaille, "Fumigation 101," *Pallet Enterprise*, February 2004.

14. Harrington, Lisa H., "The Do's and Don'ts of Packaging for Air," *Transportation and Distribution*, October 1998, pp. 59–63.

15. *Ibid*

16. Robinson, Alan, "Fixing the Cracks in the System," *Food Logistics*, October 1998, pp. 29–35.

17. Barth, Steve and Michael D. White, "Hazardous Cargo," *World Trade*, November 1998, pp. 46–48.

18. Amerman, Don, "Shippers Urged to Wrap Cargo in Anonymity," *The Journal of Commerce*, October 27, 1998, p. 1A.

19. Hamilton, David, "Untamed Frontier: PC Makers Find China Is a Chaotic Market Despite Its Potential," *The Wall Street Journal*, April 8, 1996, p. A1.

20. "Container Matters" and "Any Fool Can Stuff a Container," videos published by the Thomas Miller P&I Ltd, International House, 26 Creechurch Lane, London, EC3A 5BA, United Kingdom.

21. Armbruster, William, "To Ensure Cargo Security, Don't Leave It to Beeper," *The Journal of Commerce*, May 4, 1998, p. 1A.

22. Mottley, Robert, "Container Theft: Does Anyone Care?" *American Shipper*, June 1998, pp. 24–30.

23. Estrin, Robin, "Swissair 111 Went Down with Millions in Valuables, Including Picasso Painting," Associated Press News Release, September 4, 1998.

24. Hull, Dana, "How a Moving Company Capitalizes on Valuable Secrets," *The Washington Post*, May 5, 1997, p. F12.

25. Mottley, Robert, "Chilling Out," *American Shipper*, June 2000, pp. 43–51.

26. *Ibid*

27. Nall, Stephanie, "As Federal Rules Outlaw Fumigants, Farmers Look to High-Tech Solutions," *The Journal of Commerce*, January 7, 1998, p. 1C.

28. Mongelluzzo, Bill, "A Cool Idea," *The Journal of Commerce*, May 23, 1997, p. 1B.

29. Banham, Russ, "Foiling Spoiling," *The Journal of Commerce*, June 23, 1997, p 4C.

30. Amerman, Don, "Keeping Chiquita Sweeter Requires Atmosphere Control as Well as Reefers," *The Journal of Commerce*, June 23, 1997, p. 2C.

31. "Top 100 Importers and Exporters," *The Journal of Commerce*, Special Report, March 29, 2000.

32. Robinson, Alan, "Ports of Call," *Food Logistics*, March 1999, pp. 21–24.

Customs Clearance

Chapter Fifteen

Source: © 2007 JupiterImages Corporation.

Another aspect of international trade is the process that an importer must follow when it brings goods into a country. This process is dictated by Customs, the government office in charge of collecting taxes on imports and of enforcing a number of rules and regulations regarding what can and cannot be admitted into the country. It is generally a complex process, fraught with pitfalls and loaded with paperwork: Most countries, with very few exceptions, do not like to import goods and act accordingly. This chapter explains how the Customs system works in general but draws most of its examples on the process followed to import goods into the United States.

15-1 Duty

duty The amount of tax paid on an imported good; the duty is calculated using the tariff rate and the value of the goods.

classification The process of determining what the correct Harmonized System Number is for an import.

valuation The process of determining the value of an import, or the amount upon which the duty will be calculated.

rules of origin The rules used to determine the country of origin of a particular product.

tariff The rate at which an import is taxed; the tariff rate is dependent on the classification of the goods, as well as their country of origin. The tariff rate is also called the *duty rate*.

Duty is the tax that an importer must pay in order to bring goods into a country. Such duty is calculated in a number of different ways, generally based upon three criteria:

1. The type of goods imported, which is determined according to a number of rules of **classification** that essentially have been standardized worldwide.

2. The value of the goods imported, which is not only determined upon the invoice value, but also is calculated according to a number of rules that differ from country to country, collectively called **valuation** rules.

3. The country from which the goods are imported; this determination is made according to the **rules of origin**, a process recently simplified, but still quite cumbersome for manufactured products with components made in multiple countries.

From these three elements, Customs calculates what **tariff** will be charged on the import, or the tax that the importer will have to pay on the imported goods: It is generally a percentage of their value, but it can also be calculated with some other method, based on the number of units shipped or their weight, for example.

15-1a Classification

The classification of goods follows a coding scheme that is essentially the same worldwide, as most countries have adopted the Harmonized Commodity Description and Coding System—also called the Harmonized System (HS) of Classification—developed by the Customs Cooperation Council. The Harmonized System is used to classify both exports and imports. The fact that a trader can use the same code when it is exporting a product from one country and importing it in another is a great simplification. At one time, almost every country had its own classification and coding systems.

According to the HS, each product can have a code that uses up to ten digits. An example, taken from the tariff schedule of the United States, would be:

6402.19.05	golf shoes
30	for men
60	for women
90	for other persons

where the first six digits represent the "root" of the international coding (i.e., the code that will be identical in all the countries that have adopted the Harmonized System for the product "golf shoes"). The last four digits are "country-specific" (i.e., every country can use these to differentiate between different subcategories of the main product, as the United States does between golf shoes for men, for women, and for "other persons," presumably children rather than aliens).

The Harmonized System is divided into twenty-one sections, logically determined by the type of product and material, each divided into one or more chapters, with a total of ninety-seven chapters for the entire HS nomenclature. The chapter in which the golf shoes are classified is Chapter 64, entitled "Footwear, gaiters, and the like; parts of such articles." Each chapter is then divided into headings, which make up the first four digits of the HS number. The heading under which the golf shoes can be found is "6402 Other footwear with outsoles and uppers of rubber or plastics." Each heading is then divided into subheadings, or the six-digit code common to all HS countries ("6402.19 golf shoes" in our example).

The HS is accompanied by a series of six General Rules of Interpretation, which detail how an importer should arrive at the correct HS code for an entry:[1]

1. The section, chapter, and heading only serve as guides, and the correct classification may be in a different section, chapter, and heading altogether.

2. The classification of an incomplete or unfinished product is that of the finished product. For example, shipments that contain all of the subassemblies for a final product should be classified as the final product rather than as individual parts. This is true of chemical compounds as well.

3. When in doubt between two classifications, the one with the most specific description is the correct one. However, if the product is made up of several parts, each of which would lead to a different classification, then the classification that lends it its "essential character" is the correct one.

4. When there is no category under which a specific product can be classified, then the classification that should be used is that of a product that would be most like it.

5. Containers and packaging materials are classified with the products with which they enter: such would be the case for camera cases, for example. However, if the container has usage beyond the product itself, then it must be entered and classified separately.

6. When comparing classifications, only descriptions at the same level should be compared; it is not appropriate to compare a heading to a subheading, for example.

Nevertheless, the correct classification is always subject to some interpretation on the part of the importer and of Customs officers. Because the classification of a specific article determines at which tariff rate it will be taxed and whether it will be subjected to numerical quotas (as are some textile articles in developed countries, such as the United States; see Section 15-2a), it can be a nontrivial issue. In those cases where a U.S. importer is in doubt about a correct classification, the Customs Office will issue, prior to the entry of the goods, a **binding ruling** where it will determine the correct classification of a specific product, a decision that will be binding to both parties.[2]

In early 2000, there were efforts undertaken to simplify the ten-digit classification used by the United States and to model it after Canada's system, which uses only the six-digit subheadings of the HS.[3] However, as of 2006, the U.S. Customs' tariff schedule was still using a ten-digit-based classification system.

The correct classification of an imported good is generally made by the importer and then verified by the Customs Office; however, each country has different standards and a few put the entire classification responsibility on Customs. In any case, it is critical to have a complete description of the goods on the commercial invoice, and not just a part number or an item number. When in doubt, Customs can ask to see the merchandise before it is released, and this inspection can create substantial delays.

binding ruling
A determination, made by the United States Customs, and only applicable to the United States, which classifies a specific product and assigns it a tariff rate before the goods are imported.

Classification Quirks

Given the multitude of products imported into the United States—and given the eclectic tastes of the U.S. population—a large number of unusual products have to be classified by importers following the Harmonized System, with some decisions that can be amusing:

A novelty item called a "necktie in a bottle" was classified by Customs as a necktie—no surprise here—and therefore was made subject to numerical quotas. However, because its bottle package was unusual, it also had to be classified separately, according to General Rule of Interpretation Number 5.[4]

Some Halloween costumes have been classified as "articles of clothing" by Customs, and were therefore made subject to high tariffs and some numerical quotas. This decision obviously brought jeers on the part of importers who argue that children are unlikely to wear Dracula disguises to school, with the possible exception of a single holiday: Halloween.[5]

A novelty item, consisting of a cloth pocket that can be wrapped on a couch's armrest to hold a TV remote control or a few magazines, and sold under the trade name "TV Duck," was classified by Customs as a bedspread—Rule of Interpretation Number 4—which subjected it to

high tariffs and numerical quotas. The importer disagreed, and this protracted fight went all the way to the U.S. Court of Appeals: "You had to be in the Courtroom to appreciate the looks of disbelief that the judges directed toward [the Customs' lawyer]."[6]

Canadian exporters have drilled holes in boards to allow their construction lumber to be classified as "finished products"—because homebuilders can fit wires through them—and therefore avoid the high tariffs placed by the United States on lumber,[7] which it considers subsidized by the provincial governments of Canada. U.S. Customs and Canada fought over this issue for four years: The U.S. even suggested to Canada that it impose an export tariff on all lumber rather than face U.S. anti-dumping duties.[8]

A company importing plastic figures of mutant superheroes (X-Men, to be precise) argued that its action figures were not reproductions of human figures, which would have classified them as dolls, but rather were simply "creatures," which would classify them as toys and make them eligible for a lower tariff rate. It won its case against U.S. Customs and Border Protection.[9]

15-1b Valuation

Because most duty is collected *ad valorem* (on the value of the goods imported in a country), a correct valuation amount must be determined by the importer, following a number of valuation rules governed by the Customs office of the country in which the goods are imported.

For all member countries of the World Trade Organization, the valuation of the goods is based on the transaction value of the sale. Therefore, the valuation of the goods must start with the value presented on the invoice sent by the exporter to the importer. For most countries, the value used is the "landed" value, or the CIF/CIP value of the goods (see Sections 6-9 and 6-11 for an explanation of these Incoterms), that is, the invoice value including packaging costs, transportation costs in the exporting country, international transportation costs to the country of destination, and international insurance costs. For other countries, including the United States, the value used is the FCA or FAS value (see Sections 6-5 and 6-6 for an explanation of these Incoterms), that is, the invoice value of the goods as well as packaging costs, transportation costs in the exporting country, but excluding the costs of international shipping and insurance.

There are obvious difficulties in reaching the correct valuation unless the commercial invoice sent is detailed enough to include all of these different costs in a clear, itemized fashion, regardless of the Terms of Trade (Incoterms) used in the transaction. For example, a CIF sale to an American importer should spell out the costs of international freight and international insurance, so that they can be deducted from the invoice value for Customs purposes.

The valuation process can be much more complicated than what has been outlined so far. Some countries used to determine value based upon the Brussels Definition of Value (BDV), or the "usual" price of a commodity, based on the price at which a product would sell in a free market between an unrelated buyer and seller.

Such BDV has slowly been replaced by the transaction value since 1994.[10] In those cases where Customs suspect that valuation based on the invoice would result in undervaluation—or, possibly, overvaluation—Customs can still legitimately decide that valuation can be determined with other methods:

Comparative method: Customs determine the value of the goods based upon the value of identical or similar goods imported in similar quantity to the same country. Note that the determination of the value of the goods is made based upon importing data and that differences in exporting countries' costs are not taken into consideration.

Deductive method: Customs determine at what price identical or similar goods are sold within ninety days of importation in the importing country, and determines an entry value based upon "normal" markups in the distribution channel.

Computed or reconstructed value method: Customs determine the value of the goods by computing the manufacturing costs of the goods and adding "an amount for profit and general expenses equal to that usually reflected in the sales of goods of the same class or kind."[11]

Method of last resort: Customs use "well-trained" and "well-informed" Customs officials to determine the value of the goods imported; no specific guidelines are given, other than that the valuation cannot be "arbitrary." It is unlikely to be anything else, though.

The valuation of the goods imported can be increased by some items not included on the invoice; for example, a royalty to be paid by the importer to the exporter, a commission to be paid by the importer to a purchasing agent in the exporting country, or a percentage of the price at which the importer sells the goods to their final purchaser. The valuation can also be affected by the presence of what Customs call an **assist**, or an item that the importer provided to the exporter in order to produce the goods: for example, a mold or a die that the exporter used in manufacturing the product. The value of such an assist must be added, on a *per-item* basis, to the value of the goods imported.

assist An item provided by the importer (customer) to the exporter (seller) so that the exporter can manufacture the goods: a mold or a dye, for example.

Finally, the issue of exchange rates is relevant. Customs must arrive at the value of the goods imported in the importing country's currency, even though the invoice can be written in a different currency. Each national Customs office therefore has rules to determine what exchange rate will be used to convert an invoice issued in a foreign currency. United States Customs use the exchange rate of the date of export of the merchandise.

15-1c Rules of Origin

The third element necessary to determine the duty that will be applied to a specific import is the country of origin of the goods. Goods are given a country of origin based upon a set of rules that are known as "rules of origin," which follow one or the other of two methods, neither of which has yet been adopted universally by the World Trade Organization (WTO), despite the fact that there has been a committee working on this project since 1995.[12] So far, the committee has agreed that countries must make their rules of origin "transparent" to importers.[13]

Substantial transformation: The country of origin of a product is the country in which it acquired its most substantial transformation. The determination of the "substantial transformation" is fraught with pitfalls and can lead to widely different interpretations. For example, consider a computer assembled in Mexico from parts originating in Taiwan (memory chips), the United States (CPU), China (board and hard drive), Brazil (monitor), and so on: Where did the "substantial transformation" take place, and what is the country of origin of the product? Although vague, this is still the method followed by the United States—with the exception of textiles' country of origin determination—and it can lead to fairly interesting decisions (see the accompanying textbox).

Change in HS classification: The country of origin is the country in which the last change in Harmonized System classification occurred. This method is the one currently followed by the United States for textile products, and it has proven to be much easier to implement. Nevertheless, the decision can sometimes lead to a product's country of origin being a country in which a fairly inconsequential transformation took place, and where little value was added. Already several exceptions have been made to this rule.

Unfortunately, there seems to be no easy way to determine what the country of origin of a complex product is. The determination of a country of origin—and the markings that are associated with it—is probably one of the most difficult issues facing firms engaged in international trade today, as different duty rates are used for different countries and as numerical quotas exist for some countries but not others. An importer can be charged very different duty rates, and, in some cases, fined substantially for having hidden the actual country of origin:

> A Hong Kong clothing manufacturer was fined U.S. $388,000 for fraudulently seeking to export Chinese-made garments to the United States. [. . .] The firm pleaded guilty to ten counts of lying about the origin of 14,400 dresses. They carried Hong Kong labels but were actually made in China. The maximum penalty for such cases is U.S. $500,000 and two years in jail.[14]

U.S. Customs keeps and publishes a list of all the firms that it has found guilty of transshipping, the practice of attempting to hide the country of origin of certain products by making them transit through another country. Because of the very different conditions under which textile products from China and from Hong Kong are imported into the United States, many of these firms have been Hong Kong-based firms.[15]

In addition, the country of origin of a good can have substantial marketing consequences, as most countries require that the goods be marked with their country of origin; for obvious reasons, importers of luxury clothing items prefer a good marked "made in Italy" to one made in a country not known for its designers. However, the issue is of consequence for all sorts of products, as consumers everywhere are sensitive to what international marketers call "country-of-origin effects,"[16] the perceptions that the country of origin imparts on the product.

Finally, the rules of origin can be affected by bilateral or multilateral agreements; for example, the North American Free Trade Agreement (NAFTA) among Canada, the United States, and Mexico has its own rules of origin, and such rules differ from commodity to commodity. In general terms, a product qualifies to enter duty-free in any of the three countries if its regional content (the percentage of its value that it acquired in any of the three countries) is at least 50 percent. For some goods, though, the maximum percentage of their value that can be outside of NAFTA is 7 percent.[17] Other free-trade agreements have their own rules of origin: the Canada-Chile Free-Trade Agreement has its own rules, and so does the European Union in those agreements designed to provide EU market access to developing countries.[18] Because there are over 300 free-trade agreements worldwide, most of which have their own rules of origin, a uniform system is sorely needed.[19]

15-1d Tariffs

An importing country usually manages its imports under a tariff system that is dubbed "N-column tariff system," with N, the number of columns, corresponding to the number of different classes of countries that the importing country considers. The tariff rates would then be the same for all of the countries in a given class. As the

Made in Where?

Under the "substantial transformation" rule of origin, the United States' Customs determined that transforming steel rods into steel wire was not substantial enough to warrant changing the country of origin, but that the assembly of photo album pages into a binder was.[20] Similarly, ostrich chicks hatched in Great Britain from eggs laid in South Africa had not been subjected to "a process so substantial as to transform them into new and different articles of commerce" and therefore were coming from South Africa and subject to the then-existing embargo on imports from this country; however, ostrich feathers coming from South Africa and placed on hats made in China were considered transformed enough that their entry was permitted: They "originated" in China.[21]

Under the "change in HS number," though, there were similarly difficult situations: A pair of underwear made for Victoria's Secret, assembled into final product in a Jordanian plant from panels cut in Israel, and shipped back across the border to Israel is officially "made in Israel" as General Rule of Interpretation 2 dictates, and benefits from the free-trade agreement between Israel and the United States.[22] Silk scarves that are finished, dyed, and hand-painted in Italy, and which used to be considered "made in Italy" under the substantial transformation rule, are now considered to be originating in China, because the HS classification for a raw silk scarf and a painted one is the same.[23] Under pressure from the European Union, the United States relented, and those scarves are once again allowed to be "made in Italy" and fetch U.S. $200 prices,[24] a price difficult to obtain for a scarf made in China.

Sometimes, the rules are followed to the letter, but the results are disconcerting. The olive harvest in Italy is not sufficient to cover the Italian domestic needs for olive oil. Nevertheless, Italy exports a large amount of olive oil worldwide, clearly labeled as "imported from Italy." Most of the olives used in this oil come from Spain, Greece, and Tunisia. However, under both the "change in HS" rule and the "substantial transformation" rule, Italian olive oil can be sold as "made in Italy," even though companies report that as little as 20 percent of its oil come from Italian olives.[25] In addition, under a universal rule that anything under 7 percent of a product does not affect its country of origin, the Italian olive oil can contain as much as 7 percent of oil not even processed in Italy.

All in all, even for simple products, it's often difficult to determine where a product is truly "from." Is chocolate made in Belgium from Ivory Coast cocoa beans made in Belgium or made in the Ivory Coast? Is an espresso coffee made in the country in which the beans were roasted, ground, and steamed, or is it made in the country in which they were grown?

---

number and complexity of multilateral trade agreements increases, this terminology can sometimes be confusing, as there can be many more than "N" classes. Nevertheless, the terminology has remained, and most **tariff schedules** are known as two-, three-, or four-column schedules. For example, the United States is considered to operate under a two-column tariff schedule, with the Most-Favored Nations (MFN) subject to column one tariffs and others to column two tariffs. In 2000, the MFN designation was officially changed to Normal Trade Relations (NTR).

However, the number of columns is often quite an oversimplification of the actual tariff system. For the United States, there are only two trading partners that do not have NTR status, both of which are, at best, minor trading partners: Cuba and North Korea.[26] However, among the NTRs there are trading partners with which the United States has free-trade relations (Canada, Mexico, Israel, Chile, Jordan, Singapore, Australia, New Zealand, as well as all Caribbean countries, all Central American countries, and all sub-Sahara African countries), and several that have a special status on specific products, such as most developing countries under the Generalized System of Preference. Add to these several bilateral agreements on specific products, and the system is much more than a two-column system. Therefore the first column is actually split into two subcolumns, one labeled "general" for all NTR countries, and the other "special" for all countries for which, for a given HS number, there has been a special negotiation.

Figure 15-1[27] shows this layout, with a total of sixteen "special" tariffs. (Only two are not present in that table, the code "K" for the Agreement on Trade in Pharmaceutical Products, and "L" for the Uruguay Round Concessions on Intermediate Chemicals and Dyes.) Each product category has its own negotiated specific treatment and the Harmonized Tariff Schedule of the United States is replete with exceptions of this nature.

tariff schedule A document listing all the possible Harmonized System classification categories, as well as their associated tariff rates for the different types of countries.

Harmonized Tariff Schedule of the United States (2006) (Rev. 2)
Annotated for Statistical Reporting Purposes

XVIII

Heading / Subheading	Stat. Suffix	Article Description	Unit of Quantity	Rates of Duty		2
				1		
				General	Special	
9114		Other clock or watch parts:				
9114.10		Springs, including hairsprings:				
9114.10.40	00	For watches	No.	7.3%	Free (A+, AU, B, CA, D, E, IL, J, J+, JO, MA, MX, P, R) 1.8% (CL, SG)	65%
9114.10.80	00	Other	No.	4.2%	Free (A+, AU, B, CA, D, E, IL, J, J+, JO, MA, MX, P, R)	65%
9114.20.00	00	Jewels	No.	Free		10%
9114.30	00	Dials:				
9114.30.40	00	Not exceeding 50 mm in width	No.	0.4¢ each + 7.2%	Free (A+, AU, B, CA, D, E, IL, J, J+, JO, MA, MX, P, R) 0.1¢ each + 1.8%(CL, SG)	5¢ each + 45%
9114.30.80	00	Exceeding 50 mm in width	No.	4.4%	Free (A+, AU, B, CA, CL, D, E, IL, J, J+, JO, MA, MX, P, R, SG)	50%
9114.40		Plates and bridges:				
9114.40.20	00	Watch movement bottom or pillar plates or their equivalent	No.	12¢ each	Free (A+, AU, B, CA, CL, D, E, IL, J, J+, JO, MA, MX, P, R) 7.5¢ each (SG)	75¢ each
9114.40.40	00	Any plate, or set of plates, suitable for assembling thereon a clock movement	No.	10¢ each	Free (A+, AU, B, CA, CL, D, E, IL, J, J+, JO, MA, MX, P, R) 2.5¢ each (SG)	38¢ each
		Other:				
9114.40.60	00	For watches	X	7.3%	Free (A+, AU, B, CA, CL, D, E, IL, J, JO, MA, MX, P, SG)	65%
9114.40.80	00	Other	X	4.2%		65%
		. . . / . . .				

Legend:

A+: Generalized System of Preference
AU: United States – Australia Free Trade Agreement
B: Automotive Product Trade Act
CA: Canada
CL: United States Chile Free Trade Agreement
D: African Growth and Opportunity Act
E: Caribbean Basin Economic Recovery Act
IL: United States – Israel Free Trade Area

J: Andean Trade Preference Act
J+: Andean Drug Eradication Act
JO: United States – Jordan Free Trade Area Implementation Act
MA: United States- Morocco Freee Trade Agreement
MX: Mexico
P: Dominican Republic – Central America US Free Trade Agreement
R: United States - Carribean Basin trade Partnership Act
SG: United States – Singapore Free Trade Agreement

Figure 15-1
United States Tariff Schedule

Source: United States Tariff Schedule, 2006, Revision 2, April 1, 2006, Tariff Information Center, United States International Trade Commission, http://www.usitc.gov/tata/hts/bychapter/index_previous_sup.htm, July 22, 2006.

Tariffs are generally calculated *ad valorem* or as a percentage tax on the value of the goods imported. Nevertheless, other methods exist, such as a fixed amount per unit imported. Some others are calculated with a mixed system, such as a fixed amount per unit in addition to a percentage of the value of the goods imported; such a tariff is called a compound duty rate. Figure 15-1 illustrates all these alternatives:

- A company importing springs for watches (9114.10.4000) would have to pay 7.3 percent duty on the FCA value of the goods if they came from an NTR country, for example, Japan. If the spring came from India (Generalized System of Preference), Canada (North American Free-Trade Agreement), Haiti (Caribbean Basin Initiative), Israel (United States-Israel Free-Trade Agreement), Peru (Andean Trade Preference Act), or Mexico (NAFTA), the importer would have no duty to pay. If the spring came from North Korea, the duty rate would be 65 percent.

- A company importing small watch dials (9114.30.4000) from an NTR country, such as Germany, would have to pay U.S. $0.004 per dial, in addition to 7.2 percent of the FCA value of the dials. The same product coming from some other countries could be imported duty-free, while others—Singapore and Chile—would have to pay 1.8 percent of the FAC value of the dials. An importer obtaining these from Cuba would be saddled with a U.S. $0.05 duty in addition to 45 percent of the FCA value.

- A company importing watch plates suitable for assembling watch movements (9114.40.4000) from South Korea would pay U.S. $0.10 for each unit imported. From Chile, the same product would come in duty-free, but from Singapore, it would cost U.S. $0.025 each. Plates from North Korea would be charged U.S. $0.38 per unit.

15-1e Dumping

In some cases, Customs can determine that the invoice value is lower (in some rare cases, higher)[28] than the actual value of the goods. This is generally uncovered by comparing the value of a given invoice with a database of import entries with the same Harmonized System Number made in preceding year(s). For example, in the United States, the invoice value is systematically compared to existing valuations: This is one of the purposes of the column labeled "unit of quantity" in Table 15-1 that represents the units under which the Customs' computer keeps the values of other entries under a specific HS number to determine whether a given entry is within the bounds of "normal." Should the invoice give a value outside of these bounds, a Customs' Import Specialist will scrutinize the entry before liquidating it.

When the invoice's value is much below what Customs has historically accepted and when a much higher valuation is reached with one of the alternative valuation methods (see Section 15-1b), Customs can determine that the exporter is **dumping** the goods in the importing country (i.e., selling the goods at a price that is below their commercial value). The exact definition of "dumping" varies from country to country, but the most prevalent definition is a price that is below the wholesale price of the goods in the exporting country *and* that causes injury to competitors (or some other group, such as a labor union) located in the importing country. For some countries, such as the United States, there must be a complaint from an injured party before Customs considers that the undervaluation is a case of dumping. In addition, an organization independent from Customs—in the United States, the International Trade Commission—is asked to determine whether there is actual injury to competitors and ascertain whether the goods are sold at below their commercial value before an exporter is found guilty of dumping.

In those cases, Customs can add an additional duty to the regular duty rate of the commodity, and this duty rate is called an "anti-dumping" duty, which can range from 1 percent to several times the value of the goods imported. Unfortunately, dumping accusations have been one of the most commonly used tools of certain countries to restrict imports, and it is still one of the most commonly used methods of protectionism. In addition, Customs can also use a "countervailing" duty to tax

dumping The strategy followed by some exporters to sell the products they are exporting at a price that is considered "too low" by the importing country's Customs office.

Web Exercise

Some countries can have very unique ways of determining tariffs. Switzerland's tariff schedule stands out in that most of its tariffs are based on the gross weight of the goods imported (per 100 kg) rather than their value,[29] even for products such as computers or textiles. Most countries' tariff schedules are now published electronically and can be accessed through the World Customs Organization's website.

http://www.wcoomd.org[30]

products that the exporting government is found to have subsidized. Although there is strong support for such countervailing duties in some industries, the U.S. Commerce Department has declined to impose them on products coming from countries in which nonmarket economies prevail.[31]

In the United States, there were roughly twenty cases requesting relief from dumping practices in 2000; this lull followed a high of 105 requests in 1992.[32] Historically, most of the requests had come from the steel industry and products manufactured with steel, such as ball bearings,[33] but there is a 283 percent anti-dumping duty on raw pistachios and a 318 percent duty on roasted pistachios from Iran, due to a complaint initiated by pistachio growers in California, most of whom are, ironically, Iranian expatriates.[34]

All of this changed in May 2000, when the U.S. Congress passed what is known as the "Byrd Amendment," named after Senator Robert Byrd of West Virginia. The Byrd Amendment directed Customs to give the anti-dumping duty it collected from importers to the U.S. companies that were harmed by the dumping. In 2003, U.S. Customs and Border Protection distributed U.S. $190 million to U.S. companies (see Table 15-1),[35] U.S. $885 million in 2004, and an estimated $3.85 billion from 2005 until 2014.[36] The Timken Company, one of the largest beneficiaries of the Byrd Amendment, reported income of U.S. $66 million in 2003, which was an amount equal to 67 percent of its *operating* income of $98 million.[37] According to other sources, the U.S. Customs and Border Protection office put Timken's Byrd Amendment income at U.S. $93 million.

The Byrd Amendment triggered a rash of requests; in 2001, there were ninety-five requests for anti-dumping protection, 95 percent of which were granted.[38] The shrimp industry in the United States has been the most vocal in its requests for protection against shrimp farms in Southeast Asia.[39] Although the World Trade Organization ruled against the Byrd Amendment, by finding that it violated the rules of international trade,[40] the United States Congress had not repealed the Amendment as of July 2006.

15-1f Other Taxes

In addition to duty, several countries will perceive additional taxes based on the value of the goods; these additional taxes are a disguised way of creating additional revenues from imports while remaining within the boundaries of the General Agreement on Tariffs and Trade (GATT) and the rules of the World Trade Organization (WTO), which mandate systematic reductions in tariffs.

Such additional taxes can be labeled very creatively:

Punitive duty: The United States, unhappy about a decision by the European Union to give preferential treatment to bananas imported from former European colonies in the Caribbean and Africa, retaliated by placing a 100 percent duty on certain items coming from any of the fifteen EU countries: cashmere, blue cheese, "handbags covered in plastic sheeting," and so on.[41]

Border traffic tax: Russia, in order to "make a more accurate tally of border flows of people, cargo, and means of transportation," imposes a 1 percent tax on all goods crossing its borders. Russian travelers are taxed at 0.8 percent of their monthly income.[42]

Safeguard tax: Argentina, after being chastised by the WTO for having increased its duty rate on footwear, reduced them, and immediately re-imposed them through an emergency "safeguard tax" designed to protect its footwear industry against foreign competition.

Temporary protection tax: The United States imposed a 33 percent additional tariff on brooms from Mexico to allow U.S. manufacturers to increase their efficiency so that they could compete against imports. It repealed such tax two years later, noting that the industry had not taken advantage of this protection period to improve its efficiency.[43]

TABLE 15-1	Industries Benefiting from the Byrd Amendment (in thousands of U.S. dollars)	
Roller Bearings	112,010	58.88%
Steel	32,770	17.22%
Crawfish	9,760	5.13%
Canned Pineapples	5,360	2.82%
Polyester Fiber	4,150	2.18%
Cookware	3,760	1.98%
Candles	3,330	1.75%
Iron Products	2,790	1.47%
Pasta	2,180	1.15%
Mushrooms	2,030	1.07%
DRAMs	1,820	0.96%
Industrial Belts	1,250	0.66%
Silicon	1,170	0.61%
Pipe Fittings	1,060	0.56%
All others	677	3.56%
Total all industries	190,250	

These taxes are designed to increase revenues for the importing country, protect less efficient domestic industries, and punish importers, while respecting the letter—but certainly not the intent—of WTO agreements.

15-1g Value-Added Tax

In some countries, an additional tax is collected in addition to the duty, but is generally considered to have no bearing on importers—even if it adds up to a significant amount—because it is perceived from domestic producers as well as from importers, and is eventually only paid by consumers: the **Value-Added Tax (VAT)**. The idea of VAT is somewhat simple in its concept: The tax is perceived on the value added by each firm involved in adding value to a good, from the first one in the production chain to the last one. The implementation of a VAT is somewhat complex, though.

It is probably best to explain the VAT concept and its implementation—as it is practiced in the European Union countries, at least—with a simplified example:

1. A farmer purchases seeds, fertilizer, pesticides, and fuel to produce corn. On each of her production-related purchases, she pays the VAT. She keeps track of the VAT she has paid in a special bookkeeping account, as a "debit." She then sells the corn she has produced and collects VAT from her customer, which she also records in that account as a "credit." At the end of the quarter, she deducts the VAT she has paid from the VAT she has collected, and sends the difference to her government.

2. The corn is purchased by a mill that promptly transforms it into several products, including corn syrup. On all the products it sells to wholesalers and retailers, the mill collects VAT, an amount it records in a special bookkeeping account. At the end of the quarter, the mill deducts all the VAT it has paid to farmers for corn and all the VAT it has paid for its other purchases from the VAT it has collected from its customers and sends the difference to its government.

3. The corn syrup is purchased by a consumer who uses it for cooking. The consumer pays the VAT, but has no way to collect any, so it is the consumer who bears the tax's entire burden.

For imports, the concept is the same: The VAT is collected from the importer, but the importer can deduct the value of the VAT it has paid from the VAT it eventually

Value-Added Tax (VAT)
A tax perceived by many countries that is very similar to a sales tax, but that is collected whenever the product's value is increased. The Value-Added Tax on imports is collected at the point of entry in the country.

collects from its customers; therefore, the tax is not an actual cost to the importer. However, this is somewhat incorrect: In reality, there are substantial accounting and cash-flow costs associated with this method of garnering taxes. Nevertheless, because both domestic and imported products are taxed the same way, there are no advantages garnered by either in their final costs to the consumer. The cost is quite a substantial one for the ultimate consumer, though, as the tax rate in the European Union is approximately 20 percent.

In the European Union, the Value-Added Tax is computed on the sum of the value of the imported goods and the duty perceived at importation.

15-2 Non-Tariff Barriers

Some countries use high tariffs to attempt to limit the import of certain goods. However, steady pressure from the General Agreement on Tariffs and Trade, and now the World Trade Organization, has reduced considerably the duty paid by most goods in most countries. While there are still some exceptions, the trend is still toward ever-lower duty rates, with many countries having adopted tariffs that are rarely above 10 percent for most goods.

At the same time, the WTO has also been very active in attempting to decrease the number of non-tariff trade barriers that countries can place on imports. Nevertheless several of those alternatives are still in place, which effectively limit exporters' access to certain markets. Non-tariff trade barriers are those policies and actions that have the effect of reducing the number of items imported in a specific country. Often, not surprisingly, what is perceived as a trade barrier by an international trader is presented as an innocuous requirement by the importing country's government.

15-2a Quotas

quota A limit, set by the importing country's government, on the quantity of a specific commodity that can be imported in a given year.

The primary method used by countries to limit imports is a system of **quotas**, which limit the quantity of goods that can enter a particular country. A quota can take either of two forms:

1. An absolute quota, which places a yearly limit on the number of items entering a country under a specific HS number. On occasion, the quota can be implemented using the value of the goods imported by placing a ceiling on the total value of goods imported under a specific HS number. Once the quota is reached, goods in that category can no longer be imported. Some countries, whose products are subject to quotas, have established a system of visas to monitor how much of a given quota has been filled by its exporters (see Section 15-3g).

2. A tariff-rate quota, which places a two-tiered tariff rate on a specific category of products. Until a specific number of goods are entered, the tariff is low, but once the quota is reached, the tariff changes to a much higher percentage. Nevertheless, the goods can still be legally imported.

Quotas are usually placed on very specific items coming from a specific country of origin: For example, in 2000, no more than 147,358 dozens of articles under quota number 651-B—HS numbers 6107.22.0015 and 6108.32.0015, corresponding to boys' and girls' blanket sleepers (a type of pajamas) made of man-made fibers—could have been imported into the United States from China.[44] This complex system of quotas for textiles and apparel was followed by the United States and other developed countries for products originating from some developing countries, and was outlined in an international treaty called the Multi-Fiber Agreement (MFA). Those quotas restricted the number of textile items imported from a large number of developing countries. The WTO negotiated an Agreement on Textiles and Clothing, and all developed countries' textile quotas were supposed to have been lifted by January 1, 2005.[45]

However, within four months, both the European Union and the United States had re-imposed some quotas on textiles originating from China until 2008.[46] These quotas were established within the WTO guidelines, which allowed for some "safeguards," should the elimination of quotas be harmful to the economies of the importing countries. Mostly, the elimination of quotas was particularly harmful to the developing countries that were competing with China. Under the MFA quota system, many countries gained access to the large markets of Europe and the United States because Chinese firms were limited in the number of products they could sell. After the quotas were lifted, the Chinese firms, being the world's low-cost producer of textile apparel and having seemingly unlimited capacity, would have displaced these other countries' products and created economic hardship in those countries. Whether the imposition of quotas on Chinese goods is going to help these countries invest in increased productivity or only postpone the inevitable is unknown.

Quotas can also be aggregate quotas, applying to all imports under an HS heading, regardless of the country of origin; for example, the United States has a tariff-rate quota on milk, cream, dried milk, cheddar cheese, ice cream, peanuts, cocoa powder, sugar, and a substantial number of other food products.[47]

Quotas can also be called "voluntary quotas." Under pressure from the importing government, exporters agree to limit their exports "voluntarily" to a certain quantity. Such was the case during the early 1980s in the United States when Japanese automobile manufacturers agreed to absolute quotas for automobiles and light trucks.

Quotas can also come in the form of export quotas, when an exporting country limits the quantity of a certain type of good that firms can export from its territory (see Section 9-3f).

15-2b Adherence to National Standards

Unfortunately, quotas are hardly the only non-tariff trade barriers placed by countries to restrict imports. In many instances, countries enact "safety measures" designed to ostensibly protect their populations from defective, dangerous, or unhealthy products from abroad. While most of these restrictions are justified and necessary, some of them are based on dubious data and are simply a form of undisguised protectionism for less efficient domestic producers.

Countries certainly can demand that products sold within their borders meet the standards that their governments have enacted; for example, there are many requirements of quality for consumer products in developed countries. The most prominent ones are the Deutsche Industrie Norm (DIN) in Germany, the Japanese Industry Standards (JIS) in Japan, the Normes Françaises (NF) in France, and the American National Standards Institute (ANSI) in the United States. A few international standards exist as well, such as the ones defined by the International Organization for Standards, which laid out the ISO set of requirements. Most of these requirements are legitimate in that they reflect national preferences and sentiments toward consumer protection, health standards, and safety. For example, the European Union requires that vehicles be equipped with rear turn signals that are distinct from the brake lights, and the United States requires that automobiles be equipped with airbags. Both are worthy requirements.

The point at which these requirements become non-tariff barriers is unclear. An exporter is often unwilling to incorporate in its products an additional feature that is costly, or that it deems unnecessary, and claims that the requirement is a non-tariff barrier, when it may just be an unwillingness to deal with one of the differences and difficulties of selling a product in a foreign country.[48] In a parallel fashion, such a requirement may not be a non-tariff barrier, even if it is required only of imported products and not of domestic manufacturers, if it is to protect a country from "importing" a disease that has not yet been observed domestically. A recent example would be the so-called "mad-cow disease," against which non-European countries are trying to protect themselves.

The Sugar Quota

The United States has had a tariff-rate quota on sugar for many years. The total amount that can be imported at the low tariff rate of U.S. $0.0146 per kilogram is 1,117,195 metric tons, and any amount above that is charged U.S. $0.3387 per kilogram. The world market price for sugar is about U.S. $0.30 per kilogram, so the tariff more than doubles the cost of sugar for U.S. importers. A number of powerful groups of sugar producers in the United States are vocal supporters of this tariff-rate quota and are substantial financial backers of both political parties, so it has never been abolished, even though the WTO has ruled against it. This group is so strong that when the United States negotiated its free-trade agreement with Australia, it covered all products, but specifically excluded sugar.

Under the 2003/2004 system, which is still in place today, each producing country is allocated a given portion of the quota; for example, Mexico is allowed to import 7,258 tons, and Brazil, the world's largest producer, is allowed 152,691 tons.[49] However, these quotas are very low, especially considering that a Handysize ship can hold 35,000 tons. Essentially, the largest producer of sugar in the world (twenty-eight million metric tons) can only ship about four boatloads of sugar (0.5 percent of its produc-tion) to the largest market in the world, which has an annual consumption of 9,336,000 tons.

The quota has an impact on the sugar market in the United States. Although consumers are largely unaffected by the high price of sugar, because it represents a small portion of people's expenses, the overall market size is much smaller than it would be if there were no sugar quota; many users of sugar have substituted corn syrup (soft drink manufacturers) or moved abroad (candy manufacturers ship from Canada to the U.S. market) to circumvent the artificially high cost of sugar. This restriction also distorts the export market for American products; Mexico has a 20 percent tax on soft drinks made with corn syrup, for example.[50]

However, the impact of the sugar quota is greatest on the economies of the Caribbean and Central American countries that cannot export one of their largest agricultural crops to the United States. A possible move to sugar-based ethanol as a substitute for gasoline in automobile engines, which is common in Brazil, may change this situation, as the United States would need to import more sugar; however, as of July 2006, there were no signs that ending the quota was even being considered.

Nevertheless, countries' efforts to make imports adhere to national standards are often considered to be trade barriers: There have been lengthy spats over the safety of Mexican avocadoes in the United States, of United States' cherries in Mexico,[51] of New Zealand apples in Japan,[52] and of United States' hormone-treated beef in the European Union.[53] The dispute with Japan over the safety of U.S. tomatoes lasted forty-six years.[54]

15-2c Other Non-Tariff Barriers

Countries have enacted some very creative means to slow or restrict imports without having recourse to high tariffs, quotas, or standardization requirements. Here are several examples, which certainly do not constitute an exhaustive list:

- In the very early 1980s, France decided that it needed to protect its nascent VCR industry. It achieved this goal by requiring that every VCR entering the country be inspected, that a sticker be placed on every machine, and that the inspection take place in Poitiers, a land-locked small town about 250 miles from the port of Le Havre through which most VCRs were shipped. Moreover, the inspection station was also a *one-man* operation.[55] Countless countries have enacted similar "slow" Customs clearance processes, in order to deter imports and increase importers' costs, which need to shoulder additional storage costs and potential market delays.[56]

- Another tactic is to require a mind-numbing number of documents and approvals. For example, in India, "an exporter has to complete and process fifty-four documents [...]: twenty-seven pre-shipment documents, fourteen for Customs clearance, and thirteen for post-shipment realization of bills. As many as sixteen approvals are needed from departments of the central government."[57]

The European Union's Banana Wars

In 1993, the European Union, in an effort to support the economies of some of its members' former colonies in the Caribbean and Africa, devised a complex system of quotas, preferential tariffs, and import licenses to favor bananas imported from these countries. Even though it is not an exporter of bananas, the United States got tangled in this dispute because two of the companies that were affected by these restrictions were Dole Foods and Chiquita Brands, two American firms exporting bananas grown in Central America to Europe.[58]

Even after three rulings against this practice by the World Trade Organization, the European Union still maintained this convoluted system of preferential treatment and the United States eventually retaliated with higher tariffs on products from Europe such as pens, candles, and cheese,[59] to no avail. The "banana wars" escalated to a point where it involved the highest levels of government, and it took years to be resolved, despite WTO panels' efforts to ease the tension and resolve the issue.[60]

In early 2001, Chiquita Brands took the unusual step of suing the European Union for U.S. $525 million, which the company claims were the lost profits the company had incurred because of the restrictions, and which caused it to default on its bond payments.[61] The spat is now over, and Europeans end up paying slightly less for bananas today than they did when the trade barrier was in place.[62]

- Another way to slow Customs entries is to request additional papers that are not readily available or that are close to impossible to gather. The United States requests the "sewing tickets" for some garments, an internal work document of the garment factory, as well as the time cards of the employees working there, in an attempt to determine the country of origin of textile products.

- South Korea has been tremendously effective at keeping foreign cars out of its domestic market. In 2005, there were 800,000 Korean-made automobiles sold on the U.S. market, but only 3,900 U.S.-made automobiles sold in Korea.[63] This was achieved, despite relatively low tariffs of 8 percent, with a systematic campaign designed to portray the purchase of a foreign car as unpatriotic. To bolster this perception, the South Korean government has all but threatened all purchasers of foreign cars with an income tax audit.[64]

- Russia asked the United States' exporters of chicken parts (legs and wings) to individually inspect *every* bird—for specific diseases—before they can enter the country, effectively preventing all U.S. imports of such parts.[65]

15-2d Pre-Shipment Inspections

Pre-Shipment Inspections (PSIs) are inspections performed by independent companies at the point of departure of goods destined to be exported. The firm determines that the goods shipped are the ones ordered by the importer, in the correct quantity, and sufficiently well packed for an international shipment. When the independent firm has ascertained that all of these aspects conform to the invoice, it issues a Certificate of Inspection (see Section 9-4c) to the importer. Inspection companies have representatives in most ports and generally can handle just about any sort of shipment; on many occasions, though, the exporter experiences delays with PSIs as the workload of inspectors can be substantial, and as the expertise needed for a specific shipment may not be available.

Pre-Shipment Inspections are sometimes requested by importers to ensure that the exporter is shipping the correct product and the correct quantity; they are used when the importer is purchasing on a "Cash-in-Advance" or on a Letter of Credit basis. However, most PSIs are requested by countries that require Pre-Shipment Inspections as part of their import process. There are several reasons for that requirement:

- The country wants an expert opinion on the classification and the value of the products that are about to enter its territory.

- The country wants to fight corruption in its own ports of entry: By having a foreign, independent firm determine the classification and value of imported goods, its own Customs authorities have lost the ability to "be flexible" and change their classifications and valuations for a bribe. Such was the motivation when Indonesia demanded that any good shipped into Indonesia had to be pre-inspected by the *Société Générale de Surveillance.*[66]

- The country wants an estimate of the currency requirements it will face in the short term, and uses the value of the shipments subject to PSI to forecast its foreign currency needs.

- The country wants to generate some revenues in addition to the tariff it charges. Most of the countries requiring PSIs have long-term contracts giving an exclusive right to a single inspection company to inspect *all* of the goods about to enter its territory. Although it is pure speculation, it is likely that inspection companies compensate the country for this exclusive right by transferring a portion of the revenues generated by inspections to its Treasury.

15-3 Customs Clearing Process

The Customs clearing process differs from country to country, and tends to be arcane and cumbersome. In most countries, because of the complexity of the task, only certified Customs brokers or Customs agents are allowed to file the paperwork necessary to clear Customs. This section will only give a brief overview of the processes generally followed by Customs authorities worldwide and give examples based upon the United States system.

15-3a General Process

In some countries, the process starts with an application for an import license, a request for the express authorization to import a certain product. Import licenses are usually granted according to a number of criteria, most of which are based on the availability of foreign currency to pay for the import, and on the availability of domestic substitutes. Generally speaking, countries with scarce foreign currency resources will attempt to limit the granting of import licenses to those companies that have generated export revenues, and to those companies purchasing goods for which no close domestic substitute is available.

For most countries, however, the process starts when an importer files an **entry** (i.e., notifies the Customs authorities that it will import—or has imported—a particular product). There is usually a paper form (see Figure 15-2) that has to be filed and which must accompany all the documentation necessary for the import: invoice, Certificate of Origin, Certificate of Inspection (when required), Certificate of Insurance, and other forms as required by the Customs rules of the importing country. In most developed countries, the importer is usually responsible for classifying the goods according to the tariff schedule of the importing country, and for determining the amount of duty. In many developing countries, this task is still left to the Customs authorities, which often delays the process of clearance. In most instances, the goods are not released to the importer **cleared** until after the duty is paid or after there is evidence from the importer that it will pay, a requirement often met with a Customs bond. Generally, Customs authorities will review a percentage of the entries made by importers after the goods have been cleared and will have a few months to a few years to challenge them. If an entry is reviewed satisfactorily, the entry is deemed **liquidated**. In some countries, such as the United States, an importer dissatisfied with the final decision of Customs authorities has a brief period of time to **protest** a liquidated entry and request a review before it is finally settled.

entry The process by which an importer notifies Customs that it has imported a particular product.

cleared The term used to signify that goods were imported in a country and that the imported paid the duty that was due on those goods: The goods were released by the Customs authorities.

liquidated entry An entry that has been successfully reviewed by Customs authorities and for which duty has been paid.

protest In a Customs transaction in the United States, the formal request by an importer to have Customs reconsider its classification, its valuation, or its determination of a country of origin.

Canadian Food Inspection Agency
Agence canadienne d'inspection des aliments

IMPORT DECLARATION / DÉCLARATION D'IMPORTATION

1.
- [ ] Dairy Products / Produits laitiers
- [ ] Processed Fruits and Vegetables / Fruits et légumes transfrmés
- [ ] Honey / Miel
- [ ] Maple Products / Produits de l'érable
- [ ] Pesticides
- [ ] Seeds / Semences
- [ ] Feed / Aliments du bétail
- [ ] Fertilizer * / Engrais *

* Registrable / Sujets à l'enregistrement

2. Name and Address of Manufacturer / Nom et adresse du febricant

3. Name and Address of Exporter / Nom et adresse de l'exportateur

4. Name and Canadian Address of Importer / Nom et adresse canadienne de l'importateur

Telephone Number / Numéro de téléphone ➡

5. Name and Address of Destination (consignee) / Nom et adresse du destinataire

Telephone Number / Numéro de téléphone ➡

6. Transaction No. / N° de transaction

7. Carrier / Transporteur

9. Container No. / N° de conteneur

8. Flight No. / N°de vol

10. Trailer No. / N° de remorque

PRODUCT DESCRIPTION AND PACKAGING (ATTACH LIST IF NECESSARY)
DESCRIPTION DU PRODUIT ET DE L'EMBALLAGE (ANNEXER UNE LISTEAU BESOIN)

11. Common Name / Nom usuel	12. Brand Name / Marque	13. Grade / Catégorie	14. No. of Shipping Containers / Nbre de contenants

15. No., Type and Net Contents of Individual Containers per Shipping Container / Nbre, type et contenu net des contenants individuels par contenant d'expédition	16. Total Net Quantity / Quantité totale nette	17. Label Approval No. / N°. d'approbation de l'étiquette	18. Registration No. / N° d'enregistrement	19. Purpose of Importation / Motif de l'importation	20. Additional documentation and other references / Documents additionnels et autres références

21. Declaration / Déclaration

I, _____ the importer of the products described on this form do hereby certify that the information provided on this form is complete, correct and accurately describes the products contained in the shipment.

By signing this declaration in the case of the food products used for human consumption, I affirm that I have read the "Regulatory Requirements for Food Products Imported into Canada" set forth in the instructions to fill out this form and that the products described on this form meet those requirements.

Je, _____ , l'importateur des Produits décrits sur ce formulaire, certifie que l'information fournie sur ce formulaire est complète et qu'elle décrit avec précision les produits contenues dans cechargement.

En signant cette déclaration, dans le cas de produits alimentaires utilisés pour consommation humaine, j'affirme que j'ai lu les "Exigences réglementaires pour les produits alimentaires importés au Canada" inscrites dans les instructions pour remplir ce formulaire et que les produits décrits sur ce formulaire satisfont ces exigences.

_____ Signature   _____ Date

GOVERNMENT USE ONLY / RÉSERVÉ A L'ADMINISTRATION

22. Stamp / Estampe

23. Instructions to Customs and Importers / Directives aux douaniers et importateurs

- [ ] Au moment de l'importation, main levée et remise sous le contrôle d'AAC (pour l'inspection à l'arrivée à destination)

  Further action to be conducted on the shipment at the following place:

- [ ] _____

  Autres mesures à prendre à l'égard du chargement à l'endroit suivant :

- [ ] Other instruction / Instruction particulière

CFIA / ACIA 4560 (1999/06)

Figure 15-2
The Canadian Entry Form for Food Products

15-3b Customs Brokers

Because of the complexity and time-consuming nature of filling out Custom entries, many countries demand that importers delegate the task of interacting with Customs to a Customs broker, a representative of the importer that has acquired the knowledge and experience required to deal effectively and efficiently with Customs. In many countries, Customs brokers are the only entities qualified to enter goods (i.e., fill out the paperwork necessary to import goods). It is not the case in the United States, though, where importers can complete their own entries, as long as they have posted a Customs bond (see Section 15-3c). Customs brokers are usually compensated on a fee basis, for each entry they handle. In the United States, Customs brokers are highly qualified individuals who have to take a grueling test on issues of classification, duty computation, and quotas before being allowed to manage importers' entries.

15-3c Customs Bonds

In most countries, the importer has to pay the duty to Customs before the shipment can be legally released. However, this can be extremely unwieldy, especially in those cases where the shipment is an express package or a shipment of time-sensitive produce, for example. Therefore, Customs authorities allow importers (or Customs brokers entering goods on their behalf) to post a surety bond, which is a guarantee that the importer or the Customs broker will pay the duty due. A bond is generally a sum of money deposited with Customs, from which any unpaid duty can be withdrawn, or an insurance policy with a surety company that acts as a guarantor of the importer or the Customs broker, and which it would be required to pay if the duty were not paid on time. This process allows goods to be entered before the duty is paid. In some cases, actually, the goods are sold much before the entry is liquidated.

In the United States, the bond is not just a guarantee that the duty will be paid on time; it is also a contract that obligates the importer or the Customs broker to perform all Customs-related functions in a timely manner, such as filing entries that are complete and accurate, as well as present Customs with the goods after they have physically entered the country, generally for inspection purposes.[67]

15-3d Reasonable Care

informed compliance
A standard of behavior, set and enforced by the United States Customs Office, that is expected of importers if they want their Customs entries to be cleared quickly and if they want to keep Customs inspections to a minimum.

reasonable care A standard of behavior, set and enforced by the United States Customs Office, that is expected of importers if they want their Customs entries to be cleared quickly and if they want to keep Customs inspections to a minimum.

Out of the United States Customs Modification Act of 1993 came the concepts of **informed compliance** and **reasonable care**, neither of which can be easily defined, but which have become pivotal to the efforts of the Customs Service in the United States.

The idea behind informed compliance is that, if an importer has been found compliant, the likelihood that one of its shipments is going to be inspected is minimal, therefore minimizing delays at entry and allowing the importer to organize its supply chain more predictably. It also lowers costs, as merchandise is cleared quickly and does not languish in some bonded warehouse while the importer and Customs argue about its correct classification, valuation, or country of origin.

In order for an importer to be found compliant, it must show that it exercised reasonable care in the filing of its Customs entries. In order to demonstrate reasonable care, the importer must follow a long list of obligations that the U.S. Customs Service provides.[68] The obligations center on making sure that the importer employs a Customs specialist, who will make sure that all—including the most recent—Customs regulations are followed, and that it has put into place a process by which it correctly determines the valuation, classification, and country of origin of an import. Reasonable care is monitored through a system of compliance audits organized by the U.S. Customs.[69]

15-3e Required Documentation

The documentation required by any Customs authority can be extensive. Ideally speaking, there should be only three documents required in every country to make an entry:

- A form designated for entry (specific to the recordkeeping requirements of the importing country)
- A Certificate of Origin to ascertain the country of origin
- A Commercial Invoice with enough information to determine value and classification

However, many more can be included, from an import license to a series of certificates or other documents: Most of these documents were introduced and explained in Chapter 9. One of the worst offenders is the country of India, with about fifty-four documents, as shown in Section 15-2c. Many countries' requirements are published electronically; a good number of them can be accessed through www.tradelinks.com.

The critical element of import documentation is that it is established on a *per*-transaction basis. Every import, however small, needs to have its own specific entry, which can lead to an inordinate amount of paperwork generated, under which both the importer and the Customs authorities are drowning. For example, in order to allow a shipment that landed in any of Europe's many ports to travel to another country in the EU, a form has to be filed in quintuplicate—five copies—and there were eighteen million shipments of this nature in 1999, netting a "paper blizzard" of ninety million copies that the European Customs authorities must store in warehouses.[70]

There are several efforts made to simplify the process of importing merchandise and clearing Customs:

1. The most significant one is the automated (electronic) processing of entries, which was implemented by the U.S. Customs Service under the name of Automated Commercial System (ACS) in 1984, and is in the process of being progressively replaced with an Automated Commercial Environment (ACE), which was completed in 2005.[71] Several countries have adopted similar programs, but, to this date, they are all incompatible. The World Customs Organization, with its Kyoto Protocol, and more recently the World Trade Organization, are working on harmonizing Customs requirements worldwide, but so far these efforts have only been marginally successful.[72]

2. Great Britain's Customs Agency has developed an International Trade Prototype with the help of U.S. Customs. The idea is that the same merchandise, exported from the United States and imported into Great Britain, generates two sets of paperwork, as if it were two separate, stand-alone processes. The International Trade Prototype allows the electronic documentation used for exporting the product from the United States to be used to import the product in the United Kingdom, which reduces the amount of paper generated significantly.[73] The World Customs Organization is now considering a similar setup.[74]

3. The U.S. Customs Office is also evaluating an Entry Revision Project (ERP), which would allow an importer to file entries periodically—say, at the end of the month—rather than for every transaction. Similarly, duty could be paid for several entries at the same time.[75] Such a system would revolutionize the business of filing entries, bringing much simplification and expediency to the process.

15-3f Required Markings

Products imported in a country often require a marking—"made in [country]" or "product of [country]"—printed or affixed on the product itself or its packaging.

Rules differ from country to country on the location of the marking, its size, and whether it needs to be permanently attached to the product. The determination of the country placed on the marking is also left to the country of importation. However, there are no known instances of a country on the marking being different from the country of origin for Customs duty purposes (see Section 15-1c).

In the United States, markings are required for most products, although there is a list, maintained by the U.S. Customs Office,[76] of exceptions, mostly products on which it is difficult or impossible to place a marking. All markings must be legible, conspicuously placed, and durable. However, the United States has an additional unusual requirement. No product imported in the United States can have a name or package such that it may mislead the public as to its country of origin. It is therefore prohibited to include words such as "American, "United States," or "U.S.A." Inappropriate or missing markings are subject to penalties, liquidated damages, and seizures by U.S. Customs.[77]

Finally, there is the issue of the "made in the USA" label, which is often a marketing advantage in the U.S. market. Although the Federal Trade Commission considered lowering the minimum United States content to 75 percent of a product's value, it has maintained it at 98 percent for the foreseeable future,[78] making it all but impossible to mark a product as made in the United States unless it is entirely domestically produced.

15-3g Merchandise Visas

For those products whose importation is limited by quotas, and particularly for textile products, a bilateral monitoring system has been implemented by the importing and exporting countries.

visa A document provided by the government of an exporting country for a product that is subject to a quota in the United States. It is a document granting the exporter the "right" to export such goods.

Because there is a maximum quantity of goods that can be imported in a given country in a calendar year, the government of the country of export will grant—in some cases, sell—the right to export a set quantity of a specific good to an exporting firm. Such authorization is a **visa**. The visa specifies the type of good (by Harmonized System number), the quantity, and the destination country to which the exporter is allowed to sell.

For products for which such a system is in place, the visa is one of the required documents that must be presented to the Customs authorities of the importing countries, and often as well, to the Customs authorities of the exporting country. As the quotas are eliminated, so are the visa requirements, though, and, therefore, by 2005, visas have become obsolete.[79]

15-3h Duty Drawbacks

Several countries, including the United States, grant a substantial tax break to exporters who are using imported parts in the products they export. Such a tax break is called a **duty drawback**.

duty drawback A process by which the U.S. Customs and Border Protection Office refunds up to 99 percent of the duty it collected on goods that are imported into the United States if the same goods are later exported from the United States.

In the United States, the Customs Service will refund 99 percent of the duty paid by an importer in one of three cases:

- For merchandise that is rejected by the importer as non-conforming to the original purchase order
- For imported products that are re-exported unused
- For imported parts that are used—without substantial transformation—in the assembly or manufacturing of products that are eventually re-exported

Note that this duty drawback is not available for products exported to NAFTA countries.

This drawback can represent a considerable savings in many cases. However, few U.S. firms take advantage of this duty drawback opportunity, either because they do

Foreign Trade Zones

Another type of Foreign Trade Zone is not located in a port or cargo area, but at the place of business of a corporation, such as a plant or a refinery. In most of these types of trade zones, some economic activity beyond simple warehousing is conducted: manufacturing, assembly, repackaging, and refining, for example. The Free Trade Zone is created with the purpose of creating jobs in the host country by providing a lower cost structure to the businesses using them, because they do not have to pay duty on the goods that they are processing and eventually re-exporting. Another way a business can save money by obtaining FTZ status is when the host country has a so-called "inverted tariff structure" (i.e., the tariffs charged on parts are higher than the tariffs charged on the final product). Such FTZ locations are called "sub-zones" in the United States, as they need to be affiliated, for legal purposes, with a General Purpose Foreign Trade Zone, and because these locations are only available to one specific company and not to others.

An interesting issue arises when a substantial transformation takes place in a Foreign Trade Zone and the goods change from one Harmonized System Number classification to another. Even though the rules of origin call for the goods to be "made" in the country in which this change of HS number took place—the country in which the FTZ is located, in this case—negotiations between Customs and the company determine the country of origin that will be used for duty purposes, be it the country of origin of the parts used, or of the main component, or yet some other alternative. In any case, it is never the country in which the change in HS took place.

FTZs can be quite advantageous to hold goods in inventory until they are sold, improving the cash flow of their owner, to wait for a numerical quota to open, or to wait for an inspection by the host country's government.

However, in view of the progress made in the last few years by the WTO to lead countries to lower tariffs and increased trade, Foreign Trade Zones may have a limited future because their advantages are dwindling.

not know about it or because they fear the paperwork requirements that accompany this program.[80] Actually, the paperwork requirements used to be mind-boggling; for example, in order to take advantage of the "unused" drawback, Customs required importers to track individual items from their import to their leaving the country. However, since April 1998, the requirements have been relaxed, allowing "commercially interchangeable goods" to qualify an export for the drawback.[81] In exchange for this flexibility, Customs has substantially stiffened penalties for illegitimate drawbacks.[82]

15-4 Foreign Trade Zones

Foreign Trade Zones (FTZ) are specific locations of a country that have acquired a special Customs status. Foreign Trade Zones—sometimes called Free Trade Zones—are areas of a country that, for Customs purposes, still are located "outside" of a country. Practically, that means that goods can be shipped to the FTZ without being subject to the duties, quotas, and Customs regulations of the host country. In most countries, however, including the United States, goods admitted in an FTZ must be legal in the country in which the zone is located: The exemption applies only to Customs' purposes, not to other legal requirements. Examples of products that would not be acceptable in an FTZ would be medical devices not yet approved for use in the FTZ country, even though they can be perfectly legal in other countries.

Once in the FTZ, the goods can be warehoused until they are sent to their final destination, either in the host country or to a foreign destination. If the goods are sold in the host country, they are only dutiable at the time of that transaction. If they are sold abroad, they are dutiable only in the importing country; the country in which the FTZ is located will never collect any duty on the value of that merchandise. The country of origin used for Customs purposes remains the country from which the goods originated, and not the country in which the FTZ is located.

Foreign Trade Zones exist in one form or another in just about every country; the most common form of FTZs is that of a location where cargo transits. For example, most of the ports of the world are Foreign Trade Zones,[83] so that cargo can be unloaded from a ship, temporarily stored in a warehouse, and then loaded onto another vessel to its final destination. Such cargo, although physically present in the physical territory of the country in which the port is located, never "enters" the country and is therefore never assessed duty. Because shipping companies are moving toward a system of very large containerships serving very large "hub" ports, from which smaller, so-called feeder ships are serving smaller ports, the importance of Free Trade Zones is expected to increase. Airports, which often operate on the same concept of "hub and spoke," also often possess a few warehouses in a Free Trade Zone. Because such FTZs are available to all companies involved in international trade, the United States calls them General Purpose [Foreign Trade] Zones.[84]

Key Terms

assist (p. 337)

binding ruling (p. 335)

classification (p. 334)

cleared (p. 348)

dumping (p. 341)

duty (p. 334)

duty drawback (p. 352)

entry (p. 348)

informed compliance (p. 350)

liquidated entry (p. 348)

protest (p. 348)

quota (p. 344)

reasonable care (p. 350)

rules of origin (p. 334)

tariff (p. 334)

tariff schedule (p. 339)

valuation (p. 334)

Value-Added Tax (VAT) (p. 343)

visa (p. 352)

Review and Discussion Questions

1. What is the concept of a Harmonized System Number? How is it used? What are the advantages of such a system?

2. Explain the concept of "valuation" from the perspective of Customs. Why is it particularly important to have a detailed Commercial Invoice?

3. Explain the concept of "classification" from the perspective of Customs. Why is it particularly important to have a detailed Commercial Invoice?

4. Explain the concept of "country of origin." How is it currently determined? Why is it such a difficult concept? Why is it important?

5. What are non-tariff barriers? Why are they used? Give a few examples.

6. What types of quotas are there? How does the United States enforce the quotas it imposes? What is a "merchandise visa"?

Endnotes

1. Fisher, Donald L., "Finding the Right Classification to Determine Duty Rates Can Be a Puzzle," *The Journal of Commerce*, March 26, 1997, p. 2C. Fisher, Donald L., "Understanding Harmonized Tariffs: A Puzzle Where None of the Pieces Fit," *The Journal of Commerce*, September 16, 1998, p. 2C.

2. Fisher, Donald L., "Obtaining Customs Rulings Requires Documentation and Some Patience," *The Journal of Commerce*, November 19, 1997, p. 2C. Fisher, Donald L., "When It Comes to Customs, the Ties That Bind Can Lose You Business," *The Journal of Commerce*, November 10, 1998, p. 7A.

3. Lucentini, Jack, "Customs, Importers Urge ITC to Review Tariff Classifications," *The Journal of Commerce*, May 1, 2000, p. 3.

4. Neville, Peterson, and Williams, "Cat Antlers and 'Neckties In Bottles,'" *The Journal of Commerce*, January 14, 1998, p. 11C.

5. Green, Paula, "A Costly Halloween Question: Are Costumes Toys or Clothing?" *The Journal of Commerce*, March 26, 1998, p. 1A.

6. Rushford, Greg, "When Is a Duck Not Like a Bedspread?" *The Asian Wall Street Journal*, February 24, 1997, p. 12.

7. Ungar, Ed, "Closing a Literal Loophole," *U.S. News & World Report*, April 27, 1998, p. 32.

8. Cowan, Richard, "Weyerhauser Seeks Tax to End Canada Lumber Fight," Reuters' press release, November 20, 2002, on http://ca.news.yahoo.com/021120/5/qdat.html, December 12, 2002.

9. King, Neil Jr., "Is Wolverine Human? A Judge Answers No; Fans Howl in Protest," *The Wall Street Journal*, January 20, 2003, p. A1.

10. "Customs Valuation: Agreement on Implementation of Article VII of the General Agreement on Tariffs and Trade 1994, Within the scope of the WTO," Background Note, February 2000, Agency for International Trade Information and Cooperation [AITIC], http://www.acici.org/aitic/documents/Notes/note8ang.html, January 11, 2001.

11. "Customs Valuation: Agreement on Implementation of Article VII of the General Agreement on Tariffs and Trade 1994, Within the scope of the WTO," Background Note, February 2000, Agency for International Trade Information and Cooperation [AITIC], http://www.acici.org/aitic/documents/Notes/note8ang.html, January 11, 2001.

12. "The Agreement on Rules of Origin of the WTO," Background Note, June 1998, Agency for International Trade Information and Cooperation [AITIC], http://www.acici.org/aitic/documents/Notes/note8ang.html, January 11, 2001. Gillis, Chris, "Another Look at Product Origin," *American Shipper*, February 2004, pp. 24–26.

13. "Rules of Origin; Made in ... Where?" in "Understanding the WTO—Non-Tariff Barriers, Red Tape, etc....," World Trade Organization, http://www.wto.org/English/thewto_e/whatis_e/tif_e/agrm9_e.htm#origin, July 22, 2006.

14. Bangsberg, P. T., "Textile Dispute Impedes Hong Kong Export Growth," *The Journal of Commerce*, February 3, 1997, p. 5A.

15. Green, Paula L., "Customs Puts 63 More Firms on Violation List," *The Journal of Commerce*, November 12, 1998, p. 3A.

16. Roth, Martin S., and Jean B. Romeo, "Matching Product Category and Country Image Perceptions: A Framework for Managing Country-of-Origin Effects," *Journal of International Business Studies*, Third Quarter 1992, pp. 477–497.

17. "Rules of Origin," North American Free Trade Agreement, U.S. Customs and Border Protection, http://www.cbp.gov/nafta/docs/us/chap04.html, July 22, 2006.

18. Brenton, Paul and Miriam Manchin, "Making EU Trade Agreements Work: The Role of Rules of Origin," CEP working document no. 183, March 2002, http://129.3.20.41/eps/it/papers/0203/0203003.pdf, July 22, 2006.

19. Gillis, Chris, "Origin Compliance Challenges Shippers," *American Shipper*, March 2004, pp. 36–37. Field, Alan, "Original Sin," *The Journal of Commerce*, June 14–20, 2004, pp. 51–54.

20. Neville, Peterson, and Williams, "Meeting of the Trade Minds: Discussing the Country-of-Origin Marking Travesty," *The Journal of Commerce*, July 30, 1997, p. 13C.

21. Weiser, Steven S., and Arthur W. Bodek, "Which Came First, the Chicks Hatched in England or the South African Ostrich Eggs?" *The Journal of Commerce*, August 19, 1998, p. 11C.

22. Jehl, Douglas, "Whose Lingerie Is It? A New Mid-East Secret," *The New York Times*, December 25, 1996, p. 6.

23. Tagliabue, John, "Italian Silk Makers Upset by New U.S. Trade Law," *The New York Times*, April 10, 1997.

24. Lawrence, Richard, "U.S., EU Smooth Over Differences on Country-of-Origin Regulations," *The Journal of Commerce*, April 15, 1998, p. 4A.

25. Levy, Clifford, "The Olive Oil Seems Fine. Whether It's Italian Is the Issue," *The New York Times*, May 7, 2004.

26. *Harmonized Tariff Schedule of the United States (2006)*, United States International Trade Commission Publication 3249, United States Government Printing Office, Washington, DC 20402. Also available at http://www.customs.gov, July 21, 2006.

27. United States Tariff Schedule, 2006, Revision 2, April 1, 2006, Tariff Information Center, United States International Trade Commission, http://www.usitc.gov/tata/hts/bychapter/index_previous_sup.htm, July 22, 2006.

28. Lucentini, Jack, "Agency Takes Importer to Court for Allegedly Overvaluing Goods," *The Journal of Commerce*, October 15, 1999, p. 1. Lucentini, Jack, "Jury Exonerates Importer Who Overstated Value," *The Journal of Commerce*, October 20, 1999, p. 17.

29. Country Commercial Guide: Switzerland, Fiscal Year 2006, U.S. & Foreign Commercial Service and U.S. Department of State, March 2, 2006, http://www.stat-usa.gov, July 22, 2006.

30. Gillis, Chris, "WCO Pushes for Customs Automation," *American Shipper*, March 2002, p. 12.

31. Beadle, Andrew, "Countervailing Duty Bills Attract Support," *The Journal of Commerce*, July 19–25, 2004, pp. 38–40.

32. Lawrence, Richard, "A New Look at Laws Against Unfairly Priced Imports," *The Journal of Commerce*, April 15, 1998, p. 1C.

33. Adams, Chris, "Ailing Steel Industry Launches a Battle Against Imports," *The Wall Street Journal*, October 1, 1998. Neville, Peterson, and Williams, "Stealth Taxes: Importers Slammed with Anti-Dumping Duty without Warning," *The Journal of Commerce*, September 23, 1998, p. 12C.

34. Vardi, Nathan, "Nutty Trade," *Forbes*, October 16, 2000, p. 60.

35. Kulish, Eric, "Dumped On," *American Shipper*, July 2004, pp. 7–16.

36. *Ibid*

37. *2004 Annual Report*, The Timken Company.

38. Kulish, Eric, "Dumped On," *American Shipper*, July 2004, pp. 7–16.

39. Fritsch, Peter, "As Shrimp Industry Thrives in Vietnam, Trade Fight Looms," *The Wall Street Journal*, October 21, 2004, p. A1.

40. Meller, Paul, and Elizabeth Becker, "U.S. Loses Trade Cases and Faces Penalties," *The New York Times*, September 1, 2004.

41. Phillips, Michael M., "U.S. Plans Punitive Tariffs in Dispute with EU," *The Wall Street Journal*, December 22, 1998, p. A2.

42. Helmer, John, "Russia Imposes Tax on Border Traffic," *The Journal of Commerce*, January 27, 1997, p. 3A.

43. Lucentini, Jack, "Clinton, in Pro-Trade Move, Ends Tariffs on Brooms," *The Journal of Commerce*, December 8, 1998, p. 3A.

44. *U.S. Customs Service Textile Status Report: China*, U.S. Customs Service, http://www.customs.gov/quotas/2000/cntxtpt.htm, January 22, 2001.

45. Magnier, Mark, "Emerging Nations Wack U.S., Others over Protectionism," *The Journal of Commerce*, May 14, 1997, p. 3A.

46. Mottley, Robert, "Quota Hangover," *American Shipper*, October 2005, pp. 14–16.

47. *General Quota Information*, U.S. Customs Service, http://www.customs.gov/imp-exp2/pubform/import/special.htm, January 22, 2001.

48. Thornton, Emily, "The Japan That Says No to Cold Pills," *Business Week*, May 19, 1997.

49. "U.S. Raw Sugar Tariff Rate Quota," U.S. Department of Agriculture, http://www.fas.usda.gov/htp/sugar/2002/November/trq.pdf, July 24, 2006.

50. Malkin, Elisabeth, "In Mexico, Sugar vs. Corn Syrup," *The New York Times*, June 9, 2004.

51. DiBenedetto, William, "Mexico Says Yes to U.S. Cherries," *The Journal of Commerce*, February 12, 1997.

52. Hall, Kevin G., "Mexico Avocadoes Gain Access to U.S.," *The Journal of Commerce*, November 7, 1997, p. 3A. Shorrock, Tim, "U.S. to Investigate Japanese Barriers to Fruit Imports," *The Journal of Commerce*, October 17, 1997, p. 9A.

53. Andrews, Edmund L., "WTO Overrules Europe's Ban on U.S. Hormone-Treated Beef," *The New York Times*, May 9, 1997.

54. Linn, Gene, "U.S. Renews Attack on Asian Barriers to Food Exports," *The Journal of Commerce*, April 23, 1998, p. 1A.

55. "The Second Battle of Poitiers," *Time*, December 6, 1982, p. 31.

56. Greenberger, Robert S., "Some Asian Trade Barriers Likely to Fall," *The Wall Street Journal*, April 10, 1998, p. A2.

57. Rao, N. Vasuki, "India to Introduce EDI to Cut Paperwork," *The Journal of Commerce*, November 24, 1998, p. 3A.

58. Weinstein, Michael M., "Banana Spat Could Have Serious Consequences for World Trade," *The New York Times*, December 29, 1998.

59. Sanger, David E., "Clinton Fires First Shot in the Banana War," *The New York Times*, December 22, 1998.

60. Zaroscostas, John, "EU officials Reject Plan to Ease Banana Gridlock," *The Journal of Commerce*, January 27, 1999, p. 3A.

61. DePalma, Anthony, "Chiquita Sues Europeans, Citing Banana-Quota Losses," *The New York Times*, January 26, 2001.

62. DePalma, Anthony, "U.S. and Europeans Agree on Deal to End Banana Trade War," *The New York Times*, April 12, 2001.

63. Odessey, Bruce, "Korean, Malaysian Auto Barriers Pose Trade Negotiation Challenge," May 2, 2006, http://usinfo.state.gov/xarchives/display.html?p=washfile-english&y=2006&m=May&x=20060502145954ebyessedo0.8258783&t=ei/ei-latest.html, July 24, 2006.

64. Wright, Gregory, "South Korea Agrees to Open Market to U.S. Vehicles, Easing Threat of Sanctions," *The Journal of Commerce*, October 22, 1998, p. 2A. Schuman, Michael, "South Korea Acts to Discourage Imports," *The Wall Street Journal*, March 7, 1997, p. A8.

65. Banerjee, Neela, and Helene Cooper, "Are Russians Playing a Game of Chicken with … Chickens?" *The Wall Street Journal*, March 18, 1996.

66. Borsuk, Richard, "Changing of the Port Guards: Some Importers Fear a Return to Corruption," *Asian Wall Street Journal*, April 7, 1997, p. 14.

67. Fisher, Donald L., "Prompt, Accurate Marking Can Often Help to Avoid Liquidated Damage Claims," *The Journal of Commerce*, July 22, 1998, p. 2C.

68. *Informed Compliance*, United States Customs Service, http://www.customs.ustreas.gov/imp-exp2/pubform/import/comply.htm, October 22, 1999.

69. JBC International, "CAT Tales: All the Way from 'Gotcha' to 'Informed Compliance,' and Back Again," *The Journal of Commerce*, April 22, 1998, p. 11C. Mongelluzzo, Bill, "Reasonable Care Is Vital for Trade Arena under Mod Act," *The Journal of Commerce*, January 29, 1999, p. 6A.

70. Freudmann, Aviva, "Customs in Europe Hopes to Cyber-Melt Paper Blizzard," *The Journal of Commerce*, January 29, 1999, p. 1A.

71. Baish, Peter, "The ACE: A Good Beginning," *American Shipper*, March 2002, p. 75.

72. Freudmann, Aviva, "WTO Explores Ways to Ease Cargo Delays at Borders," *The Journal of Commerce*, October 13, 1998, p. 1A.

73. Mongelluzzo, Bill, "Customs Uniformity Urged," *The Journal of Commerce*, September 23, 1998, p. 1B. Freudmann, Aviva, "Britain Seeks Other 'Prototype' Partners," *The Journal of Commerce*, May 1, 2000, p. 1.

74. Gillis, Chris, "WCO Pushes for Customs Automation," *American Shipper*, March 2002, p. 12.

75. Mongelluzzo, Bill, "Customs Seeks a Consensus," *JoC Week*, June 12–18, 2000, p. 37.

76. *Marking*, U.S. Customs Service, http://www.customs.gov/imp-exp2/pubform/import/marking.htm, October 21, 1999.

77. Fisher, Donald L., "Prompt, Accurate Marking Can Often Help to Avoid Liquidated Damage Claims," *The Journal of Commerce*, July 22, 1998, p. 2C.

78. Hershey, Robert D, Jr., "F.T.C. Drops Plans to Relax 'Made in U.S.A.' Standard," *The New York Times*, December 2, 1997.

79. Green, Paula, "Visa Requirements on U.S. Textiles to End Jan. 1," *The Journal of Commerce*, October 9, 1998, p. 3A.

80. Imbriani, Robert, "Drawback: Learn the Rules to Earn the Refund," *Transportation and Distribution*, December 1998, p. 8.

81. Weiser, Steven S., and Ari L. Kaplan, "Unused Merchandise Drawback Offers Distinct Benefits for Importers, Exporters," *The Journal of Commerce*, May 27, 1998, p. 11C.

82. Imbriani, Robert, "Drawback: Learn the Rules to Earn the Refund," *Transportation and Distribution*, December 1998, p. 8.

83. *Index of Free Trade Zones Worldwide*, EscapeArtist.com, http://www.escapeartist.com/ftz/ftz_index.html, November 7, 2002.

84. *Foreign Trade Zones: U.S. Customs Procedures and Requirements*, http://www.customs.gov/imp-exp2/comm-imp/ftz/brochure.htm, November 7, 2002.

Using International Logistics for Competitive Advantage

Chapter Sixteen

Source: © 2007 JupiterImages Corporation.

The preceding chapters outlined many of the challenges that an international logistics manager faces in an international environment. They covered the infrastructure of international business, the management of financial and transportation risks, and the choices related to international transportation and packaging, all of which are eminently more complex than for domestic transactions.

However, a good export manager should not see these challenges as obstacles, but as opportunities to offer a higher level of service than his or her competitors. This can be done relatively simply by following a number of elementary points. The recommendations that follow may not "clinch the deal" for an exporter; however, they will certainly help in all circumstances.

Consider that an importer, in most situations, is getting several quotes from several exporters located in different countries. Although the alternative bids are likely to be evaluated on a large number of criteria (price, support, after-sale service, delivery terms, and so on), one of the most important issues will be the ease with which the purchase transaction will take place. From the importer's perspective, the easiest alternative is to purchase from a supplier who communicates clearly, who is flexible in his or her approach, who offers terms of sale that are convenient to the buyer, who is careful in handling paperwork and transportation, and who packages the goods carefully. When all else is the same, the well-prepared exporter will earn the sale by being better prepared on those logistical details.

The good management of international logistics is a competitive advantage.

16-1 Communication Challenges

One of the most challenging aspects of international business is effective communication: Conducting business with people located in a foreign country is often hampered by language barriers. It can be quite difficult to conduct business when two people from different languages and cultures are communicating. An additional challenge for the international logistics manager is that most communications with foreign counterparts are conducted in an impersonal fashion: e-mail, fax, and letters. This detached type of contact does not allow for the subtleties of in-person communication, such as tone of voice or gestures, which often help make communications more intelligible. There is also no opportunity to ask for immediate clarification as there is in verbal communication, and the possibility of errors or misunderstandings is greatly increased.

The United States Department of State classifies languages by the degree of difficulty that they present for a native English speaker intent on learning that language. Table 16-1[1] outlines these categories and languages. The greater the differences are between two persons' languages, the greater the likelihood is that communication will be difficult. Sentences can often be interpreted differently and both parties will then be left to wonder what the other person meant by a certain word, phrase, or sentence.

To the international logistician, the diversity of languages and associated possible misunderstandings means that extreme care should be extended to communication, to ensure that the correct meaning is conveyed every time. Conveniently for the native speaker of English, most international communication takes place in that language. English has become everybody's second language, mainly because it is the easiest language to learn,* but also because it is the language of the largest trade partner of most countries. However, the advantage of being able to communicate in one's own language means that there are significant responsibilities attached to it.

---

*Contrary to a commonly held belief, English actually is the easiest language to learn because of its simple grammar, its single gender, and limited number of tenses.

TABLE 16-1	Classification of Languages in Terms of Difficulty to Learn for a Native English Speaker

Category 1: Languages closest to English; easiest to learn	
Roman alphabet, similar grammar, similar syntax	Spanish, French, Dutch, Italian, Portuguese, Norwegian, Swedish, German
Category 2: Languages difficult to learn	
Roman alphabet, different grammar, different syntax	Indonesian, Turkish, Icelandic, Czech, Hungarian, Vietnamese, Polish, Slovak, Finnish
Category 3: Languages very difficult to learn	
Different alphabet, different grammar, very different syntax	Hebrew, Russian, Greek, Hindi, Thai
Category 4: Languages extremely difficult to learn	
Complex alphabet, multiple alphabets or no alphabet, very different grammar, very different syntax	Chinese (Cantonese and Mandarin), Japanese, Korean, Arabic

16-2 International English

International logistics professionals engage mostly in written communications with their counterparts abroad (by e-mail, fax, or other written documents) and therefore it is important that they communicate clearly in writing. A specific style of writing for native English speakers has developed to increase the probability that non-native speakers of English can clearly understand what was written. This technique, dubbed "**International English**" by Edmond Weiss, was outlined in his outstanding book *The Elements of International English Style* in 2005.[2]

Writing in International English means following a fairly large number of rules (Weiss lists fifty-seven of them), but the most important one is that the native English speaker should strive to make the meaning of the communication absolutely clear to the non-native speaker: "Business and technical documents intended for those who read English as their second language must be unusually simple, unambiguous, and literal. Ideally, they should be edited for ease of translation."[3] The most important rules are:

- Always assume that the person for whom English is a second language is relying on a dictionary for some words. That means that the meaning of the word used should always be (one of) the first one(s) in the dictionary and should always be unambiguous. For example: "The company sales took off 25 percent last year" should be replaced with "The company sales increased 25 percent last year," for several reasons. First, "to take" is probably one of the longest entries in the English dictionary and the meaning of "to take off" is listed way down in that entry. Another reason is that one of the first meanings listed of "to take off" is "to remove (one's clothes)"; therefore there is a strong possibility that the sentence will be understood as "sales *decreased* 25 percent." A convenience sample of foreign students reinforced this point; about 30 percent of them thought it meant a decrease. By using a precise and accurate word, "to increase," no confusion is possible. This recommendation is often contrary to the common caution to write in "simple words." In practicality, more complex words tend to be more precise and have limited alternative meanings, and therefore they are better for international English communication.

- Always proofread carefully and avoid all grammatical and spelling errors. There is a strong possibility of confusion in a sentence that reads, "The customer purchases products from company A and it's marketing services form company B." The reader is left to determine whether there are two typos or just one. Is it that the customer

International English
A technique of written communication in the English language that consists of removing all possible ambiguities, so that the communication can be understood by someone with a limited knowledge of English.

purchases products from company A and marketing services from company B, or is it that it is purchasing products from company A and providing marketing services to (for) company B? Actually, a non-native speaker would probably not understand that there are possible typos in that sentence and not "get it" at all (a correct international English sentence would have used "understand" a second time, rather than "get," even if stylistically poor; the meaning is what matters). Other common misspellings result from the confusion between *there, they're,* and *their*; between *accept* and *except*; and between *effect* and *affect*. Then there is also the frequently found "should of done..." instead of "should have done...," which is only understandable to a native speaker who "hears" English rather than reads it.

- Always make sure that quantitative information will be understood without doubt. A date of 06/12/05 can be understood three different ways: A U.S. reader will understand it as June 12, 2005; a French reader will read it as 6 décembre 2005; and a Chinese reader will understand it as the 5th of December 2006. It is best to follow the practice of spelling all dates fully: 12 June 2005 is unambiguous. A number of 10^9 is one billion to a North American reader, but 1,000 million (or a milliard) to a British or German reader, for whom a billion is 10^{12}, while 10^9 is 100 krore to an Indian. Writing the full number is always the best strategy.

- Always use simple and short sentences. As much as possible, the sentences should contain only one main idea. If there are possible "shortcuts," they should be avoided; for example, "The company requests the report be sent early in the month" should be changed to "The company requests *that* the report *should* be sent between the first and the fifth day of the month." When in doubt, punctuation should be added to enhance clarification, even if it seems too heavily punctuated to a native speaker.

- Never use idioms that are sport- or military-related, as they are rarely, if ever, understood properly. Writing that a salesperson "struck out" on a deal, or that she "hit a home run" will confuse a foreigner, who, in looking it up in the dictionary will read that she "ran around the bases with one hit."[4] A correct sentence conveying the same meaning would say that she was "unsuccessful" or "successful beyond our expectations." Military terminology should also be avoided. Terms such as "plan of attack" or "price war" tend to be difficult to translate or off-putting to some cultures.[5]

The main purpose of International English is that communication should be easy to understand and devoid of cultural references. One of the most effective ways to determine whether a particular message is written clearly enough to be understood by a foreign reader is to translate it using machine-translation software into another language (preferably one that is not a European language) and translate it back into English. It will rarely, if ever, be the same as the original text; however, if its original meaning is still understandable, then the text was written in an English that can be properly understood by a non-native speaker.

Web Exercise

Use the following websites to translate words or phrases into different languages. Translate and then back-translate some of the sentences used in this section. Compare in particular those that were used as examples of poor communication and those that were written in proper International English.

- www.babelfish.altavista.com
- www.systransoft.com
- www.google.com/language_tools

16-3 Special English

For communications conducted orally, the challenge is much greater as there is less time to refine the sentences used and to make sure that the meaning is clear. It is important to realize that one of the greatest difficulties experienced by a non-native speaker (of any language) is to work on the telephone. There are no visual cues that help communication and, on occasion, there are technical difficulties that hamper good communication.

In order to communicate clearly in English with foreigners, it is useful to become familiar with "**Special English**," a reduced-vocabulary English developed by the *Voice of America*, the U.S. government-sponsored news organization that broadcasts worldwide. While the *Voice of America* is prohibited from broadcasting in the United States,[6] it is possible to hear its broadcast on the Internet.[7] Here are the main characteristics of Special English:

- Sentences should be short and contain only one idea. It is more effective to use two sentences ("Sentences should be short. Sentences should contain only one idea.") than to confuse the listener, who is trying to understand a particular word or sentence structure and cannot remember how the sentence started. It takes a little practice, but it is certainly easy to learn to speak in such a way.

- The vocabulary should be limited to correct and accurate terms. All sorts of sports-related imagery exists in American English, but it should be avoided; stating that a contract negotiation is still "in the first inning" or that the companies competing for a particular sale are "not on a level playing field" is unlikely to ever be understood by a non-native speaker of English. The same is true of terms such as "stand up to" or "roll over," which should be replaced with their precise equivalents: "confront" or "reinvest." Even expressions that are clearly understood in one English-speaking country can be difficult for others: "carrying coals to Newcastle" makes as little sense to U.S. English speakers as "selling refrigerators to Eskimos" makes to Australians.

- The speed at which the sentences are spoken should be slower. The *Voice of America* broadcasts aim for two-thirds of the speed of normal speech. From personal experience, people from the southern part of the United States are much more easily understood than people from the north because they tend to speak at a slower pace. The "accent" is much less of an issue for foreigners, who tend to visualize the words as they are spoken.

- Finally, if a foreigner asks a native speaker to repeat a sentence, the native speaker should not repeat the sentence louder, as if the person had difficulty hearing. The issue is generally about a word that the listener did not understand or a sentence that was too complicated. It is best to just repeat the sentence using slightly different vocabulary or repeat the sentence and offer an alternative word. For example, "Our company would like to sleep on that proposal for a few days" (a sentence that violates the principle listed above, and is likely to be misunderstood) can be repeated as "Our company would like to sleep on that proposal, think about it, for a few days." In this manner, the non-native speaker better understands the sentence and gains a new bit of vocabulary.

Special English A technique of oral communication in the English language that consists of a limited vocabulary and of simplified sentences, so that the communication can be understood by someone with a limited knowledge of English.

16-4 Metric System

Communication is also better served by using what is familiar. Unfortunately for United States exporters and importers, they are using a system of measures that *no*

Calculating Conversions

There are substantial differences between the effort extended by a shipper using the metric system and that of a shipper using the English system. Two juice manufacturers, one American, the other European, need to decide whether an identical shipment of juice boxes can fit in a forty-foot container. Will the shipment weigh less than the maximum allowable weight? Will it physically fit inside the box?

Both shipments are made of 5,000 cartons of twenty-four "standard" juice boxes.

The American shipper must first determine what the weight would be of this shipment of juice boxes, each containing seven fluid ounces of apple juice. Ignoring the fact that apple juice has a slightly higher density than water, and having found that one fluid ounce weighs 1.04 *avoirdupois* ounce, he determines that each juice box weighs 7.28 ounces. The total weight of the shipment is therefore 5,000 × 24 × 7.28 = 873,600 ounces. Because a pound is sixteen ounces, he then divides that result by sixteen to obtain the total shipment's weight of 54,600 lbs. Will that shipment fit in a container whose maximum capacity is 26.29 long tons? He needs to divide 54,600 lbs by 2,240 and ends up with 24.375 long tons. Even accounting for the additional weight of packaging and dunnage, it is well within the container's weight limit.

Each juice box measures 1 5/8 in by 2 ½ in by 3 ½ in. Will this shipment fit in a regular forty-foot container whose inside measurements are 39 feet 6 in long by 7 feet 8 1/8 in wide by 7 feet 5 $^3/_4$ in high? The shipper must first determine the volume of each juice box: 1.625 × 2.5 × 3.5 = 14 cubic inches. Then, he determines the volume of the entire shipment: 5,000 × 24 × 14 = 1,680,000 cubic inches. Finally he needs to determine the volume of the container, and, for that, needs to calculate how many inches there are in each dimension: 39 feet 6 in is (39 × 12) + 6 in or 474 in

in length, 7 feet 8 1/8 in is (7 × 12) + 8.125 in or 92.125 in in width, and 7 feet 5 $^3/_4$ in is (7 × 12) + 5.75 in or 89.75 in in height. The entire volume of the container is therefore 3,919,136 cubic inches. The shipment of 1,680,000 cubic inches fits without problem, even accounting for the space taken by packaging and dunnage. Converting those dimensions to feet and calculating in cubic feet does not simplify the task at all.

Using a similar shipment, the European shipper can make these calculations much faster: The capacity of each juice box is 205 ml and therefore it weighs 205 g, if the slightly higher density of juice is ignored. The total shipment weighs 5,000 × 24 × 205 g = 24,600,000 g or 24.6 tonnes. Because the capacity of the container is 26.72 tonnes, there is no issue, even after packaging and dunnage are added.

The dimensions of each juice box are 4.1 cm by 6.3 cm by 8.9 cm. Each box therefore has a volume of 230 cm^3. (This is more than the volume of the juice itself, which is 205 cm^3, and that is due to the fact that the juice boxes tend to have sides that are slightly concave. This was also the case for the American juice boxes, but was unnoticeable because of the measure of units used.) The entire shipment is therefore 27,600,000 cm^3 or 27.6 m^3. The container is the same container, with inside dimensions of 1,204 cm (L) by 234 cm (W) by 228 cm (H). Its total volume is 1,204 × 234 × 228 = 64,235,808 cm^3 or 64.23 m^3, and therefore the shipment fits without difficulty, even after the packaging and dunnage are added.

Unless he knew it by heart, the American shipper needed a dictionary to find out that a fluid ounce weighs 1.04 oz and that a long ton is 2,240 lbs. He also needed a piece of paper to keep it all straight, as well as a calculator. The European shipper only needed a calculator.

---

one else uses,** and which is actually difficult for people who use it every day to understand. Foreigners tend to be entirely baffled by the U.S. system of measurement.

For example, within the English system of measures, there are three types of tons (the short ton, which is a measure of weight and weighs 2,000 lbs.; the long ton, also a measure of weight at 2,240 lbs; and the gross registered ton, which is a measure of volume and equal to 100 cubic feet), and there is often no indication of which ton is the "correct" one. Only "tradition" dictates which "ton" is the one that is intended.

Measurement can get much more complicated: There are five types of ounces (an *avoirdupois* weight unit weighing 437.5 grains; an apothecary or Troy weight unit weighing 480 grains; a U.S. fluid ounce, which is a measure of volume worth six teaspoons; its "equivalent" regulatory fluid ounce, which is defined as 30ml[8] or 1.5 percent more than a U.S. fluid ounce; and finally an Imperial fluid ounce, which is 4

**That is not exactly correct. There are two other countries that are not using the metric system: Liberia and Myanmar, both of which are minor world traders.

percent smaller than the U.S. unit), and there is generally no indication of which unit is the correct one in a document. If this were not enough, there are "traditional" units in some industry that use the same terminology very differently. For example, leather is measured in the United States in "ounces," which, in this case, is a measure not of weight, but of thickness: "Two-ounce leather such as calf or goat skin is about 1/32 inches thick, while 8 oz. leather is a full 1/8 inches."[9]

It is therefore to the advantage of everyone involved in a transaction to use the **metric system**, which has a very well-defined set of measures, all of which are clearly and accurately established. A kilogram is a measure of mass, a liter is a measure of volume, and a meter is a measure of distance. There are convenient ways to "cross" from one unit set to the next: One liter is exactly equal to a cube of side 0.1 meter (10^{-3} cubic meters), and a kilogram is equal to the mass of water contained in a liter. There are conventions for the name of multiples (kilo, hecto, deka) and for the names of fractions (deci, centi, and milli), all of which are decimal. More importantly, there are no ambiguous usages.

While this utilization of the metric system may represent a challenge for a U.S. exporter or importer, its customers or suppliers will understand much better what it intends to communicate, and this effort will result in a greater probability of making a sale.

Converting to the metric system, though, is more than just multiplying by the correct coefficient: Selling a product in 3.785 liter bottles (equivalent to one U.S. gallon) does not satisfy the admonition to use the metric system; while it's a convenient conversion of a common English unit, it is an unusual unit of volume for a person used to the metric system, for whom products are generally sold in one- or two-liter bottles. A correct conversion would therefore use round units of measurement rather than direct "translations" of round units in the English system into awkward units in the metric system.

> **metric system** A decimal measuring system developed in the late eighteenth century. Widely adopted worldwide, it is not commonly used in the United States.

16-5 Cultural Sensitivity

Although using International English and the metric system to convey information clearly are already great ways to become a better international logistician, it is also very valuable to become savvier about others' cultures. Unfortunately, if there is one aspect of international business about which it is difficult to generalize, it is culture. There is little to culture that can be pinpointed in a few sentences, and, when such an attempt is made, exceptions abound. In the long run, the best that an international logistician can do would be to study intercultural communication; in the meantime, however, a few of these pointers can help.

One aspect of communication that is shaped by culture is the way people address each other in person, in the mail, or over the telephone. In some cultures, the forms of address are quite formal (France), and in some others (Australia), quite informal. In some cultures, people are very sensitive to titles (Germany), in others much less (Canada). The United States culture is among the ones that care the least about titles and formalities, although there are a few notable exceptions to that "rule." In all cases, because it is difficult to offend someone by being too formal, an astute international logistics manager will therefore always err on the side of **formality**, and communicate as politely and formally as possible until there is evidence that it is appropriate to adopt a less formal tone.

Another area in which it is easy to make quick progress is in understanding the work culture of a country. First the international logistician should consider the separation between work and private life. In some countries, there is a considerable divide between work and family, and the two never or rarely intersect (Japan). In others, the two are closely tied to one another (Indonesia). When in doubt, it is generally better to consider that personal life and work life are separate, unless there is evidence on the part of the foreign interlocutor that it is appropriate to mention family and private life in business communications.

> **formality** A way for a person to interact with other individuals that uses conventions and regimented forms of address.

Another area in which there are culturally determined differences is the speed at which people operate in the workplace. In some countries, it is expected of business persons to answer an inquiry very quickly, in order to show that the inquiry is important and that it commands their full attention (Germany). A delay portrays a lack of interest. In others, it is impolite to answer too quickly, as a response should be given careful thought (Saudi Arabia). There is no specific ideal way to handle these discrepancies, but the advice for an international logistician is, again, to learn what is the appropriate response time from what his or her foreign counterpart does and mirror that behavior.

Finally, culture influences the way people spend their workday: the time at which they arrive at work, leave work in the evening, and eat during the day. Culture also influences the amount of time that they spend at each meal and the days of the week that they work. Finally, it influences the different holidays that are celebrated. Countries have different holidays, and different customs during the same holidays. Sometimes it is appropriate for an exporter or importer to send a card or a greeting; in others, it is not. In those cases, the *Culturegrams*[10] mentioned in Chapter 1 are most useful. In any case, for the international logistician, a delayed response to a request on a certain day may simply be due to a holiday rather than a lack of interest. Considering that India, due to its multiplicity of religions, has a total of forty-three official holidays, it is more likely than not that there is some celebration during a given week.

16-6 Specific Advice

In addition to the general advice presented so far, the international logistician has the opportunity to gain a competitive advantage by following a number of strategies in specific areas. Some of these strategies were presented in earlier chapters, but they bear repeating.

16-6a Terms of Payment

Although the choice of the term of sale is dependent on the level of experience of both the exporter and the importer and on the level of confidence that the exporter has in the ability of the importer to make the payment, there are some alternatives that are definitely preferable and will increase an exporter's probability to clinch the sale.

An importer, in most situations, is getting several possible quotes from several exporters located in different countries. Alternative bids are evaluated on a large number of criteria (price, specific capabilities, after-sale service, delivery terms, and so on), and on the ease with which the purchase transaction will take place. From the importer's perspective, the easiest alternative is to purchase on an Open Account basis. It is likely that at least one of the potential suppliers will offer such terms, and that others will ask for a Letter of Credit or a Documentary Collection. Therefore, the supplier offering an Open Account transaction has an advantage over the others. If that supplier has purchased credit insurance, that decision does not affect its probability of getting paid.

Therefore, an exporter intent on increasing its sales should choose to display that it is confident in the ability of the importer to pay for the goods by using an Open Account. If it is unsure about the ability of the importer to pay, it should consider purchasing a credit insurance policy.

16-6b Currency of Payment

In an international transaction, the choice of the currency exposes the exporter (or the importer) to the risk of currency exchange rate fluctuation. Rather than consider this risk to be a drawback in an international sale, a good exporter should consider it an opportunity and take advantage of the several alternatives it has to reduce its risk of currency fluctuation.

Because of the intense competition that an exporter faces in international markets, it is very likely that a significant percentage of the companies competing for the importer's business will offer quotes in the importer's currency. Because it is easier for the importer to handle a purchase in its own currency, it would place an exporter at a strategic disadvantage not to quote in that currency.

An exporter intent on increasing its sales abroad should therefore offer (all of its) quotes in the importer's currency and discuss with its banker the most appropriate hedging strategy for that particular transaction.

16-6c Incoterms

In some cases, a strategic advantage can be gained by an exporter willing to facilitate the sale of its products by assisting a novice importer in the handling of a shipment. In others, a price advantage may be obtained by an experienced importer willing to perform all or most of the tasks involved in the shipment.

Generally speaking, an exporter does not like to determine which Incoterm to use on a case-by-case basis. It adopts a "policy" to include in international quotes those services that it feels competent providing. It is difficult for an exporter to adapt its Incoterm strategy to accommodate the requirements of an importer, as it may require the exporter to be responsible for tasks that it has decided it would rather not perform. However, should the importer want to perform more tasks than what the exporter prefers, it is certainly possible for the exporter to do *less* than what it expected, and use a different Incoterm on that transaction, one for which it is responsible for less.

An exporter intent on increasing its sales should therefore offer to provide the importer with the most customer-friendly Incoterm quotes (either DDU or DDP), and, if necessary, use the services of a competent freight forwarder. Should the importer want to shoulder more responsibilities, it is always possible for the exporter to reduce its involvement and quote FCA or even EXW. The best type of quote would be one in which the exporter lists different prices for different Incoterms, leaving the importer with the decision to choose which is best for its specific case.

For example, a quote could read:

- EXW Cleveland, Ohio: $10,000
- FCA Cincinnati Airport: Covington, Kentucky: $11,000
- CIP Paris, France: $15,500
- DDU Clermont-Ferrand, France: $16,500
- DDP Clermont-Ferrand, France: $17,800

and leave the customer to decide which of the Incoterms it would like to choose.

16-6d Document Preparation

Accurate and timely document preparation and delivery are an essential part of international logistics and of the smooth transfer of goods from an exporter to an importer.

Any failure to provide complete documents in a timely manner is likely to delay a shipment, generate additional costs by requiring last-minute mailings of critical documents, or create "headaches" for one or more of the parties involved in the transaction. Because the responsibility of proper document preparation falls mostly on the exporter, regardless of the Incoterm used in a transaction, an exporter can turn its ability to do a good and thorough job in this aspect of international logistics into a marketing advantage.

An exporter intent on increasing its sales should therefore be thorough and meticulous in the way it prepares the documents that it provides to the importer. This should be reflected in the first contact, the *pro-forma* invoice, and be communicated to the importer by emphasizing the experience of the company at providing accurate and thorough documents.

16-6e Packaging

Good handling of the packaging requirements by the exporter will also help considerably in the smooth transfer of goods from the exporter to the importer.

The most important way of looking at packaging is to prepare for the worst. The exporter should truly imagine the worst-case scenarios and the roughest possible journey in packaging the goods that it ships at export. It is only under this premise that it will adequately serve the needs of the importer to receive goods in sellable and usable conditions.

Although good packaging procedures are expensive, the benefits are substantial. First, they allow the goods to arrive in perfect shape to their destination and be immediately sellable or usable by the importer. Good packaging also reduces the costs of repackaging or the costs of damaged goods. In addition, because poor packaging is always a "defense" used by insurance companies, it "pays" to have a track record of stellar packaging.

However, the greatest benefits from such a good packaging policy are the good-will that it generates between the importer and the exporter, and the marketing benefits that can be derived from it. Because the importer is obviously not interested in having to challenge invoices or having to ask for allowances for goods that were damaged in transit, it welcomes shipments that arrive packaged carefully.

Careful packaging, meticulous document preparation, and considerate choices in terms of payment and Incoterm selection will enhance the relationship between exporter and importer through goodwill and trust. Learning and understanding these skills will help an international logistician gain a substantial **competitive advantage**.

competitive advantage
A situation in which a company has acquired competencies and knowledge that give it an advantage over its competitors.

Key Terms

competitive advantage (p. 368)   International English (p. 361)   Special English (p. 363)
formality (p. 365)   metric system (p. 365)

Review and Discussion Questions

1. What are the advantages of learning to use International English and Special English in communicating with non-native speakers of English?

2. What are the advantages of using the metric system in international commerce?

3. What are the trade-offs between utilizing a standardized policy and remaining flexible for an exporter? You can choose either terms of payment or Incoterms to illustrate your points.

4. In your opinion, why is it important for an exporter to sell in the currency of the importer's country?

5. What are the advantages of having an "environmentally friendly" packaging policy for an exporter?

Endnotes

1. Adapted from "Language Learning Difficulty for English Speakers," National Virtual Translation Center, http://www.nvtc.gov/lotw/months/november/learningExpectations.html, August 15, 2006.

2. Weiss, Edmond H., *The Elements of International English Style; A Guide to Writing Correspondence, Reports, Technical Documents, Internet Pages for a Global Audience*, M.E. Sharpe Inc., Armonk, New York, 2005.

3. *Ibid*

4. *New College German Dictionary, German-English, English-German*, Langerscheidt, 1973.

5. Beamer, Linda, and Iris Varner, *Intercultural Communication in the Global Workplace*, McGraw-Hill-Irwin, New York, New York, 2001.

6. Chmela, Holli, "A Language to Air News of America to the World," *The New York Times*, July 31, 2006.

7. Special English News, Voice of America, http://www.voanews.com/specialenglish.

8. http://a257.g.akamaitech.net/7/257//01apr20051500/edocket.access.gpo.gov/cfr_2005/aprqtr/pdf/21cfr101.9.pdf.

9. "Leather and Leatherworking Tips," Legio XX Online Handbook, http://www.larp.com/legioxx/leather.html.

10. *Culturegrams*, http://culturegram.stores.yahoo.net/incul.html.

Glossary

absolute advantage An economic theory, developed by Adam Smith, that holds that when a nation can produce a certain type of goods more efficiently than other countries, it is in its best interest to manufacture more of those goods than it needs, and trade with countries that produce other goods more efficiently than that nation can.

acceptance The second step in the formation of a contract. After an offer has been made by one of the parties, the contract is formed if the other party accepts the terms of the offer. Under the Convention on Contracts for the International Sale of Goods (CISG), the second party must completely agree with all the terms presented in the offer; otherwise, it is a rejection of the offer. Under the United States' Uniform Commercial Code (UCC), however, the second party is considered to have accepted the offer if it generally agrees with its terms, even if it wants amendments to the quantity of the goods purchased, the delivery dates, and so on.

actuarial tables Tables used by insurance companies that illustrate the exact probability, based upon historical data, of a particular peril.

advertising A marketing term that includes all of the techniques that a firm uses to promote its products by using communication media, such as television, radio, and print. In advertising, the company retains total control over the content of the communication.

Advising Bank In a Letter of Credit transaction, the bank that determines whether the Issuing Bank is a legitimate bank, and whether the terms of the Letter of Credit offered by the issuing bank on behalf of the importer are appropriate. Generally, the Advising Bank is the exporter's regular bank, but in some cases, the exporter's bank will delegate this role to another bank that is more experienced in international trade.

air waybill A bill of lading used in the transportation of goods by air, domestically or internationally. An air waybill is always straight.

airfreighter An aircraft entirely dedicated to the transport of cargo. An airfreighter is either an aircraft that was originally designed as such, or a former passenger aircraft that was retrofitted as an airfreighter.

airline A company that provides regularly scheduled air transportation services for passengers or freight.

amendment A change to a Letter of Credit to which all parties to a Letter of Credit agree: the exporter, the importer, the Issuing Bank, and the Advising Bank. In general, amendments are only made if there are discrepancies, as every amendment costs the exporter and importer money.

applicant The firm asking the Issuing Bank for a Letter of Credit. Usually, the applicant is the importer.

arbitration A process by which the parties to a contract can settle a dispute, involving a panel of arbitrators who will follow most of the rules of a Court of Law, but will render a decision in a much shorter period of time. In an international contract dispute, the arbitrators will follow the laws specified in the "Choice of Law" clause. Arbitration tends to be much cheaper than litigation.

arbitration panel A group of (generally) three arbitrators who are empowered by the parties involved in a contract dispute to reach a decision on the facts of the dispute, and whose decision is binding on all parties. Generally, each of the parties chooses one arbitrator, and the third is chosen by a neutral party.

artificial currency A currency that is not in circulation. After the euro was changed into a circulating currency on January 1, 2002, the only artificial currency left was the Special Drawing Rights of the International Monetary Fund. Its value is determined by the value of a basket of four currencies: the euro (approximately 34 percent of the SDR's value), the Japanese yen (approximately 11 percent), the U.S. dollar (approximately 44 percent), and the British pound (approximately 11 percent).

assist An item provided by the importer (customer) to the exporter (seller) so that the exporter can manufacture the goods: a mold or a dye, for example. The value of an assist must be included in the valuation of the imported goods for U.S. Customs' purposes.

aval In a Documentary Collection transaction, the fact that a Presenting Bank is willing to sign the draft on behalf of the importer. An aval's existence is based on the creditworthiness of the importer.

average A loss incurred on an ocean voyage by a cargo owner. It can be further qualified as a Particular Average or as a General Average.

bale The end result of a packaging technique that consists of taking a commodity and unitizing it by compressing it and placing it into a bag or encircling it with string, metal, or plastic bands. Bales are used to transport cargo that is difficult to ship unless compressed: wool, cotton, tobacco, used clothing, scrap paper, and recycled plastic bottles or aluminum cans.

bank guarantee A contract from a bank where the bank guarantees that an exporter will perform as required by its contract with the importer. If the exporter does not perform, the bank pays a compensation to the importer. Most bank guarantees are not documentary, which means that the bank must pay without specific evidence. In other words, it pays first, and argues with the firm to which it provided a guarantee later. Bank guarantees are illegal in the United States.

banker's acceptance In a Documentary Collection transaction, the alternative where the exporter is not certain the importer will readily accept signing a draft after being notified by the Presenting Bank that the documents have arrived. It therefore asks the Presenting Bank to "accept" the draft on behalf of the importer. Generally, this is not possible without an aval from the bank.

bareboat or demise charter A lease agreement (also called a charter party) between the owner (lessor) of a bulk cargo ship and a lessee, in which the owner provides the lessee with only the ship, and no other services or supplies. See *voyage charter* and *time charter* for alternative charter party agreements for ships.

barges Flat-bottomed boats designed to carry cargo on rivers and canals, and that are designed to be pushed or pulled. Some of the barges used on the rivers and canals of Europe are self-propelled.

barratry An act of disobedience or willful misconduct by the captain or the crew of a ship that causes damage to the ship or the cargo.

beneficiary The firm named in a Letter of Credit as the firm to whom the bank is insuring payment if the importer does not pay. Usually, the beneficiary of a Letter of Credit is the exporter.

berth The location, in a port, where a ship is loaded and unloaded.

Bespoke Names In the Lloyd's of London vernacular, the individuals who take on the risks insured by syndicates, and who have unlimited liability for those risks on their personal assets.

bill of exchange In a Documentary Collection transaction, another term for a draft.

bill of lading A generic term used to describe a document issued by the carrier to the shipper. A bill of lading is: 1. a contract between the carrier and the shipper where the carrier agrees to deliver the goods for an agreed-upon price to an agreed-upon destination; 2. a receipt for the goods, where the carrier certifies that it received the goods in good condition from the shipper; and 3. a Certificate of Title, where the party in possession of the original bill of lading is the owner of the goods.

binding agent An agent that can make decisions that are binding on the principal; the principal must abide by whatever statements the representative has made.

binding ruling A determination, made by the United States Customs, and only applicable to the United States, that classifies a specific product and assigns it a tariff rate, before the goods are imported. The ruling is binding on the United States Customs, which means that it cannot "change its mind" after the product is imported.

breach In the event that one of the parties to a contract does not meet its obligation, that party can be found to have broken the terms of the contract, or to be in breach of the contract. If the party did not fulfill its obligations because of an event beyond its control, the nonperformance can be excused under the *force majeure* clause.

break-bulk cargo Cargo that is unitized in a box or crate, and that is placed directly into the hold of a ship. It is generally too large or too heavy to be placed in a container.

bunker The amount of fuel that a ship carries on board and that it needs to travel.

cabotage An ocean trade consisting of shipping between ports located in the same country.

call options See *currency options*.

carrier The transportation company that will provide transportation services to the shipper.

Certificate of Analysis A document provided by an independent inspection company that attests that the goods conform to the chemical description and purity levels contained in the invoice provided by the exporter. A Certificate of Analysis is always obtained by the exporter in the exporting country before the international voyage takes place.

Certificate of Certification A document provided by an independent inspection company that attests that the goods conform to the manufacturing standards of the importing country. A Certificate of Certification is always obtained by the exporter in the exporting country before the international voyage takes place.

Certificate of Conformity Another term for a Certificate of Certification. See *Certificate of Certification*.

Certificate of End-Use A document required by some export governments in the case of sensitive exports, such as ammunition, to ensure that the product is used for acceptable (to the exporting country's government) purposes. It is provided by the importing country's government.

Certificate of Free Sale A certificate that attests that the product that is exported conforms to all of the regulations in place in the exporting country and that it can be sold freely in the exporting country.

Certificate of Inspection A document provided by an independent inspection company that attests that the goods conform to the description contained in the invoice provided by the exporter. A Certificate of Inspection can also attest that the value of the goods is reflected accurately on the invoice. A Certificate of Inspection is always obtained by the exporter in the exporting country before the international voyage takes place. Such an inspection is called a Pre-Shipment Inspection (PSI).

Certificate of Insurance A document provided by the insurance company of the exporter that attests that the goods are insured during their international voyage. This certificate is only obtained at the request of the importer, and for transactions under certain Incoterm Terms of Trade, such as CIF and CIP.

Certificate of Manufacture A document provided by the exporter's Chamber of Commerce that attests that the goods were manufactured in the country in which the exporter is located.

Certificate of Origin A document provided by the exporter's Chamber of Commerce that attests that the goods originated from the country in which the exporter is located.

charter airplane An aircraft that is leased for a single voyage (or a limited number of voyages) under a wet lease. It can be a passenger or a freighter airplane.

charter party A type of contract of carriage between a carrier and a shipper, in which the shipper uses all or most of the carrying capacity of the ship to transport commodities such as oil, ore, grain, or polymer pellets.

classification The process of determining what the correct Harmonized System number is for an import. There are six rules of interpretation to help determine the correct classification.

Classification Society A company that is responsible for determining the seaworthiness of a particular vessel. It places a ship in a specific "class" as a function of its age, maintenance records, and the availability of on-board equipment. The premium paid by the ship's owners for hull insurance is based on its class.

clean bill of lading A bill of lading that reflects the fact that the carrier received the goods in good condition. It is characterized by the presence of only a signature of the carrier's representative, and nothing else. All Letters of Credit require a clean bill of lading. See *soiled bill of lading*.

cleared The term used to signify that goods were imported in a country and that the importer paid the duty that was due on those goods: The goods were released by the Customs authorities.

cluster An observation, first made by Michael E. Porter, that a firm can develop a substantial competitive advantage in manufacturing certain goods when a large number of its competitors and suppliers are located in close proximity, because the area then attracts the most talented employees and the extraordinary competition between the firms generates a greater need to innovate and become efficient. Such a grouping of companies is called a cluster.

combi airplane A type of airplane that is designed to carry both passengers and cargo on the main deck of the plane; generally, the front of the plane is equipped to accommodate passengers, and the rear is equipped to accommodate cargo. A combi airplane cannot carry certain hazardous cargo.

commercial invoice The invoice sent by the seller to the buyer, detailing the goods purchased and the amount due; a bill. In international trade, a commercial invoice should be quite detailed and include all of the pertinent information.

commercial risk The probability of not getting paid by a certain creditor, because this creditor does not have the funds to pay the debt or because the creditor refuses to pay the debt.

Commodity Control List A list, maintained by the Bureau of Industry and Security, that details which products cannot be exported from the United States without the express authorization of the U.S. government. Such express authorization is called an Export License.

comparative advantage An economic theory, developed by Robert Torrens and David Ricardo, that holds that nations will trade with one another as long as they can produce certain goods relatively more efficiently than one another.

competing lines In a contract between a principal and an agent or distributor, competing lines are products manufactured by a company other than the principal that compete with the products manufactured by the principal.

competitive advantage A situation in which a company has acquired competencies and knowledge that give it an advantage over its competitors.

conference A group of shipping companies (carriers) that operate vessels competing in the same trade lanes, and that have legally agreed to not compete on price and charge the same amount for the same type of cargo and the same voyage.

confidentiality In a contract between two parties, the promise by each of the parties to not divulge what it has learned about the other party's customers, manufacturing processes, and business practices.

Confirmed Letter of Credit A payment alternative in which the exporter asks a bank to provide an additional level of payment security to a Letter of Credit; should the importer not pay and should the Issuing Bank not pay, the Confirming Bank will pay.

Confirming Bank The bank providing an additional level of payment security to the beneficiary of a Letter of Credit; the Confirming Bank certifies that it will pay the Letter of Credit if the importer and the Issuing Bank do not pay.

consignee The party named on a bill of lading as the owner of the goods, or, at least, as the party to whom the goods should be surrendered at their destination. The consignee will have the original bill of lading at the point of arrival of the goods.

consular invoice A commercial invoice that is printed on stationery provided by the Consulate of the country in which the goods will be imported. The Consulate sells that stationery. Some Consular invoices need to be *visa*-ed by the Consulate as well.

container A large metal box used in international shipments that can be loaded directly onto a truck, a railroad car, or an oceangoing vessel. The most common dimensions of containers are 8 × 8 × 20 feet and 8 × 8 × 40 feet.

Container Security Initiative A program instituted by the U.S. Customs and Border Protection Agency, through which Customs agents are sent to the port of departure to inspect containers bound for the United States. Such containers are selected through screening or through suspicious activity flagged by the twenty-four-hour rule.

contract law A set of a country's laws that governs relationships and disputes between the parties who signed a contract. Contract Law essentially dictates that the Courts must settle the dispute by using the terms of the contract.

contractor When used in the context of a bank guarantee, a company fulfilling a large construction contract, usually the construction of a substantial infrastructure work or a major project.

convertible currency   A currency that can be converted into another currency. A convertible currency can be a hard currency (easy to convert) or a soft currency (not so easy to convert), but it can be converted.

Correspondent Bank   A foreign bank with which a domestic bank has a preferred business relationship.

corrugated cardboard box   A type of box made of paper fibers in which two flat sheets are glued to both sides of a "wall" made of a sinusoidally shaped sheet. If there is only one wall, it is called a "single wall" corrugated cardboard box; if there are two walls, it's a "double wall" box, and if three walls, it's a "triple wall" box.

counterfeit goods   Goods that appear to have been produced by the legitimate manufacturer, but were actually produced by another company intent on deceiving customers and imitating the genuine goods. Counterfeit goods are generally sold for a much lower price than the authentic goods.

counteroffer   An intermediary step in the formation of a contract. After an offer has been made by one of the parties, the other party may not agree with all of the terms of the offer, and may want to modify them. Under the Convention on Contracts for the International Sale of Goods (CISG), this response is construed as a counteroffer. Under the United States' Uniform Commercial Code (UCC), however, it is an acceptance of the offer.

country risk   See *political risk*.

crate   A wooden box made especially for a product to be shipped break-bulk because it does not fit into a container, or because the exporter deems that an additional level of protection is necessary.

credit insurance   An insurance policy under which commercial risk is covered; in exchange for a premium paid by the exporter, the insurance company will bear the risk of non-payment by the importer, deducting a slight percentage of the receivable. Credit insurance does not cover political risks, unless the exporter has explicitly asked for additional political coverage that is obtained through the Ex-Im Bank.

currency   The monetary unit used in a particular country for economic transactions (examples include the dollar in the United States, the British pound in the United Kingdom, the euro in Europe, and the yen in Japan).

currency block   A group of currencies whose values fluctuate in parallel fashion. The currencies within the group have a fixed exchange rate, but their exchange rates with currencies outside of the group float.

currency futures   A method used to trade currencies; the value of a fixed quantity of foreign currency for delivery at a fixed point in the future is determined by market forces. These currencies are traded as are other commodities' futures. In the United States, they are traded on the Chicago Mercantile Exchange.

currency options   A method used to speculate on the value of a currency in the future. A firm can purchase options to buy (called call options) or options to sell (called put options) a particular currency at a particular price, called the strike price, on a given date. Because the complexity of the options' market is substantial, the reader is advised to learn a lot more about this alternative before venturing into the options market.

Custom-Trade Partnership Against Terrorism (C-TPAT)   A program instituted by the U.S. Customs and Border Protection Agency, through which Customs gives preferential treatment to companies who have implemented a number of security measures in their supply chains. The shipments of companies participating in the C-TPAT program are less frequently inspected and are cleared faster than those of companies that are not participating in the program.

damp lease   A damp lease is an agreement between the owner (lessor) of an aircraft and the lessee, under which the owner provides some services in addition to the aircraft itself. For example, a damp lease could include the aircraft, maintenance, and insurance, but not the crew, which would need to be hired by the lessee.

date draft   In a Documentary Collection transaction, a date draft is a promissory note that the importer has to pay a number of days (thirty, sixty, ninety, or 180 days) after the exporter ships the goods. Because the exporter controls the date at which the goods are shipped, the draft is called a "date" draft because the date the payment is due is known ahead of time. This is in contrast to a time draft, where the importer controls the date of payment by controlling the date at which it signs the promissory note. A date draft is used in the Documentary Collection called Documents against Acceptance.

dead-weight tonnage (dwt)   The maximum weight that a ship can carry. Because the ship also carries bunker and stores, the maximum weight that a ship can actually carry is lower than its dead-weight tonnage.

Destination Control Statement   A formal statement, which an exporter has to print on its invoice and on the Shipper's Export Declaration if the goods shipped are subject to a validated export license: "This merchandise licensed by U.S. for ultimate destination [country]; diversion contrary to U.S. law prohibited."

direct quote   The value of a foreign currency expressed in units of the domestic currency; for example, the euro is worth $0.9917 as of November 15, 2002. Some currencies are traditionally expressed as direct quotes.

discrepancy   A difference between the documents required by the Letter of Credit and the documents provided by the exporter. A discrepancy can be as simple as a misspelling and as significant as a change in the invoice amount. Because Letters of Credit are documentary, any discrepancy is, in theory, a violation of the terms of the Letter of Credit and therefore invalidates it. In practice, however, 50 percent of Letters of Credit have discrepancies, which are resolved through amendments.

displacement tonnage   The total weight of the ship, when fully loaded, measured by using the weight of the water being displaced.

distribution contract   An agreement between an exporter and an intermediary; it can take the form of either an agency or a distributorship agreement.

Distribution Resources Planning (DRP) A computer-based management tool that allows a retail firm to determine what to order from its suppliers as a function of what it sells to retail customers. Such information is shared with the suppliers, so that they know, in turn, what to manufacture, and in which quantity.

dollarization A phenomenon where other countries decide to adopt the U.S. dollar as their circulating currency. Panama and Ecuador have gone through a "dollarization" of their respective economies.

draft The minimum depth of water that a ship needs in order to float.

drawee In a Documentary Collection transaction, another term for the importer who signs the draft.

dry bulk cargo Dry cargo that is loaded directly into the hold of a ship, without any form of unitization. Although dry, the cargo exhibits the properties of a liquid, in that it takes the shape of the hold. Examples of dry bulk cargo include grain, coal, plastic pellets, gravel, and iron ore.

dry lease A dry lease is an agreement between the owner (lessor) of an aircraft and a lessee, in which the owner provides only the aircraft, and no other services. See *wet lease* and *damp lease* for alternative contracts.

dumping The strategy followed by some exporters to sell the products they are exporting at a price that is considered "too low" by the importing country's Customs office. Depending on the importing country, the products' price is considered too low when it is either below their manufacturing costs or below their "normal" wholesale price.

dunnage Packaging material designed to prevent the cargo from moving while in transit.

duty The amount of tax paid on an imported good; the duty is calculated using the tariff rate and the value of the goods.

duty drawback A process by which the U.S. Customs and Border Protection Office refunds up to 99 percent of the duty it collected on goods that are imported into the United States if the same goods are later exported from the United States.

Electronic Data Interchange (EDI) A method to send documents (invoice, certificates, packing list, and so on) from one company to another, using electronic means. EDI is different from fax (facsimile transmission) in that it does not transfer a copy of a sheet of paper, but sends the information it contains, which is then used by the recipient to create a document.

entry The process by which an importer notifies Customs that it has imported a particular product. The entry process encompasses an entry form and is accompanied by a number of other documents: invoice, Certificate of Origin, Certificate of Inspection, and so on.

euro The common currency of twelve of the twenty-five countries of the European Union, developed in the early 1990s and placed in circulation on January 1, 2002.

evergreen contract A contract that, by design or by default, does not have a specific term of appointment. If a contract lapses but both parties continue acting as if the contract were still in place, the contract then can be considered "evergreen."

exclusive representative An agent or a distributor that has been granted the right of being the sole representative of the exporter in a given territory.

export quota A limit, set by the exporting country's government, on the quantity of a specific commodity that can be exported in a given year.

exposure The relative consequences of a particular risk for an exporter; the risk of a $50,000 loss would represent a greater exposure for a small exporter than for a large exporter.

facilities and activities In a contract between a principal and an agent or distributor, a clause that spells out what specific facilities each will maintain (retail store, warehouse, repair facilities) and what specific activities each will engage in (trade show participation, after-sale service, promotion).

factor endowment An economic theory, developed by Hecksher and Ohlin, that holds that a country will enjoy a comparative advantage over other countries if it is naturally endowed with a greater abundance of one of the factors of economic production, such as land, labor, capital, or entrepreneurship.

Fisher Effect An economic theory that holds that the interest rates that businesses and individuals should pay to borrow money should be uniform throughout the world and that the nominal interest rates that they actually pay in a given country are composed of this common interest rate and the inflation rate of that country.

flag of convenience A country with an open registry that has lower taxes and more lenient on-board regulations than other countries with open registries. A derogatory term.

Flexible Intermediate Bulk Container (FIBC) A type of large-capacity woven bags (polyethylene or polypropylene fibers) designed to unitize goods that would otherwise be carried as dry bulk, such as fertilizers, plastic pellets, or grain. Depending on their size and construction, FIBCs have a carrying capacity from 1,500 to 6,000 lbs (680 kg to 2,000 kg).

floating currency A currency whose value is determined by market forces. The exchange rate of a floating currency varies frequently.

force majeure An event beyond the control of any of the parties in an agreement that prevents one of the parties from fulfilling its commitment. The affected party is then not considered to be in breach of the contract.

Foreign Port Program A U.S. Customs and Border Protection (CBP) initiative under which ports abroad purchase container scanning equipment and agree to inspect cargo that the CBP considers suspicious. Cargo shipments originating from these ports get preferential treatment in the Customs inspection and clearance process in the United States.

formality A way for a person to interact with other individuals that uses conventions and regimented forms of address.

forward exchange rate The exchange rate of a foreign currency for delivery in thirty, ninety, or 180 days from the date of the quote.

forward market hedge A financial technique designed to reduce exchange rate fluctuation risks in which a business agrees to purchase (or sell) a particular currency at a predetermined exchange rate at some future time (generally thirty, sixty, ninety, 180, or 360 days later).

foul bill of lading Another term for a Soiled Bill of Lading, which is a bill of lading reflecting the fact that the carrier received the goods in anything other than good condition; it is characterized by the presence of additional comments or notes in addition to the signature of the carrier's representative.

franchise The portion of a loss, expressed as a percentage, below which a "With Average" insurance policy will not cover a partial loss. If the amount of the partial loss exceeds the franchise, then the entire costs of the partial loss are covered.

franchisee The party granted the right to use an array of intellectual property items owned by another party in exchange for the payment of royalties.

franchising A process by which a firm possessing an array of several intellectual property items (patents, copyrights, trademarks, trade secrets) grants another company the right to use these intellectual property items in exchange for royalties. In general, the firm that is granted the rights to use the items (called the franchisee) and the firm that is granting the rights to use the items (called the franchisor) are, in the eyes of their customers, indistinguishable.

franchisor The owner of an array of several intellectual property items that grants another firm (the licensee or franchisee) the rights to use that group of intellectual property items in exchange for the payment of royalties.

freight forwarder A company that specializes in shipping cargo on behalf of shippers (exporters or importers). It is a "travel agent" for freight, finding the most appropriate itinerary and carrier, given the shipper's objectives.

Full-Container-Load (FCL) A shipment whose volume and weight are close to the volume and weight limits of a container or for which the shipper requests that it be the only cargo in a container.

general average A loss incurred on an ocean voyage that involves all of the cargo owners on board, such as in the case where the captain of the ship tosses overboard some of the cargo (see *jettison*) to save the ship and the remainder of the cargo, or when the captain decides to ground the ship to prevent a total loss. The owners of the cargo saved by this action are indebted to the owners of the cargo sacrificed and to the owners of the ship.

good faith The assumption that both parties signing an agreement want to enter that agreement and have no ulterior motives. Almost all contracts have a clause specifying that the parties are entering the contract in good faith.

grain An agricultural commodity, such as corn, wheat, oats, or soybeans.

gray market A process by which entrepreneurs buy the products of a company in country A, export them to country B, and resell them to retailers and other intermediaries in country B. Because the entrepreneurs are operating outside of the normal distribution channels for these products, and

because they are not authorized distributors, the products themselves are dubbed parallel imports as well.

gross tonnage The total volume of a ship's carrying capacity, measured as the space available below deck, and expressed in hundreds of cubic feet. The gross tonnage is the basis upon which ships pay taxes or pay fees to transit through a canal.

guarantor The bank that provides a bank guarantee. If the party to which it provides a guarantee does not perform, the bank pays a compensation to the injured party. Most bank guarantees are not documentary, which means that the bank must pay without specific evidence. In other words, it pays first, and argues with the firm to which it provided a guarantee later. Bank guarantees are illegal in the United States.

Hague Rules An international liability convention for ocean-going carriers that limits their liability to $500 per package. The liability convention followed by United States' carriers.

Hague-Visby Rules An international liability convention for ocean-going carriers that limits their liability to SDR 667 per package or SDR 2 per kilogram, whichever is higher. This liability convention is the most commonly used in the world; however, the United States has not ratified this convention and therefore still abides by the Hague Rules.

Hamburg Rules An international liability convention for ocean-going carriers that limits their liability to SDR 835 per package or SDR 2.50 per kilogram, whichever is higher and eliminates most of the "defenses" a carrier could use to discharge itself of liability. The Hamburg Rules have not been ratified by many countries; the United States has not ratified this convention and therefore still abides by the Hague Rules.

hard currency A currency that can easily be converted into another currency.

hazard A situation that increases the probability of a peril and therefore of a loss. For example, a hazard would be a storm, which increases the probability of the peril of water damage, or a poorly trained crew, which increases the probability of the peril of grounding.

import license The express authorization, granted by the government of the importing country, to import a particular product in a given quantity. An import license is granted to the importer.

improper packaging The lack of appropriate packaging materials for an international shipment. The decision is oftentimes reached by an insurance company when it refuses to pay a damage claim that it considers avoidable had proper packaging procedures been followed.

inconvertible currency A currency that cannot be converted into another currency.

Incoterm An International Commerce Term, or a formalized international Term of Trade, which specifies the responsibilities of the exporter and the responsibilities of the importer in an international transaction. Incoterms were first codified by the International Chamber of Commerce in 1953, and the latest revision is dated 2000.

indirect quote The value of the domestic currency expressed in units of the foreign currency; for example, the dollar is worth

120.94 yen as of November 15, 2002. Some currencies are traditionally expressed as indirect quotes.

Individual Validated Export License The express authorization, granted by the government of the exporting country, to export a particular product, or to export to a particular country or particular individual.

informed compliance A standard of behavior, set and enforced by the United States Customs, that is expected of importers if they want their Customs entries to be cleared quickly and if they want to keep Customs inspections to a minimum.

instruction letter A document sent by the exporter to the Presenting Bank where it spells out its instructions regarding how it expects the bank to handle the documents and how it expects the bank to handle an importer who does not accept the draft sent.

intellectual property A type of intangible good that an individual or a firm can own; it is either a copyright (the rights to a work of art, a musical piece, or a written article), a patent (the rights to a process, a material, or a design), a trademark (the rights to a commercial name or slogan), or a trade secret (a unique way to manufacture a particular product). Copyrights, patents, and trademarks are protected by governments, preventing non-owners from using them without authorization. Trade secrets are protected by being kept secret.

Interest Rate Parity An economic theory that holds that the forward exchange rate between two currencies should reflect the differences in the interest rates in those two countries.

intermodal A shipment that takes several different means of transportation—road, rail, ocean, air—from its point of departure (seller/exporter) to its point of destination (buyer/importer). The meaning has evolved recently to limit the use of this term to freight for which a single bill of lading covering more than one of these alternatives is issued. Also called multi-modal.

intermodal bill of lading A bill of lading used in the intermodal transportation, domestic or international, of goods. An intermodal bill of lading is generally straight.

intermodal shipment An international shipment that will use several means (modes) of transportation (rail, road, air, ocean, barge) under a single bill of lading. In most instances today, goods shipped on an intermodal bill of lading are containerized.

International English A technique of written communication in the English language, developed by Edmond Weiss, which consists of removing all possible ambiguities so that the communication can be understood by someone with a limited knowledge of English.

international factoring A means of financing international receivable accounts. The firm can ask a factoring company to advance funds on a receivable account; the factoring firm can provide the funds with recourse, where the owner of the account receivable is still responsible for collecting it, or without recourse, where the collection responsibility shifts to the factoring house.

International Fisher Effect An economic theory that holds that the spot exchange rates between two countries' curren-cies should change as a function of the differences between these two countries' nominal interest rates.

international forfaiting A means to finance an international transaction in which an exporter collects a series of drafts from the importer, all with fairly long-term due dates. The exporter sells these receivables to a forfaiting firm that buys them without recourse, which means that the forfaiting firm is responsible for collecting the funds from the importer.

International Plant Protection Convention (IPPC) An international convention, which 144 countries have ratified, that mandates that wood used for packing or dunnage be heat-treated or treated with chemicals to prevent insect infestations. All wood materials used in international commerce must show the IPPC mark.

International Product Life Cycle An economic theory, developed by Raymond Vernon, that holds that, over its life cycle, a product will be manufactured first in the country in which it was first developed, then in other developed countries, and eventually in developing countries.

Irrevocable Letter of Credit A Letter of Credit is a document whereby a bank promises that it will pay the beneficiary (the exporter) a predetermined amount of money, should the beneficiary present a certain set of documents (bill of lading, invoice, and miscellaneous certificates) to the bank. It substitutes the credit worthiness of the importer for that of the bank. A Letter of Credit is irrevocable when it cannot be altered without the express consent of all parties involved (exporter, importer, issuing bank, and advising bank). Virtually all Letters of Credit are irrevocable, as required by the International Chamber of Commerce.

Issuing Bank The bank providing the Letter of Credit to the importer. It is that bank that, should the importer be unable to pay, and should the exporter provide all the necessary documents, has the contractual obligation to pay the beneficiary (the exporter).

jettison The act of throwing overboard part of the cargo of a ship (or of the fuel of an airplane) in an attempt to lighten the ship. The purpose of such an action is to save the ship, the remainder of the cargo, and the crew.

Just-in-Time A management philosophy that consists of planning the manufacturing of goods in such a way that they are produced just before they are needed in the next step of the assembly process, in order to minimize the amount of inventory that a firm carries. The philosophy extends to supply parts, which need to be delivered just before they are used in the assembly process as well.

labor law A set of a country's laws that governs relationships and disputes between employers and employees; it assumes that one of the parties (employee) needs to be protected from the other (employer). Labor law can be used in settling disputes between exporters and agents, at the discretion of the courts in the country in which the agent is located, regardless of the terms of the contract between the exporter and the agent. On occasion, labor law can be used to settle disputes between exporters and distributors.

laker A cargo ship designed for the Great Lakes of the United States and Canada. Its maximum size is dictated by the size of the locks through which it will travel.

land bridge A term coined to describe the practice of shipping goods from Asia to Europe through the United States. By taking the containerized goods to a West Coast port, loading them onto trains, transporting them across the United States, and loading them again on a ship from an East Coast port, shippers avoid the costs and delays of crossing the Panama Canal.

leap frogging The idea that some countries will "skip" a particular technology to adopt the most recent one available. For example, several developing countries never had a reliable telephone infrastructure; however, rather than spend funds on creating an infrastructure based on land lines, they will build a cellular-based phone system, thereby "leap frogging" the older technology.

Less-Than-Containerload (LCL) A shipment whose volume and weight are below the capacity of a container and for which the shipper does not request that it be the only cargo in a container. LCL shipments are generally "consolidated" with other shipments to form a Full-Container-Load (FCL).

Lex Mercatoria The sum total of all the international agreements, international conventions, and other international trade customs that complement the domestic laws of any given country, and to which all international trade transactions are subject. Because some countries are signatories of some treaties but not of others, the complexity associated in determining which elements of *Lex Mercatoria* apply to a given transaction can be substantial.

licensee The party that is granted the right to use an intellectual property item owned by another party, the licensor, in exchange for payment of a royalty.

licensing A process by which a firm possessing some intellectual property item (a patent, a copyright, a trademark, a trade secret) grants another company the right to use the intellectual property item in exchange for a payment called a *royalty*.

licensor The owner of an intellectual property item that grants another firm (the licensee) the right to use that intellectual property in exchange for the payment of a royalty.

light tonnage The total weight of the ship, when empty, measured by using the weight of the water being displaced.

Lighter Aboard Ship (LASH) Barge A floating container measuring eighteen meters by nine meters by three meters that can be loaded and unloaded from a LASH mothership and can be tugged to its destination in a port or to an area without port facilities.

Lighter Aboard Ship (LASH) Mothership A ship equipped with cranes that is designed to carry around eighty LASH barges and can load and unload them at anchor (i.e., without having to be in a port).

lightering The process by which a large vessel's cargo is unloaded offshore into smaller vessels that then take the cargo to nearby ports. The large vessel cannot access these ports because they are not deep enough or not equipped to handle such a large ship.

liner A ship that operates on a regular schedule, traveling from a group of ports to another group of ports.

liquidated entry An entry that has been successfully reviewed by Customs authorities and for which duty has been paid; no further processing is required when an entry is liquidated.

litigation A process by which the parties to a contract can settle a dispute, involving the courts of the country chosen in the "Choice of Forum" clause of an international contract. Litigation is considered a "last resort" option, when mediation fails and when the parties in dispute cannot agree to arbitration.

manifest A document, internal to the shipping company (the carrier), that lists all cargo onboard the transportation vehicle.

Manufacturing Resources Planning (MRP II) A computer-based management tool that uses MRP at its core, and that allows a manufacturing firm to determine what to manufacture, and in which quantity, as a function of what it sells to its customers. MRP II also includes financial and cost information and includes other functions in the firm, such as procurement and purchasing.

Materials Requirement Planning (MRP) A computer-based management tool that allows a manufacturing firm to determine what to produce, and in which quantity, in function of what it sells to its customers. Such information is shared with the suppliers, so that they know, in turn, what to manufacture, and in which quantity.

mediation A process by which the parties to a contract can attempt to settle a dispute, generally involving a third independent party who can suggest a compromise solution, acceptable to all concerned parties. Mediation is often preferred over litigation, an expensive and time-consuming process for which all judicial rules must be followed, and which cannot offer compromise solutions.

metric system A decimal measuring system developed in the late eighteenth century. Since the 1960s, it is officially known as the International System of Units (abbreviated SI, due to its French name, the *Système International d'Unités*). Widely adopted worldwide, it is not commonly used in the United States.

money market hedge A financial technique designed to reduce exchange rate fluctuation risks. When a business has to make a payment at a future date and is pursuing a money market hedge, it invests the funds in an interest-bearing account abroad. The amount invested is the amount it owes, discounted for the interest that it will earn: At maturity, the business will have sufficient funds to cover its obligations. In the case of a business anticipating a collection, the technique calls for the business to borrow from a bank abroad and reimburse the bank with the funds provided by its creditor.

multi-modal Another term for *intermodal*.

nautical fault An error in navigation made by the crew of a ship.

negotiable bill of lading A bill of lading on which the name of the consignee has been left blank, or where the words "to order" have been entered. Such a bill of lading allows the owner of the goods to sell them while in international transit.

The transfer of ownership is done with the bill of lading, because it is a Certificate of Title to the goods. Whoever has the original bill of lading when the cargo arrives in the port is the owner of the goods.

net tonnage Obtained by subtracting the volume occupied by the engine room and the spaces necessary for the operation of the ship (crew quarters, bridge) from the gross tonnage.

objective risk The chance of a loss that can be accurately calculated, because ample empirical data is available (probability of a fire causing a total loss of a residence) or because a good mathematical model has been developed.

ocean bill of lading A bill of lading used in international transportation of goods on oceangoing vessels. An ocean bill of lading can be straight or negotiable, and can be clean or soiled. See these terms for further information.

offer The initial step in the formation of a contract. When one of the parties to a potential sale contacts the other party, it does so with an offer to enter into a contract. Under the Convention on Contracts for the International Sale of Goods (CISG), the offer made by one of the parties is valid until its stated expiration date. Under the United States' Uniform Commercial Code (UCC), however, an offer can be withdrawn at any time before its expiration date, without prejudice.

on-board courier (OBC) A passenger on a regularly scheduled flight who is relinquishing his or her baggage allocation, allowing companies to ship extremely urgent cargo. Such a passenger is compensated by the cargo carrier with a discount on his or her airplane ticket.

open registry A country that allows vessels owned by companies having no business relations in its territory to be registered in that country and carry its flag.

open skies agreement An agreement between two or more countries where air carriers from one of the countries are allowed to serve any of the other countries' airports.

options market hedge A financial technique designed to reduce exchange rate fluctuation risks in which a business purchases (or sells) options in a particular currency. See *currency options.*

organized theft Theft of a cargo shipment (or part of a cargo shipment) that is due to organized criminal activity, in which one or more individuals plan and eventually commit the theft.

outright rate The exchange rate of a foreign currency for delivery in thirty, ninety, or 180 days from the date of the quote. The outright rate is the rate at which a commercial customer would purchase the currency. It has to be differentiated from the swap rate, which is the method used by banks and other financial institutions to express a forward exchange rate.

outsourcing A practice that consists of a business contracting with other businesses to have them perform some of the operations that it used to handle in-house. It decided that these operations were deemed unessential to its core competency.

overloaded A mode of transportation (truck, train, barge, ship, aircraft) that is carrying cargo of a greater weight or greater volume than it is designed to carry.

ownership of the customers' list The list of the customers of a particular company is considered a business asset. A contract between a principal and a distributor spells out which of the two parties owns that asset.

packing list A detailed list of what is contained in a shipment.

pallet An item made out of wood or plastic on which the goods are placed. The pallet allows the use of mechanical equipment to move the merchandise as a unit. Goods shipped on pallets are also called unitized packages. The pallet prevents some of the problems presented by manual handling of the goods. Pallets also offer an additional level of protection by insulating the goods from water standing on the ground.

Panamax A ship of the maximum size that can enter the locks of the Panama Canal.

particular average A partial loss incurred on an ocean voyage; the cargo may have become wet from seawater or may have been damaged from rough seas.

passenger airplane A type of airplane that is designed to carry passengers on the main deck of the plane; it can also carry cargo below the main deck, in its "belly," but the size and type of cargo are restricted.

pegged currency A currency whose value is determined by a fixed exchange rate with another, more widely traded currency. As the value of the reference currency fluctuates, so does the value of the pegged currency, but the exchange rate between the two remains constant.

peril The event that brings about a loss; for example, a fire, a collision, and a flood are all perils.

Phyto-Sanitary Certificate A document provided by an independent inspection company, or by the Agricultural Department of the exporting country's government, that attests that the goods conform to the agricultural standards of the importing country. A Phyto-Sanitary Certificate is always obtained by the exporter in the exporting country before the international voyage takes place.

piggy-back A technique, developed by railroad and trucking companies, that consists of placing truck trailers on specially designed railroad cars, so that the trailers can be carried over long distances more economically.

pilferage Theft of part of a cargo shipment (rarely the entire cargo shipment) due to "opportunity." The thief did not plan the crime; the circumstances were such that it was possible to commit it.

pipelines A mode of transportation consisting of a long series of pipes, connected end-to-end, and used for the transport of some liquid cargo (oil, refined petroleum products, water, and natural gas).

points In a forward exchange rate, the difference between the outright rate and the swap rate. Points are not fixed units; their value depends on the way a currency is expressed, but is the smallest decimal value in which that currency is traded. For example, the indirect quote U.S. $/yen exchange rate is 120.94 as of November 15, 2002; a "point" for this currency is therefore worth 0.01 yen. The direct quote for the U.S. $/euro exchange rate is 0.9917 as of the same date; a "point" for this currency is therefore worth U.S. $0.0001.

political risk The probability of not getting paid by a certain creditor, because the creditor's country does not have the funds to pay the debt (insufficient foreign exchange reserves) or because the creditor is not legally allowed to pay the debt (political embargo). Political risk can also mean the probability of nationalization of a firm's subsidiary by the host country. Political risk is also known as *country risk*.

post-Panamax A ship whose size is too large to enter the locks of the Panama Canal.

Presenting Bank In a Documentary Collection transaction, the bank that interacts with the importer on behalf of the exporter. The Presenting Bank is the one receiving the documents from the exporter or from the Remitting Bank and that holds them until the importer either signs a draft or pays the exporter.

Pre-Shipment Inspection (PSI) An inspection conducted by an independent inspection company before the goods are shipped internationally. The inspection is conducted at the request of the importer or of the importing country's government to ensure that the invoice reflects accurately the type of goods shipped by the exporter and their value. A Pre-Shipment Inspection generates a Certificate of Inspection.

principal The party represented by an agent in an international agency agreement; the exporter.

pro-forma invoice A quote provided by the exporter to the importer for the purpose of the importer obtaining a Letter of Credit. The *pro-forma* invoice should contain exactly the same information as the future commercial invoice will, for the same total cost, so as to prevent discrepancies at the time of the Letter of Credit settlement.

project cargo A type of cargo that requires more advance planning because of its size, weight, or volume. Project cargo generally moves through unconventional means.

Protection and Indemnity Club (P&I) A group of ship owners who agree to mutually share the costs of a member's liabilities to other parties; for example, the club members would be individually responsible for the costs of a single member's liability in the event of an oil spill. If the costs of the oil spill exceed the ability of a specific P&I club to cover them, other P&I clubs are contractually obligated to cover them.

protest A term with more than one meaning: 1. In a Documentary Collection transaction, if the drawee (importer) does not pay a draft that it has signed, the Presenting Bank will file a protest, a legal document that notifies other parties that the drawee is not honoring its debts. In many countries, the filing of a protest effectively cuts the drawee's ability to have access to any credit. 2. In a Customs transaction in the United States, the formal request by an importer to have Customs reconsider its classification, its valuation, or its determination of a country of origin. A protest is generally filed when an importer feels that the amount of duty paid is excessive, or when a good is not allowed in the United States because a quota has been met.

Purchasing Power Parity An economic theory that holds that exchange rates should reflect the price differences of each and every product between countries. The idea is that a set amount of money (regardless of the currency in which it is expressed) would purchase the same goods in any country of the world.

pure risk The chance or the probability of a loss only. Pure risks can be insured against (i.e., transferred to an insurance company).

put options See *currency options*.

quota A limit, set by the importing country's government (sometimes in agreement with the governments of the concerned exporting countries), on the quantity of a specific commodity that can be imported in a given year. There are two different types of quotas: 1. an absolute quota, which limits the quantity of goods imported, and beyond which no good can be imported; 2. a tariff-rate quota, which places a low duty rate on goods imported until the quota is reached, and a very high duty rate on quantities of the goods imported beyond the quota.

reasonable care A standard of behavior, set and enforced by the United States Customs, that is expected of importers if they want their Customs entries to be cleared quickly and if they want to keep Customs inspections to a minimum.

registration A process whereby an agent or a distributor has to notify the government of the importing country that it has entered into an agency agreement or a distributorship agreement with a foreign manufacturer.

rejection An intermediary step in the formation of a contract. After an offer has been made by one of the parties, the other party may not agree with all of the terms of the offer, and may want to modify them. Under the Convention on Contracts for the International Sale of Goods (CISG), this response is construed as a rejection of the original offer, to which a counteroffer can be made.

Remitting Bank In a Documentary Collection transaction, the bank that interacts with the exporter and with the Presenting Bank in the importing country. The Remitting Bank is the one that receives the documents from the exporter and then sends them to the Presenting Bank. It has no obligation to render judgment or advice on the quality of the packet of documents; it just transmits them to the Presenting Bank.

risk The chance or the probability of a loss.

risk retention A risk management strategy in which a company elects to retain a certain type of risk and decides not to insure that risk.

risk transfer A risk management strategy in which a company elects not to retain a risk and asks an insurance company to take that risk in exchange for a premium.

road-trains An Australian trucking technique, consisting of having one tractor pulling multiple trailers. Road trains are the conceptual equivalent of trains, but operating on a road. Road trains have between three and seven trailers.

roller deck The configuration of the deck of an aircraft when it is designed to accept cargo shipments; the deck is equipped with rollers and bearings that allow cargo to be moved in any direction without much friction.

royalty The amount of money paid by the licensee to the licensor for the right to use the licensor's intellectual property. Royalty fees are generally determined as a function of the number of times that the licensee or franchisee used the intellectual property.

rules of origin The rules used to determine the country of origin of a particular product. The most commonly used interpretation rule is that the country of origin is the country in which the product last changed Harmonized System Number classification.

seal Lock especially designed to be applied to containers and truck trailers and that the importer must break in order to get entry into the container or trailer. Locks have an identification number that is recorded on the bill of lading, and that number must be checked by the importer as well, to ensure that the seal was not "replaced" during the voyage. Seals can be a simple loop of braided steel or a reinforced steel pin. Some seals are electronic and record attempted entries.

secondary registry A response by developed countries to the threat of open registries and flags of convenience: They created a secondary registry with lower on-board standards and taxes to entice ship owners to carry their flag and not defect to flag of convenience countries.

ship's rail An imaginary rail that circles the entire hull of a ship. Should a cargo item fall from the crane onto the ship while it is being loaded, the determination of whose responsibility it is hinges on which side of the ship's rail it falls on. Under CIF, for example, if the cargo falls on the outside of the ship's rail, it is the exporter's responsibility; if it falls on the inside, it is the importer's.

shipper The party to an international transaction who is responsible for arranging the transportation of the goods. Depending on the Incoterm used, and depending on the leg of the journey in consideration, the shipper is either the exporter or the importer.

Shipper's Export Declaration A document collected by U.S. Customs designed to keep track of the type of goods exported from the United States, as well as their destination and their value.

Shipper's Letter of Instruction A document in which the shipper spells out how it wants the carrier to handle the goods while they are in transit.

soft currency A currency that cannot be easily converted into another currency; either it is inconvertible, or only convertible into other soft currencies, or it has an exchange rate that differs substantially between sales of the currency and purchases of the currency.

soiled bill of lading A bill of lading that reflects the fact that the carrier received the goods in anything other than good condition; it is characterized by the presence of additional comments or notes in addition to the signature of the carrier's representative.

Special Drawing Right (SDR) An artificial currency (it does not circulate; see *artificial currency*) of the International Monetary Fund. Its value is determined by the value of a basket of four currencies: the euro (approximately 34 percent of the SDR's value), the Japanese yen (approximately 11 percent), the U.S. dollar (approximately 44 percent), and the British pound (approximately 11 percent).

Special English A technique of oral communication in the English language, developed by the Voice of America, that consists of a limited vocabulary and of simplified sentences, so that the communication can be understood by someone with a limited knowledge of English.

speculative risk The chance or probability of a loss or a gain (for example, an investment in the stock market).

spot exchange rate The exchange rate of a foreign currency for immediate delivery (within forty-eight hours).

Stand-By Letter of Credit A type of Letter of Credit that covers more than one shipment; for example, a large transaction would normally necessitate a Letter of Credit for each shipment, because a separate bill of lading is generated for each shipment. A Stand-By Letter of Credit allows for multiple bills of lading, issued on different dates. A Stand-By Letter of Credit can also be used to secure the performance of the seller. Upon evidence that the seller is not performing according to the terms of the contract it has with the importer, the Issuing Bank has to pay the importer; this latter type of Stand-By Letter of Credit is often used in large construction projects involving U.S. firms, because U.S. banks cannot legally provide bank guarantees.

stevedore A company or a person whose responsibility is to load and unload ships in a port.

stores All the supplies that a ship carries and that it needs to function.

straight bill of lading A bill of lading on which the name of the consignee has been entered. Such a bill of lading is non-negotiable, which means that the ownership of the goods cannot change in transit.

strike price See *currency options*.

subjective risk The perceived risk of a loss by an individual or company. Whether this perception is correct can only be settled by calculating the objective risk.

surveyor An individual or company whose responsibility it is to determine the extent and the circumstances of a marine cargo loss. A surveyor is an independent party who is not working for the shipper, the carrier, or the insurance company.

swap rate The exchange rate of a foreign currency for delivery in thirty, ninety, or 180 days from the date of the quote. The swap rate is the difference between the current spot rate and the rate at which a commercial customer would purchase the currency. It is expressed in points that must be subtracted or added to the spot rate. The swap rate is the method used by banks and other financial institutions to express a forward exchange rate. The sum of the swap rate and the spot rate yields the outright rate, which is the rate paid by a commercial customer for the currency.

Syndicate Under the Lloyd's concept of an insurance market, a group of names who agree to insure a certain type of loss. The risks are shared by all the members of the Syndicate.

system's theft Theft that is perpetrated by someone who also gains access to a computer in the information system of the supply chain and deletes the files related to that shipment. The theft is then likely to go undetected for a period of time.

tariff A term with more than one meaning: 1. The price that conference members have agreed to charge for a specific commodity going from one specific port to another. 2. The rate at which an import is taxed; the tariff rate is dependent on the classification of the goods, as well as their country of origin. The tariff rate is also called the duty rate.

tariff schedule A document listing all the possible Harmonized System classification categories, as well as their associated tariff rates for the different types of countries. Most tariff schedules have two or more "columns," a term that refers to the number of categories of countries of origin the tariff schedule uses.

Term of Sale An element in a contract of sale that specifies the method of payment to which an exporter and an importer have agreed. Specifically, the Term of Sale will specify Cash in Advance, Letter of Credit, Documentary Collection, Open Account, or TradeCard Transaction.

Term of Trade An element in a contract of sale that specifies the responsibilities of the exporter and the responsibilities of the importer. Specifically, the Term of Trade will specify which activities must be performed by the exporter, which are performed by the importer, which activities are paid by the exporter, which are paid by the importer, and where in the international transportation process the transfer of responsibility for the merchandise takes place.

termination for convenience The unilateral decision, by one of the parties to a contract, to end a contract before its term of appointment expires, for reasons unrelated to the performance of the contract by the other party(ies). The term is also used when one party decides not to renew the contract even if the preset criteria for renewal have been met by the other party(ies).

termination for "just cause" The unilateral decision, by one of the parties to a contract, to end a contract before its term of appointment expires, because the other party has not met some of the terms of the contract that it had agreed to perform. The term is also used when one party decides to not renew the contract because the preset criteria for renewal have not been met.

time charter A lease agreement (also called a charter party) between the owner (lessor) of a bulk cargo ship and a lessee in which the owner provides the lessee with the ship, the crew, and all other services or supplies, for an agreed-upon period of time. See *voyage charter* and *bareboat charter* for alternative charter party contracts for ships.

time draft In a Documentary Collection transaction, a time draft is a promissory note that the importer has to pay a number of days (thirty, sixty, ninety, or 180 days) after it accepts the draft by signing it. A time draft is different from a date draft, because the importer controls the date at which it will sign the note, whereas in a date draft, the exporter controls the date of payment by controlling the date at which the goods are shipped. A time draft is used in the Documentary Collection called Documents against Acceptance.

to order bill of lading A bill of lading on which the name of the consignee has been left blank, or where the words "to order" have been entered. Such a bill of lading allows the owner of the goods to sell them while in international transit. The transfer of ownership is done with the bill of lading, because it is a Certificate of Title to the goods. Whoever has the original bill of lading when the cargo arrives in the port is the owner of the goods.

tractor The part of an articulated semi-truck that is in the front and whose engine pulls the trailer.

trade acceptance In a Documentary Collection transaction, the alternative where the exporter expects the importer to readily accept signing a draft after being notified by the Presenting Bank that the documents have arrived. The importer (trader) "accepts" the draft.

trademark, patent, and copyright Intangible goods (intellectual property) that an individual or a firm can own. A copyright is the term used to refer to the rights to a work of art, a musical piece, or a written article). A patent is the term used to refer to the rights to a process, a material, or a design. A trademark represents the rights to a commercial name or slogan. Copyrights, patents, and trademarks are protected by governments, preventing non-owners from using them without authorization.

trailer The part of an articulated semi-truck that is in the rear and is pulled by the tractor.

tramp A ship that does not operate on a regular schedule and is available to be chartered for any voyage, from any port to any port.

transaction exposure The risk represented by the fluctuation in exchange rates between the time at which two companies enter in an international contract and the time at which that contract is paid.

trot-on/trot-off A ship designed to carry livestock. It possesses a ramp that the animals can use to walk on board and exit the vessel.

tweendeck In a combination ship, a deck located below the main deck that is used to carry smaller size break-bulk cargo, such as vehicles.

twenty-four-hour rule A rule first instituted by the U.S. Customs and Border Protection Agency, which requires carriers to send Customs the manifest of all cargo destined for the United States twenty-four hours prior to the cargo being loaded in the port of departure. Several other countries have adopted a similar requirement.

Underwriter The company, Syndicate, or name that assumes the risk of a loss for another party, in exchange for a premium.

uniform bill of lading A bill of lading used in the transportation of goods on trucks and trains, either domestically or internationally. A uniform bill of lading is generally straight.

valuation The process of determining the value of an import, or the amount upon which the duty will be calculated. The value of an import generally includes not only the value of the goods but also the value of some of the transportation services used to get it into the importing country.

Value-Added Tax (VAT) A tax perceived by many countries that is very similar to a sales tax, but that is collected whenever the product's value is increased. Only the final consumer eventually pays the tax, but every company involved in the production or supply chain is required to collect the Value-Added Tax that its customers pay and pay the Value-Added Tax to its suppliers. The difference between what a firm collects and what it pays must be sent to the government. The Value-Added Tax on imports is collected at the point of entry in the country. The basis for the tax is the sum of the value of the goods and of the duty paid.

variant A modification to one of the Incoterms codified by the International Chamber of Commerce. Variants are generally used to further clarify the responsibilities of the exporter and of the importer in a given transaction. For example, the variant "EXW loaded" clarifies that the exporter agrees to load the goods on the vehicle provided by the importer, when the official Incoterm is silent on that specific point.

visa A term with more than one meaning: 1. A process by which the Consulate of the country in which the goods will be imported reviews and approves the Consular invoice for a fee. A visa shows on the Consular invoice as a rubber stamp or a seal. 2. A document provided by the government of an exporting country for a product that is subject to a quota in the United States. It is a document granting the exporter the "right" to export such goods. The United States Customs will not allow the import of a product subject to quotas if the shipment is not accompanied by a visa from the exporting government.

volume-weight A weight, calculated based upon the dimensions of a shipment, used by airlines to determine the tariff to be charged to a shipper, when a shipment is not very dense. The volume weight equivalency is that $6,000 \text{ cm}^3$ is one kg (or that one m^3 is 166.67 kg). In all instances, an airline charges the higher of the actual weight and the volume weight. Volume weight is also called dimensional weight.

voyage charter A lease agreement (also called a charter party) between the owner (lessor) of a bulk cargo ship and a lessee, in which the owner provides the lessee with the ship, the crew, and all other services or supplies, for a single voyage. See *time charter* and *bareboat charter* for alternative charter party contracts for ships.

wet bulk (liquid bulk) cargo Liquid cargo that is loaded directly into the hold of a ship, without any form of unitization. Examples of liquid bulk cargo include crude oil, vegetable oil, alcohol, and molasses, as well as liquid chemicals, such as chlorine or caustic soda.

wet lease An agreement under which the owner lessor of the aircraft provides the airplane, insurance, maintenance services, and a flight crew to the lessee, who has to cover all of the other variable costs (fuel and airport fees, for example).

Index

An *italic f* next to a page number (e.g., 177*f*) identifies information that appears in a figure. An *italic n* next to a page number (e.g., 177*n*) indicates information that appears in a footnote or endnote. An *italic t* next to a page number (e.g., 177*t*) identifies information that appears in a table.